Sociological Analysis

Sociological Analysis

An Empirical Approach Through Replication

Murray A. Straus
University of New Hampshire

Joel I. Nelson
University of Minnesota

Harper & Row, Publishers
NEW YORK, EVANSTON, and LONDON

Library of Congress Catalog Card Number: 68–10808

CONTENTS

V SOCIAL DIFFERENTIATION

VI GROUPS

VII INSTITUTIONS

VIII SOCIAL ORDER AND CHANGE

PREFACE

Contemporary sociology has generally moved away from a descriptive and speculative orientation. There are indications, however, that this change is not being efficiently communicated. At the graduate level, Sibley's recent comprehensive study revealed profound deficiencies in research training (Sibley, 1963). At the undergraduate level the situation may be much more serious. Despite the nearly inevitable chapter in introductory sociology books asserting that sociology *is* a science, most undergraduates do not perceive it in this light. For example, a recent study (Lewis, 1966) found that of all major disciplines, there was the greatest discrepancy between instructors and students of the social sciences in their rating of the importance of research: instructors apparently viewed research as vital, their students did not. More cursory impressions of undergraduate training in sociology has further supported this view (Page, 1959).

The reasons for the lack of a research orientation among sociology students are no doubt legion, but one part of the explanation must surely lie in the nature of the text materials available for undergraduate instruction. Even today, textbooks in sociology tend to be long on speculation and short on empirical reports and systematic theory. There are exceptions to this, but they are unfortunately too few. Consequently, scientifically minded students may come away from an introductory course with a feeling that sociology is a speculative rather than a scientific field.

In addition, undergraduate training in sociology has generally not provided an adequate parallel to the laboratory experience in the natural sciences. It is our impression that the workbooks and laboratory manuals currently available focus almost entirely on repetition, symbolic manipulation, and problems of empirical description. However important these activities may be, they do not offer any experience in empirical inference.

Adequate experience in empirical inference in sociology is surely no panacea, but it may be a step in the direction of providing to introductory students a realistic picture of sociology. The intent of *Sociological Analysis* is to provide precisely such experience. In contrast to previous laboratory attempts in sociology, all the problems contained in the present manual are both empirical and analytical: they require analysis of evidence concerning the relationship between variables. The theme of the volume is that laboratory work in sociology is both possible and necessary. Such work is possible if the aims of the laboratory are kept to the modest level of replication, as they are in the physical and biological sciences, and if the equipment is no more imposing than a questionnaire and some other mechanical guides. It is necessary if students are to have insight into sociological research—in testing theory and in contributing to an understanding of the empirical world.

In addition to meeting the scientific requirements for a laboratory experience, most of the data used for these problems are also of personal interest to students since they are obtained by questionnaires completed by the students themselves. Our experience has been that this combination of materials of personal interest, problems of scientific importance, and an objective empirical approach to their analysis constitutes a method of instruction which will provide understanding of the research process and an appreciation of attempts to make theoretical statements amenable to empirical observation and test. We believe that such an understanding and appreciation of the research process is an essential part of liberal education for a society which makes increasing use of sociological research. In addition, although it is not our primary aim, we hope that the early achievement of such an understanding will also attract research-oriented students into sociology.

Murray A. Straus
Joel I. Nelson

References

Lewis, Lionel, "Two Cultures: Some Empirical Findings," *Educational Record, 48* (Summer, 1967), pp. 260–267.

Page, Charles, "Sociology as a Teaching Enterprise," in Robert K. Merton, Leonard Broom and Leonard S. Cottrell, Jr., eds., *Sociology Today*. New York: Basic Books, Inc., 1959, pp. 579–599.

Sibley, Elbridge, *The Education of Sociologists in the United States*. New York: Russell Sage Foundation, 1963.

ACKNOWLEDGEMENTS

The development of empirical replication as an educational device was both long and sometimes painful. Since 1961, some 700 students and their instructors were subjected to the hazards of exposure to preliminary versions of this book. They suffered, although not always in silence; we thank them for their countless contributions.

In addition to the University of Minnesota, the preliminary edition was used at Indiana University by Richard Hall, at the College of St. Benedict by Sister Aquinas Nolen, and at St. John's University by Richard Devine. We are deeply indebted to each of them: for their charity and zeal in using an inadequately developed book; for the numerous deficiencies they brought to our attention. The volume was substantially enriched by their comments. Finally, we wish to acknowledge the valuable suggestions and intellectual support given by our colleague at Minnesota, Irving Tallman.

MURRAY A. STRAUS
JOEL I. NELSON

Introduction I

There are many versions of sociology. To some it is a science, to others a humanistic endeavor; to some it belabors the obvious while to others it documents the profound. Obviously, sociology is all these things and many others as well. The purpose of this volume is to introduce students to a particular, ascendant version of sociology—sociology as science. The volume will attempt to illustrate the validity of a number of sociological principles as well as some folkways of sociological research.

Contemporary sociologists are interested in explanations of the way societies and social groups behave. Explanations are scientific only if there is some evidence to indicate they are valid. Like other empirical scientists, sociologists follow the same route in assessing the validity of their thoughts: They observe. The observations may be drawn from a panorama of events, including subjects in a laboratory experiment, the behavior of an office staff, the contents of historical documents and popular fiction, or responses to questionnaires and interviews. Always, however, the question raised about these observations is the same: Of the many particular cases observed, how many were consistent with my general explanation, how many inconsistent? In microcosm, this question represents the kernel of sociological analysis: drawing inferences about some general social process from data pertaining to a specific set of events. This book is called *Sociological Analysis* because it is precisely this experience we hope to provide as part of your introduction to sociology.

The method used to provide this experience follows the form of replicating contemporary sociological research. Replication means to repeat a research study. As students in chemistry replicate the breakdown of water into hydrogen and oxygen, and as students in psychology condition the reflexes of an albino rat, so you—as students in sociology—will be asked to replicate sociological research. Hopefully, through the method of replication you will develop a feeling and an appreciation of the elementary methods of sociological research as well as an opportunity to convince yourself that sociology has a body of empirically verified knowledge.

Contained in the present volume are the key materials needed to make replication or laboratory work possible: (1) Theoretically relevant issues as posed in a collection of actual research reports provide the problems to be studied; (2) a questionnaire to be completed by each student supplies relevant and personally meaningful observations and data for replicating these studies; (3) a system for ordering the observations permits an objective and quantitative method for testing hypotheses. In short, the "replication" procedure used in this book—reading original research reports and repeating key parts of them—makes it possible for you to enjoy a meaningful laboratory experience.

The format of the book is simple. It consists of reprints of original research reports, together with directions and materials to enable you to repeat the original studies yourself. While most of the replications in this book make use of "survey" data, this limitation at least parallels the vast majority of published researches in sociology. In four of the problems, however, you will be introduced to the use of experimental methods, content analysis, participant observation, and documentary sources. The replications have been simplified so that each problem can be completed within a two-hour period. The problems are not meant to teach advanced techniques of research or to stimulate original discoveries, but to give you firsthand experience with some of the ways sociologists go about their work.

Objectives of the replication experience

Although the worth of replication as an educational tool cannot be easily gauged, there is some basis for believing it to be an efficient and satisfying form of learning. There are probably a variety of routes to acquiring knowledge, but one time-tested principle entails individual discovery. It is one thing to be told, for example, that "the power structure of the family is directly related to social class." It is quite another thing to test this proposition and find out for oneself that "it works." The thrill of independent discovery is not to be minimized in the classroom situation. It is the conviction, and of course the bias of this book, that knowledge acquired firsthand is not likely to be knowledge forgotten.

Naturally, there are potential frustrations involved in such an experience. Due to careless procedures, sampling variations, or errors in the original study, some portion of the laboratory problems will not turn out as anticipated. If and when this occurs, it is possible that some of you will follow the route taken by countless generations of freshman chemistry and physics students and "fudge" the data to "substantiate the law." Little need be said about such misguided procedures except the hope that you will not place so much emphasis on confirming hypotheses as to exaggerate this danger.

Given this possible difficulty, what other advantages are to be gained from these replications?

Hopefully, the experience provided by the projects in this volume will make more meaningful the courses in statistics and research methods which many of you will take at some time. In this book no more complicated statistics than percentages and means are used. But the experience with these projects should enable you to visualize the steps involved in quantifying and analyzing data, testing hypotheses, and interpreting findings. In addition, the experience of replicating studies in this book should place you in a better position to read and understand reports of research in sociological journals, an increasingly critical skill in light of the rapid and accelerating growth of knowledge in sociology.

Through this book you can develop some elementary mastery of research and thereby contribute to your own education and also to the long-term development of sociology: If you demand of yourself, of your instructor, and of textbooks in sociology that statements be based on objectively verifiable and verified propositions, then the entire discipline can prosper.

Finally, in addition to the educational utility of replication, it is necessary also to underline the fact that replication—the work in which you will be engaged—is among the most fundamental requisites of science. In sociology, as in all scientific endeavors, hypotheses should usually be phrased as general statements applicable to a wide variety of situations. This essentially commits the researcher to testing hypotheses again and again; that is, to replicate them within different settings if the hypothesis is to be considered confirmed with any degree of confidence. A study in Elmira, New York, found that middle class persons vote Republican more often than lower class persons. Is this true in Los Angeles, Duluth, and among your fellow students on campus? In scientific research it must be possible for any student equipped with the proper tools to restudy the problem in question. If research findings are only capable of being discovered by one man, then from the perspective of scientific worth the finding is meaningless. A scientific finding cannot be a purely personal experience, it must be reproducible.

Overview of procedures for laboratory problems

The following statement provides a general sketch of your work with this manual and hopefully anticipates some of the questions you may have.

1. *Initial laboratory period.* The first laboratory session is devoted to obtaining the data needed for most of the subsequent problems. This will be done by asking each student to complete a questionnaire. Sociology, like all sciences, depends on the analysis of observed phenomena. Each of you in the course of daily interaction has had the opportunity to make the observations necessary for the laboratory problems. In the questionnaire you can report these observations in standardized form.

2. *Second laboratory problem.* This problem is devoted to quantifying the observations in the questionnaire and recording the resulting numbers on a "code sheet." The code sheet is simply an 8½ inch by 11 inch piece of paper. This single page is more convenient to sort and tabulate than the original questionnaire. If possible, this will be done at least in part in class so that your instructor will be able to assist in coding procedures and decisions.

3. *Subsequent laboratory problems.* All subsequent problems follow a standard procedure. *First,* the research report reprinted from a sociological journal should be read in advance of the laboratory period. This is necessary because, if the article is not read in advance, replication of the problem will be difficult and probably uninteresting. *Second,* before coming to class you should write a brief hypothesis based on the article read. *Third,* using the specific instructions for each problem, data from the code sheets are tabulated to determine if the data reveal the same patterns as in the original research. *Fourth,* a laboratory report is written in which the sample, the variables used, and the findings are described, and in which you give a brief discussion and interpretation of the findings.

It is possible to do the problems in this book as outside assignments. If this is done, the code sheets will be made available to you either by placing them on reserve in the library or by allowing you to take the sheets home.

Although some of the problems use data from other sources than the code sheets, the basic pattern of tabulating data to test a hypothesis and then writing a brief laboratory report is the same for all problems except for Problem 22 (which is a demonstration of the way such analyses can be done using punched cards and computers). Once you have the knack of doing the problems, the others will be relatively easy, perhaps even repetitious for some of you. If so, it simply means that you have thoroughly mastered this elementary level of research technology. It does not mean that additional problems are not worth doing, because (1) for each study reprinted in this book we want to test its objective verifiability and (2) in each case there is something to be learned from the personal involvement which comes from actually repeating the study yourself.

Note on readings and appendixes

The reading for each problem is preceded by a brief introduction. These introductions are not intended either as reviews of the literature or as substitutes for a systematic textbook treatment of the topic. Their purpose is to sensitize you to the range of issues relating to the topic of the problem; to place the reading in the context of other related research; to alert you to some of the central issues in the article you are about to read; and, sometimes, to explain the statistical techniques used in the article if these have not already been covered in the introductory reading on "Methods and Techniques of Sociology."

If you are to get the most out of doing the problems in this book it is essential that you read the article describing the original research *before* attempting the replication. In reading these articles, bear in mind that they almost always cover far more material than is used in our simplified replication. Sociological research is actually much more complex than is appropriate for a beginning laboratory experience. While we do not expect you to do laboratory problems which include all the variations and ramifications of the original study, you should at least have read about and be aware of what is involved in typical sociological research.

In addition to the specific readings, you should also be aware of the four important appendixes contained in the back of this book; each contains material you will need to refer to throughout the course.

Appendix A explains what is required to write each laboratory report and also contains a note on interpreting cause and effect. Each replication provides special instructions which apply to a particular problem, but the general instructions are needed as a background for writing an adequate laboratory report.

Appendix B contains tables of percentages for base numbers up to 144 and thus will save much of the time required for calculation. If, for example, you want to know what percent 19 is of a group totaling 69, you can simply refer to the column headed 69 and find the answer (27.5%) without having to divide.

Appendix C contains directions for calculating the mean for grouped data, a procedure to be followed in a number of problems in this book. Since the technique is slightly different from the usual way of calculating averages, you should be sure to read these instructions for doing any problem which uses group means.

Appendix D contains notes for instructors.

INTRODUCTORY READINGS

The four readings in this introductory section were selected to provide an overview of the worth of scientific research in sociology as well as to address some technical questions to be considered in each of the subsequent replications and readings. The first two readings, by Paul F. Lazarsfeld and Glenn M. Vernon, are concerned with the most biting criticism that can be made of sociological research: that such research only documents common sense and thus does little more than belabor the obvious. This kind of criticism is neither completely true nor false. Two points, however, can be offered in rebuttal: First, there are many features of social life which men have traditionally considered to be common sense—as, for example, that Negroes are inherently ignorant—but which have no solid foundation in scientific fact. As Lazarsfeld illustrates, the list of common sense propositions proven incorrect by sociological research can readily be extended. It would appear that not every person understands enough about the complexities of his own life as well as the lives of his fellow men around the globe to be able to generalize on the intricacies of society.

The second point in rebuttal, raised in the reading by Vernon, goes one step further: Vernon implicitly admits that persons may at times be able through common sense to deduce some principle of social life; but even if they can, these principles will typically miss the subtleties and nuances of life patterns. For example, it may seem obvious that men have more power and authority in their homes than women. Is this true, however, of all men? All women? All families? In every part of the country? Among every social strata? Clearly, only detailed research can provide even an approximate answer to these questions, and to the even more important question of why this variation occurs.

Finally, we can add a third point to this list of rebuttals: Hopefully, the replication experience provided in this volume will allow you to convince yourself that not every fact about society can be gathered from common sense experience.

Given that sociological research does not merely belabor the obvious, the question still remains as to how sociologists translate their observations on social life to estimate the validity of their ideas. One method is to convert their observations into quantifiable form and actually count the number of times they have observed cases consistent with their ideas and inconsistent with their ideas. (This issue will be dealt with in more detail in the reading by James A. Quinn for Problem 1.) The most practical and reliable way of determining the number of cases consistent and inconsistent with one's ideas, that is of determining whether a relationship exists between two variables—between race and ambition, between education and income—is to organize the evidence in tabular form. Tables of scientific evidence are organized according to certain conventions. If you understand these conventions and learn to read tables of data, you will have learned a skill which is essential for further work in sociology and is also needed for many other aspects of modern life. All of you have some experience with reading tables. Usually, however, these tables are not as complex as those used for presenting research results. It is these complex, multivariable tables which W. Allen Wallis and Harry V. Roberts explain in the third reading.

Finally, the question can and should be raised as to whether, in the replications contained in this volume, it is possible to say anything general about social life. Obviously, one of the limitations of our replications is that all but a few are based on data from college students. This limitation is necessary because the task of obtaining data from a more representative sample of the population would add too much to the time and complexity of the problem for an introductory course. The question remains, however, whether it is reasonable and worthwhile to attempt to repeat studies typically based on a more representative population using only a narrow segment. Perhaps the differences which exist in the society as a whole are eliminated by the selectivity and consequent homogeneity of a college student population. In the final reading, Raymond A. Mulligan provides evidence which gives at least a partial answer to these important issues.

SOCIOLOGY vs. COMMON SENSE / *Paul F. Lazarsfeld*

Finding regularities and determining criteria of significance are concerns the social sciences have in common with the natural sciences. But there are crucial differences between the two fields of inquiry. The world of social events is much less "visible" than the realm of nature. That bodies fall to the ground, that things are hot or cold, that iron becomes rusty, are all immediately obvious. It is much more difficult to realize that ideas of right and wrong vary in different cultures; that customs may serve a different function from the one which the people practising them believe they are serving; that the same person may show marked contrasts in his behavior as a member of a family and as a member of an occupational group. The mere description of human behavior, of its variation from group to group and of its changes in different situations, is a vast and difficult undertaking. It is this task of describing, sifting and ferreting out interrelationships which surveys perform for us. And yet this very function often leads to serious misunderstandings. For it is hard to find a form of human behavior that has not already been observed somewhere. Consequently, if a study reports a prevailing regularity, many readers respond to it by thinking "of course that is the way things are." Thus, from time to time, the argument is advanced that surveys only put into complicated form observations which are already obvious to everyone.

Understanding the origin of this point of view is of importance far beyond the limits of the present discussion. The reader may be helped in recognizing this attitude if he looks over a few statements which are typical of many survey findings and carefully observes his own reaction. A short list of these, with brief interpretive comments, will be given here in order to bring into sharper focus probable reactions of many readers.

1. Better educated men showed more psycho-neurotic symptoms than those with less education. (The mental instability of the intellectual as compared to the more impassive psychology of the-man-in-the-street has often been commented on.)
2. Men from rural backgrounds were usually in better spirits during their Army life than soldiers from city backgrounds. (After all, they are more accustomed to hardships.)
3. Southern soldiers were better able to stand the climate in the hot South Sea Islands than Northern soldiers. (Of course, Southerners are more accustomed to hot weather.)
4. White privates were more eager to become non-coms than Negroes. (The lack of ambition among Negroes is almost proverbial.)
5. Southern Negroes preferred Southern to Northern white officers. (Isn't it well known that Southern whites have a more fatherly attitude toward their "darkies"?)
6. As long as the fighting continued, men were more eager to be returned to the States than they were after the German surrender. (You cannot blame people for not wanting to be killed.)

Reprinted with permission of the author and the publisher from a review of *The American Soldier,* Vols. I and II, *The Public Opinion Quarterly, 13* (Fall, 1949) pp. 378–380.

We have in these examples a sample list of the simplest type of interrelationships which provide the "bricks" from which our empirical social science is being built. But why, since they are so obvious, is so much money and energy given to establish such findings? Would it not be wiser to take them for granted and proceed directly to a more sophisticated type of analysis? This might be so except for one interesting point about the list. *Every one of these statements is the direct opposite of what actually was found.* Poorly educated soldiers were more neurotic than those with high education; Southerners showed no greater ability than Northerners to adjust to a tropical climate; Negroes were more eager for promotion than whites; and so on.

If we had mentioned the actual results of the investigation first, the reader would have labelled these "obvious" also. Obviously something is wrong with the entire argument of "obviousness." It should really be turned on its head. Since every kind of human reaction is conceivable, it is of great importance to know which reactions actually occur most frequently and under what conditions; only then will a more advanced social science develop.

From its earliest days more than a century ago down to the present, sociology has undergone a continuous and at times vehement barrage by outside critics, and sporadically even by members of the profession itself. Besides the allegation that sociology is merely common-sense observation about social behavior, four principal criticisms are directed against it.

According to the first criticism, much of sociology pretends to be science but is in fact only "scientism" or pseudoscience, lacking the objectivity, uniformity, and rigor of "real" science (that is, natural science), and dealing with erratic human beings. A second allegation, consistent with the first, is that sociology in its zeal to appear scientific has become infatuated with unnecessary jargon, and meaningless statistics. Many questions are considered under such forbidding titles as "the role of primary groups in the intergenerational transmission of sociopolitical information." In simple terms this means "what children learn about politics from their parents in contrast to what they learn from their playmates." As a consequence of this crude and pretentious language, nonprofessional popularizers in such books as *The Status Seekers, The Organization Man,* and *The Exurbanites* are replacing sociologists in publicizing social phenomena. Third, sociology is attacked for fostering the dangerous idea that its development as a science will make man ultimately predictable and therefore controllable in a new social order. Last, sociology is accused of being fundamentally unable to grasp true knowledge of man and society; this is the legitimate province only of men with wisdom and insight, such as poets, theologians, political theorists, moralists, and jurists.

SOCIOLOGY, SOCIAL ENGINEERING, AND COMMON EXPERIENCE / *Glenn M. Vernon*

Applied Sociology

In the army no one would think of adopting a new type of weapon without trying it out exhaustively on the firing range. But a new idea about handling personnel fared very differently. The last thing anybody ever thought about was trying out the idea experimentally. I recall several times when we had schemes for running an experimental tryout of an idea in the sociopsychological field. Usually one of two things would happen: the idea would be rejected as stupid without a tryout (it may have been stupid, too) or it would be seized on and applied generally and at once.

—SAMUEL A. STOUFFER[1]

An understanding of the traditional difference between a pure and an *applied* science will also enable the student to anticipate more accurately what will be covered in an introductory sociology text.[2] Let us briefly explore this distinction. It might be well to state at the beginning of the discussion, however, that the lines which will here be drawn may not always be so clear when specific college classes are considered.

The pure scientist, whatever his area of interest, is concerned primarily with gaining understanding or knowledge. He is seeking knowledge for the sake of gaining knowledge. This knowledge-for-the-sake-of-knowledge orientation is one which is generally quite foreign to the average individual who will read this text. Most individuals want to know how the new knowledge will help them. How can it be applied to make the world a better place in which to live? The pure scientist, as a scientist, does not share this orientation. He is concerned only with questions such as the following:

Why does this happen in this particular way?
What would happen if these elements were combined in such and such a fashion?
What are the component parts of X and how are they related to each other?
What is the relationship between this and that?
What happens when I do such and such?

The applied scientist is interested in applying scientific findings to specific problems which are felt to be of pragmatic value to the scientist—or to those who pay the scientist his salary. The applied scientist is action-oriented. He is concerned with making better mousetraps of one type or another. He wants to make salt water drinkable or usable as irrigation water. He wants to improve rocket performance, to improve marriages, or to reduce employee absenteeism. He applies his knowledge in an effort to achieve a goal which he has accepted as desirable. Knowledge is a means to an end, but not an end in itself.

The findings of a pure scientist are in a sense a two-edged sword. They can be used to accomplish any goal to which they are applicable, regardless of whether these goals are defined as desirable or undesirable. The principles of atomic physics can be used to build bombs which destroy human beings or to power hospital ships which save lives. The findings of the social scientist can be used by management to manipulate employees, but they can also be used by employees to manipulate management. They can be used to build strong organizations or to destroy strong organizations.

The pure scientist is not concerned *as a scientist* with how his findings will be used, although even here his research for pure knowledge may well rest upon an "applied" assumption that such activity will *in the long run* benefit mankind. Whether they actually do or not is another question and one, by the way, which the scientist *as a scientist* cannot answer for reasons that will be made clear in our subsequent discussion of values.

In the social sciences the applications of the findings of the pure scientist have been somewhat limited. This is not surprising in view of the relatively short time that the social sciences have existed. It seems safe to predict that more extensive application of existing and subsequent findings will be made in the future.

The pure-applied dichotomy can be illustrated as follows:

Pure Science	*Related Applied Science*
Astronomy	Navigation
Botany	Agriculture
Chemistry	Pharmacy
Geology	Engineering (petroleum)
Physics	Engineering
Physiology	Medicine
Sociology	Administration, social work, diplomacy, city planning
Zoology	Animal husbandry

Utility of Social Science

We already know a great deal more about man and his social relationships than most people in our casually patterned society are willing to use.

—HADLEY CANTRIL[3]

Reprinted with permission of the author and publisher from Glenn M. Vernon, *Human Interaction: An Introduction to Sociology*. Copyright © 1965 The Ronald Press Company, New York, pp. 7–12.

[1] Samuel A. Stouffer, "Some Observations on Study Design," *The American Journal of Sociology*, LV, No. 4 (January, 1950), 356.

[2] The pure-applied distinction is not as clear as it may appear in this discussion. See, for instance, the President's Science Advisory Committee, "Scientific Progress, the Universities and The Federal Government" (Washington, D. C.: Government Printing Office, 1960). For a discussion of clinical sociology, see James B. Taylor and William R. Catton, Jr., "Technical Problems of Clinical Sociology," *Sociological Inquiry*, XXXIII, No. 1 (Winter, 1963), 34–44.

[3] Hadley Cantril, "Don't Blame it on 'Human Nature'!" in John F. Cuber and Peggy B. Harroff, *Readings in Sociology* (New York: Appleton-Century-Crofts, 1962), p. 137.

Sociology, as the student will be exposed to it in this text, falls in the category of pure science. Our goal is to gain understanding of human interaction, or of man's social behavior. We are seeking knowledge, not treatment. The text is not designed to provide direct answers to the problems which beset society. The student who seeks such answers will not find them here. The information gained through such a study, however, can be utilized by anyone who does want to bring about social changes or to "improve" society.

In making this distinction, or in laying out our course of study in this way, we are not suggesting that one approach (pure or applied) is better than the other. All we are doing is establishing a division of labor and indicating what the "role" (to use a term to which we will return for extended discussion) of the pure scientist is.

Sociology then is a study of what *is*, not what *ought to be*. We are concerned only with trying to understand why human beings relate themselves to other human beings the way they do. We are not at all concerned with whether this is "as it should be."

Sociology and common experience

When we label sociology a scientific discipline we emphasize a crucial characteristic. While we have not as yet clearly stated what is specifically involved in the scientific method, it is desirable at this point to distinguish between scientific sociology and common experience or common sense. Our major purpose is to emphasize that these two are far from identical.

One of the basic premises of sociology, which will be explored in detail later, is that different individuals and/or groups may each view the same phenomenon in different ways, depending upon the experiences that each has had. The sociologist frequently views or interprets behavior quite differently from the commonly accepted views—or from common sense. Sociological interpretation and common-sense interpretation may sometimes harmonize, but they may also be contradictory. This need not necessarily disturb the student when he understands how the contradictory answers are derived. We should not in fact be surprised that different methods do not always produce identical results.

Let us look briefly at some of the characteristics of common sense. Common sense is frequently given a vague and over-simplified expression. Many popular sayings are of this type, but are repeated by some individuals as though they represent unqualified universal truths. Note, for instance, the following contradictory adages:

> Look before you leap.
> He who hesitates is lost.
>
> Repeat a lie often enough and people will believe it.
> Truth will prevail.
>
> Out of sight, out of mind.
> Absence makes the heart grow fonder.
>
> East is east, west is west, and never the twain shall meet.
> We're all brothers under the skin.
>
> You can't make a silk purse out of a sow's ear.
> Clothes make the man.
>
> Opposites attract.
> Birds of a feather flock together.

The sociologist as scientist attempts to qualify his statements, specifying, for instance, under what conditions opposites tend to attract and under what conditions "birds of a feather flock together." The student in his study of sociology should develop the habit of asking himself and others the question, "Under what conditions is such and such true?" (This may not help his popularity on campus if he does it too often in social intercourse but this further indicates the differences between sociology and common sense.) In most interaction those involved do not want to be as specific as does the sociologist. To be so would, they feel, impose limitations upon their behavior that would make them uncomfortable. Common sense, then, facilitates certain types of interaction.

Common sense may contain many beliefs that are false according to scientific information. At one time it was widely believed that the world was flat; this, however, did not make the world flat. That people have believed something for years and acted accordingly does not make the belief scientifically true. The fact that early Americans doubted that the average female—because of her "innate inferiority"—could do

Common Sense

It is common sense that leads us to think that the earth is flat; that two plumb lines are parallel (they are both directed toward the center of the earth and consequently form an angle); that motion in a straight line exists; which is absolutely false as we have to take into consideration not only the motion of the earth around its axis and around the sun, and that of the entire orbit of the earth, but also the motion of the whole solar system toward the constellation Hercules, etc. As a result a bullet, or an airplane, which seems to move in a straight line with respect to the earth, for a certain length of time, in reality follows a trajectory more closely resembling a kind of corkscrew with respect to a vaster system of reference, the nearest star, for instance. Common sense tells us that the edge of a razor blade is a continuous straight line, but if we examine it under a microscope it resembles the wavy line drawn by a child. Common sense tells us that a piece of steel is solid; X-rays show us that it is porous, and the modern theories of matter teach us that it is in reality made up of trillions of animated, miniature universes having extraordinary rapid movements and no contact with each other.

—PIERRE LECOMTE DU NOUY[4]

[4] Pierre Lecomte du Nouy, *Human Destiny* (New York: David McKay Co., Inc., 1947), pp. 5–6.

college work as well as the average male did not prove the innate (biological) inferiority of the female.

Sociology is not the same as common sense. Sociologists provide scientific checks for common sense. Many people, however, may not want such checks. Sociologists may, in fact, get into "hot water" when they challenge beliefs that have been widely accepted.

The distinction between common sense and sociological sense becomes clearer when it is recognized that "experience with" something does not necessarily produce scientific knowledge about this something even though "experience with" may have built up a store of common sense answers.

Since there are any number of things one might know about man's behavior and any number of ways of gaining such information (or information about anything else, for that matter), it follows that all experiences do not produce the same knowledge. Studying man scientifically is a unique experience. Because Citizen Jones has had considerable experience with upper-class people, it does not follow that he necessarily has scientific knowledge about them. On another level, the fact that Housewife Jones has had experience with electric refrigerators does not make her an electrical engineer. She may, in fact, have had years of experience with refrigerators without ever really understanding very much about refrigeration. Co-ed Jones is not necessarily an authority on mechanics just because she has had long experience of one type or another with cars. The fact that an individual has had considerable experience with a minority group, say, the American Indians, does not mean that his understanding of Indians is a scientific one. Ample evidence indicates that individuals with much experience with certain types of people may, in fact, believe many things about their behavior that are quite contrary to scientific findings. It is likewise true that having had extensive experience with yourself does not mean that you have scientific knowledge about yourself. The student who goes through a college course in sociology or psychology may find that his interpretations of his own behavior change considerably as he progresses through this study.

If our premise about the relationships between science and common sense is true, the typical student can anticipate having some of his beliefs about human behavior challenged and others confirmed. When such contradictions arise, the student should approach the situation with the questions: "How does the author of this text support his premise?" "What proof is there on this issue?" One of the basic purposes of science is to provide individuals who have conflicting views with a method of resolving their differences, so long as these differences apply to an area to which the scientific method is applicable.

To repeat, the scientific study of human behavior is a unique experience. To have had many non-scientific experiences with people does not qualify a person as a *scientific* student of human behavior. Becoming a social scientist is a long, difficult process.

Revised Maxims

Penny wise is inflation foolish.

Waste not and there will be no work.

A dollar saved is a quarter earned.

Honesty is the best policy without general coverage.

What goes up must come down—if it can solve the re-entry problem.

If Detroit had meant people to walk, it would have manufactured shoes.

Eyesight is only skin-deep.

Why start at the bottom of the ladder? Take the escalator.

A rolling stone gathers no pension.

Early to bed and early to rise, probably indicates unskilled employment.

A taxpayer and his money are soon parted.

—JOHN CIARDI[5]

HOW TO READ A TABLE / *W. Allen Wallis and Harry V. Roberts*

Information can be packed into a table like sardines into a can, and if you cannot read a table, it is as if you had a can of sardines but no key. Ordinary reading ability is no more effective in reading a table than an ordinary can opener in opening a can of sardines, and if you go at it with a hammer and chisel you are likely to mutilate the contents.

We will try to extract information from Table 270 about the association of illiteracy with age, color, and sex. We urge that before you read further you study Table 270 and jot down your own conclusions in the sequence in which you reach them.

You will not extract any information from the table if you continue to divert your gaze from it in embarrassed bewilderment. Don't stare at it blankly, either—focus your eyes and pick out some detail that is meaningful, then another, then compare them, then look for similar comparisons, and soon you'll know what the table says.

There are at least two good reasons for learning to read tables. The first is that once the reading of tables is mastered (and this does not take long), the reader's time is greatly economized by reversing the usual procedure, that is, by studying the tables carefully and then just skimming the text to see if there is anything there that is not evident in the tables, or not in them

[5] John Ciardi, *Saturday Review* (May 26, 1962), 194. Used with permission.

Reprinted with permission of the authors and The Free Press from W. Allen Wallis and Harry V. Roberts, *Statistics: A New Approach.* Copyright 1956 by The Free Press, pp. 270–278. The first part of the book is available as a paperback, *The Nature of Statistics,* same publisher.

EXAMPLE 270 ILLITERACY

TABLE 270. Illiteracy rates, by age, color, and sex, 1952

Based on a sample of about 25,000. Persons unable both to read and to write in any language were classified as illiterate, except that literacy was assumed for all who had completed 6 or more years of school. Only the civilian, noninstitutional population 14 years of age and over is included.

Age (years)	PERCENT ILLITERATE								
	White			Nonwhite			Both colors		
	Male	Female	Both	Male	Female	Both	Male	Female	Both
14 to 24	1.2	0.5	0.8	7.2	1.4	3.9	1.8	0.6	1.2
25 to 34	0.8	0.6	0.7	9.7	3.8	6.4	1.6	0.9	1.2
35 to 44	1.2	0.5	0.8	7.5	5.9	6.6	1.7	1.0	1.3
45 to 54	2.2	1.4	1.8	12.8	10.4	11.5	3.2	2.3	2.7
55 to 64	3.6	3.4	3.5	19.4	16.9	18.1	4.7	4.4	4.5
65 and over	5.6	4.4	5.0	35.8	31.2	33.3	7.6	6.2	6.9
14 and over	2.1	1.5	1.8	12.7	8.2	10.2	3.0	2.1	2.5

SOURCE: *Statistical Abstract: 1955,* Table 132, p. 115. Original source: Bureau of the Census. *Current Population Reports,* Series P-20, No. 45.

at all. This not only saves time but often results in a better understanding: a verbal description of any but the simplest statistical relationship is usually hard to follow, and besides, authors sometimes misrepresent or overlook important facts in their own tables. A second reason for learning to read tables is that users of research can better describe the data needed to answer their administrative or scientific problems if they can specify the types of tables needed, and this requires an understanding of tables. Research workers, in turn, can plan investigations more effectively if they visualize in advance the statistical tables needed to answer the general questions that motivate the research.

Consider, then, Table 270. By following a systematic procedure it is possible to grasp quickly the information presented. Here are the main steps:

(1) *Read the title carefully.* One of the most common mistakes in reading tables is to try to gather from a hit or miss perusal of the body of the table what the table is really about. A good title tells precisely what the table contains. In this case, the title shows that the table tells about illiteracy, in relation to age, color, and sex, in 1952, and that the data are presented as rates—percent illiterate.

(2) *Read the headnote or other explanation carefully.* In the headnote to Table 270 we get a more precise indication of the basis for classifying people as illiterate. We see, in fact, that the rates are slightly too low because it was taken for granted that any person who had completed six or more years of school was literate; but it is reasonable to suppose that the error from this source is negligible. We note also that the mentally deficient, criminals, and others in institutions have been excluded, as have the armed forces, so that the data relate to people in everyday civilian life. Finally, we note that the data are based on a sample, so we make a mental note not to attach too much importance to any single figure, or difference between figures, without first looking up the sampling error.

Information of the kind given in the headnote of Table 270 is often not attached directly to the table, but must be sought elsewhere in the text. Those who prepare reports that include statistical tables should, but frequently do not, keep in mind not only the reader who reads straight through the report without putting it down, but also the user making a quick search for a specific piece of information.

(3) *Notice the source.* Is the original source likely to be reliable? In this case, the answer is definitely "yes," for the Bureau of the Census is one of the most competent statistical agencies in the world. The secondary source, the *Statistical Abstract,* is a model of its kind. But *you* are getting the data from a tertiary source, this book. What about its reliability? Unless you have checked some of our previous data against their sources, you really do not know about that, and even if you did it would be a mistake to put complete reliance on the data without verifying them.[1] Of course *we* assure you of our reliability; but we would not trust your infallibility, or even our own, no matter who gave us assurances.

(4) *Look at the footnotes.* Maybe some of them affect the data you will study. Sometimes a footnote applies to every figure in a row, column, or section, but not every figure to which it applies has a footnote symbol.

(5) *Find out what units are used.* Reading thousands as millions or as units is not uncommon. Long tons can be confused with short tons or metric tons, meters with yards, degrees with radians (as in Example 82A), U. S. with Imperial gallons, nautical with statute miles, rates per 1,000 with rates per 100,000, "4-inch boards" with boards 4 inches wide,[2] fluid ounces with

[1] Please let us know of the inaccuracies you find, here or elsewhere in this book.

[2] A "4-inch board" is 3¾ inches wide, the 4 inches referring to the width of the rough lumber.

A useful compilation of units in common use is *World Weights and Measures: Handbook for Statisticians,* prepared by the Statistical Office of the United Nations in collaboration with the Food and Agriculture Organization of the United Nations (provisional ed.; New York: United Nations, 1955).

ounces avoirdupois, and so on. In Table 270 illiteracy is expressed in percent—incidence per 100—and age in years.

The foregoing steps are, in a sense, all for preliminary orientation before settling down to our real purpose—as a dog turns around two or three times before settling down for a nap. They do not take long, and ought to be habitual, but if you omit them you may suffer a rude awakening later—or never awaken at all.

(6) *Look at the over-all average.* The illiteracy rate for all ages, both colors, and both sexes—the whole population, in other words—is shown in the lower right hand corner of Table 270 as 2.5 percent, or one person in 40. This may surprise you, for probably not one in 400 and perhaps not even one in 4,000 of your acquaintances 14 years of age or older is illiterate. On a matter like this, for a country of 165 million people and three million square miles, neither one's own impressions nor the consensus of one's friends' impressions is valid.

(7) *See what variability there is.* It is quickly evident that there are percentages less than 1 and more than 30 in the table. There is, therefore, extraordinary variation in illiteracy among the 24 basic groups into which the population has been divided (two sexes, two colors, six age classes).

(8) *See how the average is associated with each of the main criteria of classification.*

(a) *Age.* Looking in the section for "both colors" and down the column for "both" sexes, we see that the illiteracy rate is essentially constant at about 1¼ percent from ages 14 to 44, but then rises sharply through the remainder of the age classes to a rate in the highest age class 5.7 percentage points larger than, and 5¾ times as large as, the rate in the lowest age class. (Avoid phrases such as "illiteracy increases with age," which suggest that given individuals change as they age.)

At this point, some competent table-readers, especially if they were particularly interested in the association between age and illiteracy, would pursue this path further. We shall, however, complete our survey of the gross associations with the three variables, then take up each in detail. Probably neither route has any general advantage over the other.

(b) *Sex.* In the "both colors" section, comparison of the entries at the bottoms of the "male" and "female" columns, which apply to all ages, shows that the illiteracy rate for males (3.0 percent) is over 40 percent larger than that for females (2.1 percent). In view of our finding about age, we make a mental note to consider the possibility that this is merely the association with age showing up again in the guise of a sex difference, through the medium of a difference in the age distributions of the sexes. Correspondingly, we make a note to check on the possibility that the apparent association with age is due to differences in the sex ratio at different ages. More generally, we recognize that the associations with age and sex may be *confounded*, that is, mixed together in what looks like an association with age and an association with sex.

The idea of confounding is important enough for a digression. Suppose illiteracy rates by sex and age were:

Age	*Male*	*Female*	*Both Sexes*
Young	1.0	1.0	1.0
Old	10.0	10.0	10.0

These hypothetical illiteracy rates are identical for young males and young females. They are also identical for old males and old females. But they differ greatly between the young and the old. In other words, there is a strong relation between age and illiteracy, but none at all between sex and illiteracy. Now suppose that the frequencies are as shown below:

Age	*Male*	*Female*
Young	100	300
Old	200	100

The over-all illiteracy rate for males would be (see Sec. 7.4.2)

$$\tfrac{1}{3} \times 1.0 + \tfrac{2}{3} \times 10.0 = 7.0;$$

for females it would be

$$\tfrac{3}{4} \times 1.0 + \tfrac{1}{4} \times 10.0 = 3.25.$$

Males show a higher over-all illiteracy rate, simply because relatively more of the males are old and the illiteracy rate is higher for the old of either sex. In such a case, the age and sex effects are said to be *confounded*. That is, what is really an age effect appears in the totals as a sex effect, because the age effect has had a different influence on the two sexes due to their different age distributions.

It is usual in statistics to refer to an association with, say, age, as an "age effect," or as the "effect of age," without intending the cause-and-effect implication that this term tends to carry in ordinary usage. All that is meant in statistics is association, and we will use the term "effect" that way.

(c) *Color.* To see the effect of color, we compare the entries at the bottoms of the "both" sexes columns in the "white" and "nonwhite" sections, and find the nonwhite rate (10.2 percent) to be 5⅝ times the white rate (1.8 percent). Again, however, we resolve to investigate possible confounding of all three effects.

The main effects, then, seem to be that *illiteracy rates are higher for older people, for males, and for nonwhites.*

(9) *Examine the consistency of the over-all effects and the interactions among them.*

(a) *Age.* The increase of illiteracy with age holds separately for whites and nonwhites. Some difference in detail does appear. For one thing, the nonwhite rate is not constant from ages 14 to 34, but is noticeably lower from 14 to 24. More conspicuous, the increase from the lowest to the highest age class is much larger for nonwhites than for whites: the differences are 29.4 percent and 4.2 percent, and the ratios[3] 8.5 and 6.2.

[3] Ratios are not very satisfactory for describing changes in percentages unless the percentages remain small, because of the fixed upper bound of 100. The nonwhite rate of 33.3 percent at 65 years and over, for example, could not be multiplied by

Thus, it appears that age has a greater effect on illiteracy for nonwhites than for whites. For the two sexes, on the other hand, age has about the same effect, as measured by the absolute change (5.8 percent for males and 5.6 percent for females) from the lowest to the highest age class; since females have a lower rate, this makes the ratio higher for females (10.3) than for males (4.2).

A still more careful study of the table would test whether these conclusions hold if we compare, say, the next-to-lowest age class with the next-to-highest (the conclusions are the same), thus guarding against aberrations in individual rates.

Before we italicize these conclusions derived from comparing the separate section totals, let us see whether they hold within sections, that is for each sex of a color, or for each color of a sex. Here, for the first time, we use the real core of the table, the rates for the 24 basic cells. Heretofore we have used only data combined by age, by sex, or by color, or by two of these, or (in step 6) by all three.

First, compare the males of the two colors. Then compare the females. Both comparisons confirm the conclusion that *the increases in illiteracy associated with increases in age are greater for nonwhites than for whites* and that *they are about the same for males as for females.* These statements are equivalent to saying that *the excess of nonwhite over white illiteracy rates is greater in the older age classes* and that *the difference between the sexes is not systematically related to age.*

(b) *Sex.* Similar detailed study leads to the conclusion that *the excess of the male over the female rate is higher for nonwhites than for whites.* Put the other way around, this says that *the difference between the colors is larger for males than for females.*

(c) *Color.* Our conclusions about the interaction between color and sex and between color and age have already been recorded in discussing age and sex.

(10) *Finally, look for things you weren't looking for—aberrations, anomalies, or irregularities.* The most interesting irregularity that we have noticed in Table 270 is in the age class 25–34. For white males this is below—in fact, one-third below—the rates for the preceding and following age classes. For the nonwhite males, however, the rate is above that of the adjacent age classes by about one-third. (The white females also show a higher rate in this age class than in the adjacent ones, but only by 0.1, which might be almost all due to rounding the figures to the nearest tenth of a percent, and in any case is less than the necessary allowance for sampling error.) In attempting to form a plausible conjecture to explain this peculiarity, we first note that the period when this age class was at ages 6 to 8, and therefore learning to read and write, was 1924 to 1935. This suggests nothing to us, though it might to an expert on the subject matter. As a second stab, we note that during the period of World War II, 1942–45, this age class was 15 to 27 years old. It is, therefore, the group that provided the bulk of the armed forces. This lead seems worth investigating. Did the armed forces teach many illiterates to read and write? If so, did this affect white males more than nonwhite? Even so, why would the rate for nonwhite males be increased? Could it be that mortality among whites was higher for illiterates than for literates, but for nonwhites the reverse? We should be surprised if any of these is the explanation, but investigating them would probably lead us to the explanation. A possible explanation, of course, is that the aberration is due to sampling error, or even clerical or printing error, and that the search for substantive explanations would be in vain. But such anomalies are often worth pursuing; this is one of the secrets of serendipity, from which the most fruitful findings of research often result. We would certainly pursue these questions if we were investigating illiteracy instead of explaining how to read a table.

In summary, then, here is what can be read from Table 270, and in considerably less time than it has taken us to tell about it:

Illiteracy in 1952 among the civilian, noninstitutional population 14 years of age and older—

- (i) Averaged 2.5 percent.
- (ii) Varied greatly with age, color, and sex.
- (iii) Was higher at the higher ages, for nonwhites, and for males, with
  - (a) the age differences larger for nonwhites—that is the color differences larger at the higher ages;
  - (b) the sex difference larger for nonwhites—that is, the color differences larger for males;
  - (c) no interaction between age and sex.
- (iv) Was, in the 25–34 year age class, anomalously lower for white males, but higher for colored males, than in the age classes just above and just below.

Example 277 Brains and Beauty at Berkeley

Repeating the same steps as in reading Table 270, we find at stage 8 that grades are higher in later years in college and with poorer appearance (which, to repeat earlier warnings, does not necessarily mean that given coeds get better grades as they progress in college or regress in appearance). At stage 9, however, we find it necessary to introduce such strong qualifications to the appearance effect as almost to withdraw the finding. All we can say is that for juniors grades decrease with better appearance, but for seniors and graduate students there is no systematic relation. The main effect of appearance is partly a manifestation of the year-in-college effect, in conjunction with different distributions by appearance for the three college classes.

• • •

Since the appearance effect is not present for the seniors or graduates, we conclude that its presence for all classes combined reflects partly the effect for the

8.5 again. Furthermore, the ratios depend on which percentage is used, that for occurrences or that for nonoccurrences. The literacy rates corresponding with the illiteracy rates mentioned in the text, while they have the same numerical differences as the illiteracy rates, have the ratios 1.44 and 1.04.

TABLE 277. Mean grades of college women, by appearance and year in college

Data on 643 women students of the University of California who had completed two or more years of college, classified by beauty of face. Grades averaged by scoring *A* as 3, *B* as 2, *C* as 1, *D* as 0, *E* or *F* as — 1. Frequencies on which averages are based are shown in Table 280.

Year	Homely	Plain	Good looking	Beautiful	All appearances
Junior	1.58	1.45	1.34	1.16	1.37
Senior	1.56	1.52	1.45	1.57	1.50
Graduate	1.67	1.70	1.70	1.53	1.68
All years	1.62	1.56	1.44	1.42	1.51

SOURCE: S. J. Holmes and C. E. Hatch, "Personal Appearance as Related to Scholastic Records and Marriage Selection in College Women," *Human Biology,* Vol. 10 (1938), pp. 65–76. The means shown here have been recomputed from the original data, loaned by the authors, and in a few instances differ by one unit in the last decimal place from those given in the source.

juniors and partly confounding of the class effect—that is, heavier representation in some appearance groups than in others of those classes which receive low grades. It would be possible for the appearance effect to work in one direction in all three classes, but in the opposite direction for all classes combined. For the data of Table 277 this is only barely possible, since no set of weights will result in a mean outside the range of the individual means. For the beautiful mean to exceed the homely mean, for example, virtually all of the beautiful and all of the homely would have to be seniors.

In interpreting data of this kind it is necessary to keep in mind selective factors that have determined whether individuals are available for such a sample. This is discussed in Sec. 9.4. The possibilities in connection with Table 277 are varied.

• • •

SOCIAL CHARACTERISTICS OF COLLEGE STUDENTS / *Raymond A. Mulligan*

The culture theory of class conceives of social classes as selected cultural groupings, which give to their members a similar stock of ideas, values, feelings, attitudes, and forms of behavior. It recognizes the fact that people live, work, play, and think on different class levels. The differences between classes are not merely financial or external planes of living, but they encompass the entire range of social behavior: occupation, vocation, manner of speaking, social and sexual attitudes, musical and literary tastes, and philosophy of life.

According to this theory, the culture of the lower classes obstructs the educational development of their children. The home background tends to make them critical of, or unsympathetic to, the idea of education and emphasizes the importance of going to work and contributing to the family's income at an early age. Immediate financial returns are given priority over present sacrifices for possible future gains. The culture of these classes determines to a considerable degree definitions that are unfavorable for a higher education.[1]

Nevertheless, a certain proportion of the children from the lower classes reaches college.[2] These socially mobile students have neither acquiesced in their class status nor accepted unfavorable definitions of a higher education. They have at least one thing in common with students from the other social classes in being enrolled in institutions of higher learning.

If college students from the lower socio-economic groups are atypical in their behavior, according to the culture theory of class, by attending institutions of higher learning, one wonders if they might not also deviate from their socio-economic group norm in other social characteristics. For example, do college students from the lower socio-economic groups come from the same size families as students from the upper socio-economic groups, and do they have similar religious backgrounds? McConnell[3] reports that lower class husbands have less education than their wives, and upper class husbands have more education than their wives. Would similar educational differentials be found among the parents of college students; and lastly, is there any association between rural-urban and geographical location of college students' homes and socio-economic background? The present study is an attempt to shed some light on the above questions by analyzing the socio-economic backgrounds of students at an institution of higher learning. The following data were compiled in an effort to test the hypothesis that there is no relationship between the socio-economic background of college students and family size, parental education, religion, or residence.

Reprinted with permission of the author and publisher from *American Sociological Review,* 18 (June, 1953), pp. 305–310.

[1] See James Bossard, *The Sociology of Child Development,* 1948, pp. 284–286 and 303–306.

[2] See R. Centers, "Education and Occupational Mobility," *American Sociological Review,* 14 (February, 1949), pp. 143–144; E. Havemann and R. West, *They Went to College,* 1952, p. 27; and R. Mulligan, "Social Mobility and Higher Education," *The Journal of Educational Sociology,* 25 (April, 1952), pp. 476–487, and "Socio-Economic Background and College Enrollment," *American Sociological Review,* 16 (April, 1961), pp. 188–196.

[3] J. W. McConnell, *The Evolution of Social Classes,* 1942.

Procedure

Data for the study were collected from the personnel information forms of students in the office of the Registrar at Indiana University. These forms are filled out by the individual students during registration. Only the personnel forms of male students who were in attendance at the university during the second semester of the academic year of 1946–47 were included in the study. A twenty per cent sample of the male students was secured by selecting every fifth male personnel information form alphabetically. A sample of 1,444 cases was obtained.

Occupation of the students' fathers was used as an index of socio-economic background. The classification of gainful workers into socio-economic groups developed by Edwards[4] was used for this purpose.

Findings

Number of children. Table 1 presents the number and percentage of children in the families from which the male students come, by socio-economic background. The professional and other proprietory groups on the average have the smallest families, 2.8 children, and the unskilled group has the largest, 4.3 children. The white collar groups (professional, business, and clerical) average 2.8 children per family, the blue collar groups (skilled, semi-skilled, and unskilled) average 3.6 children, and the farmers (owners and tenants) average 4 children. Excluding the farmers from Edwards' socio-economic groups, an inverse ratio exists between socio-economic background and the number of children in the families from which the students come. Many studies have established the fact that an inverse ratio exists between socio-economic background and the number of children in a family.[5] It thus appears that these relationships are also true of the families of male students who attend Indiana University.

Religion. Among the students reporting on their church associations, over 68.0 per cent classified themselves as Protestant, 11.8 per cent Roman Catholic, and 6.4 per cent Jewish.

A larger proportion of professional men, farmers, and clerks is found among the Protestant fathers than among the Catholic or Jewish fathers (Table 2). The largest proportion of business men is found among the Jews, whereas the highest proportion of skilled, semi-skilled, and unskilled labor is found among the Catholics. Approximately 79.0 per cent of the Jews come from the white collar groups, 56.4 per cent of the Protestants, and 44.2 per cent of the Catholics. Close to 11.0 per cent of the Protestant fathers are farmers, 5.3 per cent of the Catholics, and none of the Jews.

Consideration was also given to the size of families in relation to religious affiliation. Of the 1,444 students involved in the sample, 1,247 identified themselves as belonging to one of three religious categories. Table 2 indicates that the average family size of the 170 students classifying themselves as Catholic is 3.9 children. Among the Catholics, the professional group's average family size is the smallest, 2.9 children, and the farming and unskilled groups average the largest, 6.3 children. Among the Catholics, also, the white collar groups average 3.4 children, and the blue collar groups 4.6 children.

One may also calculate the average family size of Protestant students from the data presented in Table 2. The average family size is 3.0 children. Among the Protestants, the wholesale group's average family size is the smallest, 2.4 children, and the unskilled group the largest, 4.0 children. The Protestant white collar groups average 2.6 children, the blue collar groups 3.3 children, and the farming group averages 3.8 children.

The average family size of the 93 students classifying themselves as Jewish is 2.6 children. Among the Jewish students, the white collar groups average 2.6 children, and the blue collar groups 2.5 children. The latter average is not very reliable as it is based on only seventeen cases.

Although the Catholics on the average have the largest size families, 3.9 children, the Jews have the smallest average difference between the average size of their white collar families and blue collar families, —0.1. The Protestant families have an average difference of 0.7 children between their white collar and blue collar groups, and the Catholics have an average difference of 1.2 children. Stated somewhat differently, the blue collar Catholic families average over 35.0 per cent more children than the white collar Catholic families; the blue collar Protestant families average over 26.9 per cent more children than the white collar Protestant families, and the white collar Jewish families average 4.0 per cent more children than the blue collar Jewish families.

Rural-urban differences. Table 3 contains the percentage of students residing in rural-urban localities, by socio-economic group. It is evident from this table that the proportion of students belonging to the farming group decreases as the population of the rural-urban localities decreases. On the other hand, the proportion of students from the skilled group increases as population increases.

In all of the rural-urban settings the proportion of students from the white collar groups exceeds that of the blue collar groups. The smallest difference between these two categories occurs in the rural-farm setting where only 2.7 per cent separates the two groups. The largest difference occurs in the small-town rural-urban setting where the difference amounts to 34.9 per cent (white collar 63.8 per cent and blue collar 28.9 per cent).

The proportion of blue collar students increases as population increases up to 500,000. The proportion of white collar students increases from 25.9 per cent in the rural-farm setting to 64.0 per cent in the large city setting. However, for the intervening population set-

[4] Alba M. Edwards, *Comparative Occupation Statistics, U. S. 1870–1940, 16th Census,* United States Bureau of Census, 1943, p. 179.

[5] Paul H. Landis, *Population Problems,* 1943, pp. 106–125.

TABLE 1. Percentage of children in families of male students compared with percentage of male students by socio-economic group and indices, Indiana University, semester II, 1947

Socio-economic group	CHILDREN Number	CHILDREN Per cent	STUDENTS Number	STUDENTS Per cent	Index[a]	Mean
Professional	582	12.7	211	14.6	87	2.8
Farmers	506	11.1	127	8.8	126	4.0
Wholesale and retail dealers	499	10.9	175	12.1	90	2.9
Other proprietors	473	10.3	171	11.8	87	2.8
Clerical and kindred workers	723	15.8	257	17.8	89	2.8
Skilled	844	18.5	251	17.4	106	3.4
Semi-skilled	300	6.6	87	6.0	110	3.4
Unskilled	388	8.5	92	6.4	133	4.3
Unknown	257	5.6	73	5.1	110	3.6
Total	4572	100.0	1444	100.0		3.17

[a] The index is a measure of representation such that 100 would indicate a uniform distribution of socio-economic groups for both the proportion of children and the proportion of students. Therefore, an index of 87 shows that the professional group is under-represented by 13 per cent in the child population, as contrasted with the expected proportion from the student population.

Chi square is 22.02; P is less than 0.01.

TABLE 2. Percentage of children in Catholic, Protestant, and Jewish families of male students by socio-economic group, Indiana University, semester II, 1947

Socio-economic group	CATHOLIC Children	CATHOLIC Students	PROTESTANT Children	PROTESTANT Students	JEWISH Children	JEWISH Students
Professional	7.5	10.0	14.1	15.1	12.4	14.0
Farmers	8.6	5.3	13.5	10.8	0.0	0.0
Wholesale and retail dealers	11.7	11.2	7.9	10.1	39.3	34.3
Other proprietors	8.6	11.2	9.5	11.2	16.1	17.1
Clerical and kindred workers	10.7	11.8	17.5	20.0	12.4	14.0
Skilled	29.0	25.2	16.6	16.6	14.5	12.9
Semi-skilled	9.8	10.6	6.4	5.6	1.7	3.3
Unskilled	12.3	7.6	7.8	5.9	1.7	2.2
Unknown	1.8	7.1	6.5	4.7	2.1	2.2
Total percentages	100.0	100.0	100.0	100.0	100.0	100.0
Number of cases	666	170	2969	984	242	93

Chi square is 475.87; P is less than 0.001.

TABLE 3. Percentage of male students residing in rural-urban localities by socio-economic group, Indiana University, semester II, 1947

Socio-economic Group	RF	RNF	ST	MDT	CTS	LCTY
	RURAL-URBAN LOCALITIES[a]					
Professional	8.6	13.4	18.6	13.5	13.8	14.8
Farmers	45.7	13.8	3.6	2.0	1.6	0.0
Wholesale and retail dealers	4.0	17.7	12.3	13.1	11.2	11.5
Other proprietors	4.0	9.9	12.0	18.0	11.2	16.4
Clerical and kindred workers	9.3	15.1	20.9	16.3	19.9	21.3
Skilled	12.6	13.4	17.5	18.4	20.2	24.6
Semi-skilled	3.3	6.0	6.4	6.1	6.4	8.2
Unskilled	7.3	7.9	5.0	5.3	9.0	1.6
Unknown	5.3	4.4	3.6	7.3	6.7	1.6
Total percentages	100.0	100.0	100.0	100.0	100.0	100.0
Number of cases	151	232	440	245	312	61

[a] RF, Rural farm; RNF, Rural non-farm; ST, Small town (2,500–25,000 population); MDT, Middle-sized town (25,000–100,000); CTS, Cities (100,000–500,000); LCTY, Large cities (500,000 and over).

tings, the percentage of white collar students fluctuates from 56.1 per cent to 63.8, through 60.8 to 56.1.

Geographical differences. In the present study the geographical distribution of the students' homes by states was also examined.

Table 4 gives the socio-economic distribution of students with residence in Indiana and of students with residence in other states. The white collar groups in either category send more students to the university than do the blue collar groups. A larger proportion of out-of-state students comes from the white collar groups than in-state students. On the other hand, a larger proportion of in-state students comes from the blue collar groups than out-of-state students. The latter situation is also true of the farming group.

TABLE 4. Percentage of male in-state students compared with the percentage of out-of-state students by socio-economic group, Indiana University, semester II, 1947

Socio-economic group	Indiana	Out-of-state[a]
Professional	13.9	16.1
Farmers	9.4	5.1
Wholesale and retail dealers	12.4	11.1
Other proprietors	11.2	15.4
Clerical and kindred workers	17.2	20.9
Skilled	17.9	15.7
Semi-skilled	6.2	5.5
Unskilled	6.4	5.9
Unknown	5.4	4.3
Total percentages	100.0	100.0
Number of cases	1178	254

[a] Does not include foreign students.

A further analysis of the geographical distribution of the out-of-state students' homes was made by dividing the United States into two zones. All states contiguous to Indiana (Michigan, Ohio, Kentucky, and Illinois) were placed in Zone I. All other states with the exception of Indiana were placed in Zone II.

If one compares the socio-economic distribution of students with residence in Indiana with the students from states in Zone I, and Zone II (Zone I has approximately 8.0 per cent of the students, Zone II, approximately 10.0 per cent, and Indiana 80.8 per cent), it is found that the proportion of students from the white collar groups increases from 54.7 per cent in Indiana to 61.8 per cent in Zone I, to 64.0 per cent in Zone II. The proportion of students from the farming group decreases from 9.4 per cent in Indiana to 5.1 per cent in Zone I and Zone II. The proportion of students from the blue collar groups decreases from 30.5 per cent in Indiana to 27.9 per cent in Zone I, and to 26.4 per cent in Zone II.

From the above analysis it appears that the proportion of students from the white collar groups increases as the distance, when measured by states, of their homes from the university increases. On the other hand, the proportion of students from the blue collar groups decreases as the distance of their homes from the university increases. Goetsch[6] found a similar relationship between parental income and the distance students travel to an institution of higher learning. Her data reveal that the median parental income of youth who pursued a higher education in Milwaukee was 1,604 dollars; of youth who went outside of Milwaukee but remained in Wisconsin, 2,571 dollars; and of youth who went outside of Wisconsin, 3,125 dollars.

Parental education. If one considers the educational background of the students' fathers it is found that over 86.0 per cent of the professional fathers attended college, whereas only 5.4 per cent of the unskilled fathers had such an experience. Excluding the farming group, 15.7 per cent of which attended college, the proportion of fathers in each socio-economic group with college experience decreases as one moves down the socio-economic scale as follows: professional—86.7 per cent; business—66.0 per cent; clerical—26.5 per cent; skilled—12.0 per cent; semi-skilled—8.0 per cent; and, unskilled—5.4 per cent. Out of the 123 fathers who attended graduate school 102, or 82.9 per cent, belonged to the professional group.

Approximately 69.0 per cent of the professional fathers graduated from college, whereas only 1.1 per cent of the unskilled fathers, and only 3.2 per cent of the farmers completed college. The proportion of fathers in each socio-economic group having college degrees decreases as one moves down the socio-economic scale, if one excludes the farmers, as follows: professional—69.2 per cent; business—24.8 per cent; clerical—14.0 per cent; skilled—2.8 per cent; semi-skilled—1.1 per cent; unskilled—1.1 per cent. Of all the professional fathers who attended college over 80.0 per cent graduated. Only 20.0 per cent of all the unskilled fathers who attended college graduated.

It appears from the above analysis that the white collar groups have more education, by far, than the blue collar groups. However, the findings in respect to the educational achievement of the students' fathers are almost tautological. Edwards' classification of gainful workers into socio-economic groups is based on the criteria of educational achievement and amount of income.[7] Knowing this, one would obviously expect to find a close relationship between Edwards' socio-economic groups and the educational attainment of the students' fathers.

If one analyzes the educational background of the students' mothers, it is found that 55.0 per cent of the mothers in the professional group attended college. On the other hand, only 9.8 per cent of the students' mothers in the unskilled group attended college. The percentages of mothers in the other socio-economic groups who attended college are as follows: farmers—16.6 per cent; business—58.5 per cent; clerical—28.5 per cent; skilled—10.8 per cent and, semi-skilled—12.5 per cent.

[6] Helen B. Goetsch, *Parental Income and College Opportunities,* Teachers College Contributions to Education No. 795, Columbia University, 1940.

[7] See Edwards, *op. cit.,* p. 181.

Of all the mothers from the professional group, 28.4 per cent graduated from college. On the other hand, only 0.8 per cent of the mothers from the skilled group, and 1.1 per cent of the mothers from the unskilled group graduated from college. Of the twelve mothers who attended graduate school, seven, or 58.3 per cent, are members of the professional group. None of the mothers from the blue collar groups attended graduate school. In the professional group, of all the students' mothers who attended college, over 50.0 per cent graduated, whereas only 11.2 per cent of the mothers from the unskilled group who attended college graduated.

If one compares the educational backgrounds of the students' parents by college experience the following is found among the various socio-economic groups:

(1) Approximately 31.0 per cent more professional fathers than mothers attended college; 7.5 per cent more fathers from the business groups than mothers attended college; and, 1.2 per cent more fathers from the skilled group than mothers attended college.

(2) Among the parents from the farming, clerical, semi-skilled, and unskilled groups, the mothers exceed the fathers in college attendance in each of the respective socio-economic groups by the following percentages: 1.1, 2.0, 4.5, and 4.4.

(3) In all the socio-economic groups more fathers than mothers graduated from college with the exception of the unskilled and semi-skilled groups. In the unskilled group the percentage of mothers who graduated from college is matched by the percentage of fathers (1.1 per cent). In the unskilled group 1.1 per cent more mothers than fathers graduated from college.

Summary

(1) Excluding the farmers from Edwards' socio-economic groups, an inverse ratio is found between socio-economic group and the number of children in the families from which the male students at Indiana University come.

(2) The differential between blue collar and white collar family size is found to be largest among the Catholic students' families and smallest among the Jewish students' families.

(3) The differential between the proportion of students' fathers who come from the white collar groups and the proportion of students' fathers who come from the blue collar groups is smallest among the Catholics (0.7 per cent), largest among the Jews (61.5 per cent), and of median size among the Protestants (28.3 per cent).

(4) In all rural-urban settings the proportion of students from the white collar groups exceeds that of the students from the blue collar groups.

(5) A direct ratio is found between the proportion of students from the blue collar groups and size of city populations, up to a size of 500,000.

(6) The proportion of students from the skilled group increases, and the proportion from the farming group decreases, as population increases.

(7) The proportion of students from the white collar groups increases, and the proportion from the blue collar groups decreases, as distance, when measured by states, of the students' homes from the university increases.

(8) Excluding the farmers from Edwards' scale, a direct ratio is found between the proportion of students' fathers who attended college and socio-economic group.

(9) Parents from the white collar groups have more education than parents from the blue collar groups, as measured by college attendance and college graduation.

(10) Students' fathers in the white collar groups (as a whole) have more education than the mothers, but the students' mothers in the blue collar groups (as a whole) and farming group have more education than the fathers, as measured by college attendance.

Conclusions

(1) The findings of the present limited and localized study do not support the null hypothesis that there is no relationship between the socio-economic background of college students and such social characteristics as family size, parental education, religion, and residence.

(2) Many studies have reported relationships between socio-economic background and various types of social phenomena. Within the limits of the above study, certain of these relationships were, also, found to exist among college students. It thus appears that differentials in specified social characteristics exist between college students from upper and lower socio-economic groups just as it has been reported for socio-economic groups in the population as a whole.

(3) There still exists the possibility, however, that such differentials might be significantly smaller among college students than for the socio-economic groups in the population as a whole. Children from the lower socio-economic groups who reach college may have social characteristics that vary from the averages for their group in the general population in the direction of upper socio-economic group averages. The object of the present study and the nature of the data collected precluded the testing of such a hypothesis. The testing of this hypothesis might very well contribute to our knowledge of the sociology of social mobility through higher education.

Measurement and data analysis II

PROBLEM 1 MEASUREMENT

The article, "Problems and Techniques of Sociology," provides an overview of the research process in sociology. This overview is a necessary basis for understanding the way sociologists go about their research. It should be emphasized, however, that by itself the overview is not sufficient for understanding research. As noted in the introduction, understanding empirical work in sociology can probably best be acquired by carrying out actual research operations. The replications in this book are designed to provide you with such an experience.

This initial laboratory problem on measurement is devoted to the first of the three tasks of science discussed by James A. Quinn, that ". . . of classifying objects or events into categories." If classification can be done objectively and consistently, and, if numbers can be assigned to the categories, then the rudiments of measurement in sociology are established. In this laboratory problem there is the opportunity to engage in a first-hand experience in translating raw observation, that is the observations reported on the questionnaire, into measurements of behavior and belief. All of the subsequent laboratory problems contained in this volume will serve to illustrate the second and third tasks of science listed by Quinn, that of generalizing about the relationships between variables, and understanding their relevance for particular groups.

PROBLEMS AND TECHNIQUES OF SOCIOLOGY / *James A. Quinn*

The definition of sociology as "the general science of human social groups" implies that persons who enter this field should understand not only the kinds of subject matter to be examined (groups, cultures, persons) but also the method of study to be used (scientific). The present chapter considers this method. It reviews the major tasks of scientific method, makes additional comments about basic aspects of this general method, and introduces a few techniques that are used in sociology.

The tasks of scientific method

The tasks of scientific method are related, directly or indirectly, to the study of similarities of various kinds of objects or events. Three such interrelated tasks are considered in this chapter: (1) description of similarities common to all members of a category; (2) formulation and testing of generalizations about repetitive relations among variable features as related to members; and (3) interpretation of single objects or events by use of generalizations.

Reprinted with permission of the author and the publisher from James A. Quinn, *Sociology: A Systematic Analysis*. New York and Philadelphia J. B. Lippincott Company, Copyright © 1963, pp. 375–392.

DESCRIPTION OF SIMILARITIES OF MEMBERS OF A CATEGORY. One of the tasks of scientific method is that of classifying objects or events into categories and of describing the similar characteristics of members of each type. Chemists have divided material substances into categories of elements, each containing atoms that are alike in inner structure but different from those of other elements. They also classify molecules into categories on the basis of the number of various kinds of atoms they embrace (for example, H_2O, or H_2SO_4). And they often characterize categories of complex substances by describing the numbers, kinds, and arrangements of molecules typical of their respective members. Human anatomists and physiologists study similarities of men as biological organisms—including ways in which organs and tissues repeatedly are related to one another in individual bodies, repetitive arrangements of cells within each kind of tissue or organ, or the sorts of processes that operate regularly to produce a typical life-cycle of growth and decay. Sociologists have the task of classifying human social groups into categories and of describing essential similarities common to members of each of them. They divide groups into varieties, such as societies, communities, special-interest associations, families, or cliques; they subdivide larger categories into smaller ones—for example, marriages into monogamous, polygynous, and polyandrous types; and they describe similar characteristics of each variety. Sociologists also describe various processes of change or interaction that recur regularly in groups of a given kind.

Similarities of members of a category do not deny the simultaneous existence of differences among them. Scientists know that members of any category typically differ from one another in certain ways. They take some of these differences into account when distinguishing between varieties of subcategories within a more inclusive one. For example, chemists emphasize similarities common to all kinds of atoms when they contrast these smaller objects with more complex ones such as molecules; but they emphasize differences between atoms when they distinguish between lead, nitrogen, and chlorine. Sociologists emphasize similarities when they characterize human social groups as a broad category of social objects, but they utilize differences among groups as a means of distinguishing between families, gangs, or church congregations.

In contrast with uses of differences such as were described above, scientists ignore many dissimilarities as unimportant. For example, physicists generally pay no attention to contrasts in color, temperature, shape, or type of substance when studying falling bodies. In fact, the law of falling bodies is limited to the statement that, under specified conditions, every kind of physical mass falls at a similar rate and with similar acceleration. In formulating this ideal law these scientists ignore numerous differences that characterize various falling objects, and they limit their attention to the basic similarities common to all of them. Differences do not prevent the use of scientific method in studying objects provided that the latter also exhibit significant similarities. Some of the ways in which scientists deal with differences in members of a category are discussed in subsequent parts of this chapter.

GENERALIZATIONS ABOUT RELATIONS AMONG VARIABLE ASPECTS. One of the major tasks of scientific method, possibly its most important one, is that of comparing variations in two or more characteristics that are related to members of a category. Physicists know that, if other things remain constant, the volume of a gas tends to increase as its temperature rises; that a bar of iron lessens in length as its temperature drops; or that the mechanical force exerted by a moving object is equal to its mass times its velocity. Biologists know that, on the average, within the population of a society, the weight of men increases as their height becomes larger; that beyond certain limits, greater excess of weight is accompanied by shorter length of life; or that rapid increase of certain bacteria within the body is related to a rise in body temperature. Social scientists have observed that, within a free enterprise economy, the price of a commodity tends to go up if demand increases while supply remains constant; that the proportion of face-to-face contacts among members of a society decreases with larger size of population, provided other factors remain unchanged; or that the level of prestige of members of a complex community is significantly related to their degrees of legitimate control over major value satisfactions. In all of these illustrations—physical, biological, social—each of two characteristics varies from member to member, from situation to situation, or from time to time; and as one variable characteristic changes in quantity, the other also tends to change, at least under specified conditions and within certain limits. A major function of scientific method is to formulate and test such generalizations about relations among quantified variables with respect to members of categories of objects or events.

The variable features which are studied by scientists may involve diverse combinations of any or all of the following: (a) numbers and characteristics of individual component units, (b) relations among component parts of a larger unit, or (c) relations to physical or cultural environments.

A slightly different task, although somewhat similar to the one described above, may be mentioned. It involves comparisons of qualitative attributes[1] rather than quantitative variables. For example, biologists and sociologists may study differences between males and females with respect to height, weight, beliefs, incomes, and activities; and they may formulate and test generalizations about ways in which such attributes are related repeatedly to differences in other characteristics of human populations.

The discovery, formulation, and testing of generalizations about the relation among selected variables (or attributes) as related to categories of objects or events constitutes the central task of scientific method. Other tasks of science are either preliminary to this central one or involve applications of the generalizations gained through it. Such generalizations are basic to applied fields of knowledge and practice, such as engineering, medicine, or social casework.

INTERPRETATION OF SINGLE OBJECTS OR EVENTS. Some scientists spend their time in studying and interpreting single objects rather than in testing generalizations about similarities of members of a category. For example, some chemists analyze substances whose composition is unknown. These scholars may be employed by a manufacturing firm to analyze samples of raw materials or to test the quality of manufactured products. An ethnologist may spend his time in studying the

[1] An attribute is a feature that is conceived as differing in quality rather than in quantity. For example, the difference between male and female members of a population ordinarily is counted as a qualitative characteristic (an *attribute*) rather than a quantitative one (a *variable*). Similarly, differences between Jew and Gentile, alien and citizen, or vertebrate and invertebrate usually are regarded as attributes rather than as variables.

characteristics of a single society or tribe; a botanist may be asked to identify individual kinds of plants; or an astronomer may devote years to the study of a single planet.

The scientific study of individual objects is related to knowledge about similarities of members of a category. The chemist, for example, utilizes previously formulated generalizations about categories of chemicals in identifying an unknown substance, and he employs standardized techniques in determining what chemicals are present in it and in what quantities. The ethnologist depends on his previously acquired knowledge about categories of cultural objects and of whole cultures in studying and explaining the structure of and changes in a particular society. Thus some scientists have the task of applying previously tested generalizations and techniques to the interpretation of single objects, and they, themselves, do not undertake to formulate new generalizations or to test the validity of existing ones. The interpretation of single objects through the use of scientific method is an important one, but it necessarily depends on the central task described above.

Thorough studies of individual members of a category, which include aspects that appear unique to a given individual and about which generalizations have not been made, may be valuable in future scientific research in that they suggest bases for further generalizations.

Some basic aspects of scientific procedure

In order to perform the tasks of scientific method listed above, an individual may profit by considering various aspects of scientific procedure. The following pages discuss seven of these aspects as possible guides for beginning students in sociology: (1) selection of general area of inquiry; (2) tentative design of specific study; (3) nature and importance of definitions; (4) holding other factors constant; (5) selection of sample; (6) collection of data; and (7) analysis of data. The last of these topics is expanded in later sections of the chapter, which characterize several widely used techniques.

SELECTION OF GENERAL AREA OF INQUIRY. The volume of fact and theory that has accumulated in each major field of science is so great that few individuals can master all of it. In order to apply scientific procedure in his own research studies, the student ordinarily must restrict attention to a relatively narrow part of a broad field. In sociology, for example, he may limit himself to a specific kind of group such as families, gangs, or special-interest associations; he may study only one specialized aspect of group structure such as stratification or occupational specialization; or he may limit himself to analyzing relations of group structure to persons as members. In any event, a not-too-broad area of inquiry ordinarily must be selected.

After tentatively choosing his general area of study, the student may use the library to locate books or articles that deal with various aspects of it, or he may talk with instructors who are specialists in this field and who can suggest sources of information to him. Then he should read widely to learn what problems already have been attacked, what generalizations have been formulated and tentatively tested, and what data already have been collected. After he has become somewhat familiar with his general field of study, he can proceed more effectively in utilizing scientific procedure in selecting and attacking worthwhile problems.

LIMITED ASPECTS OF PROCEDURE. In carrying out a specific research study that already has been designed, five limited but important aspects of scientific procedure may profitably be kept in mind.

Nature and importance of definitions. Adequate definitions are essential to scientific study, ones that ordinarily go beyond common usage. Such definitions necessarily involve abstraction, that is, they do not include all of the features of the things which are classified together as members of a category. Instead, they are restricted to essential features common to all members. As was indicated previously, when physicists define falling objects they do not describe all of the features of any single object that is falling but only those that characterize every member of the category. Similarly, when zoologists define *men* as a type of organism they do not include all of the observable features of each unique individual but only some of those that characterize all men. Or, when sociologists define *groups* they do not include all qualities of all of the specific families, communities, or classroom groups included in this category. In short, definitions that are useful for science always involve abstraction; they make use of certain selected similarities, and they ignore other aspects of individual members.

For purposes of studying generalizations about relations among variable aspects of a category, definitions are needed both for the category as a whole and for the different variables to be compared. For example, a generalization about relations between size of community and degree of occupational specialization requires definitions of at least three terms—community, size, and occupational specialization.

(1) Definitions of categories. A good definition of a category, at least for purposes of science, enables students both to identify its members and to exclude all nonmembers.

Ordinarily, only a few characteristics are necessary in order to identify members of a category. These characteristics ideally are exhibited by all members. As defined in this text for example, all *cultural objects* are characterized by three qualities: they are (a) transmissable by language, (b) shared by members of a group, and (c) significantly shaped by man. Or, all human social groups are characterized by having (a) two or more component parts, (b) interdependence among member parts, (c) roles-played-by-members as gross components, (d) language communication among members, and (e) a distinguishable structure that exhibits qualities different from those of its individual components.

Any object that exhibits the respective features listed above may properly be identified either as a cultural object or a human social group.

In order to exclude objects that are not members of a category, the list of similar features embraced by a definition should be sufficiently complete and discriminating that only members can qualify. Any object that lacks one of the essential defining features is not counted as a member. The preceding definition of cultural objects meets this test in that any object that lacks any one of the three basic features is excluded from this category. The task of constructing a definition so that all nonmembers can be excluded, however, is often quite difficult.

Even after a definition of a category has been formulated, the decision as to whether a given object should be included in it is often difficult to make, especially if some of the identifying characteristics are variables rather than attributes. For example, if a chair is defined as an article of furniture, normally utilized for seating one person and having a back rest, it might be hard to decide whether a particular object is a chair or a stool (without a back rest). How high must a back be in order to qualify this object as a chair—twelve inches, six inches, one inch, one-tenth inch? Some articles of furniture may fall on the borderline so that they cannot with certainty be included in or excluded from a given category. In actual research, especially in its early stages, it is often desirable to concentrate on members that unquestionably belong to a category and to exclude those that are on the margin.

(2) Definition of a variable. Variables require definitions that involve some degree of quantification—that is, some judgment about the degree to which one object or event exhibits more or less of a given characteristic. For example, a number of sticks can be *ranked* in order of their *length* without using a measure such as inches or centimeters. Similarly, people or occupations can be ranked in order of *prestige*. It is important to remember, however, that such ranking indicates only that one object is higher or lower, larger or smaller than another, and not the amount by which they differ. A second variety of quantification involves the *enumeration* of discrete units. For example, the size of population of a community may be determined by counting the number of people who reside there, with every resident counted as equal without regard to his age, sex, size, or race. Thus communities may be compared with respect to the size of population. A third kind of quantification involves the *measurement* of some continuous variable by using a standard measuring device with equal intervals. For example, the height of members of a population may be measured by using a foot-inch scale or their weight by employing a pound-ounce scale. Because such variables are continuous, individual objects may be located at any point along a scale, and such objects are not divisible into distinctly separate categories as are discrete ones.

Exact characterization of the nature of certain basic variables is difficult in that the underlying qualities are hard to define. For example, height, length, mass, life, prestige, or intelligence are hard to define so that the variable quality can be measured. In fact, scientists ordinarily utilize only *operational definitions* in defining variables. Such definitions involve the use of standardized procedures, which are described and which result in similar repetitive observations. The scientist then defines the variable as that quality which this standard scale presumably measures. For example, psychologists often define intelligence as that quality which is measured by the use of certain standard operations or procedures, or physicists define electricity as the force which underlies changes in standardized instruments of a particular kind. Such definitions are valid for purposes of science if they produce results that can be repeated time and again and if they lead to increased understanding and control of a category of objects. Whatever kind of definition of a variable quality is used, however, it must be quantifiable (and preferably measurable) by use of some kind of standard repeatable operations.

Holding other factors constant. In laboratory studies a research student can keep certain influences relatively constant or unchanging while he deliberately modifies one variable and observes accompanying changes in another. For example, a bacteriologist who believes that three variable factors—temperature, light, acidity—significantly affect the speed of growth of a strain of bacteria can keep light and acidity constant while he modifies the temperature and observes accompanying changes in rate of growth; or he can hold temperature and light constant as he varies the degree of acidity, and so on. In the relay-assembly experiment conducted in the plant of the Western Electric Company changes in the rate of production of a team of six women were observed before and after controlled changes were made in various aspects of work conditions—from hourly wages to piece work, introduction of rest periods, snacks during rest periods, shorter working hours, and the like. Meanwhile, factors such as personnel, working quarters, and illumination were held constant. As previously described, however, one unknown major variable in this latter study, a social one, was not held constant by the scholars who designed this study, with the result that some quite unexpected results were obtained.

A second device for holding other factors constant involves the use of two or more samples of population which are selected as essentially similar with respect to certain characteristics. For example, zoologists sometimes utilize samples of white rats that have had similar heredity for several generations and that have been reared under similar conditions up to the time of the experiment. Thus they attempt to hold heredity and previous environmental factors constant by utilizing samples that are similar in these respects. Then they introduce a specified influence (for example, a kind of drug, a type of bacteria, or a different sort of food) into the lives of members of one sample (the experimental one) but not the other (the control sample), and they observe whether members of the former change in ways or degrees significantly different from the latter. Several of the experiments cited in earlier chapters utilize this means of holding other factors constant. For example, two samples which presumably were similar with respect to several essential characteristics were utilized in the illumination experiment, communication experiments, the study of competition and cooperation, and the study of the influences of democratic and authoritarian control.

A third means of dealing with other factors is to make allowance for their influence through mathematical computations. For example, a demographer who wants to interpret changes in the death rate of a community for two periods of time can make allowance for differences of population composition. If he wants to compare the death rate for 1960 with that of 1930, he can allow for changes in age and sex composition. To do so, he calculates the percentage of population of males and females for each age as actually reported in 1930. He redistributes the population of 1960 so that each age-sex category contains the same percentage of population as was reported in 1930. He applies the actual death rates, as reported for each age-sex category in 1960, to the population of that year as redistributed to make it comparable with 1930. He thus can determine what the death rate in 1960 would have been if the age-sex composition of the population had remained constant. If a significant difference in earlier and later death rates exists after the influences of age and sex composition have been taken into account, he can design further studies to determine how it is related to selected other variables.

Selection of a sample. Many scientific research projects, probably most of them, do not observe the entire population of a category but only a fraction of it (a sample). For example, a botanist who designs an experiment to study relations between nitrogen and the growth of red clover does not study all of the atoms of nitrogen in relation to all of the plants of this variety. Instead, he restricts his observation and experimentation to a fraction of the total, that is, to a sample. Similarly, persons who study the population of a society often utilize samples from which they infer characteristics of the whole. Or persons who study opinions, customs, or groups often observe only a fraction of the total category about which information is desired.

In order for scholars to make reliable inferences about a population by observing a sample, they must take care to insure that the latter accurately represents the larger universe (population). This can be done most reliably if every member of the population has an equal chance of being included in the sample. If, for example, the names (or identifying numbers) of every member of the total population were sealed in identical capsules and placed in a huge mixing machine and if these capsules should drop one at a time from a small opening until an adequate number were obtained, then this sample would be likely to represent the total population. This kind of sample is known as a *random*, or *probability*, sample. The size necessary to obtain a given degree of accuracy can be calculated mathematically, and its probable error (due to sampling error alone) also can be computed.

Sometimes a sample may be stratified—that is, the total population is divided into subcategories that seem to be significant, and the sample chosen so as to draw the proper proportion from each subclass. Within each subcategory, however, members should have equal chance of being chosen. A stratified sample sometimes is easier to obtain than a completely random one, and it can be designed and manipulated so that small subcategories can be represented more accurately without distorting the representativeness of the total sample.

A random sample is not a hit-or-miss one such as might be obtained by interviewing people on a street or by walking through a neighborhood and ringing doorbells here and there. Obtaining such a sample requires strict adherence to certain rules laid down by statisticians, and it involves careful consideration of the population to be studied. It is not likely that one can obtain a representative sample of the total population of a city by selecting names from a telephone directory, in that families without telephones would have no chance of being included, or by taking lists of taxpayers or registered voters because those not on such lists could not be selected. It would not be accurate to interview a single resident at each tenth house, in that a family which lives in an apartment building would have less chance of being chosen than one which lives in a single-family home. The techniques of obtaining an adequate sample are not explained here, but they can be learned in specialized courses in methods of research. It is sufficient here to emphasize the need for obtaining a representative sample and to indicate that it involves great care and adequate technical training.

Collection of data. One of the features of scientific procedure is the collection of repeatedly observable data to test hypotheses that have been formulated. Procedures for doing so, like that of obtaining an adequate sample, are subject to many possibilities of error and misuse. Mastering them ordinarily requires considerable formal training. It may be useful, however, to describe some of the ways in which social scientists obtain their data.

Scientists either make observations or ask questions. Astronomers observe the positions of heavenly bodies through telescopes; chemists weigh or measure various substances, mix them together, and observe the results; physicists use instruments to determine indirectly the action of electric currents; biologists look at the structure or the behavior of living organisms; psychologists watch the actions of rats in a maze or observe their progress in solving problems; economists record fluctuations in prices and employment; and demographers utilize census data obtained through asking questions of members of a population.

Sociologists also obtain their original data either through asking questions or observing the overt behavior of members of a group. A few general illustrations may be adequate for present purposes: Questions may be asked and answers recorded in various ways. (1) A research worker may prepare a *questionnaire* that he distributes to members of a sample. It contains questions that the respondents are requested to answer before returning the document to the researcher. These questions may either offer the respondent a list of several optional replies, so he may indicate the one he prefers, or contain spaces in which he will write his own replies. Questionnaires may be administered as tests in certain kinds of experimental studies. (2) A research worker may prepare a *schedule*, which is then placed in the hands of a trained field worker or interviewer. This worker asks questions of individual members of the sample about items covered in the schedule, and he rather than the respondent records the replies. The United States Bureau of the Census uses the schedule as a tool in collecting decennial population data. (3) Interviewers may talk at length to individual members of a sample. They may guide the conversations so as to obtain elusive data or permit the respondents to talk at random without such guidance. Sometimes an interviewer may ask a variety of questions on various topics, with members of the sample not fully aware of the specific points the researcher is trying to cover. These and other devices for asking questions may be combined in various ways depending on the nature of the research project.

Contrasting kinds of question asking techniques have different values. The questionnaire, which may be distributed by mail, does not require the services of field workers, and ordinarily costs less. The respondents can answer at their convenience and can consider their replies at length. Unfortunately, many members of a sample, usually a great majority of them, fail to reply even after receiving follow-up requests; and the research worker dare not assume that those who do reply are representative of the population. Moreover, if a respondent does not fully understand a question, he cannot ask for further guidance before making his reply. A schedule has the advantage of permitting the field worker to give further explanation or to ask additional questions in order to obtain more pertinent and complete information; but unless the data are simple and factual, the additional discussion may bias the replies. Extended interviewing permits examination of shades of attitudes and beliefs that cannot be readily reduced to schedule or questionnaire form. It also enables the interviewer to explore and evaluate qualities that are not consciously realized by the informant or fully understood by him. It is time consuming and expensive.

The types of questions to be asked and the variety of choices open for reply also differ considerably. In general those that ask for choices from a list of answers are more easily analyzed by statistical procedures, but they often do not permit the respondent to give precisely the answers he prefers. In contrast, questions that do not require standardized replies and that encourage expression of different shades of beliefs, opinions, and attitudes may be more revealing; but they are more difficult to obtain and interpret, and they usually must be restricted to smaller samples.

Sociologists may observe directly the behavior of individuals or groups, including their verbal behavior. For example, they may watch members of a group through a one-way glass (that is, a glass through which the observer can see the subjects but cannot be seen by them), or as participant observers they may record their findings in various ways by taking notes while they are making observations, by writing up their observations from memory after they leave the group, or by using wire or tape recordings or motion picture films. The latter are extremely valuable in that they enable the researcher to re-examine the situation repeatedly and they allow other scholars to hear or view the reproduction. Such data often are difficult to reduce to reliable quantitative form so that they can be used to test generalizations about relations among variables.

Analysis of data. After data have been collected and recorded, they must be analyzed by appropriate techniques in order to test generalizations. Some of the techniques widely used in sociology are described and illustrated in subsequent parts of this chapter—(a) those useful in describing single categories and in comparing two or more of them, (b) those applicable to studying relations among variable aspects of structures, and (c) those useful in studying changes.

WARNING: VARIOUS ASPECTS OF PROCEDURE INTERMINGLE. The limited aspects of scientific procedure, as discussed above, do not necessarily occur in a simple time sequence. Instead, certain of them may be reviewed and altered in the course of a research study. It is possible, for example, to further refine definitions as subsequent collection and analysis of data indicate weaknesses in the starting ones. Or, it may be desirable to modify the design of the study in order to facilitate holding other factors constant or to make use of additional techniques of analysis. In other words, all of the various aspects of scientific procedure are to be kept in mind throughout much of the entire research project, and they may be reviewed and revised at various times consistent with the finding of more adequate results.

DIFFICULTIES OF APPLICATION TO SOCIOLOGY. The application of scientific method in sociology involves some difficulties that are not encountered in equal degree in most physical and biological sciences. These difficulties inhere both in the character and complexity of the subject matter and in limitations on the use of manipulative laboratory experimentation.

Nature of subject matter. Because the subject matter of sociology is neither physical nor organic in character, it ordinarily cannot be observed directly through the senses as can physical masses, chemical elements, or living plants and animals. Much of the subject matter of sociology has no length, weight, color, odor, taste, or speed of movement, such as may be observed by physicists or zoologists. Moreover, such subject matter involves meanings that are transmissible through abstract symbols, and these symbols do not necessarily resemble the objects or events that can be observed. The meanings that underlie the social behavior of groups and persons cannot be observed directly, at least not by known techniques; and they must be inferred from observations of the behavior of individuals or groups or the manifestations of culture.

The necessity for utilizing inferences with respect to important kinds of objects or events is not restricted to the social sciences but is characteristic to some degree of physical and biological ones. Physicists do not observe electricity directly but only indirectly through its manifestations—for example, a flash of lightning, the light of an electric bulb, the tendency for pith balls to attract or repel each other, or changes in an ammeter or voltmeter. They do not observe gravity except indirectly through the behavior of physical masses in relation to one another. Zoologists do not observe *life* directly but infer it from changes in the structure and the behavior of living organisms. Similarly, sociologists do not observe directly the meanings involved in language or in social interaction, but they infer such meanings from the repetitive behavior of persons in association with one another. In making their inferences, however, sociologists face certain difficulties not experienced by scientists, in that meanings differ from society to society, from subgroup to subgroup within a society, and within one person from situation to situation.

Limitations on manipulative experiments. A high percentage of the experiments performed by physicists, chemists, and zoologists are conducted in laboratories where they can "hold constant" many of the factors that otherwise would influence their results and they can manipulate selected variables they wish to study. In contrast, sociologists cannot bring large-scale societies and associations into laboratories; and often they cannot formally manipulate the variables they desire to study. Moreover, if they bring families or other small groups into laboratories, they are likely to change the meaningful situation in which these groups operate, thus obtaining data different from those of ordinary conditions. For such reasons, sociologists ordinarily study groups outside of laboratory situations, which practice makes more difficult the tasks of holding other factors constant and of manipulating variables for experimental purposes.

Sociologists sometimes observe groups systematically, and they deliberately change selected variables in order to study their influences, as was illustrated by the "relay-assembly" experiment. They find, however, that they often overlook highly important variables that depend on meaning. For example, when members of a group become conscious of themselves as important parts of an experiment, they tend to act differently than they otherwise would. Consequently, conclusions derived from such experimental situations often cannot be applied with confidence to groups in nonlaboratory settings.

An additional difficulty with experimentation in sociology arises from the possibility that members of the experimental sample may be damaged. This difficulty does not matter greatly in physics or chemistry where the experimenter can injure or destroy his sample without too great loss. But sociologists dare not use experimentation to test the hypothesis that extreme isolation hinders the development of full human characteristics because, by doing so, the experimenter would risk serious injury to infants as members of his experimental sample.

Difficulties such as those mentioned above do not deny the possibility or the desirability of using scientific method in sociology; they only emphasize some of the difficulties of doing so. These difficulties afford challenges to the ingenuity of research workers in this field, but they do not deny the usefulness of this method in studying groups and cultures.

Techniques for describing and comparing categories

To the extent that scientific method involves something more than purely qualitative descriptions of members of a category, it makes use of various techniques and concepts that involve quantification. This section of the chapter describes briefly some of the statistical tools that are useful in characterizing the membership of categories and in comparing one category with another.

AVERAGES. When members of a group or a category differ from one another with respect to some variable characteristic, an average sometimes is used to describe these populations. For example, the people of one community may be described as having an average age of thirty years, whereas another averages forty years.

Statisticians make use of three kinds of averages—mean, median, mode—each of which may be superior under certain conditions but of less value in other instances.

The mean. The best known average, the mean, is calculated by adding the amount of any measured characteristic of all members of the population and then dividing this sum by the number of members.

Use of the mean requires that a measuring scale be used in which the units are equal (for example, pounds, inches, dollars) and that every member of the population be measured and included. It cannot be computed with accuracy except under these conditions. Once it has been determined, however, it affords a basis for certain other comparisons of categories which cannot be made by use of the median or the mode.

The median. The median represents the amount (value) of a variable quality characteristic of the middle member in a population that has been ranked from highest to lowest on the basis of this variable.

The mode. The mode represents that value of a variable characteristic which occurs most frequently among the members of a population. This average is the value that characterizes a greater number of members of the population than does any other. It often seems misleading to many people in that it may represent the highest, the lowest, or any in-between value on the variable scale.

Contrasting values of different averages. The three averages described above are not equally useful in de-

DISTRIBUTION OF 60 BOYS, BY WEIGHT

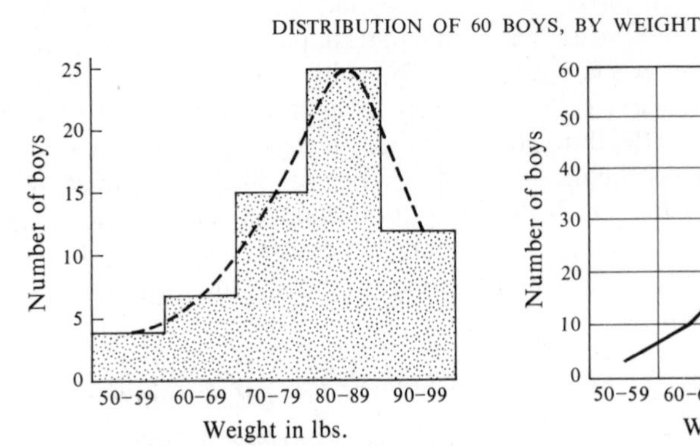

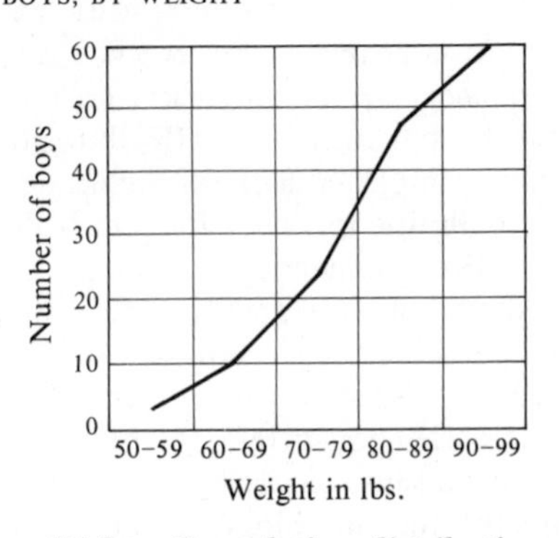

FIGURE 1. Left: Frequency distribution. Right: Cumulative distribution.

scribing the population of every category. If, for example, ten out of eleven boys have a weekly allowance of $1 each, but the other one has $45 per week, the mean would be $5. This figure does not give a very useful picture of allowances in this group. In this case it might be better to use the mode, ($1) in that ten out of eleven boys receive this amount; or possibly the median in that the middle-ranked boy also receives an allowance of $1. If, however, six boys of this population of eleven receive $1 per week, whereas five others receive $10, the median would be as misleading as the mode. Some distributions may be described as bimodal, that is as having two modes—for example, four boys receive $1 each, four others receive $5 each, and three others respectively receive $2, $3, and $4. In utilizing an average to describe or compare categories, research workers need to know which to use, and they also must keep in mind both the precise meaning of each, and the consequent limitations on its usefulness and applicability. In any event, an average never describes accurately the population of a category unless all members are identical—in which case an average is not necessary.

DISTRIBUTIONS WITHIN A CATEGORY. When a scientist wishes to gain a somewhat simplified description of a category but an average is not adequate for his purposes, he may utilize various devices for picturing the distribution of members.

One-variable distributions. When only one variable characteristic is taken into account, the population of a category may be divided into subcategories and the number in each counted. Assume, for example, that a population of sixty boys is weighed and distributed by weight into ten-pound subcategories, as shown in Table 1. These data can be as shown in Figure 1. The diagram of rectangles of different heights (a *histogram*) shows graphically the distribution of boys as distributed by subcategories, as does the smoothed curve that represents it. The curve of cumulative distribution shows the total number of boys whose weight is equal to or less than that of each successive subcategory. Tables and diagrams of these kinds are quite useful for showing more about the weights of members of this population than does any average, and yet they are much simpler to compile than a complete list of individual weights of each boy in it. Such devices also permit rough comparisons of two populations.

TABLE 1. Distribution of 60 boys, by weight

Weight in pounds	Number of boys in Subcategory	Cumulative distribution
90–99	12	60
80–89	24	48
70–79	14	24
60–69	7	10
50–59	3	3

One particular kind of distribution, known as *normal distribution*, represented by a curve of the shape shown in Figure 2, is extremely important in statistical analysis.

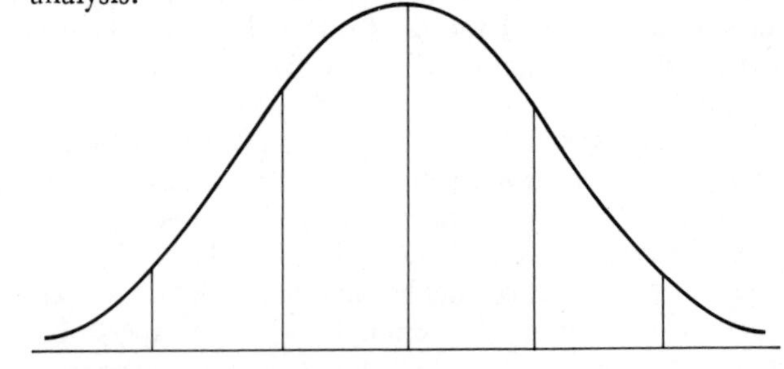

FIGURE 2. A normal distribution curve.

Two-variable distributions. Sometimes the population of a category is measured (or ranked) on the basis of two (or more) variables. When each member of the population is placed in the proper class with respect to each variable, the distribution of the total may be described as in Table 2. From this table, one may learn, for example, that among the seven boys who were 70–79 pounds in weight, one was 50–51 inches, three were 52–53 inches, two were 54–55 inches, and one was 56–57 inches. Tables showing two variable dis-

TABLE 2. Distribution of 60 boys by height and weight

		Height in inches				
Weight in pounds	Total	50–51	52–53	54–55	56–57	58–59
100–09	12	—	—	—	3	9
90–99	24	—	—	5	13	6
80–89	14	—	1	6	6	1
70–79	7	1	3	2	1	—
60–69	3	1	2	—	—	—
Total	60	2	6	13	23	16

tributions have been used in preceding chapters, especially those dealing with limited aspects of group structure. The data shown in the preceding table, when arranged in a scatter diagram, (Figure 3), enable an individual to see at a glance how individual members of this population were distributed by height and weight. Rough devices such as these afford bases for additional techniques as explained subsequently.

MEASURES OF VARIABILITY. Scientists often need measures of the degree to which members of a population differ from one another or vary from an average. They utilize measures such as *range*, *semi-interquartile range*, *average deviation*, *standard deviation*, and *variance*, which enable them to compare populations more accurately.

Range and semi-interquartile range. The range, used in relation to a one-variable distribution, equals the difference between the largest and smallest member as measured with respect to this variable. Thus, the assumed range of weight of the population of sixty boys described in Table 2 would be forty-seven pounds if the lightest one weighed sixty-one pounds and the heaviest one 108 pounds.

If a population is ranked with respect to height or weight and divided into quarters, then the points between the first and second quarters, and between the third and fourth ones embrace half of this population between them. The difference between the smallest and largest member of this central half of the population is the semi-interquartile range. This device measures the degree to which half of the population tends to cluster close to the median, and it may be used for comparing two groups with respect to their degree of variability.

Average and standard deviation. Some or all members of a category ordinarily differ in some degree from the average (mean) with respect to a given variable. For example, most of the sixty boys described in Table 1 differ from the mean weight of members of this sample. If the difference from the mean weight is measured for each boy, the mean of these individual differences is the average deviation. Thus, a population with an average deviation of five pounds is more like the average than is one with an average deviation of ten pounds. The average deviation combined with the mean gives a better picture of the category than does either measure alone.

In computing the standard deviation, the difference between each member and the mean is measured and squared. The sum of these squared deviations is then divided by the number of observations less one. The square root of this quotient is taken, and the result equals the standard deviation. This device is mathematically correct in that it does not allow negative deviations (less than the mean) to cancel out positive ones (more than the mean). The standard deviation gives greater emphasis to larger individual deviations from the mean than does average deviation, and it is more frequently used in statistical analyses.

The standard deviation may be used in describing the distribution of attributes in which each member of a population can have a value of either zero (not possessing the quality) or 1 (possessing the quality). It also may be applied within certain limits to populations that have been ranked, rather than measured accurately. It is especially important, however, when applied to populations that exhibit a "normal curve" of distribution in that a given percentage of the population ideally falls within (or outside of) a range of two times the standard deviation, and another given percentage within a range of three times the standard deviation.

Variance. Another highly useful measure of variability is merely the standard deviation squared—that is, variance. It may be employed in studying certain aspects of relations among variables. If a population is distributed among categories (cells) with respect to two variables, a comparison of deviation within cells and between cells aids in determining whether the distribution either occurred by chance or indicates that the variables are significantly related.

Measures of variability, such as those listed above, permit the scientist to describe populations of categories or groups more accurately than can be done by use of mere averages. When combined with averages they permit certain quantitative comparisons of populations that otherwise would be impossible. They also provide a basis for some techniques used in analyzing relations among variables.

Techniques of studying relations among variables

Two techniques that are widely used by scientists in studying relations among variable characteristics may be characterized briefly—Chi square (X^2) and correlation.

THE CHI SQUARE TEST. The X^2 test affords a means of determining the probability that an observed distribution of two attributes results from pure chance. It enables the research scholar to compute the number of times a given distribution would occur by random chance in a given number of samples similar to the one analyzed. If the distribution would have occurred

Weight in lbs.	Total	Height in inches				
90–99	12				I I I	I I I I I I I I I
80–89	24			I I I I I	I I I I I I I I I I I I I	I I I I I I
70–79	14		I	I I I I I I	I I I I I I	I
60–69	7	I	I I I	I I	I	
50–59	3	I	I I			
Total	60	2	6	13	23	16

FIGURE 3.

by chance no more than five times out of 100 samples the *null hypothesis* ordinarily may be rejected (that is, the hypothesis that the distribution resulted from chance), and the two variables may be regarded as significantly related.

Assume, for example, that a research scholar wishes to know whether the amount of money income of heads of families is significantly related to their graduation from high school. He selects a random sample of 200 such individuals and learns through interviews (a) the annual income of each and (b) whether he graduated from high school. Through preliminary analysis he discovers that 160 members graduated from high school and that 40 failed to do so. He also divides the population into higher and lower income categories of 100 members each. If the sample is representative and if income and education levels are not related, he would expect that approximately 80 persons of each income level would have graduated from high school and that 20 would not have graduated. If, however, his data show that 90 of 100 higher income persons as contrasted with 70 of 100 lower income ones actually had graduated, he also would want to know whether the difference was enough to be significant. By applying the proper statistical procedures to these data he could compute the X^2 value as 12.50. He could then use a standard table of X^2 values to learn that this observed distribution probably would have occurred by chance no more than five times in 100 similar samples. He would conclude, therefore, that income and level of education seem to vary together significantly and are due to reasons other than chance.

In preceding chapters several studies were cited that utilized X^2 as a basis for analyzing the probability that certain variables are related. For example, Hollingshead used this technique in testing the conclusion that clique and friendship relations are closely related to class position. Several studies dealing with communication and interaction also used this statistical device.

CORRELATIONS. Scientists often use techniques of correlation to calculate the degree to which two variable characteristics increase or decrease together. For example, they may use a correlation technique to determine the degree to which the weight of growing boys increases as their height becomes greater, as indicated by data given in Table 2. Such data consist of pairs of observations (height and weight) for each individual member of each subcategory. The observations are of the sort that can be arranged in a quantitative order. Collectively, they can be represented graphically by a curve of some sort (including a straight line).

The coefficient of correlation—r. This device measures the closeness of relation between changes in one variable, A, and corresponding changes in a second variable, B. The coefficient ranges from a value of +1.0, through 0, to a value of −1.0. If the two variables are perfectly associated so that any increase (or decrease) in A is accompanied by a proportional change in the same direction in B, the coefficient of correlation is +1.0. If, however, an increase in A invariably is accompanied by a proportional decrease in B (an *inverse* relation), the coefficient is −1.0. If differences in the two are not related, that is, if variations in one are not accompanied by corresponding changes in the other, the coefficient of correlation is 0. The closeness of the degree of association is indicated by the size of the coefficient, being closer as it approaches ±1.0. The point at which this measure indicates a significant degree of association is not identical from one research study to another, but unless stated to the contrary, it ordinarily may be counted as somewhat significant at ±.25, quite significant at ±.50, and highly significant above ±.67.

The coefficient of correlation is extremely useful when used to analyze measured data, in that it specifies both the amount and the direction of the relation between variables. But it also has certain limitations and shortcomings. It applies only to straight-line distributions and does not allow for the curvature of some distributions that do not fit straight lines. More important, however, it does not enable the research scholar to make mathematical allowance for other factors that possibly should be held constant.

Other correlation techniques. Four additional kinds of correlations may be mentioned briefly. (a) The *rank order coefficient* (symbol, r^1) may be used to test relations between observations of pairs of ranks. Because ranks do not require measurement by equal-interval scales, but involve only a distinction between greater or lesser values of a variable, this measure may be used when techniques such as the coefficient correlation are not appropriate. (b) The *correlation ratio* symbol, η, is useful in studying measured distributions that fit curved rather than straight lines. It ranges only from 0 to +1.0 and, therefore, does not distinguish between direct and inverse relations as does the coefficient of correlation. (c) *Multiple correlation* techniques permit the analysis of relations between one variable and a combination of several other variables taken together. (d) *Partial correlation* enables a research scholar to study, in turn, each of a cluster of several variables as related to an *independent* one, meanwhile holding constant each of the other dependent variables of the cluster.

Studies of changes in categories

Two preceding sections of this chapter have introduced a few techniques used in describing categories and in analyzing relations between variables, especially as observed at a given time. These techniques also may be applied to the study of changes that occur in time.

DESCRIPTIONS OF TRENDS IN AVERAGES AND DISTRIBUTIONS. Changes in the population of a group may be studied by comparing averages or degrees of variability at different periods of time. For example, changes in the size or the median age of the population of the United States may be compared by decades. Or changes in its population composition may be shown by a series of graphs or by comparison of a time series of population pyramids. Similarly, changes may be described in any variable aspect of a population or a group for which quantitative data are available at different times—for example, occupational specialization, income, mobility, net reproduction rate, spatial patterns, opinions, and so on.

A few special techniques have been developed for studying changes in averages or distributions—for example, *index numbers.* This device uses a particular period of time as a base and compares data from other periods with it. For example, a price index for selected commodities may be constructed by computing the average (mean) price for specified amounts of them during the years 1940–1944 and by using this average as equal to 100. Another period may be compared by computing its prices for these same commodities and calculating its ratio according to that of the base period. If, for example, the average price for these commodities was 21 per cent higher in 1951 than in 1940–1944 the index number would be 121 for this year.

CHANGES IN RELATIONS AMONG VARIABLES. Changes in relations between variable aspects of a population or a group may be studied by comparing them at different periods of time. This kind of research is especially adapted to groups that can be studied experimentally, particularly when one or more variables may be manipulated according to plan. It is extremely valuable in searching for causal relations in which one aspect may be modified at will, so that it will bring about desired changes in another (provided enough other factors remain constant). Studies of this type, when successful, afford valuable clues to the use of scientific generalizations in applied fields such as engineering, medicine, and social work.

Brief evaluation

This chapter on scientific method undertakes to do the following. (a) It emphasizes the essential tasks of scientific study, thus indicating how sociology, as a science, differs from social work and social reform. (b) It stresses the importance of accurate generalizations about members of categories of objects or events, statements that can be retested time and again because they are based on similarities (within given limits) and which may be applied in understanding members and perhaps in practical control of them. (c) It emphasizes the importance of exactness—in constructing definitions, in designing research studies, and in selecting adequate samples. (d) It suggests the importance of understanding a variety of techniques by which certain factors are held constant or otherwise taken into account while others vary and by use of which reliable and adequate data can be collected. (e) It describes something of the considerable stock of techniques that currently are available to sociologists and suggests the existence of many others. (f) And it warns that much additional study, far beyond the limits of an introductory course, is necessary in order to do effective work in this field. Possibly this chapter performs an additional function not previously stated—that of challenging some sincere and capable students to explore further this fascinating, important, difficult, and highly rewarding field of study.

Instructions

CODING AND INDEX COMPUTATION

Our objective in this laboratory problem is to convert the information recorded in the questionnaire into quantitative form. Quantification is desirable for most types of scientific research since it permits us to use statistics to help analyze the data. Statistical analysis is, of course, only one form of analysis, but because of its explicit and objective rules and its precision, it has many advantages, some of which were discussed in the reading for this problem.

When the terms "quantification" or "measurement" are used there is a tendency to think of these in physical terms rather than in behavioral terms. As a result, many people do not see the possibility of quantifying social behavior. But as Quinn's article makes clear, any type of behavior can be measured or quantified. While there are many complicated techniques of measurement, all that is really necessary is a system for "the assignment of numerals to objects or events according to rules" (Kogan, 1960, p. 88). This is the sense in which you will be measuring social behavior in this laboratory assignment.

The set of rules which you will use for this purpose is known as a *code*, and the process of converting the observations to numerical form by means of this set is known as coding. The code we will use starts on page 35. In modern research, coding is almost always designed to fit the data onto punched cards. This lets the researcher use computers and IBM card sorting machines to process the data. Most introductory students in sociology obviously do not have access to computer facilities. Consequently, instead of coding the data onto IBM punched cards, we will code it onto an ordinary 8½ by 11 sheet of paper which has been ruled off into boxes or cells. One item of information (in numerical form, of course) is coded into each box. What is accomplished by this process?

First, all the information from a rather long questionnaire is entered on a single sheet of paper. This is much easier to work with than the original bulky questionnaire. It will enable you to sort and tabulate the set of code sheets in a manner similar to the way IBM cards are sorted and tabulated.

Second, all the data are expressed in unambiguous numerical form. This permits use of simple statistics, such as the mean or average.

Third, in a number of cases a series of observations of the same phenomenon are combined into scales or indexes. This type of quantification usually results in a more reliable and valid measure than a single observation.

Coding instructions

1. Your instructor will shuffle and distribute the questionnaires so that each student codes a questionnaire filled out by some other individual. Coding someone else's questionnaire gives a more realistic coding experience. It also lets you sign your name as a coder, so that your coding work can be checked; at the same time there is anonymity and privacy for the content of the questionnaire.

2. Tear out page 33 which is ruled into numbered boxes and labeled "Code Sheet" (referred to as Coding Worksheet). (Do *not* use the similarly ruled ditto master code sheet at this point.)

3. The numbered boxes on this Coding Worksheet correspond to the numbers in the questionnaire and the code. The code begins on page 35.

4. Before coding, write in the upper left corner box the serial number of the questionnaire you are coding. In the next box to the right you should write today's date, and in the double box next to that, *print* your own name. Now you are ready to start coding the information from the questionnaire into the remaining boxes of the code sheet.

5. Begin coding by writing in box 1 the number of the answer circled in response to question 1. For example, if "Male" is circled you would write a "1" in box 1; if "Female," you would code a "2" in box 1. This is called a "self-coded" item. That is, the answer number is the number to be coded.

6. Question 2 (age) is coded by simply writing the age given on the questionnaire into box 2.

7. Proceed with question 3 which is coded into box 3, question 4 into box 4, etc. up through question 8 which goes into box 8. All of these are "precoded." *However*, questions 9, 10, and 11, and a number of questions from there on are not precoded. For example, in order to code question 9 you will have to make a judgment about the occupation listed in response to this question. Specifically, you will have to decide which of the 7 categories listed in the code best fits the occupation, and then code that number.

8. At various places the code gives directions for calculating indexes. The first of these is based on questions 22a through 22f. These indexes combine the answers to several questions into a summary measure. Such an index is presumably more valid and more reliable than any single item of information. These and other items which might cause difficulty in coding are printed in large letters so that you can easily identify them and take the necessary precautions.

9. Great care should be exercised in coding since all subsequent results depend on the accuracy of the coding. A high level of coding error may spoil your results on later problems.

10. After all coding has been completed, copy what you have from the Coding Worksheet onto the ditto master code sheet which your instructor will give to you. Be sure to remove the protective slip before you

begin. *Write all numbers in* LARGE, *clear, legible figures.* A ball-point pen works very well. A pencil may also be used. But whatever you use, write on a smooth surface and *press hard!* Do not make any unnecessary checks or marks on the ditto master as these will show through.

To correct on the ditto master: (A) Use a razor blade to scrape off from the back of the ditto master the incorrect number. (B) Write in the correct code number *to one side of the original number*, i.e., do not write over the corrected number because the carbon underneath it has already been used.

11. When all numbers have been copied, *replace the protective tissue* and turn in your ditto master code sheet to your instructor. He will have copies made for the class.

References

Festinger, Leon and Daniel Katz, eds., *Research Methods in the Behavioral Sciences*. New York: Dryden Press, 1953.

Francis, Roy G., *The Rhetoric of Science: A Methodological Discussion of the Two-by-Two Table*. Minneapolis: University of Minnesota Press, 1961.

Goode, William J. and Paul K. Hatt, *Methods in Social Research*. New York: McGraw-Hill, 1952.

Kogan, Leonard S., "Principles Of Measurement," in Norman A. Polansky, *Social Work Research*. Chicago: University of Chicago Press, 1960, pp. 87–105.

Riley, Matilda White, *Sociological Research: I. A Case Approach. II. Exercises and Manual*. New York: Harcourt, Brace & World, 1963.

Selltiz, Claire, Marie Jahoda, Morton Deutsch, and Stuart W. Cook, *Research Methods in Social Relations*, rev. ed. New York: Holt, Rinehart and Winston, 1959.

Straus, Murray A., "Measuring Families," in Harold T. Christensen, *Handbook of Marriage and the Family*. Chicago: Rand McNally, 1964, pp. 335–400.

Code Sheet for SOCIOLOGICAL ANALYSIS

No.	Date Mo/D/Yr	Coder		1	2	3	4	5	6
7	8	9	10	11	12	13	14	15	16
17	18	19	20	21	22a	22b	22c	22d	22e
22f	22t	23	24	25	26	26t	27	28	28t
29	30	31	32m	33m	34m	34tm	32f	33f	34f
34tf	35b	35s	35t	36	37	38	39	40a	40b
40c	40d	40e	40f	40g	40h	41	42	42t	43
44	45	45t	46	47	47t	47tt	48	49	50
51	51t	52	53	54	55	56	57	58	58t
59a	59b	59c	59d	59e	59f	59g	59h	59i	59t
60am	60bm	60cm	60tm	60af	60bf	60cf	60tf	61am	61bm
61cm	61tm	61af	61bf	61cf	61tf	62a	62b	62c	63
64a	64b	64c	64d	64e	65	66	67	68a	68b
68c	68d	68e	68f	68tc	68tc	69	70	70t	71
72	72t	73	74	75	76	77	78	79	80

General coding rules

1. Read the "Coding Instructions" on pages 30 and 31.
2. Write code numbers to fill the entire box from top to bottom.
3. All boxes *must* have a code in them. If the question was not answered, code "+".
4. "sc" means self-coding, i.e., use the number circled or written in by the respondent as the code.
5. *If a question is answered with a range* rather than a single figure, i.e., "70 to 75 years old," code the half-way point rounded to the next highest number. In this example, the half way point is 72.5, and the number to code is 73. *If two numbers are given,* i.e., 70 or 71, code the higher number, in this case 71.
6. *If two answers* to a precoded question are circled, code the higher number. *If three answers* to a precoded question are circled, code the middle answer. *However,* these two rules apply only if the answers are in some kind of rank order, and only if adjacent answer numbers are circled. In all other cases, ask your instructor what to code. It will usually be considered as "no answer" and coded as "+."
7. If a number is asked for in the question and the respondent answers "few," "many," "much," etc., this must be treated as "no answer" and coded "+."

QUES. and BOX	ITEM AND CODE
No.	Respondent Number. This is the identification number written or stamped on the questionnaire. Write it in the upper left box. Use large numbers. If the questionnaires have not been numbered your instructor will now assign numbers. Write the number on *both* the questionnaire and the code sheet.
Date	Date of Coding. (*Not* the date the questionnaire was completed.)
Coder	Name of Coder. (*Print* your name in this double box.)
1	Sex: Self-coding (sc), i.e., code the number circled or written.
2	Age: sc
3	Race: sc
4	Class in college: sc

II. MY FAMILY

5	Parents' Marital Status: sc
6	Father's Education: sc
7	Mother's Education: sc
8	Mother's Religion: sc

Note: The next five items deal with the occupations of grandparents and fathers. Occupations are difficult to code so be sure to check with your instructor if you are in doubt.

If more than one occupation is given, code the one with the lower code number.

9 Paternal Grandfather's Occupation:
1. Proprietor (except farm), i.e., owner of business
2. Manager or official, i.e., corporation or government official, department head
3. Professional, i.e., doctor, lawyer, teacher
4. Clerical and sales, i.e., salesman, bookkeeper, interviewer, postal clerk
5. Farm owner or operator
6. Skilled worker and foreman, i.e., machinist, barber, lineman, carpenter
7. Semi-skilled or unskilled, i.e., truck driver, waitress, janitor, factory worker
8. Homemaker

\+ No information

10 Maternal Grandfather's Occupation: Use same code as for question 9.

Note: Questions 11, 12, and 13 are three different ways of classifying the father's occupation. Each measures a different aspect of occupational status. They do not necessarily agree. However, you should check the coding of box 11 by comparing it with the *group letter* of question 12. They should correspond thus:

Box 11		Question 12
1	=	A
2	=	B
3	=	C
4	=	D
5	=	E
6 or 7	=	F

If they disagree, check with your instructor.

11 Father's Occupational *Group*: Use same code as for question 9.

12 Father's Occupational *Prestige*: Code the num-

QUES. and BOX	ITEM AND CODE
	ber circled in the *left* column of page 2. *Do not code the group letter*. If the question was not answered, code on the basis of the answers to questions 11 and 14. If question 11 also was not answered, code +.
13	Father's Occupational *Situs*: sc
14	Father's Employer: sc
15	Number of persons employed where father works: sc
16	Hours per week father works: sc. If a range of hours (for example, 40–45) is given, see rule 5 at the beginning of the code.
17	Job Satisfaction: sc
18	Father's social class self-conception: sc
19	Extent of mother's outside employment: sc
20	Mother's Occupation: Use same code as for question 9.
21	Father's yearly income: sc in thousands, i.e., \$8,000 = 8, \$18,000 = 18, \$105,000 = 105, no information = +.
22a	Which parent decides on car purchase: sc
22b	Which parent decides on life insurance: sc
22c	Which parent decides about vacations: sc
22d	Which parent decides residence: sc
22e	Which parent decides about mother's working: sc
22f	Which parent decides children's activities: sc
22t	RELATIVE POWER INDEX: Add the numbers coded for questions 22a through 22f and code this number in box 22t. *If ONE question is omitted*: A. Get the average of the questions which were answered. B. Round this average to the nearest whole number. C. Substitute the resulting number for the question omitted. *If two or more questions are omitted*: code this box as +.
23	Parents' marital happiness: sc
	III. ABOUT MY FATHER
24	Father's visiting with relatives: sc
25	Father's visiting with neighbors: sc
26	Father's visiting with friends: sc
26t	PRIMARY GROUP PARTICIPATION INDEX: Add the codes for questions 24, 25, and 26 and code in box 26t. If *any* of the three questions is not answered, code +.
27	Father's attendance in voluntary association: sc
28	Father's memberships in voluntary associations: sc. Answers like "very few" or "many" are coded +, no answer = +.
28t	ORGANIZATIONAL PARTICIPATION INDEX: Add the codes for questions 27 and 28 and code in box 28t. If either question is not answered, code +.
29	Father's interest in politics: sc
30	Father's political preference: sc
31	Respondent's political preference: sc
32m	Communists should *not* be allowed to speak in community: sc — Code the scores listed under ME
33m	Books should be banned: sc — Code the scores listed under ME
34m	Loyalty of college professor: sc — Code the scores listed under ME
34tm	POLITICAL TOLERANCE INDEX, RESPONDENT: Add the codes under "ME" for questions 32m, 33m, and 34m and code in box 34tm. If *any* questions were omitted, code +.
32f	Communists should not be allowed to speak in community: sc — Code the scores listed under FATHER
33f	Books should be banned: sc — Code the scores listed under FATHER
34f	Loyalty of college professor: sc — Code the scores listed under FATHER
34tf	POLITICAL TOLERANCE INDEX, FATHER: Add the codes under "FATHER" for questions 32f, 33f, and 34f and code in box 34tf. If *any* questions were omitted, code +.
	IV. CHILDHOOD AND ADOLESCENCE
35b	Number of brothers: sc
35s	Number of sisters: sc
35t	Number of siblings: add number of brothers and sisters and code: sc
36	Sex composition of sibling group: sc
37	Sibling position of respondent: sc
38	Type of residence in adolescence: sc
39	Size of community lived in during youth: sc
	Mother's value on child:
40a	working hard: sc
40b	thinking for himself: sc
40c	being considerate: sc
40d	obeying parents: sc
40e	being dependable: sc
40f	self-control: sc
40g	popularity: sc
40h	defending himself: sc

QUES. and BOX	ITEM AND CODE
41	Attachment to father: sc
42	Attachment to mother: sc
42t	ATTACHMENT TO PARENTS: Add the codes for questions 41 and 42 and code in box 42t.
43	Type of association at age 13–14: sc
44	Enjoyed being alone: sc
45	Spent more or less time alone than other children: sc
45t	AGE 13 SOCIAL PARTICIPATION INDEX: Add the codes for questions 43, 44, and 45 and code in box 45t. If a question was omitted, code this box +.
46	Extent of visiting during senior year: sc
47	Attendance at meetings during senior year: sc
47t	HIGH SCHOOL PARTICIPATION INDEX: Add the codes for questions 46 and 47 and code in box 47t. If either question was omitted, code as +.
47tt	ADOLESCENT SOCIAL PARTICIPATION INDEX: Add the codes for boxes 45t and 47t and code in box 47tt. If either of the two boxes is coded as +, code this one as +.
48	High school grades: sc
49	Critical of friends' standards: sc
50	Attempted to control temper: sc
51	Saving gave good feeling: sc
51t	DEFERRED GRATIFICATION INDEX: Add the codes for questions 49, 50, and 51 and code in box 51t. If any question is omitted, code as +.
52	Childhood happiness rating: sc
	V. HEALTH AND PERSONAL PROBLEMS
53	Trouble sleeping: sc
54	Bothered by nervousness: sc
55	Bothered by shortness of breath: sc
56	Bothered by hard heart beat: sc
57	Difficult to get up in the morning: sc
58	Couldn't get going at times: sc
58t	ANXIETY INDEX: Add the codes for questions 53 through 58 and code this number in box 58t. *If ONE question is omitted*: A. Get the score for the questions answered. B. Divide by 5. C. Round this to the *next highest* whole number. D. Add this number to the score and code. *If two or more questions are omitted:* code as +.
	VI. ATTITUDES AND OPINIONS
	Social distance from:
59a	Armenians — Code the LOWEST number circled
59b	Chinese — Code the LOWEST number circled
59c	French — Code the LOWEST number circled
59d	Germans — Code the LOWEST number circled
59e	Italians — Code the LOWEST number circled
59f	Japanese — Code the LOWEST number circled
59g	Jews — Code the LOWEST number circled
59h	Negroes — Code the LOWEST number circled
59i	Russians — Code the LOWEST number circled
59t	RACIAL DISTANCE INDEX: Add the codes in boxes 59a through 59i and code this number in box 59t. *If ONE question is omitted*: A. Get the scores for those questions which were answered. B. Divide by 8. C. Round this to the *next highest* whole number. D. Add this number to the score and code. *If more than one question is omitted*: code as +.
60am	People using me: sc — Code the scores listed under ME
60bm	Can do nothing about war: sc — Code the scores listed under ME
60cm	People are cogs in the machinery: sc — Code the scores listed under ME
60tm	POWERLESSNESS INDEX–RESPONDENT: Add the codes under ME for boxes 60am, bm, and cm and code this number. If one of the three questions is omitted, code as +.
60af	People using me: sc — Code the scores listed under FATHER
60bf	Can do nothing about war: sc — Code the scores listed under FATHER
60cf	People are cogs in the machinery: sc — Code the scores listed under FATHER
60tf	POWERLESS INDEX–FATHER: Add the codes under FATHER for boxes 60af, bf, and cf and code this number. If one of the three questions is omitted, code as +.
61am	Everything relative: sc — Code the scores listed under ME
61bm	End justifies means: sc — Code the scores listed under ME
61cm	Doubtful about religious beliefs: sc — Code the scores listed under ME
61tm	NORMLESSNESS INDEX–RESPONDENT: Add the codes under ME for boxes 61am, bm, and cm and code this number. If one of the three questions is omitted, code as +.
61af	Everything relative: sc — Code the scores listed under FATHER
61bf	End justifies means: sc — Code the scores listed under FATHER
61cf	Doubtful about religious beliefs: sc — Code the scores listed under FATHER
61tf	NORMLESSNESS INDEX–FATHER: Add the codes under FATHER for boxes 61af, bf, and cf and code this number. If one of the three questions is omitted, code as +.

QUES. and BOX	ITEM AND CODE
	VII. FAMILY AND OCCUPATIONAL PLANS
62a	Person I marry must be sexually stimulating: sc
62b	Sometimes you shouldn't confide in mate completely: sc
62c	Woman has to sacrifice more than man in marriage: sc
63	Number of children desired: sc. None = 0, but no answer = +.
	Satisfaction from:
64a	career: sc
64b	leisure time activity: sc
64c	family relationships: sc
64d	religious participation: sc
64e	community participation: sc
65	Preferred residence: sc
66	Preferred employer: sc
67	Anticipated age 40 income: sc
	Willing to:
68a	leave family: sc
68b	move a lot: sc
68c	leave community: sc
68d	leave friends: sc
68e	learn a new routine: sc
68f	take on more responsibility: sc
68tc	MOBILITY CONSTRAINTS INDEX: Count the number of items in questions 68a to 68f answered "0" and code in box 68tc. *If ONE item is omitted*: count it as an additional answer of "0." *If two or more are omitted*: code as +.
68to	ACHIEVEMENT ORIENTATION INDEX: Add the codes circled for questions 68a to 68f and code in box 68to. *If ONE item is omitted*, get the average for the six questions which were answered, round to the nearest whole number and add in this number for the missing question. *If two or more items are omitted*: code +.
	VIII. SOME PROBLEM SITUATIONS
69	Cheating on overtime work: sc
70	Claimed too much fire damage: sc
70t	STEALING ATTITUDE INDEX—LARGE BUSINESS: Add the codes for questions 69 and 70 and code in box 70t. If either of the questions is omitted, code as +.
71	Kept trousers which didn't belong to him: sc
72	Got double grocery order: sc
72t	STEALING ATTITUDE INDEX—SMALL BUSINESS: Add the codes for questions 71 and 72 and code in box 72t. If either of the questions is omitted, code as +.
73	Case A, what would you do about cheating?: sc
74	Case A, what would authorities do about cheating?: sc
75	Case B, what would you do about cheating?: sc
76	Case B, what would authorities do about cheating?: sc

(73–76: Code the HIGHEST number circled)

Concepts III

PROBLEM 2

CULTURE

Culture refers to everything people learn as a result of being members of a society—simple directions on how to brush teeth, complex calculations in nuclear physics, judgments of virtue and vice as well as desirable ways of behaving at a party or in a classroom. Sociologists, however, are generally most interested in those elements of culture which constitute the norms and rules governing social groups and social relations. As instinct guides the behavior of animals, so culture guides the behavior of men. The fact that persons share ideas about acceptable behavior makes human society possible.

Given the complexity of culture and the vast range of behavior it specifies, the study of culture has innumerable forms. Some theorists have attempted to offer typologies of aspects of culture so as to simplify and identify its various dimensions. One typology distinguishes, for example, between the general abstract level of culture, broad basic values, and the concrete level of culture with highly specific norms containing particular referents for actual behavior (Parsons, 1951). Another typology focuses on the distinction between "mores," culture that has direct relevance to the maintenance of society's foundations, and "folkways," culture that prescribes fashionable behavior, behavior that constitutes "good manners" (Summer, 1960).

An analysis of any of the innumerable typologies of culture points up how intricate culture actually is; consequently, some research has sought an understanding of these intricacies by analyzing the relationships among various aspects of culture. One such analysis examined the cultural contradictions in American society between norms specifying adult behavior from adolescents and contradictory norms expecting adolescents to remain obedient and dependent on their parents (Benedict, 1949). The author speculated that the stress and strain of teen-age life in America can be traced precisely to such contradictions. Similar analyses of cultural consistency have been applied to the success ethos (Merton, 1959), to marriage and family living (Sirjamaki, 1948), and other areas as well.

The bulk of the work on culture, however, has examined its enormous variations across various societies and traced its influence on human behavior. Although social pressures and resources sometimes mitigate its effect (see Problems 3, 7, and 21), the impact of culture is nonetheless considerable. Kluckhohn and Strodtbeck, for example, showed the relevance of cultural differences in orientations to nature, time, and lineage for an undrstanding of differences between American society and various Indian societies (Kluckhohn and Strodtbeck, 1961). Similarly, Hall has illustrated variations in the concept of space between Latin Americans and North Americans: Latin Americans tolerate standing close to each other while speaking, whereas North Americans grow uncomfortable in such situations and prefer separation of at least a few feet (Hall, 1959). These studies and numerous others that could be mentioned are important not only because they document the variability in cultural preferences, but also because they go some way to reducing the ethnocentric feeling that "our way of doing things is best."

Theodorson's research, reported in the reading for the present problem, is an excellent example of the studies in this tradition. Theodorson focuses on the cultural trait called romanticism, and he contrasts the currency attached to it in American society and three Asian societies. Each of these societies differ in the extent to which they have undergone change to an urban-industrial order. The author not only shows that romanticism is linked to the social organization of society, but also speculates on the consequences of romanticism for individual adaptation to life in an urban-industrial setting. Implicitly, of course, the article illustrates how the romantic love complex, held by most Americans to be the basic theme of family life, is rare and seen as undesirable by persons in other societies of the world.

ROMANTICISM AND MOTIVATION TO MARRY IN THE UNITED STATES, SINGAPORE, BURMA, AND INDIA / *George A. Theodorson*

Attitudes toward marriage of 3,847 American, Singapore Chinese, Burmese, and Indian students are analyzed to determine whether there is evidence of acceptance of the American type romantic orientation to marriage among the most highly educated and Westernized classes in Chinese Singapore, Burma, and India. It is found that the three groups of Asian respondents while all showing a persistence of a contractual orientation to marriage may be ranked by degree of contractualism. This ranking is related to the interaction of two analytical variables—contractualism of the traditional culture and degree of cultural change. Motivation to marry in the four cultures is then analyzed, and found to follow the same rank order as degree of romanticism.

The impact of industrialization on traditional values in non-Western societies has long been a subject of interest for social scientists as well as political leaders. There has been much discussion of whether traditional values, even in modified form, will be able to withstand the onslaught of Westernizing influences.[1] The effect of these Westernizing influences on values associated with the family is particularly crucial because of the central position of the institution of the family in maintaining the traditional social structure.

The study presented in this paper deals with respondents drawn from an urbanized, educated, and Western-influenced segment of three non-Western societies, Chinese Singapore, Burma, and India. Their attitudes toward the husband-wife relationship first will be analyzed to determine whether the impact of industrial, urban culture and Western education has led to their abandonment of the traditional contractual orientation to marriage in favor of the romantic orientation, characteristic of modern American society. Secondly, the relationship between romanticism and motivation to marry will be considered. This paper is not primarily concerned with changes in specific family norms, for example those regulating the position of women. Rather it is concerned with a broader value-orientation, contractualistic or romantic, which conceivably may change or remain constant despite changes in more specific norms.

In Singapore, Burma, and India the mass media have spread the ideals of romanticism. In all three cultures the educated youth in particular are being exposed to the romantic ideal in motion pictures, books, magazines, newspapers, and American popular songs.[2] Popular writers in these countries have expressed concern (and some alarm) about changes in traditional attitudes toward marriage and particularly about the rise of unrealistic romantic expectations of the future marriage relationship on the part of modern youth.[3] We shall start, therefore, with the following hypothesis: Due to the impact of industrialization, urbanization, Western education, and the concomitant changes and pressures accompanying these forces, no differences will be found between Indian, Burmese, and Singapore Chinese students and American students on attitudes reflecting the ideals of a romantic orientation toward marriage.[4]

Reprinted with permission of the author and publisher, University of North Carolina Press from *Social Forces, 44* (September 1965), pp. 17–27.

The author would like to acknowledge the collaborative efforts of U Maung Maung Sein, Daw Khin Mar Mar, G. C. Hallen, T. L. Green, and Miss G. K. Chew. The author also would like to thank the School of Education of the University of Singapore, the International Planned Parenthood Federation, and the Institute of National Language and Culture for sponsoring this study in Singapore. Acknowledgment also is gratefully made to the Central Fund for Research and the Social Science Research Center of The Pennsylvania State University for financial support. The author was Fulbright lecturer, University of Rangoon, Rangoon, Burma, 1958–59.

[1] See George A. Theodorson, "Acceptance of Industrialization and Its Attendant Consequences for the Social Patterns of Non-Western Societies," *American Sociological Review,* 18 (October 1953), pp. 477–484.

[2] Noel P. Gist, "Mate Selection and Mass Communication in India," *Public Opinion Quarterly,* 17 (Winter 1953), p. 482; David Mace and Vera Mace, *Marriage: East and West* (Garden City, New York: Doubleday & Co., 1959), pp. 138–142.

[3] For example see, Indira Awasty, "After the Wedding," *The Guardian* (Rangoon, October 6, 1962), p. 6.

[4] It might be noted that the hypothesis suggested by Waller and Hill, and also by Beigel, to explain the development of romanticism in the United States would also lead us to expect the spread of romanticism among the educated classes in Chinese Singapore, Burma, and India. According to this hypothesis, the development of romanticism as a dominant cultural complex in the United States basically is due to the frustration of sexual impulses in adolescence. Marriage is delayed until adult status is achieved and premarital sexual relations are frowned upon. Willard Waller and Reuben Hill, *The Family* (New York: The Dryden Press, 1951), 118–128; Hugo B. Beigel, "Romantic Love," *American Sociological Review* 16 (June 1951), pp. 326–334. Traditionally in the three Asian cultures with which we are concerned marriage took place at an early age, but in recent years average age at marriage has risen sharply, particularly among the educated youth who typically postpone marriage far

It should be recognized from the outset, however, that these three Asian groups represent three different combinations of two highly significant analytical variables—degree of contractualism of the traditional culture and degree of cultural change. Considering the first of these two variables, the degree of contractualism in marriage was very high in the traditional cultures of China and India. Parents selected suitable mates for their children on the basis of economic and social (e.g., caste in India) considerations. Since the young couple frequently did not know each other prior to marriage, romantic love played no part as the basis for marriage. In China, love before marriage was severely condemned. Romance was considered a potential enemy of filial obedience, which could create tensions destructive of family unity.[5] In India, even romantic love between husband and wife was considered dangerous, for it might cause the husband to neglect his duties toward his parents.[6] The tie between mother and son was considered more central and of deeper emotional involvement than the tie between husband and wife.

In traditional Burmese culture there was a greater element of romanticism in marriage than in India or China. Parents arranged the marriages of their children, but usually with the children's consent. The young man and woman knew each other before marriage, usually having seen each other frequently at social gatherings. In fact the young man or woman quite properly might initiate marriage proceedings by speaking to his or her parents, who, if they approved of the match, would then speak to the other parents either directly or through a matchmaker. Marriage based on romantic love was not a widespread traditional pattern, but when romantic love did occur it might be seriously considered in arranging a marriage. There was courtship, but under direct parental supervision. In the case of parental objection to a marriage, elopement was a formally disapproved but usually accepted pattern often adopted by romantically inclined young couples. However, while the element of romanticism was present, traditional Burmese expectations nevertheless were primarily contractualistic. Close scrutiny was kept over unmarried daughters, and young men and women were not permitted to be alone together. A dowry was paid by the groom to the bride's parents. As in the Indian family, the closest emotional attachment was expected to be between mother and son rather than between husband and wife.[7]

The second analytical variable to be considered is degree of cultural change. Of these three Asian societies, Burma has experienced the least change.[8] In India there is evidence of striking changes from traditional attitudes in regard to divorce, widow remarriage, intercaste marriage, and equality of the sexes.[9] However, by far the greatest change from traditional patterns has occurred among the Singapore Chinese. According to Shu-Ching Lee there was a rapid decline in the strength of the institutional family among modern educated intellectuals in the large cities of China in the early twentieth century. Since then ". . . the destruction of this system has penetrated to all groups of society and to the vast interior."[10] The Singapore Chinese have experienced family change not only insofar as they come from a background of change in China, but also because of their peculiar circumstances in Singapore. The Singapore Chinese immigrants, mostly from a rural background, experienced the impact of sudden urbanization. Secondly, they found themselves in a very heterogeneous situation, despite the fact that the majority of the population of Singapore is Chinese (78 percent in 1947) and mostly from Fukien and Kwangtung Provinces. These provinces are very diverse, and consequently there are many dialects, subdialects, and sub-sub-dialects represented. One of the most common expressions heard among the Singapore Chinese reflects a consciousness of their heterogeneity: "We Singapore people are very mixed up."[11] Thirdly, the Singapore Chinese are more mobile than they normally would be in China because a family's house cannot be its ancestral home.[12] These factors have not by any means led to an eradication of the traditional family system, but they have led to greater change and susceptibility to modern influences than in Burma or India.

In considering these two analytical variables together, it may be seen that the Singapore Chinese have a

beyond the traditional age. Cecil C. Hobbs, *Christian Education and the Burmese Family,* unpublished master's dissertation, Colgate-Rochester Divinity School, 1942, p. 110; Hannah Sen, "Our Own Times," in Tara Ali Baid (ed.), *Women of India* (Delhi: Publications Division, Ministry of Information and Broadcasting, Government of India, 1958), p. 41; Riva Tampoe, "The Women of India," *Contemporary Review,* 195 (January 1959), p. 26; Maurice Freedman, *Chinese Family and Marriage in Singapore* (London: Her Majesty's Stationery Office, "Colonial Research Studies No. 20," 1957), pp. 111–117. The three groups of Asian respondents in this study, both men and women, indicated a high ideal and a high expected age at marriage. In all three societies there are strong mores against premarital sexual relations for women, and in Burma and India for men as well.

[5] Mace and Mace, *op. cit.,* p. 134.

[6] Aileen D. Ross, *The Hindu Family in its Urban Setting* (Toronto: University of Toronto Press, 1961), p. 161.

[7] For accounts of traditional Burmese Practices of mate selection see: Sir James G. Scott (pseud., Shway Yoe), *The Burman His Life and Notions* (London: The Macmillan Co., 1896), pp. 54–57; H. Fielding Hall, *The Soul of a People* (London: The Macmillan Co., 1914), pp. 178–184; Hobbs, *op. cit.,* pp. 103–149; Mi Mi Khaing, *Burmese Family* (London: Longmans, Green, 1946), pp. 65–75; Charles S. Brant and Mi Mi Khaing, "Burmese Kinship and the Life Cycle: An Outline," *Southwestern Journal of Anthropology,* 7 (Winter 1951), pp. 449–450.

[8] See J. Russell Andrus, *Burmese Economic Life* (Stanford: Stanford University Press, 1948).

[9] See Ross, *op. cit.;* Margaret L. Cormack, *She Who Rides a Peacock* (New York: Frederick A. Praeger, 1961); G. C. Hallen and G. A. Theodorson, "Change and Traditionalism in the Indian Family: Part II of a Comparative Study of the Indian and American Family," *Indian Journal of Social Research,* 2 (July 1961), pp. 51–59. In a study of university students in Madras State, B. Kuppuswamy found a striking change from traditional attitudes toward caste intermarriage. Reported in Noel P. Gist, "Caste in Transition," *Phylon,* 15 (First Quarter 1954), p. 158.

[10] Shu-Ching Lee, "China's Traditional Family, Its Characteristics and Disintegration," *American Sociological Review,* 18 (June 1953), p. 272.

[11] Freedman, *op. cit.,* p. 27.

[12] *Ibid.,* p. 54.

highly contractualistic cultural tradition but have experienced the greatest social change. The Indians also with a highly contractualistic cultural tradition have experienced decidedly less social change. The Burmese have had the least social change, but they also have the least contractualistic cultural tradition of these three Asian groups.

Procedure

THE CROSS-CULTURAL STUDY. The data presented in this study are drawn from responses to a questionnaire completed by 4,006 students in the United States, Burma, India, and Singapore. The distribution of respondents is as follows: 1,324 students, 748 men and 576 women, from two universities in northeastern United States; 486 students, 249 men and 237 women, from the largest university in Burma; 1,240 students, 1,038 men and 202 women, from nine universities in northern India; 956 students from the university and three institutes in Singapore. Of the 956 Singapore respondents only those identifying themselves as Chinese—a total of 797, 510 men and 287 women, are included in this study. The students in the four cultural groups came from diverse curricula, with no concentration of majors in one field in any of the four groups. Burmese respondents included a larger proportion of Christians (26 percent) than are found in the total population of Burma. However, in the responses discussed in this paper there were no significant differences between Buddhists and Christians except in the one instance specifically noted below.

A basically identical questionnaire containing background questions and a series of attitude statements to which respondents indicated whether they strongly agreed, agreed, were uncertain, disagreed, or strongly disagreed, was used for all four cultural groups. For the Asian respondents high competence in English made it unnecessary to translate the questionnaire. In the case of India, where an expression might be confusing the Hindi equivalent was inserted in parentheses. The use of respondents in Burma, India, and Singapore who know English and are highly educated not only assures their understanding of the questions and familiarity with Western conceptions, but also increases the likelihood of obtaining the greatest deviation from traditional norms. These respondents are drawn from the segment of society most Westernized and most likely to have been influenced by ideas of romantic love.

THE INDICES OF ROMANTICISM. In this paper five indices are used to measure romanticism. These indices were chosen to measure crucial value differences which distinguish a romantic from a contractual orientation toward marriage.

In analyzing the literature on romanticism one finds overwhelming emphasis on physical attraction as a crucial element in the romantic complex. In discussing romantic love Parsons and Bales speak of the emphasis on "overt, specifically feminine attractiveness, with strong erotic overtones. . ."[13] Burgess and Locke write, "In romantic love the emphasis is upon sexual attraction, personal beauty, and emotional response."[14] Smith tells us that romantic love is "based on overwhelming sex attraction"[15] and that "Glamour is closely associated with romantic love . . ."[16] Harsh and Schrickel state, ". . . to love and be loved one must want intensely to possess and be possessed sexually. To that end attractive physical appearance becomes a *sine qua non*."[17] Two aspects of this emphasis on physical attraction may be distinguished. One is an emphasis on physical attraction, with strong erotic overtones, as a criterion of mate selection. The other aspect involves an emphasis on a woman's maintaining an attractive physical appearance after marriage. Recognizing these two aspects of physical attraction in romantic love, Parsons writes, "The . . . pattern . . . of the 'glamour girl,' has a tendency to predominate in the relations of the sexes in the premarital period, being deeply rooted in the youth culture. The fact that in our family system the stability of marriage must rest mainly on personal sentiment creates a tendency for this to carry over into marriage and into the adult feminine role."[18] In this paper two indices are used to measure these two aspects of the romantic value of physical attraction. They are: "The person I marry must be sexually stimulating"[19] and "A woman should be as concerned about her appearance after marriage as she was before."

A second major value in the romantic complex is the ideal of companionship between husband and wife based on a sharing of thoughts and actions, with each confiding in the other. Burgess and Locke, recognizing companionship and "freedom of communication and action" as crucial elements in romantic love, write:

> One method of gauging the depth of love of a couple is by determining the extent and intimacy of communication and behavior. In the love relationship the person may exercise even a higher degree of freedom of confiding and of acting than in a close friendship.[20]

Winch regards a belief in mutual sharing as an essential condition for mate selection to be based on romantic love. He points out that ". . . in middle-class America we have come to regard marriage as the relationship *par excellence* for the sharing of experience,

[13] Talcott Parsons and Robert F. Bales, *Family, Socialization and Interaction Process* (Glencoe, Ill.: The Free Press, 1960), p. 24.

[14] Ernest W. Burgess and Harvey J. Locke, *The Family* (New York: American Book Co., 1953), p. 327.

[15] Ernest A. Smith, *American Youth Culture* (New York: The Free Press of Glencoe, 1962), p. 117.

[16] *Ibid.*, p. 123.

[17] Charles M. Harsh and H. G. Schrickel, *Personality Development and Assessment* (New York: The Ronald Press Co., 1950), p. 248.

[18] Talcott Parsons, "The Social Structure of the Family," in Ruth Nanda Anshen (ed.), *The Family: Its Function and Destiny* (New York: Harper & Bros., 1949), p. 198.

[19] This phrase was used in the Cornell values study. See Rose K. Goldsen, Morris Rosenberg, Robin M. Williams, Jr. and Edward A. Suchman, *What College Students Think* (Princeton, New Jersey: D. Van Nostrand Co., 1960), p. 91.

[20] Burgess and Locke, *op. cit.*, p. 325.

of feelings, and hence of gratification."[21] He goes on to show that this belief which means in effect that "the marital dyad . . . [is] culturally defined as a congeniality group and the spouse as a friend" is a crucial factor in the romantic approach to mate selection.[22] The ideal romantic pair does not want to withhold secrets from each other. In contrast, under a contractual system it is usually considered proper and desirable for a husband and wife not to discuss certain matters and not to share all thoughts. Each sex may be expected to live certain areas of life apart from the opposite sex.[23] In this study those respondents who accept the ideal of total voluntary confiding will not agree with the statement, "Sometimes it is wise not to completely confide in your mate (life-partner)."

As romanticism involves the ideal of companionship between husband and wife, so it also necessarily includes a conception of the husband and wife as equal partners. Parsons points out that a marriage relationship which rests ". . . primarily on affective attachment for the other person as a concrete human individual, a 'personality' rather than on more objective considerations of status . . . puts a premium on a certain kind of mutuality and equality. . . . Each is a fully responsible 'partner' . . ." He goes on to say, "Surely the pattern of romantic love which makes his relation to the 'woman he loves' the most important single thing in a man's life, is incompatible with the view that she is an inferior creature, fit only for dependency on him."[24] Moreover, according to Benedek, the type of "psychobiological interaction" idealized in romantic love rests on an assumption of equality between the man and woman.[25] In a partnership of equals neither partner is expected to sacrifice more than the other. In contrast, in the traditional contractualism of China, India, and Burma it was considered proper for a wife to sacrifice in every way possible for her husband.[26] In this study respondents who believe that marriage is a partnership of equals based on equality of sacrifice will not agree with the statement, "Generally speaking a woman has to sacrifice more in marriage than a man."

A final essential characteristic of the romantic value complex is a de-emphasis on the fulfillment of specific expectations in the marriage relationship, and in its place an emphasis on generalized feelings of affection and trust which are combined with an idealization of the future marriage partner. Contractualism involves an orientation toward a future spouse in which the expected pattern of role relationship between husband and wife is based on the "mores, religion, and law"[27] of the cultural group. Definite, culturally defined norms of proper behavior are expected of a future mate whoever he (or she) may be. In contrast, in the case of romanticism the details of the proper marriage relationships are not as specifically determined by societal norms, but are to a much greater extent determined by the particular individuals in interaction with each other. Norms are largely dyadic and based on mutual agreement. Therefore the romantic demands of a prospective mate are relatively few in terms of formal universalistic expectations. Parsons contrasts the traditional, contractual conception of the marriage relationship which gives primary emphasis to "matters of objective status and obligations to other kin" with the romantic conception which emphasizes "subjective sen-

TABLE 1. Acceptance of romanticism

	Americans	Singapore Chinese	Burmese	Indians
MEN				
Physical attraction: As a criterion of marriage choice	133[a]	103	—	75
Physical attraction: Importance for wife after marriage[b]	164	84	88	65
Confiding valued in marriage (marriage as companionship)	168	100	86	54
Equality of sacrifice in marriage (marriage as partnership)	160	94	88	63
Trust: No compulsory explanation by husband	137	81	80	87
WOMEN				
Physical attraction: As a criterion of marriage choice	130	78	—	44
Physical attraction: Importance for wife after marriage[b]	134	81	77	57
Confiding valued in marriage (marriage as companionship)	138	67	65	81
Equality of sacrifice in marriage (marriage as partnership)	158	62	76	17
Trust: No compulsory explanation by husband	161	54	43	57

[a] $\frac{\text{observed proportion}}{\text{expected proportion}} \times 100$

[b] Based on proportions strongly agreeing.

All differences between American and Singapore Chinese men, American and Burmese men, American and Indian men, American and Singapore Chinese women, American and Burmese women, and American Indian women are statistically significant by both the chi-square test (of frequency distributions) and the Kolmogorov-Smirnov D test (one-tailed—of cumulative percentage distributions) with p's below .001 on all five indices.

[21] Robert F. Winch, *Mate-Selection* (New York: Harper & Bros., 1958), p. 70.

[22] *Ibid.*, pp. 70–71.

[23] For example in traditional India. See Ross, *op. cit.*, p. 159.

[24] Talcott Parsons, "The Kinship System of the Contemporary United States," *Essays in Sociological Theory Pure and Applied* (Glencoe, Ill.: The Free Press, 1949), pp. 245–246.

[25] Therese Benedek, "The Emotional Structure of the Family," in Anshen, *op. cit.*, p. 210.

[26] Mace and Mace, *op. cit.*, p. 67; Ross, *op. cit.*, pp. 105–06; John F. Cady, *A History of Modern Burma* (Ithaca: Cornell University Press, 1958), p. 62.

[27] Burgess and Locke, *op. cit.*, p. 23.

timent."[28] Parsons goes on to explain that in the contractual marriage relationship "Very definite expectations in the definition of the different roles, combined with a complex system of interrelated sanctions, both positive and negative, go far to guarantee stability and the maintenance of standards of performance." Since this is lacking in the American kinship system Parsons suggests that romanticism provides a "functionally equivalent substitute in motivation to conformity with the expectations of the role. . . ." "Hence it may be suggested that the institutional sanction placed on the proper subjective sentiments of spouses, in short the expectation that they have an obligation to be 'in love,' has that significance."[29] This means, in effect, that the romantic attitude toward one's future spouse holds that he (or she) will do "the right thing" because "he loves me" not because of societal norms and sanctions. This belief is strengthened by the romantic tendency to idealize one's future spouse, a romantic tendency often discussed,[30] and by the romantic myth of a mysterious predetermined destiny for each other.[31] Thus the romantic emphasis is on trust, on the voluntary fulfillment of one's role because of love. As Parsons says, ". . . affective devotion . . . is linked to a presumption of the absence of any element of coercion."[32] Respondents who accept the ideal of the absence of coercion, the romantic value of trust with role fulfillment based on love will not agree that "A husband is obliged to tell his wife where he has been if he comes home very late."

Results

The results are summarized in Table 1. Table 1 presents normed indices based on the observed proportion of each group of respondents who agree (or do not agree if not agreeing indicates a romantic orientation) with each statement divided by the proportion of that group that would be expected to agree (or not agree)—that is the proportion the group is of the total number of men or women—multiplied by 100. Thus in all cases a higher index score indicates a more romantic orientation. On all five indices American respondents are significantly more romantic (at the .001 level) than any of the three Asian groups. This is true of both men and women. However, the three Asian groups tend to follow a consistent pattern with the Singapore Chinese most romantic, the Burmese intermediate, and the Indians least romantic.

PHYSICAL ATTRACTION. The Indian and Singapore Chinese respondents show significantly less concern with physical attraction as a criterion of mate selection than do American respondents. An overwhelming majority of Americans agree that "The person I marry must be sexually stimulating." In contrast, a majority of the Indians do not agree. Many more Indian women disagree than agree. The Singapore Chinese are in an intermediate position. It was not permissible to ask this question in Burma.

This difference between the Indian and American respondents does not reflect a more puritanical attitude on the part of the Indians. Traditional Indian culture stressed the importance of sex in marriage. Moreover, 79 percent of the Indian men and 68 percent of the women agree that "Sex is one of the most important aspects of marriage." This is an even greater proportion of agreement than among the Americans. (Sixty-two percent of the American men and 55 percent of the women agree.) Indian respondents do not refuse to recognize the role of sex, rather they are less concerned with physical attraction as a criterion in mate selection. Thus they tend to believe that concern with sex should follow rather than precede marriage.

The Americans also place greater emphasis on the desirability of a wife's maintaining continued concern with her physical attractiveness. The Americans express almost unanimous agreement with the statement, "A woman should be as concerned with her appearance after marriage as she was before marriage." While the Indians, Burmese, and Singapore Chinese are not opposed to a wife's maintaining an attractive appearance, they are far less likely than the Americans to strongly agree. This is not a crucial and highly valued norm for them as it is for the romantically oriented Americans.

CONFIDING. Indian, Burmese, and Singapore Chinese respondents show significantly less acceptance than do American respondents of the romantic ideal of total voluntary confiding in marriage. A majority of the Indians, Burmese, and Singapore Chinese express a belief, characteristic of a contractual system, in the desirability of a husband and wife not discussing certain matters and not sharing all thoughts. A particularly large proportion of the Indian men agree that it is wise not to confide (82 percent). This is in accordance with the findings of Ross who reports in her study of India that husbands frequently withhold secrets from their wives and that there is very little companionship between husbands and wives even in the cities.[33]

EQUALITY OF SACRIFICE. An overwhelming majority of the Indians (90 percent of the women) agree that "Generally speaking, a woman has to sacrifice more in marriage than a man." In contrast, more Americans (a majority of the men) disagree than agree. A majority of the Burmese and Singapore Chinese agree, but the lower percentage of the Indians places them in an intermediate position. (Among the Burmese, more Buddhists, 65 percent, than Christians, 50 percent, agree.) Responses to this question do not differentiate

[28] Parsons, "The Social Structure of the Family," *op. cit.*, p. 183.

[29] *Ibid.*, p. 184.

[30] Howard Becker and Reuben Hill, *Family, Marriage, and Parenthood* (Boston: D. C. Heath & Co., 1955), pp. 217 and 223; William N. Stephens, *The Family in Cross-cultural Perspective* (New York: Holt, Rinehart & Winston, 1963), p. 204; Burgess and Locke, *op. cit.*, pp. 322 and 324; Smith, *op. cit.*, pp. 123–124; Harsh and Schrickel, *op. cit.*, p. 248.

[31] Becker and Hill, *op. cit.*, p. 222; Smith, *op. cit.*, p. 118.

[32] Parsons, "The Social Structure of the Family," *op. cit.*, p. 184.

[33] Ross, *op. cit.*, pp. 127 and 159.

TABLE 2. "Ideally, if it were up to you, would you like to get married?"

	Yes	No	N.A.	Total	Number
MEN					
Americans	86.5%	1.6%	11.9%	100%	748
Singapore Chinese	86.9	8.8	4.3	100	510
Burmese	81.5	8.8	9.7	100	249
Indians	50.0	19.6	30.4	100	1038
WOMEN					
Americans	94.4%	1.4%	4.1%	100%	576
Singapore Chinese	80.5	12.5	7.0	100	287
Burmese	75.5	18.6	5.9	100	237
Indians	48.5	28.2	23.3	100	202

American and Singapore Chinese men: $\chi^2 = 30.97$; d.f. = 1; $p < .001$
American and Burmese men: $\chi^2 = 28.73$; d.f. = 1; $p < .001$
American and Indian men: $\chi^2 = 181.41$; d.f. = 1; $p < .001$
American and Singapore Chinese women: $\chi^2 = 49.01$; d.f. = 1; $p < .001$
American and Burmese women: $\chi^2 = 85.02$; d.f. = 1; $p < .001$
American and Indian women: $\chi^2 = 181.21$; d.f. = 1; $p < .001$

between traditional and modern evaluations of the desirability of feminine sacrifice. Agreement on the part of the Indians, Burmese, and Singapore Chinese, first of all may represent approval of the traditional Indian, Burmese, and Chinese point of view that it is proper for a woman to sacrifice more than her husband. On the other hand, feminists may also agree, feeling that while it is not morally right, it is nevertheless true that women must sacrifice more than men. However, the question does differentiate between the romantic and the non-romantic orientation. The majority of Indian, Burmese, and Singapore Chinese respondents do not accept the romantic view that marriage involves equal sacrifice for husband and wife.

TRUST: ROLE CONFORMITY THROUGH AFFECTION. Indian, Burmese, and Singapore Chinese respondents show a greater orientation in terms of specific expectations, whereas American respondents show a greater emphasis on the ideal of trust. Significantly more Indians, Burmese, and Singapore Chinese than Americans agree that "A husband is obliged to tell his wife where he has been if he comes home very late." There is a particularly striking difference between the women in the strongly agree category. Only 14 percent of the American women strongly agree compared to 39 percent of the Singapore Chinese, 44 percent of the Indian, and 47 percent of the Burmese women. Whether or not an American wife would in fact like an explanation if her husband came home late, the significantly lower percentage of American agreement must be understood primarily in terms of a projection of the romantic ideal. The Indian, Burmese, and Singapore Chinese responses indicate the persistence of a contractualistic orientation, with concrete universal expectations rather than a romantic orientation with an emphasis on trust.

The five indices point to a rejection of the null hypothesis. Despite the impact of industrialization, urbanization, and Western education, despite changes in specific traditional family norms and despite the sexual frustrations which result from delayed marriage combined with premarital sexual taboos, Indian, Burmese, and Singapore Chinese respondents have maintained a contractualistic value-orientation toward marriage and basically have not accepted the ideals of the romantic orientation. However, the three Asian groups are not equally contractualistic. On the five indices they follow a rank order directly related to the two analytical variables discussed above. The Singapore Chinese, who have experienced the most social change are the least contractualistic. The Burmese, with the least contractualistic cultural tradition, rank second. The Indians express the most contractualistic value-orientations.

Romanticism and motivation to marry

Since the publication of E. W. Burgess' paper on romanticism and family disorganization in the nineteen twenties,[34] most sociological analysis has emphasized the dysfunctions of romanticism. However, there also has been some recognition of possible positive functions of romanticism. Parsons suggests that romanticism may serve a positive function in motivating choice of a marriage partner in the absence of coercion or a system of arranged marriages.[35] This function also is mentioned by Waller and Hill who see romanticism functioning as a motivation to marriage counteracting certain pressures of modern life against marriage.[36] The data in this study tend to support this hypothesis. More specifically these data suggest that romanticism may function to promote a greater motivation to marry than does contractualism during a period of rapid social change.

A significantly greater percentage of the American

[34] E. W. Burgess, "The Romantic Impulse and Family Disorganization," *Survey,* 57 (1927), pp. 290–294.
[35] Parsons, "The Kinship System of the Contemporary United States," *op. cit.,* p. 241.
[36] Waller and Hill, *op. cit.,* pp. 174–175.

respondents than of the Indian, Burmese, and Singapore Chinese respondents express a desire to marry. The difference is particularly great among the women, with 28 percent of the Indian women, 19 percent of the Burmese women, 13 percent of the Singapore Chinese women, and only one percent of the American women not wishing to marry. (Table 2.) The large percentage of Indian respondents who do not wish to marry reflects the strains in the Indian family and a radical departure from traditionalism. Marriage, according to the traditional Indian conception was accepted as a natural, necessary and inevitable part of life. For women, a husband was the only means for respectable status in this world and salvation in the next.[37] The proportion of Burmese respondents who do not wish to marry, although less than the Indians, also indicates a weakening of the traditional system. One of the five specific duties of parents, according to Burmese Buddhism, is to provide their children with suitable wives and husbands, while one of the duties of children is to maintain the lineage and tradition of the family.[38] It has been noted in the literature that Western education has increased the number of unmarried men and women in Burma. In traditional Chinese culture also marriage was regarded as essential. A girl's life was without significance unless she married and had a son. In the tradition of Mencius, of the three unfilial acts, the worst is to have no posterity.[39] Thus, in all three cultures traditionally motivation to marry was supported by strong sanctions. The large percentages of respondents in these cultures expressing a desire not to marry indicate a decline in the strength of traditional motivations for marriage.

The greater motivation to marry of the American respondents suggests a possible positive function of the romantic approach to marriage under conditions of rapid social change.[40] The continuing contractualistic orientation of the Indian, Burmese, and Singapore Chinese respondents may be less functional than the romantic orientation in maintaining high morale toward marriage in an urban setting amid rapid social change. In the contractualistic orientation marriage expectations are in keeping with institutionally expected norms. In a period of rapid social change, with the emerging of new definitions to challenge the old ones, demoralization may be greater with a contractual orientation than with the more fluid romantic orientation. During periods of social change, traditional expectations come into conflict with new expectations, as for example, husband dominance vs. equalitarian husband-wife relationships. (Men may fear feminist wives, while women may fear patriarchical husbands.) Various traditional and modern norms are unevenly accepted by the two sexes, as well as by different individuals. In the romantic marriage, the rejection of traditional universalistic definitions of the marriage relationship may provide less confusion and demoralization because the definition of what is proper is primarily to be decided through husband-wife interaction. This may eliminate much of the possibility of a conflict of past family traditions with newly emerging definitions. The problem of defining the precise relationship is ultimately and ideally to be decided only in marriage and in the dyadic relationship itself.

It might be suggested that the larger proportion of Asian women not wishing to marry is due to the greater career orientation of college women in these countries than in the United States. However, it must be recognized that while only one percent of the American women do not wish to marry, obviously a far larger percentage than this are career oriented. Romanticism permits the combination of a career for the wife with marriage far more readily than does contractualism. It is the contractual orientation placing as it does primary emphasis on the performance of traditional role expectations that makes marriage unattractive to career minded women. Thus whether or not Asian college women are more career oriented than American college women does not diminish the significance of the relationship between romanticism and motivation to marry. Quite clearly, the difference in desire to marry of the men is not a matter of a difference in career orientation.

In considering the relationship between romanticism and motivation to marry suggested by the data presented in this paper, it must be recognized that group correlations are not synonomous with individual correlations.[41]

However, it is not possible with these data to establish for each cultural group significant positive individual correlations between romanticism and motivation to marry. In the case of the American respondents there are too few who do not wish to marry to permit any significant comparison. In the contractualistically oriented societies, factors such as poor opportunity to find romantically oriented marriage partners may adversely affect the motivation to marry of romantically oriented individuals. The specific factors involved are beyond the scope of the data available in this study, but provide a valuable area for further investigation.

As Menzel has pointed out, group correlations, while not establishing individual correlations, may in them-

[37] Ross, *op. cit.*, p. 154.

[38] Hobbs, *op. cit.*, pp. 76–77.

[39] Shu-Ching Lee, *op. cit.*, p. 275; Mace and Mace, *op. cit.*, pp. 28–29; Hsiao-Tung Fei, "Peasantry and Gentry: An Interpretation of Chinese Social Structure and Its Changes," in Reinhard Bendix and Seymour M. Lipset (eds.), *Class, Status and Power* (Glencoe, Ill.: The Free Press, 1953), p. 633.

[40] It might seem at first that the lower morale of the Asian students may be due to their poorer economic situation compared to the American students. However, it must be recognized that the students in this study are on the higher rungs of the social ladder, and that while many of them may be slated only for clerical positions in government service, their position in relation to the mass of the Indian, Burmese, and Singapore populations is quite enviable. Their lower morale is a function of their changing urban conceptions of marriage which also involves a rapidly dissolving extended family system that traditionally functioned in a more socially and economically satisfactory and morale maintaining manner despite even lower standards of living. Hence their lower morale with regard to the future and present realities of married life is not purely economic in origin. In addition, the percentage of Indians, Burmese, and Singapore Chinese who "ideally" do not want to marry is greater than the percentage who "realistically" do not expect to marry.

[41] W. S. Robinson, "Ecological Correlations and the Behavior of Individuals," *American Sociological Review*, 15 (June 1950), pp. 351–357.

TABLE 3. Romanticism and disinterest in marriage

	Mean of romanticism indices	Desire not to marry
MEN		
Americans	152	14
Singapore Chinese	92	69
Burmese	85	73
Indians	69	209
WOMEN		
Americans	144	12
Singapore Chinese	68	111
Burmese	65	167
Indians	51	304

selves provide valuable information.[42] In Table 3 it may be seen that there is a perfect inverse rank order correlation for the four cultural groups (in the case of both the men and the women) between the means of the five normed indices of romanticism and normed index scores of desire not to marry. These data suggest that romanticism promotes a milieu in which, despite the absence of traditional pressures, and despite the conflicts inherent in rapid social change, marriage is highly valued and viewed optimistically. It is significant to know that a greater degree of optimism toward marriage permeates a culture in association with the diffusion of the ideals of romanticism regardless of the nature of the psychological relationship between romanticism and motivation to marry in various social and cultural contexts.

It is recognized, of course, that we are concerned here with a highly Westernized segment of the three Asian cultures studied, and it is not suggested that traditional pressures motivating a desire to marry are equally weakened in the population at large.

Conclusion

Indian, Burmese, and Singapore Chinese respondents, although from the segment of their societies most subject to Western influences, do not show an acceptance of the American type romantic orientation to marriage. Consistently large significant differences were found between the American respondents on the one hand, and the Indian, Burmese, and Singapore Chinese respondents on the other hand, on attitudes reflecting the romantic or contractualistic orientation to marriage. Singapore Chinese attitudes were closest to the romantic American attitudes, with the Burmese attitudes next, and the Indian attitudes the most contractualistic. This has been explained in terms of the interaction of two analytical variables—degree of contractualism in the traditional cultures and of contractualism in the traditional cultures and degree of cultural change.

The data also support Parsons and Waller and Hill's hypothesis that romanticism functions to maintain high motivation to marry with the decline of traditional sources of motivation. The data suggest that contractualism when combined with the rejection of traditional norms may be less functional than romanticism in maintaining high motivations to marry. The four cultural groups follow the same rank order on romanticism and on desire to marry. This relationship requires further and more specifically focused investigation.

Replication

CULTURAL DIFFERENCES IN ROMANTICISM

To fully replicate Theodorson's study it would be necessary to give the questionnaire containing the items measuring romanticism to a sample of students in Burma, India, and Singapore, as well as to an American sample. Since this is obviously not practical for a class laboratory problem, we will have to content ourselves with comparing the responses of the American sample (whose questionnaires are represented in our set of code sheets) with the data for Asian students supplied by Theodorson. Therefore, strictly speaking, we are only replicating the American student part of Theodorson's study.

[42] Herbert Menzel, "Comment on Robinson's 'Ecological Correlations and the Behavior of Individuals,'" *American Sociological Review,* 15 (October 1950), p. 674.

Hypothesis

1. Before coming to class or doing the tabulations, write your hypothesis on the "Laboratory Report Form." State whether you expect American students to be different from Asian students in their support of romantic attitudes, and, if so, in what way?
2. *Important:* Read Appendix A for general information on writing a hypothesis.

Empirical indicator for this problem

62. Here is a list of things which some people consider important for their husband or wife. For

each one, please circle a number to show the extent to which YOU agree or disagree.

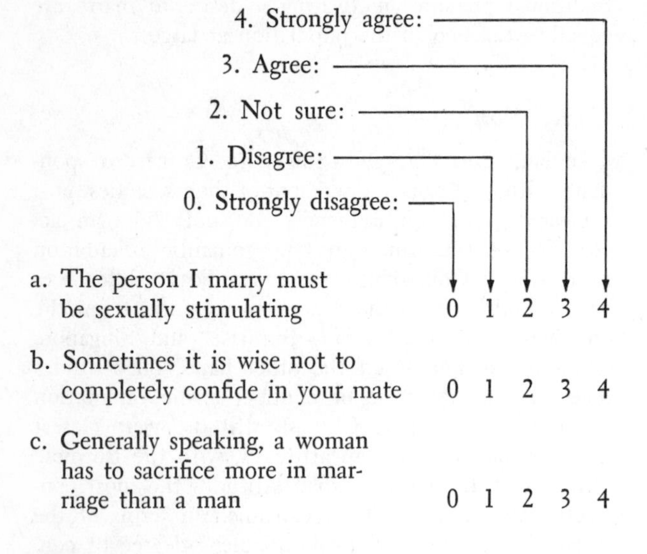

4. Strongly agree:
3. Agree:
2. Not sure:
1. Disagree:
0. Strongly disagree:

a. The person I marry must be sexually stimulating	0	1	2	3	4
b. Sometimes it is wise not to completely confide in your mate	0	1	2	3	4
c. Generally speaking, a woman has to sacrifice more in marriage than a man	0	1	2	3	4

Data analysis

1. *Tally* (onto Tables 1, 2, and 3 of the tabulation form) the codes for the three questions used to index romanticism. These codes are in boxes 62a, 62b, and 62c. Use tally marks (𝍸 ///) entered in the place headed "Number."

2. *To be most efficient*: (A) Tally the codes for all three boxes at one time. (B) Divide up the code sheets so that you and your partner can each tally half of the code sheets and then combine your tallies. An alternative way to divide up the work is to have one person read out the codes as the other person tallies them.

3. *Note* that to simplify the analysis, each of the questions is tallied into only two groups: a "romantic response" group, and a residual group.

4. *Combine* your results with those of your partner (if each of you tallied half of the code sheets).

5. *Add* the tally marks for each row and then add the rows to get the total number of cases. Do not include the "no information" (+) cases in the total.

6. *Compute* the percentage of cases in the romantic group for each question (by dividing the number of cases in the romantic group by the total number of cases or by looking them up in the percentage tables in Appendix B), and then enter them under "This Study" in Table 4. (Your instructor may put the results obtained by several different students on the blackboard so that you can check your results.)

Lab report

1. *Important*. Read the directions for writing laboratory reports in Appendix A before attempting to write your own report.

2. You may encounter some difficulty in this first problem in determining the INDEPENDENT and DEPENDENT VARIABLES. For our present purpose, the independent variable is degree of industrialization and urbanization of the *society* (from most to least industrialized these are: U.S.A., Singapore, India, and Burma as measured by the nationality of students completing the questionnaire), and the dependent variable is *romantic culture* or culturally patterned behavior current in these societies as measured by the percentage supporting a romantic conception of marriage in response to three questions in the questionnaire.

3. In describing the SAMPLE give the number of cases and characteristics of both the cases obtained by Theodorson and the cases obtained for your replication of the American part of his study. Mention any characteristics (in addition to nationality) which might influence the results.

4. Base your write-up of the FINDINGS on a comparison of the percentages you have just computed for American students with the percentages Theodorson obtained for students in India, Burma, and Singapore, as given in Table 4. See the article "How To Read A Table" (Pages 9–13).

5. Gives special attention to the DISCUSSION. Be sure to give possible reasons for the differences found. In addition to arguing from various readings, do not hesitate to advance your own reasoning.

References

Benedict, Ruth, "Continuities and Discontinuities in Cultural Conditioning," in Logan Wilson and William L. Clob, eds., *Sociological Analysis*. New York: Harcourt, Brace & World, Inc., 1949, pp. 223–231.

Hall, Edward T., *The Silent Language*. Garden City, N. Y.: Doubleday, 1959.

Kluckhohn, Florence, Fred Strodtbeck *et al.*, *Variations in Value Orientations*. New York: Harper & Row, 1961.

Merton, Robert K., "Social Structure and Anomie," in *Social Theory and Social Structure*. New York: Free Press, 1959, pp. 131–160.

Parsons, Talcott, *The Social System*. New York: Free Press, 1951.

Sirjamaki, John, "Culture Configurations in the American Family," *American Journal of Sociology*, 53 (May 1948), pp. 464–470.

Summer, William G., *Folkways*. New York: A Mentor Book, 1960.

Name____________________

Date____________________

TABLE 1. Physical attraction as a criterion for marriage

PHYSICAL ATTRACTION (Box 62a)	Tally of number of cases below	Percent
"Others" (codes of 0, 1, & 2)		
"Romantics" (codes of 3 & 4)		
TOTAL		100%
+ (No info.)		

TABLE 2. Confiding in spouse

CONFIDE IN SPOUSE (Box 62b)	Tally number of cases below	Percent
Romantics (0 and 1)		
Others (2, 3, and 4)		
TOTAL		100%
+ (No info.)		

TABLE 3. Equality of sacrifice in marriage

SACRIFICE IN MARRIAGE (Box 62c)	Tally number of cases below	Percent
Romantics (0 and 1)		
Others (2, 3, and 4)		
TOTAL		100%
+ (No info.)		

TABLE 4. Percentage supporting romanticism in four societies[a]

ROMANTICISM INDICATOR	MOST URBAN AND INDUSTRIALIZED ← Americans: Theodorson's results	Americans: Your results	Singapore Chinese	Indians	→ LEAST URBAN AND INDUSTRIALIZED Burmese
Physical attraction	83%	———	60%	44%	—
Confide in spouse	43%	———	21%	15%	13%
Equality of sacrifice	48%	———	23%	15%	19%

[a] The percentages in this table were supplied through the courtesy of Professor Theodorson to enable you to avoid the more complex calculation of the romanticism indexes used in his article.

LABORATORY REPORT FOR PROBLEM ____________

Course or
Section ____________ Date ____________ Name ____________

HYPOTHESIS: ____________

SAMPLE: ____________

INDEPENDENT VARIABLE(S): ____________

DEPENDENT VARIABLE(S): ____________

OTHER FACTORS: ____________

LABORATORY REPORT FOR PROBLEM ____________

SUMMARY OF FINDINGS: ____________

DISCUSSION: ____________

PROBLEM 3

SOCIAL STRUCTURE

Culture represents one of the key explanations of social behavior. Yet it is neither the only nor at times even the most important explanation that can be offered. Merely a cursory observation of activities in any society will readily illustrate a wide variety of behaviors which are often outside general cultural prescriptions—murder, theft, and suicide are some obvious examples. Having an inordinately large family (see Problem 15) or the growth of red tape in large-scale formal organizations are two less obvious examples. Such behaviors exist, and to explain them requires a step beyond purely cultural analysis.

In human society, men share not only a variety of common symbolic expectations but patterns of social relationships and interaction as well. The kernel of sociological analysis is to understand the particular consequences of interaction patterns and group membership for other activities. It has been suggested, for example, that suicide is a function of economic reversals as well as relative isolation from friends and relatives. The argument holds that the reversals strain an individual's personality, and the absence of social relations leaves him without resources to discuss and ultimately bolster his depressed feelings. Consequently, for such persons the probability of suicide is increased (Durkheim, 1951; Henry and Short, 1954). Note that nowhere in this theory is recourse made to the phenomenon of culture, although in fact, most societies maintain strong prescriptions against suicide. The key explanation offered, aside from the allusion to economic reversals, has to do with the presence and absence of social relationships. Consider another example, one provided by Myrdal in the analysis of race relations in America. Myrdal notes that American culture has a strong equalitarian bias, a bias most persons readily accept. Nonetheless, in their behavior few persons practice this equalitarian preference in regard to Negroes, in part for fear of economic or violent reprisals from others in the community (Myrdal, 1944). Similar examples could be cited, but a more important point is at stake: Resources, power, subtle pressures and the other things that are part and parcel of human interaction represent a distinctive explanation of human behavior.

In reality, all human behavior has roots in both social relations and in culture. Some sociologists use the term "socio-cultural" as a means of illustrating this duality (Kroeber and Parsons, 1958). But the distinction between social relations and culture is a viable one precisely because the pressures emanating from each are not always consistent with one another. For this reason, attempts to understand the influence of social interaction, or more broadly, social structure, have typically focused on showing that particular behaviors are carried out regardless of whether or not persons have values consonant with such behavior (Blau, 1960). The research reported by Blood and Wolfe as the reading for the present problem illustrates this strategy.

Specifically, Blood and Wolfe's study deals with the distribution of power in the family and the relationship of this distribution to a variety of indicators of social class. From a cultural perspective, it might be argued that differences in family behavior between middle-class and working-class individuals are a result of the different attitudes, values, and norms of the two classes. It is known, for example, that the middle-class subculture specifies an equalitarian relationship between husband and wife, that is, shared decisions on all important family matters. In contrast, the working-class subculture values male dominance, the feeling that "the husband should wear the pants" (Hoffman, 1960; Komarovsky, 1964). Thus, on the basis of differences in subcultural preferences one would expect to find that working-class husbands have higher power scores than middle-class husbands.

However intriguing this argument may appear, it ignores the structural perspective that power is a function of the resources a person has available by virtue of his position in the class structure. Obviously a middle-class man has available a wider range of resources in the form of a higher education, more earning power in the market place, and a more prestigious occupation. This would argue for a hypothesis in the direction opposite to the one specified by the subcultural perspective, namely, that middle-class men have more power in their family than working-class men. In fact, this is precisely the hypothesis supported by Blood and Wolfe's data: Despite the cultural preference for equalitarianism in the middle class and male dominance in the working class, power follows resources, and it is the middle-class husband who exerts more power in the family.

THE POWER TO MAKE DECISIONS / *Robert O. Blood and Donald M. Wolfe*

The methods of this study

While our over-all approach throughout this book is to provide a general and theoretical discussion of family structure and process, of the problems families face and the services they perform for their members, it is essential to base this discussion on empirical evidence. Thus, this book is also a report of a major research project on the modern American family.

The data presented in the tables and text come from a systematic probability-sample survey of families in the Detroit metropolitan area and from a comparable survey of farm families in southeastern Michigan. Structured and controlled interviews, lasting more than an hour each, were conducted with 731 urban and suburban wives and with 178 farm wives. Where comparable data are available, these data match very well the findings of the 1950 U.S. Census for the same geographical areas; the samples seem to be quite representative of the populations from which they were drawn.

It may seem strange that in a study of marriage only one partner should be interviewed. However, many previous studies have shown a close correlation between what husbands and wives say about their marriages, making it possible to rely on one partner's responses. There are undoubtedly individual cases where the husband would have given a different picture from the one the wife gave us, but these differences tend to get lost in the shuffle when large numbers of cases are considered.

Wives, in general, probably look at marriage somewhat differently from husbands. Hence, it should be remembered that this is a wife's-eye view of marriage. But we assume that when we make comparisons between groups of wives—as between middle-class wives and working-class wives—the sex bias cancels out and the differences which emerge are real differences between families.

The selection of wives instead of husbands was largely a question of productivity. Wives are more easily located at home so that more interviews can be obtained from them. In addition, to the extent that wives invest more time and effort in family matters, they may provide more complete and useful data. Although unavailable at present, a comparable study based on interviews with husbands would nevertheless add valuable detail.

Two theories about the sources of power

No change in the American family is mentioned more often than the shift from one-sided male authority to the sharing of power by husband and wife. Perhaps no change is more significant, either. The balance of power between husband and wife is a sensitive reflection of the roles they play in marriage—and, in turn, has many repercussions on other aspects of their relationship.

Power and authority. Power may be defined as the potential ability of one partner to influence the other's behavior. Power is manifested in the ability to make decisions affecting the life of the family.

Authority is closely related to power. Authority is legitimate power, i.e., power held by one partner because both partners feel it is proper for him to do so. The family authority pattern is prescribed by the society at large in such forms as: "the man should be the head of the house"—or "husbands should not dictate to their wives."

Power, on the other hand, refers to the way in which husbands and wives actually deal with each other. Caspar Milquetoast, as a man, may be supposed to have considerable authority, but in practice he exercises very little power. Power and authority do not necessarily coincide.

The power to make decisions is influenced by the prescribed authority pattern. In a patriarchal system both the husband and the wife will ordinarily take for granted that the husband should make most of the decisions. He derives a measure of assertiveness from the social norm, and she, a corresponding measure of deference. But even in a tradition-bound society, there are variations between couples. Indeed, the whole conception of a hen-pecked husband implies a norm that is being violated.

The existence of such discrepancies suggests that there must be other sources of marital power besides authority. In the world at large, the illegitimate seizure of power usually rests on military might. But husbands and wives do not ordinarily point guns at each other. Even rolling pins and fists are more often preludes to the disintegration of marriage than the basis on which a balance of power is worked out.

The sources of power in so intimate a relationship as marriage must be sought in the comparative resources which the husband and wife bring to the marriage, rather than in brute force. A resource may be defined as anything that one partner may make available to the other, helping the latter satisfy his needs or attain his goals. The balance of power will be on the side of that partner who contributes the greater resources to the marriage.

Marriage itself may be thought of as an institution designed to meet certain vital needs of the participants. People get married because they believe that they will find sexual fulfillment, emotional response, companionship, and the new experience of parenthood, in living together. Both partners hope to attain these goals through the same marriage. Insofar as both partners contribute to each other's satisfaction in life, they build up a mutual respect that expresses itself naturally in mutual consultation. As one partner is able to contribute more than his share to the marriage, he acquires the basis for a more than fifty-fifty say in decisions. This is seldom a conscious process of weighing the balance. It is an automatic readjustment which occurs as the contributing partner discovers that he has a lot to offer to the marriage, while the receiving partner feels indebted for what has already been given and dependent upon what he hopes to receive in the future. Control over future resources is especially crucial, since decision-making involves the allocation of resources within the family. The partner who may provide or withhold resources is in a strategic position for influencing their disposition. Hence, power accrues spontaneously to the partner who has the greater resources at his disposal.

A second factor is closely related to resources. Anyone who is able to make a contribution is, almost by definition, a competent person—i.e., someone with special skills. To possess a skill enables the individual to make a contribution; in addition, it implies special competence in decision-making as such. Thus, a wife may not only depend on her husband for "bringing home the bacon" but recognize that in his work he becomes familiar with some of the complexities of life outside the home. Therefore, she may defer to his superior knowledge in decisions about politics, taxes, and cars.

The chief objective of this chapter is to look at the comparative competence of the two partners and their relative contributions to marriage, as explanations for the variations which occur between couples' balance of power. According to this hypothesis, Caspar is henpecked because he is incompetent and makes very little contribution to the life-satisfactions of his wife.

CULTURE OR COMPETENCE? If authority patterns and personal resources both influence the balance of power, are they equally important? There are two different theories: according to one, families do what the culture tells them to do; the other states that they do what their own characteristics dictate. In a stable society, the two sources of power will coincide. American society, however, has not been stable. Everybody knows that the balance of power between men and women has been changing. Has it changed because our ideas about how men and women ought to treat each other have changed? Or has it changed because the comparative resources of American men and women have changed?

The answer is not likely to be completely one or the other—since changes in one are bound to affect the other sooner or later. If husbands become infected with democratic ideas and start giving their wives more freedom, the wives will gain more competence. On the other hand, if wives gain increased resources, old patriarchal notions are not likely to remain unaffected for very long.

Despite this interdependence of ideological and pragmatic sources of power, there may still be an important difference in their potency. Historical analyses may show that one changes first and the other follows after. Contemporary analysis may show patriarchal norms continuing to influence the balance of power under changing circumstances, or it may show families adapting rapidly to new conditions no matter their ideological training.

The ideological theory will be tested first by looking for patriarchal subcultures in the Detroit area. If culture is more than just a rationalization of existing circumstances, Detroit families should be more traditional if they grew up on farms, or in "the old country," or in "the old days." This search will prove fruitless; the alternative pragmatic theory of the basis of power will have to be tested to show its usefulness. The evidence from Detroit in support of competence as the chief basis for power will be cumulatively impressive.

According to the resource theory, statements about patriarchal authority patterns or equalitarian ones are chiefly rationalizations of existing practice—like codifications of the common law. As people grow up under a husband-dominant family system, they come to take that balance of power for granted—and even to feel that it is right. Henceforward, the idea of patriarchy acquires momentum and influence in its own right, shaping generations to come until it is undermined by new conditions. At first, only the innovators in society see the handwriting on the wall and begin talking about new beliefs to fit new circumstances. For the rest of society, the old system hangs on by a kind of cultural lag, although increasingly paid only lip service. Finally, the social change is consolidated, and new ideas about marriage spread through the society to all but the most conservative.

From this analysis, it is clear that culture is not a sufficient explanation for power. It is not enough to say that wives used to be submissive to their husbands because they lived under a patriarchal system, or because that was the custom. The search must be pushed further into why the patriarchal system arose in the first place. The same search for "basic" causes will be necessary if we are to understand the modern pattern of decision-making.

The contemporary pattern of power

In order to measure the precise balance of power between husbands and wives one would have to assess their influence in all the family decisions which had even been made—or at least all those which had been made over a considerable period of time. Such an exhaustive undertaking would exceed the capacities of husbands' and wives' memories.

Since a complete record of decisions is unobtainable, any study of marriage must rely on a sample of decisions to represent the larger whole. In this study, eight decisions were selected to provide an estimate of the relative balance of power between husband and wife.

The eight decisions are:

1. What job the husband should take.
2. What car to get.
3. Whether or not to buy life insurance.
4. Where to go on a vacation.
5. What house or apartment to take.
6. Whether or not the wife should go to work or quit work.
7. What doctor to have when someone is sick.
8. How much money the family can afford to spend per week on food.

These eight were selected because they are all relatively important (compared to deciding whether to go to a movie tonight). They are also questions which nearly all couples have to face. (This is why no questions were asked relating to children.) Only three per cent of the couples at most answered any question in hypothetical terms (the three per cent who had never bought a car and the similar number who hadn't yet taken a vacation). The remaining criterion for these questions was that they should range from typically masculine to typically feminine decisions—but should always affect the family as a whole.

It was assumed in advance that contemporary husbands and wives would often talk things over in the process of arriving at a decision. Even a patriarchal husband may consult his wife as one source of opinion and one factor to be taken into consideration while he makes up his mind. The crucial question is not who takes part in the discussion but who makes the final decision. To get this information the lead-in statement to the battery of questions was as follows:

"In every family somebody has to decide such things as where the family will live and so on. Many couples talk such things over first, but the *final* decision often has to be made by the husband or the wife. For instance, who usually makes the final decision about . . . ?"

In order to provide comparable answers, the respondents were given a choice of "husband always," "husband more than wife," "husband and wife exactly the same," "wife more than husband," and "wife always" as response categories.

WHO DECIDES? The wives' answers to the eight questions are shown in Table 1 with the items arranged in order of decreasing male participation.

Two decisions are primarily the husband's province (his job and the car), two the wife's (her work and the food), while all the others are joint decisions in the sense of having more "same" responses than anything else. Even the wife's working turns out to be a quite middling decision from the standpoint of the mean score, leaving only the food expenditures preponderantly in the wife's hands. Only the two male decisions are made more than half the time by a particular partner.

Sex roles. The distribution of decisions by sex is not surprising. The husband's work is his chief role in life. From it he derives his greatest sense of well-being or malaise, and there he invests the greatest part of his energies. His work is so one-sidedly important to him that almost all the wives leave him alone for his final decision.

Automobiles are associated with the mechanical aptitude of males (Scheinfeld, 1943). Moreover, a large proportion of the driving in the United States is done by males, giving them added interest in the choice of car.

At the other extreme, meal-planning is part of the wife's role in the division of labor (as will be documented in the next chapter), giving to the wife the major responsibility for food expenditures.

The choice of doctor falls to the wife especially often where there are dependent children in the home, so that it is associated with her role as mother. However, it also reflects the general tendency of women to play a nurturant role for the sick and helpless.

The family vacation and the choice of house are most frequently joint decisions. Is this because they most clearly affect both partners equally?

The fact that insurance decisions are made somewhat more often by the husband may reflect the technical financial questions involved. If so, the financial training involved in his money-earning role gives him extra competence.

That the husband should be more involved in his wife's job decisions than she with his is understandable. For one thing, her work is seldom her major preoccupation in life the way it is for a man. Even if she works just as many hours a week, she does not usually make the same life-long commitment to the world of work. Nor is her pay check as indispensable to the family finances (if only because it is usually smaller). In such ways the choice whether to work or not is less vital to a woman than to a man.

In addition, the wife's decisions about working have repercussions on the husband. If his wife goes to work, he will have to help out more around the house. If he is a business executive, he may prefer to have her concentrate her energy on entertaining prospective clients at home. As a small businessman or independent professional, he may need her services in his own enterprise. On the other hand, regardless of his own occupation, he may want her to work in order to help him buy a house or a business or pay for the children's education.

It may be, then, that the work role is so much the responsibility of the husband in marriage that even the wife's work is but an adjunct of his instrumental leadership, leaving this decision frequently in his hands.

THE BALANCE OF POWER. Whether families are patriarchal in general is far more important than whether they sometimes conform to patriarchal norms in a single area of decision-making. With eight ques-

TABLE 1. Allocation of power in decision-making areas (731 Detroit families)

	Decision							
Who decides?	Husband's job	Car	Insurance	Vacation	House	Wife's work	Doctor	Food
(5) Husband always	90%	56%	31%	12%	12%	26%	7%	10%
(4) Husband more than wife	4	12	11	6	6	5	3	2
(3) Husband and wife exactly the same	3	25	41	68	58	18	45	32
(2) Wife more than husband	0	2	4	4	10	9	11	11
(1) Wife always	1	3	10	7	13	39	31	41
N.A.	2	1	2	3	1	3	3	3
Total	100	99	99	100	100	100	100	99
Husband's mean power[a]	4.86	4.18	3.50	3.12	2.94	2.69	2.53	2.26

[a] The mean for each column is computed on the basis of the weights shown, e.g., "husband always" = 5.

tions so widely distributed between masculine and feminine roles, the Detroit families as a whole could not look very patriarchal when their answers to the whole battery of questions are totalled up. Even so, there might still be considerable variation between families, if in some the husbands consistently make the decisions while in others wives consistently do.

In actual practice, such consistency is rare. Less than one half of one per cent of the Detroit husbands make all eight decisions and a similarly small proportion of wives are all-powerful. Nevertheless such extremes do exist and exemplify the fact that it is possible to find all kinds of power-balances from the most patriarchal to the most matriarchal.

Given these eight particular questions, the aggregate balance of power falls slightly in the husband's direction. When the total scores for the eight questions, weighted as shown in Table 1, are converted into a ten-point scale reflecting the amount of influence exerted by the husband, the average score for all families is 5.09 (whereas a score of 4.00 is the equivalent of "husband and wife exactly the same").

Although families can be found varying all the way from one extreme to the other, most families bunch together around this mean score. Forty-six per cent of all the Detroit families have scores of four to six. Though slightly skewed to the husband's side in absolute terms, it seems preferable to label these as relatively equalitarian couples. This leaves twenty-two per cent with scores of seven or more who can be called relatively male dominant and another twenty-two per cent with scores of three or less who are relatively female-dominant.[1] Even these extreme groups cluster close to the central group. This means that Detroit families, on the whole, are extraordinarily alike when it comes to the balance of decision-making.

The middle group of equalitarian marriages can be differentiated further according to whether they make most of their decisions jointly or whether they assign equal numbers of separate decisions to both partners. The former type is called "syncratic" and the latter "autonomic" (Herbst in Oeser and Hammond, 1954). Despite the fact that these four types (husband-dominant, syncratic, autonomic, and wife-dominant) are concentrated in the middle range of power, they still differ enough from each other to provide important distinctions between families in many respects.

The impression that the average Detroit marriage is properly labelled equalitarian is supported by answers to the question: "When you and your husband differ about something, do you usually give in and do it your husband's way, or does he usually come around to your point of view?" Thirty-four per cent say that they usually or always give in under these circumstances, twenty-four per cent say the husband does, but the remaining forty per cent (two per cent, no answer) give equalitarian responses. This forty per cent undoubtedly underestimates the proportion of equalitarian marriages because many wives made it entirely clear that they and their husbands agree on most things most of the time, leaving this question to apply only to marginal disagreements. When viewed against the relatively small margin of husband-winning over wife-winning cases, Detroit marriages have clearly moved a long way from nineteenth century patriarchalism.

The sources of power in marriage

Having designated some marriages as relatively husband-dominant, let us search for the segments of the population in which the patriarchal tradition apparently still survives. Presumably it should be found intact among those families which have been less exposed to urban, industrial, and educational influences.

WHERE IS THE PATRIARCHAL FAMILY? The groups which would be expected to be patriarchal are families now or formerly living on farms, immigrant families, old couples, uneducated couples, and Catholic marriages (because of the Catholic advocacy of the patriar-

[1] The remaining 10 per cent are unknown because they failed to answer one or more of the eight decision questions.

chal ideal). However, none of these expectations is confirmed.

Farm families? The typical number of decisions made by Michigan farm husbands is exactly the same as the score for city husbands. This does not necessarily mean that living on a farm no longer contributes to the husband's power. But it certainly means that its influence may be entirely nullified by other factors, at least on farms that are within the sphere of influence of a giant metropolis.

With no difference between the families living on farms and those living in the city, patriarchal survivals cannot be expected among people within the city who grew up on farms. The differences between migrants and Detroit-born families actually lie in the opposite direction from what was expected (with migrant wives making more rather than less of the decisions). This is probably due to their low social status rather than a reflection of any matriarchal cultural pattern.

Immigrant families? A second place where patriarchal culture might survive is among immigrants from the old country. Families brought up under patriarchal norms would be expected to live by the ideals that they learned in their youth even after moving to a new country.

These expectations are refuted, again. Immigrants turn out to be less patriarchal than native Americans (see Table 2). Again the differences which exist in this table are probably not a reflection of different ideas but of the relatively low-status position which immigrants hold in our society.

TABLE 2. Husband's power in native-born and foreign-born families

	Wife's Place of Birth	
	Native-born	Foreign-born
Husband's mean power[a]	5.24	4.94
Number of families	494	60

[a] Those interested in the statistical significance of differences between means of subsamples on this power index (assuming that the variance of the subsamples is the same as that of the total sample) may keep in mind that the probability is less than .05 of finding as great as .34, when the subsamples are around 200 cases each, or .69 when the subsamples are around 50 cases each, in size. In all cross-tabulations, cases not ascertained on either variable have been omitted for the sake of simplicity.

Uneducated couples? The final place where a lingering patriarchy might be found is among couples who haven't been exposed to the unsettling influences of modern education, especially higher education. Supposedly, equalitarianism is the new enlightened norm which grade school graduates are unfamiliar with, but to which college students especially subscribe. This is the theme of many textbooks on marriage, under such meaningful titles as *Marriage for Moderns* (Bowman, 1960).

Table 3 shows that there is indeed a relationship between exposure to education and the amount of power the husband has—but that it is in the opposite direction from the theory of eroding patriarchalism. As usual, the opposite conclusion does not follow—that high schools and colleges are teaching their graduates (especially their male graduates) to be patriarchal. The contribution of education to the power structure seems likely to be non-ideological in nature (see below). For both husbands and wives, education seems to be a source of personal power vis-à-vis the partner. This will become clearer later when the relationship of the comparative education of husband and wife to power is explored.

We have looked in five directions for evidence that patriarchal subcultures still linger in contemporary American society—and without success. Neither the farm families, nor immigrants from other countries, nor Catholic families, nor the older generation, nor poorly educated families adhere to a patriarchal way of life. In some cases, they are no different from the families which were expected to be more "modern" in their decision-making. In other cases, they are significantly less patriarchal than those which were supposed to be most "emancipated" from the bonds of tradition.

Under these circumstances, the weight of evidence suggests that the patriarchal family is dead. This does not mean there is no such thing as an American family in which the husband makes most of the decisions. Nor does it mean that no *groups* of American families can be found in which the husbands have a great deal of power. What it does mean is that wherever husbands exercise power today, it is not because they and their wives subscribe to a patriarchal belief system which says that it is only right and proper to have this kind of marriage.

PRAGMATIC SOURCES OF POWER. Having exhausted the fruitfulness of the ideological theory of power, it is desirable to turn to the pragmatic theory. To restate it simply, this proposes that the balance of power in particular families and in whole categories of families is determined by the comparative resourcefulness of the two partners and by the life circumstances within which they live.

Some husbands today are just as powerful as their grandfathers were—but they can no longer take for granted the *authority* held by older generations of men. No longer is the husband able to exercise power just because he is "the man of the house." Rather, he must prove his right to power, or win power by virtue of his own skills and accomplishments in competition with his wife.

This reflects a new unpredictability in family life. Under former historical circumstances, the husband's economic and social role almost automatically gave him pre-eminence. Under modern conditions, the roles of men and women have changed so much that husbands and wives are potential equals—with the balance of power tipped sometimes one way, sometimes the other. It is no longer possible to assume that just because a man is a man, he is the boss. Once upon a time, the function of culture was to rationalize the predominance of the male sex. Today the function of culture is to develop a philosophy of equal rights under which the

TABLE 3. Husband's power, by husband's and wife's education

Husband's mean power	Years of education					
	Under 6	7–8	9–11	12	13–15	16+
By husband's education	4.87 (53)	4.73 (98)	5.17 (121)	5.41 (173)	5.70 (54)	5.46 (50)
By wife's education	4.83 (46)	5.07 (82)	5.10 (136)	5.43 (229)	5.25 (36)	4.87 (23)

saying goes, "May the best man win!"—and the best man is sometimes a woman. The role of culture has shifted from sanctioning a competent sex over an incompetent sex to sanctioning the competent marriage partner over the incompetent one, regardless of sex.

Under these circumstances, it seems wise to abandon the use of the term "patriarchal" because of its implication of prescribed authority. Preferable instead is the term "husband-dominant" which is the modern equivalent of the old patriarchate, minus the supporting sanctions.

THE HUSBAND'S POSITION IN THE COMMUNITY. Although society no longer insists upon a particular balance of power in marriage, the larger community still affects husband-wife relationships. Today, the more successful the husband is in the eyes of the community, the more dominant his part in marital decision-making.

Earlier it was suggested that the low social status of Southern farm migrants, foreign immigrants, and poorly educated husbands might account for their low power. Now it is desirable to look directly at indices of success in the community.

Occupation. Table 4 shows that generally speaking, the higher the husband's occupational prestige, the greater his voice in marital decisions.[2] The major break comes between white-collar occupations and blue-collar occupations.

TABLE 4. Husband's power, by occupational status

	Husband's occupation			
	Blue collar		White collar	
	Low[a]	High	Low	High
Husband's mean power	5.07	4.98	5.36	5.52
Number of families	162	161	78	151

[a] Low-blue-collar jobs are semi-skilled, unskilled, and service. High-blue-collar: skilled workers and foremen. Low-white-collar: sales and clerical. High-white-collar: busines and professional.

Why should the average white-collar husband have more say at home than blue-collar ones? Perhaps the prestige of white-collar work provides self-confidence in his own eyes and respect in the eyes of his wife. In addition, white-collar work involves reliance on the interpersonal skills of discussion and argument which are involved in decision-making. Moreover, husbands accustomed to responsible roles on the job would understandably be inclined to take responsibility in the home. As a result of such factors, white-collar husbands are extra-equipped with the knowledge and skills required for decision-making, and their wives correspondingly inclined to recognize their husband's competence along these lines.

Income. Because his work is his chief role in life, occupational success is the crucial index of a man's competence. But the kind of job a man has is not the only measure of occupational achievement. After all, many men simply follow in their fathers' footsteps. The son of a professional man will usually be a white-collar worker too, and though this gives him prestige in the eyes of the community, it may not reflect an unusually competent personality.

A better measure of success on the job is how much money the husband earns. In part, this is simply a reflection of occupation. But extreme income differences go beyond this to sort out the most successful from the least successful workers.

TABLE 5. Husband's power, by income

	Husband's income				
	Under $3,000	$3,000 –4,999	$5,000 –6,999	$7,000 –9,999	$10,-000+
Husband's mean power	4.58	5.00	5.25	5.38	5.83
Number of families	57	165	185	84	48

Table 5 shows that the husband's earnings are an even more sensitive indicator of his power than his occupation. Partly this is because the families are now split into five groups instead of four. Mostly this is because small groups are separated out at both extremes. Husbands with less than $3,000 income are the least successful of the low-blue-collar workers, and those earning more than $10,000 the most successful of the high-white-collar workers (such as doctors and big businessmen).

Bringing home the bacon is a prime example of contributing a resource to marriage. That top-income-bracket husbands should be most influential in marriage reflects the magnitude of their contribution to the family exchequer. By contrast, where the total income of the family (rather than the husband's alone) is taken into consideration, the balance of power is altered in the wife's direction. As a result of the supplementary contribution of other family members (principally the wives themselves), the number of families

[2] The generalization that husband's power is correlated with occupational status also holds within the Negro race (4.31, 4.60, no cases, and 5.00 respectively).

When controls for the wife's employment are instituted, there is one reversal at the blue-collar level among housewife families: 5.31, 5.16, 5.50, 5.68, while working-wife families show no difference at the blue-collar level: 4.22, 4.22, 4.77, 4.85.

in the $7–10,000 income bracket jumps from 84 to 131 while the husband's power falls drastically from 5.38 to 4.85. Above the $10,000 mark there are 78 multiple-income families compared to 48 one-income units, and the husband's power is reduced from 5.83 to 5.41. This comparison shows how the balance of power reflects the husband's resources alone only as long as other things are equal. So, high-income husbands are most powerful if their wives contribute no income.

Social status. Income and occupation are interrelated variables. The husband's education is also related [illegible] amount of power that he has. These are the [illegible] variables that sociologists often group together to summarize the social position or status of a family in the community. The Social Status Index used here is an aggregate of these three factors (occupation, income, and education) plus the prestige-ranking of the husband's ethnic or nationality background. The combined index gives a rough picture of a family's over-all prestige in the eyes of the community from the standpoint of these four characteristics.[8]

For the community as a whole, the husband's power is directly related to his social status: 4.39, 4.79, 5.00, 5.33, 5.56. However, the few white husbands in the lowest social status group differ sharply from their powerless Negro counterparts. . . . If this small group is dismissed as likely to be affected by factors other than status alone, the general conclusion from Table 6 is that the higher the husband's social status, the greater his power.

TABLE 6. Husband's power, by social status

	Percentile ranking on social status index				
	0–19	20–39	40–59	60–79	80–99
Husband's mean power	5.33	5.02	4.97	5.37	5.57
Number of families	12	87	194	174	84

Do high-status husbands exercise control equally over all eight decision areas? Examination of the relationship between social status and the eight separate decisions shows that high-status husbands make more decisions in only three areas: whether to buy life insurance, what house or apartment to get, and especially whether the wife should go to work or quit work. Actually what happens is not that more high-status husbands make these decisions unilaterally, but that fewer wives do. In other words, high-status husbands take a more active part rather than the wife making the decision by herself.

[8] Income and education scores were assigned on the basis of the percentiles of the Detroit population falling at the various rank levels. Occupation scores used the percentile prestige ratings developed by the National Opinion Research Center. The ethnic scale was developed from ratings by 195 University of Michigan students from the Detroit area. The over-all score is a simple average of these four individual scores. Examples of scores are: $5,000 income, 61 points; factory worker, 26 points; 11 years of schooling, 42 points; Polish ancestry, 34 points. Such a family would have a Social Status Index of 40.75. (Further details are given in Lenski, 1954.)

Are there any reasons why high-status husbands would want to control these particular areas? Chapter 3 will show that high-status husbands are more apt to handle the money and bills. The reason for this appears to be that there is a larger increment of money involved beyond the level of daily necessities. At high-status levels, insurance correspondingly becomes more than burial insurance. As a major expenditure, it necessarily interests the husband. Such husbands are also making a major investment when it comes to choice of a house, whereas for low-status families one flat is about as good as another. Finally, the low-status wife more often feels she has a right to decide for herself whether she will go to work or not, whereas the high-status husband again takes more of an interest in these matters. This does not necessarily mean that high-status husbands are worried about a threat to their prestige if their wives go to work, but that they are concerned about the problems involved in the reorganization of their family life around a working wife. If such reasoning is sound, insurance, housing, and the wife's employment are all matters of special interest to the high-status husband.

In general then, social-status differences in decision-making lie in the more active sharing of responsibility by high-status husbands, whereas low-status men more often fail to take part in the decision-making process. This is the first of many signs which will appear of patterns of sharing in the middle class and of *apartheid* in the working class. The latter pattern often orients the husband outside the family, leaving the wife saddled with the burden of making family decisions unaided. In terms of the four kinds of decision-making, this means that middle-class families are more often syncratic (shared-equal), whereas working-class families tend to be more wife-dominant in their power structure.

Education. Table 3 showed that the more education the husband had, the greater his power. However, for wives the relationship seems to be curvilinear. By putting the education of the husband and the wife together, it is possible to resolve this apparent contradiction.

The Detroit data show that where the wife has at least five more years of schooling than the husband his power is only 4.29, but when the tables are reversed, his power is 5.68. The conclusion is clear that the more one partner's education exceeds that of the other, the larger his share in marital decision-making will be.

Such a relationship might be due simply to the fact that only comparatively high-status (and therefore powerful) husbands exceed their wives in education by five or more years, while it takes a comparatively low-status husband to be that much inferior to his wife. However, controlling by the husband's occupation does not wipe out the relationship (see Table 7). Instead, high-white-collar husbands continue to gain power if they exceed the wife's education, and to lose it if they fall short of the wife. And the same trends hold within the low-white-collar and the high-blue-collar groups, leaving only one low-blue-collar reversal.

Since comparative education influences marital decision-making at all occupational levels, it proves to be a highly consistent resource for marital power.

TABLE 7. Husband's power, by comparative education of husband and wife within occupational strata

Husband's mean power by husband's occupation	Comparative education		
	Wife more	Equal	Husband more
High-white-collar	5.32 (31)	5.45 (42)	5.65 (78)
Low-white-collar	4.92 (12)	5.20 (30)	5.59 (37)
High-blue-collar	4.80 (117)	5.08 (84)	5.28 (82)
Low-blue-collar	4.79 (14)	5.44 (16)	4.88 (8)

Schooling trains people in verbal skills and knowledge which facilitate decision-making quite directly. In addition, schooling contributes to the effective participation of the individual in the community (through paid or voluntary participation) which in turn strengthens the power position of the individual. So whether directly or indirectly, the better-educated partner brings greater resources to the decision arena.

Organizational participation. Activity in a formal organization provides the wife with a resource analogous to the husband's success on the job. Getting outside the home brings knowledge pertinent to settling household issues. Moreover, a person who has enough initiative to be active in the community seems also more likely to participate actively in family decision-making. By contrast, stay-at-home spouses may lack the personal and community-derived resources to play as active a role in making decisions.

Unfortunately, the questionnaire used in this study did not include information on the frequency with which husbands attend organizational meetings. However, it does yield the number of types of organizations both partners belong to.[4] Table 8 shows that the partner who belongs to more types of organizations—aside from a church—takes a more active part in family decisions. At the extremes, wives who belong to at least two more organizations depress the husband's power to 4.45 whereas the converse husbands raise it to 5.45. Presumably knowledge of the partners' comparative degree of activity in their organizations would yield an even better picture of the skills and resources they bring to the marriage.

Church membership was excluded from Table 8 because sociologists have traditionally viewed church membership as a conventional matter unlikely to signify

TABLE 8. Husband's power, by comparative organizational membership of husband and wife

	Comparative organizational membership		
	Wife more	Equal	Husband more
Husband's mean power	5.05	5.14	5.36
Number of families	85	216	250

much about the persons involved. The separate analysis of comparative church attendance in Table 9 suggests that separation is unnecessary—churches should be looked upon as another example of a formal organization. (Indeed labor unions with their much lower percentage of attendance at meetings are correspondingly less meaningful organizations to the rank and file.)[5]

Table 9 shows that the more often the husband attends church, the more power he has. Churches are not unique in this respect. This is another example of the kind of influence attached to participation in any organization outside the home. Perhaps in a society where church-going is so much the norm, we should put it the other way around and say that individuals who attend *less* often than their partners tend to put themselves at a disadvantage and weaken their basis for participating in family decisions.

TABLE 9. Husband's power, by comparative church attendance of husband and wife (same church only)

	Comparative frequency of church attendance		
	Wife more	Equal	Husband more
Husband's mean power	4.72	5.21	5.70
Number of families	99	370	20

Work. Participation in organizations is in many ways the equivalent of holding a job. Both involve coming to the family from a point of independent leverage. Both involve outside contacts which bolster the resources in knowledge and interpersonal skill which the participating partner brings to the marriage. Working, of course, involves the additional contribution of money—the most tangible of all resources. For both reasons, we would expect the comparative work participation of the two partners to affect the balance of power.

Table 10 shows that whichever partner works more gains power thereby. This is true not only for working wives versus non-working wives but even reflects the number of hours the husband works, with overtime husbands edging out husbands who work only a forty-hour week.

It is difficult to know where to place in this series the families in which neither partner is employed. In

[4] Most Detroiters belong to very few organizations aside from a church. Forty-two per cent of the wives and 19 per cent of the husbands belong to no non-church organizations at all, while 28 per cent and 40 per cent respectively belong to only one type (e.g., labor unions or lodges). Even this membership is often nominal, for almost a fourth of those women who belong to one or more organizations hadn't attended a single meeting in the three months prior to being interviewed.

[5] The median Detroit wife attends church every week, the typical husband about every two weeks.

TABLE 10. Husband's power, by comparative work participation of husband and wife

	Comparative work participation					
	WIFE NOT EMPLOYED			WIFE EMPLOYED		
	Husband overtime	Husband full-time	Husband none	Husband overtime	Husband full-time	Husband none
Husband's mean power	56.2	5.28	4.88	4.50	4.46	2.67
Number of families	195	218	25	44	57	3

some respects, they might seem equivalent to couples where both partners work full time. However their equality in not working is tempered by the fact that many of these wives never worked. This may be why the husband's power is greater than that of two-income families.

Marital power reflects not only the current working relationship of the partners but the length of time the wife works after marriage. The more years the wife has worked since marriage, the more power she has (see Table 11). Only one-third of the wives who have ever worked since marriage are currently employed. Nevertheless, the number of years worked correlate with the wife's power regardless of whether she is still working.[6]

TABLE 11. Husband's power, by length of wife's work participation since marriage

	Wife's work participation in years				
	0	Under 1	1–4	5–9	10+
Husband's mean power	5.80	5.65	4.97	4.66	4.29
Number of families	154	85	183	70	55

The relationship between the wife's employment and her power is complicated by the fact that more wives are employed in the wife-dominant, low-status segment of the community. Indeed this is one reason why low-status husbands on the whole have less power. However, controlling on social status and race shows that working wives have substantially more power on the average than non-working wives at all status levels. Indeed the comparative work participation of husband and wife is related far more closely to the balance of power in marriage than is the social status of the husband in the community taken by itself. This is not, however, to reject the importance of considering the husband's social position, for both his own community role and his wife's comparative resources contribute to the over-all balance of power in marriage.

The power to make decisions

In summary, the power to make decisions stems primarily from the resources which the individual can provide to meet the needs of his marriage partner and to upgrade his decision-making skill. Because it is based on such tangible and relevant criteria, the balance of power may be said to be adapted to the interpersonal relationship of the two partners involved.

Contemporary married couples are freed from the "dead hand" of patriarchal tradition to work out their own destiny in the way best suited to them. This does not mean that they can work out their decision-making pattern in any fashion whatever, but that they are not bound by any "cake of custom" which arbitrarily installs one sex in power. Whereas in the past, custom often dictated that all families should be patriarchal, today the rise of women produces considerable variation between families (and even within families with the passage of time). With less sex-linked cultural norms, such variation incurs less penalty than it once would have. Indeed, the emerging norm may not be a particular pattern of male-dominance or equalitarianism but, rather, the idea of appropriateness. If a wife is working today, it is appropriate that she should have more voice in decisions, rather than be subjugated to an arbitrary standard.

Only at the wife-dominant extreme is there evidence of deviance from the norm today. It may be appropriate for the wife who is the sole support of her family to make most of the decisions, but it certainly is not normal for the marital roles to be reversed in this way. We will find throughout this study dissatisfaction associated with wife-dominance. This is not, however, simply a reflection of breaking social rules. Rather, the circumstances which lead to the wife's dominance involve corresponding inadequacies and incompetencies on the husband's part. An inadequate husband is by definition unable to make a satisfactory marriage partner. So the dominant wife is not exultant over her "victory," but exercises power regretfully by default of her "no good" or incapacitated husband.

Within the range from husband-dominance to extreme equalitarianism, appropriateness appears to be linked with satisfaction. A wife who doesn't get to make many decisions does get to have her needs met by a resourceful husband, and the husband who "has to" share his power with his wife has the compensation of her greater contributions to the marriage.

Under these circumstances, power in American marriages is not a matter of brute coercion and unwilling defeat so much as a mutual recognition of individual skills in particular areas of competence and of the partners' dual stake in areas of joint concern. Given such a natural working out of particular decisions under varying circumstances, it is no wonder that most wives

[6] This generalization applies primarily to wives who work apart from their husbands. Gold and Slater (1958) find that young independent businessmen and professionals are more often patriarchal than junior corporation executives, despite the fact that the formers' wives often assist them in their work, whereas the latter do not. Apparently helping one's husband involves submission to his leadership and therefore should not be considered an independent resource for the wife in the same sense that working for someone else is.

cannot say *why* they make decisions at home the way they do.[7] All they are aware of is that somehow their balance of power "just growed" and that it is right.

Only when American marriages are looked at *en masse* is it clear why power is patterned the way it is—and why it seems right to the couples involved. The answer lies in the tangible resources and skills which the two partners pool in marriage. Today's marriages have a variable balance of power which is not determined by the assignment of authority to one sex, but by the interplay of dynamic forces which affect the marriage from within and without.

Replication

SOCIAL CLASS AND POWER WITHIN THE FAMILY

This replication will focus on the relationship between the husband's position in the community and the power he exercises in the family. To simplify the tabulations, the husband's position in the community will be measured only by the prestige of his occupation. Given the high correlation between prestige and the other indicators that Blood and Wolfe use, as for example education or income, this simplification should not drastically alter the logic of the analysis.

The measure of power used for our replication closely approximates Blood and Wolfe's, namely, a summary score of the frequency of times husbands or wives "had the final say" in a sample of household decisions. However, as Heer (1963) has observed, there are many aspects of power, each of which requires a different measurement technique. For example, there is an important difference between the *authority* of a member of the family, which is the legitimacy or the social recognition of that person's right to exercise power, and the power actually exercised. Thus, in a society such as India where the husband is vested with almost absolute authority, the wife or son, in practice, are frequently very influential. For purposes of this replication, we are concerned with the latter phenomena: Specifically, the question of the balance of power between husband and wife in terms of who has the final say on a number of important decisions.

Hypothesis

1. State which of the following social class groups you think will be shown by this study to have the highest, and which the lowest, average score for father's decision power: working class, lower middle class, or upper middle class.

2. For a second hypothesis, state what you think the results will show for farmers.

3. See Appendix A for general information on writing a hypothesis.

Empirical indicators for this problem

11. Father's Occupation:

    1. Proprietor (except farm)
    2. Manager or official
    3. Professional
    4. Clerical and sales
    5. Farm owner or operator
    6. Skilled worker and foreman
    7. Semi-skilled and unskilled worker

12. Occupational Prestige:

    1. Proprietor of a large business (valued at $100,-000 or more); Top-level executive in large organization; Top-level professional

    2. Proprietor of a medium business (valued at $35,000 to $100,000); Middle-level executive or official, or top level of a small organization; Lower-level professional; Sales representative of manufacturer or wholesaler or other senior salesmen earning $10,000 or more per year; Farmer of farm worth $100,000+

    3. Proprietor of a small business (valued at $6,000 to $35,000); Lower-level official and manager; Semi-professional; Sales representative (as above) earning $7,000 to $10,000 per year; Farmer of farm worth $35,000 to $100,000

    4. Proprietor of a very small business (valued under $6,000); Technician; Sales clerk and salesman earning *less* than $7,000 per year and clerical workers; Farmer of farm worth $15,000 to $35,000

    5. Farmer of farm worth under $15,000; Skilled manual worker and foreman

    6. Farmer, sharecropper or tenant with little stock or equipment; Semi-skilled worker and machine operator

    7. Unskilled worker.

22. During your last year in high school, WHICH PARENT HAD THE FINAL SAY on the things listed below? Circle one number for each of the decisions listed. If the decision never came up, guess which parent would have had the final say.

[7] This question proved completely unworkable in early pretests of the questionnaire.

5. Father always had final say
4. Father more than Mother
3. Father and Mother exactly the same
2. Mother more than Father
1. Mother always

a. What car to get?	1	2	3	4	5
b. Whether or not (or how much) life insurance to buy?	1	2	3	4	5
c. Where to go on vacation?	1	2	3	4	5
d. What house or apartment to take?	1	2	3	4	5
e. Whether Mother should go to work or quit work?	1	2	3	4	5
f. Things concerning the children's activities (getting special privileges, discipline)?	1	2	3	4	5

Data analysis

1. *Sort* the code sheets according to *box 11* into two groups:

   Farmers = all those coded "5"
   Others = all other first-digit codes

2. *Sub-sort* the "Others" according to *box 12* into social class groups as follows:

   Upper middle class = "1" or "2"
   Lower middle class = "3" or "4"
   Working class = "5," "6," or "7"

3. *Tally* (~~////~~ ///) onto the tabulation form the "Relative Power Index" scores (box 22t) of each of the four social class groups into which you have just divided the code sheets.

4. *Compute* the average (in this case the "mean") Relative Power Index of each social class group. See Appendix C for computing instructions. The calculation must be repeated four times to obtain the mean for each social class group (each column) of the table.

Lab report

1. Reread the direction for writing laboratory reports in Appendix A before writing your report.
2. Give special attention to the DISCUSSION. Be sure to discuss possible reasons for the findings. In addition to arguing from (or with) Blood and Wolfe and other material you have read, do not hesitate to advance your own reasoning.

References

Blau, Peter, "Structural Effects," *American Sociological Review, 25* (April 1960), pp. 178–193.

Bowman, Henry A., Marriage for Moderns. New York: McGraw-Hill, 1960.

Durkheim, Emile, *Suicide*. New York: Free Press, 1951.

Gold, Martin and Carol Slater, "Office, Factory, Store—and Family: A Study of Integration Setting," *American Sociological Review, 23* (1958), pp. 64–74.

Heer, David M., "Measurement and Bases of Family Power," *Marriage and Family Living, 25* (May 1963), pp. 133–139.

Henry, Andrew F. and James F. Short, Jr., *Suicide and Homicide*. New York: Free Press, 1954.

Hoffman, Lois W., "Effects of Employment of Mothers on Parental Power Relations and the Division of Household Tasks," *Marriage and Family Living, 22* (February 1960), pp. 27–35.

Komarovsky, Mirra, *Blue Collar Marriage*. New York: Random House, 1964, chapter 10.

Kroeber, A. L. and Talcott Parsons, "The Concepts of Culture and of Social System," *American Sociological Review, 23* (October 1958), pp. 582–583.

Lenski, Gerhard E., "Status Crystallization: A Non-vertical Dimension of Social Status," *American Sociological Review, 19* (1954), pp. 405–413.

Myrdal, Gunnar *et al., An American Dilemma*. New York: Harper & Row, 1944.

Scheinfeld, Amram, *Women and Men*. New York: Harcourt, Brace & World, 1943.

Name________________________

Date________________________

TABLE 1. Relative power index by social class

RELATIVE POWER INDEX (Box 22t)	Farmer (All those coded 5 in Box 11)		NON-FARM OCCUPATIONAL CLASS (Box 12)					
			Upper Middle (Box 12 = 1, 2)		Lower Middle (Box 12 = 3, 4)		Working class (Box 12 = 5, 6, 7, 8)	
x	f	fx	f	fx	f	fx	f	fx
6–8								
9–11								
12–14								
15–17								
18–20								
21–23								
24–26								
27–30								
TOTAL								
Mean =								
+ (No info.)		X		X		X		X

LABORATORY REPORT FOR PROBLEM ________

Course or Section ________ Date ________ Name ________

HYPOTHESIS: ________

SAMPLE: ________

INDEPENDENT VARIABLE(S): ________

DEPENDENT VARIABLE(S): ________

OTHER FACTORS: ________

LABORATORY REPORT FOR PROBLEM ____________

SUMMARY OF FINDINGS: ____________

DISCUSSION: ____________

PROBLEM 4

ROLES

The sociological perspective seeks to explain behavior as a consequence of interaction, that is, a consequence of the way individuals respond to one another. This perspective does not deny that other types of causal factors, such as physiological and psychological factors, also influence behavior; it merely directs attention to a particular type of explanation.

Sociologists are especially interested in the uniformities in interaction which result from being the occupant of a particular position or status. Thus, individuals are studied as occupants of a status: as fathers, as workers, as community leaders, or as church members. Attached to each such status are norms or expectations which define what is held to be the correct, appropriate behavior for a person occupying that particular status. Although these expectations vary according to the situation, within a given type of situation, the expectations provide a blueprint of behavior for persons of similar status. This blueprint is generally what is meant by the term *role* (Parsons and Shils, 1951). From this view, it is apparent that the concept of a role occupies a fundamental place in sociological analysis: By focusing attention on behavior in response to others, the concept underlines the importance of fulfilling mutual expectations as the basis of human society.

In most situations, conformity to role expectations is in fact the rule rather than the exception simply because individuals generally want to do what others expect them to do. However, for a variety of reasons, it may happen that the normal performance of an expected role does not occur. A number of possibilities can cause such deviations in role performance: (1) expectations may conflict to the point where performing one role is tantamount to disregarding another; (2) expectations may be consistent but overburdening to an individual's resources of time and energy; (3) expectations may be beyond realistic possibilities for achievement (Davis, 1948). In these and other instances, it becomes difficult—if not impossible—for individuals to carry out their roles as anticipated. These considerations have led some theorists to speculate that an element of strain is inherent in the performance of any role (Merton, 1957; Goode, 1960). Faced with such "role strain," an individual may attempt to reorganize his system of roles. For example, he might curtail or eliminate particular role relationships. In the event, however, that this or other alternatives are not possible, persons may become subject to the sanction of others for inadequate role performance and may also internalize the strain to the extent that they become mentally ill.

In reality, the blueprint for behavior which is called a role would be almost impossible to diagram in simple form, for the blueprint actually specifies not one behavior but almost an infinite series of variations. For example, the blueprint calls for differences in behavior according to such things as (1) the status of the others with whom the person is interacting, (2) the nature of the relationship between the actors and the others, and (3) the fact that persons always have more than one status, each with an accompanying (and sometimes conflicting) set of role expectations to be balanced against one another. Consequently, to diagram a blueprint specifying behavior would require complex multidimensional geometry or graph theory (Harary, Norman, and Cartwright, 1965; Tallman, 1967).

The reading for the present problem illustrates both the elementary notion of roles as a blueprint for behavior and also some of the factors which enter into the actual complexity of role analysis. The research clearly shows that role expectations and behavior are not absolute; rather, they vary according to the relationship of those involved in a given situation. Specifically, the data illustrate the way in which a person in his status as student is expected to modify his behavior to take into account his status as friend and roommate, and how he expects others to modify their expectations of him as well.

AN ANALYSIS OF CONFLICTING SOCIAL NORMS / *Samuel A. Stouffer*

This paper illustrates an empirical procedure for studying role obligations, with particular reference to simultaneous role obligations which conflict.

The writer became especially interested in the problem when considering the strains to which the non-commissioned officer in the Army was subjected. On the one hand, the non-com had the role of agent of the command and in case the orders from above conflicted with what his men thought were right and necessary he was expected by his superiors to carry out the orders. But he also was an enlisted man, sharing enlisted men's attitudes, often hostile attitudes, toward the commissioned ranks. Consequently, the system of informal controls was such as to reward him for siding with the men in a conflict situation and punish him if he did not. There was some evidence that unless his men had confidence that he could see their point of view, he was an ineffective leader; on the other hand, open and flagrant disobedience by him of an order from above could not be tolerated by the command.[1]

The general theoretical viewpoint behind this paper involves several propositions:

1. In any social group there exist norms and a strain for conformity to these norms.

2. Ordinarily, if the norms are clear and unambiguous the individual has no choice but to conform or take the consequences in group resentment.

3. If a person has simultaneous roles in two or more groups such that simultaneous conformity to the norms of each of the groups is incompatible, he can take one of only a limited number of actions, for example:

(1) He can conform to one set of role expectations and take the consequences of non-conformity to other sets.
(2) He can seek a compromise position by which he attempts to conform in part, though not wholly, to one or more sets of role expectations, in the hope that the sanctions applied will be minimal.

It need hardly be pointed out that conflicts of role obligations are a common experience of all people, especially in our complex Western society. The foreman in industry, like the non-com in the Army, is an obvious example; the "marginal man," as represented by the second-generation foreign born, for example, has been much studied. But role conflicts are not limited to such situations. Every adolescent is certain to experience situations in which his family and his peer group are in conflict, such that conformity to the norms of the one is incompatible with conformity to the norms of the other. Most adults are subject to strains to conformity to norms incompatible from one group to another; although, often enough to make life tolerable, either the conflicts do not arise simultaneously or there is a broad enough range of tolerated behavior to provide some flexibility.

In any authoritarian situation, it is axiomatic that adherence to the rules prescribed by the authority depends to no small extent on the compatibility of the rules with dominant values of those who must obey them. It is likely, in most social situations, that the compatibility is not absolute but a matter of degree. There may be variability among members of the group in the extent to which a given value is held in common. The existence of such variability is a factor which should weaken the sanctions against any particular act and facilitate compromise solutions.

With respect to any social value, there are at least two classes of variability which need to be distinguished.

(1) Each individual may perceive a narrow range of behavior as permissible, but for different individuals the ranges, though small, may constitute different segments of a continuum.
(2) Each individual may perceive a rather wide range of behavior as permissible, even though there is considerable consensus as to the termini of this range.

It is the viewpoint of this paper that the *range* of approved or permissible behavior as perceived by a given individual is an important datum for the analysis of what constitutes a social norm in any group, and especially for the analysis of conflicting norms.

In order to illustrate some of these concepts and to make some preliminary attempts to define them such that statistical operations could be performed with them, an empirical study was made of conflicting role expectations in a sample of 196 Harvard and Radcliffe students, mostly undergraduates. Since the concern was wholly methodological, no effort was made to obtain a random or representative sample of the student body, and the data here reported cannot necessarily be regarded as typical of how a properly drawn sample would respond. The students were all taking the same course, Social Relations 116. The data were collected on the first day of the course, without any explicit prior discussion of the theoretical problems involved.

Each student filled out a brief questionnaire, anonymously. He was told first:

> Imagine that you are proctoring an examination in a middle-group course. About half way through the exam you see a fellow student openly cheating. The student is copying his answers from previously prepared notes. When he sees that you have seen the notes as you walked down the aisle and stopped near his seat, he whispers quietly to you, "O. K., I'm caught. That's all there is to it."
>
> *You do not know the student.* What would you as proctor do:
>
> If you knew that, *except for your action*, there could be very little chance that either the authorities or your student friends would hear about your part in the incident, which of

Reprinted with permission of the publisher from *American Sociological Review, 14* (December 1949), pp. 707–717.

This study was made at the Harvard Laboratory of Social Relations, in connection with research sponsored by the RAND Corporation under Air-Force Project RAND.

[1] Stouffer, Suchman, DeVinney, Star, and Williams, *The American Soldier,* Vol. I, chapter 8.

the following actions (see *Table 1*) would you as proctor be most likely to take? Next most likely? Least likely? Next least likely?

After he had finished checking these questions he was presented with a new complication, as follows:

Now, assume that *except for your action*, there could be very little chance that your student friends would hear about your part in the incident. But assume that, for some reason, there is a good chance, whatever you do, of the authorities finding out about it. Which of the following actions would you as proctor be most likely to take? Next most likely? Least likely? Next least likely?[2]

This was followed by exactly the same check list as before.

Next the respondent was asked to fill out the following check list:

A. Suppose now that a proctor's action would be: *Take away his notes and exam book, dismiss him, and report him for cheating.*

How would the university authorities feel if they knew you as proctor did this? (check one)

— Would expect one to do something like this
— Would not necessarily expect one to do this, but would not disapprove
— Would disapprove
— Would not tolerate it

How would your friends in the student body feel if they knew you did this? (check one)

— Would expect one to do something like this
— Would not necessarily expect one to do this, but would not disapprove
— Would disapprove
— Would not tolerate it

B. Suppose that a proctor's action would be: *Take away his notes, let him finish the exam, but report him for cheating.*

C. Suppose now that a proctor's action would be: *If he can be led to withdraw from the exam on some excuse, do not report him for cheating; otherwise report him.*

D. Suppose now that a proctor's action would be: *Take away his notes, but let him finish the exam, and not report him for cheating.*

E. Suppose now that a proctor's action would be: *Act as if nothing had happened and not report him for cheating.*

(For B, C, D, and E, the same check lists were used as for A, but are here omitted to save space.)

Next the respondent was confronted with what it was hoped, for the methodological purposes of this illustrative study, would be more of a dilemma. He was told:

Now suppose the facts in the case in which you as proctor see a fellow student are exactly the same as in the first case, except for one difference. The student you as proctor see cheating is *your own roommate and close friend.* You know that your roommate is a hard working, though not a brilliant, student and desperately needs a good grade in this course.

If you knew that, *except for your action*, there could be very little chance that either the authorities or your student friends would know about your part in the incident, which of the following actions would you as proctor be most likely to take? Next most likely? Least likely? Next least likely?

The check list was the same as in the ordinary case presented first. This was followed by:

Now assume that *except for your action*, there could be very little chance that your student friends would hear about your part in the incident. But assume that, for some reason, there is a good chance, whatever you do, of the authorities finding out about it. Which of the following actions would you as proctor be most likely to take? Next most likely? Least likely? Next least likely?

Again the check list was the same.

Finally, the identical series of questions about expectations on the part of authorities and students was repeated for this roommate-friend situation.

The five actions described were designed to constitute, from A to E, an ordered sequence along a dimension of *degree of punitiveness*. That they were so perceived generally by the respondents can be shown easily. To illustrate: If a person said that the authorities, for example, would expect or approve more than one act, it is necessary for unidimensionality that the two or more acts be contiguous (for example, A and B, or B and C, or A, B, and C, but not A and C only). Actually, as we shall see, most students reported at least two acts which would be either expected or approved by the authorities; likewise most reported at least two acts which would be either expected or approved by their friends in the student body. In all, there were 4 chances for each respondent to designate such ranges. Of the 744 responses designating ranges of two or more, the acts checked were entirely contiguous in all but 41; in other words, 95 per cent of the responses were consistent with the perception of the sequence of acts as a continuum.[3]

Attention should be called to the likelihood that the responses as to the approval or disapproval of the authorities or of one's friends in the student body to a given act have an intrinsic merit which for our purposes could be superior to the merit of the estimates of one's own probable action in a hypothetical case. In any social situation, we have some kind of awareness of the group expectations as to an act affecting the group. We can verbalize those, and these responses when tabulated are *primary data* as to the agreement among group members concerning such expectations. On the

[2] The questionnaire also contained a parallel set of answer categories for the situation where he was asked: Now assume that, *except for your action*, there could be very little chance that the authorities would hear about your part in the incident. But also assume that there is a good chance that whatever you do your student friends would hear of it. Which of the following actions would you as proctor be most likely to take? Next most likely? Least likely? Next least likely?

However, only the situations indicated above will be used in the present paper.

[3] To simplify the subsequent presentation the inconsistencies are here treated as checking errors, although in some cases the respondent may actually have perceived an act as not fitting into an ordered sequence (for example, when he said A and C would be approved, but B would be disapproved, he may really have viewed B in a different way from other respondents). Fortunately, the inconsistencies were so few that it is possible to edit them without appreciable effect one way or another, except to simplify the ensuing presentation materially.

TABLE 1.

	My *most* likely action (check one)	My next most likely action (check one)	My *least* likely action (check one)	My next least likely action (check one)
A. Take away his notes and exam book, dismiss him and report him for cheating	—	—	—	—
B. Take away his notes, let him finish the exam, but report him for cheating	—	—	—	—
C. If he can be led to withdraw from the exam on some excuse, do *not* report him for cheating; otherwise report him	—	—	—	—
D. Take away his notes, but let him finish the exam, and *not* report him for cheating	—	—	—	—
E. Act as if nothing had happened and *not* report him for cheating	—	—	—	—

other hand, a guess as to what one would do one's self in a particular hypothetical conflict situation has a more "iffy" quality which, though possibly quite highly correlated with actual behavior, need not necessarily be so correlated. The main stress in the present paper, it will be seen, is on the reported *role expectations*. The hypothetical personal action is introduced mainly to suggest how concepts like role expectations, when adequately measured, can be applied in the study of an individual's behavior in that role. Ideally, in place of the individual's hypothetical behavior we would like to substitute actual behavior, either in a natural or experimental situation, or reported past behavior. Studies may be devised in the future with such improvements, but in any case the basic sorting variables would be the reported role expectations as perceived by different group members.

Figure 1 is a picture of social norms, as perceived and reported by the respondents in this study. At the left, we see (heavy line) that almost all of the respondents thought the authorities would approve acts A and B, about a fifth thought the authorities would approve act C, and almost nobody thought the authorities would approve acts D and E.[4] Also at the left we see (dotted line) that the majority of the respondents felt that their friends in the student body would approve the most punitive acts, namely, A and B. But, in addition we see that three-fourths of the respondents thought act C would be approved and a bare majority said the same for act D. Only a few felt E would meet student approval. In other words, if a proctor took action consistent with the authorities' expectations he would not be in conflict with student expectations, although the range of expectations is wider for students than for the authorities.

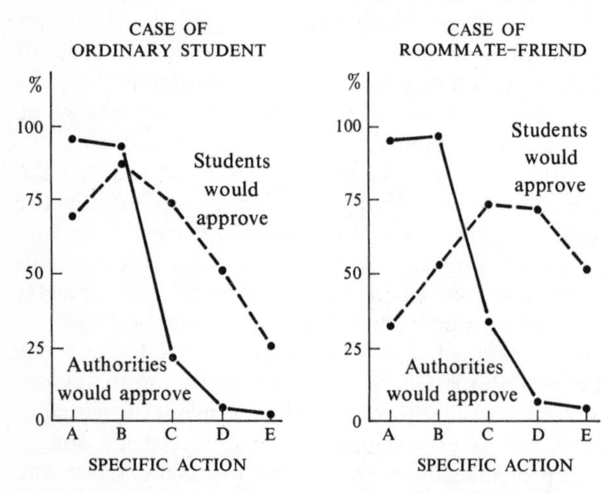

FIGURE 1. Percentage saying that a specific action as a proctor would be approved by authorities and by fellow students, respectively.

The left diagram in Figure 1 portrayed the estimate of the situation where the offender was an ordinary student. By contrast, the right-hand diagram shows far less overlap in expectations imputed to authorities and students respectively. The offender in this case was one's roommate and friend. Feelings that the proctor in punishing an ordinary offender was behaving consistently with the long-range interest of the students are now overshadowed by the obligations involved in codes of personal friendship: "You can't rat on a friend; you can't let a friend down."

In the case of the friend, the respondents perceived the authorities' position to be about the same as in the case of the ordinary student, except that about a third now thought the authorities might let the proctor get away with C in view of the proctor's personal dilemma. But only a third of the respondents thought the students would approve act A. The modal acts are C and D. About half believed that the least punitive of all, E, would be approved by most of the students.

In Table 2 each act (separately for the case of the ordinary student and the friend, respectively) is broken down according to the percentage who think it would be approved by (a) the authorities only, (b) both the authorities and students, (c) students only, and (d) by neither the authorities nor students.

Let us now examine the relationship between these

[4] To simplify the presentation, "approval" is here taken to mean that the respondent checked either of the following categories:
—Would expect one to do something like this
—Would not necessarily expect one to do this, but would not disapprove

TABLE 2. Percentage who attribute given role expectations on the part of authorities and/or students with respect to each specific act

	Percentage distribution for each specific action					
	A	B	C	D	E	All actions
CASE OF ORDINARY STUDENT						
Think given action would be approved by:						
Authorities only	28	12	3	—	—	9
Both authorities and students	68	81	19	4	2	35
Students only	1	6	55	48	24	27
Neither authorities nor students	3	1	23	48	74	29
	100	100	100	100	100	100
CASE OF ROOMMATE-FRIEND						
Think given action would be approved by:						
Authorities only	63	44	9	1	—	24
Both authorities and students	33	53	25	6	4	24
Students only	—	—	49	66	48	33
Neither authorities nor students	4	3	17	27	48	19
	100	100	100	100	100	100
N = 196						

role expectations and the respondent's own hypothetical behavior as proctor. It will be recalled that in both the case of the ordinary student and the roommate-friend, the respondent was asked what he personally would do under two hypothetical conditions: (1) if neither the authorities nor his student friends would hear about his part in the incident; and (2) if there could be very little chance that the authorities would hear about his part in the incident.

In Table 3 we have a percentage distribution of the acts which each student said he would be *most* likely to choose in the given situation. In the case of the ordinary student, as Table 3 shows, the majority of respondents say they would be most likely to employ acts A or B, the most punitive. There is not a large difference between the hypothetical behavior in private or in public (public only in the restricted sense that the authorities would hear about it in any case, though students need not). The main difference is a small increase, from a private 21 per cent to a public 30 per cent, in first choices for the most severe act A. However, the hypothetical behavior in the roommate-friend case shows a very different pattern. As can be seen in Table 3, nearly two-thirds of the respondents elect acts D or E as their first preferences in private action, and only 16 per cent say they would employ as first choice punitive acts A or B. But if the authorities were sure to find out about it, the picture changes. Less than a third would elect D or E as first choice and 40 per cent would prefer A or B. Yet this is still only about half as large as the proportion who would prefer A or B in comparable circumstances in the case of the ordinary student.

Table 3, while of a good deal of interest in itself, is subject to the caveats entered earlier in this paper against taking reports on such hypothetical behavior too literally. But the main purpose for introducing the material in Table 3 is to enable us to see how such hypothetical behavior is related to the reported perceptions of authorities' and students' expectations, respectively, of proper behavior from a proctor. The data in Table 3 are, therefore, next broken down according to the categories used in Table 2. Here we see in Table 4, as we doubtless would expect to see, that most students who chose acts A or B as their first preference if they themselves were proctors, also tended to perceive such acts as one which *both* the authorities and students would approve. But that tended to be true of several of the respondents who would take less punitive action —they had a different perception of expectations and thus thought they were avoiding conflict. In the case of the ordinary student, only 43 of the 196 respondents indicated a private action which was perceived to be acceptable to students only, and only 27 a public action. Contrast this with their hypothetical behavior when the offender was a roommate-friend. Of the 196 respondents, 118 preferred a private action tolerated by the students only. This number was reduced to 74, who would still stick by their friend even if they knew the authorities would find out about their action, or rather, inaction.

Figure 1, it will be recalled, indicated quite a marked range of tolerance in imputed student expectations, especially in the roommate-friend situation. But it is not possible to tell directly from Figure 1 the extent to which this is due to (a) different respondents visualizing different role expectations, or to (b) respondents generally agreeing that a wide range of role expectations existed. Let us now look at Table 5, where the frequency with which each range of expectations was indicated is shown. We see here quite clearly the degree of consensus among respondents as to what the authorities would approve. Among the 196 respondents, 134, or two-thirds, checked A, B identically for the case of

TABLE 3. Percentage distribution of hypothetical actions which the respondents say they would be most likely to take as proctor

Action	In case of ordinary student		In case of roommate-friend	
	Private[a]	Public[b]	Private	Public
A	21	30	4	6
B	47	48	12	34
C	16	13	18	31
D	15	7	38	18
E	1	2	28	11
	100	100	100	100

N = 196

[a] "If you knew that, *except for your action* there could be very little chance that either the authorities or your student friends would hear about your part in the incident."

[b] "If you knew that, *except for your action* there could be very little chance that your student friends would hear about your part in the incident, but that there is a good chance, whatever you do, of the authorities finding out about it."

TABLE 4. Respondents whose own most likely hypothetical action as proctor is as indicated, broken down by expectations attributed to authorities and/or students

		Would be approved by			
		Authorities only	Both authorities and students	Students only	Neither
CASE OF ORDINARY STUDENT					
(Private Act)	A	6	35	—	—
	B	3	86	3	—
	C	—	13	17	1
	D	—	5	21	4
	E	—	—	2	—
		9	139	43	5
(Public Act)	A	9	50	—	—
	B	5	87	3	—
	C	—	13	13	—
	D	—	4	9	1
	E	—	—	2	—
		14	154	27	1
CASE OF ROOMMATE-FRIEND					
(Private Act)	A	1	7	—	—
	B	2	20	—	1
	C	—	14	17	5
	D	—	4	62	9
	E	—	3	39	12
		3	48	118	27
(Public Act)	A	2	10	—	—
	B	14	50	—	2
	C	4	21	30	5
	D	—	4	29	3
	E	—	4	15	3
		20	89	74	13

the ordinary student; 120 checked A, B, for the case of the roommate-friend. The majority of the remainder checked A, B, C, in both cases.

Far different is the picture from Table 5 in the case of imputed student expectations. The majority settled for a range of either two or three acts in both of the situations, but within a given range there were all possible variations. For example, in the roommate-friend

TABLE 5. Frequency with which various ranges of acts are perceived as approved by authorities and students, respectively

	Range	Case of ordinary student acts approved by		Case of roommate-friend acts approved by	
		Authorities	Students	Authorities	Students
1	A	13	4	4	3
	B	5	1	4	3
	C	—	—	—	2
	D	—	3	—	2
	E	—	—	—	4
		18	8	8	14
2	AB	134	37	120	12
	BC	3	10	2	10
	CD	—	7	—	14
	DE	—	5	—	26
		137	59	122	62
3	ABC	33	42	52	20
	BCD	—	14	—	18
	CDE	—	7	1	42
		33	63	53	80
4	ABCD	5	27	8	11
	BCDE	—	14	1	11
		5	41	9	22
5	ABCDE	3	25	4	18
	Totals	196	196	196	196

TABLE 6. An illustration of hypothetical actions of respondent as proctor, as related to specific ranges of student approval in case of roommate-friend[a]

Range of student approval	Private behavior							Public behavior						
	A	B	C	D	E	Total frequency	Average rank[b]	A	B	C	D	E	Total frequency	Average rank
A	1	—	—	—	—	1	1.0	1	—	—	—	—	1	1.0
AB	2	3	2	2	2	11	2.9	2	6	2	—	1	11	2.3
B	—	—	1	—	1	2	4.0	—	1	—	—	1	2	3.5
ABC	2	5	4	2	2	15	2.7	5	4	4	1	1	15	2.3
BC	—	—	3	2	—	5	3.4	—	3	2	—	—	5	2.4
ABCD	—	1	3	3	1	8	3.5	1	3	4	—	—	8	2.4
C	—	—	2	—	—	2	3.0	—	2	—	—	—	2	2.0
BCD	—	4	1	8	—	13	3.3	—	9	3	1	—	13	2.4
ABCDE	—	3	1	7	3	14	3.7	—	9	2	1	2	14	2.7
CD	1	—	1	4	2	8	3.8	1	—	4	3	—	8	3.1
BCDE	—	1	1	3	1	6	3.7	—	3	1	1	1	6	3.0
CDE	—	1	1	10	9	21	4.3	—	6	9	4	2	21	3.1
DE	—	—	—	6	7	13	4.5	—	2	2	4	5	13	4.0
E	—	—	—	—	1	1	5.0	—	—	—	—	1	1	5.0
					Total	120						Total	120	

[a] (These data are for 120 respondents who said the authorities would approve the range AB only.)
[b] A, B, C, D, E ranked 1, 2, 3, 4, 5, respectively.

situation there were 80 who indicated a range of student approval covering 3 acts, but of these, 20 perceived the range as A, B, C; 18 perceived it as B, C, D; and 42 as C, D, E. Clearly there is an absence of consensus here, and it is not a mere uniform coverage of the whole range of possibilities by all individuals.

TABLE 7.

	Student expectations which have identical midpoints but different ranges	
	Those with minimum range	Those with greater than minimum range
PRIVATE ACT		
Own behavior more severe than any act within the *minimum* range of student expectation	2	12
Own behavior within *minimum* range	31	20
Own behavior less severe than any act within *minimum* range	8	34
	41	66
PUBLIC ACT		
Own behavior more severe than any act within the *minimum* range of student expectation	5	29
Own behavior within *minimum* range	32	21
Own behavior less severe than any act within *minimum* range	4	16
	41	66

If we take, for illustration, the 120 respondents who perceived the range of acts approved by the authorities in the case of the roommate-friend as A, B, and order the ranges approved by students, according to these same respondents, we see in Table 6 the ways in which these different specific ranges are related to one's personal hypothetical behavior as proctor. Here we show for *each pattern* of role expectation the hypothetical private and public behavior respectively. For convenience, these hypothetical acts A, B, C, D, E have been ranked 1, 2, 3, 4, and 5, respectively, and average ranks computed.

As we move from role expectations A to E we see how the average ranks of the students' hypothetical behavior increase. It is interesting to note that, at least in the present example, this progressive increase seems to depend more on the midpoint of the range than on the termini. For example, if the expectation is BC the average rank of the hypothetical behavior is just about the same as when the expectation is A, B, C, D. In some cases the pattern with the longer range has higher average rank than its counterpart with the same midpoint but shorter range; in other cases the reverse is true. The number of cases available in the present data is, however, exceedingly small for this kind of comparison.

While the average rank of hypothetical acts did not tend to differ consistently when we compared two or more ranges with the same midpoint in Table 6, there is a hint that differences in the *range* of hypothetical acts vary with the *range* of role expectations which have the same midpoint. It doubtless would be expected that if a respondent perceived the range of approved behavior to be B, C, D, he would be more likely to choose *either* B or D for his own act than if he perceived the range to be only C. Take the following from Table 6.

	A	B	C	D	E	
C	—	—	2	—	—	2
BCD	—	4	1	8	—	13
ABCDE	—	3	1	7	3	14

Most of the other examples in Table 6 are less neat than this and the number of cases is distressingly few, but if we form other tables like Table 6 for other values of the range of expected approval by the authorities and take all possible matched comparisons thus available (for example, authorities ABC; students BC vs. ABCD) we obtain a rather convincing overall result, in the roommate-friend situation:

The same tendency is also seen, though somewhat less strikingly, in the case of the ordinary student.

While interpretation of such a finding should be indulged in only with caution, the results are sufficient to suggest the importance of taking into account not only the midpoints of a given range of role expectations, but the magnitude of the range as well.

We have now completed the analysis of the present data except for one further observation which has implications for further research.

In such a study as this, it would be interesting first to differentiate individuals into types according to the way they perceive conflicting role expectations and then to ask how these different types of persons vary according to other social and psychological characteristics. Information of the latter type was not collected in the present study. However, the foregoing analysis has suggested how typologies could be set up and related to such outside variables. To take a simple illustration from the roommate-friend situation:

One could classify most of our respondents into three main types according as they perceived the role conflict.

Type I—Those who thought the range of approved

acts identical from the point of view of authorities and students. (21 cases) For such respondents the problem of conformity in their own hypothetical acts could not have been difficult.

Type II—Those who thought the range of acts approved by the authorities did not overlap in any way with the range of acts approved by the students. (56 cases) For them simultaneous conformity to both was impossible. It is noteworthy, parenthetically, that 51 of the 56 said their own private act would be one conforming to student expectation, though 16 of these 51 shifted their act to a non-student position in the public situation.

Type III—Those who perceived a difference in the range of authorities' and students' expectations but who found at least one act which would be tolerated by both. (119 cases) Privately, only 36 of these individuals would take an action satisfactory to both. Publicly, however, 73 out of the 119 were able to find in an act perceived to be mutually acceptable the basis for their own hypothetical solution.

Why did these three types differ so markedly in their definition of the situation? Why, within these types did different subtypes prefer different solutions? These are the kinds of questions which subsequent research can explore. But first we must have a way of defining and classifying the role expectations relevant to our problem and the purpose of the present study is to illustrate a technique for accomplishing this first step.

From the theoretical standpoint, the most important implication of this paper may stem from its stress on variability. In essay writing in this field it is common and convenient to think of a social norm as a point, or at least as a very narrow band on either side of a point. This probably is quite unrealistic as to most of our social behavior. And it may be precisely the ranges of permissible behavior which most need examination, if we are to make progress in this realm which is so central in social science. For it may be the very existence of some flexibility or social slippage—but not too much—which makes behavior in groups possible.

Replication

SOCIAL RELATIONSHIPS AND VARIATIONS IN ROLE PERFORMANCE

The logic of this replication will partly follow Stouffer's design in the original study. We will attempt to see whether students serving as proctors tend to be more lenient, and if university officials expect the proctor to be more lenient, in handling friends who have cheated as opposed to strangers who have cheated. To clarify the comparisons to be made we have separated the respondents into two groups: proctors who catch a friend cheating and proctors who catch a stranger cheating.

The three variables used in the partial replication are: role expectations, status of offender, and status of person holding the expectations (see Table 1). To determine which variables are the independent and dependent variables, you must decide which of the variables comes first chronologically, or, which is likely to be the cause of the others. See the "Note on Interpreting Cause and Effect" in Appendix A.

Hypothesis

1. State whether there is greater leniency or severity in handling friends who have cheated as opposed to strangers who have cheated.

2. State your anticipation regarding university officials—do *they* expect the proctor to act more or less leniently with a close friend than with strangers?

3. See Appendix A for general information on writing an hypothesis.

Empirical indicators for this problem

Imagine that you are proctoring an examination (i.e., in charge of keeping order during one exam) for a university course. About halfway through the exam you see a fellow openly cheating. The student is copying his answers from notes. When he sees that you have seen the notes, he whispers quietly to you, "Okay, I'm caught. That's all there is to it." What would you do?

IMPORTANT: If your *birthday* is on an *odd-numbered* day, answer only for "Case A" and skip "Case B." If your birthday is on an *even-numbered* day, skip "Case A" and answer only "Case B."

Case A (Odd-numbered birthdays only)

73. Assume that there would be very little chance that either the authorities or your friends would know about your part in the incident, and that you do not know the student who is cheating. What would you do? Circle as many of the following as you would do (i.e., more than one action may be circled).

    1. Nothing
    2. Tell him to stop copying
    3. Take away his notes
    4. Let him withdraw from the exam on some excuse such as sickness
    5. Dismiss him from the exam room
    6. Report him for cheating

74. In this situation which of these actions do you think the university authorities would most likely want you to take? (More than one action may be circled.)

    1. Nothing

2. Tell him to stop copying
3. Take away his notes
4. Let him withdraw from the exam on some excuse such as sickness
5. Dismiss him from the exam room
6. Report him for cheating

Case B (Even-numbered birthdays only)

75. Assume that there would be very little chance that either the authorities or your friends would know about your part in the incident, and that the student who is cheating is your own roommate and close friend. You know that your friend is a hard working, though not a brilliant student and desperately needs a good grade in this course. What would you do? Circle as many of the following as you would do (i.e., more than one action may be circled).

    1. Nothing
    2. Tell him to stop copying
    3. Take away his notes
    4. Let him withdraw from the exam on some excuse such as sickness
    5. Dismiss him from the exam room
    6. Report him for cheating

76. In this situation which of these actions do you think the university authorities would most likely want you to take? (More than one action may be circled.)

    1. Nothing
    2. Tell him to stop copying
    3. Take away his notes
    4. Let him withdraw from the exam on some excuse such as sickness
    5. Dismiss him from the exam room
    6. Report him for cheating

Data analysis

1. *Sort* the code sheets into two groups according to whether the student answered in response to Case A (strangers) or Case B (friends):

Case A: Strangers = Boxes 73 and 74 have scores, whereas boxes 75 and 76 are coded +

Case B: Friends = Boxes 75 and 76 have scores, whereas boxes 73 and 74 are coded +

2. *Tally* onto the tabulation form the actions for Case A, i.e., the actions individual students would take in reaction to a stranger cheating (box 73). At the same time also tally the action he thinks the university would expect him to take (box 74).

3. *Compute* the percentage of students who would take each action and the percentage of students who think the university would expect each action. Use the percentage tables in Appendix B to save time.

4. *Repeat* steps 2 and 3, this time using the data in boxes 75 and 76 for actions in respect to a student who is also a friend (Case B).

Lab report

1. Base your statement of the findings on a comparison of the percentage who would take the most severe action.

2. State whether the findings pertaining to hypothesis 1 and hypothesis 2 are consistent, i.e., do the students in this sample expect that university officials will also take into account whether or not the student caught cheating is a friend. Discuss the relevance of any consistency or inconsistency for a broader understanding of role performance.

3. See Appendix A for general information on writing laboratory reports.

References

Davis, Kingsley, *Human Society*. New York: Macmillan, 1948, chapter 10.

Goode, William J., "A Theory of Role Strain," *American Sociological Review*, 25 (August 1960), pp. 483–496.

Harary, Frank, Robert Z. Norman, and Dorian Cartwright, *Structural Models: An Introduction to the Theory of Directed Graphs*. New York: Wiley, 1965.

Merton, Robert K., *Social Theory and Social Structure*. New York: Free Press, 1957, pp. 368–380.

Parsons, Talcott and Edward Shils, eds., *Toward a General Theory of Action*. Cambridge, Mass.: Harvard University Press, 1951.

Tallman, Irving, "The Balance Principle and Normative Discrepancy," *Human Relations*, 20 (November 1967), pp. 341–355.

Name________________

Date________________

TABLE 1. Role expectations by status of offender and state of person holding the expectation

EXPECTED ACTION	CASE A — STRANGER				CASE B — FRIEND			
	Action student expects to take (Box 73)		Action university expects of student (Box 74)		Action student expects to take (Box 75)		Action university expects of student (Box 76)	
	Tally	%	Tally	%	Tally	%	Tally	%
1. Nothing								
2. Tell him to stop copying								
3. Take away his notes								
4. Let him withdraw on some excuse								
5. Dismiss him from the exam room								
6. Report him for cheating								
TOTAL		100%		100%		100%		100%
+ (No info.)		X		X		X		X

LABORATORY REPORT FOR PROBLEM ______

Course or Section ______ Date ______ Name ______

HYPOTHESIS: ______

SAMPLE: ______

INDEPENDENT VARIABLE(S): ______

DEPENDENT VARIABLE(S): ______

OTHER FACTORS: ______

LABORATORY REPORT FOR PROBLEM ______

SUMMARY OF FINDINGS: ______

DISCUSSION: ______

Processes IV

PROBLEM 5 HUMAN INTERACTION

In the normal course of everyday activities, men are placed in face to face contact with one another. They may interact as members of a family, as friends, casual acquaintances, or strangers; they may show deference or arrogance to one another. Yet, whatever the relationship may be, or whatever attitude may be taken, a normal pattern is learned when young and continued as an everyday activity throughout life. As is true of most things considered "normal," interaction is usually not subject to objective examination and analysis. We tend to learn a language without an ability to articulate grammatical structure; similarly, we learn to interact without understanding the rudiments of interaction situations themselves.

Sociologists have a vested interest in studying interaction situations, for these situations, in the form of communications or symbolic exchanges, are the basis of society itself. These exchanges can be analyzed at a variety of levels. Sociologists have been prone to observe the levels which are not necessarily stressed by the participants engaged in interaction. Thus, a sociological analysis of cocktail hours or coffee breaks focuses on these less as occasions for consuming liquids and more as periods for sociability (Riesman, 1960). Similarly, sports events, such as wrestling, can be viewed not merely in terms of competition but as a means of sustaining codes basic to social morality (Stone and Oldenburg, 1967; Matza, 1964).

Much of the research in interaction analysis owes intellectual debt to the pioneering observations of Georg Simmel. It was Simmel's conviction that interaction in social situations took particular forms, forms which were both stable and amenable to systematic analysis (Simmel, 1950). It is this stable feature of social life which makes possible a science of society. Since Simmel's work, a large number of studies have been devoted to codifying the patterns of social interaction. Among the most important examples of these efforts are Goffman's attempt to illustrate the way everyday interaction situations parallel the theater—complete with props, rehearsals, and on-stage and off-stage presentations (Goffman, 1959), and Parsons and Bales' (1953) observations in small group laboratory settings of the systematic cycle between conflict and cooperation.

The reading by Harold Garfinkel for the present problem is an excellent example of contemporary work on interaction. Garfinkel's major point is that interaction rests on a series of "common understandings" between participants. These understandings take the form of mutual expectancies: Some expectancies are social and require, for example, that participants do not take each other's communications too seriously, or that participants acknowledge their common history of role relations. Other expectancies, although socially defined, center on physical relations, as for example the understanding that persons maintain a distance of at least a few feet when in conversation. Such expectancies, Garfinkel maintains, are largely invisible and are taken for granted by the participants. However, it is possible to bring these expectancies to visibility by modifying them, that is, by not meeting expectancies at all. When this is done, as Garfinkel illustrates in a series of delightful vignettes, persons react—by withdrawal, suspicion, fear, and anger. These consequences are striking confirmation in support of the idea that interaction is sustained only by observing highly specific yet unnoticed rules of "proper" behavior. In reading Garfinkle's paper you should pay particular attention to pages 84–88 which reports the parts of his study we will replicate.

STUDIES OF THE ROUTINE GROUNDS OF EVERYDAY ACTIVITIES / *Harold Garfinkel*

The problem

For Kant the moral order "within" was an awesome mystery; for sociologists the moral order "without" is a technical mystery. From the point of view of sociological theory the moral order consists of the rule governed activities of everyday life. A society's members encounter and know the moral order as perceivedly normal courses of action—familiar scenes of everyday affairs, the world of daily life known in common with others and with others taken for granted.

They refer to this world as the "natural facts of life" which, for members, are through and through moral facts of life. For members not only are matters so about familiar scenes, but they are so because it is morally right or wrong that they are so. Familiar scenes of everyday activities, treated by members as the "natural facts of life," are massive facts of the members daily existence both as a real world and as the product of activities *in* a real world. They furnish the "fix," the "this is it" to which the waking state returns one, and are the points of departure and return for every modification of the world of daily life that is achieved in play, dreaming, trance, theatre, scientific theorizing, or high ceremony.

In every discipline, humanistic or scientific, the familiar common sense world of everyday life is a matter of abiding interest. In the social sciences, and in sociology particularly, it is a matter of essential preoccupation. It makes up sociology's problematic subject matter, enters the very constitution of the sociological attitude, and exercises an odd and obstinate sovereignty over sociologists' claims to adequate explanation.

Despite the topic's centrality, an immense literature contains little data and few methods with which the essential features of socially recognized "familiar scenes" may be detected and related to dimensions of social organization. Although sociologists take socially structured scenes of everyday life as a point of departure they rarely see[1] as a task of sociological inquiry in its own right the general question of how any such common sense world is possible. Instead, the possibility of the everyday world is either settled by theoretical representation or merely assumed. As a topic and methodological ground for sociological inquiries, the definition of the common sense world of everyday life, though it is appropriately a project of sociological inquiry, has been neglected. My purposes in this paper are to demonstrate the essential relevance to the program of sociological inquires of a concern for common sense activities as a topic of inquiry in its own right and, by reporting a series of studies, to urge its "rediscovery."

Making commonplace scenes visible

In accounting for the stable features of everyday activities sociologists commonly select familiar settings such as familial households or work places and ask for the variables that contribute to their stable features. Just as commonly, one set of considerations are unexamined: the socially standardized and standardizing, "seen but unnoticed," expected, background features of everyday scenes. The member of the society uses background expectancies as a scheme of interpretation. In their terms, actual appearances are for him recognizable and intelligible as the appearances of familiar events. Demonstrably he is responsive to this background. At the same time he is at a loss to tell us what specifically the expectancies consist of. When we ask him about them he has little or nothing to say.

For these background expectancies to come into view one must either be a stranger to the "life as usual" character of everyday scenes, or become estranged from them. As Alfred Schutz pointed out, a "special motive" is required to make them problematic. In the sociologist's case this "special motive" consists in the programmatic task of treating a societal member's practical circumstances, which include from the member's point of view the morally necessary character of many of its background features, as matters of theoretic interest. The seen but unnoticed backgrounds of everyday activities are made visible and are described from a perspective in which persons live out the lives they do, have the children they do, feel the feelings, think the thoughts, enter the relationships they do, all in order to permit the sociologist to solve his theoretical problems.

Almost alone among sociological theorists, the late Alfred Schutz, in a series of classical studies[2] of the

Reprinted with permission of the author and publisher from *Social Problems, 11* (Winter 1964), pp. 225–250.

This investigation was supported by a Senior Research Fellowship, SF-81 from the U. S. Public Health Service. I am indebted to Egon Bittner, Craig MacAndrew, Edward Rose, Harvey Sacks, and Eleanor Sheldon for their many criticisms and suggestions.

[1] The work of Alfred Schutz, cited in footnote 2, is a magnificent exception. Readers who are acquainted with his writings will recognize how heavily this paper is indebted to him.

[2] Schutz, Alfred, *Der Sinnhafte Aufba Der Sozialen Welt,* Wein: Verlag von Julius Springer, 1932; "The Problem of Rationality in the Social World," *Economica,* 10 (May, 1943), pp. 130–149; "Some Leading Concepts in Phenomenology," *Social Research,* 12 (1945), pp. 77–97; "On Multiple Realities," *Philosophy and Phenomenological Research,* 4 (June, 1945), pp. 533–575; "Choosing Among Projects of Action," *Philosophy and Phenomenological Research,* 12 (December, 1951), pp. 161–184; "Common Sense and Scientific Interpretation of Human Action," *Philosophy and Phenomenological Research,* 14 (September, 1953), pp. 1–37; "Concept and Theory Formation in

constitutive phenomenology of the world of everyday life, described many of these seen but unnoticed background expectancies. He called them the "attitude of daily life." He referred to their scenic attributions as the "world known in common and taken for granted." Schutz' fundamental work makes it possible to pursue further the tasks of clarifying their nature and operation, of relating them to the processes of concerted actions, and assigning them their place in an empirically imaginable society.

The studies reported in this paper attempt to detect some expectancies that lend commonplace scenes their familiar, life-as-usual character, and to relate these to the stable social structures of everyday activities. Procedurally it is my preference to start with familiar scenes and ask what can be done to make trouble. The operations that one would have to perform in order to multiply the senseless features of perceived environments; to produce and sustain bewilderment, consternation, and confusion; to produce the socially structured affects of anxiety, shame, guilt, and indignation; and to produce disorganized interaction should tell us something about how the structures of everyday activities are ordinarily and routinely produced and maintained.[3]

A word of reservation. Despite their procedural emphasis, my studies are not properly speaking experimental. They are demonstrations, designed, in Herbert Spiegelberg's phrase, as "aids to a sluggish imagination." I have found that they produce reflections through which the strangeness of an obstinately familiar world can be detected.

Some essential features of common understandings

Various considerations dictate that common understandings cannot possibly consist of a measured amount of shared agreement among persons on certain topics. Even if the topics are limited in number or scope and every practical difficulty of assessment is forgiven, the notion that we are dealing with an amount of shared agreement remains essentially incorrect. This may be demonstrated as follows.

Students were asked to report common conversations by writing on the left side of a sheet what the parties actually said and on the right side what they and their partners understood that they were talking about. A student reported the following colloquy between himself and his wife.

HUSBAND: Dana succeeded in putting a penny in a parking meter today without being picked up.	This afternoon as I was bringing Dana, our four year old son, home from the nursery school, he succeeded in reaching high enough to put a penny in a parking meter when we parked in a meter parking zone, whereas before he has always had to be picked up to reach that high.
WIFE: Did you take him to the record store?	Since he put a penny in a meter that means that you stopped while he was with you. I know that you stopped at the record store either on the way to get him or on the way back. Was it on the way back, so that he was with you or did you stop there on the way to get him and somewhere else on the way back?
HUSBAND: No, to the shoe repair shop.	No, I stopped at the record store on the way to get him and stopped at the shoe repair shop on the way home when he was with me.
WIFE: What for?	I know of one reason why you might have stopped at the shoe repair shop. Why did you in fact?
HUSBAND: I got some new shoe laces for my shoes.	As you will remember I broke a shoe lace on one of my brown oxfords the other day so I stopped to get some new laces.
WIFE: Your loafers need new heels badly.	Something else you could have gotten that I was thinking of. You could have taken in your black loafers which need heels badly. You'd better get them taken care of pretty soon.

An examination of the colloquy reveals the following. (a) There were many matters that the partners understood they were talking about that they did not mention. (b) Many matters that the partners understood were understood on the basis not only of what was actually said but what was left unspoken. (c) Many matters were understood through a process of attending to the temporal series of utterances as documentary evidences of a developing conversation rather than as a string of terms. (d) Matters that the two understood in common were understood only in and through a course of understanding work that consisted of treating an actual linguistic event as "the document of," as "pointing to," as standing on behalf of an underlying pattern of matters that each already supposed to be the matters that the person, by his speaking, could be telling the other about. The underlying pattern was not only derived from a course of individual documentary evidences but the documentary evidences in their turn were interpreted on the basis of "what was known" and anticipatorily knowable about the underlying patterns.[4] Each was used to elaborate the other. (e) In attending to the utterances as events-in-the-conversation each party

the Social Sciences," *American Journal of Philosophy,* 51 (April, 1954), pp. 257–274; "Symbol, Reality and Society," *Symbols and Society,* Fourteenth Symposium of the Conference on Science, Philosophy, and Religion, edited by Lyman Bryson and others, New York: Harper and Brothers, 1955, pp. 135–202; *Collected Papers: I. The Problem of Social Reality,* edited by Maurice Natanson, The Hague: Martinus Nijhoff, 1962.

[3] Obversely, a knowledge of how the structures of everyday activities are routinely produced should permit us to tell how we might proceed for the effective production of desired disturbances.

[4] Karl Mannheim, in his essay "On the Interpretation of Weltanschauung," *Essays on the Sociology of Knowledge,* translated and edited by Paul Kecskemeti, New York: Oxford University Press, 1952, pp. 33–83, referred to this work as the "documentary method of interpretation." Its features are detailed in my article, "Common Sense Knowledge of Social Structures: the Documentary Method of Interpretation," in *Towards a Definition of Mind,* edited by Jordan M. Scher, Glencoe: The Free Press, 1962, pp. 689–712.

made reference to the biography and prospects of the present interaction which each used and attributed to the other as a common scheme of interpretation and expression. (f) Each waited for something more to be said in order to hear what had previously been talked about, and each seemed willing to wait.

Common understandings would consist of a measured amount of shared agreement if the common understandings consisted of events coordinated with the successive positions of the hands of the clock, i.e., of events in standard time. The foregoing results, because they deal with the exchanges of the colloquy as events-in-a-conversation, urge that one more time parameter, at least, is required: the role of time as it is constitutive of "the matter talked about" as a developing and developed event over the course of action that produced it, as both the process and product were known *from within* this development by both parties, each for himself as well as on behalf of the other.

The colloquy reveals additional features. (1) Many of its expressions are such that their sense cannot be decided by an auditor unless he knows or assumes something about the biography and the purposes of the speaker, the circumstances of the utterance, the previous course of the conversation, or the particular relationship of actual or potential interaction that exists between user and auditor. The expressions do not have a sense that remains identical through the changing occasions of their use. (2) The events that were talked about were specifically vague. Not only do they not frame a clearly restricted set of possible determinations but the depicted events include as their essentially intended and sanctioned features an accompanying "fringe" of determinations that are open with respect to internal relationships, relationships to other events, and relationships to retrospective and prospective possibilities. (3) For the sensible character of an expression, upon its occurrence each of the conversationalists as auditor of his own as well as the other's productions had to assume as of any present accomplished point in the exchange that by waiting for what he or the other person might have said at a later time the present significance of what had already been said would have been clarified. Thus many expressions had the property of being progressively realized and realizable through the further course of the conversation. (4) It hardly needs to be pointed out that the sense of the expressions depended upon where the expression occurred in serial order, the expressive character of the terms that comprised it, and the importance to the conversationalists of the events depicted.

These properties of common understandings stand in contrast to the features they would have if we disregarded their temporally constituted character and treated them instead as precoded entries on a memory drum, to be consulted as a definite set of alternative meanings from among which one was to select, under pre-decided conditions that specified in which of some set of alternative ways one was to understand the situation upon the occasion that the necessity for a decision arose. The latter properties are those of strict rational discourse as these are idealized in the rules that define an adequate logical proof.

For the purposes of *conducting their everyday affairs* persons refuse to permit each other to understand "what they are really talking about" in this way. The anticipation that persons *will* understand, the occasionality of expressions, the specific vagueness of references, the retrospective-prospective sense of a present occurrence, waiting for something later in order to see what was meant before, are sanctioned properties of common discourse. They furnish a background of seen but unnoticed features of common discourse whereby actual utterances are recognized as events of common, reasonable, understandable, plain talk. Persons require these properties of discourse as conditions under which they are themselves entitled and entitle others to claim that they know what they are talking about, and that what they are saying is understandable and ought to be understood. In short, their seen but unnoticed presence is used to entitle persons to conduct their common conversational affairs without interference. Departures from such usages call forth immediate attempts to restore a right state of affairs.

The sanctioned character of these properties is demonstrable as follows. Students were instructed to engage an acquaintance or a friend in an ordinary conversation and, without indicating that what the experimenter was asking was in any way unusual, to insist that the person clarify the sense of his commonplace remarks. Twenty-three students reported twenty-five instances of such encounters. The following are typical excerpts from their accounts.

Case 1

(S) Hi, Ray. How is your girl friend feeling?
(E) What do you mean, how is she feeling? Do you mean physical or mental?
(S) I mean how is she feeling? What's the matter with you? (He looked peeved.)
(E) Nothing. Just explain a little clearer what do you mean?
(S) Skip it. How are your Med School applications coming?
(E) What do you mean, "How are they?"
(S) You know what I mean.
(E) I really don't.
(S) What's the matter with you? Are you sick?

Case 2

On Friday night my husband and I were watching television. My husband remarked that he was tired. I asked, "How are you tired? Physically, mentally, or just bored?"
(S) I don't know, I guess physically, mainly.
(E) You mean that your muscles ache, or your bones?
(S) I guess so. Don't be so technical. (After more watching)
(S) All these old movies have the same kind of old iron bedstead in them.
(E) What do you mean? Do you mean all old movies, or some of them, or just the ones you have seen?
(S) What's the matter with you? You know what I mean.
(E) I wish you would be more specific.
(S) You know what I mean! Drop dead!

Background understandings and "adequate" recognition of commonplace events

What kinds of expectancies make up a "seen but unnoticed background of common understandings, and how are they related to persons' recognition of and stable courses of interpersonal transactions? Some information can be obtained if we first ask how a person will look at an ordinary and familiar scene and what will he see in it if we require of him that he do no more than look at it as something that for him it "obviously" and "really" is not.

Undergraduate students were assigned the task of spending from fifteen minutes to an hour in their homes viewing its activities while assuming that they were boarders in the household. They were instructed not to act out the assumption. Thirty-three students reported their experiences.

In their written reports students "behaviorized" the household scenes. Here is an excerpt from one account to illustrate my meaning.

> A short, stout man entered the house, kissed me on the cheek and asked, "How was school?" I answered politely. He walked into the kitchen, kissed the younger of two women, and said hello to the other. The younger woman asked me "What do you want for dinner, honey?" I answered, "Nothing." She shrugged her shoulders and said no more. The older woman shuffled around the kitchen muttering. The man washed his hands, sat down at the table, and picked up the paper. He read until the two women had finished putting the food on the table. The three sat down. They exchanged idle chatter about the day's events. The older woman said something in a foreign language which made the others laugh.

Persons, relationships, and activities were described without respect for their history, for the place of the scene in a set of developing life circumstances, or for the scenes as texture of relevant events for the parties themselves. References to motives, propriety, subjectivity generally, and the socially standardized character of the events were omitted. Descriptions might be thought of as those of a keyhole observer who puts aside much of what he knows in common with subjects about the scenes he is looking at, as if the writer had witnessed the scenes under a mild amnesia for common sense knowledge of social structures.

Students were surprised to see the ways in which members' treatments of each other were personal. The business of one was treated as the business of the others. A person being criticized was unable to stand on dignity and was prevented by the others from taking offense. One student reported her surprise at how freely she had the run of the house. Displays of conduct and feeling occurred without apparent concern for the management of impressions. Table manners were bad, and family members showed each other little politeness. An early casualty in the scene was the family news of the day which turned into trivial talk.

Students reported that this way of looking was difficult to sustain. Familiar objects—persons obviously, but furniture and room arrangements as well—resisted students' efforts to think of themselves as strangers. Many became uncomfortably aware of how habitual movements were being made: of *how* one was handling the silverware, or *how* one opened a door or greeted another member. Many reported that the attitude was difficult to sustain because with it quarreling, bickering, and hostile motivations became discomfitingly visible. Frequently an account that recited newly visible troubles was accompanied by the student's assertion that his account of family problems was not a "true" picture; the family was *really* a very happy one. Several students reported a mildly oppressive feeling of "conforming to a part." Several students attempted to formulate the "real me" as activities governed by rules of conduct but gave it up as a bad job. They found it more convincing to think of themselves in "usual" circumstances as "being one's real self." Nevertheless one student was intrigued with how deliberately and successfully he could predict the others' responses to his actions. He was not troubled by this feeling.

Many accounts reported a variation on the theme: "I was glad when the hour was up and I could return to the real me."

Students were convinced that the view from the boarder's attitude was not their real home environment. The boarder's attitude produced appearances which they discounted as interesting incongruities of little and misleading practical import. How had the familiar ways of looking at their home environments been altered? How did their looking differ from usual?

Several contrasts to the "usual" and "required" way of looking are detectable from their accounts. (1) In looking at their home scenes as boarders they replaced the mutually recognized texture of events with a rule of interpretation which required that this mutual texture be *temporarily* disregarded. (2) The mutually recognized texture was brought under the jurisdiction of the new attitude as a definition of the essential structures of this texture. (3) This was done by engaging in interaction with others with an attitude whose nature and purpose only the user knew about, that remained undisclosed, that could be either adopted or put aside at a time of the user's own choosing, and was a matter of willful election. (4) The attitude as an intention was sustained as a matter of personal and willed compliance with an explicit and single rule, (5) in which, like a game, the goal of the intention was identical with looking at things under the auspices of the single rule itself. (6) Above all, looking was not bound by any necessity for gearing one's interests within the attitude to the actions of others. These were the matters that students found strange.

When students used these background expectancies not only as ways of looking at familial scenes but as grounds for acting in them, the scenes exploded with the bewilderment and anger of family members.

Students were required to spend from fifteen minutes to an hour in their homes imagining that they were boarders and acting out this assumption. They were instructed to conduct themselves in a circumspect and polite fashion. They were to avoid getting personal, to use formal address, to speak only when spoken to.

In nine of forty-nine cases students either refused to do the assignment (five cases) or the try was "unsuccessful" (four cases). Four of the "no try" students said they were afraid to do it; a fifth said she preferred to avoid the risk of exciting her mother who had a heart condition. In two of the "unsuccessful" cases the family treated it as a joke from the beginning and refused despite the continuing actions of the student to change. A third family took the view that something undisclosed was the matter, but what it might be was of no concern to them. In the fourth family the father and mother remarked that the daughter was being "extra nice" and undoubtedly wanted something that she would shortly reveal.

In the remaining four-fifths of the cases family members were stupefied. They vigorously sought to make the strange actions intelligible and to restore the situation to normal appearances. Reports were filled with accounts of astonishment, bewilderment, shock, anxiety, embarrassment, and anger and with charges by various family members that the student was mean, inconsiderate, selfish, nasty, or impolite. Family members demanded explanations: What's the matter? What's gotten into you? Did you get fired? Are you sick? What are you being so superior about? Why are you mad? Are you out of your mind or are you just stupid? One student acutely embarrassed his mother in front of her friends by asking if she minded if he had a snack from the refrigerator. "Mind if you have a little snack? You've been eating little snacks around here for years without asking me. What's gotten into you?" One mother, infuriated when her daughter spoke to her only when she was spoken to, began to shriek in angry denunciation of the daughter for her disrespect and insubordination and refused to be calmed by the student's sister. A father berated his daughter for being insufficiently concerned for the welfare of others and of acting like a spoiled child.

Occasionally family members would first treat the student's action as a cue for a joint comedy routine which was soon replaced by irritation and exasperated anger at the student for not knowing when enough was enough. Family members mocked the "politeness" of the students—"Certainly, Mr. Herzberg!"—or charged the student with acting like a wise guy and generally reproved the "politeness" with sarcasm.

Explanations were sought in previous, understandable motives of the student: the student was working too hard in school; the student was ill; there had been "another fight" with a fiancee. When offered explanations by family members went unacknowledged, there followed withdrawal by the offended member, attempted isolation of the culprit, retaliation, and denunciation. "Don't bother with him, he's in one of his moods again"; "Pay no attention but just wait until he asks me for something"; "You're cutting me, okay I'll cut you and then some"; "Why must you always create friction in our family harmony?" Many accounts reported versions of the following confrontation. A father followed his son into the bedroom. "Your mother is right. You don't look well and you're not talking sense. You had better get another job that doesn't require such late hours." To this the student replied that he appreciated the consideration, but that he felt fine and only wanted a little privacy. The father responded in a high rage, "I don't want any more of *that* out of you and if you can't treat your mother decently you'd better move out!"

There were no cases in which the situation was not restorable upon the student's explanation. Nevertheless, for the most part family members were not amused and only rarely did they find the experience instructive as the student argued that it was supposed to have been. After hearing the explanation a sister replied coldly on behalf of a family of four, "Please, no more of these experiments. We're not rats, you know." Occasionally an explanation was accepted but still it added offense. In several cases students reported that the explanation left them, their families, or both wondering how much of what the student had said was "in character" and how much the student "really meant."

Students found the assignment difficult to complete. But in contrast with on-lookers' accounts students were likely to report that difficulties consisted in not being treated as if they were in the role that they were attempting to play, and of being confronted with situations but not knowing how a boarder would respond.

There were several entirely unexpected findings. (1) Although many students reported extensive rehearsals in imagination, very few mentioned anticipatory fears or embarrassment. (2) On the other hand, although unanticipated and nasty developments frequently occurred, in only one case did a student report serious regrets. (3) Very few students reported heartfelt relief when the hour was over. They were much more likely to report partial relief. They frequently reported that in response to the anger of others they became angry in return and slipped easily into subjectively recognizable feelings and actions.

In contrast to the reports of the on-looking "boarders" very few reports "behaviorized" the scene.

Background understandings and social affects

Despite the interest in social affects that prevails in the social sciences, and despite the extensive concern that clinical psychiatry pays them, surprisingly little has been written on the socially structured conditions for their production, while the role that a background of common understandings plays in their production, control, and recognition is almost *terra incognita*. This lack of attention from experimental investigators is all the more remarkable if one considers that it is precisely this relationship that persons are concerned with in their common sense portrayals of how to conduct one's daily affairs so as to solicit enthusiasm and friendliness or avoid anxiety, guilt, shame, or boredom. The relationship between the common understandings and social affects may be illustrated by thinking of the acting out student-boarders' procedure as one that involved the production of bewilderment and anger by treating an important state of affairs as something that it "obviously," "naturally," and "really" is not.

The existence of a definite and strong relationship between common understandings and social affects can be demonstrated and some of its features explored by the deliberate display of distrust, a procedure that for us produced highly standardized effects. The rationale was as follows.

One of the background expectancies Schutz described concerns the sanctioned use of doubt as a constituent feature of a world that is being understood in common. Schutz proposed that for the *conduct of his everyday affairs* the person assumes, assumes the other person assumes as well, and assumes that as he assumes it of the other person the other person assumes it of him that a relationship of undoubted correspondence is the sanctioned relationship between the actual appearances of an object and the intended object that appears in a particular way. For the person conducting his everyday affairs, objects, for him as he expects for others, are as they appear to be. To treat this relationship under a *rule* of doubt requires that the necessity and motivation for such a rule be justified.

We anticipated that because of the differing relationship of an exhibited rule of doubt (distrust)[5] that the other person was as he appeared to be to the legitimate texture of common expectancies, there should be different affective states for the doubter and the doubted. On the part of the person distrusted there should be the demand for justification and when it was not forthcoming, as "anyone could see" it could not be, anger. For the experimenter we expected embarrassment to result from the disparity that the distrusting procedure would create between the lesser thing that the experimenter's challenges of "what anyone could see" made him out to be under the gaze of his victim, and the competent person he with others knew himself "after all" to be but which the procedure required that he could not claim.

Like Santayana's clock, this formulation was neither right nor wrong. Although the procedure produced what we anticipated, it also furnished us and the experimenters with more than we had bargained for.

Students were instructed to engage someone in conversation and to imagine and act on the assumption that what the other person was saying was directed by hidden motives which were his real ones. They were to assume that the other person was trying to trick them or mislead them.

In only two of thirty-five accounts did students attempt the assignment with strangers. Most students were afraid that such a situation would get out of hand so they selected friends, roommates, siblings, and family members. Even so they reported considerable rehearsal in imagination, much review of possible consequences, and deliberate selections among eligible persons.

The attitude was difficult to sustain and carry through. Students reported acute awareness of being "in an artificial game," of being unable "to live the part," and of frequently being "at a loss as to what to do next." In the course of listening to the other person experimenters would lose sight of the assignment. One student spoke for several when she said she was unable to get any results because so much of her effort was directed to maintaining an attitude of distrust that she was unable to follow the conversation. She said she was unable to imagine how her fellow conversationalists might be deceiving her because they were talking about such inconsequential matters.

With many students the assumption that the other person was not what he appeared to be and was to be distrusted was the same as the attribution that the other person was angry with them and hated them. On the other hand many victims, although they complained that the student had no reason to be angry with them, offered unsolicited attempts at explanation and conciliation. When this was of no avail there followed frank displays of anger and "disgust."

Anticipated and acute embarrassment swiftly materialized for the two students who attempted the procedure with strangers. After badgering a bus driver for assurances that the bus would pass the street that she wanted and receiving several assurances in return that indeed the bus did pass the street, the exasperated bus driver shouted so that all passengers overheard, "Look lady, I told you once, didn't I? How many times do I have to tell you!" She reported, "I shrank to the back of the bus to sink as low as I could in the seat. I had gotten a good case of cold feet, a flaming face, and a strong dislike for my assignment."

There were very few reports of shame or embarrassment from students who tried it with friends and family. Instead they were surprised, and so were we, to find as one student reported that "once I started acting the role of a hated person I actually came to feel somewhat hated and by the time I left the table I was quite angry." Even more surprising to us, many reported that they found the procedure enjoyable and this included the real anger not only of others but their own.

Although students' explanations easily restored most situations, some episodes "turned serious" and left a residue of disturbance for one or both parties that the offered explanation did not resolve. This can be illustrated in the report of a student housewife who at the conclusion of dinner, and with some trepidation, questioned her husband about his having worked late the night before and raised a question about his actually having played poker as he claimed on an evening of the week before. Without asking him what he had actually done she indicated an explanation was called for. He replied sarcastically, "You seem to be uneasy about something. Do you know what it might be?

[5] The concepts of "trust" and "distrust" are elaborated in my paper, "A Conception of and Experiments with 'Trust' as a Condition of Stable Concerted Actions," in *Motivation and Social Interaction,* edited by O. J. Harvey, New York: The Ronald Press, 1963, pp. 187–238. The term "trust" is used there to refer to a person's compliance with the expectancies of the attitude of daily life as a morality. Acting in accordance with a rule of doubt directed to the correspondence between appearances and the objects that appearances are appearances of is only one way of specifying "distrust." Modifications of each of the other expectancies that make up the attitude of everyday life, as well as their various sub-sets, furnish variations on the central theme of treating a world that one is required to know in common and take for granted as a problematic matter. See footnote 2 for references to Schutz' discussions of the attitude of daily life. The attitude's constituent expectancies are briefly enumerated below, p. 91.

This conversation would no doubt make more sense if *I* knew too." She accused him of deliberately avoiding the subject, although the subject had not been mentioned. He insisted that *she* tell *him* what the *subject* was. When she did not say, he asked directly, "Okay, what's the joke?" Instead of replying "I gave him a long hurt look." He became visibly upset, became very solicitous, gentle, and persuasive. In response she acknowledged the experiment. He stalked off obviously unhappy and for the remainder of the evening was sullen and suspicious. She, in the meanwhile, remained at the table piqued and unsettled about the remarks that her statements had drawn forth about his not being bored at work "with all the insinuations it might or could mean," particularly the insinuation that he was not bored at work but he *was* bored with her and at home. She wrote, "I was actually bothered by his remarks . . . I felt more upset and worried than he did throughout the experiment . . . about how imperturbable he seemed to be." Neither one attempted nor wanted to discuss the matter further. The following day the husband confessed that he had been considerably disturbed and had the following reactions in this order: determination to remain calm; shock at his wife's "suspicious nature"; surprise to find that cheating on her was liable to be hard; a determination to make her figure out her own answers to her questions without any denial or help from him; extreme relief when the encounter was revealed to have been experimentally contrived; but finally a residue of uneasy feelings which he characterized as "his shaken ideas of my (the wife's) nature which remained for the rest of the evening."

Background understandings and bewilderment

Earlier the argument was made that the possibility of common understanding does not consist in demonstrated measures of shared knowledge of social structure but consists instead and entirely in the enforceable character of actions in compliance with the expectancies of everyday life as a morality. Common sense knowledge of the facts of social life for the members of the society is institutionalized knowledge of the real world. Not only does common sense knowledge portray a real society for members but in the manner of a self-fulfilling prophecy the features of the real society are produced by persons' motivated compliance with these background expectancies. Hence the stability of concerted actions that occur under the auspices of this compliance as well as the extent and severity of disturbances in concerted actions should vary directly with whatsoever are the real conditions of social organization that guarantee persons' motivated compliance with this background texture of relevances as a legitimate order of beliefs about life in society seen "from within" the society. Seen from the person's point of view, his commitments to motivated compliance consist of his grasp of and subscription to the "natural facts of life in society."

Such considerations suggest that the firmer a societal member's grasp of What Anyone Like Us Necessarily Knows, the more severe should be his disturbance when "natural facts of life" are impugned for him as a depiction of his real circumstances. To test this suggestion a procedure would need to modify the *objective* structure of the familiar, known-in-common environment by rendering the background expectancies inoperative. Specifically, this modification would consist of subjecting a person to a breach of the background expectancies of everyday life while (a) making it difficult for the person to interpret his situation as a game, an experiment, a deception, a play, i.e., as something other than the one known according to the attitude of everyday life as a matter of enforceable morality and action, (b) making it necessary that he reconstruct the "natural facts" but giving him insufficient time to manage the reconstruction with respect to required mastery of practical circumstances for which he must call upon his knowledge of the "natural facts," and (c) requiring that he manage the reconstruction of the natural facts by himself and without consensual validation.

Presumably he should have no alternative but to try to normalize the resultant incongruities within the order of events of everyday life. Under the developing effort itself, events should lose their perceivedly normal character. The member should be unable to recognize an event's status as typical. Judgments of likelihood should fail him. He should be unable to assign present occurrences to similar orders of events he has known in the past. He should be unable to assign, let alone to "see at a glance," the conditions under which the events can be reproduced. He should be unable to order these events to means-ends relationships. The conviction should be undermined that the moral authority of the familiar society compels their occurrence. Stable and "realistic" matchings of intentions and objects should dissolve, by which I mean that the ways, otherwise familiar to him, in which the objective perceived environment serves as both the motivating grounds of feelings and is motivated by feelings directed to it, should become obscure. In short, the members' real perceived environment on losing its known in common background should become "specifically senseless."[6] Ideally speaking, behaviors directed to such a senseless environment should be those of bewilderment, uncertainty, internal conflict, psychosocial isolation, acute and nameless anxiety along with various symptoms of acute depersonalization. Structures of interaction should be correspondingly disorganized.

This is expecting quite a lot of a breach of the background expectancies. Obviously we would settle for less if the results of a procedure for their breach was at all encouraging about this formulation. As it hap-

[6] The term is borrowed from Max Weber's essay, "The Social Psychology of the World Religions," in *From Max Weber: Essays in Sociology,* translated by H. H. Gerth and C. Wright Mills, New York: Oxford University Press, 1946, pp. 267–301. I have adapted its meaning.

pens, the procedure produced convincing and easily detected bewilderment and anxiety.

To begin with, it is necessary to specify just what expectancies we are dealing with. Schutz reported that the feature of a scene, "known in common with others," was compound and consisted of several constituents. Because they have been discussed elsewhere[7] I shall restrict discussion to brief enumeration.

According to Schutz, the person assumes, assumes that the other person assumes as well, and assumes that as he assumes it of the other person the other person assumes the same for him:

1. That the determinations assigned to an event by the witness are required matters that hold on grounds that specifically disregard personal opinion or socially structured circumstances of particular witnesses, i.e., that the determinations are required as matters of "objective necessity" or "facts of nature."

2. That a relationship of undoubted correspondence is the sanctioned relationship between the-presented-appearance-of-the-object and the-intended-object-that-presents-itself-in-the-perspective-of-the-particular-appearance.

3. That the event that is known in the manner that it is known can actually and potentially affect the witness and can be affected by his action.

4. That the meanings of events are products of a socially standardized process of naming, reification, and idealization of the user's stream of experience, i.e., are the products of a language.

5. That present determinations of an event, whatsoever these may be, are determinations that were intended on previous occasions and that may be again intended in identical fashion on an indefinite number of future occasions.

6. That the intended event is retained as the temporally identical event throughout the stream of experience.

7. That the event has as its context of interpretation: (a) a commonly entertained scheme of interpretation consisting of a standardized system of signals and coding rules, and (b) "What anyone knows," i.e., a preestablished corpus of socially warranted knowledge.

8. That the actual determinations that the event exhibits for the witness are the potential determinations that it would exhibit for the other person were they to exchange positions.

9. That to each event there corresponds its determinations that originate in the witness's and in the other person's particular biography. From the witness's point of view such determinations are irrelevant for the purposes at hand of either and both he and the other have selected and interpreted the actual and potential determinations of events in an empirically identical manner that is sufficient for all their practical purposes.

10. That there is a characteristic disparity between the publicly acknowledged determinations and the personal, withheld determinations of events, and this private knowledge is held in reserve, i.e., that the event means for both the witness and the other more than the witness can say.

11. That alterations of this characteristic disparity remain within the witness's autonomous control.

It is *not* the case that what an event exhibits as a distinctive determination is a condition of its membership in a known-in-the-manner-of-common-sense-environment. Instead the conditions of its membership are the attributions that its determinations, *whatever they might substantively consist of*, could be seen by the other person if their positions were exchanged, or that its features are not assigned as matters of personal preference but are to be seen by anyone, i.e., the previously enumerated features. These and only these enumerated features *irrespective* of any other determinations of an event define the common sense character of an event. Whatever other determinations an event of everyday life may exhibit—whether its determinations are those of persons' motives, their life histories, the distributions of income in the population, kinship obligations, the organization of an industry, or what ghosts do when night falls—if and only if the event has for the witness the enumerated determinations is it an event in an environment "known in common with others."

Such attributions are features of witnessed events that are seen without being noticed. They are demonstrably relevant to the common sense that the actor makes of what is going on about him. They inform the witness about any particular appearance of an interpersonal environment. They inform the witness as to the real objects that actual appearances are the appearances of, but without these attributed features necessarily being recognized in a deliberate or conscious fashion.

Since each of the expectancies that make up the attitude of daily life assigns an expected feature to the actor's environment, it should be possible to breach these expectancies by deliberately modifying scenic events so as to disappoint these attributions. By definition, surprise is possible with respect to each of these expected features. The nastiness of surprise should vary directly with the extent to which the person as a matter of moral necessity complies with their use as a scheme for assigning witnessed appearances their status as events in a perceivedly normal environment. In short, the realistic grasp by a collectivity member of the natural facts of life, and his commitment to a knowledge of them as a condition of self-esteem as a bona-fide and competent collectivity member,[8] is the

[7] Schutz, *op. cit.*, "On Multiple Realities," and "Common Sense and Scientific Interpretation of Human Action." Garfinkel, *op. cit.*, "A Conception of and Experiments with 'Trust' . . ." and "Common Sense Knowledge of Social Structures," *Transactions of the Fourth World Congress of Sociology*, Milan, 1959, Vol. 4, pp. 51–65.

[8] I use the term "competence" to mean the claim that a collectivity member is entitled to exercise that he is capable of managing his everyday affairs without interference. That members can take such claims for granted I refer to by speaking of a person as a "bona-fide" collectivity member. More extensive discussion of the relationships between "competence" and "common sense knowledge of social structures" will be found in the Ph.D. dissertation by Egon Bittner, "Popular Interests in Psy-

condition that we require in order to maximize his confusion upon the occasion that the grounds of this grasp are made a source of irreducible incongruity.

I designed a procedure to breach these expectancies while satisfying the three conditions under which their breach would presumably produce confusion, i.e., that the person could not turn the situation into a play, a joke, an experiment, a deception and the like, or, in Lewinian terminology, that he could not "leave the field"; that he have insufficient time to work through a redefinition of his real circumstances; and that he be deprived of consensual support for an alternative definition of social reality.

Twenty-eight pre-medical students were run individually through a three hour experimental interview. As part of the solicitation of subjects as well as at the beginning of the interview, the experimenter identified himself as a representative of an Eastern medical school who was attempting to learn why the medical school intake interview was such a stressful situation. It was hoped that identifying the experimenter as a person with medical school ties would make it difficult for students to "leave the field" once the expectancy breaching procedure began. How the other two conditions of (a) managing a redefinition in insufficient time and (b) not being able to count on consensual support for an alternative definition of social reality were met will be apparent in the following description.

During the first hour of the interview the student furnished to the "medical school representative" the medical interview facts-of-life by answering for the representative such questions as "what sources of information about a candidate are available to medical schools?", "What kind of man are the medical schools looking for?", "What should a good candidate do in the interview?", "What should he avoid?" With this much completed the student was told that the representative's research interests had been satisfied. The student was then asked if he would care to hear a recording of an actual interview. All students wanted very much to hear the recording.

The recording was a faked one between a "medical school interviewer" and an "applicant." The applicant was a boor, his language was ungrammatical and filled with colloquialisms, he was evasive, he contradicted the interviewer, he bragged, he ran down other schools and professions, he insisted on knowing how he had done in the interview. Detailed assessments by the student of the recorded applicant were obtained immediately after the recording was finished.

The student was then given information from the applicant's "official record." Performance information and characterological information were furnished in that order. Performance information dealt with the applicant's activities, grades, family background, courses, charity work and the like. Characterological information consisted of character assessments by "Dr. Gardner, the medical school interviewer," "six psychiatrically trained members of the admissions committee who had heard only the recorded interview," and "other students."

The information was deliberately contrived to contradict the principal points in the student's assessment. For example, if the student said that the applicant must have come from a lower class family, he was told that the applicant's father was vice president of a firm that manufactured pneumatic doors for trains and buses. Was the applicant ignorant? Then he had excelled in courses like The Poetry of Milton and Dramas of Shakespeare. If the student said the applicant did not know how to get along with people, then the applicant had worked as a voluntary solicitor for Sydenham Hospital in New York City and had raised $32,000 from 30 "big givers." That the applicant was stupid and would not do well in a scientific field was met by citing A's in organic and physical chemistry and graduate level performance in an undergraduate research course.

Students wanted very much to know what "the others" thought of the applicant and had he been admitted? The student was told that the applicant had been admitted and was living up to the promise that the medical school interviewer and the "six psychiatrists" had found and expressed in a strong recommendation of the applicant's characterological fitness which was read to the student. As for the views of other students, the student was told (for example) that thirty other students had been seen, that twenty-eight were in entire agreement with the medical school interviewer's assessment, and the remaining two had been slightly uncertain but at the first bit of information had seen him just as the others had.

Following this the student was invited to listen to the record a second time, after which he was asked to assess the applicant again.

RESULTS. Twenty-five of the twenty-eight students were taken in. The following does not apply to the three who were convinced there was a deception. Two of these are discussed at the conclusion of this section.

Students managed incongruities of performance data with vigorous attempts to make it factually compatible with their original and very derogatory assessments. For example, many said that the applicant sounded like or was a lower class person. When they were told that his father was vice president of a national corporation which manufactured pneumatic doors for trains and buses, they replied like this:

> "That explains why he said he had to work. Probably his father made him work. That would make a lot of his moans unjustified in the sense that things were really not so bad."

When told he had a straight A average in physical science courses, students began to acknowledge bewilderment openly.

chiatric Remedies: A Study in Social Control," University of California, Los Angeles, 1961.

The concepts of "collectivity" and "collectivity membership" are intended in strict accord with Talcott Parsons' usage in *The Social System*, Glencoe: The Free Press, 1951, and in the general introduction to *Theories of Society*, by Talcott Parsons, Edward Shils, Kaspar D. Naegele, and Jesse R. Pitts, New York: The Free Press of Glencoe, 1961.

"Well! I think you can analyze it this way. In psychological terms. See—one possible way—now I may be all *wet* but this is the way I look at *that*. He probably suffered from an inferiority complex and that's an over compensation for his inferiority complex. His *great* marks—his *good* marks are a compensation for his failure—in social dealings perhaps, I don't know."

Attempts to resolve the incongruities produced by the character assessment of "Gardner" and "the other six judges" were very much less frequent than normalizing attempts with performance information. Open expressions of bewilderment and anxiety interspersed with silent ruminations were characteristic:

(Whistles.) I—I don't think he sounded well bred at all. That whole tone of voice! ! —I— Perhaps you noticed though, when he said "You should have said in the first place," *before* he (the recorded medical school examiner) took it with a smile. — But even so! No, no I can't see that. "You should have said that before." Maybe he was being funny though. Exercising a — No! To me it sounded impertinent!

Soon after the performance data produced its consternation, students occasionally asked what the other students made of him. Only after they were given "Dr. Gardner's" assessment, and their responses to it had been made, were the opinions of "the other students" given. In some cases the subject was told "Thirty-four out of thirty-five before you agreed with Dr. Gardner," sometimes forty-three out of forty-five, nineteen out of twenty, fifty-one out of fifty-two. All the numbers were large. For eighteen of the twenty-five students the delivery hardly varied from the following protocol:

(36 out of 37) I would go back on my former opinion but I wouldn't go back too far. I just don't see it. — Why should I have these different standards? Were my opinions more or less in agreement? (No.) That leads me to think. — That's funny. Unless you got thirty-six unusual people. I can't understand it. Maybe it's my personality. (Does it make any difference?) It does make a difference if I assume they're correct. What I consider is proper, they don't. — It's my attitude — Still in all a man of that sort would alienate me, a wise guy type to be avoided. Of course you can talk like that with other fellows—but in an interview? . . . Now I'm more confused than I was at the beginning of the entire interview. I think I ought to go home and look in the mirror and talk to myself. Do you have any ideas? (Why? Does it disturb you?) Yes it *does* disturb me! It makes me think my abilities to judge people and values are way off from normal. It's not a healthy situation. (What difference does it make?) If I act the way I act it seems to me that I'm just putting my head in the lion's mouth. I did have preconceptions but they're shattered all to hell. It makes me wonder about myself. Why should I have these different standards. It all points to me.

Of the twenty-five subjects that were taken in, seven were unable to resolve the incongruity of having been wrong about such an obvious matter and were unable to "see" the alternative. Their suffering was dramatic and unrelieved. Five more resolved it with the view that the medical school had accepted a good man; five others with the view that it had accepted a boor. Although they changed they nevertheless did not abandon their former views. For them Gardner's view could be seen "in general" but it was a grasp without conviction. When their attention was drawn to particulars the general picture would evaporate. These subjects were willing to entertain and use the "general" picture but they suffered whenever indigestible particulars of the same portrait came into view. Subscription to the "general" picture was accompanied by a recitation of characteristics that were not only the opposite of those in the subject's original assessment but were intensified by superlative adjectives so that where previously the candidate was gauche, he was now "supremely" poised; where he had been boorish, he was "very" natural; where he had been hysterical, he was "very" calm. Further, they saw the new features through a new appreciation of the way the medical examiner had been listening. They *saw*, for example, that the examiner *was smiling* when the applicant had forgotten to offer him a cigarette.

Three more subjects were convinced that there was a deception and acted on the conviction through the interview. They showed no disturbance. Two of them showed acute suffering as soon as it appeared that the interview was finished, and they were being dismissed with no acknowledgement of a deception.

Three others, by suffering in silence, confounded the experimenter. Without giving any indication to the experimenter, they regarded the interview as an experimental one in which they were required to solve some problems and thought therefore they were being asked to do as well as possible and to make no changes in their opinions for only then would they be contributing to the study. They were difficult for the experimenter to understand during the interview because they displayed marked anxiety yet their remarks were bland and were not addressed to the matters that were provoking it. Finally three more subjects contrasted with the others. One of these insisted that the character assessments were semantically ambiguous and because there was insufficient information a "high correlation opinion" was not possible. A second, the only one in the series, according to his account found the second portrait as convincing as the original one. When the deception was revealed he was disturbed that he could have been as convinced as he was. The third one in the face of everything showed only slight disturbance of very short duration. However, he alone among the subjects had already been interviewed for medical school and had excellent medical school contacts. Despite a grade point average of less than C, he estimated his chances of admission as fair and had expressed his preference for a career in the diplomatic service over a career in medicine.

As a final observation, twenty-two of the twenty-eight subjects expressed marked relief—ten of them with explosive expressions—when the deception was disclosed. Unanimously they said that the news of the deception permitted them to return to their former views. Seven subjects had to be convinced that there had been a deception. When the deception was revealed they asked what they were to believe. Was the experimenter telling them that there had been a deception in order to make them feel better? No pains were

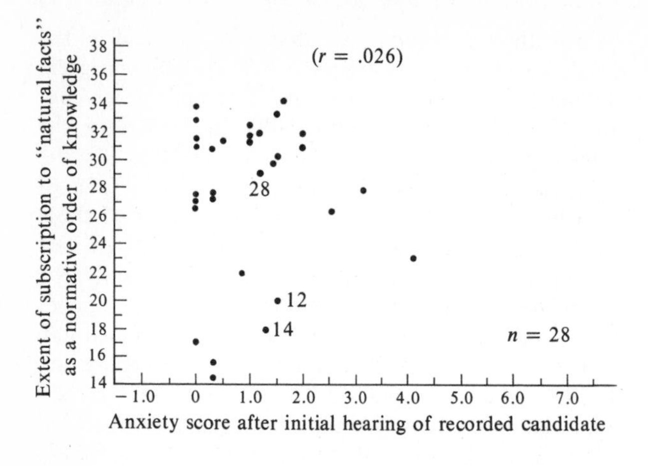

FIGURE 1. Correlation of the extent of subject's subscription of the "natural facts" as an institutionalized order of knowledge about pre-medical circumstances and initial anxiety score.

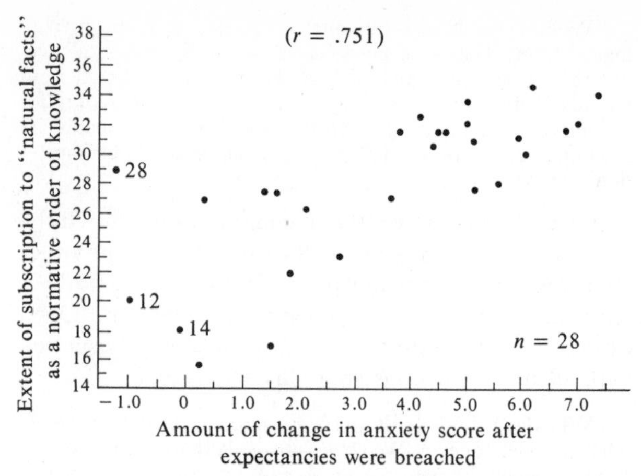

FIGURE 2. Correlation of the extent of subject's subscription of the "natural facts" as an institutionalized order of knowledge about pre-medical circumstances and relative anxiety score.

spared and whatever truth or lies that had to be told were told in order to establish the truth that there had been a deception.

Because motivated compliance to the expectancies that make up the attitude of daily life consists from the person's point of view of his grasp of and subscription to the "natural facts of life," variations in the organizational conditions of motivated compliance for different collectivity members would consist of members' differential grasp of and subscription to the "natural facts of life." Hence the severity of the effects described above should vary directly with the enforceable commitments of members to a grasp of the natural facts of life. Further, because of the *objective* character of the grasped common moral order of the facts of collectivity life, the severity should vary with their committed grasp of the natural facts of life and independently of "personality characteristics." By personality characteristics I mean all characteristics of persons that investigators use methodologically to account for a person's courses of action by referring these actions to more or less systematically conceived motivational and "inner life" variables while disregarding social and cultural system effects. The results of most conventional personality assessment devices and clinical psychiatric procedures satisfy this condition.

Thereby, the following phenomenon should be discoverable. Imagine a procedure whereby a convincing assessment can be made of the extent of a person's committed grasp of the "natural facts of social life." Imagine another procedure whereby the extent of a person's confusion can be assessed ranging through the various degrees and mixtures of the behaviors described before. For a set of unselected persons, and independently of personality determinations, the initial relationship between the committed "grasp of natural facts" and "confusion" should be random. Under the breach of the expectancies of everyday life, given the conditions for the optimal production of disturbance, persons should shift in exhibited confusion in an amount that is coordinate with the original extent of their grasp of the "natural facts of life."

The type of phenomenon that I propose is discoverable is portrayed in Figures 1 and 2 which are based on the study of the twenty-eight pre-medical students reported above. Prior to the introduction of incongruous material, the extent of students' subscription to a common moral order of facts of pre-medical school life and the students' anxiety correlated −.026. After the incongruous material had been introduced and unsuccessfully normalized, and before the deception was revealed, the correlation was .751. Because assessment procedures were extremely crude, because of serious errors in design and procedure, and because of the *post hoc* argument, *these results do no more than illustrate what I am talking about. Under no circumstances should they be considered as findings.*

The relevance of common understandings to the fact that models of man in society portray him as a judgmental dope

Many studies have documented the finding that the social standardization of common understandings, irrespective of what it is that is standardized, orients persons' actions to scenic events, and furnishes persons the grounds upon which departures from perceivedly normal courses of affairs are detectable, restoration is made, and effortful action is mobilized.

Social science theorists—most particularly social psychiatrists, social psychologists, anthropologists, and sociologists—have used the fact of standardization to conceive the character and consequences of actions that comply with standardized expectancies. Generally they have acknowledged but otherwise neglected the fact that by these same actions persons discover, create, and sustain this standardization. An important and prevalent consequence of this neglect is that of being misled about the nature and conditions of stable actions. This occurs by making out the member of the society to be a judgmental dope of a cultural and/or psychological sort with the result that the *unpublished* results of any accomplished study of the relationship between actions and standardized expectations will invariably contain enough incongruous material to invite essential revision.

By "cultural dope" I refer to the man-in-the-sociologist's-society who produces the stable features of the society by acting in compliance with pre-established and legitimate alternatives of action that the common culture provides. The "psychological dope" is the man-in-the-psychologist's-society who produces the stable features of the society by choices among alternative courses of action that are compelled on the grounds of psychiatric biography, conditioning history, and the variables of mental functioning. The common feature in the use of these "models of man" is the fact that courses of common sense rationalities[9] of judgment which involve the person's use of common sense knowledge of social structures over the temporal "succession" of here and now situations are treated as epiphenomenal.

The misleading character of the use of the judgmental dope to portray the relationship between standardized expectancies and courses of action goes to the problem of adequate explanation as the controlling consideration in the investigator's decision to either consider or disregard the common sense rationalities when deciding the necessary relationships between courses of action, given such problematic considerations as perspectival choice, subjectivity, and inner time. A favored solution is to portray what the member's actions will have come to by using the stable structures—what they came to—as a point of theoretical departure from which to portray the necessary character of the pathways whereby the end result is assembled. Hierarchies of need dispositions, and common culture as enforced rules of action are favored devices for bringing the problem of necessary inference to terms, although at the cost of making out the person-in-society to be a judgmental dope.

How is an investigator *doing* it when he is making out the member of a society to be a judgmental dope? Several examples will furnish some specifics and consequences.

I assigned students the task of bargaining for standard priced merchandise. The relevant standardized expectancy is the "institutionalized one price rule," a constituent element, according to Parsons,[10] of the institution of contract. Because of its "internalized" character the student-customers should have been fearful and shamed by the prospective assignment, and shamed by having done it. Reciprocally, anxiety and anger should have been commonly reported for sales persons.

Sixty-eight students were required to accomplish one trial only for any item costing no more than two dollars, and were to offer much less than the asking price. Another sixty-seven students were required to accomplish a series of six trials: three for items costing two dollars or less, and three for items costing fifty dollars or more.

FINDINGS. (a) Sales persons can be dismissed as either having been dopes in different ways than current theories of standardized expectancies provide, or not dopes enough. A few showed some anxiety; occasionally one got angry. (b) Twenty percent of the single tries refused to try or aborted the effort, as compared with three percent of those who had been assigned the series of six trials. (c) When the bargaining episode was analyzed as consisting of a series of steps—anticipation of the trial, approaching the sales person, actually making the offer, the ensuing interaction, terminating the episode, and afterwards—it was found that fears occurred with the greatest frequency in both groups in anticipating the assignment and approaching the sales person *for the first try*. Among the single trials the number of persons who reported discomfort declined with each successive step in the sequence. Most of the students who bargained in two or more trials reported that by the third episode they were enjoying the assignment. (d) Most students reported less discomfort in bargaining for high priced than low priced merchandise. (e) Following the six episodes many students reported that they had learned to their "surprise" that one could bargain in standard priced settings with some realistic chance of an advantageous outcome and planned to do so in the future, particularly for costly merchandise.

Such findings suggest that one can make the member of the society out to be a cultural dope (a) by portraying a member of the society as one who operates by the rules when one is actually talking about the anticipatory anxiety that prevents him from permitting a situation to develop, let alone confronting a situation in which he has the alternative of acting or not with respect to a rule; or (b) by overlooking the practical and theoretical importance of the mastery of fears. (c) If upon the arousal of troubled feelings persons avoid tinkering with these "standardized" expectancies, the standardization could consist of an *attributed* standardization that is supported by the fact that persons avoid the very situations in which they might learn about them.

Lay as well as professional knowledge of the nature of rule governed actions and the consequences of breaching the rules is prominently based on just such procedure. Indeed, the more important the rule, the greater is the likelihood that knowledge is based on avoided tests. Strange findings must certainly await anyone who examines the expectancies that make up routine backgrounds of common place activities for they have rarely been exposed by investigators even to

[9] Common sense rationalities are discussed at length in Schutz, *op. cit., Economica,* and in my article, "The Rational Properties of Scientific and Common Sense Activities," *Behavioral Science,* 5 (January, 1960), pp. 72–83. The common sense rationalities were made the basis of a radical criticism and reconstruction of sociological interests in mental illness in Egon Bittner, *op. cit.*

[10] Parsons, Talcott, "Economy, Policy, Money, and Power," dittoed manuscript, 1959.

as much revision as an imaginative rehearsal of their breach would produce.

Another way in which the member of the society can be made a judgmental dope is by using any of the available theories of the formal properties of signs and symbols to portray the way persons construe environmental displays as significant ones. The dope is made out in several ways. I shall mention two.

(a) Characteristically, formal investigations have been concerned either with devising normative theories of symbolic usages or, while seeking descriptive theories, have settled for normative ones. In either case it is necessary to instruct the construing member to act in accordance with the investigator's instructions in order to guarantee that the investigator will be able to study their usages as instances of the usages the investigator has in mind. But, following Wittgenstein,[11] person's actual usages are rational usages in *some* "language game." What is *their* game? As long as this programmatic question is neglected, it is inevitable that person's usages will fall short. The more will this be so the more are subjects' interests in usages dictated by different practical considerations than those of investigators.

(b) Available theories have many important things to say about such sign functions as marks and indications, but they are silent on such overwhelmingly more common functions as glosses, synecdoche, documented representation, euphemism, irony, and double entendre. References to common sense knowledge of ordinary affairs may be safely disregarded in detecting and analyzing marks and indications as sign functions *because* users disregard them as well. The analysis of irony, double entendre, glosses, and the like, however, imposes different requirements. Any attempt to consider the related character of utterances, meanings, perspectives, and orders necessarily requires reference to common sense knowledge of ordinary affairs.

Although investigators have neglected these "complex" usages, they have not put their problematic character entirely aside. Instead, they have glossed them by portraying the usages of the member of a language community as either culture bound or need compelled, or by construing the pairing of appearances and intended objects—the pairing of "sign" and "referent"—as an association. In each case a procedural description of such symbolic usages is precluded by neglecting the judgmental work of the user.

Precisely this judgmental work, along with its reliance upon and its reference to common sense knowledge of social structures, forced itself upon our attention in every case where incongruities were induced. Our attention was forced *because* our subjects had exactly their judgmental work and common sense knowledge to contend with as matters which the incongruities presented to them as practical problems. Every procedure that involved departures from an anticipated course of ordinary affairs, regardless of whether the departure was gross or slight, aroused recognition in subjects that the experimenter was engaged in double talk, irony, glosses, euphemism, or lies. This occurred repeatedly in departures from ordinary game play.

Students were instructed to play ticktacktoe and to mix their subjects by age, sex, and degree of acquaintance. After drawing the ticktacktoe matrix they invited the subject to move first. After the subject made his move the experimenter erased the subject's mark, moved it to another square and made his own mark but without giving any indications that anything about the play was unusual. In half of 247 trials students reported that subjects treated the move as a gesture with hidden but definite significance. Subjects were convinced that the experimenter was "after something" that he was not saying and whatever he "really" was doing had nothing to do with ticktacktoe. He was making a sexual pass; he was commenting on the subject's stupidity; he was making a slurring or an impudent gesture. Identical effects occurred when students bargained for standard priced merchandise, or asked the other to clarify his commonplace remarks, or joined without invitation a strange group of conversationalists, or used a gaze that during an ordinary conversation wandered "randomly" by time to various objects in the scene.

Still another way of making the person out for a cultural dope is to simplify the communicative texture of his behavioral environment. For example, by giving physical events preferred status one can theorize out of existence the way the person's scene, as a texture of potential and actual events, contains not only appearances and attributions but the person's own lively inner states as well. We encountered this in the following procedure.

Students were instructed to select someone other than a family member and in the course of an ordinary conversation and, without indicating that anything unusual was happening, to bring their faces up to the subject's until their noses were almost touching. According to most of the 79 accounts, regardless of whether the pairs were the same or different sexes, whether they were acquaintances or close friends (strangers were prohibited), and regardless of age differences except where children were involved, the procedure motivated in *both* experimenter and subject attributions of a sexual intent on the part of the other though confirmation of this intent was withheld by the very character of the procedure. Such attributions to the other were accompanied by the person's own impulses which themselves became part of the scene as their not only being desired but their desiring. The unconfirmed invitation to choose had its accompanying conflictful hesitancy about acknowledging the choice and having been chosen. Attempted avoidance, bewilderment, acute embarrassment, furtiveness, and above all uncertainties of these as well as uncertainties of fear, hope, and anger were characteristic. These effects were most pronounced between males. Characteristically, experimenters were unable to restore the situation. Sub-

[11] Wittgenstein, Ludwig, *Philosophical Investigations*, Oxford: Basil Blackwell, 1959.

jects were only partially accepting of the experimenter's explanation that it has been done "as an experiment for a course in Sociology." They often complained, "All right, it was an experiment, but why did you have to choose *me?*" Characteristically, subject and experimenter wanted some further resolution than the explanation furnished but were uncertain about what it could or should consist of.

Finally, the member may be made out to be a judgmental dope by portraying routine actions as those governed by prior agreements, and by making the likelihood that a member will recognize deviance depend upon the existence of prior agreements. That this is a matter of mere theoretical preference whose use theorizes essential phenomena out of existence can be seen by considering the commonplace fact that persons will hold each other to agreements whose terms they never actually stipulated. This neglected property of common understandings has far reaching consequences when it is explicitly brought into the portrayal of the nature of "agreements."

Apparently no matter how specific the terms of common understandings may be—a contract may be considered the prototype—they attain the status of an agreement for persons only insofar as the stipulated conditions carry along an unspoken but understood *et cetera*[12] clause. Specific stipulations are formulated under the rule of an agreement by being brought under the jurisdiction of the *et cetera* clause. This does not occur once and for all, but is essentially bound to both the inner and outer temporal course of activities and thereby to the progressive development of circumstances and their contingencies. Therefore it is both misleading and incorrect to think of an agreement as an actuarial device whereby persons are enabled as of any Here and Now to predict each other's future activities. More accurately, common understandings that have been formulated under the rule of an agreement are used by persons to normalize whatever their actual activities turn out to be. Not only can contingencies arise, but persons know as of any Here and Now that contingencies can materialize or be invented at any time that it must be decided whether or not what the parties actually did satisfied the agreement. The *et cetera* clause provides for the certainty that unknown conditions are at every hand in terms of which an agreement, as of any particular moment, can be retrospectively reread to find out in light of present practical circumstances what the agreement "really" consisted of "in the first place" and "all along." That the work of bringing present circumstances under the rule of previously agreed activity is sometimes contested should not be permitted to mask its pervasive and routine use as an ongoing and essential feature of "actions in accord with common understandings."

This process, which I shall call a method of discovering agreements by eliciting or imposing a respect for the rule of practical circumstances, is a version of practical ethics. Although it has received little if any attention by social scientists, it is a matter of the most abiding and commonplace concern in everyday affairs and common sense theories of these affairs. Adeptness in the deliberate manipulation of *et cetera* considerations for the furtherance of specific advantages is an occupational talent of lawyers and is specifically taught to law school students. One should not suppose, however, that because it is a lawyer's skill, that only lawyers are skilled at it, or that only those who do so deliberately, do so at all. The method is general to the phenomenon of the society as a system of rule governed activities.[13] It is available as one of the mechanisms whereby potential and actual successes and windfalls, on the one hand, and the disappointments, frustrations, and failures, on the other, that persons must inevitably encounter by reason of seeking to comply with agreements, can be managed while retaining the perceived reasonableness of actual socially organized activities.

A small scale but accurate instance of this phenomenon was consistently produced by a procedure in which the experimenter engaged others in conversation while he had a wire recorder hidden under his coat. In the course of the conversation the experimenter opened his jacket to reveal the recorder, saying, "See what I have?" An initial pause was almost invariably followed by the question, "What are you going to do with it?" Subjects claimed the breach of the expectancy that the conversation was "between us." The fact that the conversation was revealed to have been recorded motivated new possibilities which the parties then sought to bring under the jurisdiction of an agreement that they had never specifically mentioned, and that indeed did not previously exist. The conversation, now seen to have been recorded, thereby acquired fresh and problematic import in view of unknown uses to which it might be turned. An agreed privacy was thereupon treated as though it had operated all along.

[12] The *et cetera* clause, its properties, and the consequences of its use have been prevailing topics of study and discussion among the members of the Conferences on Ethnomethodology that have been in progress at the University of California, Los Angeles, and the University of Colorado since February, 1962, with the aid of a grant from the U. S. Air Force Office of Scientific Research. Conference members are Egon Bittner, Harold Garfinkel, Craig MacAndrew, Edward Rose, and Harvey Sacks. Published discussions of *et cetera* by conference participants will be found in Egon Bittner, "Radicalism: A Study of the Sociology of Knowledge," *American Sociological Review* (in press); Harvey Sacks, "On Sociological Description," *Berkeley Journal of Sociology,* 8 (1963), pp. 1–16; Harold Garfinkel, "A Conception and Some Experiments With Trust . . . ," *op. cit.* Extended studies dealing with coding procedures, methods of interrogation, lawyers' work, translation, model construction, historical reconstruction, "social bookkeeping," counting, and personality diagnosis will be found in unpublished papers by Bittner, Garfinkel, MacAndrew, Rose, and Sacks; in transcribed talks given by Bittner, Garfinkel, and Sacks on "Reasonable Accounts" at the Sixteenth Annual Conference on World Affairs, University of Colorado, Boulder, April 11–12, 1963; and in Conference transcriptions. Publication of these materials is planned by the group for 1964.

[13] Insofar as this is true, it establishes the programmatic task of reconstructing the problem of social order as it is currently formulated in sociological theories, and of criticizing currently preferred solutions. At the heart of the reconstruction is the empirical problem of demonstrating the definitive features of "et cetera" thinking.

Concluding remarks

The expectancies that make up the attitude of everyday life are constitutive of the institutionalized common understandings of the practical everyday organization and workings of society as it is seen "from within." Modification of these expectancies must thereby modify the real environments of the societies' members. Such modifications transform one perceived environment of real objects into another environment of real objects.

Each of many kinds of modifications of the background of everyday expectancies furnish an area of needed further work. Each modification has as its counterpart transformed objective structures of the behavioral environments that each modification produces. It is disconcerting to find how little we know about these different sets of background expectancies and the different objective environments that they constitute.

One such modification consists of the ceremonial transformation of one environment of real objects into another. Such modifications occur in play, theatre going, high ceremony, religious conversion, convention going, and scientific inquiry. A second modification consists of instrumental transformations of environments of real objects such as occur in experimentally induced psychosis, extreme fatigue, acute sensory deprivation, brain injuries, prefrontal lobotomies, and the use of hallucinogenic drugs. A third transformation consists of neonate learning which quite literally entails the growth of a world and is directed to the production of objective features of the persons' environment that "any competent member can see." The growth of the world is necessarily accompanied by the progressively enforced and enforceable compliance of the developing member to the attitude of daily life as a competent societal member's way of "looking at things." A fourth set of modifications is involved in adult socialization, distinguishable from neonate learning by the absence of radically naive expectancies. Other modifications are those of estrangement, which must include the various phenomena intended under the currently popular theme of "alienation," as well as the phenomena of the cultural stranger, of the major and minor forms of mental illness, of the degradation that accompanies charges of criminality and the fates of social incompetence found in mental retardation and old age. Modifications occur through mischief, playful and serious; through the subtle psychopathic effects of aging as one comes to learn that one may sin, cause others harm, and not "pay"; and through the discovery that the common societal orders which in adolescence appear so massive and homogeneous not only have their interstices but depend for their massiveness upon persons' continual improvisations. Finally, there is the modification that consists in the discovery and rationalization of the common sense world through the growth of social science as a social movement.

I have been arguing that a concern for the nature, production, and recognition of reasonable, realistic, and analyzable actions is not the monopoly of philosophers and professional sociologists. Members of a society are concerned as a matter of course and necessarily with these matters both as features and for the socially managed production of their everyday affairs. The study of common sense knowledge and common sense activities consists of treating as problematic phenomena the actual methods whereby members of a society, doing sociology, lay or professional, make the social structures of everyday activities observable. The "rediscovery" of common sense is possible perhaps because professional sociologists, like members, have had too much to do with common sense knowledge of social structures as both a topic and a resource for their inquiries and not enough to do with it only and exclusively as sociology's programmatic topic.

Replication

CONSEQUENCES OF DEVIATION FROM ROLE-EXPECTATIONS IN EVERYDAY INTERACTION

Garfinkel's research emphasizes the use of everyday activities and common sense notions as *phenomena to be studied*. He does *not* argue that sociological analysis and conclusions should be based on common sense. His work, in fact, demonstrates the scientist's insistence on empirical data as the basis for conclusions. Nevertheless, in the form in which he carried out his studies, Garfinkel notes that they ". . . are not properly speaking experimental. They are demonstrations . . . through which the strangeness of an obstinately familiar world can be detected."

Our replication is in part intended to give you a personal experience in detecting some of these essential but largely unperceived rules which make social interaction possible. In addition, we will slightly enlarge on Garfinkel's demonstration by converting it into an experiment in the literal sense of that term. We will do this by gathering data for a "control group" as well as an "experimental group." The experimental group will be asked to interact with their parents, roommate, or spouse as though they were a boarder. Such a role is perfectly polite and legal, but inappropriate to one's status in this relationship. Thus, in technical terms, the "experimental treatment" or variable of this study is the failure to carry out role-expectations, and the students who will do this make up the "experimental group" of the study. The need for a control group arises because many other factors can also influence the responses of the parents, roommates, or spouses. Consequently, the control group will gather the same data as the experimental group, but without the experimental treatment. We can then compare the two sets of data to see if the experimental treatment does in fact produce a difference in the behavior of others.

To facilitate this comparison, the responses of the person with whom each student is interacting will be recorded in terms of a widely used set of categories, called the "Interaction Process Analysis" (Bales, 1950). The Interaction Process Analysis (IPA) consists of twelve categories designed so that all behavior can be classified into one or the other of these categories. The IPA categories will be described in more detail below. To write your hypothesis it is only necessary to bear in mind that three of the categories represent "negative reactions," three "positive reactions," and the other six deal with information seeking and giving.

Hypothesis

1. State what differences you expect to find in the responses of the parents, roommates, or spouses to students who play the role of a boarder as compared to the control group of students. For purposes of this hypothesis, state the differences in terms of the three main groups of Interaction Process Analysis scores: Negative Acts, Positive Acts, and Information Seeking Acts.

2. See Appendix A for general information on writing a hypothesis.

Experimental procedure

1. *Experimental and Control Groups.* Your instructor will assign you to either the experimental or the control group. In either case you will record data concerning the first thirty minutes of interaction when you first come home for the evening. This interaction can be between you and your parents, brother or sister, roommate, or husband or wife. IMPORTANT: Be sure to read and become familiar with the Interaction Process categories given on Raw Data Form A before participating in the thirty minute sample of interaction.

2. *Experimental Treatment.* If you are assigned to the experimental group, you are to imagine that you are a boarder in the house and base all your actions on this assumption. For example, you should conduct yourself in a circumspect and polite fashion. Use formal address such as Mr. or Mrs., speak only when spoken to unless the situation demands otherwise, and above all avoid getting personal. Act on the assumption that you know nothing about the habits, interests, or preferences of others, and that they are similarly ignorant of your behavior. You should try to maintain this role for 30 minutes.

3. *Interaction Recording.* As soon as possible after the thirty minute sample of interaction, record the nature of the interaction on Raw Data Form A, and give examples on Raw Data Form B. On Form A you should rate each of the types of behavior which occurred in response to your actions during this thirty minute period. Use the scale from 0 (no response of this type) to 5 (entire response was of this type) given on the form.

If the person with whom you are interacting just gives up and leaves or tries to ignore you this should be counted as an instance of category k.

4. *Specific Examples.* On Raw Data Form B give an example of an interaction which was classified under the two categories which occurred most frequently. Write the description of your action on the left side of the page, and write the response which this action evoked on the right side. Then give an example of an interaction which you classified into the second-ranked category.

Data analysis

1. *Enter Ratings on Blackboard.* On the day this problem is to be done your instructor will have a copy of Table 1 on the blackboard. (The blackboard version of the table should omit the "fx" columns.) As soon as you arrive in class, go up to the blackboard and enter a tally mark for each category in the row corresponding to the rating you gave this category on your Raw Data Form A. Be sure you always put your tally marks in the columns headed "Exp." if you were part of the experimental group, or in the column headed "Cont." if you were part of the control group. You should put a total of twelve tally marks on the blackboard—one for each category of Interaction Process.

NOTE: For the next two steps of the Data Analysis, your instructor might assign Categories a, b, and c to one part of the class; d, e, and f to another part; g, h, and i to another part; and j, k, and l to still another part of the class. Each student will then have six frequency distributions to copy and six means to calculate (i.e., three experimental and three control).

2. *Copy* from the blackboard onto your tabulation form the frequency (f) with which each category for which you are responsible was rated 1, 2, 3, 4, or 5.

3. *Compute* the mean rating for each of the categories for which you are responsible. See Appendix C for instructions concerning how to calculate the mean. Your instructor may put the results obtained by other students on the blackboard so that you can check your results. If the work of computing means was divided among the members of the class, he will put the means obtained by the other students on the blackboard so that you will have a full set of results to use as the basis for the laboratory report.

4. *Copy* the mean ratings onto the Summary Table.

5. *Compute* the mean rating assigned to each of the four main groupings by first adding the mean rating for the three categories included in each group and then dividing this total by three.

Lab report

1. Reread the general directions for writing laboratory reports in Appendix A before writing your report.

2. Under the heading INDEPENDENT VARIABLE, identify this variable and describe the way in which it was experimentally manipulated.

3. Base your SUMMARY OF THE FINDINGS on a comparison of the mean scores of the experimental and the control groups for the four summary categories, with special emphasis on groups I and IV.

4. Give special attention to the DISCUSSION, including factors which could account for the findings and for the implications of the findings.

References

Goffman, Erving, *The Presentation of Self in Everyday Life.* Garden City, N. Y.: Doubleday, 1959.

Matza, David, "Position and Behavior Patterns of Youth," in Robert E. L. Faris, ed., Handbook of Modern Sociology, Chicago: Rand-McNally, 1964, pp. 203–207.

Parsons, Talcott, Robert Bales, and Edward Shils, *Working Papers in the Theory of Action.* New York: Free Press, 1953.

Riesman, David, Robert S. Potter, and Jeanne Watson, "The Vanishing Host," *Human Organization, 19* (Spring 1960), pp. 17–27.

Simmel, Georg, *The Sociology of Georg Simmel,* trans. by Kurt H. Wolff. New York: Free Press, 1950.

Stone, Gregory P. and Ramon Oldenburg, "Wrestling," in Ralph Slovenko and James A. Knight, eds., *Motivations in Play, Games and Sports.* Springfield, Ill.: Charles C Thomas, Publishers, 1967, pp. 503–532.

Name_______________________

Date_______________________

Circle one: 1. Experimental
2. Control

About how many minutes were you able to maintain this role? ____________

Circle the person or persons to whom these data apply (more than one may be circled)

1. Father
2. Mother
3. Brother
4. Sister
5. Roommate
6. Husband
7. Wife
8. Other ____________ specify

INTERACTION PROCESS CATEGORY	RATING
I. POSITIVE REACTIONS	
a. *Shows solidarity,* affection, liking for other, raises other's status, gives help, reward:	______
b. *Shows tension release,* jokes, laughs, shows satisfaction:	______
c. *Agrees,* shows passive acceptance, understands, concurs, complies:	______
II. ATTEMPTED ANSWERS	
d. *Gives suggestion,* direction, implying autonomy for other:	______
e. *Gives opinion,* evaluation, analysis, expresses feeling, wish:	______
f. *Gives orientation,* information, repeats, clarifies, confirms:	______
III. QUESTIONS	
g. *Asks for orientation,* information, repetition, confirmation, explanation of behavior:	______
h. *Asks for opinion,* evaluation, analysis, expression of feeling:	______
i. *Asks for suggestion,* direction, possible ways of action:	______
IV. NEGATIVE REACTIONS	
j. *Disagrees,* shows passive rejection, formality, withholds help, doubts genuineness of behavior:	______
k. *Shows tension,* embarrassment, asks for help, withdraws out of field:	______
l. *Shows antagonism,* anger, irritation, deflates other's status, defends or asserts self:	______

RATE EACH CATEGORY USING THE FOLLOWING SCALE:

0. No response of this type accurred
1. Very little occurred
2. Some of this occurred
3. Quite a bit occurred
4. A great deal of this occurred
5. Entire response was of this type

Example of response classified under

IPA category: ______ (give letter of category)

Role of person making the response:

____

MY STATEMENT OR ACTION

RESPONSE

Example of response classified under

IPA category: ______

Role of person making the response:

____

MY STATEMENT OR ACTION

RESPONSE

Name________________

Date________________

TABLE 1. Mean interaction process category scores of experimental and control groups

Rating (x)	a. SOLIDARITY				b. TENSION REL.				c. AGREES				d. SUGGESTIONS				e. OPINION				f. ORIENTATION			
	Exp.		Cont.		Exp.		Cont.		Exp.		Cont.		Exp.		Cont.		Exp.		Cont.		Exp.		Cont.	
	f	fx	f	fx	f	fx	f	fx	f	fx	f	fx	f	fx	f	fx	f	fx	f	fx	f	fx	f	fx
0																								
1																								
2																								
3																								
4																								
5																								
TOTAL																								
Mean																								

TABLE 1. *(Continued)*

Rating (x)	g. ASKS FOR ORIEN. Exp.		Cont.		h. ASKS FOR OPIN. Exp.		Cont.		i. ASKS FOR SUGGES. Exp.		Cont.		j. DISAGREES Exp.		Cont.		k. SHOWS TENSION Exp.		Cont.		l. ANTAGONISM Exp.		Cont.	
	f	fx	f	fx	f	fx	f	fx	f	fx	f	fx	f	fx	f	fx	f	fx	f	fx	f	fx	f	fx
0																								
1																								
2																								
3																								
4																								
5																								
TOTAL																								
Mean																								

Name ____________________

Summary table	Mean rating Exp.	Mean rating Cont.
I. POSITIVE REACTIONS		
a. Shows solidarity	______	______
b. Shows tension release	______	______
c. Agrees	______	______
TOTAL	______	______
MEAN	______	______
II. ATTEMPTED ANSWERS		
d. Gives suggestion	______	______
e. Gives opinion	______	______
f. Gives orientation	______	______
TOTAL	______	______
MEAN	______	______
III. QUESTIONS		
g. Asks for orientation	______	______
h. Asks for opinion	______	______
i. Asks for suggestion	______	______
TOTAL	______	______
MEAN	______	______
IV. NEGATIVE REACTIONS		
j. Disagrees	______	______
k. Shows tension (or withdraws)	______	______
l. Shows antagonism	______	______
TOTAL	______	______
MEAN	______	______

LABORATORY REPORT FOR PROBLEM ______

Course or Section ______ Date ______ Name ______

HYPOTHESIS: ______

SAMPLE: ______

INDEPENDENT VARIABLE(S): ______

DEPENDENT VARIABLE(S): ______

OTHER FACTORS: ______

LABORATORY REPORT FOR PROBLEM________

SUMMARY OF FINDINGS: ________

DISCUSSION: ________

PROBLEM 6

COMMUNICATION

Symbolic communication is one of the chief characteristics differentiating human from animal society. Animals communicate in terms of signals, non-differentiated responses to stimuli in the immediate environment. In contrast, human communication is symbolic, permitting exchanges about feelings, sentiments, and other similar things which may not be immediately observable.

Clearly, human society as we know it would not be possible without this symbolic nature of communication. For example, culture—the blueprint of human behavior—is merely a logical juxtaposition of symbols; the dictum that "man should be good" has no clear empirical referent. Similarly, socialization and most other forms of human interaction rest almost wholly on man's capacity for symbolic exchange.

While communication is a universal process, it exhibits marked variations in different segments of society. For example, there are well-known variations in language usage: thus, a creek in one part of the country is called a "branch" in another part of the country, a "stream" in a third part, and a "brook" in a fourth (Lundberg, Schrag, and Larsen, 1958). Perhaps more important is the notable variation in communicative skills. Thus, it has been well documented that lower class persons lack complexity in their speech: they tend not to generalize from concrete activities, use limited perspectives, and lack richness and subtlety in describing events (Schatzman and Strauss, 1955; Bernstein, 1961).

Equally as interesting as the variations in communicative skill is the selective nature of communication. Even in purportedly objective reports, communication is rarely a mechanical or passive process. Persons tend, by and large, to report the things consonant with their own feelings and experience. The reading by Allport and Postman for the present problem is a classic study on the selective aspect of communication. Their research shows that errors or distortions in transmitting a message are neither accidental nor random, but reflect the social roles and values of the society as well as the personality of the communicators and recipients of the message. The design of the research is a simple variation of the children's party game in which a message is given to one person who in turn gives it to another and so on until it reaches the end of a chain. As the authors clearly illustrate, the final version of the message differs in a number of basic ways from the original: the message tends to be shorter, sharper in focus on some particular detail, and assimilated around the cultural expectations of the persons engaged in the communication.

In reading Allport and Postman's study, attention should be given to their research methodology. Their research, and also our replication of the Garfinkel study in the previous problem, both illustrate the possibilities of laboratory experimentation in sociology. This method contrasts with the interview and questionnaire data used in most other studies reprinted in this book. To the extent that experimentation can be developed to deal with the problems of sociology, there is great advantage to its use. First, the researcher does not have to depend on untrained and possibly biased observers (i.e., the person completing the questionnaire or answering the interview) for his data. Instead, events can be recorded more objectively. Second, there is an opportunity to gain further insights from direct observation of the behaviors being studied. Finally, the experimental method has the advantage of allowing the researcher to more definitely establish cause-and-effect relationships (see the "Note on Interpreting Cause and Effect" in Appendix A).

THE BASIC PSYCHOLOGY OF RUMOR / *Gordon W. Allport and Leo J. Postman*

Rumors in wartime

During the year 1942, rumor became a national problem of considerable urgency. Its first dangerous manifestation was felt soon after the initial shock of Pearl Harbor. This traumatic event dislocated our normal channels of communication by bringing into existence an unfamiliar and unwelcome, if at the same time a relatively mild censorship of news, and it simultaneously dislocated the lives of millions of citizens whose futures abruptly became hostages to fortune.

Reprinted by permission of the authors and the publisher from *Transactions of The New York Academy of Sciences, Series II, VIII* (1945), pp. 61–81.

This combination of circumstances created the most fertile of all possible soils for the propagation of rumor. We now know that *rumors concerning a given subject-matter will circulate within a group in proportion to the importance and the ambiguity of this subject-matter in the lives of individual members of the group.*

The affair of Pearl Harbor was fraught with both importance and ambiguity to nearly every citizen. The affair was important because of the potential danger it represented to all of us, and because its aftermath of mobilization affected every life. It was ambiguous because no one seemed quite certain of the extent of, reasons for, or consequences of the attack. Since the two conditions of rumor—importance and ambiguity—were at a maximum, we had an unprecedented flood of what became known as "Pearl Harbor rumors." It was said that our fleet was "wiped out," that Washington didn't dare tell the extent of the damage, that Hawaii was in the hands of the Japanese. So widespread and so demoralizing were these tales that, on February 23, 1942, President Roosevelt broadcast a speech devoted entirely to denying the harmful rumors and to reiterating the official report on the losses.

Did the solemn assurance of the Commander in Chief restore the confidence of the people and eliminate the tales of suspicion and fear? It so happens that a bit of objective evidence on this question became available to us almost by accident. On the twentieth of February, before the President's speech, we had asked approximately 200 college students whether they thought our losses at Pearl Harbor were "greater," "much greater," or "no greater" than the official Knox report had stated. Among these students, 68 percent had believed the demoralizing rumors in preference to the official report, and insisted that the losses were "greater" or "much greater" than Washington admitted. Then came the President's speech. On February 25 an equivalent group of college students were asked the same question. Among those who had not heard or read the speech the proportion of rumor-believers was still about two thirds. But among those who were acquainted with the President's speech, the number of rumor-believers fell by 24 percent. It is important to note that, in spite of the utmost efforts of the highest authority to allay anxiety, approximately 44 percent of the college population studied were too profoundly affected by the event and by the resulting rumors to accept the reassurance.

The year 1942 was characterized by floods of similar fear-inspired tales. Shipping losses were fantastically exaggerated. Knapp records one instance where a collier was sunk through accident near the Cap Cod Canal. So great was the anxiety of the New England public that this incident became a fantastic tale of an American ship being torpedoed with the loss of thousands of nurses who were aboard her.[1]

Such wild stories, as we have said, are due to the grave importance of the subject for the average citizen and to the ambiguity to him of the objective situation. This ambiguity may result from the failure of communications, or from a total lack of authentic news, a condition that often prevailed in war-torn countries or among isolated bands of troops who had few reliable sources of news. Again, the ambiguity may be due to the receipt of conflicting news stories, no one more credible than another; or it may be due (as in the case of the Pearl Harbor rumors) to the distrust of many people in the candor of the Administration and in the operation of wartime censorship. As the war progressed, a higher degree of confidence in our news services was rapidly achieved, and rumors concurrently subsided.

In addition to the fear-rumors of 1942, which persisted until the tide of victory commenced to turn, there was a still more numerous crop of hostility-rumors whose theme dealt always with the shortcomings, disloyalty, or inefficiency of some special group of cobelligerents. The Army, the Navy, the Administration, our allies, or American minority groups were the most frequent scapegoats in these rumors. We were told that the Army wasted whole sides of beef, that the Russians greased their guns with lend-lease butter, that Negroes were saving icepicks for a revolt, and that Jews were evading the draft.

These hostility rumors were the most numerous of all. An analysis of 1,000 rumors collected from all parts of the country in 1942[2] revealed that they could be classified fairly readily as:

Hostility (wedge-driving) rumors	=	66 percent
Fear (bogey) rumors	=	25 percent
Wish (pipe-dream) rumors	=	2 percent
Unclassifiable rumors	=	7 percent

To be sure, the proportion of fear and wish rumors soon altered. As victory approached, especially on the eve of V–E and V–J day, the whirlwind of rumors was almost wholly concerned with the cessation of hostilities, reflecting a goal-gradient phenomenon whereby rumor under special conditions hastens the completion of a desired event. But, throughout the war and continuing to the present, it is probably true that the majority of all rumors are of a more or less slanderous nature, expressing hostility against this group or that.

The principal reason why rumor circulates can be briefly stated. It circulates because it *serves the twin function of explaining and relieving emotional tensions felt by individuals.*[3]

The Pearl Harbor rumors, for example, helped to *explain* to the teller why he felt such distressing anxiety.

[1] R. H. Knapp, "A Psychology of Rumor," *Pub. Op. Quart.*, 1944, VIII, 22–37.

[2] R. H. Knapp, *ibid.*, 25.

[3] This brief formula leaves out of account only the relatively few rumors which seem to serve the purpose of "phatic communication"—a form of idle conversation to facilitate social intercourse. When a lull occurs in a conversation, an individual may "fill in" with the latest bit of gossip that comes to mind, without being motivated by the deeper tensions that underlie the great bulk of rumor-mongering.

In this paper we cannot enter into a fuller discussion of the reasons why people believe some rumors and not others. This question is carefully studied by F. H. Allport and M. Lepkin, "Wartime Rumors of Waste and Special Privilege: Why Some People Believe Them," *J. Abnorm. & Soc. Psychol.*, 1945, XL, 3–36.

Would his jitters not be justified if it were true that our protecting fleet was "wiped out" at Pearl Harbor? Something serious must have happened to account for his anxiety. Families deprived of sons, husbands, or fathers vaguely cast around for someone to blame for their privation. Well, the Jews, who were said to be evading the draft, were "obviously" not doing their share and thus the heavy burden falling on "good citizens" was explained. True, this draft-evasion charge did not last very long, owing, no doubt, to the inescapable evidence of heavy enlistments among Jews and of their heroic conduct in the war. But when shortages were felt, the traditional Jewish scapegoat was again trotted out as a convenient explanation of the privations suffered. Their operation of the black market "explained" our annoying experiences in the futile pursuit of an evening lamb chop.

To blame others verbally is not only a mode of explanation for one's emotional distress, but is at the same time a mode of *relief*. Everyone knows the reduction of tension that comes after administering a tongue lashing. It matters little whether the victim of the tongue lashing is guilty or not. Dressing down *anyone* to his face or behind his back has the strange property of temporarily reducing hatred felt against this person or, what is more remarkable, of reducing hatred felt against any person or thing. If you wish to deflate a taut inner tube you can unscrew the valve or you can make a puncture. Unscrewing the valve corresponds to directing our hostility toward the Nazis or Japanese, who were the cause of our suffering. Making a puncture corresponds to displacing the hostility upon innocent victims or scapegoats. In either case, the air will escape and relaxation follow. To blame Jews, Negroes, the Administration, brass hats, the OPA, or the politicians is to bring a certain relief from accumulated feelings of hostility, whatever their true cause. Relief, odd as it may seem, comes also from "bogey" rumors. To tell my neighbor that the Cape Cod Canal is choked with corpses is an easy manner of projecting into the outer world my own choking anxieties concerning my son or my friends in combat service. Having shared my anxiety with my friend by telling him exaggerated tales or losses or of atrocities, I no longer feel so much alone and helpless. Through my rumor-spreading, others, too, are put "on the alert." I therefore feel reassured.

Experimental approach

Leaving now the broader social setting of the problem, we ask ourselves what processes in the human mind account for the spectacular distortions and exaggerations that enter into the rumor-process, and lead to so much damage to the public intelligence and public conscience.

Since it is very difficult to trace in detail the course of a rumor in everyday life, we have endeavored by an experimental technique to study as many of the basic phenomena as possible under relatively well controlled laboratory conditions.

Our method is simple. A slide is thrown upon a screen. Ordinarily, a semidramatic picture is used containing a large number of related details. Six or seven subjects, who have not seen the picture, wait in an adjacent room. One of them enters and takes a position where he cannot see the screen. Someone in the audience (or the experimenter) describes the picture, giving about twenty details in the account. A second subject

FIGURE 1. A sample of pictorial material employed in the experiments. Here is a typical terminal report (the last in a chain of reproduction): "This is a subway train in New York headed for Portland Street. There is a Jewish woman and a Negro who has a razor in his hand. The woman has a baby or a dog. The train is going to Deyer Street, and nothing much happened."

enters the room and stands beside the first subject who proceeds to tell him all he can about the picture. (All subjects are under instruction to report as "accurately as possible what you have heard.") The first subject then takes his seat, and a third enters to hear the story from the second subject. Each succeeding subject hears and repeats the story in the same way. Thus, the audience is able to watch the deterioration of the rumor by comparing the successive versions with the stimulus-picture which remains on the screen throughout the experiment.

This procedure has been used with over forty groups of subjects, including college undergraduates, Army trainees in ASTP, members of community forums, patients in an Army hospital, members of a Teachers' Round Table, and police officials in a training course. In addition to these adult subjects, children in a private school were used, in grades from the fourth through the ninth. In some experiments, Negro subjects took part along with whites, a fact which, as we shall see, had important consequences when the test-pictures depicted scenes with a "racial angle."

All of these experiments took place before an audience (20–300 spectators). By using volunteer subjects, one eliminates the danger of stage fright. There was, however, a social influence in all the audience situations. The magnitude of this influence was studied in a control group of experiments where no one was present in the room excepting the subject and the experimenter.

At the outset, it is necessary to admit that in five respects this experimental situation fails to reproduce accurately the conditions of rumor-spreading in everyday life. (1) The effect of an audience is considerable, tending to create caution and to shorten the report. Without an audience subjects gave on the average twice as many details as with an audience. (2) The effect of the instructions is to maximize accuracy and induce caution. In ordinary rumor-spreading, there is no critical experimenter on hand to see whether the tale is rightly repeated. (3) There is no opportunity for subjects to ask questions of his informer. In ordinary rumor-spreading, the listener can chat with his informer and, if he wishes, cross-examine him. (4) The lapse of time between hearing and telling in the experimental situation is very slight. In ordinary rumor spreading, it is much greater. (5) Most important of all, the conditions of motivation are quite different. In the experiment, the subject is striving for accuracy. His own fears, hates, wishes are not likely to be aroused under the experimental conditions. In short, he is not the spontaneous rumor-agent that he is in ordinary life. His stake in spreading the experimental rumor is neither personal nor deeply motivated.

It should be noted that all of these conditions, excepting the third, may be expected to enhance the accuracy of the report in the experimental situation, and to yield far less distortion and projection than in real-life rumor-spreading.

In spite of the fact that our experiment does not completely reproduce the normal conditions for rumor, still we believe that all essential changes and distortions are represented in our results. "Indoor" rumors may not be as lively, as emotionally toned, or as extreme as "outdoor" rumors, and yet the same basic phenomena are demonstrable in both.

What happens in both real-life and laboratory rumors is a complex course of distortion in which three interrelated tendencies are clearly distinguishable.

Leveling

As rumor travels, it tends to grow shorter, more concise, more easily grasped and told. In successive versions, fewer words are used and fewer details are mentioned.

The number of details *retained* declines most sharply at the beginning of the series of reproductions. The number continues to decline, more slowly, throughout the experiment. Figure 2 shows the percentage of the details initially given which are retained in each successive reproduction.

The number of items enumerated in the description from the screen constitutes the 100 percent level, and all subsequent percentages are calculated from that base. The curve, based on 11 experiments, shows that about 70 percent of the details are eliminated in the course of five or six mouth-to-mouth transmissions, even when virtually no time lapse intervenes.

The curve is like the famous Ebbinghaus curve for decline in individual retention, though in his experiments the interval between initial learning and successive reproduction was not as short as under the conditions of our experiment. Comparing the present curve with Ebbinghaus's, we conclude that *social memory accomplishes as much leveling within a few minutes as individual memory accomplishes in weeks of time.*

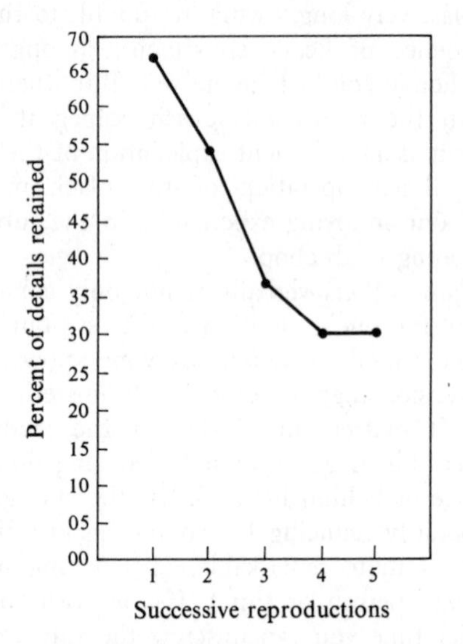

FIGURE 2. Percentage of details originally given which are retained in each successive reproduction.

Leveling (in our experiments) never proceeds to the point of total obliteration. The stabilization of the last part of the curve is a finding of some consequence. It indicates (1) that a short concise statement is likely to be faithfully reproduced; (2) that when the report has become short and concise, the subject has very little detail to select from and the possibilities of further distortion grow fewer; (3) that the assignment becomes so easy that a virtually rote memory serves to hold the material in mind. In all cases, the terminal and the anteterminal reports are more similar than any two preceding reports.

The reliance on rote is probably more conspicuous in our experiments than in ordinary rumor-spreading, where accuracy is not the aim, where time interval interferes with rote retention, and where strong interests prevent literal memory. There are, however, conditions where rote memory plays a part in ordinary rumor-spreading. If the individual is motivated by no stronger desire than to make conversation, he may find himself idly repeating what he has recently heard in the form in which he heard it. If a rumor has become so crisp and brief, so sloganized, that it requires no effort to retain it in the literal form in which it was heard, rote memory seems to be involved. For example:

The Jews are evading the draft;
The CIO is communist controlled;
The Russians are nationalizing their women.

We conclude that whenever verbal material is transmitted among a group of people whether as rumor, legend, or history, change will be in the direction of greater brevity and conciseness. Leveling, however, is not a random phenomenon. Our protocols show again and again that items which are of particular interest to the subjects, facts which confirm their expectations and help them to structure the story, are the last to be leveled out and often are retained to the final reproduction.

Sharpening

We may define sharpening as the selective perception, retention, and reporting of a limited number of details from a larger context. Sharpening is inevitably the reciprocal of leveling. The one cannot exist without the other, for what little remains to a rumor after leveling has taken place is by contrast unavoidably featured.

Although sharpening occurs in every protocol, the same items are not always emphasized. Sometimes, a trifling detail such as a subway advertising card becomes the focus of attention and report. Around it the whole rumor becomes structured. But, in most experiments, this same detail drops out promptly, and is never heard of after the first reproduction.

One way in which sharpening seems to be determined is through the retention of odd, or attention-getting words which, having appeared early in the series, catch the attention of each successive listener and are often passed on in preference to other details intrinsically more important to the story. An instance of this effect is seen in a series of protocols where the statement, "there is a boy stealing and a man remonstrating with him" is transmitted throughout the entire series. The unusual word "remonstrate" somehow caught the attention of each successive listener and was passed on without change.

Sharpening may also take a *numerical* turn, as in the experiments where emphasized items become reduplicated in the telling. For example, in reports of a picture containing the figure of a Negro, whose size and unusual appearance invite emphasis, we find that the number of Negroes reported in the picture jumps from one to "four" or "several."

There is also *temporal* sharpening manifested in the tendency to describe events as occurring in the immediate present. What happens *here* and *now* is of greatest interest and importance to the perceiver. In most instances, to be sure, the story is started in the present tense, but even when the initial description is couched in the past tense, immediate reversal occurs and the scene is contemporized by the listener. Obviously, this effect cannot occur in rumors which deal specifically with some alleged past (or future) event. One cannot contemporize the rumor that "the *Queen Mary* sailed this morning (or will sail tomorrow) with 10,000 troops aboard." Yet it not infrequently happens that stories gain in sharpening by tying them to present conditions. For example, a statement that Mr. X bought a chicken in the black market last week and paid $1.50 a pound for it may be (and usually is) rendered, "I hear they are charging $1.50 a pound on the black market for chicken." People are more interested in today than in last week, and the temptation, therefore, is to adapt (assimilate) the time of occurrence, when possible, to this interest.

Sharpening often takes place when there is a clear implication of movement. The flying of airplanes and the bursting of bombs are frequently stressed in the telling. Similarly, the falling flower pot in one picture is often retained and accented. Indeed, the "falling motif" may be extended to other objects such as the cigar which a man in the picture is smoking. In one rumor, it is said to be falling (like the flower pot), though in reality it is quite securely held between his teeth.

Sometimes sharpening is achieved by ascribing movement to objects which are really stationary. Thus, a subway train, clearly at a standstill at a subway station, is frequently described as moving.

Relative size is also a primary determinant of attention. Objects that are prominent because of their size tend to be retained and sharpened. The first reporter calls attention to their prominence and each successive listener receives an impression of their largeness. He then proceeds to sharpen this impression in his memory. The large Negro may, in the telling, become "four Negroes," or may become "a gigantic statue of a Negro."

There are verbal as well as physical determinants of attention. Thus, there is a pronounced tendency for *labels* to persist, especially if they serve to set the stage for the story. One picture is usually introduced by some version of the statement, "This is a battle scene," and this label persists throughout the series of reproductions. Another story usually opens with the statement, "This is a picture of a race riot."

To explain this type of sharpening, we may invoke the desire of the subject to achieve some spatial and temporal schema for the story to come. Such orientation is essential in ordinary life and appears to constitute a strong need even when imaginal material is dealt with.

An additional factor making for preferential retention of spatial and temporal labels is the *primacy* effect. An item that comes first in a series is likely to be better remembered than subsequent items. Usually, the "label" indicating place and time comes at the beginning of a report and thus benefits by the primacy effect.

Sharpening also occurs in relation to familiar symbols. In one series of reports, a church and a cross are among the most frequently reported items, although they are relatively minor details in the original picture. These well-known symbols "pack" meaning and are familiar to all. The subject feels secure in reporting them because they have an accustomed concreteness that the other details in the picture lack. Retention of familiar symbols advances the process of conventionalization that is so prominent an aspect of rumor-embedding. In two of our pictures are a night stick, symbol of police authority, and a razor, stereotyped symbol of Negro violence. These symbols are always retained and sharpened.

Explanations added by the reporter to the description transmitted to him comprise a final form of sharpening. They represent a tendency to put "closure" upon a story which is felt to be otherwise incomplete. They illustrate the "effort after meaning" which customarily haunts the subject who finds himself in an unstructured situation. Such need for sharpening by explanation becomes especially strong when the story has been badly distorted and the report contains implausible and incompatible items. As an example, one subject who received a badly confused description of the subway scene (Figure 1) inferred that there must have been "an accident." This explanation seemed plausible enough to successive listeners and so was not only accepted by them but sharpened in the telling.

In everyday rumors, sharpening through the introduction of specious explanations is very apparent. Indeed, as we have said, one of the principal functions of a rumor is to explain personal tensions. To accept tales of Army waste or special privilege among OPA officials could "explain" food shortages and discomfort. Such stories, therefore, find wide credence.

Here, perhaps, is the place to take issue with the popular notion that rumors tend to expand like snowballs, become overelaborate, and verbose. Actually, the course of rumor is toward brevity, whether in the laboratory or in everyday life. Such exaggeration as exists is nearly always a sharpening of some feature resident in the original stimulus-situation. The distortion caused by sharpening is, of course, enormous in extent; but we do not find that we need the category of "elaboration" to account for the changes we observe.

Assimilation

It is apparent that both leveling and sharpening are selective processes. But what is it that leads to the obliteration of some details and the pointing-up of others; and what accounts for all transpositions, importations, and other falsifications that marks the course of rumor? The answer is to be found in the process of *assimilation*, which has to do with the powerful attractive force exerted upon rumor by habits, interests, and sentiments existing in the listener's mind.

Assimilation to principal theme. It generally happens that items become sharpened or leveled to fit the leading motif of the story, and they become consistent with this motif in such a way as to make the resulting story more coherent, plausible, and well-rounded. Thus, in one series of rumors, the war theme is preserved and emphasized in all reports. In some experiments using the same picture, a chaplain is introduced, or people (in the plural) are reported as being killed; the ambulance becomes a Red Cross station; demolished buildings are multiplied in the telling; the extent of devastation is exaggerated. All these reports, false though they are, fit the principal theme—a battle incident. If the reported details were actually present in the picture, they would make a "better" *Gestalt*. Objects wholly extraneous to the theme are never introduced—no apple pies, no ballet dancers, no baseball players.

Besides importations, we find other falsifications in the interest of supporting the principal theme. The original picture shows that the Red Cross truck is loaded with explosives, but it is ordinarily reported as carrying medical supplies which is, of course, the way it "ought" to be.

The Negro in this same picture is nearly always described as a soldier, although his clothes might indicate that he is a civilian partisan. It is a "better" configuration to have a soldier in action on the battlefield than to have a civilian among regular soldiers.

Good continuation. Other falsifications result from the attempt to complete incompleted pictures or to fill in gaps which exist in the stimulus field. The effort is again to make the resulting whole coherent, and meaningful. Thus, the sign, "Loew's Pa . . .," over a moving picture theater is invariably read and reproduced as "Loew's Palace" and Gene *Antry* becomes Gene *Autry*. "Lucky Rakes" are reported as "Lucky Strikes."

All these, and many instances like them, are examples of what has been called, in *Gestalt* terms, "closures." Falsifications of perception and memory they are, but they occur in the interests of bringing about a more coherent, consistent mental configuration. Every detail is assimilated to the principal theme, and "good continuation" is sought, in order to round out meaning where it is lacking or incomplete.

Assimilation by condensation. It sometimes seems as though memory tries to burden itself as little as possible. For instance, instead of remembering two items, it is more economical to fuse them into one. Instead of a series of subway cards, each of which has its own identity, reports sometimes refer only to "a billboard," or perhaps to a "lot of advertising" (Figure 1). In another picture, it is more convenient to refer to "all kinds of fruit," rather than to enumerate all the different items on the vendor's cart. Again, the occupants of the car come to be described by some such summary phrase as "several people sitting and standing in the car." Their individuality is lost.

Assimilation to expectation. Just as details are changed or imported to bear out the simplified theme that the listener has in mind, so also many items take a form that supports the agent's habits of thought. Things are perceived and remembered the way they *usually* are. Thus a drugstore, in one stimulus-picture, is situated in the middle of a block; but, in the telling, it moves up to the corner of the two streets and becomes the familiar "corner drugstore." A Red Cross ambulance is said to carry medical supplies rather than explosives, because it "ought" to be carrying medical supplies. The kilometers on the signposts are changed into miles, since Americans are accustomed to having distances indicated in miles.

The most spectacular of all our assimilative distortions is the finding that, in more than half of our experiments, a razor moves (in the telling) from a white man's hand to a Negro's hand (Figure 1). This result is a clear instance of assimilation to stereotyped expectancy. Black men are "supposed" to carry razors, white men not.

Assimilation to linguistic habits. Expectancy is often merely a matter of fitting perceived and remembered material to preexisting verbal clichés, which exert a powerful influence in the conventionalization of rumors. Words often arouse compelling familiar images in the listener's mind and fix for him the categories in which he must think of the event and the value that he must attach to it. A "zoot-suit sharpie" packs much more meaning and carries more affect than more objective words, such as, "a colored man with pegged trousers, wide-brimmed hat, etc." (Figure 1). Rumors are commonly told in verbal stereotypes which imply prejudicial judgment, such as "draft dodger," "Japanese spy," "brass hat," "dumb Swede," "long-haired professor," and the like.

More highly motivated assimilation

Although the conditions of our experiment do not give full play to emotional tendencies underlying gossip, rumor, and scandal, such tendencies are so insistent that they express themselves even under laboratory conditions.

Assimilation to interest. It sometimes happens that a picture containing women's dresses, as a trifling detail in the original scene, becomes, in the telling, a story exclusively about dresses. This sharpening occurs when the rumor is told by groups of women, but never when told by men.

A picture involving police was employed with a group of police officers as subjects. In the resulting protocol, the entire reproduction centered around the police officer (with whom the subjects undoubtedly felt keen sympathy or "identification"). Furthermore, the nightstick, a symbol of his power, is greatly sharpened and becomes the main object of the controversy. The tale as a whole is protective of, and partial to, the policeman.

Assimilation to prejudice. Hard as it is in an experimental situation to obtain distortions that arise from hatred, yet we have in our material a certain opportunity to trace the hostile complex of racial attitudes.

We have spoken of the picture which contained a white man holding a razor while arguing with a Negro. In over half of the experiments with this picture, the final report indicated that the Negro (instead of the white man) held the razor in his hand, and several times he was reported as "brandishing it widely" or as "threatening" the white man with it (Figure 1).

Whether this ominous distortion reflects hatred and fear of Negroes we cannot definitely say. In some cases, these deeper emotions may be the assimilative factor at work. And yet the distortion may occur even in subjects who have no anti-Negro bias. It is an unthinking cultural stereotype that the Negro is hot tempered and addicted to the use of razors as weapons. The rumor, though mischievous, may reflect chiefly an assimilation of the story to verbal-clichés and conventional expectation. Distortion in this case may not mean assimilation to hostility. Much so-called prejudice is, of course, a mere matter of conforming to current folkways by accepting prevalent beliefs about an out-group.

Whether or not this razor-shift reflects deep hatred and fear on the part of white subjects, it is certain that the reports of our Negro subjects betray a motivated type of distortion. Because it was to their interest as members of the race to deemphasize the racial caricature, Negro subjects almost invariably avoided mention of color. One of them hearing a rumor containing the phrase, "a Negro zoot-suiter," reported "There is a man wearing a zoot suit, *possibly* a Negro."

For one picture, a Negro reporter said that the colored man in the center of the picture "is being maltreated." Though this interpretation may be correct, it is likewise possible that he is a rioter about to be arrested by the police officer. White and Negro subjects are very likely to perceive, remember, and interpret this particular situation in quite opposite ways.

Thus, even under laboratory conditions, we find assimilation in terms of deep-lying emotional predispositions. Our rumors, like those of everyday life, tend to fit into, and support, the occupational interests, class or racial memberships, or personal prejudices of the reporter.

Conclusion: the embedding process

Leveling, sharpening, and assimilation are not independent mechanisms. They function simultaneously, and reflect a singular subjectifying process that results in the autism and falsification which are so characteristic of rumor. If we were to attempt to summarize what happens in a few words we might say:

Whenever a stimulus field is of potential importance to an individual, but at the same time unclear, or susceptible of divergent interpretations, a subjective structuring process is started. Although the process is complex (involving, as it does, leveling, sharpening, and assimilation), its essential nature can be characterized as an effort to reduce the stimulus to a simple and meaningful structure that has adaptive significance for the individual in terms of his own interests and experience. The process begins at the moment the ambiguous situation is perceived, but the effects are greatest if memory intervenes. The longer the time that elapses after the stimulus is perceived the greater the threefold change is likely to be. Also, the more people involved in a serial report, the greater the change is likely to be, until the rumor has reached an aphoristic brevity, and is repeated by rote.

Now, this three-pronged process turns out to be characteristic not only of rumor but of the individual memory function as well. It has been uncovered and described in the experiments on individual retention conducted by Wulf, Gibson, Allport,[4] and, in Bartlett's memory experiments carried out both on individuals and on groups.[5]

Up to now, however, there has been no agreement on precisely the terminology to use, nor upon the adequacy of the three functions we here describe. We believe that our conceptualization of the three-fold course of change and decay is sufficient to account, not only for our own experimental findings and for the experiments of others in this area, but also for the distortions that everyday rumors undergo.

For lack of a better designation, we speak of the three-fold change as the *embedding* process. What seems to occur in all our experiments and in all related studies is that each subject finds the outer stimulus-world far too hard to grasp and retain in its objective character. For his own personal uses, it must be recast to fit not only his span of comprehension and his span of retention, but, likewise, his own personal needs and interests. What was outer becomes inner; what was objective becomes subjective. In telling a rumor, the kernel of objective information that he received has become so embedded into his own dynamic mental life that the product is chiefly one of projection. Into the rumor, he projects the deficiencies of his retentive processes, as well as his own effort to engender meaning upon an ambiguous field, and the product reveals much of his own emotional needs, including his anxieties, hates, and wishes. When several rumor-agents have been involved in this embedding process, the net result of the serial reproduction reflects the lowest common denominator of cultural interest, of memory span, and of group sentiment and prejudice.

One may ask whether a rumor must always be false. We answer that, in virtually every case, the embedding process is so extensive that no credibility whatever should be ascribed to the product. If a report does turn out to be trustworthy, we usually find that secure standards of evidence have somehow been present to which successive agents could refer for purposes of validation. Perhaps the morning newspaper or the radio have held the rumor under control, but when such secure standards of verification are available, it is questionable whether we should speak of rumor at all.

There are, of course, border-line cases where we may not be able to say whether a given tidbit should or should not be called a rumor. But if we define rumor (and we herewith propose that we should), as a *proposition for belief of topical reference, without secure standards of evidence being present*—then it follows from the facts we have presented that rumor will suffer such serious distortion through the embedding process, that *it is never under any circumstances a valid guide for belief or conduct.*

Replication

DISTORTION IN THE COMMUNICATION PROCESS

The replication of Allport and Postman's experiment will entail the passage of a controversial news story through a chain of seven individuals. The first person will listen to the story and transmit it verbally to the second individual, and so on until it reaches the last person in the chain.

Clearly, this replication of the experiment cannot use the picture illustrated in Allport and Postman's article because, by reading their report, you have already been alerted to the outcome of the experiment. Instead, the material to be communicated from one person to another is a brief newspaper story summarizing the results of a ten-year follow-up study of city neighborhoods. (Copies of this article are supplied to instructors using this book.) Some of the findings reported in this story are "controversial" in that they contradict popular prejudices; other findings tend to be consistent with the way most people see things. The experimental variable therefore consists of differences in the nature of the material to be transmitted. We will seek to determine if there are differences in the accuracy with which these two types of material are transmitted. More detailed instructions on the experiment are given below.

Hypothesis

1. A brief article containing "controversial" and "noncontroversial" material will be given to the first person in chains of seven persons. State what differences you expect to find in the accuracy with which these two types of material are transmitted through the chain.

2. See Appendix A for general information on writing a hypothesis.

The experiment

1. The instructor will divide the class into groups of seven students each. Each student will be assigned a number from one to seven. This is his "carrier number."

2. The passage of controversial material (supplied to instructors using this manual) will be read to carrier number one of each group.

[4] Conveniently summarized in K. Koffka, *Principles of Gestalt Psychology* (New York: Harcourt, Brace and Co., 1935).

[5] F. C. Bartlett, *Remembering* (Cambridge, England: Cambridge University Press, 1932).

3. After carrier number one has heard the passage, he should attempt to repeat it as accurately as possible to carrier number two. Of course, the others in the chain should not listen.

4. Carrier number two should then transmit the message to number three, carrier three to carrier four, etc., until the message reaches the seventh person of each group.

5. After the last person in each group has received the message, your instructor will give the class a brief test to determine how much each person in the chain learned. Use a sheet of notepaper to record your answers to the questions your instructor will ask about the message.

Data analysis

1. Exchange answer papers with another student and mark each question with a "+" if the answer is correct or approximately correct (your instructor will give you the correct answers), or a "0" if the answer is wrong.

2. Your instructor will ask you to indicate with a show of hands all those with correct and incorrect answers to question one. After recording the number of correct and incorrect answers on the blackboard, he will go on to question 2, then question 3, etc.

3. *Add* each row of the table.

4. *Compute* the percent of correct answers for each question. Use the number of students participating in the experiment as the base for these percents. To avoid dividing these numbers by hand, use the percentage tables (Appendix B).

Lab report

1. For purposes of your report consider as the experimental or causal variable the odd-numbered questions compared with the even-numbered questions. The odd-numbered questions all deal with findings from the survey which can be considered as desirable consequences of integrated neighborhoods; the even-numbered questions all refer to racial-integration consequences which most Americans have traditionally regarded as undesirable consequences. After the tabulations have been completed, your instructor will list these questions for you so that you will know what is in each set of questions.

2. If the type of material which is most accurately transmitted is different from that which you expected, discuss possible reasons for this, including the particular characteristics of the sample used for the replication, social change between the time of the original experiment (1944) and the present, etc.

3. See Appendix A for general instructions on writing laboratory reports, and the "Note on Interpreting Cause and Effect" in that appendix for a discussion of experimental variables.

References

Bernstein, Basil, "Social Class and Linguistic Development: A Theory of Social Learning," in A. H. Halsey *et al.*, *Education, Economy, and Society*. New York: Free Press, 1961, pp. 288–314.

Bram, Joseph, *Language and Society*. New York: Random House, 1955.

Hertzler, Joyce O., *A Sociology of Language*. New York: Random House, 1965.

Lundberg, George A., Clarence C. Schrag, and Otto N. Larsen, *Sociology*. New York: Harper & Row, 1958, pp. 208–212.

Mead, G. H., *Mind, Self, and Society*. Chicago: University of Chicago Press, 1934.

Osgood, Charles E. and Thomas A. Sebeok, *Psycholinguistics, a Survey of Theory and Research Problems*, rev. ed. Bloomington, Ind.: Indiana University Press, 1965.

Schatzman, Leonard and Anslem Strauss, "Social Class and Modes of Communication," *American Journal of Sociology*, *60* (January 1955), pp. 329–338.

Name______________________________

Date______________________________

TABLE 1. Percent of correct answers by type of material communicated

Type of material communicated as measured by question number:	Number of answers:			Percent of correct answers
	Correct	Incorrect	Total	
Question 1				
Question 2				
Question 3				
Question 4				
Question 5				
Question 6				

LABORATORY REPORT FOR PROBLEM ________

Course or
Section ________ Date ________ Name ________

HYPOTHESIS: ________

SAMPLE: ________

INDEPENDENT VARIABLE(S): ________

DEPENDENT VARIABLE(S): ________

OTHER FACTORS: ________

LABORATORY REPORT FOR PROBLEM ____________

SUMMARY OF FINDINGS: ____________

DISCUSSION: ____________

PROBLEM 7
SOCIALIZATION

Socialization is the process by which persons take on the language and the culture of their social setting. Although socialization is continuous through the life span of an individual, the bulk of learning occurs in childhood and adolescence. It is at this time that basic cultural products are transmitted across generations, so that the young can acquire the wisdom of society without having to invent for themselves a language, a code of behavior, or any other past innovation. Without this transmission societies would have no continuity, and individuals—without language and without culture—would have no identity.

Peer groups, schools, literature all contribute to socialization, but in most societies it is the family which has clear-cut responsibility for socializing the young and also represents the most influential and important socializing agency. This influence is understandable because of a combination of factors. Among these factors is the almost exclusive control of the child during his earliest years, and the power inherent in the family's control of the affection and material resources needed by the growing child. The influence of the family is further enhanced because families are one of the rare instances of a social unit in which nearly every status and role of an individual is known and accounted for. In schools we are recognized as students, in teams as athletes, in offices as workers; but in families we are seen as students, athletes, workers, community members and from nearly every other side of the huge array of statuses a person may occupy. This characteristic has led one observer to refer to the family as a "role budget center" (Goode, 1960).

Families are the key units in socializing children, but they may be profitably viewed as reflections or mediators of their cultural setting. Thus, it has been well established that working-class families transmit different values than middle-class families (Bronfenbrenner, 1958), that Jews differ in socialization practices from Protestants and Catholics (Strodtbeck, 1958), that rural families differ from families in metropolitan communities (Straus, 1962). These differential practices determine in large part the conception children develop of themselves, as well as their ambitions regarding occupational success, notions of family life, and the number of children they want to have. Socialization is not the only determinant of behavior (Wrong, 1961) but its influence is considerable.

The process of socialization itself is of course more complex than a mere transmission of ideas. Various sources of disturbance may affect both the effectiveness of the agent and the receptiveness of the child. Families, for example, like other groups, experience conflict, and when they do children may react to their parents by adapting contrary beliefs and opinions. In the article for the present problem, Middleton and Putney illustrate the pervasive influence of families in determining the political preferences of their children and *also* the factors which mitigate this influence. In American society, with a highly individualistic ethos, political preferences are purportedly made on the basis of rational decisions. Middleton and Putney's data, however, show that despite the range of political postures available, the majority of children adopt the preference of their parents. The authors make one other important point. In families where politics is important, the emotional climate of the family becomes a critical determinant of political conformity or deviance from the parents' views. Children who feel close to their parents overwhelmingly identify with their political views, but children who feel rejected or distant from their parents rebel by adopting contrary political postures. Thus, influential as families may be in political socialization, in transmitting the preferences of one generation to another they may also contain the seeds of social change.

POLITICAL EXPRESSION OF ADOLESCENT REBELLION / *Russell Middleton and Snell Putney*

The relationship between deviation from parental political viewpoints and parent-child relationships is explored in a sample of 1,440 students in sixteen colleges and universities across the United States. Males are more likely to deviate from the political positions of their parents than females. A significant association is not found between a history of defiance of parents and political rebellion, suggesting that adolescent rebellion in America is expressed primarily in non-political ways. Rebellion is associated, at least for female students, with discipline in the home that is perceived as either strict or permissive, whereas those who report average discipline are less likely to rebel politically. Perceived extremes of parental discipline (strict or permissive) are associated for both males and females with lack of closeness between parent and child, which, in turn, is associated with political rebellion. This is particularly true when the student perceives his parent as being interested in politics. Political rebellion, then, appears most likely to occur when parent and child are emotionally estranged, when the child believes parental discipline is non-typical, and when the parent is interested in politics.

In his pioneer psychoanalytic study of political attitudes Lasswell pointed out that, although political beliefs may be expressed in a highly rational form, they are often developed in highly irrational ways. "When they are seen against the developmental history of the person, they take on meanings which are quite different than the phrases in which they are put."[1] Using a series of case studies, he attempted to demonstrate that family relationships were one of the non-rational determinants of whether or not an individual became an anarchist, a socialist, a highly conservative Republican, or a political assassin.

Political beliefs can be influenced by family relationships through rebellion; a youth may, for example, express rebellion against his parents by rejecting their political beliefs and adopting a divergent set. The probability of such political rebellion is enhanced by the fact that adolescence, which most authors regard as a period of generalized rebellion in American society,[2] is also the age at which most individuals seem to crystallize their political viewpoints.[3]

Clearly, adolescent rebellion cannot be attributed solely to the biological maturation process, for adolescence is not a period of storm and stress in every society.[4] Rather, there appear to be structural features in American society conducive to youthful rebellion. Parsons, for example, argues that, since there is a sharp limitation of "objects of cathexis" in the isolated conjugal family typical of American society, children tend to be highly dependent emotionally on their parents, especially on the mother.[5] As the individual nears adulthood, however, he is expected to break this dependency and choose his occupation and sexual partner with little adult support. In adolescence, therefore, a reaction formation may be generated against the dependency needs and may find expression in a rebellious youth culture, compulsively independent and defiant of parental norms and authority, and, at the same time, compulsively conformist to the peer group that satisfies individual dependency needs. Parsons maintains that the rebellion is especially strong among adolescent boys because of an additional reaction formation of compulsive masculinity against an original identification with the mother.

The question remains, however, whether the adolescent is likely to use political beliefs as an instrument of rebellion. Hyman believes that he is not: "The almost complete absence of negative correlations [between the political attitudes of parents and children] provides considerable evidence *against* the theory that political attitudes are formed *generally* in terms of rebellion and opposition to parents."[6] The absence of negative correlations between the political beliefs of adolescents and their parents, however, does not demonstrate that rebellion tends to be non-political. It might simply indicate a relative lack of rebellion, even though such rebellion as occurred might often be political.

A recent study by Lane based on depth interviews

Reprinted from "Political Expression of Adolescent Rebellion" by Russell Middleton and Snell Putney from *The American Journal of Sociology*, LXVII (March 1963), pp. 527–535 by permission of The University of Chicago Press. Copyright 1963 by The University of Chicago Press.

[1] Harold D. Lasswell, *Psychopathology and Politics* (Chicago: University of Chicago Press, 1930), p. 153.

[2] Kingsley Davis, "The Sociology of Parent-Youth Conflict," *American Sociological Review*, V (August, 1940), 523–35; Kingsley Davis, "Adolescence and Social Structure," *Annals of the American Academy of Political and Social Science*, CCXXVI (November, 1944), 8–15; Ernest A. Smith, *American Youth Culture* (Glencoe, Ill.: Free Press, 1962); Florence Kluckhohn and John P. Spiegel, *Integration and Conflict in Family Behavior* (Group for the Advancement of Psychiatry, Report No. 27 [Topeka, August, 1954]); P. Blos, *The Adolescent Personality* (New York: Appleton-Century-Crofts, Inc., 1941); Ruth Benedict, "Continuities and Discontinuities in Cultural Conditioning," in Clyde Kluckhohn and H. A. Murray (eds.), *Personality in Nature, Society and Culture* (New York: Alfred A. Knopf, Inc., 1955), pp. 522–31. For a variant view, however, see Frederick Elkin and W. A. Westley, "Myth of Adolescent Culture," *American Sociological Review*, XX (December, 1955), 680–84, and William A. Westley and Frederick Elkin, "The Protective Environment and Adolescent Socialization," *Social Forces*, XXXV (March, 1957), 243–49.

[3] See Herbert H. Hyman, *Political Socialization* (Glencoe, Ill.: Free Press, 1959), pp. 51–68, and Robert E. Lane, *Political Life: Why People Get Involved in Politics* (Glencoe, Ill.: Free Press, 1959), p. 217.

[4] Margaret Mead, *Coming of Age in Samoa* (New York: William Morrow & Co., 1928); Margaret Mead, "Adolescence in Primitive and in Modern Society," in Eleanor E. Maccoby, T. M. Newcomb, and E. L. Hartley (eds.), *Readings in Social Psychology* (3d ed.; New York: Henry Holt & Co., 1958), pp. 341–49; and Yehudi A. Cohen, " 'Adolescent Conflict' in a Jamaican Community," in *Social Structure and Personality* (New York: Holt, Rinehart & Winston, 1961), pp. 167–82.

[5] Talcott Parsons, "Psychoanalysis and the Social Structure," in *Essays in Sociological Theory* (rev. ed.; Glencoe, Ill.: Free Press, 1954), pp. 336–47.

[6] Hyman, *op. cit.*, p. 72.

with fifteen working-class and lower-middle-class men selected at random from an eastern housing development focused on how often rebellion against the parent was expressed politically.[7] Concentrating on rebellion against the father, he found that only four of his subjects had impaired relationships with their fathers. In none of these cases did the rebellion take a political form, and the subjects' general level of interest in politics was low. On the basis of these scant but suggestive data, Lane argues that, compared with other Western cultures, American culture (because it is more permissive and the father is less dominant) tends to discourage youthful rebellion against the father. Moreover, when such rebellion does occur, it tends to discourage its expression in political terms because politics is relatively unimportant to the father, making other forms of rebellion more appealing.[8]

Maccoby, Matthews, and Morton conducted a study of the circumstances under which political rebellion against the parent was most likely to occur in American society.[9] Seeking to test the hypothesis that the young tend to become radical in their political views because of adolescent rebellion against strict parental authority and discipline, they interviewed 339 first-time voters between the ages of twenty-one and twenty-four in Cambridge, Massachusetts, immediately after the 1952 presidential election. Each respondent was asked: "In your case, when you were in your teens, did your family want to have quite a lot to say about your friends and the places you went and so on, or were you pretty much on your own?" They found that there was maximum political conformity to parents among those subjects who said that their parents had "about an average amount to say." Those who reported that their parents "had a lot to say" and those who said their parents left them "on their own" were both more likely to deviate politically from their parents. The researchers thus concluded that political rebellion was correlated with the type of discipline prevalent in the adolescent's family.

On the other hand, Nogee and Levin, in a study of 314 Boston University students eligible to vote for the first time in the 1956 presidential election, found no evidence of any relationship between strict parental control in early adolescence and political rebellion: "Although a small number do 'revolt' against their parents' political views, there is no evidence that the likelihood of such revolt is related to the strictness of parental control."[10] This study, like the previous study by Maccoby, Matthews, and Morton, did not investigate whether strictness of discipline was correlated with estrangement between the youth and his parents; rather they implicitly assumed such a relationship and concentrated on measuring the degree to which it might be expressed politically.

Previous research thus presents an incomplete and contradictory picture of adolescent political rebellion. It is generally agreed that adolescence is a period of general rebellion in American society. Hyman and Lane, however, are doubtful that this rebellion is likely to take a political form in the context of American culture. And when political rebellion occurs, Maccoby, Matthews, and Morton disagree with Nogee and Levin as to whether it is associated with the perceived degree of strictness of parental control.

In the present study we have attempted to investigate further some of the problems raised by the earlier studies. Are youths who are estranged from their parents no more likely to deviate from parental political views, as Lane suggests, than youths who are close to their parents? Does parental indifference to politics, as Lane further suggests, inhibit the political expression of rebellion by those who are estranged from their parents?

Our basic hypothesis is that estrangement from parents is associated with political rebellion if the parents are interested in politics, and perceived extremes of parental discipline (strict or permissive) are associated with lack of closeness between parent and child and thus with political rebellion.

Methods

Anonymous questionnaires were administered late in 1961 to classes of students in sixteen colleges and universities in the United States. A state university, a state college, a private university, and a private leberal arts college were included in each of four regions—Far West, Middle West, Northeast, and South. Four of the institutions were church affiliated. Thus, although the individual subjects were not selected in a strictly random fashion, the sample does include a broad range of types of institutions and regions. Caution should be used in generalizing the findings on this sample to American college students in general, but analysis of the sample has not revealed any marked biases correlated with political rebellion or adolescent rebellion.

A total of 1,440 completed questionnaires was obtained from students attending the sixteen colleges and universities included in the survey. Almost all the subjects were between the ages of seventeen and twenty-two, a group in transition to young adulthood. At their age, the storms of adolescence are recent enough to be recalled, but distant enough to be viewed with a certain objectivity. Fully three-fourths of these students reported that they had fairly clear political views while still in high school, and it can be assumed that the effects of adolescent rebellion on their political beliefs are now largely complete.

There were 824 males and 616 females in the sample. Since the relations of males and females to their mothers and fathers are somewhat different—especially in psychoanalytic theory, but also in terms of culturally

[7] Robert E. Lane, "Fathers and Sons: Foundations of Political Belief," *American Sociological Review,* XXIV (August, 1959), 502–11.

[8] *Ibid.,* p. 510.

[9] Eleanor E. Maccoby, Richard E. Matthews, and Anton S. Morton, "Youth and Political Change," *Public Opinion Quarterly,* XVIII (Spring, 1954), 23–39.

[10] Philip Nogee and M. B. Levin, "Some Determinants of Political Attitudes among College Voters," *Public Opinion Quarterly,* XXII (Winter, 1958–1959), 463.

defined relations between the sexes—we have considered the sexes separately throughout the analysis.

Each student was asked how close he was to each of his parents (response categories: "Very close," "Fairly close," "Not very close," and "Hostile"). If a parent died early in a child's life, lack of closeness is hardly indicative of rebellion, nor is the parent likely to have had a significant influence on the child's political views. When examining the personal nexus between parent and child in relation to political rebellion, therefore, we have excluded those cases in which the parent died before the child entered high school.

In order to measure political views, each respondent was presented with a set of five political categories and asked: "Which of these political positions is closest to your own views?"

1. Socialist
2. Highly liberal
3. Moderately liberal
4. Moderately conservative
5. Highly conservative
6. I have no political views

Extensive pretesting indicated that this set of categories was meaningful to American college students, involving as it does an extremely simple left-to-right continuum, and few students experienced any difficulty in characterizing their views in terms of the categories. At the same time, this approach avoided some of the knotty methodological problems involved in the use of political party affiliation or attitudes on substantive political issues as indexes of political position.[11]

To determine whether or not the student was deviating from his parents' political views, he was also asked to use the same categories to characterize the views of his mother and his father. In many cases the students' perceptions of their parents' views may have been incorrect. Yet it is precisely the perceived rather than the actual views of the parent that are of crucial importance in the present study. As the Thomas theorem states, "If men define situations as real, they are real in their consequences."

For purposes of this study a student was defined as a political rebel if he placed himself to the left or right of his parent. If the student agreed with his parent, had no political views, or simply remained unaware of the views of his parent, he was considered a non-rebel.

Each student was asked, "How close are (were) you to your father?" and "How close are (were) you to your mother?" Further, in a question patterned after that used by Maccoby, Matthews, and Morton, we asked each student to report on the strictness of his parents' discipline: "When you were in high school, did your parents want to have quite a lot to say about your friends and the places you went and so on, or were you pretty much on your own?" (Response categories: "Parents had a lot to say," "Parents had an average amount to say," and "Parents left me pretty much on my own.")

As a rough index of generalized rebellion against the parent, each student was asked: "When you were in high school, how often did you defy your parents and do things contrary to their instructions or wishes?"

Finally, each student was asked how much interest he thought each of his parents took in political matters. Parents were classified as interested in politics if the student reported that they were very much interested or moderately interested most of the time. If the student believed that they were only slightly interested or not at all interested, they were classified as not interested in politics. Once again, it is the student's perception of his parent that might influence the pattern of his rebellion, not necessarily the actual views or interests of the parents.

The χ^2 test of significance was applied throughout the analysis, and the rejection level for the null hypothesis was set at .05.

Findings

As shown in Table 1, approximately half the students hold political views different from those they attribute to their fathers, and nearly half hold political views different from those they attribute to their mothers. Male students are more likely than female students to deviate from the political views of their fathers and also from those of their mothers, and these tendencies are statistically significant beyond the .05 level ($P < .001$).

TABLE 1. Percent rebelling from political views of parents, by sex of student and parent

	From position of father		From position of mother	
	Per cent	*N*	Per cent	*N*
Male students	54	781	49	812
Female students	42	584	38	605
Total	49	1,365	45	1,417

Thus our findings indicate that divergence from parental political views, as measured by our categories, is fairly common, especially among male students. The question remains as to how much of this difference between viewpoints can be attributed to the nature of parent-child relationships. If deviation from parental political viewpoints is motivated by rebellion against the parents, it might be expected that those students who have a history of conflict with the parents would deviate more often than those who do not. In Table 2, the students who report that they defied their parents often or very often while in high school are compared to those who report that they did so only occasionally or rarely. Except in the case of male students in relation to their mothers (where there is no

[11] For a detailed discussion of the problems of measuring variations in political views and the rationale for the particular categories we have selected, see Russell Middleton and Snell Putney, "Student Rebellion against Parental Political Beliefs," *Social Forces,* 41 (May, 1963), pp. 377–383.

difference), those who report frequent defiance deviate from the parental political viewpoints more often than those who do not. However, the differences observed in the sample are small, and none are significant at the .05 level. It might, nevertheless, be expected that when the parents of defiant students were interested in politics, there would be markedly more political rebellion than when the parents were indifferent to political issues. However, when the data are broken down according to the degree of perceived parental interest in politics, no consistent pattern emerges, and no statistically significant relationships are found. Our data thus lend little support to the contention that political rebellion is related to a generalized rebellion against the parents, and are consistent with Lane's contention that generalized rebellion in America is likely to be expressed primarily in non-political terms.

TABLE 2. Relation of defiance of parental wishes while in high school to political rebellion, by sex

	Per cent	N
REBELLING FROM POLITICAL VIEWS OF FATHER:		
Male students:		
Defied parents often or very often	56	130
Defied parents occasionally or rarely	53	650
Female students		
Defied parents often or very often	48	71
Defied parents occasionally or rarely	41	515
REBELLING FROM POLITICAL VIEWS OF MOTHER:		
Male students:		
Defied parents often or very often	49	135
Defied parents occasionally or rarely	49	678
Female students:		
Defied parents often or very often	44	73
Defied parents occasionally or rarely	37	533

Nevertheless, political rebellion might occur under particular circumstances. Following Maccoby, Matthews, and Morton, we therefore examined the relation of parental discipline to political deviation (Table 3). In every case, there is a maximum of political rebellion in students who perceive their parents as having imposed strict discipline. Moreover, we find (as did Maccoby, Matthews, and Morton) that those who perceive their parents' discipline as average are least likely to rebel politically (except in the case of males in relation to their mothers). However, the association between political rebellion and parental discipline is significant at the .05 level only for females ($P < .01$ for rebellion against the father's political views and $P < .02$ for rebellion against the mother's political views). Moreover, the percentages do not differ sufficiently to suggest that parental discipline is generally a decisive factor in determining whether or not the student deviates from the political views of the parents.

Discipline, however, is likely to influence the degree of closeness between parent and child. Accordingly, we examined the relation between the student's perceptions of his parents' discipline and his degree of closeness with his parents (Table 4). The relationship revealed is non-linear, with those students who regard their parents' discipline as average having stronger emotional ties than those who regard it as either strict or permissive. All of the relationships are significant at the .05 level ($P < .001$ for male students in relation to their fathers, and $P < .01$ for the other three). This finding may explain why Maccoby, Matthews, and Morton found a maximum of political conformity among those young people who perceived their parents' discipline as average. These are the young people who are likely to be closest to their parents, and if nexus to parents is related to political conformity, there would thus be an indirect relationship between discipline and political rebellion. It must first be established, however, that closeness between parent and child is related to political conformity.

In general, there is a linear relationship between parent-child nexus and conformity to parental political views (Table 5). The associations are significant at the .05 level, except in the case of male students in relation to their mothers where it is nonlinear and not significant. The factor of parental interest in politics needs to be explored, however, inasmuch as politics is a relatively pointless instrument of rebellion unless it is of some importance to the parents.

Accordingly, the factor of perceived parental interest in politics is introduced into the examination of the relationship between parent-child closeness and political rebellion (Table 6). When the student perceives his parent as not interested in politics, no consistent relationship emerges between closeness to the parent and political rebellion, and none of the comparisons are statistically significant at the .05 level. When the student perceives his parent as interested in politics, however, a linear relationship is observed in all cases between political rebellion and estrangement of the student and his parent. Three of these four relationships are significant beyond the .05 level ($P < .01$ for male students and fathers, $P < .01$ for female students and fathers, and $P < .05$ for male students and mothers).

Conclusions

The data thus support our basic hypothesis that deviation from parental political viewpoints is associated with estrangement between parent and child—if the parent is interested in politics. This finding is consistent with Lane's contention that parental indifference to politics inhibits adolescent political rebellion. In general, the association between estrangement and rebellion is more marked in relation to fathers than in relation to mothers, perhaps because enough of the traditional male predominance in politics remains to render the father's political views a more obvious basis for rebellion than those of the mother.

Our data, moreover, generally support the conclusions of Maccoby, Matthews, and Morton (as against

TABLE 3. Relation of perceived strictness of parental discipline to political rebellion, by sex

	Strict discipline		Average discipline		Permissive discipline	
	Per cent	N	Per cent	N	Per cent	N
Rebelling from political views of father:						
Male students	56	97	53	379	54	304
Female students	55	104	36	315	46	166
Rebelling from political views of mother:						
Male students	53	102	50	393	47	318
Female students	49	106	34	331	40	168

TABLE 4. Relation of perceived strictness of parental discipline to closeness of relation with parent, by sex

	Strict discipline		Average discipline		Permissive discipline	
	Per cent	N	Per cent	N	Per cent	N
Feel close to father:						
Male students	73	97	86	379	70	304
Female students	73	104	83	315	70	166
Feel close to mother:						
Male students	87	102	94	392	88	317
Female students	85	106	94	331	86	167

TABLE 5. Relation of closeness to parent to political rebellion, by sex

	Per cent of students rebelling from political position of parents			
	Father		Mother	
	Per cent	N	Per cent	N
Male students:				
Very close to parent	46	210	46	311
Fairly close to parent	56	399	53	424
Not very close or hostile to parent	57	172	47	77
Female students:				
Very close to parent	37	205	34	333
Fairly close to parent	43	249	41	211
Not very close or hostile to parent	50	130	49	61

TABLE 6. Relation of closeness to parent to political rebellion by interest of parent in politics, and by sex

	PER CENT OF STUDENTS REBELLING FROM POLITICAL POSITION OF PARENT							
	Father interested in politics		Father not interested in politics		Mother interested in politics		Mother not interested in politics	
	Per cent	N	Per cent	N	Per cent	N	Per cent	N
Male students:								
Very close to parent	44	165	53	45	50	165	40	146
Fairly close to parent	57	263	54	136	63	165	56	259
Not very close or hostile to parent	63	80	53	92	74	19	38	58
Female students:								
Very close to parent	35	188	53	17	36	214	32	119
Fairly close to parent	44	193	38	56	40	108	42	103
Not very close or hostile to parent	58	76	39	54	50	22	49	39

those of Nogee and Levin) that deviation from parental political views is related to the kind of discipline experienced in the home. However, the associations observed are not extremely high, a point consistent with Hyman's contention that political attitudes in America are not in general generated by adolescent rebellion.

Some caution should be observed in imputing a causal relationship to the associations observed between impairment of parent-child relationships and deviations from parental political views. Rebellion against the parent, arising from strained parent-child relationships, may provoke political deviation. But it may also be the case that political deviation arising from factors unrelated to the parent may be the source of alienation between parent and child. For example, one of our subjects reports that he and his father have drifted apart in large measure because he acquired different political views while attending college. When he visits home he and his father now become involved in bitter arguments over political questions, although once they were fairly close. Here the causal sequence seems clearly reversed.

One unexpected finding adds another dimension to the picture of political attitudes and parent-child relationships. Our data disclose a positive relationship between parental interest in politics and closeness of the student to the parent. In fact this tendency of students to feel closer to parents who are interested in politics is significant well beyond the .001 level in all four relationships: father and son, father and daughter, mother and son, and mother and daughter. Any interpretation of this finding is necessarily ex post facto, but a plausible explanation would be that there is a relation between frequent and rewarding parent-child communication and the student's perception of the parent as interested in politics. In many cases of alienation between parent and child there may be too little communication for the student to perceive clearly his parents' political interests, whereas when the parent and child are close, communication of political viewpoints may be facilitated.

In any case, our data suggest that, while some students express rebellion against their parents in political terms, many, if not most, do not. Family relationships are an influence on political attitudes, as Lasswell suggested, but many other factors, including education, reference groups outside the home, mass media, and perhaps even rational evaluation of issues, may influence political beliefs.

Replication

FAMILY INTERACTION AND POLITICAL SOCIALIZATION

Middleton and Putney obtained their most striking findings when they controlled for both the sex of the child and the parent's interest in politics (Table 6). However, since the problems in this book are generally carried out with a sample only about one tenth as large as theirs, such small breakdowns are not possible. Consequently, for this replication we will omit the control for sex of the child and simply relate the degree of parent-child closeness to political rebellion, taking into account whether or not the father was interested in politics.

Hypothesis

1. State whether there is likely to be more agreement or more disagreement between fathers and their children regarding their political beliefs.

2. State the relationship you anticipate finding between father-child closeness and agreement with father's political views, and whether you feel this will be the case when the father is not interested in politics as well when he is interested.

3. See Appendix A for general instructions on writing a hypothesis.

Empirical indicators for this problem

29. How much interest did your father take in politics during your last year in high school?

    1. None at all
    2. Very little interest
    3. Somewhat interested
    4. Moderately interested
    5. Very much interested

30. Which of the following comes closest to your FATHER'S political beliefs:

    1. Socialist
    2. Liberal Democrat
    3. Conservative Democrat
    4. Liberal Republican
    5. Conservative Republican

31. Which of the following comes closest to YOUR OWN beliefs:

    1. Socialist
    2. Liberal Democrat
    3. Conservative Democrat
    4. Liberal Republican
    5. Conservative Republican

41. How close was the attachment between you and your father?

    0. None at all
    1. A little
    2. Somewhat
    3. Considerable
    4. Very close
    5. Extremely close

Data analysis

1. *Sort* the code sheets on box 29 into two groups:

Father *not* interested in politics = 1, 2, or 3
Father *is* interested in politics = 4 or 5

2. *Sub-sort* the "not interested" fathers into two groups on the basis of box 41:

Not close to child = 0, 1, 2, or 3
Close to child = 4 or 5

3. *Tally* onto the tabulation form for the "not close" group the number of cases in which the father and the child agree and disagree on political beliefs. Agreement is to be scored if the numbers in boxes 30 and 31 are the same. Disagreement is to be scored if the numbers in boxes 30 and 31 are different. Repeat this procedure for the "close to child" group.

4. *Repeat* steps 2 and 3 for the "father is interested in politics" group.

5. *Compute* the percentage of children who agree and disagree with their father's political views. Use the percentage tables in Appendix B to save time.

Lab report

1. Put the main emphasis of your report on a comparison of those who were close to their father versus those who were not close, but also take into account how the father's interest in politics affects the relationship between these two variables.

2. See the "Note on Interpreting Cause and Effect" in Appendix A for help in determining which is the independent variable and which is the control variable.

References

Bronfenbrenner, Urie, "Socialization and Social Class in Time and Space," in Eleanor E. Maccoby, Theodore M. Newcomb, and Eugene L. Hartley, eds. *Readings in Social Psychology*. New York: Holt, 1958, pp. 400–425.

Goode, William J., "A Theory of Role Strain," *American Sociological Review*, 25 (August 1960), pp. 483–496.

Straus, Murray A., "Work Roles and Responsibility in the Socialization of Farm, Fringe, and Town Boys," *Rural Sociology*, 27 (September 1962), pp. 257–274.

Strodtbeck, Fred L., "Family Interaction, Values, and Achievement," in David C. McClelland, *et al.*, *Talent and Society*. Princeton, N.J.: Van Nostrand, 1958, pp. 135–194.

Wrong, Dennis, "The Oversocialized Conception of Man," *American Sociological Review*, 26 (April 1961), pp. 183–193.

Name________________

Date________________

TABLE 1. Agreement in political preference by closeness to father and father's interest in politics

POLITICAL AGREEMENT (Box 30 and 31)	Father NOT INTERESTED in politics (Box 29 = 1, 2, or 3)				Father is INTERESTED in politics (Box 29 = 4 or 5)			
	Not close to father (Box 41 = 0 to 3)		Close to father (Box 41 = 4 or 5)		Not close to father (Box 41 = 0 to 3)		Close to father (Box 41 = 4 or 5)	
	Tally	%	Tally	%	Tally	%	Tally	%
AGREE: Codes in Boxes 30 & 31 are identical								
DISAGREE: Codes in Boxes 30 & 31 are different								
TOTAL		100%		100%		100%		100%
+ (No info.)		X		X		X		X

LABORATORY REPORT FOR PROBLEM ________

Course or
Section ________ Date ________ Name ________

HYPOTHESIS: ________

____

____

____

____

____

SAMPLE: ________

____

____

____

____

INDEPENDENT VARIABLE(S): ________

____

____

____

____

DEPENDENT VARIABLE(S): ________

____

____

____

____

OTHER FACTORS: ________

____

____

____

____

LABORATORY REPORT FOR PROBLEM ____________

SUMMARY OF FINDINGS: ____________

DISCUSSION: ____________

Social Differentiation V

PROBLEM 8 STRATIFICATION

Socio-economic status is the general term used for the position a person occupies in the prestige hierarchy of a society. As far as can now be determined, all societies have such a hierarchy, usually in the form of a social class system (Davis and Moore, 1945). In addition to being a near universal aspect of human social structure, socio-economic ranking is one of the most important determinants of behavior. There have been so many empirical studies relating socio-economic status to a diversity of phenomena that a catalog of these findings would be a considerable undertaking. Only a casual review of this literature, however, would reveal a general lack of agreement on what socio-economic status is and, further, on how it is to be measured. This poses definite problems for research.

One problem relates to whether persons of similar socio-economic status actually form a social class—that is, a group of individuals who engage in common interaction, share similar beliefs, and present a distinctive life style to the larger community. Research on this issue has been carried out in a variety of small communities. Hollingshead, in a study of one midwestern community, simply asked residents how many social classes existed and which people in the community belonged to each class (Hollingshead, 1949). His results show surprising agreement on both the perception of the number of existing classes and the more difficult task of placing individuals into classes. Hollingshead's results were confirmed for the same community by W. Lloyd Warner (Warner, 1949).

The evidence, however, is not clear cut. Laswell, in a study of "Citrus City" (1954), found no agreement on the number of classes or the placement of individuals; Lenski (1952) similarly discovered high ambiguity in an analysis of the class structure of Danielson, Connecticut. Both Lenski and Laswell arrived at the same conclusion: In the absence of community-wide agreement on social class, the most strategic alternative is to consider the American class structure as statistical strata—that is, as aggregates in which the researcher himself groups persons of similar status and arbitrarily divides them into some such classification as lower, middle and upper class. The implication of this view is that classes (at least in the United States) are not entities with distinct boundaries; rather, they are heuristic concepts introduced for purposes of research. Much additional research, however, is needed to resolve these issues of the existence of social classes.

It should be clear that the option of asking persons to place others into various classes does not exist in large metropolitan communities. Many persons do not even know their neighbors, and they would thus be virtually ignorant of the class standing of representative members of the community. An alternative is to forgo the possibility of asking others about class and instead to group individuals, as Lenski and Laswell implicitly suggest, on the basis of similar status characteristics. This alternative, however, creates a new set of issues. For example, in determining an individual's niche in the stratification structure, is it more revealing to look at the style of life he maintains (as indicated, for example, by the value of his residence), the resources he commands (income), the potential he possesses (education), the work he experiences (occupation)? Second, if all of these can be interpreted as proper indicators of socio-economic status, then does the use of one of these indicators in one study and another in a different study lead to different substantive conclusions? Third, how does one decide on what is and is not a proper indicator?

In the reading for the present problem, Kahl and Davis explore the relationships between nineteen different indicators of socio-economic status, ranging from impressionistic ratings of interviewers, to income, to self-reported class identification. They find that nearly all such indicators tap two basic dimensions—one related to husband's occupation and the other to residential area. Moreover, the indicators of each separate dimension are highly correlated with one another. The implication of the high correlations for the strategy of research is this: It may not make a great deal of difference which indicator is selected, for all appear to reflect a similar underlying factor.

In order to deal with a large number of indicators at once, Kahl and Davis use a rather complicated statistical technique known as "factor analysis." The calculation of a factor analysis is complex, but for present purposes it is not essential that you understand the details. You need only bear in mind that factor analysis is a technique to determine whether, among a large group of variables, any of them form clusters in which all the variables in the cluster are more closely related to each other than to the variables in another cluster. Each of these clusters or groups of variables is known as a factor.

A COMPARISON OF INDEXES OF SOCIO-ECONOMIC STATUS / *Joseph A. Kahl and James A. Davis*

In the past twenty years many indexes have been devised as measures of the socio-economic status of individuals. The task has been complicated by the fact that investigators have not agreed upon precise definitions of the term "socio-economic status" (or its several synonyms); therefore they sought a short and usable index for a loosely defined and unmeasured variable.[1]

This variable has been conceived of in different ways: as a unidimensional attribute that could be directly measured if we had adequate tools; as a unidimensional attribute, but one that must be measured indirectly; as a unidimensional composite that cannot be directly measured, made up of several interrelated attributes that are measurable and can be combined in an index; as a complex of attributes that are interrelated, but do not form a single dimension and thus should not be measured, directly or indirectly, as a totality. Many researchers have avoided the logical and definitional problems by using a measurement that supposedly maximized prediction of certain behavioral consequences of status position, however it be defined. Usually these investigators have offered a new index that proved useful in the context of a given research situation without indicating how it was related to other measurement devices. The result has been proliferation and confusion, with only a few attempts to study the relations among the indexes themselves.[2]

This article reports an additional study of the inter-correlations among standard measurement tools. Information was collected from over two hundred adult men; 19 scores were computed for each respondent which measured some aspect of his socio-economic status; these scores were then inter-correlated and subjected to factor and cluster analysis. The 19 measures were not all independent; many were simply alternative ways of scoring the same variable (such as occupation), for the field worker needs guidance about their relative efficiency. Some additional data are presented comparing open-ended and closed questions on the status self-identification of the respondents.

Reprinted with permission of the authors and publisher from *American Sociological Review,* 20 (June 1955), pp. 317–325.

The authors are grateful for the support of the Harvard Laboratory of Social Relations, the assistance of Mrs. Hope Leichter, and the advice of Professors Peter H. Rossi, Ray Hyman, and Daniel O. Price.

[1] For a brief discussion of the logical problems involved and references to many attempts to solve them in practical situations, see the section on Methodology in Harold W. Pfautz, "The Current Literature on Social Stratification: Critique and Bibliography," *American Journal of Sociology,* LVIII 1953), pp. 394–99.

[2] Among them are: George A. Lundberg, "The Measurement of Socio-Economic Status," *American Sociological Review,* V (1940), pp. 29–39; Louis Guttman, "A Revision of Chapin's Social Status Scale," *ibid.,* VII (1942), pp. 362–69; Raymond B. Cattell, "The Concept of Social Status," *Journal of Social Psychology,* XV (1942), pp. 293–308; G. A. Lundberg and P. Friedman, "A Comparison of Three Measures of Socio-Economic Status," Rural Sociology, VIII (1943), pp. 227–36; Genevieve Knupfer, *Indices of Socio-Economic Status: A Study of Some Problems of Measurement.* New York: author, 1946; Ph.D. Thesis, Columbia University; Richard Centers, "Toward an Articulation of Two Approaches to Social Class Phenomena, Parts I and II," *International Journal of Opinion and Attitude Research,* IV (Winter, 1950–51), pp. 499–514, V (Summer, 1951), pp. 159–78; Otis Dudley Duncan and Jay W. Artis, *Social Stratification in a Pennsylvania Rural Community,* State College, Pa.: Bulletin 543, Pennsylvania State College of Agriculture, October, 1951; F. H. Finch and A. J. Hoechn, "Measuring Socio-Economic or Cultural Status: A Comparison of Methods," *Journal of Social Psychology,* XXXIII (1951), pp. 51–67; Neal Gross, "Social Class Identification in the Urban Community," *American Sociological Review,* XVIII (1953), pp. 398–404.

The data

Using students in a 1953 Harvard University course on social stratification as interviewers, we approached 219 men in their homes in Cambridge, Massachusetts, and asked them for the information needed to compute scores on most of the indexes of stratification position used in contemporary research. We restricted our sample to men between the ages of 30 and 49 in order to get persons who were at the peaks of their occupational careers, thus minimizing the effects of differential positions in the life cycle. And to reduce ethnic variations, we eliminated all Negroes and those whites who did not complete their educations in the United States.

Cambridge is a mixed industrial and residential area contiguous to Boston. We first rank-ordered the 30 census tracts by average monthly rent; next chose 15 alternating tracts on the list, eliminating those immediately adjacent to the University; then gave each interviewing team of two students a specific tract to cover, and instructed the team to choose any available 16 respondents who could be found in their homes within the tract boundaries. There were 219 usable schedules out of a possible 240. Obviously, we were not seeking a random sample of any specified universe, but rather a sample with sufficient representation of all levels of the status hierarchy to permit various internal comparisons. When the occupational distribution of the men in our sample is compared to that for all employed men in the Boston metropolitan area, as given in Table 1, it can be seen that the sample is over-weighted

TABLE 1. Percentage distribution among occupations, research sample and employed men in Boston metropolitan area

Occupation	Sample	Employed men[a]
	Per Cent	Per Cent
Professional, technical and kindred	19	11
Proprietors, managers and officials	10	13
Sales workers	9	9
Clerical and kindred	8	9
Craftsmen, foremen and kindred	24	21
Operatives and kindred	17	20
Service, exc. private household	7	9
Laborers, inc. private household	5	7
Never in labor force, or uncodeable	1	1
Total	100	100

[a] Source: U. S. Bureau of the Census, *1950 Census of Population,* Vol. II, Part 21, Table 35, Washington: Government Printing Office, 1952.

at the professional level, but otherwise does not differ markedly.

Our schedule included questions about the respondent's three best friends (chosen by the respondent from among his friends and defined as those with whom house visits were exchanged at least once a month). Each friend was given an occupational code (North-Hatt—see below) and the scores for the three (or fewer, if less than three were mentioned) were averaged. This average score for each respondent was used as a measure of his level of social participation in the community—a useful substitute in the metropolitan community for the information that investigators in small towns get through sociometric questions and interviews concerning personal reputation. In some of the interpretations below, this score is used as a criterion measurement of current behavior to be predicted by other indexes.

Tetrachoric correlations were used for convenience in machine tabulation. The inter-correlations among the indexes are shown in Table 2. The nineteen measures were dichotomized as close to the median as possible, in the following ways:

1. Warner occupational category:[3] 1–4 vs. 5–7
2. Occupation of friends, North-Hatt category:[4] approximately: average scores of 75–96 vs. 33–74
3. Subject's education: some training beyond high school vs. high school graduation or less
4. Census occupational category of subject:[5] clerical and above vs. craftsman or below
5. North-Hatt occupational category of subject:[4] scores 63–96 vs. 33–62
6. Wife's father's occupation, Census category:[5] clerical and above vs. craftsman or below
7. Interviewer's impressionistic rating of subject:[3] in Warner terms: upper, upper-middle, lower-middle vs. common man (undifferentiated), upper-lower, lower-lower
8. Self-identification (Centers) of subject:[6] upper, upper-middle, undifferentiated middle, lower-middle vs. working and lower
9. Subject's mother's education: part high school or more vs. grade school or less
10. Source of income (Warner):[3] wealth, profits and fees, salary vs. wage or relief
11. Census tract, mean monthly rent:[7] tract ranks 1–12 vs. 13–30
12. Interviewer's rating of residential area, Warner category:[3] 1–4 vs. 5–7
13. Subject's father's occupation, Census category:[5] clerical and above vs. craftsman or below
14. Interviewer's rating of house, Warner category:[3] 1–4 vs. 5–7
15. Subject's father's education: part high school or more vs. grade school or less

[3] W. Lloyd Warner, *et al., Social Class in America,* Chicago: Science Research Associates, 1949.

[4] National Opinion Research Center (C. C. North and P. H. Hatt), "Jobs and Occupations: A Popular Evaluation," in *Class, Status and Power,* Reinhard Bendix and Seymour M. Lipset (eds.), Glencoe, Illinois: The Free Press, 1953, pp. 411–26. This article gives a rank order of the "general standing" of 90 occupations as judged by a national sample of American adults. In our coding we divided it into seven levels, and scored occupations not on the list by analogy. We predicted that this particular occupational code would maximize prediction of related variables as it was based on public (rather than armchair) opinion; we were wrong.

[5] U. S. Bureau of the Census, *1950 Census of Population, Classified Index of Occupations and Industries,* Washington: Government Printing Office, 1950. We reversed the order of clerks and salesmen. Thus the dichotomy we used was professionals, proprietors and managers, salesmen and clerks vs. craftsmen, operatives, service workers, and laborers.

[6] Richard Centers, *The Psychology of Social Classes,* Princeton: Princeton University Press, 1949.

[7] U. S. Bureau of the Census, *1950 Census of Housing,* Vol. V, Part 26, Washington: Government Printing Office, 1951.

TABLE 2. Tetrachoric correlation matrix; nineteen status indexes

	1	2	3	4	5	6	7	8	9	10	11	12	13	14	15	16	17	18	19
1																			
2	.80																		
3	.77	.81																	
4	.93	.70	.70																
5	.81	.70	.65	.50															
6	.57	.63	.52	.59	.49														
7	.75	.69	.53	.74	.63	.34													
8	.73	.69	.75	.71	.63	.59	.60												
9	.48	.57	.60	.39	.55	.65	.41	.53											
10	.78	.59	.65	.86	.54	.62	.62	.60	.39										
11	.53	.36	.41	.47	.46	.64	.50	.43	.38	.41									
12	.54	.48	.45	.43	.51	.48	.50	.32	.30	.34	.76								
13	.54	.60	.53	.53	.48	.65	.44	.41	.57	.30	.33	.28							
14	.49	.46	.43	.39	.36	.50	.38	.30	.35	.45	.62	.92	.49						
15	.37	.48	.54	.36	.46	.48	.47	.40	.86	.23	.45	.37	.61	.40					
16	.43	.39	.45	.40	.44	.68	.43	.47	.49	.35	.43	.62	.54	.46	.29				
17	.49	.82	.59	.50	.43	.45	.40	.40	.39	.47	.39	.20	.25	.37	.29	.16			
18	.51	.34	.36	.41	.42	.34	.56	.34	.39	.34	.63	.35	.30	.22	.21	.35	.23		
19	.29	.45	.41	.22	.29	.48	.35	.32	.48	.20	.36	.27	.52	.14	.52	.44	.20	.13	

16. Wife's father's occupation, North-Hatt category:[4] scores 63–96 vs. 33–62

17. Subject's wife's education: high school graduate or more vs. part high school or less

18. Annual family income: $5,000 or over vs. less than $5,000

19. Subject's father's occupation, North-Hatt category:[4] scores 63–96 vs. 33–62

Table 2 is useful as it stands. For instance, if one is interested in the average occupational level of a man's three best friends as a criterion of status participation, he can immediately rank order the various indexes according to their power as predictors thereof. (Incidentally, additional data not published in this article show that approximately the same rank order of indexes holds for the prediction of certain aspects of ideology that are class-related.) Or, one can observe that the subject and the interviewer equally use occupation as an important clue to status position, but the subject weights education more than the interviewer does. However, it is possible to analyze the information in the table more systematically, and we used two alternative but complementary methods to do so: factor analysis and cluster analysis.

Factor analysis

The relatively high positive correlations among the variables suggest that they all may be indexes of the same underlying factor but measure it with varying degrees of approximation: that is, each measures (in differing proportions) both the general factor and idiosyncratic attributes specific to itself. This situation presents an exact parallel to the one which results from a battery of intelligence tests, and we can use the procedure that the psychologists developed to study I.Q.: factor analysis.

This technique allows us to identify indirectly the general component, subtract its contribution to the observed inter-correlations, and see what remains. If the remaining correlations are small, we conclude that there exists a single dimension of socio-economic status distributed among our measures. But if the remaining correlations are large, we conclude that there are two or more separate components to socio-economic status, and we can then search for the best measures of each of them. The technique is far from automatic and definitive; decisions based on judgment are involved in its application, for instance, the judgment of when to stop extracting additional common factors. Furthermore, it should be noted that all our results are but approximations, for some of the conditions for factor analysis are not fully met by our data.

Our first approximation, using the centroid method,[8] did indeed reveal a general factor with high correlations with many of our variables, ranging from .88 with the Warner occupational scale to .49 with subject's father's occupation on the North-Hatt scale. (See the column headed "k" in Table 3.) This approximates the best single dimension accounting for the inter-correlations among the variables. But it was possible to control more variance by extracting two common factors instead of one general factor. The two common factors taken together accounted for most of the variance of the original variables, so it was not worth while to seek a third factor.

The details are shown in Table 3. The column headed "h^2" (the "communality") gives a rough estimate of the proportion that can be accounted for by its relationship to all potential common factors combined ($1 - h^2$ includes variance due to the specificity of the given variable plus measurement error). The column "k" shows the "loading" or correlation of a

[8] J. P. Guilford, *Psychometric Methods,* New York: McGraw-Hill, 1936, Chapter 14.

TABLE 3. Results of factor analysis

Variable	h^2	$h^2-(k_1^2+k_2^2)$	k	k_1	k_2
1. Warner occupation	.86	−.04	.88	.88	.36
4. Census occupation	.86	+.07	.80	.84	.29
2. Friends' occupations	.67	−.16	.85	.83	.37
10. Source of income	.74	+.07	.72	.78	.24
3. Subject's education	.66	−.07	.82	.75	.41
8. Self-identification	.56	−.05	.74	.71	.33
7. Interviewer's rating of subject	.56	−.04	.75	.67	.39
5. North-Hatt occupation	.66	+.06	.77	.64	.44
17. Wife's education	.67	+.23	.59	.63	.20
11. Census tract	.58	−.02	.70	.26	.73
12. Area rating	.85	+.28	.67	.22	.72
6. Wife's father's occupation, Census	.46	−.18	.77	.37	.71
9. Subject's mother's education	.74	+.16	.72	.33	.69
15. Subject's father's education	.74	+.21	.65	.23	.69
14. House rating	.85	+.33	.65	.24	.68
16. Wife's father's occupation, North-Hatt	.46	−.04	.63	.22	.67
13. Subject's father's occupation, Census	.42	−.08	.67	.32	.63
19. Subject's father's occupation, North-Hatt	.27	−.03	.49	.18	.52
18. Income	.40	+.12	.53	.36	.39

given variable with the one general factor. Columns "k_1" and "k_2" show the loadings with each of the two common factors. Since the communality of a given variable equals the sum of its squared loadings on all potential common factors ($h^2 = k_1^2 + k_2^2 \ldots + k_n^2$), the column "$h^2 - (k_1^2 + k_2^2)$" shows the residual communality after that due to the two common factors has been removed.[9] The table was computed after a 45-degree rotation of axes; plotting suggests that a slightly better fit could be obtained by the use of oblique axes.

The factor analysis shows that the first common component (k_1) in our indexes is most closely related (in rank order) to the Warner occupational scale, the Census occupational scale, occupation of friends, source of income, education of subject, self-identification of subject, interviewer's impressionistic judgment of subject, the North-Hatt occupational scale, and wife's education—the top half of Table 3. Naturally, we expected the various scales for the subject's occupation to measure the same thing with slightly different degrees of approximation. Since source of income (wage vs. salary) is in fact another form of occupational scale, it too should fit here. Education of subject belongs because it is the best single predictor of occupation that is available, and the education of the wife usually comes close to that of her husband. Apparently these factors combined determined choice of friends. Finally, the inclusion here of the interviewer's impression of the subject and the latter's own self-identification indicate that both used the aforementioned "objective" characteristics as the basis of their judgments. Note that most of these variables may be considered as measures, causes or consequents of occupational position; the first common factor "makes sense."

The second common factor (k_2) is most closely related to the various measures of the house and the residential area, and to those of the status of the parents of the subject and his wife—the bottom half of Table 3. It is not immediately apparent why these two types of variables should be so closely related, and why they should be clearly distinguishable from the items in the first factor. One possible explanation is in terms of life cycle sequences, particularly for socially mobile persons. A man makes a basic decision about his career by deciding how long to stay in school. After he is educated, he picks a wife of roughly the same schooling, and enters an occupational level that is largely determined by his training in school. Presumably, he chooses friends appropriate to his own level, and begins to think of himself in terms of that level. But there may well be a lag with respect to his housing; a cautious man will not buy a big new house until his career is far enough advanced that he is sure he can afford to pay the mortgage. Consequently, measures of his housing may not be too closely related to those of his occupation but may reflect an earlier period of his career: he may live for a while as did his parents. Is this an instance of "cultural lag" within the life

[9] Tetrachoric correlations standardize the distributions of the variables, giving each a variance of 1. Therefore, the variances of the 19 measures sum to 19. Since the square of a correlation coefficient is an estimate of the proportion of the variance accounted for by the correlation, the sum of k^2 (9.63) is an estimate of the proportion of the total variance accounted for by k. It equals 51 per cent of 19. Likewise, k_1 accounts for 31 per cent, k_2 for 28 per cent, and ($k_1 + k_2$) for 59 per cent of the total variance. Since the square of the guessed communality is an estimate of the proportion of the total variance accounted for by all possible factors, the ratio of h^2 to the squares of the factor loadings gives an estimate of the proportion of the total common factor variance controlled by the various factors. Thus, k accounts for 80 per cent, k_1 for 48 per cent, k_2 for 44 per cent, and ($k_1 + k_2$) for 92 per cent of that part of the total variance which can be explained by common factors.

cycle? This argument applies particularly to young professionals, and our sample is over-loaded with them. (And there may be "status consciousness" differences that will make some people more concerned than others with having their status symbols harmoniously matched.)

The research man who wants to use our results as a guide for his procedures must remember that our sample is small and somewhat biased, that inductive statistics capitalize on chance, that the technique of factor analysis has limitations, that our tetrachoric correlations are based on dichotomies and thus overemphasize cases in the middle of the distribution. But pending replication, he can tentatively conclude that "socio-economic status" is an accurate though clumsy term: there is a composite of social and economic attributes that tend to cluster together, and we can measure the composite fairly well. For many purposes, it is practical to treat this composite as one dimension—the general factor. The best single index of it is an occupational scale. (Warner's has a higher loading, but the Census Bureau gives details that make coding more reliable.) Some improvement in measurement can be had by combining occupation and one of the variables from the second common factor, such as Census tract, with a heavier weight given to the former. It is probably not practical in most instances to add more variables to a composite index.

For some purposes the researcher might prefer an index of a somewhat purer dimension, the first common factor, which is concerned more closely with occupation and its satellite variables. If so, he should use an occupational scale as his main index, with either source of income or education as a secondary criterion.

Income stands in sulking isolation. It has an equal loading on both common factors, and not a very high one at that. Why is the amount of family income a poor measure of socio-economic status? Observation suggests that the core of status is a culturally defined, group-shared style of life, and income is a necessary but not a sufficient condition thereof. Values intervene between the receipt of a paycheck and its expenditure in conspicuous consumption. A satisfied blue collar worker and an ambitious clerk may have the same income but a different mode of living. The former is likely to have a bigger house in a cheaper neighborhood, to spend more on automobiles, to save less, and to have working class friends and beliefs. There is a great deal of overlap and variability at precisely this point of the stratification hierarchy, and it is at this point that we had to arbitrarily dichotomize our variables. Income is probably a good index at the extremes, but weakens as one approaches the great "common man" group at the middle of our system.[10]

Our results partially support the study of the small town of Jonesville, reported by Warner in *Social Class in America*. He was able to predict Evaluated Participation (EP), a complex rating of social reputation and participation based on free interviews, by the Index of Status Characteristics (ISC), which consisted of occupation, source of income, house type, and dwelling area, weighted 4, 3, 3, and 2, respectively. He got a product moment correlation of .91 between occupation and EP, and a startling multiple correlation of .97 between the entire ISC and EP. However, his sample was highly biased with extreme cases that inflated the coefficients (about half were upper or upper-middle class). We were able to get a product moment correlation of .74 between occupation (Warner) and status of friends, and a multiple correlation of .80 between occupation plus education and status of friends. (The partial correlation between occupation and friends was .43, between education and friends was .21.) The important comparison is the relative rank of predicting indexes, not the absolute size of the correlations, and our data agree with Warner's that occupation (as he measures it) is the best predictor of either social participation or the whole socio-economic cluster represented by the general factor. He found that amount of income, source of income, house type, dwelling area and education (in that order) were the next best predictors of EP. Our order was slightly different: after occupation as a measure of the general factor came education, source of income, dwelling area, house type, and amount of income.

Cluster analysis

While factor analysis partitions a set of inter-correlations into a few basic components and shows the relationship of each variable to those components, cluster analysis directly groups together those variables whose inter-correlations are especially high and offers a standard criterion for rejecting other variables which come close to those in a cluster but are not as intimately related to them as they are to each other.[11] The cluster is based on the ratio of the correlations of two or more variables with each other to their correlations with all the variables outside the cluster. High inter-correlations will *not* produce a cluster if the related variables share high correlations with outside variables —in other words, if their relationship is primarily a result of shared loadings on common factors. Therefore, our results may be thought of as producing sub-groupings *within* each of the two major groupings indicated by the two common factors, sub-groupings which have some *additional* close relationship *after* the common factor has been controlled.

Table 4 shows the clusters that meet the criterion; the higher the B-coefficient the tighter the special relationship between the variables in the cluster. The conventional minimum for this measure is 1.300.

[10] Kahl has offered a description of the "common man" way of life in the Boston area, based on free interviews, in "Educational and Occupational Aspirations of 'Common Man' Boys," *Harvard Educational Review,* XXIII (1953), pp. 186–203.

[11] Robert C. Tryon, *Cluster Analysis,* Ann Arbor, Michigan: Edwards Bros., 1939. For an interesting example of the use of the method to identify culture areas by the clustering of traits (with full details on procedure) see Forrest E. Clements, "Use of Cluster Analysis with Anthropological Data," *American Anthropologist,* LVI (1954), pp. 180–99.

TABLE 4. Results of cluster analysis

Cluster	Variables	B-Coefficient
1	12. Area rating 14. House rating	2.233
2	15. Subject's father's education 9. Subject's mother's education	1.969
3	2. Friends' occupations 17. Wife's education	1.748
4	4. Subject's occupation, Census 1. Subject's occupation, Warner 10. Source of income	1.696
5	16. Wife's father's occupation, North-Hatt 6. Wife's father's occupation, Census	1.478
6	11. Census tract 18. Income	1.463
7	3. Subject's education 8. Subject's self-identification	1.427
8	19. Subject's father's occupation, North-Hatt 13. Subject's father's occupation, Census	1.319

The close relationship between house and area scores (cluster 1) is not surprising, for they are both impressionistic ratings by the same interviewer, made by looking at the house and the neighborhood before interviewing the subject. The relationship is the result of ecological patterning plus interviewer effect.

Clusters 4, 5, and 8 are replicating measures of the same variable. Cluster 2 indicates that a man's father married his mother partly because she had an education similar to his. (The relation between subject's education and that of his wife is not reflected in a cluster because of their high shared loadings on the first common factor.) Cluster 3 suggests that although a couple choose friends of similar occupational level, the wife has some additional voice in the matter. Cluster 6 indicates that family income and average rent of census tract are especially close. Finally, Cluster 7 indicates that education is a variable that is closely related to a man's vision of himself.

Self-identification

In this final section we take a closer look at one of our measures of status: the respondent's conception of himself. Many investigators have been interested in subjective identification as a criterion of class membership because it may be the key intervening variable between objective indexes like occupation and specific attitudes and behavior. However, various ways of asking the question "Who are you?" produce varying results. The Warner school maintains that the question cannot be directly put because the American value system of equality leads people to deny differentiation. Consequently, they recommend that we listen to a wide range of verbalizations, observe behavior in many situations, and then abstract out the *implied* self-identifications by noting the invidious distinctions that appear. Centers, in *The Psychology of Social Classes*, was more direct; he bluntly asked a man whether he was upper, middle, working, or lower class. But critics said that this told us too much about the categories in Centers' mind and not enough about those of his respondents. Gross (cited above) approached the problem by first using an open-ended question about class membership, and then following it with the Centers' question. The results were disparate, and he remained unhappy about the validity of closed items. We followed a procedure similar to that of Gross but took the additional step of cross-classifying the answers.

We first asked this question:

> There has been a lot of talk recently about social classes in the United States. I wonder what you think about this. What social classes do you think there are in this part of the country?

We followed that by a series of items designed as standardized probes:

> Which social class do you think you are in?
> What puts you in that class?
> Which class is next below yours in social standing?
> In what ways are people in that class different from people in your class?
> Which class is next above yours in social standing?
> In what ways are people in that class different from people in your class?

Finally, we asked the Centers' question, along with an additional probe:

> If you were asked to use one of these four names for your social class, which would you say you belonged in: the middle class, the lower class, the working class, or the upper class?
> If *middle*: Would you say you were in the upper-middle or the lower-middle? (If no discrimination, answer was coded "middle.")

These questions came after those on the subject's occupation, income, and education, so our respondent was somewhat warned of the areas of our interest. In coding the replies, we combined information from the whole battery of open-ended questions. We found that 12 per cent of our respondents had no conception of a class order; 6 per cent understood the questions well enough to explicitly deny that a class order existed in the United States; 5 per cent recognized a class order, but either disapproved of it so strongly that they did not want to describe it, or said it was too complex to describe; 10 per cent said it contained two strata; 42 per cent claimed it consisted of three strata; 20 per cent recognized four strata; and 5 per cent detected five or more strata.

Of those who described a system with a given number of strata, 61 per cent used as the main criterion of differentiation income and/or the style of life it bought; 8 per cent mentioned a specific occupational level as the main criterion (such as "professionals"); 9 per cent used morals (including motivation to work); 16 per cent insisted that there was no single criterion; and the few remaining answers were scattered among family background, education and training, and innate ability. Ethnic criteria were seldom used. The category of morals was most popular as the secondary criterion. As has been noticed before, there was a slight tendency for those lower on the socio-economic scale to stress income, and those higher on the scale to stress quality and morals.[12]

In describing their own class position 69 per cent of our respondents spontaneously used labels that approximated the ones which appear on the Centers' list (as amended by us). The details are shown in Table 5, which cross-classifies the open and closed

TABLE 5. Class self-identification: open and closed questions

Identification on open questions	N	Identification on closed questions: U	UM	M	LM	W	L	N.A.
Upper	3	2	....	....	....	1	....	....
Upper-middle	9	2	6	....	1	....	....	....
Middle or synonym	97	1	23	19	18	36	....	....
Lower-middle	7	1	....	....	4	2	....	....
Working or synonym	30	....	....	2	....	27	....	1
Lower	5	....	....	....	....	....	5	....
Intellectual or professional	9	2	6	....	1	....	....	....
Other occupational categories	5	1	1	1	....	2	....	....
Other	15	1	2	3	....	8	....	1
Denies class, or no conception, or no answer	39	....	3	2	2	27	2	3
Total	219	10	41	27	26	103	7	5

responses. There are several interesting patterns: those who spontaneously used labels at the extremes (upper-middle, working, or lower) were consistent, and gave the same reply when re-questioned with fixed alternative answers. However, those who spontaneously called themselves middle class wavered on the closed question, *with over a third changing their answers to working class.* Half of those who gave varied labels on the open question (classified as "other"), and over two-thirds of those who denied the existence of class or could not give any answer at all on the open question, called themselves working class when given the fixed alternatives.

When we examined the occupations of the various types of respondents, we found that those who called themselves upper or upper-middle were mostly professional men; those who called themselves middle or lower-middle on both the open and closed questions tended to be professional men, businessmen, salesmen, or clerks; whereas those who called themselves middle on the open but working on the closed questions tended to be skilled or semi-skilled workers. The respondents who chose working on both sets of questions tended to be skilled workers, the confused men who denied or had no conception of class or used a special label for their position on the open questions and used middle on the closed tended to be small businessmen, whereas the persons who gave those answers on the open questions but switched to working on the closed were mostly semi-skilled operatives.

It appears, then, that if sufficient probes are used it is possible to get a description of the class system with open-ended questions. Although there is some denial and much variation, there is also a core of consensus. The majority of our respondents saw the system as a rough division of the population into three or four strata representing occupation-consumption levels. Almost half spontaneously put themselves into the middle, but when specific alternatives were forced on them, they made finer distinctions and further divided themselves into a lower-middle range of white collar workers and an upper working class range of successful blue collar workers. The closed answers provided more information than the open because they forced the common man group to sub-divide themselves and the doubters to commit themselves. Yet these forced answers appeared consistent with the earlier free answers if interpreted with occupational data at hand.[13]

Summary

Factor analysis of scores on 19 stratification indexes for 219 men showed that the indexes were highly correlated because they all, in varying degrees, measured the same underlying dimension. For rough purposes, this common component could be conceived of as a single dimension or general factor. However, a more precise statement would be that the battery of indexes showed two common factors. The first was composed of the various measures of occupation, plus certain variables closely related to occupation, such as education, self-identification, and the interviewer's impressionistic rating of the subject. The second factor was composed of ecological measures plus those of the status of the parents of the subject and his wife.

The two common factors accounted for most of the mutual variance of the original indexes. The little that remained was studied via cluster analysis. It revealed certain subgroupings of variables that were highly related to each other after their mutual relationships to the common factors were controlled. These turned out to be mainly clusters of indexes that were replicating measures of the same variable, a further indication of the fact that the two common factors "explained" most of the important relationships among the 19 indexes.

[12] Hadley Cantril, "Identification with Social and Economic Class," *Journal of Abnormal and Social Psychology,* XXXVIII (1944), pp. 74–80.

[13] For a parallel study in Britain, see F. M. Martin, "Some Subjective Aspects of Social Stratification," in *Social Mobility in Britain,* D. V. Glass, ed., London: Routledge and Kegan Paul, 1954.

The findings suggest that a non-verbal instrument might avoid some of the difficulties of this approach. A study in preparation by J. A. Davis indicates that if subjects are asked to place themselves "higher" or "lower" in social standing than photographs of people and living rooms, acceptable Guttman scales of up to 23 scale types result (which show strong association with standard measurement indexes).

The two techniques were applied independently; each started with the inter-correlation matrix. They proved to be complementary ways of reducing the matrix to simpler and more understandable form.

Finally, the answers of the respondents to a series of open-ended questions about their conceptions of the class system and their own positions within it were compared to their answers to the Centers' closed item on self-identification. It was found that the majority of respondents in their free answers agreed about the basic outlines of a three or four class system of occupation-consumption strata. Almost half put themselves into the middle level. When faced with the closed alternatives, a third of these changed their minds and called themselves working class. The meaning of this inconsistency was explored.

Replication

MEASUREMENT OF SOCIO-ECONOMIC STATUS

This replication simplifies the procedures in the original study for two basic reasons. First, the factor analytic technique used by Kahl and Davis to determine the relationship among different measures of socio-economic status is extremely involved and complex in its calculation. Second, it would be both tedious and time consuming to cross-tabulate the nineteen variables with each other. To make the problem manageable, we have selected three of the most widely used indicators of socio-economic status—occupation, education, and subjective class identification. Your problem will be to determine whether these three are correlated (e.g., related) with each other, as well as to determine whether any one of these measures tends on the average to be most highly correlated. Since our purpose is to look at the interrelation of three indicators rather than to test hypotheses of cause and consequence, you should regard all three variables as, in turn, both independent and dependent variables.

Hypothesis

1. State whether you think there is a relationship between the three indicators of social class.

2. For a second hypothesis, state which of these indicators you anticipate will be most strongly related to the other two and which will be least strongly related to the other two.

Empirical indicators for this problem

6. Please circle the HIGHEST LEVEL of education completed by your FATHER:
   1. Some grade school
   2. Completed grade school
   3. Some high school
   4. Completed high school
   5. Completed high school, and also had other training, but not college, e.g. technical
   6. Some college
   7. Completed college
   8. Some graduate work
   9. Graduate degree, M.D., M.A., Ph.D., etc.

12. Occupational Prestige:
    1. Proprietor of a large business (valued at $100,-000 or more); Top-level executive in large organization; Top-level professional
    2. Proprietor of a medium business (valued at $35,000 to $100,000); Middle-level executive or official, or top-level of a small organization; Lower-level professional; Sales representatives of manufacturers or wholesalers or other senior salesmen earning $10,000 or more per year; Farmer of farm worth $100,000+
    3. Proprietor of a small business (valued at $6,000 to $35,000); Lower-level official and manager; Semi-professional; Sales representative (as above) earning $7,000 to $10,000 per year; Farmer or farm worth $35,000 to $100,000
    4. Proprietor of a very small business (valued under $6,000); Technician; Sales clerk and salesman earning *less* than $7,000 per year and clerical workers; Farmer of farm worth $15,000 to $35,000
    5. Farmer of farm worth under $15,000; Skilled manual worker and foreman
    6. Farmer, sharecropper or tenant with little stock or equipment; semi-skilled worker and machine operator
    7. Unskilled worker

18. If your father were asked to use one of these five names for his social class, which one do you think he would be more likely to choose?
    1. The lower class
    2. The working class
    3. The lower-middle class
    4. The upper-middle class
    5. The upper class

Data analysis

To compare all the possible combinations of indicators will require three separate tabulations. To simplify things we will divide each indicator into "lower," "middle," and "upper" thirds. The "cutting points" to do this for each of the indicators are as follows:

		Socio-economic groups		
INDICATOR	BOX NUMBER	UPPER	MIDDLE	LOWER
Occupation	12	1,2	3,4	5,6,7
Education	6	6,7,8,9	4,5	1,2,3
Subjective identification	18	4,5	3	1,2

1. Correlation of Occupation and Education:
   A. *Sort* the code sheets on occupation (box 12) into lower, middle, and upper levels, using the groupings or "cutting points" shown above.
   B. *Tally* onto Table 1 of the tabulation form the educational levels as given in box 6 (e.g., lower, middle, upper), for each occupational level.
   C. *Compute* the "Percentage Correlation" by first adding the number of cases from the tabulation sheet falling into the "major diagonal" of Table 1, that is, the cases in the upper occupation-upper education cell, the middle occupation-middle education, and the lower occupation-lower education cell. These three cells are double ruled on the tabulation form. This sum represents the number of cases similarly classified by the occupation and education variables. Divide this sum by the total number of cases to obtain the percentage (see tables in Appendix B). The resulting statistic, the Percentage Correlation, is a rough measure of the degree of association between the two variables. Enter it into the space below Table 1.

2. Occupation and Subjective Identification: Repeat the procedure outlined in steps 1B and 1C, but this time tallying subjective class identification (box 18) onto Table 2.

3. Education and Subjective Identification:
   A. *Sort* the code sheets on education (box 6) into lower, middle, and upper levels.
   B. *Tally* onto Table 3 of the tabulation form the subjective identification codes (box 18) for each educational group.
   C. *Compute* the percentage correlation and enter it below Table 3.

4. Compute the "Combined Percentage Correlation" for each of the three indicators of socio-economic status:
   A. *Copy* the Percentage Correlations from Tables 1, 2, and 3 into the first two rows of the summary table (Table 4). Note that each Percentage Correlation is entered twice in Table 4.
   B. *Add* the two Percentage Correlations for each indicator and divide by two to get the Combined Percentage Correlation. This is a rough measure of how closely the indicator is correlated with the other indicators.

Lab report

1. Follow the directions for writing laboratory reports as outlined in Appendix A.

2. In writing your report consider the extent to which the Combined Percentage Correlations differ and try to explain these differences if they are sizeable.

References

Davis, Kingsley and Wilbert E. Moore, "Some Principles of Stratification," *American Sociological Review, 10* (April 1945), pp. 242–249.

Haer, John L., "Predictive Utility of Five Indices of Social Stratification," *American Sociological Review*, 22 (October 1957), pp. 541–546.

Hollingshead, August B., *Elmtown's Youth: The Impact of Social Classes on Adolescents*. New York: Wiley, 1949.

Laswell, Thomas E., "A Study of Social Stratification Using an Area Sample of Raters," *American Sociological Review, 19* (June 1954), pp. 430–437.

Lenski, Gerhard E., "American Social Classes: Statistical Strata or Social Groups," *American Journal of Sociology, 58* (September 1952), pp. 139–144.

Lundberg, George A. and Pearl Friedman, "A Comparison of Three Measures of Socio-Economic Status," in Paul F. Lazarsfeld and Morris Rosenberg, eds. *The Language of Sociological Research*. New York: Free Press, 1962, pp. 66–73.

Warner, W. Lloyd, *et al., Democracy in Jonesville*. New York: Harper & Row, 1949.

Name________________________

Date________________________

TABLE 1. Education by occupation

Education (Box 6)	OCCUPATION (BOX 12)		
	Upper Middle (Box 12 = 1 & 2)	Lower Middle (Box 12 = 3 & 4)	Working (Box 12 = 5, 6 & 7)
Upper = 6, 7, 8 or 9			
Middle = 4 or 5			
Low = 1, 2 or 3			

Percent correlation = ____________

TABLE 2. Subjective identification by occupation

Subjective identification (Box 18)	OCCUPATION (BOX 12)		
	Upper Middle (Box 12 = 1 & 2)	Lower Middle (Box 12 = 3 & 4)	Working (Box 12 = 5, 6 & 7)
Upper and Upper Middle = 4 or 5			
Lower Middle = 3			
Working or Lower = 1 or 2			

Percent correlation = ____________

TABLE 3. Subjective identification by education

Subjective identification (Box 18)	EDUCATION (BOX 6)		
	Upper (Box = 6, 7, 8 or 9)	Middle (Box = 4 or 5)	Low (Box = 1, 2 or 3)
Upper and Upper Middle = 4 or 5			
Lower Middle = 3			
Working or Lower = 1 or 2			

Percent correlation = ______

TABLE 4. Combined percent correlations

Occupation & Education = ______	Education & Occupation = ______	Subjective & Occupation = ______
Subjective & Occupation = ______	Education & Subjective = ______	Subjective & Education = ______
COMBINED	COMBINED	COMBINED
for Occupation = ______	for Education = ______	for Subjective = ______

LABORATORY REPORT FOR PROBLEM ____________

Course or
Section ____________ Date ____________ Name ____________

HYPOTHESIS: ____________

SAMPLE: ____________

INDEPENDENT VARIABLE(S): ____________

DEPENDENT VARIABLE(S): ____________

OTHER FACTORS: ____________

LABORATORY REPORT FOR PROBLEM __________

SUMMARY OF FINDINGS:

DISCUSSION:

PROBLEM 9

OCCUPATIONS

In an industrial society a man's work is the most valuable and efficient predictor of his life chances and life style. To know, for example, that a man is a professional or a manual worker is to know something about the number of children he may have, the neighborhood he will tend to live in, the styles of leisure he will likely enjoy. Obviously, professionals command more prestige and income than manual workers, and these differentials are important clues to the patterns of social activities.

Although income and prestige are important, occupations differ in other significant ways. One study, for example, considered the relevance of working night shifts. The research showed that because night workers are cut off from typical primary group attachments among family and friends, they are more likely to seek out colleagues at work and also more likely to participate in union affairs (Lipset, Trow, and Coleman, 1962). Another study contrasted the differences in leisure activity between those who worked many hours a week as opposed to those who worked few hours a week. Persons on short-hour schedules tended to watch television more indiscriminantly and generally participate in "lowbrow culture" (Wilensky, 1964). The author argued that mass culture serves to fill in the empty hours away from work—a point certainly relevant to any considerations of large-scale reductions in the workweek. Other studies have focused on unique features in the work tasks of particular occupations such as janitors, boxers, jazz musicians, etc. (Weinberg and Arond, 1952; Gold, 1952; Becker, 1951). Each such study suggests that, in addition to income and prestige, it is necessary to analyze working hours, work schedules, and work tasks if the full impact of occupation on life styles is to be understood. Further, all research on occupations implicitly plays on the same central theme: An activity such as work that demands the great majority of each day's energy and awareness is likely to have broad ramifications for one's life.

In the reading for the present problem, Murphy and Morris suggest that a novel aspect of occupations—the dimension of situs—is directly involved in shaping class identification and political party preference. *Situs* refers to the primary work functions of work organizations, the objective of the organization's central task. Manufacturing is one example of a situs, transportation is a second example, entertainment, a third. It must be stressed that classifying individuals in a situs has nothing to do with *status*, which refers to the income or prestige of a particular job. Thus a legal secretary and a supreme court justice are placed in a situs of legal authority; similarly, the airplane mechanic and the president of a national network of railroads are both classified in a situs of transportation.

The implication of situs for political preference and class identification is drawn in the following way. The authors argue that each situs has a particular social class stamp. Legal work and work in finance and records entail much symbolic manipulation and consequently promote an image of thinking, studying, discussing—in brief, an image of a white-collar world. Alternatively, manufacturing, with its emphasis on putting materials together, manual skills, and technology evokes an image of a blue-collar world. Murphy and Morris hypothesize that both political preference and class identification are shaped by the class image of a situs regardless of an individual's particular status. To support this point they show that individuals in situses with a blue-collar image tend to identify with the working class and vote Democratic, whereas individuals in situses with a white-collar image tend to identify with the middle class and vote Republican even though both groups possess similar educational levels and command similar incomes. In brief, the contribution of their research is to illustrate the effects of situs on class identification and politics even when typical indicators of social class such as education and income are controlled.

OCCUPATIONAL SITUS, SUBJECTIVE CLASS IDENTIFICATION, AND POLITICAL AFFILIATION / *Raymond J. Murphy and Richard T. Morris*

The effects of occupational situs and socio-economic level (measured by income and education) on subjective class identification and political party affiliation are examined. The data represent a secondary analysis of interview materials collected in four San Francisco census tracts in 1953. The findings indicate a positive relationship between socio-economic level and identification with middle class. Similarly, those in higher positions tend to affiliate with the Republican party. Individuals in the Finance and Records and Commerce situses tend to see themselves as middle class and favor the Republican party, while those in Manufacturing and Building and Maintenance identify typically with the working class and prefer the Democratic party. These situs differences remain statistically significant when socio-economic level is controlled, suggesting the independent influence of type of work on these aspects of behavior. We suggest that the findings may be explained in terms of historical definitions of work in American society. The results indicate the utility of considering the situs dimension in the analysis of occupational structure.

A persistent theme running through the literature on the sociology of work concerns the notion that a man's occupation exerts a compelling influence on his behavior, both off and on the job. Knowing a person's occupation, it is argued, will enable us to make a number of reasonably accurate predictions about his attitudes, life style, and central values. Edwards' view is typical of this position:[1]

> The most nearly dominant single influence on a man's life is probably his occupation. . . . More than anything else, perhaps, a man's occupation determines his course and contribution in life . . . A man's occupation not only tells, for each workday, what he does during one-half of his waking hours, but it indicates, with some degree of accuracy, his manner of life during the other half—the kind of associates he will have, the kind of clothes he will wear, the kind of house he will live in, and even, to some extent, the kind of food he will eat. And, usually, it indicates, in some degree, the cultural level of his family.

Similarly Anderson and Davidson assert that:[2]

> The work a man does to earn his livelihood stamps him with mental and physical traits characteristic of the form and level of his labor, defines his circle of friends and acquaintances affects the use of his leisure, influences his political affiliations, limits his interests and the attainment of his aspirations, and tends to set the boundaries of his culture.

In one of his earliest essays, Everett Hughes discusses the effects of the occupational life on personality and comments that, "In relation to its technique and the interests of those who use that technique, the occupational group tends to build up a set of collective representations, more or less peculiar to the occupation and more or less incomprehensible to the community. . . . This culture and technique, the etiquette and skill of the profession, appear in the individual as personal traits."[3]

From a number of detailed case studies of particular occupations,[4] the empirical validity of this notion becomes evident, yet in a broader sense a number of theoretical and practical questions remain unanswered: Do all occupations (or types of occupations) exert such a compelling influence, or does this vary with certain characteristics inherent in the requisites and qualities of the occupation? In what sectors of social behavior does the occupation exert influence? How does this vary by occupation or occupational type? What is the relationship between length of time in the job and mobility history and occupational influence? To what extent are the influences noted a function of the specific occupation and to what extent might they be a function of the more general life chances of the individual at the particular socio-economic level characteristic of the occupation?

Hypothetical answers exist to some of these questions. For example, both Hughes and Caplow suggest that occupations involving considerable training and a long initiation period are most likely to influence behavior both on and off the job. Caplow hypothesizes that:

> Other things being equal, we should expect to find the strictest control of nonoccupational behavior attached to those occupations which have important role-setting obligations, are identified with sacred symbols, and have relatively low status. We should expect least control in connection with those occupations which enjoy high status without the involvement of sacred elements.[5]

Thus it may be concluded that professional occupa-

Reprinted with permission of the authors and publisher from *American Sociological Review,* 26 (June 1961), pp. 383–392.

[1] Alba M. Edwards, *Comparative Occupation Statistics for the United States, 1870–1940,* Washington, D.C.: Government Printing Office, 1943, p. XI.

[2] H. Dewey Anderson and Percy E. Davidson, *Occupational Trends in the United States,* Palo Alto: Stanford University Press, 1940, p. 1.

[3] Everett C. Hughes, "Personality Types and the Division of Labor," *American Journal of Sociology,* 33 (March, 1928), p. 765.

[4] See, for example: Howard S. Becker, "The Professional Dance Musician and His Audience," *American Journal of Sociology,* 57 (September, 1951), pp. 136–144; Theodore Caplow, *The Sociology of Work,* Minneapolis: University of Minnesota Press, 1954, esp. Ch. 6, "Occupational Ideologies"; W. F. Cottrell, *The Railroader,* Palo Alto: Stanford University Press, 1940; Frances R. Donovan, *The Woman Who Waits,* Boston: Richard G. Badger, 1920; James C. Healey, *Foc's'le and Glory Hole: A Study of the Merchant Seaman and His Occupation,* New York: Merchant Marine Publishers Association, 1936; Morris Janowitz, *The Professional Soldier,* Glencoe, Ill.: The Free Press, 1960; Louis Kriesberg, "The Retail Furrier: Concepts of Security and Success," *American Journal of Sociology,* 57 (March, 1952), pp. 478–485, S. Kirson Weinberg and Henry Arond, "The Occupational Culture of the Boxer," *American Journal of Sociology,* 57 (March, 1952), pp. 460–469; Logan Wilson, *The Academic Man: A Study in the Sociology of a Profession,* New York: Oxford University Press, 1942.

[5] Caplow, *op. cit.,* p. 129.

tions, particularly those associated publicly with "sacred" or basic values, such as the clergy or school teaching, are more likely to make demands upon their incumbent's lives than are non-professional or less sacred types of work.

In our opinion, one of the major limitations of such theorizing has been the almost exclusive concentration on the correlates of the socio-economic characteristics of the occupation, namely income and education. Edwards' statement quoted above is presented in the context of his discussion of "Social-Economic" groups—categories widely used by sociologists as occupational strata. The same may be said for Davidson and Anderson.

There are many other occupational features which theoretically should have an influence on the attitudes and behavior of individuals. Among these are institutional setting,[6] practitioner-client relationship, working conditions, and the nature and function of the work itself. What is needed is an investigation of the relative contribution of several occupational characteristics to the attitudes and behavior of a single population. We hope in this paper to offer a beginning in this direction by investigating two of these characteristics simultaneously: socio-economic level and primary work function.

In an earlier paper[7] the authors presented the rationale for utilizing a separate dimension of analysis, situs, to explore non-stratified aspects of the occupational structure. Situs categories represent groups of occupations, covering theoretically equal status ranges, classified in terms of primary work function. Ten situs categories were proposed: Legal Authority; Finance and Records; Manufacturing; Transportation; Extraction; Building and Maintenance; Commerce; Arts and Entertainment; Education and Research; and Health and Welfare. In discussing the potential utility of this dimension of occupational structure we expressed the notion that:

> ". . . situses, as well as strata, form characteristic subcultures expressed in common values, norms, understandings, and attitudes . . . The basic prediction here is that the functional context of an occupation may make as much difference for the behavior or life style of the incumbent as the general prestige or socio-economic level of that occupation. As with strata, occupational situses may be expected to influence formal and informal group membership, common interests, goals, tastes, and so on."[8]

The use of the situs dimension provides us with a technique to assess the relative effect of *type* of work as well as socio-economic *level* on attitudes and behavior. By statistically controlling for one of these dimensions, one can observe whether the other has any effect.

As a means of testing the empirical relevance of this idea, we have selected two variables that are known to be related to occupational strata: subjective class identification and political party affiliation. Considerable literature has shown that both variables are related to the socio-economic position of individuals.[9] In general, as socio-economic level increases, identification with middle or upper class also increases and there is a greater likelihood for individuals to claim affiliation with the Republican party.

The problem we seek to explore here is the extent to which subjective class identification and political party affiliation are a function of the occupational *situs* of the individual. The relationship between these variables and socio-economic level has already been established. If we can demonstrate that situs makes a difference, *even when controlling for strata,* we can make a strong argument for the independent operation of the situs dimension.[10]

The data for our study are based on a secondary analysis of interview materials collected by Wendell Bell in four census tracts in San Francisco in 1953.[11] The tracts were selected so that they would vary widely in terms of economic and family characteristics, but would be essentially homogeneous in terms of nationality and racial characteristics. Within each of the four tracts area probability samples were drawn from a complete list of all residential dwellings in the area. The respondents were white males over the age of 21. A total of 701 interviews was obtained. In this paper the data for the four tracts were combined to comprise an analytic sample with respect to family and economic characteristics. The occupation of each respondent was classified into one of the 10 situs categories.[12] Two measures of socio-economic position were utilized: income and educational attainment. Because of the size of the sample and the occupational distribution, only four situs groups contained numbers sufficient for statistical analysis: Commerce, Finance and Records, Manufacturing, and Building and Maintenance. Accordingly,

[6] See the discussion of the Enterprise or institutional setting dimension in Donald E. Super, *The Psychology of Careers,* New York: Harper, 1957.

[7] Richard T. Morris and Raymond J. Murphy, "The Situs Dimension in Occupational Structure," *American Sociological Review,* 24 (April, 1959), pp. 231–239.

[8] *Ibid.,* p. 239.

[9] For subjective class identification see: Richard Centers, *The Psychology of Social Classes,* Princeton: Princeton University Press, 1949, pp. 110, 114, 202–204, 230; for party see: Heinz Eulau, "Perceptions of Class and Party in Voting Behavior: 1952," *American Political Science Review,* 49 (June, 1955), pp. 364–384; Angus Campbell, Gerald Gurin, and Warren E. Miller, *The Voter Decides,* Evanston, Ill.: Row, Peterson, 1954; Paul F. Lazarsfeld, Bernard Berelson, and Hazel Gaudet, *The People's Choice,* New York: Duell, Sloan and Pearce, 1944; Bernard R. Berelson, Paul F. Lazarsfeld and William N. McPhee, *Voting,* Chicago: University of Chicago Press, 1954.

[10] We do not mean to suggest here that there will be no range of opinion within an occupational group. Even the most ardent supporters of occupation as the "key" to human understanding are willing to admit other influences on attitudes and subjective perspectives.

[11] For a discussion of the sample, see Wendell Bell, "The Utility of the Shevky Typology for the Design of Urban Sub-Area Field Studies," *Journal of Social Psychology,* 47 (1958), pp. 71–83. The original study was sponsored by the Carnegie Corporation of New York and the Stanford University Committee for Research in the Social Sciences. We acknowledge with thanks the use of Professor Bell's interview schedules.

[12] The procedure for making this classification is described in Richard T. Morris and Raymond J. Murphy, *Theoretical Situs Location of Selected Occupations,* Department of Anthropology and Sociology, University of California, Los Angeles, 1959, 12 pp. (mimeo).

TABLE 1. Socio-economic strata and subjective class identification

	Income				Education			
	Under $4000	$4000–5999	$6000 and over	Total	Elem. educ.	H.S. educ.	College[a] educ.	Total
Middle class[b]	34%	31%	72%	50%	28%	52%	76%	50%
Working class	66	69	28	50	72	48	24	50
Total per cent	100	100	100	100	100	100	100	100
N	131	166	224	521	156	248	127	531
	$\chi^2 = 78.81$, df = 2, $P < .001$.				$\chi^2 = 66.96$, df = 2, $P < .001$.			

[a] Elementary education includes those who report no formal education, some elementary education, or completion of elementary education. High school education includes all those reporting from one to four years of high school. College education includes one to four years undergraduate work and graduate training.

[b] Class identification was measured by asking the respondent to choose one of the following words, "upper class, middle class, working class, lower class," to describe his class. Since only small numbers identified with upper or lower class, we report only on middle and working class responses.

we report situs differences among these four groups only.[13]

According to the theory of situs analysis, each situs should represent an equal range of status characteristics, i.e., each situs category should contain occupations which range from high to low on the income, education, prestige or other stratification scales. This does not mean that the *distribution* of occupations by income, etc. need be the same in each situs, but rather that the ranges be equally extended. In the present study, for example, respondents in the Commerce and Finance and Records situses tended to represent higher socio-economic levels than did those in the Building and Maintenance and Manufacturing situses. While only 6 per cent of those in Finance and Records had less than a high school education, 42 per cent of those in Building and Maintenance had a similar education level. As for income, 71 per cent of those in Commerce earned over $6,000, while only 34 per cent of those in Manufacturing earned this amount. It should be emphasized, however, that in each situs sufficient numbers of respondents were found at all levels to satisfy our theoretical requirements.

Socio-economic strata and subjective class identification

Based on the work of Centers and others, we expected to find, and did find (see Table 1), a correlation between socio-economic strata and subjective class identification, for both indicators: education and income. Those in higher socio-economic positions tend to identify with the middle class, while those in the lower positions typically indicate a working class identification.

[13] The Commerce situs is defined as including "all occupations primarily concerned with the buying, selling, exchange or marketing of goods or persons." Finance and Records includes "all occupations primarily concerned with the handling of monetary affairs or the processing of records, accounts or correspondence." Manufacturing includes "all occupations primarily concerned with the fabrication of articles or the processing of raw materials on a production-line basis." Building and Maintenance includes "all occupations primarily concerned with the construction of buildings or other non-massproduced units, or the installation, maintenance or repair of equipment, property or facilities."

Occupational situs and subjective class identification

We have suggested that situses form sub-cultures, based upon important contextual differences in work. One of these is the relative emphasis upon what is being worked on or with. Popularly, middle class membership has been associated with "clean," paper-people work, while working class membership has been associated with "dirty" manual work with tools. Even though there are non-manual occupations in the Manufacturing and Building and Maintenance situses, particularly in the higher strata, we expected that individuals in these situses would tend to identify with the working class because of closer contact with, past experience in, or control over, manual or tool work. Conversely, those engaged in the Finance and Records or Commerce situses are less apt in their daily rounds to be in close contact with or in supervision over manual work, and should therefore more closely identify themselves with the middle class. In Table 2, the relation between situs and subjective class identification is shown to be as expected.

Controlling for income, situs differences still persist, as shown in Table 3. To compare the extremes, 94 per cent of those in the Commerce situs who make under $4,000 per year identify with the middle class. Conversely, over half of those in the Building and Maintenance situs at the highest income level maintain a working class identification. In every group, with the exception of high-income Manufacturing, the majority identify with class according to the situs hypotheses at every income level.[14]

Controlling for education, situs differences are still apparent at the lower educational levels, but begin to disappear at the college level, as seen in Table 4. Why this should be is not known, particularly in view of the fact that situs differences in class identification do hold up at the highest income level. There may be

[14] When subjective class identification is examined by income levels *within* each situs, there is a significant difference in the expected direction in three out of four situses: the higher the income, the more the middle class identification. (Finance and Records: $x^2 = 4.90$, $P < .10$; Commerce: $x^2 = 9.34$, $P < .01$; Manufacturing: $x^2 = 17.66$, $P < .001$; Building and Maintenance: $x^2 = 17.58$, $P < .001$).

TABLE 2. Occupational situs and subjective class identification

	Commerce	Finance and Records	Manu-facturing	Bldg. and Maint.	Total
Middle class	81%	71%	38%	24%	50%
Working class	19	29	62	76	50
Total per cent	100	100	100	100	100
N	134	91	94	202	521
$\chi^2 = 125.55$, df = 3, $P < .001$.					

TABLE 3. Occupational situs and subjective class identification: income controlled

	Commerce	Finance and Records	Manu-facturing	Bldg. and Maint.	Total
Under $4000					
Middle class	94%	58%	30%	15%	34%
Working class	6	42	70	85	66
Total per cent	100	100	100	100	100
N	17	19	27	68	131
$\chi^2 = 34.19$, df = 3, $P < .001$.					
$4000–5999					
Middle class	60%	62%	19%	19%	31%
Working class	40	38	81	81	69
Total per cent	100	100	100	100	100
N	25	24	36	81	166
$\chi^2 = 28.93$, df = 3, $P < .001$.					
$6000 and over					
Middle class	84%	81%	68%	45%	72%
Working class	16	19	32	55	28
Total per cent	100	100	100	100	100
N	92	48	31	53	224
$\chi^2 = 27.23$, df = 3, $P < .001$.					

TABLE 4. Occupational situs and subjective class identification: education controlled

	Commerce	Finance and Records	Manu-facturing	Bldg. and Maint.	Total
Elementary education					
Middle class	73%	[a]	26%	13%	27%
Working class	27	[a]	74	87	73
Total per cent	100	[a]	100	100	100
N	26	[a]	39	85	150
$\chi^2 = 36.88$, df = 2, $P < .001$.					
High school education					
Middle class	85%	64%	40%	26%	52%
Working class	15	36	60	74	48
Total per cent	100	100	100	100	100
N	71	44	38	95	248
$\chi^2 = 59.87$, df = 3, $P < .001$.					
College education					
Middle class	81%	84%	65%	61%	76%
Working class	19	16	35	39	24
Total per cent	100	100	100	100	100
N	43	44	17	23	127
$\chi^2 = 6.40$, df = 3, $P < .10$.					

[a] Too few cases for χ^2 analysis.

something about moving into a job from the college level, e.g., in engineering, construction, etc., that prevents the usual association and socialization into situs attitudes that have a chance to operate in other mobility patterns typified by on-the-job training and experience.

Socio-economic strata and political affiliation

As indicated above, many empirical studies have found a consistent relationship between socio-economic level and political affiliation—the higher the level, the greater the Republican affiliation. The data from the

TABLE 5. Socio-economic strata and political affiliation

	Income				Education			
	Under $4000	$4000–5999	$6000 and over	Total	Elem. educ.	H.S. educ.	College educ.	Total
Republican[a]	36%	30%	60%	45%	33%	42%	67%	46%
Democrat	64	70	40	55	67	58	33	54
Total per cent	100	100	100	100	100	100	100	100
N	131	149	238	518	150	241	138	529
	$\chi^2 = 39.40$, df = 2, $P < .001$.				$\chi^2 = 36.72$, df = 2, $P < .001$.			

[a] The data here were obtained in answer to the question, "Generally what is your political preference?"

TABLE 6. Occupational situs and political affiliation

	Commerce	Finance and Records	Manu-facturing	Bldg. and Maint.	Total
Republican	69%	60%	36%	26%	45%
Democrat	31	40	64	74	55
Total per cent	100	100	100	100	100
N	139	94	92	193	518
$\chi^2 = 72.00$, df = 3, $P < .001$.					

TABLE 7. Occupational situs and political affiliation: income controlled

	Commerce	Finance and Records	Manu-facturing	Bldg. and Maint.	Total
Under $4000					
Republican	75%	50%	30%	26%	45%
Democrat	25	50	70	74	55
Total per cent	100	100	100	100	100
N	16	18	27	70	131
$\chi^2 = 9.86$, df = 3, $P < .02$.					
$4000–5999					
Republican	52%	43%	28%	20%	36%
Democrat	48	57	72	80	64
Total per cent	100	100	100	100	100
N	25	21	32	71	149
$\chi^2 = 11.00$, df = 3, $P < .02$.					
$6000 and over					
Republican	72%	69%	49%	35%	56%
Democrat	28	31	51	65	44
Total per cent	100	100	100	100	100
N	98	55	33	52	238
$\chi^2 = 14.02$, df = 3, $P < .01$.					

present study also show this relationship for both income and education, as indicated in Table 5.

Occupational situs and political affiliation

There is a prevalent public image that identifies the two major political parties as spokesmen of various occupational groups. Republicans in the popular mind represent the white collar worker and the businessman, while the Democrats stand up for the working man. Although these images are partly a reflection of perceived strata differences, we felt that situses should also vary in the degree to which the two parties are represented. Commerce and Finance and Records should be more Republican, Manufacturing and Building and Maintenance should be more Democratic. The results as shown in Table 6 are as expected.

Controlling for income, the situs differences in political affiliation still generally hold at each income level as shown in Table 7, although there is one reversal in the Finance and Records situs at the middle income level, with a predominance of Democrats in this group. To compare the extremes, 75 per cent of those in the Commerce situs who make under $4,000 per year are Republicans. On the other hand, 65 per cent of those in the Building and Maintenance situs who make $6,000 or over per year are Democrats.[15]

[15] When political affiliation is examined by income levels *within* each situs, there is no statistically significant difference shown, thus suggesting that situs is a better predictor of political affiliation than is socio-economic level.

TABLE 8. Occupational situs and political affiliation: education controlled

	Commerce	Finance and Records	Manu-facturing	Bldg. and Maint.	Total
Elementary education					
Republican	73%	[a]	24%	21%	31%
Democrat	27	[a]	76	79	69
Total per cent	100	[a]	100	100	100
N	26	[a]	37	81	144
$\chi^2 = 25.94$, df = 2, $P < .001$.					
High school education					
Republican	67%	51%	31%	22%	42%
Democrat	33	49	69	78	58
Total per cent	100	100	100	100	100
N	70	45	36	90	241
$\chi^2 = 36.10$, df = 3, $P < .001$.					
College education					
Republican	72%	67%	63%	61%	67%
Democrat	28	33	37	39	33
Total per cent	100	100	100	100	100
N	50	46	19	23	138
$\chi^2 = 1.08$, df = 3, $P < .80$.					

[a] Too few cases for χ^2 analysis.

Controlling for education, political affiliation seems to be associated with situs at the elementary and high school level, but again, as with class identification, the relationship disappears at the college level, as shown in Table 8. Perhaps the same *ex post facto* explanation applies: political socialization takes place in the educational setting or in any case prior to, rather than on the job for these college-trained people.

We have shown above that situs is related to subjective class identification and to political affiliation even when the socio-economic strata variables of income and education are controlled (with the exception of the college-educated respondents). In part this is a duplication of effects, since party affiliation is strongly related to class identification. As Centers has reported,[16] people who identify themselves with the middle class are more apt to be Republicans than those who say they are members of the working class. Table 9 indicates that this same relationship holds for our sample.

TABLE 9. Political affiliation and subjective class identification

	Working Class	Middle Class	Total
Republican	25%	63%	44%
Democrat	75	37	56
Total per cent	100	100	100
N	241	254	495
$\chi^2 = 69.63$, df = 1, $P < .001$.			

It is possible to view subjective class identification as a third stratification variable, in addition to income and education. If despite the strong relationship between class and party, we still find situs making a difference in political affiliation, while *controlling* for subjective class identification, we can make two points at once: that situs is predictive of political behavior, over and above both subjective and objective strata differences, and, secondly, that the relationship between class and party is not strong enough to prevent their use as separate effect variables. Results are shown in Table 10: situs is significantly related to party affiliation in both working class and middle class groups.

Summary and conclusion

The primary purpose of this paper was to investigate the effects of two dimensions of occupation, socio-economic level and situs classification, upon subjective class identification and political affiliation. We found additional support for the expected relationship between socio-economic level and the dependent variables and also found that situs was significantly related to both class and party, controlling for income and education. These findings suggest that occupational situs does exert an independent influence upon these aspects of behavior.

This finding is of some significance, since it supports the notion that the behavioral influences of an occupation may be tapped by more than one dimension. In the above quotations from Edwards and Anderson and Davidson, assumptions were made as to the effects of *type of work* on the individual's beliefs and actions. Interestingly enough, however, when these authors classify occupations for the purpose of demonstrating such influence, they typically consider not type of work *per se*, but the socio-economic level of the occupation. Thus any correlates reported are those of the socio-economic dimension. Through the use of the situs dimension, based on primary work function as measured through an analysis of what the worker does,

[16] Centers, *op. cit.*, p. 131.

TABLE 10. Occupational situs and political affiliation: subjective class identification controlled

	Commerce	Finance and Records	Manu-facturing	Bldg. and Maint.	Total
Middle class					
Republican	72%	66%	56%	42%	63%
Democrat	28	34	44	58	37
Total per cent	100	100	100	100	100
N	108	64	34	48	254
$\chi^2 = 14.16$, df = 3, $P < .01$.					
Working class					
Republican	54%	36%	26%	20%	25%
Democrat	46	64	74	80	75
Total per cent	100	100	100	100	100
N	24	25	53	139	241
$\chi^2 = 14.64$, df = 3, $P < .01$.					

the investigator is better able to assess the contributions of type of work to aspects of behavior. In our opinion, therefore, the use of the situs dimension represents a much more direct test of the influence of the nature of work than does a stratification classification.

There is no reason to believe that class and party are the most important correlates of occupational situs. It is possible that a number of other variables may show an even clearer relation to the primary function of work, for example: definitions of success, mobility perceptions and aspirations, alienation, types of mental disorder, rates of deviant behavior. We suggested in the earlier paper that the situs dimension may be important and have demonstrated in the present article that it is important, for two variables at any rate, but we still do not know why. To frame the question for discussion: What is there about occupational situs that makes a difference in behavior?

There are a number of possibilities that suggest themselves with regard to the present set of dependent variables. (1) Situs differences may simply be a carry-over from an earlier system of stratification. The old head-hands, or clean-dirty, hierarchy that operated most clearly prior to World War I has gradually shifted its axis until many white-collar and blue-collar jobs form parallel status ladders in income, prestige, and life style. Perhaps the old ideology lingers on, even after the objective conditions have changed. (2) Situs differences in class and party may be a function of differential rates and nature of unionization. It is probable that occupations in the Manufacturing and Building and Maintenance situses have been more strongly organized for a longer period of time than those in the Commerce or Finance and Records situses. This may well have an effect upon class identification and political affiliation. (3) It is possible that there is a differential distribution of entrepreneurial vs. bureaucratic jobs in the various situses. This may explain the greater tendency toward Republican party affiliation and middle class identification in the Commerce situs as compared with the Finance and Records situs, as shown above. The Manufacturing situs shows the same bias when compared with the Building and Maintenance situs for perhaps the same reason.[17] (4) The mobility characteristics of the various situses may help explain the class and party correlates. The Horatio Algers of our society typically have been squarely placed in Commerce or Finance and Records. The way to the top may be smoother and more clearly marked in some situses than in others. Given differential rates of mobility discouragement or ambiguity in each situs, political consequences should follow.

We have limited our analysis and discussion to only four of the ten situs categories. If we consider, for example, the political implications of belonging to the Arts and Entertainment situs as opposed to the Legal Authority situs, a number of speculations leap to mind, e.g., is there something about creative work which makes for more liberal attitudes as compared with work which involves a central concern with normative enforcement?

These alternative interpretations of why situs might operate as it does do not add up to any coherent or systematic theory of the effects of occupation on social behavior. Such a theory has not been developed as yet, but its construction, we believe, will be best carried out on three levels: first, a further extension of the empirical investigation of other correlates of situs; second, the further conceptualization and operationalizing of other aspects of occupation in addition to situs and stratum; and third, the enlargement and codification of imaginative insights into the nature of occupational effects through increasing use of intensive case studies of particular occupations, an area of research which has grown consistently in the past few years.

[17] The variable of self versus salaried employment may also help explain the fading of situs differences in the highest educational category on both political affiliation and subjective class identification, i.e., the highly educated self-employed are more apt to identify themselves as Republicans and with the middle class, than the salaried individuals with the same educational attainment. Thus any differences in the ratio of self to salaried employed in the various situses might obscure situs differences.

Replication

OCCUPATIONAL SITUS AND POLITICAL PREFERENCE

The research to be replicated for this problem will closely follow the design of the original study: first, classifying persons into various situs groupings; second, classifying those in each situs into similar income groupings; finally, comparing the differences in political party preferences among persons in different situses with similar incomes. To simplify the analysis, education as a control variable and class identification as a dependent variable have been omitted.

It should be noted that the use of income as a control variable is an integral part of the research design. The need to use a control variable arises because the average income of persons in a situs such as manufacturing, with its predominance of manual workers, is generally less than the average income in a situs such as legal authority, with its predominance of professional personnel. Consequently any overall comparison of persons in these two situses might reflect the effects of income. To eliminate this confounding feature, the control variable confines comparisons to persons in different situses with similar incomes, thus ruling out income as a possible explanation of situs differences.

One other feature of the design should be noted. Although Murphy and Morris present impressive evidence on situs differences controlling for education and income, the real and most critical test of their hypothesis would rest on examining whether *situs* effects override the effects of an individual's *status* as a blue-collar or white-collar worker. That is, they would have to show that blue-collar workers in white-collar situses more closely resemble white-collar workers in white-collar situses than blue-collar workers in blue-collar situses. The task of implementing such research is difficult simply because an enormously large sample would be necessary to obtain a sufficient number of blue-collar workers in white-collar situses. Nonetheless, the evidence they do present, and which we will replicate, suggests that if enough cases were available the influence of situs might be confirmed.

Hypothesis

1. State the political preferences (e.g., Republican or Democratic) you think predominate in the following situses even with income differences controlled: Commerce, Finance and Records, Manufacturing, and Building and Maintenance.

2. State similar hypotheses for any other situs which has a sufficient number of cases for analysis (as determined from step 1, Data Analysis).

Empirical indicators for this problem

13. Now classify your father's occupation according to the *purpose* of the organization or company for which he works. For example, if your father is a janitor for a bank circle *Finance and Records;* if he is an accountant for a shoe factory circle *Manufacturing.* If no group fits exactly, circle the one which comes closest:

    0. *Legal Authority:* Organizations primarily concerned with the formulation, arbitration, interpretation, or enforcement of the custody of law-breakers

    1. *Finance and Records:* Organizations primarily concerned with the handling of monetary affairs or the processing of records, accounts, or correspondence

    2. *Commerce:* Organizations primarily concerned with the buying, selling, exchange, or marketing of goods or persons

    3. *Manufacturing:* Organizations primarily concerned with the fabrication of articles or the processing of raw materials on a production-line basis

    4. *Transportation:* Organizations primarily concerned with the movement of persons or goods from one location to another

    5. *Extraction:* Organizations primarily concerned with the extraction, procurement, or production of raw materials

    6. *Building and Maintenance:* Organizations primarily concerned with the construction of buildings or other non-mass produced units, or the installation, maintenance, or repair of equipment, property facilities

    7. *Arts and Entertainment:* Organizations primarily concerned with the creation of art forms or with the provision of entertainment, recreation, information, or aesthetic satisfaction for the public

    8. *Education and Research:* Organizations primarily concerned with formal instruction or training or with the acquisition of knowledge as an end in itself.

    9. *Health and Welfare:* Organizations primarily concerned with the detection, prevention, or alleviation of illness, hazard, or distress

21. Please estimate to the nearest $1,000 your *father's* yearly income (as opposed to total family income). $______thousand dollars per year

30. Which of the following comes closest to your FATHER'S political preference:

    1. Socialist
    2. Liberal Democrat
    3. Conservative Democrat
    4. Liberal Republican
    5. Conservative Republican

Data analysis

1. *Sort* the code sheets on box 13 into the following situs groups:
   Finance and Records = 1
   Commerce = 2
   Manufacturing = 3
   Building and Maintenance = 6
   Any other situs *provided* there are at least 10 cases in that situs.

2. *Sub-sort* each situs on box 21 into the following income groups:
   High Income = 9 and above
   Low Income = 8 and below

3. *Tally* onto the tabulation form the political party preference of the father as indicated in box 30 for each situs and income group.

4. *Compute* the percentage Republican and Democratic in each situs-income group. Use the percentage tables in Appendix B to save time.

5. *Combine* the percent "Liberal Republican" and "Conservative Republican" and enter this percentage in the Summary Table (Table 2).

Lab report

Treat income as a "control variable" and focus on interpreting the comparison of people of similar incomes but in different situses. See the "Note on Interpreting Cause and Effect" in Appendix A and the article "How to Read a Table' in the Introduction.

References

Becker, Howard S., "The Professional Dance Musician and His Audience," *American Journal of Sociology*, 57 (September 1951), pp. 136–144.

Gold, Ray, "Janitors Versus Tenants: A Status-Income Dilemma," *American Journal of Sociology*, 57 (March 1952), pp. 486–493.

Lipset, Seymour, Martin Trow, and James Coleman, *Union Democracy*. Garden City, New York: Anchor Books, 1962, pp. 153–159.

Weinberg, S. Kirson and Henry Arond, "The Occupational Culture of the Boxer," *American Journal of Sociology*, 57 (March 1952), pp. 460–469.

Wilensky, Harold, "Mass Society and Mass Culture: Interdependence or Independence?" *American Sociological Review*, 29 (April 1964), pp. 173–197.

Name________________

Date________________

TABLE 1. Political preference of father by father's occupational situs and income level

FATHER'S POLITICAL PREFERENCE (Box 30)	OCCUPATIONAL SITUS (BOX 13)																			
	Finance = 1				Commerce = 2				Manufacturing = 3				Building = 6				=			
	Income High = 09 +		(Box 21) Low = 00 − 08		Income High = 09 +		(Box 21) Low = 00 − 08		Income High = 09 +		(Box 21) Low = 00 − 08		Income High = 09 +		(Box 21) Low = 00 − 08		Income High = 09 +		(Box 21) Low = 00 − 08	
	Tally	%	Tally	%	Tally	%	Tally	%	Tally	%	Tally	%	Tally	%	Tally	%	Tally	%	Tally	%
1 = Socialist																				
2 = Liberal Democrats																				
3 = Conservative Democrats																				
4 = Liberal Republicans																				
5 = Conservative Republicans																				
TOTAL		100 %		100 %		100 %		100 %		100 %		100 %		100 %		100 %		100 %		100 %
+ = (No info.)																				

TABLE 2. Percent Republican by occupational situs and income

Income group	Finance	Commerce	Manufacturing	Building	
High					
Low					

LABORATORY REPORT FOR PROBLEM ______________

Course or
Section ______________ Date ______________ Name ______________

HYPOTHESIS: ______________

SAMPLE: ______________

INDEPENDENT VARIABLE(S): ______________

DEPENDENT VARIABLE(S): ______________

OTHER FACTORS: ______________

LABORATORY REPORT FOR PROBLEM ______

SUMMARY OF FINDINGS: ______

DISCUSSION: ______

PROBLEM 10
MOBILITY

Social mobility, the movement of persons from one class to another, injects a degree of fluidity into the stratification structure of society. Research in this area has shattered the many myths that frequently attend so important an activity as movement within the economic system. Contrary to popular belief, it has been well established, for example, that the United States offered no greater possibility for mobility two generations ago than it does today; that industrialized societies—Japan, Great Britain, France, Denmark—have as much mobility as does the United States; and that even purportedly rigid caste systems, as in India or medieval China, are remarkably open in terms of the opportunities for mobility they provide (Lipset and Bendix, 1960). Given this amount of mobility, the appearance of new men in new positions and the decline of others, it is little wonder that each generation brings with it social change.

The uniformities in the data on national mobility, however, do not suggest that mobility is available to all persons in society and hence equally distributed throughout the social structure. Careful and extensive research has shown the existence of marked inequality. Individuals are more likely to be upwardly mobile if they lived in urban areas (Lipset and Bendix, 1960), come from families with high status (Caro and Pihlblad, 1964), and have parents who were vitally concerned about their occupational prospects (Kahl, 1953).

These findings, and others similar to them, are best interpreted as a means of identifying the conditions facilitating access to the channels of mobility—that is, to education, the major vehicle in most societies for maintaining past and prospective occupational gains. Usually the educated man is more likely to advance than the noneducated man. It is necessary to stress, however, that education is not a sufficient cause or a guarantee of upward mobility. Many persons who have access to educational channels of mobility never capitalize on their advantaged position. Therefore, one of the most interesting and important issues in the study of social mobility is to establish the factors facilitating educational success. One condition of success in school systems is certainly the complex biological and social trait called "intelligence." The more intelligent the individual, the more likely he will succeed (Sewell, Haller, and Straus, 1957; Sewell and Armer, 1966).

In the reading for the present problem, another social psychological characteristic is introduced to explain the process by which some persons with access to channels of mobility capitalize on their superior position and others with similar access do not. The characteristic is called "deferred gratification" and refers to a complex psychological pattern of seeking long-term goals, even at the cost of deferring immediate rewards. The rationale underlying the hypothesized relationship between educational achievement and deferred gratification is simply that success in school is often predicated on concentration, hard work, concerted study, and other patterns requiring an ability to renounce the disruptive pull of gratifying but short-term pursuits. Therefore, those persons capable of deferring gratification should also be most successful in school. To test this hypothesis, the author shows that deferred gratification in four areas—sex, consumption, affiliation, and aggression—is related to academic success as well as to another measure of achievement, occupational aspirations. As the data in the study illustrate, the deferred gratification argument is not meant to replace other explanations: it merely identifies the process by which the intelligent, the wealthy, the educated, translate their position into capital for mobility.

DEFERRED GRATIFICATION, SOCIAL CLASS, AND THE ACHIEVEMENT SYNDROME / *Murray A. Straus*

The theoretical and research literature on self-imposed postponement of gratifications or satisfactions is reviewed with emphasis on the relation of such a "Deferred Gratification Pattern" (DGP) to social class and social mobility. Three

Reprinted with permission of the author and publisher from *American Sociological Review*, 27 (June 1962), pp. 326–335.
Paper read at the 1961 Meeting of the American Sociological Association. This investigation was carried out with the aid of funds granted under National Institute of Mental Health, Research Grant No. M-4060 (A); and by the Department of Child Development and Family Relationships, Cornell University. I wish to express my appreciation to Edward C. Devereux Jr. and Harry Levin of Cornell University, and to Louis Schneider of the University of Illinois, for critical comments on an earlier draft.

hypotheses growing out of this review were tested on 338 male high school students. The hypothesis of a deferred gratification pattern received some support from the fact that scales with reproducibilities from .92 to .96 were developed for deferment of five adolescent needs (affiliation, aggression, consumption, economic independence, and sex); and by the intercorrelation of these scales. The hypothesis of positive correlation between socioeconomic status and DGP was not supported. The hypothesis of positive correlation between the DGP scales and achievement role-performance and role-orientation was supported. These relationships were not eliminated by controls for socioeconomic status and intelligence. Findings are interpreted as supporting the theory that need deferment is functional for social mobility in American society.

The term "deferred gratification pattern" was introduced by Schneider and Lysgaard to designate the phenomenon of "impulse-renunciation" or "self-imposed postponement of gratifications or satisfactions."[1] This phenomenon is one of the classic foci of sociological and social psychological analysis. For example, the concept of deferred gratification pattern substantially overlaps Max Weber's key concept of "inner-worldly asceticism." Similarly, Freud and his followers emphasized the early learning of impulse-renunciation (particularly sphincter control) as providing the foundation for the "acquisitive character structure" of the entrepreneur;[2] and Parsons' "instrumental orientation" is at one point defined in terms of renunciation of immediate gratifications in favor of disciplined seeking of larger future gains.[3]

Perhaps the most extensive contemporary sociological literature on the deferred gratification pattern (hereafter abbreviated as DGP) is to be found in attempts to understand social class and color differences in behavior, particularly the work of Davis, Dollard, Havighurst, Drake and Cayton, Hollingshead, and Lewis.[4] Dollard, for example, devotes considerable space to describing the relatively uninhibited aggressiveness and sexuality of the lower class, and the Negro lower class in particular. All of these studies point to the DGP as one of the major cultural and personality patterns which establish and maintain boundaries between social class and racial subsegments of American society. Similarly, Schneider and Lysgaard view the DGP as a middle class normative pattern. More important, the studies reviewed suggest that the ability to defer gratification is functional for movement into or maintenance of middle class status.[5]

An important recent treatment of the deferred gratification concept occurs in Miller and Swanson's *The Changing American Parent*.[6] They present data to show that the "entrepreneurial" occupational groups allow their children less immediate and complete satisfaction of basic physiological needs than do the contrasting "bureaucratic" groups. They interpret this denial and deferment as training which ". . . lays a foundation for teaching him that giving up immediate pleasures can lead to future gains" (page 40). They further speculate that as American society becomes increasingly mass-organization-dominated, training for self-denial, and the prevalence of persons who have internalized this pattern, will (and indeed ought to) decline. In effect, they argue that the DGP is anachronistic and dysfunctional in what they call our contemporary "welfare bureaucracy." Certainly, more evidence is needed before conclusions of this magnitude can be accepted.

Further studies of the DGP are also needed because of methodological limitations inherent in the studies cited. First, most of the literature is at the theoretical and case study levels of empiricism, and relatively few studies report quantitative data. Second, most of what quantitative data is available refers to the behavior of parents. The Miller and Swanson study, for example, contains no evidence of the *child's* impulse-renunciation. Similarly, although the data for Schneider and

[1] Louis Schneider and Sverre Lysgaard, "The Deferred Gratification Pattern: A Preliminary Study," *American Sociological Review*, 18 (April, 1953), pp. 142–149.

[2] Sigmund Freud, "Character and Eroticism," in *Collected Papers*, Vol. II, London: Hogarth, 1925; F. S. Perls, *Ego, Hunger, and Aggression*, London: George Allen & Unwin, 1947, Chapter 11.

[3] Talcott Parsons, *The Social System*, Glencoe, Ill.: Free Press, 1951, pp. 48–49.

[4] Allison Davis and John Dollard, *Children of Bondage*, Washington, D. C.: American Council on Education, 1940; Allison Davis and Robert J. Havighurst, "Social Class and Color Differences in Child-Rearing," *American Sociological Review*, 11 (December, 1946), pp. 698–710; St. Clair Drake and Horace R. Cayton, *Black Metropolis*, New York: Harcourt, Brace, 1945; John Dollard, *Caste and Class in a Southern Town*, New York: Harper, 1949; August B. Hollingshead, *Elmtown's Youth*, New York: Wiley, 1949; Oscar Lewis, *Five Families: Mexican Case Studies in the Culture of Poverty*, New York: Basic Books, 1959.

[5] This is most explicitly stated in studies of "time orientation" (e.g., past, present, and future) and social class. The concepts of "future orientation" and DGP overlap substantially since the idea of deferment, as here conceptualized, implies future satisfaction of the deferred need. See the studies reviewed in Melvin Wallace and Albert I. Rabin, "Temporal Experience," *Psychological Bulletin*, 57 (May, 1960), pp. 213–236; also Orville G. Brim, and Raymond Rorer, "A Note on the Relation of Values and Social Structure to Life Planning," *Sociometry*, 19 (March, 1956), pp. 54–60; Lawrence H. LeShan, "Time Orientation and Social Class," *Journal of Abnormal and Social Psychology*, 47 (July, 1952), pp. 589–592; Bernard C. Rosen, "The Achievement Syndrome: A Psycho-cultural Dimension of Social Stratification," *American Sociological Review*, 21 (April, 1956), pp. 203–211; and Fred L. Strodtbeck, "Family Interaction, Values, and Achievement," in David C. McClelland, *et al.*, *Talent and Society*, Princeton, N. J.: Van Nostrand, 1958, pp. 135–194.

A dissenting note is introduced by Beilin who views the deferment element in future time orientation studies as an interpretation ". . . the observer introduces to explain apparent differences in behavior although the actors themselves do not perceive . . . [deferment]. To the college going youth from the lower socio-economic classes, going to college involves the *gratification* of values he has developed rather than relinquishing of valued behavior." See Harry Beilin, "The Pattern of Postponability and its Relation to Social Class Mobility," *Journal of Social Psychology*, 44 (August, 1956), pp. 33–48. It will take carefully designed research to determine which of these imputed meanings tends actually to be experienced. Fortunately, resolution of this ambiguity concerning the subjective meaning experienced by the actors is not crucial for the central problems of this paper, namely, (1) whether middle class persons tend to choose temporally more distant goals and to control impulse expression to a greater degree than do other classes; and (2) whether the presence of such tendencies is related to achievement for both middle and lower socio-economic levels.

[6] Daniel R. Miller and Guy E. Swanson, *The Changing American Parent*, New York: Wiley, 1958.

Lysgaard's study were gathered from adolescents, a number of the items do not refer to the *adolescent's* deferment of gratification, but rather to the *parents'* deferment, or to the *parents'* demands for deferment on the part of the child.[7] Third, the quantitative evidence of relationship between DGP and social mobility is primarily for deferment of adolescent needs for economic independence as measured by delaying entry into the labor force in order to secure higher education. Since numerous studies of reasons for attending college have shown the primary motivation to be preparation for a desirable occupation, this evidence is open to the charge of circularity.[8] Fourth, Schneider and Lysgaard contend that the deferment of such diverse needs as those for affiliation, aggression, material goods, independence, and sex ". . . fall into a *pattern*. . . ." They imply that deferment of any one of these needs tends to be correlated with deferment of the others, particularly in the middle class. However, they present no direct evidence in support of the pattern concept. The data which they report simply relate discrete indicators of deferment to social class position, and no "pattern" is actually demonstrated.

This brief review of prior studies points up both the theoretical importance of the phenomenon of deferred gratification, and important empirical gaps and methodological problems in existing studies. The present study is intended to help fill some of these gaps by testing the following three interrelated hypotheses:

1. There is a general tendency to defer gratification which can be expressed as a unidimensional variable within and across five types of adolescent needs.
2. The higher the socioeconomic level, the greater the tendency to defer gratification.[9]
3. The greater the tendency to defer gratification, the higher the performance on two measures of the "achievement syndrome."

[7] These criticisms do not apply to the psychological literature on time orientation (see footnote 5) or to studies of preference for "delayed reinforcement." See especially the work of Walter Mischel in four articles forthcoming in the *Journal of Abnormal and Social Psychology,* and his "Preference for Delayed Reinforcement: An Experimental Study of a Cultural Observation," *Journal of Abnormal and Social Psychology,* 56 (January, 1958), pp. 57–61. Other research in this tradition includes: Alvin Mahrer, "The Role of Expectancy in Delayed Reinforcement," *Journal of Experimental Psychology,* 52 (August, 1956), pp. 101–105; Levon Melikian, "Preference for Delayed Reinforcement: An Experimental Study Among Palestinian Refugee Children," *Journal of Social Psychology,* 50 (August, 1959), pp. 81–86; and Jerome L. Singer, Harold Wilensky, and Vivian G. McGraven, "Delaying Capacity, Fantasy and Planning Ability: A Factorial Study of Some Basic Ego Functions," *Journal of Consulting Psychology,* 20 (October, 1956), pp. 375–383.

[8] The Kinsey data showing that the *pre-mobility* sexual behavior of socially mobile persons tends to resemble the sexual patterns of the strata of destination, are not subject to this charge. See Alfred C. Kinsey, Wardell B. Pomeroy, and Clyde E. Martin, *Sexual Behavior in the Human Male,* Philadelphia: Saunders, 1948, Chapter 11; and Alfred C. Kinsey, *et al., Sexual Behavior in the Human Female,* Philadelphia: Saunders, 1953, pp. 182 and 338.

[9] With the exception of groups comparable to Warner's "upper-upper class." This exception will not be tested due to limitation of the sample. It is indicated here to make explicit this limitation of the study. This qualification is based on the theoretical reasoning that deferred gratification has little or no function in preserving or acquiring class status for the top group; it is also based on the many suggestions in the stratification literature indicating that the upper class neither values nor practices gratification deferment to the same extent as the middle class.

Since it is known that achievement orientation increases with both socioeconomic status and intelligence,[10] zero order relationships in support of the third hypothesis could be interpreted as a function of socioeconomic status, intelligence, or both. Consequently, in testing Hypothesis 3, both SES and intelligence will be controlled.

Sample and method

Data to test these hypotheses were obtained from school records and by questionnaire. The sample consists of 338 boys attending the junior and senior classes of the four high schools of one Wisconsin county in the last week of March, 1950.[11]

Five adolescent needs were chosen for study: the need for affiliation, aggression, consumption, economic independence, and sexual expression.[12] For each of

[10] For evidence on this point, see, for example, Bernard C. Rosen, *op. cit.,* and William H. Sewell, Archibald O. Haller, and Murray A. Straus, "Social Status and Educational and Occupational Aspiration," *American Sociological Review,* 22 (February, 1957), pp. 67–73.

[11] Of the 490 boys enrolled, 41 were lost to the study because of absence during the interview week, and another 121 because of incomplete school record or questionnaire data. The county studied is adjacent to the city of Milwaukee. It contains a considerable variety of within-county industry, as well as farmers (approximately one-quarter of the sample), and residents who commute to Milwaukee for employment. Forty-five per cent of the sample are sons of blue collar workers, including 20 per cent sons of semiskilled or unskilled workers. Nevertheless, it should be noted that any sampling of youth using the high school as the primary sampling unit underrepresents the lower socioeconomic levels. This results from differential school leaving and differential absentee rates. This underrepresentation of the lowest socioeconomic levels stacks the cards against finding support for the hypotheses posed. However, if the hypotheses are supported, they can be interpreted as probably understating the true difference between socioeconomic groups.

TABLE 1. Deferred gratification scales for five adolescent needs

Deferment scale	Score range	Rep.
Affiliation	0–3	.93
Aggression	0–4	.93
Consumption	0–3	.92
Independence	0–3	.96
Sex	0–4	.95

[12] Ideally, these should represent universal human needs, or as a second best, needs that are known to be general in the society studied. Clearly, the sexual and affiliative need categories meet the universality criteria. Many sociologists and psychologists would also include aggression in this group. See, for example, the treatment of control of aggression as a universal step in socialization in Robert R. Sears, Eleanor F. Maccoby, and Harry Levin, *Patterns of Child Rearing,* Evanston, Ill.: Row, Peterson, 1957; also, Norman Livson and Wanda C. Bronson, "An Exploration of Patterns of Impulse Control in Early Adolescence," *Child Development,* 32 (March, 1961), pp. 75–88; and Bryon Sutton-Smith and B. G. Rosenberg, "A Scale to Identify Impulsive Behavior in Children," *Journal of Genetic Psychology,* 95 (December, 1959), pp. 211–216. The needs for material goods and services (consumption) and for economic independence are more culture-specific, and

these needs, four items designed to indicate deferment of the need were included in the questionnaire. For example, one of the items used to tap aggressive needs was "Since school started last fall, how many of your arguments have led to fights? None, One or Two, Three or more." Using these items, gratification deferment scales were computed with the ranges and reproducibilities presented in Table 1.[13]

Unidimensionality of deferred gratification

The coefficients of reproducibility shown in Table 1 provide at least minimal evidence in support of that part of the first hypothesis which specifies that a general tendency to defer gratification exists as a unidimensional variable within each of these five types of adolescent needs. However, this evidence is not impressive since, with three and four item scales, the possibility of obtaining reproducibilities of this size by chance alone must be borne in mind. Thus, the limitations of the data available permit no broader conclusion than the statement that the findings of the study do not refute the idea of unidimensionality for each of these kinds of need deferment.

Hypothesis 1 also specifies a tendency for deferment of any one of these needs to be related to deferment of the others. To test this hypothesis, the intercorrelation of the five deferred gratification scales was computed. The results are presented in Table 2.

TABLE 2. Intercorrelations of deferred gratification scales (N = 338)

Deferment scale	Total DGP[a]	Aggr.	Sex	Affil.	Cons.
Aggression	.65				
Sex	.61	.21[b]			
Affiliation	.53	.08	.14[b]		
Consumption	.43	.05	−.03	.03	
Econ. independence	.21	.09[c]	.01	.16[b]	.24[b]

[a] Coefficients in this column are inflated because the Total DGP Scale is the sum of the first four scales listed. The correlations are presented here simply to provide an indication of internal consistency for the Total DGP Scale.
[b] P≤.01 (one-sided tests).
[c] P≤.05.

The correlations enclosed within the upper left triangle of Table 2 indicate that deferment of sexual needs tends to be associated with a small but statistically significant tendency also to defer affiliative and aggressive needs. The consumption deferment scale on the other hand, is significantly correlated with the economic independence scale, but not with any of the first three scales. The correlation matrix, therefore, shows a tendency for the deferred gratification scales to fall into two clusters, one representing deferment of interpersonal interaction needs, and the other representing deferment of material needs.

It is concluded that this study does provide some evidence in support of the hypothesis predicting a deferred gratification pattern or generalized disposition to defer need satisfaction. However, this conclusion carries two important qualifications. First, there seem to be two deferred gratification patterns rather than one. Secondly, the correlations within each of these two factors, while statistically significant, are low, indicating relatively little common trait variance. However, in view of the crudity of the measures employed, they are at least sufficient to support the theory under test.

Additional support for the pattern hypothesis comes from the results of attempting to combine the separate need deferment scales into a Total DGP Scale. This scale was constructed primarily to enable an overall test of Hypothesis 3 without the cumbersome calculations involved in a five variable multiple correlation.[14]

nothing is claimed for them beyond their prevalence in the youth culture of contemporary United States. See in this connection Ruth C. Strang, *The Adolescent Views Himself,* New York: McGraw-Hill, 1957.

[13] In constructing these scales, an attempt has been made to use only items that deal with the respondent's specific deferment actions or beliefs. However, the third item in the Aggression Scale (see below) does not meet this criterion. Moreover, it would have been preferable to avoid mixing what Brim calls "role prescription" with "role performance" type items, since there is no empirical evidence that both can serve as indicators of the same phenomenon. (See Orville G. Brim, "Parent-Child Relations as a Social System: I. Parent and Child Roles," *Child Development,* 28 [September, 1957], pp. 343–364.) It should be obvious, then, that these scales are not presented as instruments for general use, and that research is needed on the development of techniques for the measurement of DGP and related phenomena. In this connection, the work of Mischel, *op. cit.,* is particularly promising, since it almost completely avoids the difficulties inherent in self-report based measures such as are used in this paper.

The items comprising the scale used in this paper are: 1. *Affiliation.* "For the most part, I enjoy being together with friends who come from families at least as nice and successful as my own, rather than being together with just anybody." (Agree = 57%); "I have certain standards which my friends must meet." (Yes = 59%); "Teenagers have to be careful about the behavior of the crowd they go with." (Yes = 90%); 2. *Aggression.* "When I get angry at a person, I generally prefer . . ." (To let my temper quiet down before I try to settle the argument = 61%); "Since school started last fall, how many of your arguments have led to fights?" (None = 70%); "Since last fall, how many adult arguments have you seen end in a real fight?" (None = 79%); "From what you have experienced, who would you say usually wins in settling arguments?" (The smart and tactful = 91%); 3. *Consumption.* "Money is made to spend not save." (Disagree = 60%); "Nowadays with world conditions the way they are, the wise person lives for today and lets tomorrow take care of itself." (Disagree = 72%); "The money I save gives me at least as good a feeling as things I buy." (Not sure or agree = 84%); 4. *Economic Independence.* "How much education do you definitely plan to get?" (College degree or higher = 30%); "If a fellow can get a good job when he graduates from high school, he is foolish to go to college." (Disagree = 82%); 5. *Sex.* "I think the ideal age for a boy to marry is:" (Age 25 or older = 10%); "Girls would rather go out with boys who do not try to make love until they have been going steady for at least a month." (Yes = 35%); "People usually fear going too far while out on a date." (Yes = 59%); "A boy has as much responsibility as a girl in seeing that necking does not go too far." (Agree = 87%).

[14] Guttman states: "If an area is scalable . . . the simple correlation of any outside variable with the [scale] is equivalent to the multiple correlation on the [items] . . ." See "Questions and Answers about Scale Analysis," Report No. D-2, I. and E. Division, Army Service Forces, Washington, D. C., July, 1945.

This was accomplished by treating each scale as a dichotomous item. The resulting scale has a coefficient of reproducibility of .92, and therefore provides some additional evidence in favor of the pattern hypothesis.[15]

Socioeconomic status and deferred gratification

For purpose of testing Hypothesis 2, which specifies a positive association between socioeconomic status and tendency to defer gratification, each student was scored on a seven item socioeconomic status scale.[16] The correlations of this scale with the five specific need deferment scales and the Total DGP Scale are presented in Table 3. These coefficients show that the deferment of aggressive, sexual, and consumption needs by this sample of adolescent boys is unrelated to the socioeconomic status of the boy's family of orientation. Deferment of affiliative needs does tend to increase slightly as socioeconomic status increases. This is probably the result of the first affiliation item (see footnote 12), which, hindsight reveals, has a built in "class bias." This is enough to introduce a correlation between the affiliation deferment scale and SES. However, when the affiliation scale is combined with the aggression, sex, and consumption scales to form the Total DGP Scale, the influence of this one item is slight. The Total DGP Scale is therefore shown in Table 3 to be unrelated to SES.[17]

TABLE 3. Correlation between socioeconomic status and gratification deferment scales

Deferment scale	Correlation with SES (N = 338)
Affiliation	.12[a]
Aggression	−.02
Sex	−.04
Consumption	.04
Econ. independence	.26[a]
Total DGP scale	.04

[a] $P \leq .01$ (one-sided tests).

There remains only the Economic Independence Scale. This scale was omitted from the Total DGP Scale because of the tautology involved in correlating desire for prolonged education with measures of occupational aspiration and academic achievement (see footnote 14). The correlation of the Economic Independence deferment scale with SES is also information of little value since the variable measured is confounded with SES. This results from the fact that a boy's deferment of his needs for economic independence is in large part dependent on the ability of the parents to maintain him as a dependent through a college education. Consequently, it is likely that the correlation between SES and the Economic Independence deferment scale shown in Table 3 is largely a result of differential ability to afford prolonged dependence on parents.[18]

[15] The primary purpose of this Total DGP Scale is to provide an instrument for testing relationship to the achievement syndrome. The Economic Independence Scale was therefore omitted, since there is a tautology involved in correlating plans for prolonged education (the essential content of this scale) with, for example, occupational aspiration. Cutting points used to dichotomize each component scale are as follows: Sex: scale type III or higher = 29%; Consumption: III or higher = 41%; Affiliation: II or higher = 79%; and Aggression: II or higher = 90%. However, to provide a more normally distributed and less attenuated variable for use in correlation analysis, the simple sum of the four component scales was employed rather than the scale type scores. This procedure was felt justified because, as Guttman notes, "If an area is scalable, then arbitrary weights . . . will yield the proper scale order." See "Questions and Answers about Scale Analysis," *op. cit.*

[16] This is a Guttman scale, with a coefficient of reproducibility of .91. The items comprising the scale, in order of decreasing marginal frequency, are: Family income $4,000 or higher; possession of five or more of a list of ten level-of-living items; father has at least some high school education; mother high school graduate or more; paternal grandfather professional, proprietor or manager; and maternal grandfather professional, proprietor or manager.

The choice of this scale as the measure of SES was based on results of previous analyses which indicated it to be a more sensitive measure than any available alternatives, such as father's occupation. Correlations subsequently computed support this decision. For example, the correlation between the SES Scale and the two dependent variables of this paper are shown below, along with the correlations for five single dimensional indicators of SES:

SES measure	*Correlation with:* Academic achievement	Occupational aspiration
SES scale	.28	.30
Mother's education	.25	.25
Father's occupation	.20	.23
Father's education	.16	.23
Family income	.17	.09
Items possessed from list of ten	.00	.01

It can be seen that the SES Scale yields higher correlations than any of the single indicators of SES. See, however, footnote 17.

[17] The tables were examined for possible curvilinear relationships which, of course, would produce low or zero product-moment correlations, and none was found. In a further effort to check on the unanticipated lack of relationship between SES and DGP, the hypothesis was re-tested using five other indicators of SES: father's occupational prestige rating (as measured by the Empey modification of the North-Hatt and Smith Scales. See LaMar T. Empey, "Social Class and Occupational Aspirations: A Comparison of Absolute and Relative Measurement," *American Sociological Review*, 21 [December, 1956], pp. 703–709), father's education, mother's education, level of living index, and family income. Except for mother's education and father's occupation, correlations were almost always lower than those in Table 3. The coefficients for mother's education (in the order in which they appear in Table 3) are: .18, .05, .04, .10, .30, and .16; and for father's education: .11, .10, .00, .02, .27, and .10. It can be seen that mother's education yielded higher correlations with five of the DGP scales, and father's occupation with three of the scales; but the differences are not large. Since, as noted in footnote 16, the SES Scale appears to have a somewhat higher validity than any of the single factor indicators, it was decided to retain the SES scale as the measure of SES used in the remainder of the analysis.

[18] The correlation between social status and educational plans is already well documented and conceptualized, and little seems to be gained by conceptualization in terms of deferred gratification. See the studies cited in William H. Sewell, Archie O. Haller, and Murray A. Straus, "Social Status and Educational and Occupational Aspiration," *American Sociological Review*, 22 (February, 1957), pp. 67–73.

Except in the dubious area of economic independence, the findings of this study provide no evidence in support of the hypothesis of positive correlation between SES and deferred gratification. These negative results are probably, at least in part, a function of the attenuated SES composition of the sample and the fact that the sample excludes those who have dropped out of school. They cannot, therefore, be interpreted as refuting findings based on data for such truly poverty-stricken groups as Davis, Havighurst, Dollard, Drake and Cayton, and Lewis studied. However, this sample is reasonably comparable to the populations studied by Hollingshead, and by Schneider and Lysgaard; yet the findings seem to be contradictory. Closer examination reveals only minimal contradiction, since almost all of the significant associations between SES and need deferment items reported by Hollingshead and Schneider and Lysgaard fall into the category here labeled Economic Independence. The present study also finds that Economic Independence is related to SES.

Hollingshead's and Schneider and Lysgaard's findings for other need areas either: (1) agree with those of the present study in finding no association with SES (for example the sex items in the Schneider and Lysgaard study); (2) are conflicting (for example, Hollingshead, who indicates that the lowest SES groups do not defer sexual needs by late marriage, but that the upper groups "exploit" lower class girls sexually); (3) represent trivial amounts of covariance (for example, Schneider and Lysgaard's data on deferment of aggressive needs); or (4) report parents' rather than children's behavior (as in Schneider and Lysgaard's data on table manners).

Indicators of the achievement syndrome

Two measures are used in this study to index what Rosen has aptly termed "the achievement syndrome."[19] These measures and the rationale for their choice are as follows:

Academic achievement. High school grades were selected as an indication of the boys' current level of actual achievement, since they represent perhaps the most important instrumental activity that adolescent boys are called upon to perform in American society.[20]

Despite the importance of academic performance it is well known that such performance is only a very imperfect indicator of either achievement disposition or later actual achievement. Therefore, to provide another test of the hypothesis that deferred gratification is functionally related to achievement, a measure designed to indicate presence or absence of achievement orientation is employed:

Occupational aspiration. If academic achievement is to be translated into actual achievement, as socially defined, the boy must internalize culturally appropriate achievement goals or aspirations. One index of such aspirations is provided by the occupation stated in response to the question "What job do you think you will actually make your life's work?" These occupations were coded by use of the Empey modification of the North-Hatt and Smith occupational prestige scales to provide a measure of occupational aspiration.[21]

Deferred gratification and achievement

The correlations of the four need deferment scales and the Total DGP Scale with the measures indexing the achievement syndrome, are shown in Table 4.[22]

TABLE 4. Correlations between deferred gratification and achievement measures

Need deferred	Correlation (r) with: Academic achievement	Occupational aspiration
Affiliation	.21[a]	.18[a]
Aggression	.15[a]	.19[a]
Consumption	.16[a]	.10[b]
Sex	.08	.03
Total DGP	.26[a]	.23[a]

[a] p≤.01 (one-sided tests).
[b] p≤.05.

It can be seen that each of the deferred gratification measures, except sexual deferment, tends to be correlated with the achievement measures. These correlations are low but statistically significant. As expected, the largest correlations are with the Total DGP Scale, since use of this scale represents an approximation to the multiple correlation of the four component scales. Table 4, then, provides evidence in support of the hypothesis of positive relation between deferred gratification and achievement, particularly if the combined effect of deferment of all four needs is considered.[23]

The correlations in Table 4 may be interpreted as providing evidence of functional interrelation between

[19] Bernard C. Rosen, "The Achievement Syndrome," *op. cit.*

[20] In computing this measure, grades for physical education and driver training were omitted but vocational subjects were included. To standardize for school-to-school variation in grading system and standards, the grade point average distribution for each school and class was normalized using the Sten score system. This provides a variable ranging from 0 to 9, with each step in the scale representing one-half standard deviation above or below the mean.

[21] See LaMar T. Empey, *op. cit.*

[22] The Economic Independence Scale is omitted due to the tautology inherent in correlating this score with measures of academic performance and occupational aspiration as noted in footnote 14. These coefficients, however, were computed and, of course, are considerably higher than those shown for the other scales.

[23] No explanation for the failure of sexual deferment to follow the same pattern as the other three types of deferment has as yet been formulated. In view of the fact that previous studies have found significant relationships between sexual deferment and social mobility, one likely explanation is invalidity of the scale due to the circumspect sexual deferment items to which the study was limited by virtue of being administered through the school system. See Kinsey, *et al., op. cit.*, and Frank A. Linderfeld, "A Note on Social Mobility, Religiosity, and Students' Attitudes Towards Premarital Sexual Relations," *American Sociological Review,* 25 (February, 1960), pp. 81–84.

DGP and the achievement syndrome. Specifically, learning to defer any one of these needs except sex may be viewed as providing a prototype for the future-oriented behavior needed for achievement in American society. The increase in the correlation resulting from the Total DGP Scale further suggests that the larger the number of needs the boy has learned to defer, the more potent the behavioral model, and hence the greater the achievement potential.[24]

A controlled analysis

Although SES was found to be essentially unrelated to DGP in this study, the first rows of Table 5 show

TABLE 5. Total, multiple, and partial correlation analysis for the relationship of SES, intelligence, and deferred gratification to two achievement measures[a]

Independent variables	Correlation (r) with: Academic achievement[b]	Occupational aspiration[b]
SES	.25	.34
Intelligence	.59	.42
DGP	.26	.23
DGP (intel. and SES held constant)	.48	.23
Intel. plus SES	.59	.45
Intel. plus SES plus DGP	.71	.51

[a] The full matrix of intercorrelations of the variables used in this table is given in this or previous tables and footnotes, except for the following: Intelligence with DGP = .16, and Academic Achievement with Occupational Aspiration = .40.

[b] All correlations are significant ($P \leq .01$).

that SES *is* importantly related to both achievement measures, as is also intelligence.[25] Moreover, intelligence tends to be slightly related to the need deferment measures. This raises the possibility that the relationships between DGP and achievement are really due to the covariance of both independent and dependent variable with intelligence. To explore this possibility, partial correlations were computed between the Total DGP Scale and the dependent variables, in each case holding constant both SES and intelligence.[26] These coefficients are shown in the fourth row of Table 5. By comparing the partial coefficients with the zero order coefficients in the third row, one can see that holding SES and intelligence in one case increases, and in the other does not alter, the magnitude of the correlation between DGP and achievement.[27] Thus, the results of this partial correlation analysis provide further support for Hypothesis 3, since they show that even when that portion of the variance in achievement that is associated with SES and intelligence is partialed out, there is still a significant relationship between DGP and achievement.

The independent contribution of deferred gratification to achievement can also be shown by comparing successively higher order multiple correlations. Row five of Table 5 shows the combined relation of SES and intelligence to achievement. The coefficients in the bottom row show that addition of the deferred gratification pattern measure to the equation accounts for a significantly larger proportion of the explained variance in the two achievement measures than is obtained by the use of SES and intelligence alone.[28]

[24] The fact that the correlations are low reflects the dependence of academic achievement and occupational aspiration on many other factors in addition to those represented by the DGP scales, and particularly intelligence. In a theoretical analysis such as this, low correlations (provided they are not chance artifacts) are a secondary consideration, unless, of course, the theory under test is both deterministic, necessary, and sufficient. See Hans L. Zetterberg, *On Theory and Verification in Sociology*, New York: Tressler Press, 1954.

[25] As measured by the Henmon-Nelson test, with raw scores normalized into "Sten" score distributions for the population, see V. A. C. Henmon and M. J. Nelson, *The Henmon-Nelson Test of Mental Ability*, Boston: Houghton Mifflin, 1942.

[26] SES is employed in the multiple and partial correlation analysis despite the non-significant relation with DGP because of its correlation with the dependent variables, and in order to act as a "suppressant." See Quinn McNemar, *Psychological Statistics*, Second edition, New York: Wiley, 1955, pp. 188–189.

[27] The theoretical basis of the study, together with the results of another similar analysis, suggested a reason for this increase. Assume that the factors supporting the achievement syndrome can be divided into two groups: cultural and economic means, and intrapsychic organization. On the one hand, it can be reasoned that the relationship between DGP and achievement should decline as SES increases because the cultural and economic means needed for achievement are more readily accessible to the upper groups almost regardless of personality (see Sewell, Haller, and Straus, *op. cit.*, for evidence on this point). On the other hand, it also seems likely that among the low SES groups, the difficulty of access to these cultural and economic means exerts a depressing effect which interferes with a boy's making full use of his potentialities. The middle SES group, on the other hand, has access to the cultural and economic means necessary for achievement, but not such ready access that intrapsychic organization becomes relatively unimportant. These considerations lead to the hypothesis that the highest correlation between DGP and achievement is found among the middle SES group. To test this hypothesis, the sample was divided into a low, middle, and high SES group. Correlations between DGP and achievement variables were then computed separately for each SES group. The results supported the reasoning just presented: The highest correlations between DGP and achievement variables occur for the middle group, followed by the low SES group; and the lowest correlations occur in the high SES group. The effect of partialing out SES, then, is to prevent the low relationship between DGP and achievement for the high SES part of the sample from obscuring the higher relationships found elsewhere in the sample. For another example of this type of relationship, see Murray A. Straus and Allan J. Estep, *Education For Technological Change Among Wisconsin Farmers*, Madison, Wisconsin: Wisconsin Agricultural Experiment Station Research Bulletin 214, 1959.

[28] The formula for testing the significance of the increment stemming from the addition of another variable to a multiple correlation is given in footnote 3 of David R. Saunders, "Moderator Variables in Prediction," *Educational and Psychological Measurement*, 16 (Summer, 1956), pp. 209–222. In the case of the addition of the third predictor variable, this formula becomes:

$$t = \sqrt{\frac{N-4(R^2 1.234 - R^2 1.23}{1-R^2 1.23}}$$

Using this formula, all coefficients shown in row six of Table 5 are significantly different from those shown in row five with probabilities of less than .001.

Testing the significance of difference between correlation coefficients usually assumes that the coefficients were observed in different samples. Such an assumption is obviously impossible for the present purpose. In response to an inquiry concerning

Summary and conclusions

This study investigated the tendency to postpone gratification of five adolescent needs among a sample of 338 male high school students, with particular emphasis on socioeconomic status as an antecedent variable, and achievement as a consequence variable.

Of the five adolescent needs chosen for study, all proved scalable. Correlations between the five scales, although low, suggest two rather than one "deferred gratification pattern": The Affiliation, Aggression, and Sex scales form one cluster, indicative of tendencies to defer interpersonal needs. The Consumption and Economic Independence scales form a second cluster, representing tendencies to defer *material* needs. At the same time, the specific need deferment scales were found to constitute a general Deferred Gratification Pattern Scale, with a reproducibility of .92. The hypothesis of a deferred gratification *pattern* was therefore judged to be supported by these data, but with important qualifications.

Except for deferment of needs for economic independence, no evidence was found in support of the hypothesis of positive correlation between SES and deferred gratification. Possible reasons for these negative results were discussed, including the nature of the population studied, and over-generalization from the economic independence area in previous studies.

Although deferred gratification was not found to be related to SES in this population, each of the specific need deferment scales, except sexual deferment, was found to be significantly correlated with measures of achievement role performance and role disposition. A partial correlation analysis, holding constant SES and intelligence, showed the relation of the DGP Scale to achievement to persist independently of these two factors. Similar results were obtained by multiple correlation. That is, SES and intelligence accounted for a considerable proportion of the variance in achievement, but addition of the DGP Scale to the equation resulted in a significant increase in the proportion of achievement variance accounted for in this population.

It is concluded that the results of this study provide at least some evidence in support of a general deferred gratification pattern, but fail to support the view that this is a peculiarly middle-class normative pattern.[29] Learning to defer need gratification seems to be associated with achievement at all levels of the status hierarchy represented in this sample, and hence can probably best be interpreted as one of the personality prerequisites for achievement roles in contemporary American society.

Replication

DEFERRED GRATIFICATION, ACADEMIC ACHIEVEMENT, AND ACHIEVEMENT ORIENTATION

The replication for this problem will simplify the original study by concentrating on the relationship of deferred gratification to achievement orientation and grade-point average. Considerations of the contribution of intelligence to mobility are omitted. It should be noted that the original study handles the overlap of the independent and dependent variables with socioeconomic status by using "partial correlations." This is a technique for examining the strength of a relationship between two variables by statistically controlling or "partialling out" the effects of a third variable. Since the calculation of a partial correlation requires considerable statistical sophistication, our replication will use the more straightforward technique of subdividing the sample into roughly equivalent socioeconomic status groups and then examining the relationship between deferred gratification and mobility indicators within each of these status groups.

Hypothesis

1. State whether grade-point averages and achievement orientation will be higher among a high deferred gratification group or a low deferred gratification group.
2. State whether the relationships hypothesized above will be different in any way within the following three social class groups: "Upper Middle," "Lower Middle," and "Working Class." (The procedure you will use to test this hypothesis is to repeat the analysis done for Hypothesis 1 for each of the three social class groups. This is an example of use of a third variable as a "control." See "Note on Interpreting Cause and Effect" in Appendix A for a discussion of control variables.)
3. See Appendix A for general information on writing a hypothesis.

the rationale of this formula, Saunders notes: "Remember that t is also the square root of F, when the numerator has just one degree of freedom. The F involved in the present instance is the ratio of the variance per degree of freedom accounted for by the addition of one more constant to the regression equation divided by the variance per degree of freedom still unpredicted. It does not matter whether the new constant belongs to a linear or a product term or what—it is still just one constant, and so the number of degrees of freedom is one and appears implicitly in the denominator of the formula. You will see that the formula could *only* apply when the correlations *are* from the same sample and would break down in case two samples were involved."

[29] It must again be noted that the sample studied virtually excludes the "lower-lower" class, who best represent the "impulse-following" as opposed to the deferment pattern. But while the lower-lower vs. the upper-middle probably represents the most crucial comparison, the literature reviewed also suggests that similar differences of lesser magnitude should be evident in less extreme comparisons such as those reported in this paper.

Empirical indicators for this problem

12. Occupational Prestige:

    1. Proprietor of a large business (valued at $100,-000 or more); Top-level executive in large organization; Top-level professional
    2. Proprietor of a medium business (valued at $35,000 to $100,000); Middle-level executive or official, or top-level of a small organization; Lower-level professional; Sales representatives of manufacturers or wholesalers or other senior salesmen earning $10,000 or more per year; Farmer of farm worth $100,000+
    3. Proprietor of a small business (valued at $6,000 to $35,000); Lower-level official and manager; Semi-professional; Sales representative (as above) earning $7,000 to $10,000 per year; Farmer of farm worth $35,000 to $100,000
    4. Proprietor of a very small business (valued under $6,000); Technician; Sales clerk and salesman earning less than $7,000 per year and clerical workers; Farmer of farm worth $15,000 to $35,000
    5. Farmer of farm worth under $15,000; Skilled manual worker and foreman
    6. Farmer, sharecropper or tenant with little stock or equipment; semi-skilled worker and machine operator
    7. Unskilled worker

48. During my last year of high school, my grade average was:

    0. D– or lower
    1. D
    2. C–
    3. C
    4. C+
    5. B–
    6. B
    7. B+
    8. A–
    9. All or almost all A's

49. If a person didn't meet certain standards I didn't have too much to do with him (or her) even if I liked the person:

    0. Never
    1. Sometimes
    2. Frequently
    3. Usually
    4. Always

50. When you got angry with a person that year, to what extent did you prefer to let your temper quiet down before trying to settle the argument:

    0. Never
    1. Sometimes
    2. Frequently
    3. Usually
    4. Always

51. When you were a high school senior, to what extent did the money you saved give you as good a feeling as the things you bought:

    0. Not at all
    1. A little
    2. Somewhat
    3. Almost as much
    4. As much or more

68. Here is a list of things which might stop some people from taking a new job. Suppose you were offered an opportunity to make a substantial advance in a job or occupation. Circle a number for each item in the list to show how important it would be in stopping you from making that advance. (If you are a woman, please answer in terms of the advice you would give your husband.)

	0 Might stop me from making the change:	1 Would be a serious consideration but wouldn't stop me:	2 Wouldn't matter at all:
a. Leave your family for some time	0	1	2
b. Move around the country a lot	0	1	2
c. Leave your community	0	1	2
d. Leave your friends	0	1	2
e. Learn a new routine	0	1	2
f. Take on more responsibility	0	1	2

Data analysis

1. *Sort* the code sheets according to "Occupational Prestige" (Box 12) into three groups:
Upper Middle = 1, 2
Lower Middle = 3, 4
Working Class = 5 through 7

2. *Sub-sort* the Upper Middle group according to Box 51t into two groups:
High deferred gratification (DGP) = 7 and above
Low deferred gratification (DGP) = 6 and below
NOTE: It will be less time consuming for half of the

class to carry out the tallying procedures specified in Step 3 and half to carry out the tallying procedures specified in step 3a.

3. *Tally* onto Table 1 the high school grade average (Box 48). Do this separately for each of the deferred gratification groups.

3a. *Tally* onto Table 2 the "Achievement Orientation Index" (68 to) for each of the deferred gratification groups.

4. Repeat steps 2 and 3 (or 3a) for the "Lower Middle" group and then for the "Working Class" group.

5. *Compute* the mean grade-point average (or the mean achievement orientation score) for the Low Deferred Gratification group and the High Deferred Gratification group for each social class. See Appendix C for instructions on computing the mean.

Lab report

1. Place the emphasis of your report on the comparison of deferred gratification groups within each social class group. However, you should also pay attention to the effect of using social class as a "Control Variable," i.e., are different results obtained for each of the social class groups? How are these differences to be explained?

2. See Appendix A for general information on writing laboratory reports.

References

Caro, Francis G. and C. Terence Pihlblad, "Social Class, Formal Education, and Social Mobility," *Sociology and Social Research, 48* (July 1964), pp. 428–437.

Kahl, Joseph A., *The American Class Structure*. New York: Holt, Rinehart and Winston, 1953.

Lipset, Seymour and Reinhard Bendix, *Social Mobility In Industrial Society*. Berkeley: University of California Press, 1960.

Sewell, William H., A. O. Haller, and Murray A. Straus, "Social Status and Educational and Occupational Aspirations," *American Sociological Review, 22* (February 1957), pp. 67–73.

Sewell, William H. and J. Michael Armer, "Neighborhood Context and College Plans," *American Sociological Review, 31* (April 1966), pp. 159–168.

Name________________ Date____________

TABLE 1. Grade point average score by deferred gratification and social class

Score x	HIGH SCHOOL GRADES (Box 48)	Upper Middle (Box 12 = 1 or 2)				Lower Middle (Box 12 = 3 or 4)				Working (Box 12 = 5, 6, or 7)			
		Low DGP (Box 51t=0–6)		High DGP (Box 51t=7+)		Low DGP (Box 51t=0–6)		High DGP (Box 51t=7+)		Low DGP (Box 51t=0–6)		High DGP (Box 51t=7+)	
		f	fx	f	fx	f	fx	f	fx	f	fx	f	fx
0	D– or lower												
1	D												
2	C–												
3	C												
4	C+												
5	B–												
6	B												
7	B+												
8	A–												
9	All or almost all A												
TOTAL													
Mean													
+ (No info.)			X		X		X		X		X		X

Name____________________ Date____________________

TABLE 2. Achievement orientation index by deferred gratification and social class

ACHIEVEMENT ORIENTATION INDEX (Box 68to)	Upper Middle (Box 12 = 1 or 2)				Lower Middle (Box 12 = 3 or 4)				Working (Box 12 = 5, 6, or 7)			
	Low DGP (Box 51t=0–6)		High DGP (Box 51t=7+)		Low DGP (Box 51t=0–6)		High DGP (Box 51t=7+)		Low DGP (Box 51t=0–6)		High DGP (Box 51t=7+)	
	f	fx	f	fx	f	fx	f	fx	f	fx	f	fx
0												
1												
2												
3												
4												
5												
6												
7												
8												
9												
10												
11												
12												
TOTAL												
Mean												
+ (No info.)		X		X		X				X		X

LABORATORY REPORT FOR PROBLEM ____________

Course or
Section ____________ Date ____________ Name ____________

HYPOTHESIS: ____________

SAMPLE: ____________

INDEPENDENT VARIABLE(S): ____________

DEPENDENT VARIABLE(S): ____________

OTHER FACTORS: ____________

LABORATORY REPORT FOR PROBLEM ____________

SUMMARY OF FINDINGS: ____________

DISCUSSION: ____________

PROBLEM 11

RACE AND ETHNIC PREJUDICE

Prejudice is usually defined as an underlying feeling of hostility or resentment directed towards particular groups. The hostility typically focuses on a stereotyped version of the group's characteristics, such as the "greedy Jew" or the "lazy Negro." More often than not, the object of prejudice tends to be a minority group.

Many of the theories advanced to explain the origins of prejudice draw their predictive capacity from the concept of frustration. The concept enters into the theory in the following way: Individuals who are consistently thwarted from fulfilling their aspirations will evidence frustration; frustration is an unstable set of circumstances making for ill-feelings and general resentment; to stabilize the situation, resentment and antagonism are vented on convenient minority groups—groups which at times falsely symbolize the original reason for failure (e.g., the "rich" and "crafty" Jew, blamed for economic reversals). From this view, prejudice is a safety-valve permitting the frustrated to release hostility. The existing evidence does appear to indicate that prejudice is most frequently found among the frustrated: the lower class (Kornhauser, 1950); the downwardly mobile (Greenblum and Pearlin, 1953); and generally persons in economically deprived circumstances (Hovland and Sears, 1940).

Given such predispositions towards predjudice, an additional question remains to be answered—why does prejudice persist? What are the mechanisms in the structure of society which sustain stereotyped and uninformed views of minority members? A partial answer may lie in the sequence of events a prejudiced attitude sets into motion. Robert K. Merton has recognized this possibility as an aspect of the "self-fulfilling prophecy." The reasoning of the perspective is as follows (1) an originating attitude defines the Negro, for example, as ignorant; (2) this definition gains currency and is ultimately translated into action—if Negroes are ignorant, why appropriate sufficient funds for Negro education?; (3) insufficient school funds deprive most Negroes of the possibility of an adequate education; (4) consequently, on standardized measures of academic aptitude the Negro does show up as less intelligent than his Caucasian counterpart. The original prejudiced definition, in brief, is fulfilled (Merton, 1959).

This example furnishes only an inkling of the possible complex mechanisms at work giving widespread currency to race and ethnic prejudice in American society. There is sufficient evidence to show that the requisites of prejudice—an awareness and devaluation of distinguishing characteristics—are well established in childhood. One study showed that as early as three or four years of age, white and Negro children show a definite preference for white rather than colored dolls (Clark and Clark, 1958). The reading for the present problem points up one of the key mechanisms for teaching and promoting prejudice on a large scale—the perpetuation in the mass media of stereotypical images of minority groups. Literature is one of the means by which cultural elements such as prejudice are taught and maintained. Consequently, the presence of an unfavorable image of racial and ethnic groups in popular literature may be part of the reason why prejudice remains an aspect of the culture.

In their analysis of stories published in 1943, Berelson and Salter found considerable evidence of such prejudice. Much has happened since then in race relations. In this problem, then, we will not only have an opportunity to see if racial and ethnic prejudice is transmitted as part of the popular literature of our society, but also to determine if the extent to which it is transmitted has increased or decreased since 1943. Specifically, the study explores whether various racial and ethnic groups are consistently given an unfavorable image in popular literature. If prejudice is inoperative in various popular stories, the authors argue, there should be no greater tendency for minority group members to occupy low statuses, to have unpleasant personalities, or possess any other negatively valued traits. Conversely, if prejudice were operative, minority members should possess these traits more frequently than the majority group, the white Anglo-Saxon American. To provide evidence on these points the authors systematically analyzed the content of various popular stories: They classified the characters involved according to minority-majority group status and then, on a variety of dimensions, coded the image of the character as positive or negative.

Popular fiction has an additional relation to the question of race prejudice. Such stories may reflect the values of the audience which reads it. Research using "content analysis," including the present replication of Berelson and Salter as well as many other similar studies (Albrecht, 1956; Straus and Houghton, 1960), usually makes this assumption. However, Berelson and Salter's research does not provide evidence on whether popular literature reflects the values of the wider society or even the particular audience to which it is directed. This would require additional study. Nonetheless, it would appear that literature is a means for teaching various elements of culture, and further, that the presence of an unfavorable image of minority members in popular literature may be part of the reason prejudice remains an integral aspect of American culture. Similarly, if the fictional portrayal of a minority group becomes favorable, this can both reflect changes in the popular image and also reinforce and spread such change.

Important: The data for this problem must be obtained *before* coming to class to do the problem, see page 187.

MAJORITY AND MINORITY AMERICANS: AN ANALYSIS OF MAGAZINE FICTION / *Bernard Berelson and Patricia J. Salter*

This is a study of prejudice—of unintentional but consistent discrimination against minority groups of hyphenate Americans in one of the last fields one might think to look for it: popular magazine fiction. The fact that it is unconscious prejudice does not mitigate its corrosive effects on the tolerance of readers: it steals in without warning when they are relaxed and unsuspecting.

This article is based on a research analysis originally made for the Writers' War Board in 1945. It appears as a publication[1] of the Bureau of Applied Social Research, Columbia University, with which the authors are associated.

Prejudice against minority peoples in this country is widespread. It embraces a large number of groups: American Negroes and Jews are disapproved; Mexicans, Italian-Americans, Japanese-Americans are rejected as "out-group"; and even Irish-Americans are sometimes not accepted as "good Americans." Common to all these prejudices against minorities is the other side of the coin—prejudice in favor of the majority and approval of the "100% Americans."

Discrimination based upon these prejudices is expressed in many ways. Negroes are often the last to be hired and the first to be fired; people of "pure American stock"—white, Protestant, Anglo-Saxons—often have the best chance at better jobs. The Epsteins and the Goldbergs are often barred from hotels which are glad to welcome the Smiths and the Joneses. The sons of South European or Oriental parents are less apt to be put up for Congress than their "100% American" neighbors.

The fight against prejudice and discrimination is most likely to take place in areas where they are the most overt and intentional. But it is not only these overt and intentional areas of attack upon minority groups and support of "Americans" which serve as sources of such discrimination. Prejudice also finds its way into innocuous areas where people are exposed to them without consciousness that an ethnic problem is being raised at all.

This is a study of the latter kind of exposure to anti-minority and pro-majority discrimination: the treatment of majority and minority groups in the popular fiction appearing in mass magazines. How do people meet the various ethnic and religious groups of this country in this channel of communication, which reaches a large number of people in their relaxed, leisure hours? Are some groups presented as more important or more personable or wealthier than others? Do some groups in these stories get more of society's rewards, such as love or high position? What picture is presented of the relationships between different ethnic groups? In short, what kinds of people appear in typical magazine short stories in terms of their racial, religious, and national backgrounds, and how are they treated?

The sample and the stories

The sample. The object of analysis was a sample of 198 short stories published in eight of the country's most widely read magazines in 1937 and 1943: The magazines included in the study are the following:[2]

General Weeklies:	*Saturday Evening Post*
	Collier's
General Monthlies:	*American*
	Cosmopolitan
Women's:	*Woman's Home Companion*
	Ladies' Home Journal
Confessionals:	*True Story*
	True Confessions

The years 1937 and 1943 were selected in order to investigate the effect of World War II upon the fictional treatment of various groups. The standard analy-

Reprinted with permission of the authors and publisher from *The Public Opinion Quarterly, 10* (Summer 1946), pp. 168–190.

[1] Number A-75.

[2] The results reported in this paper are substantially the same for each magazine, so they are presented for the group as a whole.

sis was done for a total of 185 stories—those with a United States locale or a "transferred" U.S. locale (i.e., the fifteen or so stories laid outside the United States but containing a predominantly American cast of characters). A special analysis was done for the thirteen stories in the sample which were laid in foreign countries and peopled with predominantly foreign characters. For each magazine for each year, four issues were selected at regular intervals (in order to avoid the possible bias of seasons or events), and the first, third, and fifth short stories were analyzed in each of the selected issues (in order to avoid the possible bias of placement in the magazine).[3] Serials and "short short stories" were omitted altogether.

The stories. The majority of the analyzed stories were of the romantic love, boy-meets-girl type. Others dealt with family or domestic or marital problems, and there were some adventure and mystery stories. In the 1943 sample, several war-related stories appeared, but their plots were usually the standard romantic models with military personnel or settings appended, rather than treatments of wartime or military problems. On the whole, the stories were light-hearted in tone and were designed primarily if not solely for purposes of entertainment. They were chosen exclusively as a representative sample of the short stories appearing in such popular magazines and *not* with reference to their treatment of ethnic problems. Some representative plots:

A wealthy young society girl becomes infatuated with a handsome married man, although she is loved by a fine young man of her own set. She recognizes her foolishness when the wife appears, and returns to her young man.

A man who thinks he wants complete freedom discovers true happiness with the woman he loves and a place of his own.

A cab driver protects a beautiful woman who faces danger and death. Through his heroism he gets rid of her pursuers and wins her for himself.

The only son of an Irish family becomes involved in a murder as an accomplice. Through his mother's faith and the strong support of the family, he wins a new chance.

A shallow, dissipating girl who has led a glamorous New York life finds comfort, love, and peace of mind with a quiet Western rancher who sees what she is really like, underneath.

Almost all the stories (about 90%) were laid in the contemporary world. Their locale strongly favors the East Coast, especially New York City, and discriminates against the South.[4]

[3] This procedure calls for a total of 192 stories but it could not be fulfilled in seven instances, leaving a total of 185 stories actually analyzed.

[4] The distribution of the population in magazine fiction and the actual population of the country is as follows:

	United States	*Magazine Fiction*
New York City	5%	34%
East Coast	24	30
Middle West	30	17
West Coast	11	12
South	30	7

The method

The analysis procedure. The central problem of the study was to investigate the existence and nature of differential treatment accorded various ethnic groups in magazine fiction. The procedures and techniques of the analysis can be described in the following stages, listed here in roughly chronological order.

1. On the basis of general knowledge of such stories, supplemented by the focussed reading of a few of them, a set of hypotheses dealing with the problem at hand was formulated. For the sake of simplicity, the hypotheses were formulated in terms of two major groups—the "Anglo-Saxons" and the "foreigners"—with the understanding that the actual analysis would establish empirically the ethnic composition of these two groups in the stories. The hypotheses dealt with the frequency of appearance of various groups, their characteristics, cultural contributions, relative status positions, and social interaction. In addition, hypotheses on time and locale differences were also formulated. From time to time during the study, some of the hypotheses were modified and a few were added.[5]

2. The conversion of the hypotheses into analytic operations took two forms, based upon two different units of analysis. The first unit was a character in the story and the second was the story as a whole.

The first called for the coding of eight characteristics for each of the speaking characters (or groups) in the story.[6] The eight characteristics for which data were secured whenever possible were the following: *Role* in the story (major, submajor, minor; hero, heroine, villain); *Sex; Status position* (occupation, economic status, educational level, "class"); *Social origin* (nationality, race, religion); *Personality traits; Goals or values* (the ends the characters were trying to realize, such as economic advancement, romantic love, settled marriage state, social position, etc.); *Plus-minus position* (the approval or disapproval of the character: sympathy-hostility, liking-disliking, desirability-undesirability, pleasantness-unpleasantness, etc.); *Summary identification* by ethnic groups (using both explicit and implicit indicators).

The analysts not only checked each of these categories for each speaking character, whenever applicable, but also documented their entry with a brief summary of or quotation from the appropriate story content, which were used to standardize the indices used by the analysts for certain categories.

The second form of analysis dealt with the story as a whole. The hypotheses not covered directly by the character analysis—e.g., the hypothesis that the stories do not *explicitly* deal with problems of ethnic relationships in American life—were listed, with five possible entries for each: confirmed; refuted; both confirmed and refuted in the same story; indeterminate as between confirmation and refutation; not applicable. An

[5] A set of the initial hypotheses, the code sheets, and the analysis' instructions for the study are available on request.

[6] In the 185 stories, a total of 889 characters and groups were identifiable by racial, religious, or national origins. Of these, only 25, or less than 3%, were groups.

entry for each hypothesis for each story was required, together with full documentation of the basis for decision.

3. After a period of instruction in the procedures of the study, the eight analysts (all graduate students in sociology) coded the same story. Differences in interpretation were discovered and minimized through re-definition of the disputed categories. In addition, the supervisor of the analysts checked a random sample of each analyst's work during the early stages of the study and standardized analytic procedures among the workers.

4. After the analysis of the story had been completed, codes were inductively constructed for the "open" categories in the character analysis, such as goals and traits. The codes were based upon a total of about a third of the analysis sheets; at about that point, additional analyses failed to yield additional categories for the code. The character analysis was coded for transfer to punch cards. The story analysis was hand-tallied because of the progressive re-definition of hypotheses in the course of the study and the necessity for standardization.

So much for the procedures. Now let us turn to the findings of the study. Did magazine short stories "prefer" some kinds of people to other kinds? If so, how did such preferential treatment operate? We shall present the results of our analysis in five main sections:

The distribution of the characters
Their role
Their appearance
Their status
Their goals

Distribution of characters

What was the composition of the fictional population? What groups of people appeared more and less frequently in the stories? The brief answer is that characters identifiable only as "Americans" more than filled the center of the stage.

The Americans and the field. Of all the identifiable speaking characters, fully 84% were presented just as Americans (Table 1). The others were about equally divided between the various American minorities on the one hand and various foreign groups on the other. The nearly 200 stories, containing nearly 900 identifiable characters, included only sixteen Negroes and only ten Jews. On the whole, this small number of minority and foreign characters is spread very thin throughout the stories. Very seldom did more than one of them appear in a single story. They typically filled isolated roles in order to provide background or "tone" or some other specialized function within the stories. The "Americans," on the other hand, appeared not only in almost every story but also in whole aggregates of characters.

But what about the ethnic composition of the characters as compared to the ethnic composition of the people of the United States? Perhaps the distribution of the fictional characters simply reflected census statistics. Actually, however, census data only accentuate the differential treatment accorded "natives" and "minorities" in the stories. Although the "minorities" (as here defined) make up 40% of the population of the United States, they make up only 10% of the population of the short stories (Figure 1). Every "minority" group appears less frequently in the stories than in the country. Only the "Americans" appear more frequently.

Thus we start with a fundamental conclusion: in popular magazine short stories laid in the United States, minority and foreign groups were seldom represented. The American minorities appeared much less frequently in magazine fiction than in the population. Overwhelming attention was given to the "Americans." The stage and the spotlight belonged to them.

TABLE 1. Minority and foreign groups in magazine short stories are dwarfed by the "American" giant[a]

"Americans"		84.0%
American minorities		8.5
Anglo-Saxon and Nordic hyphenates	3.0%	
Other hyphenates	2.5	
Negroes	2.0–	
Jews	1.0+	
Foreigners		7.5
Anglo-Saxon and Nordic groups	4.0	
Other foreign groups	3.5	
Total number of identifiable characters (equalling 100%)		889

[a] Since relatively few of the characters were explicitly identified by national origin, it was necessary to classify them by other indicators. The following sources of identification were used (the total is more than 100% because some characters were identified in more than one way):

Explicit Identification	21%
Identified by: Name	58
Language	21
Appearance	17
Position	8
Other indicators	2

Examples of names used for purposes of identification:
American: Julie Britton, Eleanor Madison, Doris Baldwin, Martha Langford, Dorothy Green, Dick Ferris, Steve Kennedy, Perry West, Bill Davis, Joe Blake.
Italian: Mr. Casparri, Marty Spinelli, Louis di Paolo. *Jewish:* Max Betterman, Chick Bernstein. *Scandinavian:* Sven Borsen, Fred Gorse. *Irish:* Marty Flanagan, Officer Flaherty. *German:* Adolph Hertz. *Polish:* Anna Krupek. The assumption here is that such names would be similarly identified by typical readers.
In both the American minority and the foreign groups the following classification is used:
Anglo-Saxon and Nordic: English, Irish, Scotch, Canadian, Scandinavian (Norwegian, Swedish, Finnish, Danish).
Other: German, Polish, Italian, Russian, Austrian, Czech, Portuguese, Spanish, Latin-American, Oriental.

The three basic groups of characters. Three ethnic groups of characters in these stories were accorded differential treatment. The first group is composed of *The Americans*—white Protestants with no distinguishable ancestry of foreign origin. They are called

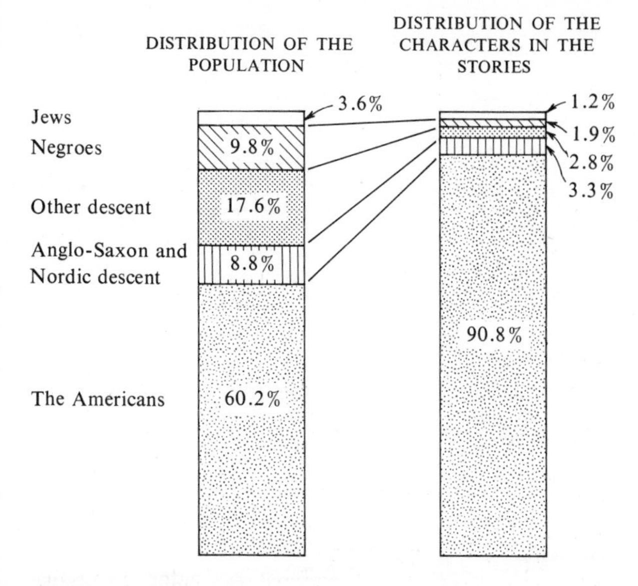

FIGURE 1. There are many more Americans in the stories than in the population. The foreigners in the stories are omitted here. The data are not strictly comparable but provide the best comparison which could be secured from available information. The population data, taken from the *World's Almanac* for 1944 are from the 1940 census (except for the figures for Jews, which came from the Jewish Statistical Bureau). The data on hyphenates represent the foreign-born and the native-born of foreign and mixed parentage. (In this report, there is a bias against the distribution of minority characters in the stories, who are of any generation.) The figures for the Americans were secured by subtracting the total for the other groups from the total population.

"The Americans" here because that is the stereotypic designation for this type of "unadulterated" person.

Not all the non-Americans were treated alike, and the other two groups are composed of sub-groups within the minorities, and foreigners. The basic distinction is *not* that between all American minorities on the one hand and all foreigners on the other; these two groups were approved and disapproved to the same extent. Rather, the important distinction appeared between those American hyphenates and foreigners with Anglo-Saxon and Nordic backgrounds, on the one hand, and the Jews, the Negroes, and the hyphenates and foreigners with other European, Latin-American, and Oriental backgrounds, on the other. On all the important considerations, the former group showed up to better advantage than the latter.

Accordingly, the findings shall be presented as comparisons of these three groups:

The Americans—84% of the total group of characters

Anglo-Saxon and Nordic minorities and foreigners (abbreviated *The AS&Ns*)—7% of the total

Other minorities and foreigners—Jews, Negroes, Italians, Germans, Poles, Orientals, etc. (abbreviated *The Others*)—9% of the total

Since World War II did not serve to increase or otherwise modify the treatment of minority and foreign characters in these stories, the data reported in this study include both the 1937 and the 1943 samples.[7]

The roles of the characters

The characters in these stories play all sorts of parts, ranging from the central and highly approved figure appearing throughout the action to the marginal and unsympathetic figure appearing only for a few lines. What about the importance to the story of our three basic groups of characters?

The majors and the minors. The characters in these stories can be conveniently classified into three groups—major, sub-major, minor—in terms of their importance to the story (as measured by the amount of attention given to them). Those playing the most important roles, i.e., given the most space, are the major characters. The characters given a medium amount of space in the stories are the sub-major and those who appear in incidental roles are the minor characters.

The Americans appeared as major characters just over half the time and as minor characters only about a third of the time (Table 2). But *The AS&Ns* appeared slightly more frequently in minor roles than major, and *The Others* much more frequently. Not only did *The Americans* appear more often than the rest, but they also got more than their share of the important roles. When *The AS&Ns* and *The Others* did get into the stories, they were placed in smaller roles.

TABLE 2. The Americans appeared more often in the major roles

	The Americans	*The AS&Ns*	*The Others*
Major characters	52%	38%	30%
Sub-major characters	16	18	14
Minor characters	32	44	56
Total no. of identifiable characters (equalling 100%)	745	61	77

The heroes and heroines occupy the best roles of all. Again *The Americans* furnished more than their share, and so did *The AS&Ns*. About 35% of all *The Americans* and 31% of *The AS&Ns* were heroes or heroines, as against only 10% of *The Others*. In other words, the heroes and heroines in these stories were almost exclusively either of "pure" American or else of Anglo-Saxon or Nordic stock. *The Others*—Italian-

[7] Only about 5% of the stories in these magazines were laid in foreign countries. In such stories, too, the Americans and the Anglo-Saxons received preferential treatment. If anything, the descriptions of the foreigners were even more stereotyped in these stories than in those laid in the United States.

Americans, Jews, Negroes, et al.,—rarely reached such lofty positions.

The approved and the disapproved. Similarly, the characters can be differentiated on the basis of the approval or disapproval attached to their roles in the stories. The approved characters were likeable, personable, wise, desirable, respectable, honest, upright; the disapproved characters were the opposite. In such "light" fiction as these magazine stories—which are entertaining and pleasant rather than "realistic" or "serious"—the large majority of the characters are approved. This was true, in this sample, for all three groups—but not equally true (Table 3). Here *The Americans* and *The AS&Ns* were approved more often than *The Others*. Incidentally, the heavy appearance of neutral characters among the minority and foreign groups reflects the colorless roles to which they were assigned.

This tendency of the minority and foreign groups to draw minor, less approved roles and seldom to reach the positions of hero or heroine obviously places serious limitations on the extent to which their personalities can be developed. Space limitations together with the general lack of sophistication of these stories, impose a low level of complexity for all characters, and have a particularly strong impact upon the minority and foreign groups. Since they were more often hand-maidens to the plot, they must more often be one-dimensional in personality. They were usually developed only in that aspect of their personalities necessary to their dramatic function, namely, the most obvious or stereotypic aspect which made the author's point facilely and quickly.

Indeed, some of the minor non-Americans, falling even lower on a scale of personalities-in-their-own-right, came to serve the function of *things* in the stories. That is, they merely provided atmosphere and mood or dramatized the broadminded or cosmopolitan nature of *The Americans*. A typical case, for example, was the American heroine who was seen "talking charmingly to the quaint Italian flower vendor," who in that sentence fulfilled his role in the story.

TABLE 3. The characters were differentiated by their approval in the stories, with *The Others* the least approved of all

	The Americans	*The AS&Ns*	*The Others*
Approved characters	80%	78%	62%
Neutral characters	4	14	14
Disapproved characters	16	8	24
Total no. of identifiable characters (equalling 100%)[a]	726	60	77

[a] These figures are not exactly alike from table to table because of varying numbers of indeterminate characters for the different categories.

The appearance of the characters

By its nature, this sort of magazine fiction capitalizes on quick stereotypic delineations of characters. Such delineations apply to most of the characters in the stories—whether major or minor, approved or disapproved, American or not. The easy description of personality *types* which are considered desirable or acceptable, rather than the difficult and complicated elaboration of an individual *personality*, is the custom. As a result, some facets of the characters—those which are thought to be representative or at least familiar to a wide audience—are often made to serve as the complete personality.

For example, the American heroes in the stories were typically tall, blond, and handsome in the best Hollywood tradition, and the American heroines were stereotyped in similar fashion. Other American characters were similarly drawn from standard patterns—the "darling" Southern girl, the "stalwart" college athlete, the "efficient" career girl, the "modern" housewife and mother. However, such stereotypes are seldom invidious or even implicitly disparaging and, more important, they are not attached to socially distinctive groups in the sense in which that term applies to Negroes or Jews or Italian-Americans.

But this function of the stereotype to compress the members of a group into a common mold operates in these stories not only artistically as the enemy of individuality in fictional characters. When the stereotype applies to ethnic groups like Negroes or Jews or Italian-Americans, it also operates socially as a stimulus of xenophobia. Studies of popular attitudes have repeatedly shown that people hold certain settled opinions about the traits and behavior of members of "outgroups"—mental pictures of what other "different" kinds of people believe and do. Such stereotypes, to which they think the others actually correspond, may arise from personal contact with some individuals in the other group, or from general hearsay, or from reading and listening, or from some other source. But whatever their source, their function is to label the "outsider" as an outsider, so that he may be easily identified, appropriately reacted to, and conveniently rejected.

Minority and foreign characters described stereotypically. The representatives of minority and foreign groups were usually tailored to the stereotypic dimensions of their respective groups. Of all the stories including one or more minority or foreign characters, familiar and usually disparaging stereotypic descriptions were employed in fully three-fourths.[8]

Stereotypes were found for virtually every minority and foreign group in the fictional population. The Negro, the Irishman, and the Italian appeared most frequently in this connection, but many others were given the same sort of treatment: Jews, Poles, Filipinos, French, Chinese, Scandinavians, and even South Sea island natives. (Of the very few non-stereotypic de-

[8] A character delineation was accepted as a stereotype when a sizeable proportion of the American public would have identified it as such according to our assumption based upon knowledge of the experimental studies. The examples cited in the text are typical illustrations.

scriptions, half involved Canadians, the out-group closest to *The Americans*.) The following are only a few examples of the stereotypic treatment found in the sample of stories:

The amusingly ignorant Negro: Rosemary is a "generously upholstered" maid who "cackles" and "rocks back and forth from her rounded hips." Her "golden eye-teeth" reveal themselves "in an affectionate smile, her flat feet toed out at a forty-five degree angle, her bulgy body solid enough but looking perilously safety-pinned together." She leaves a note for her mistress: " 'I taken the gray evening dress like you said. Will leave it at the diars on my way home tonite. I allso taken some of your lonjourey and your lecktrick ion because I got time to do some wash on my oather job. Will bring the ion in the mourning. If you needed it tonite you find me att my oather place till 8 clock.' "

The Italian gangster: Louie di Paolo, an amiable racketeer with a debt of loyalty to an heiress, furnishes her with money and a kidnapping so that she can get her own way with a young man. Louie is "a sinister-looking individual with a white scar over one eye . . . known as Blackie, Two Rod, and Smart 'Em Up in various police precincts, and among the underworld citizenry. . . ." Says he: " 'Beer was my racket. I made my pile and been layin' low ever since. If you want twenty-five G's, all I got to do is stick up my own safe-deposit box.' " He drives "a coupe with bulletproof glass and a specially built steel body, ready for anything."

The sly and shrewd Jew: Jew Jake, manager of a troop of barnstorming stunt flyers, shows greater concern for money than for the safety of his employees. He has an "ungainly and corpulent figure" and he rubs his hands "in a familiar and excited gesture." In answer to his question, " 'Maybe you'd like to make five bucks easy?' ", the hero says: " 'Jake, you would not put out five bucks for anything less than a suicide.' " Another character says: " 'You ought to know the way Jake is. He'd like it better if I did not pull it (the parachute cord) at all. It would give the customers a thrill.' "

The emotional Irish: Ellen, an Irish cook, is overwhelmed by her first sight of the new baby: "Ellen—who, being a Celt, was easily moved—flew out of the kitchen, saw a fraction of David's face, and burst into a flood of tears."

The primitive and "backward" Pole: A Polish-American girl thinks of escape from her national community. "I began to despise our way of life. . . . The American men did not value a wife who could work all day on her knees at his side, taking only a day or two off to bear a child. They love the weakness, not the strength in their women; love the job of looking after and supporting them."

The patronized native of a Pacific island: The orientation of a white planter in the Pacific world is set at the beginning of the story. After a few years on an island, the planter learns the native patois, "mixed with a smattering of Mother English to justify their white skins." Then, "after the coconut planter completes the metamorphosis, he takes on a native mistress who develops gradually into a native wife. Still more gradually the house begins to fill with brown mestizo children. Upon reaching this stage of little brown souvenirs of his exile, the planter passes into that broad classification of 'one who has missed too many boats.' Eventually he misses his final boat."

In addition to these, there are the humorous Chinese servant, the correct Filipino houseboy, the volatile Latins, the extravagantly romantic Frenchman, the hard-working and thrifty Scandinavian. And in most of the cases, there is also a patronizing tone in these stereotypic descriptions of minority and foreign characters.

The status of the characters

Now let us turn to the characters' position in the socio-economic hierarchy. Did differences appear between *The Americans* and the rest in the possession of man's worldly goods? What kinds of jobs were held by what kinds of people? What sort of social interaction, if any, occurred between different groups of characters?

Status—possessed and deserved. The general economic level of characters in these stories was assessed as an interviewer for an opinion survey would assess the economic level of a respondent—by the person's appearance, clothes, home, possessions, etc. The characters were classified on four levels, designated A, B, C, and D. The A people have the most money, influence and prestige and the D people have the least.

Again, *The Americans* showed to better advantage than *The AS&Ns* or *The Others* (Table 5). Almost three-fourths of the former fell on the upper two levels of this status index as against less than half of the latter. This simple index reflects substantial differences in characters' standards of living. *The Americans* lived better in various ways: they ate better food, wore better clothes, resided in better homes, and generally enjoyed more material conveniences and luxury possessions.

TABLE 5. *The Americans* enjoyed higher socio-economic status than the rest[a]

Socio-economic status	*The Americans*	*The AS&Ns*	*The Others*
A	39%	24%	16%
B	33	18	28
C	23	49	37
D	5	9	19
Total no. of identifiable characters (equalling 100%)	722	55	76

[a] These status differences are not simply a reflection of the differences in role among our three basic groups of characters. The status differences remain even when role is held constant. The data:

Role	Percentage with A & B Status: *The Americans*	*The AS&Ns* and *The Others*
Major	71% (387)	58% (46)
Sub-major and minor	68% (353)	32% (94)

There was thus a stronger association between *The Americans* and high status than between major role and high status. Similarly, it can be shown that *The AS&Ns* and *The Others* were approved less than *The Americans* when status is held roughly constant; thus, the fact that they were approved less is not simply the result of their lower status. (Although similar control tables do not appear in the text in connection with other tables, the differences have all been tested in this way.)

Not only that, they also seemed to *deserve* their higher status; it was usually taken for granted. People can achieve wealth, power and prestige in a variety of ways—through fortunate birth or fortunate marriage or hard work or crooked dealing or luck. In these stories, only infrequently were the sources of *The Americans'* high status positions explicitly mentioned. However, when the representatives of minority and foreign groups appeared in high status positions, *their* paths to power—whatever they were—were more often explicitly mentioned (Table 6). In other words, the

TABLE 6. Fewer explanations were forthcoming of *The Americans'* high status positions

	The Americans	*The AS&Ns and The Others*
Source of high status not explained in the story	78%	43%
Source of high status explained in the story	22	57
Total number of stories with characters in high status positions (equalling 100%)	93	14

claim of *The Americans* on society's rewards was presented much less as a matter for explanation or justification. Their acceptance at the top, without elaboration, subtly suggested that they belonged there. But when the rest appeared at the top, their rise had to be explained more often, because they did not belong there.

Occupational level—"positions" and "jobs". *The Americans* also engaged in pleasanter and more desirable work than the members of minority and foreign groups. For the sake of convenience, the occupations have been grouped in a few major categories. Once more *The Americans* came off best, *The AS&Ns* next, and *The Others* worst (Table 7). Not only did *The*

TABLE 7. *The Americans* had more desirable occupations than the other groups[a]

	The Americans	*The AS&Ns*	*The Others*
High occupations	59%	29%	20%
Middle occupations	19	23	20
Low occupations	11	27	36
Illegal and "suspect" occupations	1	2	15
Members of the armed forces	10	19	9
Total no. of identifiable characters (equalling 100%)	602	52	66

[a] *The high occupations:* Business executives; the "idle rich"; parent-supported college students; lawyers, doctors, professors, ministers, architects, artists, musicians, and other professions; entertainers; major government officials; "luxury" housewives.

The middle occupations: White-collar workers, minor government officials, small businessmen, farmers, housewives who do their own housework.

The low occupations: Fishermen, skilled laborers, servants, building maintenance workers, unskilled laborers.

The illegal and "suspect" occupations: Racketeers, thieves, gamblers, night club proprietors (suspect in these stories).

Others contain many more characters in illegal and "suspect" occupations; in addition, they were more likely to be enlisted men rather than officers in the armed forces (two-thirds of *The Others*, one-half of *The AS&Ns*, and one-fourth of *The Americans*). Thus the distinctions among the groups extend even into the military hierarchy.

Social interaction—the upper and the lower. These stories contain whole networks of personal interactions, some conducted on a basis of equality but others serving to place one character in a lesser position relative to another. Such social interaction varies from the intimate to the incidental; that is, two characters can marry each other or they can have a chance meeting in a restaurant when one serves the other. How did such social interaction take place among our groups of characters?

The distribution of occupations suggests the answer. Whenever social interaction in these stories occurred *on the job*, it was the members of minority and foreign groups who were found in the subordinate roles. They were the servants, the dressmakers, the liverymen, the restaurateurs, the peddlers. The "quaint flower vendor" was Italian; Mr. Beilstein was a butcher; Mr. Casparri ran a restaurant; Silva was a Filipino houseman; Ella was an Irish cook and Hong a Chinese cook; Rosemary and Bessie and Sidonia, and many others, were Negro servants. They worked for, and served, *The Americans.*

In some cases, the minority and foreign representatives appeared subordinate to *The Americans* in non-occupational roles. For example, an Irish mother pleaded with a wealthy American for her criminal son; an Italian gangster was slavishly devoted to an American heroine who once helped him; Tanya Verriki was an inmate of a home for delinquent girls where all the staff members were Americans. And when social interaction between *The Americans* and the rest did occur on a basis of equality, it was usually *The AS&Ns* who participated. The English girl entertained American soldiers; British army officers (aristocrats) were invited to dinner; the Irish-American flyer became his ship's hero; the Scotch-American photographer won the motion picture actress; the Irish sea captain was fully accepted and admired by his American fellows. Only occasionally did *The Americans* associate with *The Others* on an equal basis and even in such cases it was usually the former who monopolized the spotlight.

But the acid test for personal relations is courtship and marriage. Who married whom in these stories? What boys won what girls? The distribution of marriages and successful courtships in these stories, closely paralleling the distribution of characters, reveals the slight extent to which *The Americans* courted or married members of minority and foreign groups (Table 8). It also shows the still smaller extent to which either *The Americans* or *The AS&Ns* courted or married *The Others.* Inter-love and inter-marriage were not sanctioned in magazine fiction.

In sum, then, not only did *The Americans* play the leading roles in the stories. In addition, they were also represented as getting more of the world's material values and they occupied the superordinate roles in most of the human relationships. They made more money, lived more comfortably, had better occupations,

TABLE 8. On the whole, courtship and marriage were intra-group

Love or marriage partners	Frequency
The Americans—The Americans	85%
The Americans—The AS&Ns	5
The Americans—The Others	4
The AS&Ns—The AS&Ns	3
The AS&Ns—The Others	2
The Others—The Others	1
Total identifiable courtships and marriages (equalling 100%)	153

gave more orders. In these stories, the world belonged to them, and they ran it.

The goals of the characters

Finally, what were the different groups of characters striving for in these stories? What did they want from life? People in magazine fiction pursue a variety of goals—romantic love, settled marriages, money, power, prestige, idealism, and a few more. These goals were classified into two broad categories—"heart" goals, which are emotional and affective, and "head" goals, which are rational and calculating. These specific goals subsumed under each category, and the frequency with which they appeared, are these:

"Heart" Goals	"Head" Goals
Romantic love (231)	Solution of an immediate concrete problem (94)
Settled marriage state (190)	Self-advancement (92)
Idealism (74)	Money and material goods (58)
Affection and emotional security (62)	Economic and social security (51)
Patriotism (57)	Power and dominance (22)
Adventure (20)	
Justice (9)	
Independence (8)	

The "heart" goals are "in the clouds" and the "head" goals are "down-to-earth." In these stories, *The Americans* were less encumbered with such down-to-earth goals (Table 9). Their goals were more frequently pleasant and idealistic and "pure." Particularly *The Others* were bound to mundane and calculating aims.

Summing up

This concludes the analysis of the differential treatment of characters in magazine fiction. On the whole, life in the United States as reflected in these stories was lived differently by our three basic groups. On almost every index—frequency, role, delineation, status, goals —*The Americans* received better treatment, both qualitatively and quantitatively, than the minority and foreign groups. And within the latter, a preference operated in behalf of *The AS&Ns*. The rules seem to be that the character receives better treatment the

TABLE 9. *The Americans* pursue "heart" goals more than the other two groups

	The Americans	*The AS&Ns*	*The Others*
"Heart" goals	69%	61%	49%
"Head" goals	31	39	51
Total no. of identifiable goals (equalling 100%)	793	57	53

closer he is to the norm of *The American*, i.e., white, Protestant, English-speaking, Anglo-Saxon. Common ancestry and common characteristics are decisive.

And even within *The Others* some kinds of people came off better than others. The minority and foreign groups from the other European and Oriental countries, deprived as they were, received preferential treatment in these stories over two critical American minorities—the Negroes and the Jews. On several characteristics this distinction held up. The Negroes and Jews never appeared as heroes and heroines. No Negroes or Jews were depicted as members of the armed forces. They had the lowest occupational rating. They constituted the only group with more disapproved than approved traits. In short, of all the distinguishable groups of characters in magazine fiction, the Negroes and the Jews were depicted least favorably.

Intent and effect

Such a description of magazine fiction (or of any other communication content) supports two sets of interpretations. One set deals with the *intent* behind the communication; how did it get that way? The second set deals with the *effects* of the communication; what difference does it make in the readers' attitudes? The communication itself—in this case short stories in popular magazines—occupies a midway position between the writers and the readers.

Presumable intents. How do these stories happen to be written in this way? We can undoubtedly discount at once any malice on the part of the writers and editors responsible for these stories.

First, it is a convenient method of writing. Such short stories call for brief, compact plots in which the action begins immediately and moves rapidly, and any techniques which facilitate "getting the character across" easily and immediately are at a premium. Thus, many stock roles must be filled by stock characters, and they are often conveniently found in minority groups. For example, whenever the plot requires a gangster it is the simple and "natural" thing to cast an Italian in the role and put it up to the reader to fill in the overtones for himself on the basis of the familiar stereotypes. Although this practice makes for shallow and cliché-filled writing, it does save time and space in the development of the story.

Secondly, the standard pattern for such short stories demands, and gets, conformity. Inertia on the one hand and fear of changing a "successful" formula on the other, combine to keep the stories within designated bounds. Just as certain language is proscribed, so are certain ("controversial") topics and certain uses of fictional characters. An editor or publisher who would eagerly accept another variant of the typical boy-meets-girl story starring Julie Britton and Bill Davis would not consider printing the same story if the leading figures in it were called Sadie Horowitz and Abe Goldstein, or Lorenzina Sereno and Sebastian de Grazia.

Further, the heterogeneity of the audience to whom such stories are directed may necessitate the use of the broadest symbols of identification. As the types of readers in an audience increase in diversity, both the variety and the complexity of communicable ideas decrease. Heterogeneity breeds generality, and thus the leading characters become members of the dominant and presumably the best-recognized group.

Finally, insofar as the leading roles are taken by members of probably the most respected and certainly the most envied group in the community, these stories correspond to the historical bias of literature in centering upon the economic-, prestige-, and power-elites of every age. On the one hand they have traditionally been considered the people most worth writing about, and on the other hand, as the people most deferred to, they present a convenient focus of attention for large groups of readers who seek to identify themselves with the rich and the powerful.

Presumable effects. These stories are probably offered and accepted purely as entertainment. Their typical effect upon readers is a respite effect; that is, they normally provide a satisfying and enjoyable vacation from daily routines and daily cares. That may be the typical effect, but it is certainly not the only one. Many communications have other than their intended effects upon readers or listeners and this is probably such a case. In all likelihood, the consistent deprivation of *The AS&Ns* and especially *The Others* in these stories, over a long period of time, serves to activate the predispositions of a hostile or even an indifferent audience. Readers with latent tendencies to assign the usual stereotypic descriptions to groups whom they do not know, or toward whom they are unsympathetic, or with whom they do not come in personal contact, can find support for their convenient tags, labels, and aggressions in such magazine fiction. And this is all the more striking as a result of the implicit comparison with *The Americans*. Thus the condition and behavior of fictional characters can readily be used to "prove" that the Negroes are lazy or ignorant, the Jews sly, the Irish superstitious, the Italians criminal, and so on.

The implicit yes and the explicit no

The nature of these stories, then, tends to perpetuate the myth of the "100% American" by differentiating, subtly and consistently, between *The Americans* and the representatives of other groups. Such differentiation in itself constitutes an implicit recognition of a "minority problem" in this country. What about the *explicit* handling of the problem in these stories? Was the direct relationship between various ethnic groups overtly discussed in these stories, and if so, how?

One of this country's favorite ideologies claims equality for the diverse national, racial, and religious strains which make up the United States. In one sense, it is "immoral" to suggest that inequality actually exists or, if that is acknowledged, that it cannot be attributed to biological factors or individual inadequacies. This ideology is not challenged in these stories. Minority differences are regularly recognized but the minorities are not *overtly* depreciated.

Of our sample of 185 stories, only four contained a direct reference of any kind to this problem area in American life. Only four brought the issue into the open:

An Indian girl is subject to conflict between loyalty to and marriage into her own people and assimilation into the American culture. Her ambivalence is resolved by acceptance of Indian social life (marriage to an Indian) and by acceptance of material conditions characteristic of American life (clothes, household appliances, etc.). Caste lines are maintained.

A Polish girl rebels against the traditional life of the American-Polish community, notably by dating an outsider. She is shamed by her people, almost loses her fiancé, acknowledges her mistake, and ends by accepting the traditional life of her community.

An upper-class American girl tries to evade jury duty and is chastised: " 'This country would get into a pretty mess if a girl of the more intelligent class, why, she just checked aside and let the foreign element administrate justice in our courts.' "

An "American-born" man protests against being identified with French-Canadians living in New England: " 'But I'm an American.' " A character refers to such French-Canadians as " 'kind of American—but ain't.' "

The latter two references were only incidental comments on the problem. Only the first two—involving the adjustment problems of the Indian and Polish girls —contained "serious" and extended considerations of the problem itself. And in each case, the "out-group" heroine solved her problem by remaining within her own group. In each case, social assimilation was unsuccessful—although in each case the material trappings of American civilization, such as washing machines and radios, were secured. The moral for these stories was sounded by an Indian character: " 'We want to win a place among the white people by our efforts and our determination, but we can never hope to be accepted socially.' "

Thus the consistent deprivation of the minority groups is indirect; it is present in the stories but only seldom is it directly acknowleged or its implications discussed. The readers of short stories in popular magazines are constantly exposed, implicitly, to the prejudices and stereotypes attached to minority problems in the United States. But they are almost never exposed to serious and direct presentation of the problems themselves. Minority representatives are consistently deprived within an atmosphere which acknowledges no basis for such deprivation.

Minority problems in the United States are serious and deep-rooted. They will not be solved by symbols alone, but symbols will help. So will recognition of the pervasiveness of the problems. Even here, in ephemeral fiction fashioned of sweetness and light and designed purely for entertainment and divertissement, a subtle discrimination against minorities and foreigners has found its way. Even here, there are different classes of citizenship for different classes of people.

Replication

ETHNIC PREJUDICE IN POPULAR LITERATURE

In this replication, data will be obtained by coding the content of a sample of popular fiction rather than the questionnaire data used for preceding problems. This method was chosen not only to conform to Berelson and Salter's analysis, but for a number of other reasons as well: to introduce content analysis as another method for establishing knowledge in sociology, to explore the theoretical importance of mass media for the issue of race prejudice, and to examine changes since 1943 in the status of minority group members in popular fiction. Thus, in a single laboratory problem you will deal with three important topics in sociology: race and ethnic group prejudice, the interrelation of mass media and mass culture, and social change.

The replication itself will closely follow the analysis provided in the original study: sorting characters into minority and majority group membership and comparing their socio-economic status, their role in the story, their goals, and whether or not the characters are approved. Particular attention should be paid to identifying which is the independent variable. To prevent unnecessary anguish it should be noted that the designation, if it can be made at all, is by no means obvious. Therefore, when you identify the independent variable provide a brief justification for your view.

Hypothesis

1. State which racial or ethnic group or groups you think will be presented most favorably and which groups will be presented least favorably. Alternatively, you may hypothesize that there is no prejudice expressed in the fiction examined in this problem.

2. State whether you think the amount of prejudice expressed in popular fiction has increased or decreased since 1943, and, very briefly, give a reason for this hypothesis.

Assignment of stories

Your instructor will assign the stories to be coded the week before this problem is scheduled so that you can come to class with the necessary data. A sample of 50 or more stories should be coded. Therefore in a class of 25, each of you will code at least two stories.

1. *Sign the assignment sheet* (supplied to instructors using this book) indicating which magazine and which months you will code, and *copy these down* on your tabulation sheet. The magazines should be from the list of those studied by Berelson and Salter. Since some of these magazines are no longer published, substitute magazines such as *Redbook* or *Argosy*. However, do not substitute "highbrow" magazines such as *Harpers* or the *Saturday Review* since in this problem we are interested in mass culture rather than "high culture". If the magazine is not in your college library, try the public library, a secondhand magazine store, or buy a copy on the newsstand.

2. *Buy some 3-by-5 inch ruled file cards.* You will need about twenty, so a package of one hundred can be shared with other students.

3. *Selection of the stories.* In issues assigned to you, do your analysis of the first story which has the following characteristics:

A. Is fictional (except for *True Story* and *True Confessions*).
B. Is complete in that issue, i.e., avoid serials, but also avoid one or two page "short short" stories.
C. Takes place in a predominantly American locale, i.e., avoid stories taking place in foreign countries.
D. Code only one story per issue of a magazine. The story does *not* have to deal with race or ethnic issues to be eligible for analysis.

4. Enter onto the tabulation sheet the author, title, pages, etc. for each of your stories.

Content analysis coding

The unit of coding is a "character" in the story. Make out one 3-by-5 code card for *each* character who appears in the story. Five variables are to be coded onto this card for each character. The code numbers or initials should be written across the top line of the card as in the example below, and the story number (from your tabulation sheet) should be written in the lower right corner along with your name and the date.

1. *Ethnic group* of the character. Classify each character into one of the following five ethnic groups and write the code initial for that group in the upper left corner of the file card.

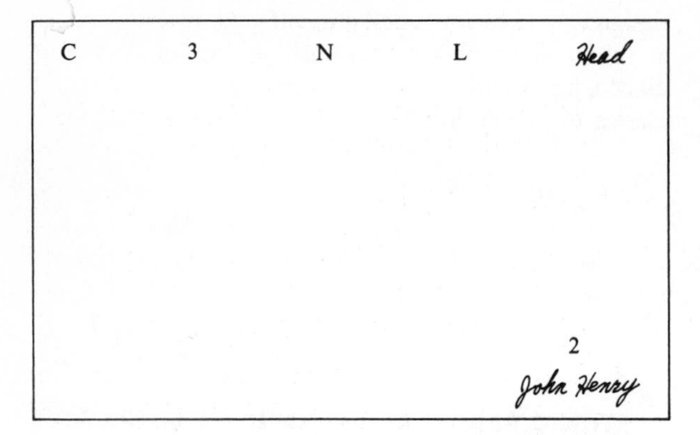

A = Americans: Any character with an English name (provided he is not identified as an ethnic minority person) or any person who is explicitly identified as an "American" without qualification as to national origin or race.

ASN = Anglo-Saxon and Nordic Hyphenates: Any character who is described as an "Irish-American," "Swedish-American," etc. The idea here is that the character's identification as an American is qualified by his national origin also being identified.

OH = Other Hyphenates (except colored persons): Any character whose ancestry is any country in Europe except Scandinavia and the British Isles. This may be indicated explicitly or inferred from a distinctive name (see Berelson and Salter, footnote 7). Jews are included in this group no matter what their national origin.

C = Colored Persons: Negro, Chinese, Japanese, American or East Indian, Burmese, Korean, Polynesian, etc.

O = Other: Characters who cannot be classified into one of the above groups. Include in this group foreigners who are temporarily in the United States. If this code is used, write the name of the ethnic group in the center of the card.

You will need to consult Berelson and Salter for a discussion of things to look for to be able to determine the ethnic group of a character.

2. *Major versus Minor Role.* Classify each character according to the amount of attention (as measured by the amount of space given to them) in the story as follows:

1 = Major role: those characters given the most space.

2 = Sub-major role: those given a medium amount of space.

3 = Minor characters: those who appear incidentally and briefly.

3. *Approval versus Disapproval.* Classify each character as either:

A = Approved, as indicated by being depicted as likeable, personable, wise, desirable, respectable, honest, upright, etc.

N = Neutral, i.e., depicted without evaluating adjectives or description.

D = Disapproved, as indicated by the opposite of the traits listed under "Approved."

Code this in the center position on the file cards. NOTE: If the evaluation of the characters change, as for example when the villain turns out to be a hero and vice versa, code the final evaluation.

4. *Socio-economic Status (SES).* Classify each character into one of the following socio-economic levels, as indicated by the character's occupation (or if a non-college student or non-employed woman, as indicated by the father's occupation or the husband's occupation):

H = High Occupations: business executives, the "idle rich," parent-supported college students, doctors, professors, ministers, architects, artists, musicians and other professions, star entertainers, major government officials, housewives living in "luxury" (if the husband's occupation is not given).

M = Middle Occupations: clerical and sales workers (except obviously upper income sales agents), minor government officials, small businessmen, farmers, housewives without a servant (if the husband's occupation is not mentioned).

L = Low Occupations: manual workers of all kinds, including foremen, servants, "orderlies," and aids.

\+ = No occupation given or inferable.

5. *Goals of the Characters.* Use the following categories to classify goals, and code in the right corner of the file card.

"Head": to indicate "head" goals, such as:
- Solution of an immediate concrete problem
- Self-advancement
- Money and material goods
- Economic and social security
- Power and dominance

"Heart": to indicate "heart" goals, such as:
- Romantic love
- Settled marriage state
- Idealism
- Affection and emotional security
- Patriotism
- Adventure
- Justice
- Independence

The example given of the way file cards should be

coded represents a character whose ethnic group is C (colored), whose role in the story is 3 (minor character), who is given neither approval nor disapproval in the story and is therefore coded N (neutral), whose socioeconomic status is L (low), and whose goals are classified Head (since he seeks only to wait on tables and receive a tip). Cards like this are to be made out for each character in the stories you analyze.

Data analysis

1. Before coming to class:

   A. *Sort* the cards into the five ethnic groups.

   B. *Tally* the frequency of the other four variables for each ethnic group.

2. In class:

   A. Your instructor will have on the blackboard a large version of Table 1. As soon as you come to class copy the numbers from your Table 1 onto the blackboard table. Do this neatly with the numbers lined up in columns so that the results can be added together accurately.

   B. Your instructor will assign one quarter of the class the job of adding up the figures for Socioeconomic level (SES), one quarter Major versus Minor Roles, one quarter Approval versus Disapproval, and one quarter to add up the results for Goals.

   C. Enter the frequency distributions resulting from Step B in the left column of Table 2.

   D. Compute the percent that this combined frequency is of the total number of characters for each ethnic group (each column) and enter in the appropriate cells of Table 2. This job will be easier if you use the percentage tables in Appendix B.

   E. Your instructor will put these results on the blackboard so that you can copy down the results obtained for the other three variables.

Laboratory report

1. Provide a reason for your designation of the independent and dependent variable.
2. Under summary of findings, report the evidence you found in support or in opposition to your hypotheses. Do this in words only, referring to Table 2 for specific figures. See Appendix A for general information on writing laboratory reports.
3. Under DISCUSSION, take into account the distinction between "intent" and "effect" when you discuss the role of the mass media in establishing and maintaining prejudice as an element in American culture.
4. Hand in the cards and the Tabulation Form along with your Laboratory Report.

References

Albrecht, M. C., "Does Literature Reflect Common Values?," *American Sociological Review, 21* (December 1956), pp. 722–729.

Berelson, Bernard, *Content Analysis*. New York: Free Press, 1952.

Clark, Kenneth B. and Marnie P. Clark, "Racial Identification and Preference in Negro Children" in Eleanor E. Maccoby, Theodore M. Newcomb, and Eugene L. Hartley, eds., *Readings in Social Psychology*. New York: Holt, Rinehart and Winston, 1958, pp. 602–611.

Greenblum, Joseph and Leonard I. Pearlin, "Vertical Mobility and Prejudice: A Socio-Psychological Analysis," in Reinhard Bendix and Seymour M. Lipset, eds., *Class, Status and Power*. New York: Free Press, 1953, pp. 480–491.

Hovland, C. I. and R. R. Sears, "Minor Studies of Aggression: Correlation of Lynching with Economic Indices," *Journal of Psychology* 9 (April 1940), pp. 301–310.

Kornhauser, Arthur, "Public Opinion and Social Class," *American Journal of Sociology, 55* (January 1950), pp. 333–345.

Merton, Robert K., *Social Theory and Social Structure*. New York: Free Press, 1959, pp. 421–436.

Straus, Murray A. and Lawrence J. Houghton, "Achievement, Affiliation and Cooperation Values as Clues to Trends in American Rural Society, 1924–1958," *Rural Sociology, 25* (December 1960), pp. 394–403.

Name____________________

Date____________________

Magazine____________________Year________Volume________

Story no.	Month	Page	Author	Title
1				
2				
3				
4				
5				

TABLE 1. Characteristics of characters *in stories listed above,* by ethnic group

Characteristic		ETHNIC GROUP				
		A	ASN	OH	C	O
ROLE	1. Major					
	2. Sub-Maj.					
	3. Minor					
	TOTAL					
APPROVAL	A					
	N					
	D					
	TOTAL					
SES	H					
	M					
	L					
	+					
	TOTAL					
GOAL	Head					
	Heart					
	TOTAL					

TABLE 2. Characteristics of characters for *all stories combined,* by ethnic group

Characteristic		ETHNIC GROUP									
		A		ASN		OH		C		O	
		f	%	f	%	f	%	f	%	f	%
ROLE	1. Major										
	2. Sub-Maj.										
	3. Minor										
	TOTAL		100%		100%		100%		100%		100%
APPROVAL	A										
	N										
	D										
	TOTAL		100%		100%		100%		100%		100%
SES	H										
	M										
	L										
	+										
	TOTAL		100%		100%		100%		100%		100%
GOAL	Head										
	Heart										
	TOTAL		100%		100%		100%		100%		100%

LABORATORY REPORT FOR PROBLEM ________

Course or
Section ________ Date ________ Name ________

HYPOTHESIS: ________

SAMPLE: ________

INDEPENDENT VARIABLE(S): ________

DEPENDENT VARIABLE(S): ________

OTHER FACTORS: ________

LABORATORY REPORT FOR PROBLEM ____________

SUMMARY OF FINDINGS: ____________

DISCUSSION: ____________

Groups VI

PROBLEM 12

PRIMARY GROUPS

A primary group is a highly personal, inclusive relationship evoking strong feelings of mutual identification among its members. As originally envisioned by Cooley (1909), the primary group was a basic feature of all societies, providing individuals with their first and most meaningful experience of social life. In accord with this speculation, Murdock has found that families, which usually incorporate primary group behavior, are found in every known society (Murdock, 1949); similarly, Axelrod (1956) and Stone (1954) have shown that much primary group interaction exists even in the purportedly anonymous metropolis; and in such unlikely places as factories, armies, and governmental agencies, the primary group has been discovered time and again (Shils, 1951).

Given the apparent universality of the primary group, what vital role does it play in the maintenance of individual behavior and social patterns? The sociological perspective on this role is perhaps nowhere more succinctly phrased than in Emile Durkheim's classic study of suicide. Noting the relevance of primary groups to forms of suicide, Durkheim argued that these groups provide a

> . . . constant interchange of ideas and feelings from all to each and each to all, something like a mutual moral support, which instead of throwing the individual on his own resources, leads him to share in the collective energy and supports his own when exhausted (Durkheim, 1951, p. 210).

The primary group, in brief, integrates individuals into a social unity. To the sociologist, it represents the critical structure tying individuals to the fabric of society. Without these groups, be they composed of family members or peers, individuals stand outside the society, lacking both the social support and the social controls and expectations provided by primary groups. Moreover, as Durkheim so poignantly illustrated, the absence of primary group ties has dramatic implications: Individuals without group support more frequently take their own lives.

Considerable research has validated Durkheim's theory. Individuals learn their culture within a primary group setting, typically composed of fathers and mothers acting as agents of the wider society. The evidence indicates that if such agents are not present, individuals may never fully develop their mental capacity (Yarrow, 1961). At a later stage of individual development, it has been shown that primary group interaction is necessary to *sustain* personality, not merely to bring it about. For example, Faris and Dunham's research, conducted in Chicago in the early thirties, suggested that social isolation breeds mental disorders (Faris and Dunham, 1939). Jaco has shown a direct relationship between isolation and schizophrenia (Jaco, 1954). These and other findings point to the same conclusion: In isolation from primary group interaction, individuals are not responsive to the expectations of the society; they thus tend to develop differently from other persons. This "difference" is labeled by the society as mental illness.

In the research to be replicated for this laboratory problem, Kohn and Clausen continue Durkheim and Cooley's concern with the integrative functions of the primary group. The question they raise is a simple one: Is isolation from peers in adolescence (an indicator of infrequent primary group interaction) connected with various forms of mental disorder? To test the hypothesis of a relationship between isolation and mental illness, the authors compare the rates of adolescent interaction of mentally ill individuals with normal individuals. To refine their comparisons and to eliminate other possible explanations, the authors selectively sample the two populations so that the composition of each group is roughly similar on five dimensions: age, sex, father's occupation, family composition, and area of residence.

It is necessary to foreshadow the author's conclusions and direct attention to their summary remark that "the data do not support the hypothesis that social isolation in adolescence is a predisposing factor in either schizophrenia or manic-depressive psychosis." From one point of view Kohn and Clausen are correct: Isolation does not completely explain all the variability in rates of mental illness. Nonetheless, their data do in fact show that isolation explains *some* of the variability. This suggests that isolation *is* a factor connected with mental illness, but it is one among many.

SOCIAL ISOLATION AND SCHIZOPHRENIA / *Melvin L. Kohn and John A. Clausen*

Of the several hypotheses relating the frequency of mental disorders to social conditions, none has been more persistently enunciated than that which proposes that schizophrenia is the outgrowth of social isolation. First stated by Faris in 1934,[1] this hypothesis subsequently seemed consistent with, and indeed explanatory of, the findings of Faris and Dunham's classic ecological study of mental disorder. Faris and Dunham ascertained that high rates of first hospital admissions for schizophrenia are found in areas of the city characterized by high residential mobility and low socio-economic status, among ethnic group persons living in non-ethnic areas, and among the foreign-born populations of the slums.[2] All of these indices were regarded as reflecting tendencies toward the social isolation of certain segments of the population.

In earlier statements of the hypothesis, Faris suggested that "any form of isolation that cuts the person off from intimate social relations for an extended period of time may possibly lead to this form of mental disorder."[3] More recent statements have suggested that isolation is a result of incongruent intra-familial and extra-familial orientations toward the child and represents a stage in a "typical process" for schizophrenics. Briefly this typical process is said to involve the following stages:

(1) "Parental oversolicitude produces the 'spoiled child' type of personality," and leads to

(2) "a certain isolation from all but the intimates within the family."

(3) "The next stage is persecution, discrimination or exclusion by children outside the family."

(4) "The most usual reaction to this persecution is to feel unhappy but with no immediate depreciation of establishing friendships."

(5) "Often the children try for years to make friends. . . . Eventually there is a resignation—a withdrawal from a hopeless goal . . . From this time on their interest in sociability declines and they slowly develop the seclusive personality that is characteristic of the schizophrenic."

(6) Finally, the symptoms of schizophrenia are ascribed to the lack of social experience in the person so isolated: "Not being experienced in intimate personal contacts with a larger number of other persons he is deficient in his understanding of the reactions of others, and responds unconventionally and inappropriately to them."[4]

Reprinted with permission of the authors and publisher from *American Sociological Review, 20* (June 1955), pp. 265–273. Paper read at the annual meeting of the American Sociological Society, September, 1954.

The authors are indebted to the Maryland State Department of Mental Hygiene, and its Commissioner, Dr. Clifton Perkins, for making available its patient-files, granting access to patients at State hospitals, and aiding our research with a grant-in-aid; to the hospitals of the State of Maryland, especially Springfield State Hospital and Brooklane Farm Hospital for contributing their case records, and enabling us to interview their patients and former patients; to the physicians of Washington County for aid in arranging interviews and in providing valuable data; and to the Public Health Methods Division of the USPHS (especially Dr. Philip Lawrence, Chief of the Familial Studies Unit in Hagerstown) for granting access to their files of Morbidity Studies (basic to our control-group selection) and for valuable suggestions and aid in the field work.

[1] Robert E. L. Faris, "Cultural Isolation and the Schizophrenic Personality," *American Journal of Sociology,* XL (September, 1934), pp. 155–164.

[2] Robert E. L. Faris and H. Warren Dunham, *Mental Disorders in Urban Areas,* Chicago: University of Chicago Press, 1939. In this volume, Faris and Dunham base the case for the social isolation hypothesis primarily on the findings of high rates in areas of high residential mobility and among ethnic group persons living in non-ethnic neighborhoods (*ibid.,* pp. 173–177). Faris' hypothesis that peer-group rejection leads to isolation and consequent psychosis is developed in his chapter, "Ecological Factors in Human Behavior," in J. McV. Hunt (ed.), *Personality and the Behavior Disorders,* 2 vol. New York: Ronald Press, 1944, II, pp. 736–757; and in *Social Psychology,* New York: Ronald Press, 1952, especially pages 338–365. Dunham has further hypothesized that the harsh, competitive character of life in the foreign-born slum communities, particularly for persons already sensitive, self-conscious, or timid, is productive of isolation and thus of schizophrenia. See H. Warren Dunham, "The Current Status of Ecological Research in Mental Disorder," *Social Forces,* 25 (March, 1947), pp. 321–326. We have discussed a number of questions relating to interpretations made in these studies and to the clarification of the concept, social isolation, in "The Ecological Approach in Social Psychiatry," *American Journal of Sociology,* LX (September, 1954), pp. 140–151.

[3] Faris, "Cultural Isolation and the Schizophrenic Personality," *op. cit.,* p. 157.

[4] This statement of Faris' hypothesis of a typical process is abstracted from "Ecological Factors in Human Behavior," *op. cit.,* pp. 752–753.

This view holds that social isolation—that is, the diminution or total absence of social interaction with peers—enters the schizophrenic process as a directly predisposing or "causative" factor. The bizarre behavior of the schizophrenic is attributed to social inexperience stemming from isolation. Presumably then, such isolation should underlie all schizophrenic disorders. Supporting evidence for this hypothesis was provided in a study by Dunham of the early social experience of catatonic schizophrenes who grew up in areas of high delinquency rates.[5] On the other hand, Weinberg found little evidence of social isolation in the childhood histories of a sample of acute schizophrenics (called by him transient schizophrenics), more than half of whom were catatonics.[6]

The present paper reports findings of a study designed to ascertain the extent and significance of social isolation in adolescence in a sample group of schizophrenic patients and a matched group of normal controls. A small group of manic-depressive patients, together with controls for these patients, was also studied.

Sample and method of data collection

The sample of patients interviewed consists of 45 schizophrenic and 13 manic-depressive patients who were first admitted to mental hospitals in Maryland during the period 1940–1952. These comprise 58 out of a total of 79 first admissions from Hagerstown, Maryland, who were diagnosed either schizophrenic or manic-depressive during this period. Of the 21 patients not interviewed at the time of the research, 11 were too ill, 6 had moved too far from the site of the research, and 4 refused to be interviewed. Thus interviews were secured with 73 per cent of the total sample and 94 per cent of those patients who can be regarded as having been physically and psychologically accessible. In 15 of the 21 cases where an interview with the patient was not possible, we were able to interview a close relative. Analysis of these interviews demonstrates that the non-interviewed patients do not differ appreciably from the interviewed patients with respect to their social participation as adolescents.

Controls were individually paired with the patients on the basis of age, sex, and occupation (or father's occupation), using records derived from Public Health Service morbidity studies conducted periodically in Hagerstown since 1921. By this method it was possible to accomplish matching as of a period well before the onset of illness—on the average, 16 years before hospitalization. In roughly half of the cases the patient and his control had attended the same class in public school. In addition to individual matching on the characteristics mentioned, overall frequencies were balanced with respect to family composition and area of residence.[7]

The interview schedule covered the following topics: residential and occupational history, relationships in the parental family, friendship and activity patterns in early adolescence, dating patterns, social participation as an adult, and a brief psychosomatic inventory.

All interviews with patients were conducted by one of the authors, as were approximately one-fifth of the interviews with controls. The balance of the controls were interviewed by another staff member after a period of training and with careful check to insure comparability of approach.

Extent of social isolation among schizophrenics

Assessment of social isolation was accomplished by the use of an index of social participation based upon the respondents' answers to two types of questions. The first ascertained *with whom* the respondent played when he was 13–14 years old, the second *what types* of activities he engaged in at that age.[8] We first asked:

> "(When you were 13 or 14 years old) did you usually hang out with the crowd, with one or two close friends, with your brothers or sisters, or did you stay by yourself most of the time?"

Both schizophrenic and manic-depressive patients more frequently than their controls replied that they stayed by themselves, controls that they played with a crowd or with close friends.[9] (See Table 1.)

To determine the *types* of social activities in which respondents engaged, we asked a series of questions:

[5] H. Warren Dunham, "The Social Personality of the Catatonic-Schizophrene," *American Journal of Sociology,* XLIX (May, 1944), pp. 508–518.

[6] S. Kirson Weinberg, "A Sociological Analysis of a Schizophrenic Type," *American Sociological Review,* XV (October, 1950), pp. 600–610.

[7] Our intent in pairing patients and controls on some variables and balancing frequencies on others was to hold constant several variables known to relate significantly to the frequency of schizophrenia, and then to examine the relationship between presence or absence of this illness and other characteristics or experiences of the two groups, especially with reference to social isolation. This is, of course, quite different from the intent and assumptions involved in matching for an experimental design entailing "before" and "after" measures.

[8] It was necessary to delimit the time period about which we asked in order to secure reasonably comparable data from all respondents. It was difficult to determine, however, which time period was most important. In all probability the crucial phases of personality development do not occur at the same age for all persons. It is also probable that some important events in the individual's relations with his peers occur at so early an age that we cannot expect an adult to remember them. Thus, our selection had to be to some degree arbitrary. Age 13–14 had the two virtues of being a period of high peer-group activity and of being quite definitely marked in the respondent's memory by virtue of the transition from grade school to high school.

We shall show, later in this paper, that the age range selected affects the number of isolates we distinguish in a group of patients, but that it does not affect the question of the possible etiological importance of isolation.

[9] The significance of differences between the patient and control groups has been tested by the method suggested by McNemar for comparisons between samples whose means are intercorrelated. See Quinn McNemar, *Psychological Statistics,* New York: John Wiley and Sons, 1949, pp. 71–82. The chi-square test was used for testing the significance of differences between the proportions of isolated and non-isolated patient groups. The five per cent level has been used as the criterion of significance.

(1) What were your favorite activities or pastimes when you were 13 or 14 years old?
(2) What sorts of things did you and your friends do together?
(3) What were the types of things you most enjoyed doing *alone* when you were 13 or 14?
(4) Did you enjoy (the things you did alone) as much as you enjoyed playing with other children?
(5) Thinking back to whomever it was you considered your closest friend about the time you were 13 or 14, can you tell me what sorts of things you most enjoyed doing together?
(6) Did you belong to the scouts, the "Y," or any clubs in school, or Sunday School? Which clubs?

TABLE 1. Usual play patterns of patients and controls in adolescence

Usually played	Schiz.	Controls	Manic-Dep.	Controls
With crowd or close friends	20	37	6	11
With siblings	5	6	1	2
Alone	8	1	4	—
Primarily alone, but occasionally with crowd, close friends, or siblings	12	1	2	—
Total	45	45	13	13

This material was then coded without knowledge of any respondent's replies to other questions, or whether the respondent was a patient or a control.[10] Four categories were used: (a) activities primarily social, with few or no solitary activities; (b) both social and solitary activities; (c) activities primarily solitary, with few or no social activities; and (d) ambiguous cases. (See Table 2.)

TABLE 2. Type of activities participated in by patients and controls in adolescence

	Schiz.	Controls	Manic-Dep.	Controls
Activities primarily social, few or no solitary activities	15	21	4	5
Both social and solitary activities	19	20	6	6
Activities primarily solitary, few or no social activities	9	3	3	1
Ambiguous cases	2	1	0	1
Total	45	45	13	13

[10] The answers to these particular questions were transcribed onto separate sheets of paper, without identifying information and without the answers to any other questions. Patients and controls were randomly interspersed. Two coders working independently agreed 94 per cent of the time on the categories in which they would place respondents. We attempted to code this same material along several other continua (for example, physical-sedentary, competitive-non-competitive, structured-non-structured) but coding reliability was too low, approximating only 60 per cent. Interviewing specifications had not been drawn up with such dimensions clearly envisaged.

Finally, these two aspects of social participation—*with whom* the individual played and the *types* of activities in which he engaged—were combined to form a single index. In schematic form, this *Index of Social Participation*[11] is found on page 199.

Comparing patients to controls on the basis of this Index, we find a significantly larger proportion of both the schizophrenics and the manic-depressives than of the controls have been isolates or partial-isolates. However, this is by no means true of all patients—only one-third of the schizophrenics and one-third of the manic-depressives had been isolated or partially-isolated at this age. Finally, patients and controls do *not* differ with respect to the proportion who played only with siblings.[12] For two-thirds of the patients, then, retrospective reports show no discernible social isolation in early adolescence. (See Table 3.)

In the present state of psychiatric knowledge, there is considerable question whether either schizophrenia or manic-depressive psychosis is a single disease of common etiology or a group of similar appearing diseases of differing etiology. For this reason, even though two-thirds of the patients were not isolated as adolescents, there remains the possibility that isolation was a predisposing factor for the remaining one-third; these may constitute a distinct sub-group whose etiology differs from that of other patients. If so, this sub-group cannot be defined according to the usual diagnostic criteria. Schizophrenics are no more likely to have been isolates than are manic-depressives: the proportion of manic-depressives who were classified as having been isolates or partial isolates is 38 per cent, the proportion of schizophrenics 34 per cent. Similarly, within the schizophrenic group the proportion of isolates is approximately the same among paranoids (42 per cent) as it is among catatonics (31 per cent).[13]

Therefore, it appears that, for the cases here studied, social isolation in early adolescence is not a necessary condition for any subtype of schizophrenia. There remains, however, the task of examining the conditions leading up to isolation and the consequences of isolation. We turn to a direct comparison of the adolescent social experiences of the isolated and the non-

[11] Evidence on the consistency of responses to items in this index with related items not included in the index is provided by the answers to the question, "(At the age of 13–14) did you spend more or less time alone than most other children your age did (or did you spend the same amount of time alone?)" The isolates without exception replied, "more time alone." Nine of the eleven partial-isolates replied "more time alone" and the other two replied, "The same amount of time as the average." Among the non-isolates, eight replied that they spent more time alone, 35 that they spent the average time alone, and 27 that they spent less time alone than other children their age.

[12] The most important fact about the persons who played only with siblings is that all of the patients and all but one of the controls in this category are female.

[13] Though the number of cases on which these percentages are based is small, the consistency is so striking that it seems justified to conclude that there are no appreciable differences in the proportion of isolates and partial-isolates in these diagnostic groups. (These percentages are based on 26 cases of paranoid schizophrenia and 16 cases of catatonic schizophrenia.) Nor is isolation a sex-linked phenomenon: the proportion of females among isolates is 55 per cent, among non-isolates, 64 per cent. (Based on 20 male cases and 38 female cases.)

INDEX. Pattern of association in play activities (at age 13–14)

Types of activities	"Alone"	"Alone, but occasionally with friends or crowd"	"With siblings," or "Alone, but occasionally with siblings"	"With close friends" or "crowd"
Social	X	X	Played only with siblings	Non-isolates
Both social and solitary	X	Partial isolates		
Solitary	Isolates	X	X	X

(X = Ambiguous classification)

TABLE 3. Classification of social participation of patients and controls

	Schizophrenics		Controls		Manic-Depres.		Controls	
	Number	Per cent	Number	Per cent	Number	Per cent	Number	Per cent
Isolates	7	16	1	2	3	23	0	0
Partial-isolates	8	18	1	2	2	15	0	0
Played only with siblings	9	20	6	14	1	8	2	15
Non-isolates	19	42	36	80	6	46	9	70
Ambiguous cases	2	4	1	2	1	8	2	15
Total	45	100	45	100	13	100	13	100

isolated patients. Because the proportion of isolates and partial-isolates among the manic-depressives is so similar to the proportion among schizophrenics, the two diagnostic groups will be considered together. The results that will be presented are almost precisely the same as those for the schizophrenic group alone, because empirically the manic-depressive isolates and partial-isolates behaved similarly to the schizophrenic isolates and partial-isolates, and the manic-depressive non-isolates behaved similarly to the schizophrenic non-isolates.

Conditions leading to isolation

There are several possible reasons why the isolates might have been prevented from playing with other children—for example, childhood illness, living on out-of-the-way farms, great residential mobility. But a systematic comparison shows that these factors were no more applicable to the isolated and partially isolated patients than to the non-isolated patients. A slightly higher proportion of the isolates report fewer than five available playmates, but the difference does not approach statistical significance and even among the isolates 14 in 20 report there were five or more children of their age living in the neighborhood. (See Table 4.)

The isolates were not prevented by serious illness from playing with other children: isolates and partial-isolates do not differ significantly from non-isolates with respect to the proportion who report having been very sickly or rather sickly, either in the first decade of life or as a teenager.[14]

[14] Furthermore, those patients who had been included in the Public Health morbidity records did not differ from their controls with respect to the number of days they were absent from school.

TABLE 4. Number of children of similar age reported to have been living in the neighborhood when patient was 13–14 years old

	Isolated and partially-isolated patients[a]	Non-isolated patients[b]
	(20) Per cent	(25) Per cent
None	5	0
One or two	10	4
Three to five	15	4
More than five	70	88
Can't say	0	4
Total	100	100

[a] Isolated and partially-isolated patients have been combined in all tables because empirically they behaved almost identically.

[b] Ambiguous cases and persons who played only with their siblings are excluded from these comparisons. The isolates and partial-isolates are compared only to the clear-cut non-isolated cases.

Finally, the isolates were not prevented by excessive residential mobility from interacting with other children: isolates and partial-isolates do not differ significantly from non-isolates with respect to the proportions who lived in five or more residences, four or more neighborhoods, or four or more cities up to the age of fifteen.[15]

These factors, then, do not explain why the isolates became isolated. Non-isolates and controls who lived on out-of-the-way farms apparently managed to play in the school yard after school hours or to have their

[15] Comparisons of residential mobility are based upon complete residential histories secured from all patients. These histories were checked against past Hagerstown City Directories and found to be highly consistent with Directory listings.

classmates visit them at home. The isolates did not do this. Non-isolates and controls whose families moved around frequently nevertheless managed to find playmates where they moved; isolates did not.

Nor is social isolation the result of parental restrictions upon the activities of the child: no greater proportion of isolates and partial-isolates than of non-isolates report parental restrictions either on physical activities or on choice of friends.

Isolation and family relationships

How about the patterning of familial relationships? Let us state, first, that a larger proportion of *patients* than of *controls* recall their mothers as having been more easily angered, more dominating, more anxious for the children to get ahead, less likely to be satisfied with the children's behavior, and more restrictive than their fathers. Correspondingly, a larger proportion of patients recall their fathers as having been more likely in case of disagreement to give in, less certain of themselves and less strict than their mothers.[16]

We present a comparison of patients to controls on three of these items as an illustration: a larger proportion of patients than of controls recall their mothers as having been more easily angered, more dominating, and more restrictive than their fathers. (See Table 5.)

TABLE 5. Recollections of parental behavior by patients and controls[a]

Respondent recalls mother as	Patients	Controls
	(52) Per cent	(52) Per cent
More easily angered than father	50	17
More dominating than father	46	19
More likely to restrict the children's freedom than father	38	6

[a] Excludes those patients and controls raised by only one parent.

But *isolated* and *partially-isolated* patients do not differ significantly from *non-isolate* patients in their comparisons of mother to father on these same items. (See Table 6.)

TABLE 6. Recollections of parental behavior by isolated and non-isolated patients

Respondent recalls mother as	Isolated and partially-isolated patients	Non-isolated patients
	(18) Per cent	(23) Per cent
More easily angered than father	44	48
More dominating than father	49	40
More likely to restrict the children's freedom than father	32	43

The same is true of all other aspects of family functioning that the patients report differently from the controls: in no case do the isolated and partially-isolated patients differ from the non-isolated patients. This is true, for example, of their perceptions of how well their parents got along; how close they felt to each of their parents; to which parent they turned when in trouble; and which parent made the day-to-day decisions, the major decisions, and the decisions that particularly affected the children. Nor do isolated patients differ from non-isolated patients on a number of other aspects of family structure and functioning with respect to which patients do not differ from controls—such as family composition; deaths, illnesses, or divorce of parents; occupations of parents; parental aspirations for the children; or the respondents' relations with their siblings. In summary we find no evidence that the social isolation of one third of the patients was a resultant of, or even a correlate of, the familial relationships studied.

[16] We have analyzed these data in detail in "Parental Authority Behavior and Schizophrenia," *American Journal of Orthopsychiatry,* in press.

Isolation and withdrawal

We have been unable to find any evidence that the isolates have been prevented from social participation because of lack of available playmates, residential mobility, illness, or parental restrictions. Nor have we been able to find any evidence that the isolation of one third of the patients resulted from the particular nature of their family relationships. Did the isolates and partial-isolates become isolated, then, because they withdrew from social relationships? Here our primary sources of information are the hospital case-records, based on interviews with family respondents, together with supplementary research interviews that we have conducted with the siblings of still hospitalized patients.

Information indicating that the patient's isolation could be viewed as an expression of his shy, timid, or fearful personality was reported for seven of the ten persons whom we have classified as *isolates*. The pattern is quite different for those patients classified as partial-isolates: family respondents almost uniformly stated that these patients appeared normal and sociable at age 13 or 14. This was true also of the patients classified as *non-isolates,* none of whose case-records gives evidence that his relatives considered him shy, withdrawn, or at all disturbed at age 13–14. But relatives of three of these patients state that subsequent to that age the patients definitely withdrew from normal social participation.

It would seem, then, that the patients whom we have classified as *isolates* had already manifested signs of personality disturbance sufficient to be noted by family respondents by the time they were 13 or 14 years old. Patients whom we have classified as *partial-*

isolates appeared normal to their relatives at that age, even though they report that they had already begun to withdraw from social activities by that age. Presumably the isolation process had not proceeded as far. This process had proceeded least far for the patients classified as *non-isolates*.

The significance of social isolation

We had anticipated that patients who had been isolated from an early age would either have been hospitalized earlier than other patients or would have suffered a more long-lasting illness. Neither of these is the case. Isolates and partial-isolates were hospitalized at approximately the same ages as were non-isolates. (See Table 7.)

TABLE 7. Age at first hospitalization

	Isolated and partially-isolated patients	Non-isolated patients
	(20) Per cent	(25) Per cent
Under 25	15	28
25–34	40	28
35–44	40	36
45–49	5	8
Total	100	100

Nor did the isolates and partial-isolates require longer hospitalization, or respond less adequately to hospitalization, than did the non-isolates. (See Table 8.)

At the time of the research interview, we were unable to discern any important differences in the current functioning of the two groups of patients. Furthermore the two groups do not differ with respect to their current patterns of social relationships—how they spend leisure time, whether or not they belong to formal groups, and how frequently they get together informally with friends. These data all lead to the conclusion that social isolation in this early period does not seem to have appreciably influenced the development of the illness.

Summary and theoretical implications

We may summarize our findings as follows: (a) approximately one-third of the schizophrenic and manic-depressive patients give evidence of having been socially-isolated at age 13–14, whereas appreciably none of the normal controls gives evidence of having been isolated at that age; (b) we have been unable to find any evidence that the isolated patients had been prevented from interacting with their peers because of a lack of available playmates, excessive residential mobility, severe illness, or parental restrictions; (c) we have been unable to find any evidence of a correlation between social isolation and familial relationships—that is, we have been unable to ascertain any appreciable difference between the perceptions of their relationships with parents and siblings held by the isolated patients and those held by the non-isolated patients.

These data, it must be recognized, are based on the retrospective impressions of a group of persons who have undergone the severely disorienting experience of psychosis. But a systematic comparison of the research interviews with the patients to prior hospital interviews with their relatives shows a high level of consistency for 26 of the 30 patients whose hospital records contain data on this topic.

Our general conclusion must be, then, that for the group here studied the data do not support the hypothesis that social isolation in adolescence is a predisposing factor in either schizophrenia or manic-depressive psychosis. Only a third of the patients were isolated in adolescent life, and even for them isolation does not seem to have been instrumental in predisposing them to psychosis. Nor does it seem to increase the duration of hospitalization.

In early statements of the social isolation hypothesis, it was posited that isolation of any person for an extended period of time results in schizophrenia. Later the process was seen as far more complex: a particular type of person, living in a particular social setting, becomes rebuffed and rejected by his peers; after fruitless attempts to gain acceptance, he finally withdraws into a shell of isolation.

One wonders why, if this complex series of events is seen as necessary to the schizophrenic process, isolation is seized upon as the crucial element that leads to schizophrenia. Why was the individual rebuffed in the first place? Why did he react so extremely to rebuff as to withdraw from all social interaction? Does not his behavior before he became isolated indicate that his personality development was already quite abnormal? A far simpler explanation of the isolation experience was afforded by Bleuler as long ago as 1908 in his classic volume on schizophrenia: "The overt symptomatology certainly represents the expression of a more or less successful attempt to find a way out of an intolerable situation."[17]

An interpretation in harmony with the findings of this study is that as a result of inadequacies in their social relationships, both within and outside the family, certain individuals come to feel that they do not really belong to their peer-groups—that is, they become *alienated* from their peers. Under severe enough conditions, alienation may lead to a withdrawal from social interaction, that is, to isolation. But it need not do so; it might lead, for example, to compulsive interaction such as that engaged in by some manic patients, or it might not lead to abnormal behavior at all. In any case, isolation does not seem to be the crucial experience in predisposing the individual to illness.

Thus, in terms of process, social isolation is to be viewed as a sign that the individual's interpersonal

[17] Eugen Bleuler, *Dementia Praecox, or the Group of Schizophrenias*, English edition translated by Joseph Zinken, New York: International Universities Press, 1950, p. 460.

TABLE 8. Status of isolated and non-isolated patients at yearly intervals following date of first admission[a]

	ONE YEAR		TWO YEARS		THREE YEARS	
	Isolated and partially-isolated patients	Non-isolated patients	Isolated and partially-isolated patients	Non-isolated patients	Isolated and partially-isolated patients	Non-isolated patients
	(20) Per cent	(25) Per cent	(19) Per cent	(22) Per cent	(17) Per cent	(18) Per cent
Patient resident in a mental hospital	30	16	26	22	18	22
Patient discharged, occupation similar to that prior to illness	45	60	48	60	47	56
Patient discharged, functioning at markedly reduced level	20	24	26	18	29	22
Patient discharged, but no data available as to level on which he is operating	5	0	0	0	6	0
Total	100	100	100	100	100	100

[a] The number of patients included beyond the first year decreases because some of the patients had been admitted to the hospital less than two years prior to the time of data collection.

difficulties have become so great that he is no longer capable of functioning in interpersonal relationships. The question of how he got that way is not a question of social isolation, *per se*. It is rather a series of problems, starting with the question of what are the conditions that produce alienation, and continuing with the processes by which subsequent interpersonal experiences transform this base of interpersonal difficulty into interpersonal failure.

Replication

MENTAL DISORDER AND THE PRIMARY GROUP

The replication will entail the same major comparison illustrated in the original study: an analysis of the covariation between illness and adolescent participation. However, a number of departures from the original should be noted. First, our measure of mental illness, the anxiety scale, is best interpreted as an indicator of neurosis rather than psychosis. The rationale for using such a measure in this laboratory problem is the view that the difference between them may be a matter of degree. This is a necessary substitution in that psychosis is difficult to measure and we do not have easy access to a group diagnosed as psychotic. Also, Kohn and Clausen's comparisons were drawn between mentally ill individuals and a carefully matched group of normal individuals. Limitations in the size of the sample for this replication do not permit such rigor. We will only crudely approximate matched groups by making separate comparisons for males and females. Finally, Kohn and Clausen's comparisons were not only between ill and normal persons but between institutionalized and noninstitutionalized people as well. Could this affect your findings, or theirs? You may want to consider this question in your write-up.

Hypothesis

1. State whether social isolates will have higher, the same, or lower scores on the anxiety scale than non-isolates.

2. As an additional hypothesis, state whether you think the predicted relationship between isolation and anxiety will be different for males and females.

3. See Appendix A for general information on writing hypotheses.

Empirical indicators for this problem

1. Sex:

   1. Male
   2. Female

43. Try to think back to when you were 13 to 14 years old. At this age did you usually:

   1. Stay alone
   2. Stay alone, but occasionally hang out with friends or a crowd

3. Hang out with brothers and sisters
4. Hang out with close friends or a crowd

44. At age 13 to 14, to what extent did you enjoy the things you did alone as much as the things you did playing with other children:

1. Enjoyed things alone more
2. About the same
3. Enjoyed things with other children more

45. At age 13 to 14, did you spend more or less time alone than most other children your age:

1. More time alone than most
2. About average
3. Less time alone than most

46. During your senior year in high school, about how often did you visit friends (or have friends over to your house):

0. Never
1. Only once that year
2. Two or three times
3. Four to eight times
4. About once a month (9 to 12 times)
5. Two or three times a month
6. About once a week
7. A few times a week (2 to 4 times)
8. Almost every day or more often

47. About how often during your senior year in high school did you attend meetings of clubs and organizations:

0. Never
1. Only once that year
2. Two or three times
3. Four to eight times
4. About once a month (9 to 12 times)
5. Two or three times a month
6. About once a week
7. A few times a week (2 to 4 times)
8. Almost every day or more often

53. Do you ever have any trouble getting to sleep or staying asleep?

1. Never
2. Not very much
3. Pretty often
4. Nearly all the time

54. Have you ever been bothered by nervousness, feeling fidgety or tense?

1. Never
2. Not very much
3. Pretty often
4. Nearly all the time

55. Have you ever been bothered by shortness of breath when you were not working hard or exercising?

1. Never
2. Hardly ever
3. Sometimes
4. Many times

56. Have you ever been bothered by your heart beating hard?

1. Never
2. Hardly ever
3. Sometimes
4. Many times

57. Do you find it difficult to get up in the morning?

1. Never
2. Not very much
3. Pretty often
4. Nearly all the time

58. Have there ever been times when you couldn't take care of things because you just couldn't get going?

1. Never
2. Hardly ever
3. Sometimes
4. Many times

Data analysis

1. *Sort* the code sheets into rank order on the basis of box 47tt, the "Adolescent Social Participation Index."

2. *Divide* the code sheets into the following three groups:

High social participation: These should be the third of the code sheets with the highest scores

Medium social participation: The code sheets with scores in the middle

Low social participation: The lowest scoring one-third of the sample

Be sure that everyone with the same score is in the same group.

3. *Sub-sort* each of these three groups by sex according to box 1:

1 = Males
2 = Females

4. *Tally* the male group's "Anxiety Index" scores (box 58t) into the "f" column of Table 1. Do this for each of the three social participation categories.

5. *Compute* the mean anxiety score for each participation group. See Appendix C for instructions.

6. *Repeat* steps 3, 4 and 5 for females, entering the data on Table 2.

Lab report

1. See the "Outline for Laboratory Reports" in Appendix A for general directions.
2. Give primary attention to the differences between

social participation groups. However, you should also consider whether there are differences between males and females in the way social participation is related to anxiety. If differences are obtained, attempt to explain why. One of the most important contributions of empirical research is to "specify" theories—that is, to determine the conditions under which they hold and do not hold.

References

Axelrod, Morris, "Urban Structure and Social Participation," *American Sociological Review, 21* (February 1956), pp. 13–18.

Cooley, Charles H., *Social Organization*. New York: Scribner's, 1909.

Durkheim, Emile, *Suicide*, trans. by George Simpson. New York: Free Press, 1951.

Faris, Robert E. L. and H. Warren Dunham, *Mental Disorders in Urban Areas*. Chicago: University of Chicago Press, 1939.

Jaco, E. Gartley, "The Social Isolation Hypothesis and Schizophrenia," *American Sociological Review, 19* (October 1954), pp. 567–577.

Murdock, George P., *Social Structure*. New York: Macmillan, 1949.

Shils, Edward A., "The Study of the Primary Group," in Daniel Lerner and Harold D. Laswell, eds., *The Policy Sciences*. Stanford University Press, 1951, pp. 44–69.

Stone, Gregory P., "City Shoppers and Urban Identification: Observation on the Social Psychology of City Life," *American Journal of Sociology, 60* (July 1954), pp. 36–45.

Yarrow, Leon, "Maternal Deprivation: Toward an Empirical and Conceptual Re-evaluation," *Psychological Bulletin, 63* (November 1961), pp. 459–490.

Name________________________

Date________________________

TABLE 1. Anxiety score by group participation, males

ANXIETY SCALE (Box 58t) x	MALES (1 in Box 1) ADOLESCENT SOCIAL PARTICIPATION GROUP (Box 47t)					
	High = upper third		Medium = middle third		Low = lower third	
	f	fx	f	fx	f	fx
20 and over						
19						
18						
17						
16						
15						
14						
13						
12						
11						
10						
9						
8						
7						
6						
TOTALS						
Mean =						
+ (No info.)		☒		☒		☒

TABLE 2. Anxiety score by group participation, females

ANXIETY SCALE (Box 58t) x	FEMALES (2 in Box 1) ADOLESCENT SOCIAL PARTICIPATION GROUP (Box 47t)					
	High = upper third		Medium = middle third		Low = lower third	
	f	fx	f	fx	f	fx
20 and over						
19						
18						
17						
16						
15						
14						
13						
12						
11						
10						
9						
8						
7						
6						
TOTALS						
Mean =						
+ (No info.)		☒		☒		☒

LABORATORY REPORT FOR PROBLEM ______

Course or
Section ______ Date ______ Name ______

HYPOTHESIS: ______

SAMPLE: ______

INDEPENDENT VARIABLE(S): ______

DEPENDENT VARIABLE(S): ______

OTHER FACTORS: ______

LABORATORY REPORT FOR PROBLEM

SUMMARY OF FINDINGS:

DISCUSSION:

PROBLEM 13

ORGANIZATIONS

Persons in contemporary society are increasingly involved in large-scale social organizations. As consumers they deal with giant industries; as citizens they join national political parties; as students they increasingly enter large colleges and universities. The benefits of participation in organizations are many, but the most obvious is that certain objectives can only be attained when individuals commit themselves to working together and in this way reap advantages beyond those any one individual could gain by himself (Greer, 1961). Size, pooled resources, and reduced operating costs are but a few of the direct benefits foreseen. However, once an organization is created or joined, the attainment of organizational goals is far from certain. Difficulties such as poor coordination, red tape, inadequate personnel, and poor management are some of the many internal problems which may make organizations ineffective in achieving the very goals they were designed to attain.

Max Weber, one of the founders of modern sociology, attempted to identify the cause of organization ineffectiveness by specifying exactly what an organization required to rationally and efficiently achieve its goals (Weber, 1958). Weber considered a number of factors: clear lines of authority and responsibility, unbiased decisions, rules to govern all organizational activity, and the possibility for participants in the organization to commit themselves to a career in their work. Each of these things, Weber felt, would maximize the rationality of the organization and the dedication of its members. For example, clarifying lines of authority would locate power in specific offices and thus avoid commonplace tendencies to "pass the buck"; or, unbiased decisions would have the presumed effect of narrowing judgments to the work situation alone, rather than permitting consideration of personal likes, dislikes, and other factors irrelevant to the task at hand.

In reality, few organizations resemble the ideal model Weber portrayed. Sometimes the very conditions specified in the model create unanticipated circumstances which work against efficiency (March and Simon, 1958). For example, in an analysis of a federal agency Blau found that clear-cut lines of authority were at the root of irrational behavior (Blau, 1956). The blueprint of this organization required the workers to report to their supervisors if they were unable to handle a problem. The workers, however, felt that asking their supervisors for aid was tantamount to an embarrassing admission of ignorance. Instead, they turned to their fellow workers, thereby avoiding the specified lines of formal authority and responsibility. Some theorists, in fact, have speculated that wherever there is a high emphasis on rationality, a countervailing emphasis on irrationality will also be found (Udy, 1959).

In some instances Weber's criteria for organizational effectiveness are totally abandoned. Mayors of various-sized cities, for example, are at times removed from office every two years with little thought given to the disruption of governmental organization. Many unions still retain rules creating nepotism and thus dispense with the idea that persons be hired according to their skill rather than kinship connections. The reading for the present problem illustrates the consequences of abandoning the notion of "career commitment"—a factor considered by Weber to be of central importance in maintaining organizational effectiveness. The formal organizations considered are baseball teams.

Baseball, in contemporary America, is a multimillion-dollar industry with large profits or losses at stake. How well a team is faring in the league standings generally affects attendance and income. This means that teams performing poorly are also likely to be financial risks. One reaction to this is that the club's administration will frequently fire the manager—the person they see as responsible for the team's performance. It is precisely this issue of managerial succession and, more generally, personnel turnover, to which Grusky, the author of the study for this problem, directs attention. His argument is clear: While dismissal may appear at the moment to be desirable, one of its consequences is to reduce continuity of experience and increase strain within the organization, thus impairing the organization's effectiveness in winning games. To support this point, Grusky shows that a high turnover of managers is inversely related to a team's league standing.

It should be noted that questions have been raised about the evidence in support of Grusky's argument. Gamson and Scotch (1964), for example, argue for the more common-sense perspective that an ineffective team will likely fire its manager, rather than the organization perspective that turnover reduces effectiveness. Grusky's data do show a *correlation* or association between turnover of managers and organizational effectiveness, but despite his disclaimers they do not establish which is cause and which is effect.

Important: The data for this problem must be looked up in the library *before* coming to class to do the problem. See the first step under DATA ANALYSIS.

MANAGERIAL SUCCESSION AND ORGANIZATIONAL EFFECTIVENESS / *Oscar Grusky*

A negative correlation is found between (1) rates of managerial succession and effectiveness and (2) change in succession rate and change in organizational effectiveness among sixteen professional baseball teams examined over two time periods, 1921–41 and 1951–58.

A set of ten variables from organization theory is applied to the analysis of team performance and administrative succession. A number of illustrative propositions are presented.

The major purpose of this study was to test two related hypotheses: (1) that rates of administrative succession and degree of organizational effectiveness are negatively correlated, and (2) that a change in the rate of administrative succession is negatively correlated with a change in organizational effectiveness.[1] The hypotheses are deliberately stated so as not to attribute causality solely to either succession or effectiveness. We assumed that the variables induce reciprocal effects. High rates of succession should produce declining organizational effectiveness, and low effectiveness should encourage high rates of administrative succession.

To obtain anything resembling an adequate field test of these hypotheses required a substantial number of formal organizations that, ideally, were identical in official goals, size, and authority structure. If the objectives of the organizations were not similar, then obviously it would not be feasible to compare their relative effectiveness, since this concept refers to the extent to which an organization is able to move toward the accomplishment of its official aims. We know that for business organizations and certain public agencies, and perhaps for other kinds as well, rates of succession are positively related to organizational size.[2] Therefore, we sought a sample of organizations of similar size.

There is some evidence, although it is highly limited, that organizations with different types of authority structures respond in very different ways to personnel changes at top levels in the hierarchy.[3] Hence, organizations with similar types of structures of authority were desirable.

In addition, a relatively "clean" field test of the hypotheses demanded reliable and valid measures of rates of administrative succession and organizational effectiveness. Since the sixteen organizations selected for study, professional baseball teams, met all the relatively stringent requirements described, a second objective of this research was to illustrate some of the potentialities of sports organizations as objects of sociological investigation.

Methods and findings

All data for this study were gathered by means of secondary analysis of published documents.[4] Baseball teams and, in fact, most professional sports clubs offer the research advantages of public records of team personnel and team performance. This fact, as we shall see, also has important implications for the behavior of the organization.

Two time periods, 1921–41 and 1951–58, were selected for study. It was deemed wise to skip the

Reprinted from "Managerial Succession and Organizational Effectiveness" by Oscar Grusky from *The American Journal of Sociology,* LXIX (July 1963) pp. 21–31 by permission of The University of Chicago Press.

A number of people have contributed to this study. I am grateful to Judith Kairath for doing the coding and to John Vincent and Jerry King for computational work. The Helms Athletic Foundation was most gracious in permitting use of its library and records. I am also indebted to the members of the Department of Sociology, University of California, Davis, for their numerous helpful comments when an earlier version of this paper was presented at a seminar. Professors Mayer Zald, Charles R. Wright, and Fritz J. Roethlisberger and an anonymous reviewer gave much constructive advice. This is an expanded version of a paper read at the annual meetings of the American Sociological Association in Washington, D.C., 1962.

[1] This hypothesis was discussed in my "Administrative Succession in Formal Organizations," *Social Forces,* XXXIX (December, 1960), 105–15.

[2] See my "Corporate Size, Bureaucratization, and Managerial Succession," *American Journal of Sociology,* LXVII (November, 1961), 261–69, and L. Kriesberg, "Careers, Organization Size, and Succession," *American Journal of Sociology,* LXVIII (November, 1962), 355–59. For a comprehensive discussion of other variables related to size see T. Caplow, "Organizational Size," *Administrative Science Quarterly,* II (March 1957), 484–505.

[3] D. M. Sills, *The Volunteers* (Glencoe, Ill.: Free Press, 1957); W. A. Lunden, "The Tenure and Turnover of State Prison Wardens," *American Journal of Corrections,* XIX (November-December, 1957), 14–15; and A. Etzioni, "Authority Structure and Organizational Effectiveness," *Administrative Science Quarterly,* IV (June, 1959), 43–67.

[4] H. Hurkin and S. C. Thompson, *The Official Encyclopedia of Baseball* (2d rev. ed.; New York: A. S. Barnes & Co., 1959); H. Johnson, *Who's Who in Baseball* (New York: Buston Publishing Co., 1953); F. Menke, *The Encyclopedia of Sports* (2d rev. ed.; New York: A. S. Barnes & Co., 1960); *1958 Baseball Guide and Record Book* (St. Louis, Mo.: Sporting News, 1958); T. Spink and Son, *Baseball Register,* compiled by T. Spink and P. Rickart (St. Louis, Mo.: Sporting News, 1940–41, 1951–58).

World War II and immediate post–World War II periods.

The structure of baseball organizations is such that ultimate responsibility for the performance of the team is almost always fixed on one position, that of field manager. At the same time, official authority is generally concentrated in this position. Therefore, it was clear that personnel changes among field managers rather than club presidents, general managers, or team captains were central to the study. The number of managerial changes for each time period or the average length of managerial tenure constituted the rate of succession for each team.

The measure of organizational effectiveness was team standing, based on the number of games won and lost at the completion of the season. This might be considered analogous in some respects to productivity in industrial organizations. Georgopoulos and Tannenbaum's study of thirty-two similar suborganizations or stations demonstrated significant correlations between their various measures of organizational effectiveness: expert assessment of station effectiveness, productivity, intragroup strain, and flexibility.[5] It would certainly be safe to say that, among baseball experts, team standing is the most widely accepted criterion of effectiveness. Financial profit is also an important criterion. It would appear that the profitability of a baseball club is highly related to its team standing. Consistent with this assumption, we found a strong positive correlation between team standing and yearly attendance.[6]

Table 1 presents the basic data of the study. The data for Periods I and II taken separately or together strongly supported the hypothesized negative correlation between rates of managerial succession and organizational effectiveness. The correlations were considerably greater in the second time period, 1951–58, than in the earlier one. Rates of succession and team standing correlated − .40 in the first period and − .60 in the second. One team that contributed to the lower correlation in the earlier period was the Philadelphia Athletics. Despite the fact that the team consistently finished in the second division between 1921 and 1941, no managerial successions took place during this period. Undoubtedly, manager Connie Mack's ownership of the club assisted his long tenure. The Athletics experienced frequent managerial succession during 1951–58 with the departure of Mack from the scene.

In contrast, the Yankees, as Table 1 suggests, contributed to the magnitude of the correlation in both time periods. Not only were they highly effective, but they also experienced few managerial changes.

The second hypothesis was tested by examining the relationship between changes from Period I to Period II in the average length of time a manager retained his position with a team and changes in the team's standing. That is, we wanted to see if teams that kept their managers for shorter periods (experienced more succession) in Period II than they had in Period I were less effective in the later period and vice versa. In fact, the average tenure for managers declined in Period II for all but two clubs. As Table 2 demonstrates, our hypothesis was again strongly supported.[7] All eight teams that increased considerably their rate of managerial succession over that of the earlier period experienced a decline in average team standing. Moreover, the two clubs that decreased their rate of succession increased their effectiveness. However, it was evident that those teams that had experienced frequent and infrequent succession in the original period needed to be analyzed separately. Therefore, we controlled for average length of managerial tenure in Period I (a control for average team standing in Period I also would have been desirable, but we did not have a sufficient number of cases). The hypothesis was partially supported when the relationship was examined separately for teams that were below and above the median with respect to rates of succession in the first period (Table 3). Moreover, it should be noted that one deviant case in Table 3 (the St. Louis Cardinals) was the team with the *lowest managerial tenure of any team in Period I*. This low rate remained about the same in Period II, although team effectiveness declined somewhat. We might speculate that perhaps (1) the very slight alteration of the club's policy of frequent succession was not above the threshold necessary to raise the organization's effectiveness, and/or (2) the slight decrease in the club's effectiveness did not encourage the owners to alter their policy of frequent succession.

The findings of this study may be compared with a recent laboratory investigation by Trow.[8] Using Leavitt's Common-Symbol problem and the five-position chain organizational network, Trow found no significant linear relationship between mean rate of succession and long-run organizational performance. He did find that the mean performance of the twelve teams with the lowest replacement rates was signifi-

[5] B. S. Georgopoulos and A. S. Tannenbaum, "A Study of Organizational Effectiveness," *American Sociological Review*, XXII (October, 1957), 534–40.

[6] Profitability, attendance, and effectiveness are related in part because prolonged increases in profits tend to yield increases in organizational control over the market for new talent and therefore tend to produce a more effective farm system. Interpretation of the correlation between team standing and attendance should be approached cautiously. Attendance may also be a function of variables such as the total population of the metropolitan area, its particular age and sex distribution, and, of course, the number of professional baseball teams in the community.

[7] We realize some of the interpretative limitations of utilizing team averages as measures of succession. A study comparing the "effectiveness" and length of tenure of the successor and his managerial predecessor is in progress. In this investigation the object of study is the manager and not the team. Some limitations in our measure of effectiveness also should be noted. Team standing may not reflect perfectly the ability of the team, just as fielding and batting averages are not ideal measures of individual performance. E.g., a team may improve over the course of a season and because of a poor start finish only second, although it is the best team by other standards. And the bias of the official scorer has a lot to do with the players' fielding and batting averages.

[8] D. B. Trow, "Membership Succession and Team Performance," *Human Relations*, XIII, No. 3 (1960), 259–68. An immediate problem in making such a contrast is the critical difference in the objects of study. Trow applies his findings to "self-organizing" groups and points out several limitations of the experimental situation relevant to generalizing the findings. Formal organizations typically possess properties that laboratory organizations such as Trow's do not possess, such as: a formal system of authority, at least three levels of authority, and

TABLE 1. Measures of succession and effectiveness for sixteen professional baseball organizations over two time periods[a]

Team	NO. OF SUCCESSIONS Period I (1)	Period II (2)	Periods I and II (3)	AVERAGE TEAM STANDING[b] Period I (4)	Period II (5)	Periods I and II (6)
Phillies	7	3	10	7.2	4.8	6.5
Giants	1	1	2	2.7	3.4	2.9
Cardinals	10	4	14	3.0	3.8	3.2
Braves	7	3	10	6.3	2.8	5.3
Pirates	6	3	9	3.2	6.9	4.2
Cubs	8	3	11	3.5	6.2	4.4
Dodgers	4	1	5	4.9	2.2	4.2
Reds	7	3	10	4.9	4.9	4.9
Athletics	0	4	4	4.8	6.6	5.3
Nats	6	3	9	4.2	6.8	4.9
Yankees	2	0	2	1.8	1.2	1.6
White Sox	8	2	10	5.6	2.9	4.9
Red Sox	8	2	10	6.0	3.9	5.4
Indians	6	1	7	3.9	2.6	3.6
Browns (Orioles)	9	5	14	5.6	6.8	5.9
Tigers	4	4	8	3.9	5.4	4.3

[a] Period I, 1921–41; Period II, 1951–58. Rank-order correlations (Kendall's tau) and one-tail p values are: cols. (1) and (4), −.40 ($p < .02$); cols. (2) and (5), −.60 ($p < .001$); and cols. (3) and (6), −.43 ($p < .001$).

[b] A numerically high team standing meant low effectiveness.

TABLE 2. Relationship between change in average length of managerial tenure and average team standing from period I to period II for fifteen professional baseball teams[a]

Change in average managerial tenure	CHANGE IN AVERAGE TEAM STANDING Increased effectiveness	Decreased effectiveness
Tenure longer	2	0
Tenure about same[b]	4	1
Tenure much shorter	1	7

[a] $P = .009$ by Fisher's Exact Test if the categories "Longer tenure" and "Tenure about same" are combined. One team (Reds) that did not change its average team standing was excluded.

[b] Defined as a decrease of 0.3 year or less.

planned task differentiation. Moreover, when laboratory investigations have attempted to manipulate some of these differentiating variables, important results have been indicated. Hence, H. H. Kelley found that the existence of a hierarchy influenced communication ("Communication in Experimentally Created Hierarchies," *Human Relations,* IV, [1951], 39–56), and I. D. Steiner and W. I. Field found that the assignment of roles to persons in laboratory groups affected persons' perceptions of and reactions to one another ("Role Assignment and Interpersonal Influence," *Journal of Abnormal and Social Psychology,* LX, No. 2 [1960], 239–45). Of course, there are outstanding examples of experimental studies that have attempted to establish structures which legitimately could be called formal organizations. See, e.g., W. M. Evan and M. Zelditch, Jr., "A Laboratory Studv on Bureaucratic Authoritv," *American Sociological Review,* XXVI, No. 6 (1961), 883–93.

TABLE 3. Relationship between change in average length of managerial tenure and average team standing from period I to period II for fifteen professional baseball teams, controlling for average length of managerial tenure in period I[a]

Change in average managerial tenure	CHANGE IN AVERAGE TEAM STANDING Increased effectiveness	Decreased effectiveness	One-tail p level[b]
A. Short tenure in Period I (below median):			
Tenure longer or about same[c]	3	1	.45
Tenure much shorter	1	2	
B. Long tenure in Period I (above median):			
Tenure longer or about same	3	0	.018
Tenure much shorter	0	5	

[a] One team (Reds) that did not change its average team standing was excluded.

[b] By Fisher's Exact Test.

[c] "About same" was defined as a decrease of 0.3 year or less.

cantly superior to the mean performance of the twelve teams with the highest rates of succession. Trow discovered that *variability* in the rate of succession was a more important factor in team performance, noting that "whatever the average rate of succession, an increase in the rate, i.e., a temporal clustering of succession, tends to bring about a decrease in the level of organizational performance." In addition, he found that ability of the successor was a major factor in organizational performance. Thus, despite considerable differences between the techniques of secondary analysis and contrived experimentation, the findings of the two studies appear to be consistent at least with respect to the second hypothesis.

Succession and effectiveness

It is apparent that theoretical explanations for the findings of this study may be pursued from two opposite directions; it may be assumed that either effectiveness or succession functions as the primary independent variable. Our data demonstrate only the existence of an association, not its cause. Logic or common knowledge will not permit us to decide the issue. However, there is no intrinsic reason why a particular variable, such as rate of succession, could not be *both* a cause and an effect of effectiveness. This may very well be so in this instance.

A common-sense explanation for our results might suggest that effectiveness alone is the cause. The manager is fired because the team performs badly. Not only is the simplicity of this explanation appealing, but the negative correlation between succession and effectiveness is fully consistent with it. However, if taken by itself, this approach possesses all the deficiencies properly attributed to orientations that rest only on common knowledge: they typically do not stimulate careful empirical test; they typically do not suggest additional propositions which might be worthy of examination; they typically do not fit in systematically to a comprehensive body of generalizations in the field of interest. Naturally, we prefer explanations that can meet these and other criteria described by Nagel somewhat more adequately.[9]

If we assume that effectiveness and succession influence each other by contributing to managerial role strain, it is possible to formulate an alternative explanation for the major findings, one that ties in with a growing body of theory and research. It was this assumption that originally provoked this study. Succession, because it represents a universal organizational process, and effectiveness, because all formal organizations tend to strive toward the attainment of their official objectives, are strategic concepts for studying organizations within a comparative framework. Numerous studies conducted in the laboratory as well as in the field suggest that these variables produce reciprocal effects. For example, both Gouldner's and Guest's field research as well as Trow's experiment indicate that succession influences organizational effectiveness.[10] On the other hand, Hamblin's laboratory study suggests that the ineffectiveness of the group contributes to high rates of succession among the leaders. When the leader could not solve a crisis problem confronting the group, he was replaced.[11] Accordingly, the relationship between rates of succession and organizational effectiveness was analyzed within the context of a conceptual scheme that focused on their interrelationships with a number of other variables: managerial (or executive) role strain, expectation of replacement, style of supervision, subgroup stability, morale, clientele support, degree of discrepancy between managerial authority and responsibility, and availability of objective assessment of organizational performance.

Figure 1 presents the proposed network of interrelations of the variables. The arrows indicate the direction of influence. Key propositions discussed below are followed by a numerical reference to the relevant variables. Of course, no attempt was made to exhaust the logical possibilities in the formation of propositions.

The magnitude of managerial role strain is a general factor conditioning the nature of the relationship between succession and effectiveness.[12] By role strain is meant the extent to which role performance produces stress for the occupant of a position that cannot be fully relieved by institutionally legitimated means. Hence, this concept refers to the amount of tension with which a person is confronted as a result of occupying a particular office in an organization. The sources

[9] Ernest Nagel in a recent book provides an excellent discussion of the elements of the scientific and common sense approaches. He observed that "the sciences seek to discover and to formulate in general terms the conditions under which events of various sorts occur, the corresponding happenings. This goal can be achieved only by distinguishing or isolating certain properties in the subject matter studied and by ascertaining the repeatable patterns of dependence in which these properties stand to one another. In consequence, when the inquiry is successful, propositions that hitherto appeared to be quite unrelated are exhibited as linked to each other in determinate ways by virtue of their place in a system of explanation" (*The Structure of Science* [New York: Harcourt, Brace & World, 1961], p. 4).

[10] A. Gouldner, *Patterns of Industrial Bureaucracy* (Glencoe, Ill.: Free Press, 1954); R. H. Guest, *Organizational Change* (Homewood, Ill.: Dorsey Press, 1962); and Trow, *op. cit.* See also W. F. Whyte, "The Social Structure of the Restaurant Industry," *American Journal of Sociology,* LIV (January, 1949), 302–10; C. R. Christiansen, *Management Succession in Small and Growing Enterprises* (Boston: Graduate School of Business Administration, Harvard University, 1953); E. Dale, "Du Pont: Pioneer in Systematic Management," *Administrative Science Quarterly,* II (June, 1957), 26–30; O. Grusky, "Role Conflict in Organization: A Study of Prison Camp Officials," *Administrative Science Quarterly,* III (March, 1959), 463–467; and R. H. McCleery, *Policy Change in Prison Management* (East Lansing: Michigan State University, 1957), pp. 10–27.

[11] R. L. Hamblin, "Leadership and Crisis," *Sociometry,* XXI (December, 1958), 322–35.

[12] Position or office refers to a category that is located in the formal social structure of an organization. In a formal organization the category is defined in terms of its relationship with other positions that in turn are organized around the official objectives of the system. By role is meant a "set of evaluative standards applied to an incumbent of a particular position" (see N. Gross, W. S. Mason, and A. W. McEachern, *Explorations in Role Analysis* [New York: John Wiley & Sons, 1958], p. 60). Role strain is viewed in the present study as a more inclusive concept than role conflict. The latter is limited to situations of strain produced by incompatible expectations. W. J. Goode defines role strain as "the felt difficulty in fulfilling role obligations." Our definition differs in that it does not require a perfect association between perceived and objective role strain ("A Theory of Role Strain," *American Sociological Review,* XXIV [August, 1960], 483–96).

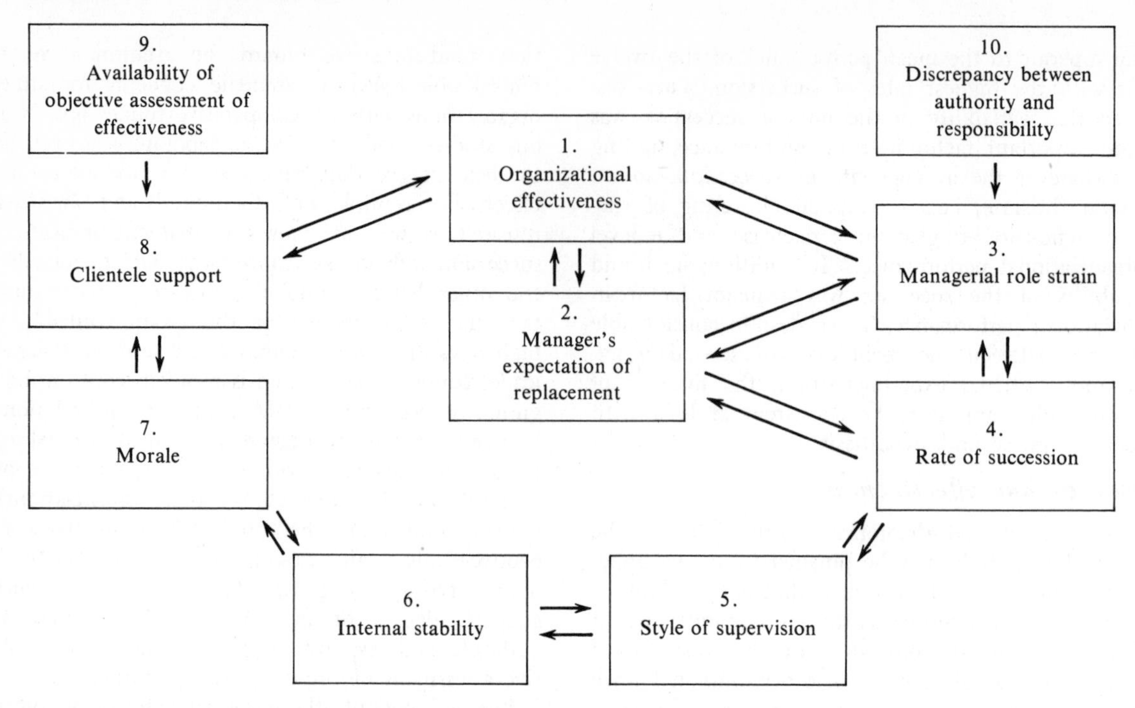

FIGURE 1. Organizational factors in team performance.

of strain will vary, of course, with the nature of the organizational setting, rank of the position, experience of the person, and so on. In general, organizational effectiveness should be inversely related to strength of managerial role strain (*1* and *3*); high levels of effectiveness (of the manager's unit) should be associated with low managerial strain and low levels of effectiveness correlated with high managerial strain. Perhaps, however, some optimum level of managerial strain is associated with maximum organizational effectiveness. At the same time, again assuming all else equal, the magnitude of managerial role strain should be positively correlated with rates of succession (*3* and *4*). Low strain defines a position as desirable. If the strain is too high, the manager searches for opportunities elsewhere, or redefines previous opportunities as attractive and eventually leaves the organization. Once again a simple monotonic relationship may be an oversimplification; too little strain may indicate a lack of "challenge" to the manager and thereby also stimulate turnover.

If rates of succession in a position have been high, and expectation of replacement arises, this, in turn, should contribute to managerial role strain. All else being equal, the stronger the expectation of replacement, the greater the role strain (*2* and *3*). Organizational effectiveness should be inversely related to strength of expectation of replacement; if the organization is performing well, the manager would not normally expect to be replaced (*1* and *2*). Strength of managerial role strain should also be related to style of supervision. All else being equal, the greater the role strain, the greater the likelihood that supervision will be close (*3* and *5*).[13] There are numerous studies relating closeness of supervision, morale, and organizational effectiveness (*1* and *7*; *1* and *5*).[14] Judging from Guest's study, we would expect that the greater the rate of succession in an organization, the greater would be the tendency to supervise closely (*4* and *5*). There is evidence suggesting that closeness of supervision is associated with degree of internal organizational stability (*5* and *6*).[15]

Two special sources of strain seemed pertinent to the analysis of the managerial role in baseball organizations: (1) the discrepancy between official responsibility and authority (we assumed that, in general, the greater this discrepancy, the greater the role strain [*3* and *10*]) and (2) the availability of objective assessment of managerial and team performance to the organization's clientele and higher levels of authority. We would expect that when objective assessment is available, the negative correlation between effectiveness and managerial role strain should be higher than when such objective assessment is not available (*8* and *9*). The first attribute concerns primarily the nature of the internal structure of baseball organizations, the second the relationship between the organization and its interested public.

Many of the role strains of the field manager emerge from the fact that he alone is acknowledged to be officially responsible for team performance. Therefore, it is defined as illegitimate for him to delegate ultimate responsibility for results either upward to the "Front Office" or downward to the coaches and individual players. At the same time, however, he depends, par-

[13] Guest, *op. cit.*, chap. iii.

[14] Many of these studies are discussed in P. Blau and W. R. Scott, *Formal Organizations* (San Francisco: Chandler Publishing Co., 1962), pp. 140–64.

[15] Gouldner, *op. cit.*, and R. O. Carlson, *Executive Succession and Organizational Change* (Chicago: Midwest Administrative Center, University of Chicago, 1962).

ticularly over the long run, upon the front office for assistance by providing a strong farm system and advantageous trades, and, at all times, upon the quality of performance of the lower-level members of the hierarchy, the players. If they perform well, his position is secure; if they do not, it is in jeopardy.

However, although other managerial positions, such as those in business, often carry responsibility for results, what distinguishes the baseball manager is the fact that not only is he acknowledged to be responsible, but his superiors have objective data with which they can readily evaluate his performance. Unlike the typical business executive, for whom few clear standards of performance tend to exist, the baseball manager is exposed continually to seemingly unassailable comparative measures of effectiveness.[16] Moreover, the effects of many of the manager's daily decisions are a matter of public record. This means that every managerial decision that turns out to be an unfortunate one for the team, such as substituting in a key situation a mediocre left-hand hitting pinch batter for the team's star right-hand hitting slugger, is immediately "second-guessed" by the players, coaches, the front office, and the fans. The manager is constantly open to criticism, public and private.

The relationship between the field manager and his subordinates, upon whom he depends so heavily, is also influenced by the availability of public and objective measures of performance. Outstanding performance on the part of individual players insures their remaining with the club, and, importantly, the evaluation of this performance rests *not* with managerial subjective judgment as it does frequently in business firms, but instead is based largely on relatively objective standards of performance. Hence, the player in many respects is independent of managerial control. Where the ballplayer tends to resemble the traditional entrepreneur, the manager resembles the bureaucrat.[17] But the manager is a bureaucrat stripped of many vital bureaucratic controls. For example, the typical manager in a bureaucracy possesses power because he can limit the access of his subordinates to higher positions. However, the average ballplayer does not anticipate upward mobility in the ordinary sense within the structure of the professional baseball organization. In his case, upward career mobility applies primarily to the income and popularity rank systems; the players' major sources of reward are external to managerial control.

To a certain extent each manager develops his own inimitable way of handling players. After a while, the players feel comfortable with this style, and the younger ones in particular may feel that no successor can quite measure up to the standard (Willie Mays's reported fondness for Leo Durocher is a case in point). A managerial change inevitably upsets old patterns of behavior. New organizational policies, a different style of leadership, perhaps new players, and the addition of new coaches produce changes of great magnitude in the internal structure of the team. Members are forced to adapt not only to the successor's new ways of doing things but also to the new informal coalitions that inevitably develop. The recruitment of the successor from the present staff or from outside the organization may be an important factor affecting the degree of instability created by succession.[18] Moreover, a high rate of managerial succession on a team tends to generate expectations, especially during a losing streak, that the current manager's job is in danger. This may encourage dissatisfied players to challenge the manager's authority and increase even more the felt discrepancy between his responsibility and authority. The result is greater managerial role strain.

In addition to the internal sources of tension, constant pressure on both the manager and the ordinary team members emanates from the organization's clientele. Unlike many other kinds of organizations, professional baseball teams must deal with a clientele that is both highly committed and highly informed. The strong emotional identification of the fan with "his" professional baseball or football club is often a part of the resident's identification with his local community. In some locales, such as Los Angeles, comprised of a large number of suburban subcommunities, it probably represents one of the more important integrative symbols. In the Green Bay area, the Green Bay Packers football team is referred to as a "regional religion."

Not only are the clientele strongly committed but in addition, as we suggested, they can readily and continually evaluate the effectiveness of the team since

[16] See F. X. Sutton, S. E. Harris, C. Kaysen, and J. Tobin, *The American Business Creed* (New York: Schocken Books, 1962), pp. 336–38. In this study the authors point out how the *lack* of clear standards of performance can contribute to role strain. It should be pointed out that the skill of the baseball manager also is greatly affected by subjective judgments. As Sutton *et al.* point out, it often matters not that the effectiveness of the organization was in fact unrelated or only slightly related to the behavior of the manager. It is typically assumed in business, in baseball, and elsewhere, that a strong correlation exists between organizational effectiveness and the performance and ability of the manager in charge.

[17] Recently (April 1, 1962), sports columnist Frank Finch of the *Los Angeles Times* reported the difficult problem of control confronting Coach Pete Reiser of the Dodgers. Although Reiser is referred to as Howard's "father-confessor," it appears that the player refused to alter his batting stance to fit the coach's demands. "I'd like to have the authority to tell Frank to hit the way I say or else not play," the exasperated Reiser is quoted as saying, "but in baseball you just don't order people to do anything in a certain way." Of course, the fact that Howard in 1961 hit fifteen home runs and batted .296 contributed to his independence. Howard's reported point of view in this dispute parallels the individualistic spirit of the traditional entrepreneur: "I appreciate advice, and I accept it if it will help me, but Frank Howard, and nobody else, is going to help Frank Howard hit the ball on the button. When you step into the batter's box you're on your own. . . . This is a game made up of individuals." It would be a gross exaggeration to assert that Howard's attitude is universally found among ballplayers. Obviously, co-operation is common, perhaps especially among infielders who tend not to have high batting averages. Their skills are more likely to lie with the kinds of plays that require smooth co-ordination and not with the bat. For this and other related reasons, we hypothesized in another study that infielders and catchers would be more likely than outfielders and pitchers to become managers.

[18] See Carlson, *op. cit.*

performance criteria are public knowledge.[19] In other types of organizations, the clientele cannot evaluate the effectiveness of the system with comparable precision. Consumers of an industrial corporation's products, for example, typically possess neither the propensity nor the knowledge to compare objectively the quality of the products they purchase or the "efficiency" of the corporation's employees. Accordingly, public relations and advertising men are probably able to manipulate the image of the corporation and its products much more effectively than can professional baseball teams.[20] Not even the best advertising men could have undone the damage to the Philadelphia Phillies' game attendance between 1934 and 1941 when they finished in last or next to last place every year.

Clientele support is critical because of its close relationship to morale and team effectiveness (*8* and *7*; *8* and *1*); it is important in two ways. First, attendance is ostensibly highly related to profitability, and a drop in profitability produces strong pressures for managerial change. Second, high rates of attendance, by raising team morale, may contribute to team effectiveness as well as being affected by it. Our data revealed a strong correlation between effectiveness based on team standing and ranked yearly attendance. The zero-order correlations, by Kendall's tau, were as follows: for Period I, $T = .60$, $p < .0007$; for Period II, $T = .44$, $p < .009$; for Periods I and II combined, $T = .58$, $p < .001$. These data, of course, do not allow us to separate cause and effect. Mosteller's statistical study of the effects of playing "at home" and "away" upon winning World Series games found no significant differences in performance under the two conditions.[21] However, as he pointed out, outcomes of regular season games might still be influenced by this factor. He noted: (1) Baseball teams are often tailored to the home park because half the games are played there. Perhaps league champions are more skilful hitters and therefore less limited by the dimensions of a particular park. (2) Fatigue from excessive traveling may disadvantage the away team to a greater extent during the regular season than during the World Series. Still another possibility is that clientele support is less critical for team performance during World Series competition than during the day-in-day-out play of the regular season. The extensive publicity and assured popular interest in the World Series generates sufficient enthusiasm on the part of the player whether he is playing at home or away. We suspect that the home crowd can exercise considerable influence on player performance during a regular season game. Under these conditions, enthusiastic support from the crowd may stimulate the player to "put out" more in the same way that a responsive audience can help produce scintillating dramatic performances on the stage. The ineffective team is less likely to receive this added inducement to perform well.

To summarize briefly: Our orientation focused on a set of ten variables. Analysis of the situation of the ineffective team may be used illustratively. If a team is ineffective, clientele support and profitability decline. Accordingly, strong external pressures for managerial change are set in motion and, concomitantly, the magnitude of managerial role strain increases. A managerial change may be viewed in some quarters as attractive in that it can function to demonstrate publicly that the owners are taking concrete action to remedy an undesirable situation.[22] The public nature of team performance and the close identification of community pride with team behavior combine to establish a strong basis for clientele control over the functioning of the team. These external influences tend to increase the felt discrepancy between managerial responsibility and actual authority. Since the rewards of popularity are controlled externally, individual rather than team performance may be encouraged. Similarly, the availability of objective performance standards decreases managerial control and thereby contributes to role strain. The greater the managerial role strain, the higher the rates of succession. Moreover, the higher the rates of succession, the stronger the expectations of replacement when team performance declines. Frequent managerial change can produce important dysfunctional consequences within the team by affecting style of supervision and disturbing the informal network of interpersonal relationships. New policies and new personnel create the necessity for restructuring primary relationships. The resulting low primary-group stability produces low morale and may thereby contribute to team ineffectiveness. Declining clientele support may encourage a greater decline in team morale and performance. The consequent continued drop in profitability induces pressures for further managerial changes. Such changes, in turn, produce additional disruptive effects on the organization, and the vicious circle continues.

Our findings demonstrating a negative correlation between rates of succession and effectiveness and a positive correlation between clientele support and

[19] Manager Freddie Hutchinson of the Cincinnati Reds once rather grimly described baseball as "the only sport in the world where everybody thinks he is an expert." No wonder several managers feel, as does Hutchinson, that fans are much too preoccupied with baseball statistics: "Now every club has to have a statistician, ours included. The statistician gives his figures to the newsmen and the broadcasters and now he's got everybody conscious of them."

[20] I am indebted to Professor R. J. Murphy for this observation.

[21] F. Mosteller, "The World Series Competition," *Journal of the American Statistical Association,* XLVII (September, 1942), 355–80.

[22] Although officially the manager may be held responsible for a team's poor showing, the fact that managers frequently are hired later by other clubs would suggest that their alleged ineptness is partly a screen. It is not easy for the front office to resist public pressures even if they might feel that the decision to replace the manager is unwise. The case of Mike Higgins and the Boston Red Sox is instructive, for it is one where the owner really did not want to fire the manager but did so anyway. Yawkey, the owner, and Higgins, the manager, were the best of friends. Yet a few years back when the Red Sox were doing very poorly, Yawkey gave in to public criticism and replaced Higgins. However, he kept Higgins on in the rather vague position of "troubleshooter." When the team still did poorly under Billy Jurges, Higgins was rehired. A new manager at least provides the fans with some hope for the coming season. Professor Gerard Brandmeyer kindly provided this example.

effectiveness constitute only two connections of the chain depicted in Figure 1. The methodological weaknesses of studies such as the present one, based wholly on official documents, should not be underestimated. Clearly, such inquiries are not adequate substitutes for well-designed field and laboratory investigations. Systematic research examining, for example, the nature of the relationship between morale and effectiveness in baseball teams (morale and productivity studies of industrial organizations have produced contradictory findings[23]), morale and strength of clientele support, and managerial role strain and team effectiveness, would be highly desirable.

Several years ago Herbert A. Simon pointed out that the problem of organizational effectiveness was essentially an empirical one. He observes: "What is needed is empirical research and experimentation to determine the relative desirability of alternative administrative arrangements."[24] In addition, he emphasized two canons of research design: "First, it is necessary that the objectives of the administrative organization under study be defined in concrete terms so that results, expressed in terms of these objectives, may be accurately measured. Second, it is necessary that sufficient experimental control be exercised."[25] As an approximation to these principles, this study, by means of secondary analysis of published documents, has, in effect, compared the performance of professional baseball teams operating under contrasting administrative arrangements, the conditions of frequent and relatively infrequent managerial succession.

Replication

CHANGE IN MANAGERS AND THE PERFORMANCE OF MAJOR LEAGUE TEAMS

Grusky's data were drawn from league standings in 1921 to 1941 and in 1951 to 1958. The data to be used in this replication supplement the original data; they will be taken from the years 1958 to 1965. In addition, to provide better evidence on cause and effect, there will be a slight modification in the research design. In lieu of using the team's standing in the year the manager was replaced, we will note whether hiring a new manager is associated with a *shift* in league standings between the preceding year under the old manager and the first year under a new manager. This permits a slightly better test of the causal sequence Grusky suggests, namely, that turnover *leads* to ineffectiveness.

Hypothesis

1. State whether you think the study will show that managerial succession increases, reduces, or does not affect a team's league standing.

Data analysis

1. *Secure data on teams.* The week before this problem is to be done your instructor will assign to each student (or to each group of students) one or more teams from the following clubs in existence as of 1957.

NATIONAL LEAGUE	AMERICAN LEAGUE
Milwaukee Braves	New York Yankees
Pittsburgh Pirates	Chicago White Sox
San Francisco Giants	Boston Red Sox
Cincinnati Reds	Cleveland Indians
Chicago Cubs	Detroit Tigers
St. Louis Cardinals	Baltimore Orioles
Los Angeles Dodgers	Kansas City Athletics
Philadelphia Phillies	Washington Senators

Copy onto the "Raw Data Sheet" for the team assigned to you the name of the manager (or managers) and the league standing for each year for at least eight years, starting with the earliest year. In addition to the sources noted in footnote 4 of Grusky's article, the following references may be helpful: *One For the Book* (St. Louis: *The Sporting News*, 1966); *The Little Red Book of Baseball* (New York: Elias Sports Bureau, Inc., 1966); *Information Please Almanac*, and newspapers and sports periodicals such as *Sports Illustrated* for the particular years in question.

2. *Code* each year of the Raw Data Sheet for:

A. Whether the manager was *succeeded* by another manager (= code of S), or remained constant (= code of C)

B. Whether the team's standing Increased (code "+"), Decreased (code "−"), or remained Constant ("0") for each year

In most instances this procedure will be relatively simple. However, some difficulties will arise in situations where a team has more than one manager during the year. The general rule to be employed is as follows:

[23] E.g., R. L. Kahn and N. C. Morse, "The Relationship of Productivity to Morale," *Journal of Social Issues*, VII, No. 3 (1951), 8–17; D. Katz, N. Maccoby, and N. C. Morse, *Productivity, Supervision and Morale in an Office Situation* (Ann Arbor, Mich.: Institute of Social Research, 1950); D. Katz, N. Maccoby, and L. G. Floor, *Productivity, Satisfaction and Morale among Railroad Workers* (Ann Arbor, Mich.: Institute of Social Research, 1951); and N. C. Morse, *Satisfactions in the White-Collar Job* (Ann Arbor, Mich.: Institute for Social Research, 1953); H. Wilensky's paper in C. Arensberg *et al.* (eds.) *Research in Industrial Human Relations: A Critical Appraisal* (New York: Harper & Bros., 1957), pp. 25–50.

[24] *Administrative Behavior* (2d ed.; New York: The Macmillan Co., 1958), p. 42.

[25] *Ibid.*

"Management constant" (C) should be scored if a manager continues throughout a season and at least some part of the following season; "management succession" (S) should be scored if a new manager is appointed in the middle of a season regardless of whether he continues for all, some, or none of the next season.

3. *Tally* the codes for each year into Table 1. For example, if for 1963 there was no change in management (coded C) and the team's league standing was the same as in 1962 (coded 0), one tally should be entered in the center cell of the first row of Table 1. However, if the standing of the team increased (coded +), the tally should be in the left-hand cell of the first row; and if it decreased (coded −), it should go in the right-hand cell.

4. *Write on the blackboard* the number of cases in each cell of Table 1. Your instructor will have drawn a large version of Table 1 on the blackboard. The numbers should be written *in neat columns* so that they can be added. If data for the same team was looked up by two or more persons, they should compare figures and agree on the number to put on the blackboard.

5. *Add* the figures on the blackboard and enter them in Table 2.

6. *Compute* the percents for each row of Table 2.

Lab report

1. In your opinion, do the findings provide a firm test of the hypothesis that managerial succession *leads* to ineffectiveness? See in this connection the "Note On Interpreting Cause and Effect" in Appendix A.

2. What other information should be gathered about the teams to more adequately test the hypothesis?

References

Blau, Peter, *Bureaucracy in Modern Society*. New York: Random House, 1956, chapter 3.

Gamson, William A. and Norman A. Scotch, "Scapegoating in Baseball," *American Journal of Sociology, LXX* (July 1964), pp. 69–72.

Greer, Scott, *Social Organization*. New York: Random House, 1961.

Grusky, Oscar, "Reply to Gamson and Scotch," *American Journal of Sociology, LXX* (July 1964), pp. 72–76.

March, James G. and Herbert A. Simon, *Organizations*. New York: Wiley, 1958, chapter 3.

Udy, Stanley H. Jr., "'Bureaucracy' and 'Rationality' in Weber's Organization Theory," *American Sociological Review, 24* (December 1959), pp. 791–795.

Weber, Max, "Bureaucracy," in H. H. Gerth and C. Wright Mills, eds. and trans., *From Max Weber*. New York: A Galaxy Book, 1958.

Name____________________

Date____________________

Name of team____________________

Year[a]	Manager	Succession code (C or S)	League standing	Standing code (+, 0, or −)

[a] List earliest year first.

TABLE 1. League standing by management change for ______________________ (name of team)

Succession	+ Increased	0 No change	– Decreased	Total
	LEAGUE STANDING			
C = Management constant				
S = Management succession				

TABLE 2. League standing by management change for all teams

Succession		+ Increased	0 No change	– Decreased	Total
		LEAGUE STANDING			
C = Constant	Number				
	%				100%
S = Succession	Number				
	%				100%

LABORATORY REPORT FOR PROBLEM________

Course or Section________ Date________ Name________

HYPOTHESIS:________

____

____

____

____

____

SAMPLE:________

____

____

____

____

INDEPENDENT VARIABLE(S):________

____

____

____

____

DEPENDENT VARIABLE(S):________

____

____

____

____

OTHER FACTORS:________

____

____

____

____

LABORATORY REPORT FOR PROBLEM________

SUMMARY OF FINDINGS: ________

DISCUSSION: ________

PROBLEM 14

COMMUNITIES

One of the earliest and most important contributions of sociology has been the analysis of different types of communities and the discovery of behavior which is typical of each of these types. This is well-illustrated in the work of a founding father of sociology, Ferdinand Tonnies (Tonnies, 1940). He distinguished two types of communities: the *gemeinschaft* and the *gesellschaft*. The *gemeinschaft*, according to Tonnies, described a network of warm, friendly social relationships where action was predicated on natural sentiments; conversely, the *gesellschaft* purportedly contained cold and distant social relationships resting on a base of rational, calculating sentiments. The prototype of the *gemeinschaft* was the rural community, and the prototype of the *gesellschaft* was the urban community. All things considered, Tonnies had a marked personal preference for the *gemeinschaft*. Since the writing of Tonnies' pioneering treatise, his distinction has been taken up time and again and been recast in different forms; it is present in Simmel's essay on the metropolis (Simmel, 1957), in Redfield's distinction regarding folk and urban communities (Redfield, 1947), and others as well.

Tonnies' concepts gained their force in American sociology largely through the works of Louis Wirth and his colleagues and the University of Chicago. Wirth saw the city as embodying *gesellschaft*-like relationships: formal patterns of interaction, an underemphasis on kinship relations, and a general decline in primary group bonds (Wirth, 1957). Further, as other sociologists at Chicago later pointed out, the lack of informal interaction was instrumental in causing a variety of social problems in the metropolis (Faris and Dunham, 1939; Shaw and McKay, 1942), thus reaffirming Tonnies' dislike of the urban life.

Recent research has shown that many of Tonnies' notions, as well as those presented by Wirth and his colleagues, were inaccurate. It appears, for example, that urban areas are in fact not anonymous; they tend rather to be marked by an abundance of sociable relations (Bell and Boat, 1957; Litwak, 1960; Stone, 1954). In addition, it also seems that rural areas do not contain the virtues frequently attributed to them. The farm, for example is frequently depicted as an ideal environment for raising children. But the empirical evidence shows the farm to be less suitable than urban areas since these studies reveal that farm-reared children lag behind their urban peers in such things as intelligence, school and occupational achievement (Burchinal, 1966; Straus, 1962), parent-child adjustment (Nye, 1950), and health (Burchinal, 1966).

It is difficult to explain why Tonnies' stereotyped preference for the *gemeinschaft*-rural community as an ideal environment went unchecked for nearly a generation. Part of the reason probably lies in the lack of good comparative research. Part also may be because American culture *and* American sociologists have an agrarian bias (Mills, 1943). An "agrarian bias" refers to the tendency to attribute good things to the rural way of life, even in the absence of clear evidence on rural superiority. It should be noted that in the United States as recently as 1920, half of all Americans lived in rural areas. In the 1930s and 1940s, the era when Wirth's work was being supplemented, much of this changed, but most persons were still born on farms and raised in rural areas generally. In light of this recent rural past, it should not be too surprising to discover agrarian biases in American culture and American sociology.

The reading for the present problem continues the classical forms of community analysis suggested by Tonnies, Wirth, and others. It is directed towards the possible differences in the interpersonal contacts of persons in rural communities and urban communities. Through the use of time budgets—actual estimates of time spent in personal and impersonal interaction—the interaction profiles of rural and urban residents are charted. Further, by comparing the profiles of persons of different communities of residence but of identical class background, the author is in position to reliably answer the time-honored question of whether urbanites are indeed hard and aloof and whether rural dwellers are warm and sociable.

RURAL-URBAN AND STATUS DIFFERENCES IN INTERPERSONAL CONTACTS / *Albert J. Reiss, Jr.*

In a pilot study to test differences in types of personal contacts among urban, rural-non-farm, and rural-farm residents of high and low status, the time-budget was used as a means of gathering data. There are no significant differences of status in types of interpersonal contact or time spent in contact which are independent of residential settings. Among the residential groups, classified by contacts, significant differences in exposure to mass media, secondary-group situations, time spent at work and in isolation were found. Urban males spent a greater average time in primary contacts than rural-non-farm or rural-farm males, but this was due largely to differences in primary contacts at work. Urban and rural-non-farm males are more likely to have a greater mean amount of impersonal contact in their workday than are rural-farm males.

Sociologists customarily describe the ideal type of personal contacts in cities as anonymous, segmental, and impersonal and contrast them with the intimate and personal type in rural areas.[1] A large number of studies offer general support for this description, but most give data for only a rural or an urban setting.[2] Comparisons between the two settings are therefore made by inferring the characteristics for one of them.

This paper reports the results of a pilot study to test several hypotheses about differences in types of interpersonal contacts among urban, rural–non-farm and rural-farm residents, the time-budget being used in gathering data. Sorokin and Zimmerman, who provide the most precise statement of supposed differences in the quality and quantity of social contact or interaction of rural and urban residents,[3] state a single hypothesis as to quantitative aspects: "the number of contacts per individual in a given unit of time is greater in urban than rural life." Qualitative differences are described in five hypotheses:

1. The area of the contact system of a member of a rural community, as well as that of the rural community as a whole, is spatially more narrow and limited than the area of a member of an urban community and of the urban community as a whole.

2. . . . Face to face relations occupy a less [sic] proportion of the whole interaction system of an urbanite than of a rural individual.

3. . . . The interaction system of an urbanite is woven, to a greater proportion than in the case of a rural individual, out of impersonal and to a less degree out of personal relations.

4. . . . In the totality of relations which compose the network of the interaction system of an urban individual, the part composed of casual, superficial and short-lived relations, in contrast to permanent, strong, and durable relations, occupies a much more conspicuous place than in the interaction system of a rural dweller.

5. . . . The relations are more flexible, less durable, and more impersonal; the whole network of this system of interaction is to be marked by greater complexity, greater plasticity, differentiation, manifoldness, and, at the same time by greater superficiality, "standardization," and mechanization than the network of the interaction system of a rural dweller.

The data from this pilot study permit only a partial test of the first four hypotheses. A sixth hypothesis, which follows from several of the postulates underlying these hypotheses, is also tested. Since agricultural work is less often organized on the basis of personal contacts than is non-agricultural and since in rural areas contacts are relatively fewer in frequency than in non-rural, the rural person is expected to spend a greater part of his time in isolation.

A growing body of evidence shows that the quantity and quality of social interaction is a function of socio-economic status, as well as of residential location. The major hypothesis advanced in sociological literature is that the amount of impersonal contact varies directly with socio-economic status. A corollary is that formal group participation varies more or less directly with socio-economic status, while informal varies inversely among the urban.[4] This paper also examines status, within each residential category, as a further test of the hypotheses.

Residents of high and low socio-economic status classified as rural-farm (RF), rural–non-farm (RNF), and urban residential, comprise the six populations.[5]

Reprinted from "Rural-Urban and Status Differences in Interpersonal Contacts" by Albert J. Reiss, Jr. from *The American Journal of Sociology,* LXV (September 1959), pp. 182–195 by permission of The University of Chicago Press. Copyright 1959 by The University of Chicago Press.

Financial support from the Institute of Research in the Social Sciences of Vanderbilt University and the assistance of A. Lewis Rhodes in gathering data and in statistical computations are gratefully acknowledged.

In this paper the now fashionable term *inter*personal is used interchangeably with the more acceptable *personal,* which seems to cover the ground quite adequately.

[1] The statement by Georg Simmel generally serves as a prototype; cf. his "The Metropolis and Mental Life," trans. in Kurt H. Wolff, *The Sociology of Georg Simmel* (Glencoe, Ill.: Free Press, 1950).

[2] For a fairly complete summary of the early literature see P.A. Sorokin and C. C. Zimmerman, *Principles of Rural-urban Sociology* (New York: Henry Holt & Co., 1929), and P. A. Sorokin and Clarence Q. Berger, *Time-Budgets of Human Behavior* (Cambridge: Harvard University Press, 1938).

[3] Sorokin and Zimmerman, *op. cit.,* pp. 48–49, 51–54.

[4] Among the most recent representative urban studies in this area, pertinent are Morris Axelrod, "Urban Structure and Urban Participation," *American Sociological Review,* XXI (February, 1956), 13–18, and Wendell Bell and Maryanne T. Force, "Urban Neighborhood Types and Participation in Formal Associations," *American Sociological Review,* XXI (February, 1956), 25–34. This relationship, commonly observed in urban areas, is not always verified in rural community studies; for example: "The white-collar groups had the highest scores for all three types of participation, although their superiority was less marked for informal than for formal and semiformal participation" (Otis Dudley Duncan and Jay W. Artis, *Social Stratification in a Pennsylvania Rural Community* [Pennsylvania State College School of Agriculture, AES Bull. 543 (1951)], p. 38).

[5] Among urban and RNF males, professional, technical, and kindred workers; proprietors, managers, and officials; sales workers; and clerical and kindred workers are the white-collar, non-agricultural occupations designated as "high status." All other occupations are "low status." Among RF males, all farm proprietors and managers are designated "high status"; all tenants, sharecroppers, and laborers "low status."

They were not selected by uniform sampling criteria.

The urban population of the Nashville, Tennessee, Standard Metropolitan Area (SMA) was classified into white-collar and manual-worker census tracts and four white-collar and three manual-worker tracts were randomly selected. A 25 per cent random sample of dwelling units was selected in each of these tracts and a respondent twenty years old and over was interviewed. The RNF and RF respondents were selected from a county south of the Nashville SMA. Two village communities located at maximum distance from the city center were selected, the rural area within a four-mile radius of them, and the major traffic artery from the central city to the areas. A respondent twenty years old or over in every fourth dwelling unit with a male head of household was then interviewed. The place of work of RNF respondents was not held constant. Some worked in the SMA, while others were employed in the villages or in rural locations, such as motel and dam sites, and so on. The population for which comparisons are made is white married males, age twenty to sixty-five, with a regular full-time job. These criteria were imposed to eliminate known sources of variation by sex, marital status, age, and employment status.

Time-budgets. The allocation of an individual's time during a single day was chosen as the measure of the amount and kind of personal contact. A budget of time was obtained for the nearest previous workday and the last full day off. This paper reports the data for only the workday.

The time-budget opened with the statement: "Now, we would like to know how you spent your time yesterday. We want to know just how much time you spent doing different things during the day and whom you spent it with. Suppose we begin with the time you got up yesterday: what time did you get up?" This was followed by, "What did you do when you first got up? Did you spend the time with anyone, or were you more or less alone? Whom were you with? and, how close are they to you?" Each new activity or block of time was similarly explored until the person said he went to sleep. Interviewers were specifically instructed to get the information so that it could be coded into one of the following mutually exclusive categories:

1. *Intimate kinship,* such as nuclear family members and extended kin members.
2. *Close intimate friends,* friends defined as "very close," "my best friend," etc.
3. *Close associate or client,* a close friend deriving from a work context, whether or not actually seen at work.
4. *Good friend,* a friend defined as "close," "just a good friend," etc.
5. *Distant associate or casual acquaintance,* either a fellow worker who is not defined as a friend or a person with whom one has a "speaking acquaintance."
6. *Cordial recognition,* defined as a person whom one recognizes in address, or "just someone to whom I say, 'hello.' "
7. *Pure client,* defined as a person whom one doesn't know personally, but one with whom contact is made, or with whom interaction takes place in a client relationship.

For analytical purposes, Nos. 1–4 are defined as "primary contacts"; Nos. 5–7 as "secondary contacts", Nos. 6 and 7 as "impersonal contacts." As the total time awake was obtained, most persons also had some time with "no personal contact."

Part of the daily activity was also allocated to one of three contexts: time spent at work on a job; time spent in exposure to mass media; and time spent where secondary contacts are probable. Persons need not have experienced any personal contact to be coded active in that situation. Classification into these three situations is independent of the classification for interpersonal contacts. The same period of time, therefore, may be coded in both the contact and the situation class.

There are, of course, many problems of classification in allocating time to social situations and types of contact. Several types of contact may occur at a single time, for example, or the situation may include more than one type of activity. This problem was met by asking each respondent to allocate the time among the various types of persons with whom contemporaneous contact was made. It is clear from the time-budgets that urban dwellers spend more time in situations with more than one type of contact than do rural dwellers; the criterion adopted here masks this difference. Similarly, social contact among persons with whom the most intimate relationships are maintained may vary from mingling to copulation. In a strict sense, this study simply allocates daily contact time to persons with whom one has a particular *qualitative* relationship and to types of social situations, given certain *structural* characteristics. The quality and content of the interaction are not usually known.[6]

The time at which a time-budget is obtained affects the allocation of daily time. Seasonal and weekly differences in work influence both the amount of time spent at it, the situation, and the kind of daily contacts. The allocation of time also varies for individual households, owing to such circumstances as the temporary presence of guests or the temporary absence of a member. Such shifts in the daily round cannot be considered atypical and deserve analysis in themselves. They are not controlled in this study, except insofar as the interviewing of all urban respondents in April or May and of all RNF and RF respondents in May or in July allows gross seasonal variations.

Structural characteristics of the society likewise affect the social allocation of time. Age, sex, marital and occupational status are roughly controlled in this study either by selection of respondents or by statistical procedure. Others, such as the size of the family, the

[6] The conclusions of this study are limited by the selection of the particular population and by the criteria of allocating time among types of contact and types of situations. Alternative measures of contact or measures of interaction might easily result in different conclusions. Suppose, for example, that one knew the total number of persons seen (or met) during a day; urban persons probably have more such contacts in a day. Or suppose that the urban person works with a close friend more often than does a rural person; this does not preclude his also having a large number of indirect social contacts at work or contacts with persons he never even sees. While not all forms of social contact which are said to discriminate among persons in different environments are analyzed here, it should be clear that concepts like impersonal and personal contacts or indirect and direct contacts permit meaningful comparisons only if their operational referents are specified.

presence of preschool children, religious affiliation, the availability of mass media, and type of work are not controlled. A partial listing of some forty structural correlates of time-allocation was made for this study. Obviously, it would take simultaneous study of a very large population of respondents to control variation from all these sources.

Testing procedures. The time-budget was recorded in minutes for the waking hours of the day. Respondents erred sometimes in the allocation of minutes spent in a particular activity or relationship, since each was asked to recall the previous day. The error is readily apparent in their frequent "rounding" of numbers of minutes to figures ending in 0 and 5. The allocation of time is perhaps more reliable for activities represented in the "daily round" than for others. Pretests showed that the procedure of having respondents "follow the clock" with their report of daily activity provides a more reliable estimate of time than is obtained if the respondent is simply asked to "recall his day."

The mean and standard deviation were chosen as the measures of central tendency and dispersion for each group, and the null hypothesis of differences in means and variances was tested. The comparison of variances of rural and urban residential contexts is open to question on the grounds that one might logically expect greater variation within urban than rural contexts, since the urban is more heterogeneous in occupational composition. Ideally, occupational composition should be more satisfactorily controlled in comparisons than it is in this study, but our sample size does not permit a more detailed occupational classification. The difference between means was tested by the conventional *T*-test, which assumes that the populations do not differ significantly with respect to their variances. When the variances differed significantly, unless n_1 was equal to n_2, the standard error of the difference between means was calculated by using the estimates of the two population variances rather than a common estimate of the population variances. A two-tailed test of significance was used only when direction was not predicted.

There are 225 comparisons of types of interpersonal contact and contact situation for high- and low-status urban RNF and RF categories in Tables 2 and 4 involving tests of significance for proportions, for means, and for variances. For purposes of testing the hypotheses in this study, however, attention is directed to the *pattern* of significant differences among the comparisons by residence and status for a type of interpersonal contact or contract situation rather than on each significant comparison.

Tables 1–4 in this paper provide data and statistical tests for fifteen residential area-status group comparisons, but the tests of particular hypotheses do not refer to all comparisons. Zero-order comparisons of either status or residential categories with respect to type of interpersonal contact or situation can be made by recombining information in the tables.

The present study relies solely on a cross-section comparison to test the hypotheses, and historical inferences, therefore, should be drawn only with extreme caution. Conclusions from a comparison of an urban community of today with an ideal typical description of a rural or urban community of a century ago may be highly misleading. Differences in personal contacts among urbanites of one hundred years ago and today could be greater, in fact, than the difference between residents of rural and urban areas at either time, for variation over time in some types of contact may be greater than that between categories at a particular time.

Sorokin and Zimmerman's first hypothesis states that the urban individual and the urban area have a more extensive spatial contact system than do rural persons and rural areas. The distance between workplace and residence is one rough measure, assuming that the greater the distance between the two, the greater the territory over which contact obtains. Using this rough measure of spatial contact, the three residential settings are ranked thus: RNF, urban, and RF; and the hypothesis is not accepted. It seems likely that urban inhabitants may have a larger spatial area of contact if all modes of communication are mapped in territorial space. If this is true, then we might say that city people spread their daily symbolic contacts but not their direct physical contacts over a larger territory than do RNF inhabitants.

If we postulate that contacts with mass media are a measure of an extensive spatial contact system, we have a second test of the hypothesis. Every household in the study had either a radio or a television set and often a telephone and a daily newspaper. Every male, therefore, was potentially exposed to the mass media. The data show a higher proportion of urban than of RNF or RF males exposed to mass-media situations, irrespective of status. Mean exposure time was significantly greater for urban males than for RF males or RNF males of low status. But there are no significant differences by status either in the proportion of males who spend some time in daily contact with mass media or in mean amount of contact with media within the RNF and RF residence categories (see Tables 1–4). This result is consistent with the expectation that urban persons would have a greater range of contact than rural persons, except that RNF males of high status are more like urban than rural males in their exposure time to mass media.

Significantly more of the urban and RNF than RF males, regardless of status, had some exposure to secondary situations (line 16 in Tables 1 and 2). Urban and RNF males, likewise, have a higher mean exposure and variance in exposure to secondary situations than do RF males, but no significant differences of this kind are found between urban and RNF males (line 16, Tables 3 and 4). If we postulate that secondary contacts are generally spatially more diffuse than primary ones—a questionable postulate—it appears that non-agricultural workers have a more extensive spatial contact system than do those in agriculture.

These tests of our first hypothesis suggest that residential setting may be less important than occupational situs in determining the range of social contact. Men with non-agricultural employment, even when they re-

TABLE 1. Per cent reporting some workday contact or situations, by residence and status

Type of interpersonal contact or contact situation	URBAN High	URBAN Low	RNF High	RNF Low	RF High	RF Low
No. of cases	176	75	27	24	28	21
Per cent reporting any contact with:						
1. Intimate kinship	97	99	90	100	100	100
2. Close intimate friend	33	39	80	42	36	24
3. Close associate or client	71	59	25	13	14	[a]
4. Good friend	32	37	30	38	18	10
5. Distant associate or client	43	44	65	38	46	33
6. Cordial recognition	10	12	[a]	4	4	[a]
7. Pure client	45	33	40	29	4	19
Per cent reporting workday time in:						
8. No interpersonal contact	86	81	90	92	82	71
9. Primary contact (1–4)	100	100	100	100	100	100
10. Secondary contact (5–7)	76	68	95	58	50	43
11. All impersonal contact (6–7)	51	41	40	33	7	19
12. All interpersonal contact (1–7)	100	100	100	100	100	100
13. Total waking time	100	100	100	100	100	100
Per cent of total waking time in:						
14. Job situations	100	100	100	100	100	100
15. Mass-media situations	87	88	55	45	61	53
16. Secondary situations	95	87	90	79	36	24

[a] No time reported for any respondent.

side in village or open country, more often are exposed to secondary contact situations than are males in agriculture. There are probably two main reasons for this: the nature of their job situations and their movement to and from places of work.

Primary social relations are said to be involved in a smaller proportion of the total interaction system of an urban than of a rural individual. There are a number of ways to test this second hypothesis, and much depends upon the definition of an "indirect interaction system" as part of the total system of social interaction. Sorokin and Zimmerman argue, by deduction, that the interaction system of an urbanite consists of a larger network of indirect contacts—persons whom one never sees—than does that of the typical rural person; hence the actual face-to-face, or primary, relations of an urbanite are a smaller proportion of the total interaction system. No data are available on the amount of indirect interaction contacts, since no satisfactory operational definition of them was developed when the study was designed. It is difficult to say, for example, whether a rural dweller's indirect contact with a state or federal authority is greater or less than that of an urban resident, in view of agricultural subsidies, flood-control programs, and the like. The tests of the hypothesis, therefore, were limited to measures based on the actual amount of time spent in interaction.

All the respondents had some primary contact on the workday as shown by line 9 of Tables 1 and 2. This follows from the fact that all respondents were married males. While all men had some exposure to primary contacts during the day, the average urban male reported a significantly greater number of minutes of primary contact than did the average RNF or RF person, regardless of status (see Tables 3 and 4). There are no significant differences between RNF and RF males in total time spent in primary contacts. Table 4 also shows that there are no significant differences between any of the groups in variances in amount of daily primary contacts, despite differences in mean contact. Urban males, on the whole, exhibited no greater variability in this respect than did the RNF or RF. On the average, an urban employed, married male spends over 10 hours a day in primary interaction as compared with, roughly, 8 hours for the low-status RNF or RF male. Urban males, therefore, spend more actual time in primary contacts than do the RNF or RF. But urban males also spend more time on *all* personal contacts than do the low-status RNF and all RF. If one computes a ratio of the average time in primary contact to the average time in all personal contact (ratio of line 9 to line 12 in Table 3) for each residence-status group, the ratios for high- and low-status groups, respectively, are 0.73 and 0.76 for urban, 0.62 and 0.68 for RNF, and 0.76 and 0.79 for RF males. The differences are not particularly large. Certainly, the average urban male does not spend considerably less of his total time in interaction in primary contacts than does the average rural male. It appears that RNF males spend the least part of the total time in interaction in primary contacts, but this difference cannot be attributed to any single type of primary contact.

The third hypothesis—that the interaction system of the urban as compared with the rural individual is, to a greater degree, made up of impersonal relations—is a corollary of hypothesis 2. The types of impersonal relations defined for this study were those of cordial recognition and pure-client relations. The major finding is that urban and RNF males have a higher average amount of impersonal contact than do RF males (line 11, Tables 3 and 4). Only about one-tenth or fewer of the men in any residential setting or status group had contacts of cordial recognition on their workday, as Table 1 shows. It is not surprising, therefore, that there

TABLE 2. Significant residence and status group differences in proportions of respondents reporting contact for types of interpersonal contacts and situations (P values)[a]

Type of interpersonal contact or contact situations	Urban high status VERSUS					Urban low status VERSUS				RNF high status VERSUS			RNF low status VERSUS		RF high status VERSUS
	Urban low	RNF high	RNF low	RF high	RF low	RNF high	RNF low	RF high	RF low	RNF low	RF high	RF low	RF high	RF low	RF low
1. Intimate kin	−	+	−	−	−	+	−	−	−	−	−	−	=	=	=
2. Close intimate friend	−	−[b]	−	−	+	−[b]	−	+	+	+[c]	+[b]	+[b]	+	+	+
3. Close associate or client	+	+[b]	+[b]	+[b]	+[b]	+[b]	+[b]	+[b]	+[b]	+	+	+[b]	−	+[c]	+[c]
4. Good friend	−	+	−	+	+[c]	+	−	+	+[c]	−	+	+	+	+[c]	+
5. Distant associate or client	−	−	+	−	+	−	+	−	+	+	+	+[b]	−	+	+
6. Cordial recognition	−	+[b]	+	−	+	+[b]	+	+	+[b]	−	−	=	=	+	+
7. Pure client	+	+	+	+[b]	+[c]	+	+	+[b]	+	+	+[b]	+	+[c]	+	−
8. No interpersonal contact	+	−	−	+	+[c]	−	−	−	+	−	+	+	+	+	+
9. Primary contact (1–4)	=	=	=	=	=	=	=	=	=	=	=[b]	=[b]	=	=	=
10. Secondary contact (5–7)	+	−[c]	+	+[c]	+[b]	−[b]	+	+	+[c]	+[b]	+[b]	+[b]	+	+	+
11. All impersonal contacts (6–7)	+	+	+	+[c]	+[b]	+	+	+[b]	+[c]	+	+[c]	+	+[c]	+	−
12. All interpersonal contacts (1–7)	=	=	=	=	=	=	=	=	=	=	=	=	=	=	=
13. Total time awake (1–8)	=	=	=	=	=	=	=	=	=	=	=	=	=	=	=
14. Total time in job situation	=	=	=	=	=	=	=	=	=	=	=	=	=	=	=
15. Total time in mass-media situations	−	+[b]	+[b]	+[b]	+[b]	+[c]	+[b]	+[c]	+[b]	+	−	+	−	−	+
16. Total time in secondary situations	+	+	+[c]	+[c]	+[b]	+	+	+[b]	+[b]	+	+[b]	+[b]	+[b]	+[b]	+

[a] The significance of the difference between proportions was determined from nomographs (Joseph Lubin, "Nomographs for Determining the Significance of the Differences between the Frequencies of Events in Two Contrasted Series or Groups," *Journal of the American Statistical Association,* XXXIV (September, 1939), 540–41. The nomographs report P levels for only a critical ratio of 2 (0.0455) and of 3 (0.0027); levels are reported as 0.05 and 0.003, respectively, in the body of the table. The +, −, and = signs refer to the direction of the difference in each comparison.

[b] 0.005 level of significance.

[c] 0.05 level of significance.

TABLE 3. Mean and standard deviation of time spent in specified types of interpersonal contact situations by residence and status

Type of interpersonal contact or contact situation	Means (in minutes)						Standard deviations (in minutes)					
	URBAN		RNF		RF		URBAN		RNF		RF	
	High	Low	High	Low	High	Low	High	Low	High	Low	High	Low
1. Intimate kinship	322	355	282	285	334	401	125	102	176	158	222	255
2. Close intimate friend	43	35	117	93	72	79	108	86	134	140	141	195
3. Close associate or client	223	191	54	21	33	[a]	215	224	125	66	109	[a]
4. Good friend	34	54	51	89	64	8	82	114	112	155	173	25
5. Distant associate or client	113	134	215	140	155	123	181	193	239	220	204	201
6. Cordial recognition	8	20	[a]	27	2	[a]	31	81	[a]	120	11	[a]
7. Pure client	111	48	87	53	1	7	190	117	135	89	4	16
8. No interpersonal contact	119	133	181	241	297	311	140	167	168	234	286	291
9. Primary contact (1–4)	622	634	498	485	507	488	256	251	226	266	281	271
10. Secondary contact (5–7)	233	202	308	222	158	130	225	219	205	222	207	202
11. All impersonal contact (6–7)	120	68	87	81	3	7	193	140	135	139	12	16
12. All interpersonal contact (1–7)	855	836	806	707	665	618	156	181	182	244	291	293
13. Total time awake	974	968	985	948	962	928	92	76	64	76	86	70
14. Total time in job situations	498	491	539	514	641	640	131	77	155	98	138	142
15. Total time in mass media situations	121	125	71	70	62	44	85	89	111	87	65	53
16. Total time in secondary situations	367	324	378	269	71	20	197	242	227	259	111	48

[a] No time reported for any respondent.

are no sizable significant differences in mean duration of contact in cordial relationships.

The pure-client relationship, however, is clearly not rural. The RF males have pure-client contacts much less often than do urban and RNF males, although the results are not statistically significant for all status categories (line 7 of Table 2). A separate tabulation also shows that no RF male had a pure-client relationship on the job, in contrast to at least two-fifths of the high-status and one-fifth of the low-status urban and RNF males. Urban and RNF males, regardless of status, have a significantly higher mean duration of pure-client contacts than do RF males (line 7 of Tables 3 and 4). The high-status urban male, as expected, has the greatest average contact in a client role, averaging almost 2 hours a day. This average, in fact, is significantly and appreciably above that of all categories except RNF persons of high status. There is also a significantly higher variance for pure-client contacts for urban and RNF than for RF males. High-status urban and RNF males, in fact, tend to have significantly greater variance in pure-client contacts than do the other residence-status groups, although the comparisons are not always statistically significant (line 7 of Tables 3 and 4). This apparently higher variance for high-status urban and RNF males is probably accounted for largely by differences in occupational role composition and job context. Some white-collar jobs—particularly professional and sales occupations—require almost exclusive contact with clients, while others require little, if any.

Sorokin and Zimmerman's fourth hypothesis also is closely related to the second and third hypotheses: that casual, superficial, and short-lived relationships comprise a greater proportion of the total of interaction relations than do the permanent, strong, and durable relationships. Lines 1–7 in all the tables provide comparisons for four types of primary and three types of secondary relationships which permit a partial test; they lend only parital support to it. RF males may have a somewhat greater proportion of their total contact in a primary interaction relationship than RNF males and perhaps urban males of high status, but the differences are small and certainly do not warrant a conclusion that the hypothesis is sustained. The findings on amount of time actually spent in primary and secondary situations tend to support the hypothesis. Urbanites increase their primary contact time over that of their rural counterparts by having primary contacts at their work—an opportunity usually denied to rural males on small farms. Moreover, urban males make more personal contacts of the distinctly impersonal type—the pure-client relationship—than do the rural. These two types of relationships, then, are the major differentia. Yet, lest these differences be interpreted out of context, it must be remembered that the average urban person of high status—the extreme type—spends less than 2 hours a day in a pure-client relationship and only about 4 hours in all secondary contacts, while he spends over 10 hours in all types of primary interaction. His interaction time, therefore, is spent predominantly in primary relationships. These two types of relationships also appear clearly to reflect differences in opportunity for contact at work. Both the differences in primary contact with associates or clients and in the secondary pure-client type occur primarily at work. Non-agricultural work often provides opportunities for both types

TABLE 4. Significant residence and status group differences in interpersonal contacts and situations (P values)[a]

Type of interpersonal contact or situation	Urban high status VERSUS					Urban low status VERSUS				RNF high status VERSUS			RNF low status VERSUS		RF high status VERSUS
	Urban low	RNF high	RNF low	RF high	RF low	RNF high	RNF low	RF high	RF low	RNF low	RF high	RF low	RF high	RF low	RF low
1. Intimate kinship	−	+	+	(−)	(−)	(+)	(+)	(+)	(−)	−	−	−	−	−	−
2. Close intimate friend	(+)	−[b]	−	−	(−)	−[b]	(−)	(−)	(−)	(−)	+	+	+	+	−
3. Close associate or client	+	(+)[c]	(+)[c]	(+)[c]	[d]	(+)[c]	(+)[c]	(+)[c]	[d]	+	+	[d]	−	[d]	[d]
4. Good friend	(−)	(−)	(−)	(−)	(+)[c]	+	−	(−)	(+)[b]	−	−	(+)	+	(+)[b]	(+)
5. Distant associate or client	−	−[b]	−	−	−	−	−	−	+	+	+	+	−	+	+
6. Cordial recognition	(−)	[d]	−	(−)	[d]	[d]	−	(+)	[d]	[d]	[d]	[d]	(+)	[d]	[d]
7. Pure client	(+)[b]	+	(+)[b]	(+)[c]	(+)[c]	−	−	(+)[b]	(+)[b]	+	(+)[b]	(+)[b]	(+)[b]	(+)[b]	−
8. No interpersonal contact	+	−	(−)[b]	(−)[b]	(−)[b]	−	−[b]	(−)[b]	(−)[b]	−	(−)	(−)[c]	−	−	−
9. All primary contact (1–4)	−	+[b]	+[b]	+[b]	+[b]	+[b]	+[b]	+[b]	+[b]	+	−	+	−	−	+
10. All secondary contact (5–7)	+	−	+	+	+[b]	−	−	+	+	+	+[b]	+[b]	+	+	+
11. All impersonal contact (6–7)	(+)[b]	+	+	(+)[c]	(+)[b]	−	−	(+)[c]	(+)[b]	+	(+)[b]	(+)[b]	(+)[b]	(+)[b]	−
12. All interpersonal contact (1–7)	+	+	(+)	(+)[b]	(+)[b]	+	+[b]	(+)[b]	(+)[b]	+	+[b]	+[b]	+	+	+
13. Total time awake (1–8)	+	−	+	+	+[b]	−	+	+	+[b]	+	+	+[b]	−	+	+
14. Total time in job situation	(+)	−	−	−[c]	−[c]	(−)	−	(−)[c]	−[c]	+	−[b]	−[b]	−[c]	−[b]	+
15. Total time in mass media situations	−	+	+[b]	+[c]	(+)[c]	+	+[b]	+[c]	(+)[c]	+	(+)	(+)	+	+	+
16. Total time in secondary situations	+	−	+	(+)[c]	(+)[c]	−	+	(+)[c]	(+)[c]	+	(+)[c]	(+)[c]	(+)[c]	(+)[c]	(+)

[a] The + and − signs refer to the direction of the difference in each comparison. Parentheses indicate that the variances differ significantly at the 0.02 level.
[b] Means differ significantly at the 0.05 level.
[c] Means differ significantly at the 0.001 level.
[d] No time is reported for any respondent in at least one of the groups; the mean difference, therefore, is not calculated.

of contact—a primary friendship relation with a fellow or co-worker at the same or adjacent status levels and a secondary relationship with a member of the public or a client.

The final hypothesis is that the RF male spends a greater part of his waking time without any personal contact, given less opportunity for group contact in both work and non-work situations. There are no significant residence differences in the percentage of persons who spent some time in isolation (line 8 of Tables 1 and 2); however, RF males spend significantly more time in isolation and show greater variance than do urban (but not RNF) males, regardless of status (line 8, Tables 3 and 4).

The mean time spent in social isolation by the several residence-status groups can be expressed as a proportion of the mean time awake. These proportions, for high and low status, respectively, are 12.2 and 13.6 for urban, 18.4 and 25.4 for RNF, and 30.9 and 32.5 for RF males. It is readily seen that the average RF employed married male spends about a third of his day without any personal contact, as compared with only one-seventh of the waking time of urban employed married males, regardless of status; the RNF proportions are in between. It may be true that for single persons the urban environment is more conducive to living in almost complete isolation from social contact, but the typical urban married male in this study is less likely to spend part of his day isolated from social contact than is the typical RF married male. The average urban married male has more of primary contact and less of isolation than does the average married RNF or RF. The variance in amount of time spent without personal contact also is greater for RF than for urban married males. This at least suggests that the extremes of isolation (other than with intimate kin) are approached more closely by the RF than by the urban married male.

The modern period of Western society is often referred to as an age of potential leisure. This is attributed to the historical change in the amount of time spent at work by both agricultural and non-agricultural workers. The average time spent on the job was significantly longer for RF males than for RNF or urban males, regardless of status (line 14 of Tables 3 and 4). The average agricultural worker spent between 8 and 9 hours a day at work. The fact that the lowest variance for time spent on the job (line 14, Table 4) occurs for the non-agricultural worker of low status follows from the prevalence of a workday and week standardized by contract. The variance in length of work-day for urban workers of low status, in fact, is significantly below that of urban and RNF workers of high status and all RF workers.

The reduction in working hours provides considerable opportunity for persons to divide their waking hours among other activities (line 13 of Tables 3 and 4). There are a few significant differences between residence-status groups in the average duration of waking hours and no significant differences in variance. The mean waking interval is a little over 16 hours a day, with a standard deviation of 60–90 minutes, except for low-status RF persons. If one takes as a very crude measure of potential leisure the ratio of working hours to total hours awake, almost half the waking time of urban and RNF married males is spent outside the work context. These ratios for high- and low-status groups, respectively, are 51 and 51 for urban, 55 and 54 for RNF, and 67 and 69 for RF males. By contrast, roughly two-thirds of the waking time of RF persons is spent at work. Since, with the exception of RF persons of low status, there are no significant differences in total waking hours (and this is not enough to account for the observed differences), it is clear that the non-agricultural worker has a longer potential time for leisure than does the agricultural worker, at least on the workday.

Some attention was given to status differences in types of contact in referring to a combined residential area-status group difference. The status differentials in interpersonal contact are now examined within each of the three residential areas, though it is recognized that each test is not independent of the others in a sampling sense.

First of all, there are few status differences by residence in the proportion reporting some daily contact or in mean time spent in the several types of personal contact or contact situations (Tables 1–4). None of these status differences is significant in more than one of the three residential contexts. Urban groups of high and low status, in fact, show no significant differences in exposure to types of contact, and there are no significant differences in average time spent in personal contacts or contact situations between RNF or RF males of high and low status. Among urban inhabitants, males of high status have a greater mean contact in a pure-client relationship, and consequently in all impersonal contacts, than do urban males of low status. The same status differential is observed for RNF males, but it is not statistically significant. As noted, this probably is largely a consequence of differences in exposure to clients when at work.

There are somewhat more significant differences between high- and low-status groups in variances of time spent in personal contact and contact situations, even though there are few significant differences between them in average time spent in types of contact. None of the differences is observed in all residential settings, however.

Urban males of high status have a greater variance in contact with close intimate friends than do those of low status, but the latter have a greater variance in contact with good friends than do those of high status. The status difference in variance for all friendship contacts therefore disappears. High-status RF males, in contrast to high-status urban males, have a greater variance for contact with good friends than do those of low status; but the reverse, although not significant, is found for close intimate friends among RF males, so that the status difference in variance for all friendships also disappears for RF males. The apparent pattern then seems to be one where high-status urban and low-status

RF males show higher variance for contacts with good friends. This difference could well be a function of how high- and low-status males define "good' as compared with "close" friends—the distinction is difficult, in any case.

Urban males of high status have substantially greater variance in all impersonal contacts than do males of low status, but the difference is accounted for by the fact that high-status males have a greater variance in pure-client contacts, since low-status males have a substantially greater variance in contact in patterns of cordial recognition. Urban males of high status also show greater variance in the total time on their job than do those of low status. Both these patterns occur for RNF males, although they are not statistically significant. Hence white-collar workers are probably less homogeneous in their personal relations than are manual workers (in the non-agricultural situs).

The failure to reject the major null hypothesis about status differentials in interpersonal contact or in exposure to types of situation, independent of residence, is a surprising one, given both a general expectation of class differentials and the existing literature on them.

Only a few of the many possible reasons for this failure are mentioned here. The first is that differences in measurement account for the difference in conclusions. Most previous studies use some attribute of persons, such as their membership in certain groups, or a characteristic of their behavior, such as number of personal visits or meetings attended, as measures of personal contact and participation, and they also focus more on organizational structure. The present study measures times spent by the individual in a type of contact or situation. These are different dimensions of behavior. The time spent in many activities can be a negligible proportion of one's day: for example, the time spent in voluntary associations or in formal community organizations usually occupies only a very small proportion of a man's weekly, much less daily, time.

A second explanation is that our data are for very small samples, so that real, but small, differences may go undetected. Moreover, we examined only employed married males aged twenty to sixty-five; other age-sex-marital-status groups may show these expected differences. If this is the case, generalizations must be appropriately qualified. Fourth, the selection of our population in a southern locale may account for some differences, since it might be argued that the "more rural South" places high emphasis on primary relationships. This, conceivably, could affect the absolute allocation of time to a particular type of contact; but just how such an argument would apply to a failure to secure relative differences in residence-status comparisons is far from clear. Fifth, the limitation of our data to a single workday may limit our conclusion—the day-off could show a quite different pattern, although preliminary analysis suggests that this is not the case. Furthermore, a record of activity over an extended period might conceivably confirm the differences found in other studies in our population. Many previous studies measure contact for weekly, monthly, and even longer intervals. Generally, the longer the time, however, the less time "other-than-daily contact" will occupy of a person's total interaction time. A once-a-week contact with a friend, on the average, should account for less of the total weekly time than a daily contact, unless the time spent in the weekly contact is considerably longer. Finally, our measure of status is a simple dichotomy of white-collar and manual-worker status groups. Such a gross distinction may mask true differences in status. On the other hand, the more status is refined in terms of specific operational indicators such as occupation, the more it may reflect non-status differences in the indicator.

The major findings with respect to status differences in types of interpersonal contact and exposure to contact situations are as follows:

1. There are no significant status differences in the proportion of respondents who had some contact or exposure, mean amount of contact or exposure, or variance in contact or exposure in types of interpersonal contact or time spent in contact, independent of residence.
2. When only the non-agricultural residential settings are considered (urban and RNF), there similarly are no clear-cut significant differences in the proportion with contact, mean amount, and variance in interpersonal contact or exposure to contact situations. High-status urban and RNF males both may have a greater mean contact and variance in a pure-client relationship and in total time in job situations than do low-status ones. These differences may be a function of only some white-collar jobs, however.

With respect to residence differences in exposure to different types of contact situations the major findings are as follows:

1. A higher proportion of urban employed married males than of RNF or RF males, regardless of social status, as exposed to mass media on their workday, and with greater mean exposure time.
2. Significantly more of the urban and RNF males (non-agricultural workers) than of RF males, regardless of social status, had some exposure to secondary situations, and they likewise had both higher mean exposure and variance in exposure to secondary situations.
3. There are no significant differences by residence in the proportion of persons who spent some time in isolation. But all RF males, regardless of status, spend significantly more time in isolation than do urban males, and they have a significantly greater variance in isolation as well.
4. The average time spent on the job was significantly greater for RF than for RNF or urban males, regardless of status.

Differences in types of interpersonal contacts for residential settings may be summarized as follows:

1. While almost all men had some exposure to primary contacts during the workday, the average urban employed male had a significantly greater average time in primary contact than did his RNF or RF counterpart, regardless of status. There was no such significant difference between RNF and RF males. Primary contact time *may* occupy a somewhat smaller proportion of the total interaction time for urban and RNF males than it does for RF males.
2. Urban males do not show a greater amount of primary contact in all specific types of primary contacts, however. There is almost no significant variation in average daily contact with intimate kin and association with close intimate friends by residence. The major differentiating type is contact

with a work associate or client. A significantly larger proportion of the urban than of the RNF or RF males, regardless of status, had contact with a close work associate or client on their workday, and they spent a greater average amount of their daily time in such contacts.

3. Urban and RNF males are more likely to have a greater mean amount of impersonal contact on their workday than are RF males. This impersonal contact consists largely of contact in the client-role relationship.

Sociologists who speculate about the findings of this paper may be tempted to use the findings to show that the differences between residential groups in the United States have almost disappeared, but, of course, the study was not designed to demonstrate this, since no comparative historical data are available. Others may use them to show that the ideal typical description of the decline of the kinship relationship in urban areas has been exaggerated, much as Axelrod has done in a recent paper.[7] This interpretation is similarly suspect, inasmuch as no bench-mark data are available for temporal comparison.

For those inclined to speculate about the theoretical implications of the findings, two conclusions appear of special relevance. The first is that the agricultural—non-agricultural situs distinction appears to discriminate better with respect to differences in personal contact than does the type of residential settlement. This observation is in keeping with that made by Sorokin and Zimmerman about thirty years ago:

> . . . Rural sociology is in the first place a sociology of an occupation group, namely the sociology of the agricultural *occupation*. Such is the first and fundamental criterion of differences between the rural and other, particularly urban, communities. From it follow a series of other differences between the rural and the urban communities, most of which are causally connected with the above difference in occupation.[8]

The second observation is that the theoretical constructs conventionally employed to type urban and rural interpersonal relations and contexts do not lend themselves too readily to research. And, when they are translated into operational terms, the findings apparently vary for subclasses of a general construct. Thus, for example, only the "pure-client" relationship appears to have much discriminatory power in the "secondary" or "impersonal" relations construct. It is not maintained here that these operational constructs are the most satisfactory for theory—they probably are not—but rather that more attention must be given to the analytical discrimination of constructs in theoretically based research investigations on differences in interpersonal contacts or relationships.

Replication

SOCIAL INTERACTION IN RURAL AND URBAN COMMUNITIES

In this replication we will examine the extent to which people living in rural communities differ from urban people in respect to the frequency of social interaction.

The replication will necessarily require simplifying the array of indicators of social participation used in the original research. Two broad measures of interaction will be employed: one, a summary measure of informal interaction with friends, relatives and neighbors; the second, a measure of formal participation in voluntary organizations. Despite this simplification, the logic of the analysis remains the same: comparisons, with class background controlled, of the frequencies of interaction among persons in rural and urban communities.

Hypothesis

1. State which of the following groups you think has the highest and which the lowest amount of "informal social participation" (i.e., interaction with friends, neighbors, and relatives): farmers, rural nonfarm residents, city or suburban residents.

2. State a similar hypothesis for "formal social participation" (i.e., membership and attendance in voluntary clubs and other organizations).

3. Socio-economic level should also affect the amount and type of social interaction. Do you think the differences you anticipated in your previous hypotheses will be the same in the working class and the middle class?

Empirical indicators for this problem

11. My father's main occupation is (or was): ______

During the last year you were in high school, about how often did YOUR FATHER participate in each of the activities listed in the next four questions?

24. Visited his relatives (or had visits from them):

0. Not at all
1. Only once a year
2. Two or three times a year
3. Four to eight times a year
4. About once a month (9 to 12 times)
5. Two or three times a month
6. About once a week
7. A few times a week (2 to 4 times)
8. Almost every day or more often

[7] *Op. cit.*, pp. 17–18.

[8] *Op. cit.*, p. 16.

25. Visited neighbors (or had visits from them):

    0. Not at all
    1. Only once a year
    2. Two or three times a year
    3. Four to eight times a year
    4. About once a month (9 to 12 times)
    5. Two or three times a month
    6. About once a week
    7. A few times a week (2 to 4 times)
    8. Almost every day or more often

26. My father visited (or had visits from) his other friends:

    0. Not at all
    1. Only once a year
    2. Two or three times a year
    3. Four to eight times a year
    4. About once a month (9 to 12 times)
    5. Two or three times a month
    6. About once a week
    7. A few times a week (2 to 4 times)
    8. Almost every day or more often

27. My father attended meetings of organizations and clubs such as fraternal orders, church groups (but do not count Sunday services), business organizations, unions, recreation groups such as bowling teams, scouts, and any other nonprofit voluntary group having a recognized organization and officers:

    0. Not at all
    1. Only once a year
    2. Two or three times a year
    3. Four to eight times a year
    4. About once a month (9 to 12 times)
    5. Two or three times a month
    6. About once a week
    7. A few times a week (2 to 4 times)
    8. Almost every day or more often

28. About how many different clubs and organizations did *your father* belong to when you were a high school senior:

    ________ organizations

38. What kind of place did you live in, for the most part, during your childhood and adolescence:

    1. *Farm* (father was a farmer)
    2. *Fringe:* the open country but father was employed in *non*farm work
    3. *Suburb* or small town near a city
    4. *Within the city limits* of a city, town, or village

Data analysis

1. *Sort* the code sheets on the basis of box 11 into the following occupational class groups:

1, 2, 3 or 4 = White collar
5 = Farm
6 or 7 = Blue collar

2. *Sub-sort* the "white-collar" and the "blue-collar" groups according to box 38 into the following residential groups:

1 or 2 = Rural
3 or 4 = Suburb and city

3. *Tally* onto the Tabulation Form each of the resulting five groups according to either the Primary Group Participation Index (box 26t) or the Organizational Participation Index (box 28t). Your instructor will assign half the class to tally one of these measures and the other half to tally the other measure. However, both sets of data will be put on the blackboard to be used for your lab report.

4. *Compute* the mean Primary Group Participation (or the Organizational Participation Index). See Appendix C for instructions on computing the mean. Use the "upper limits' as the "x" value in calculating the mean (see "Note" in Appendix C).

5. *Compute* the mean for all the blue-collar groups by combining the Total "fx" for the blue-collar-rural-nonfarm and the blue-collar-urban groups and dividing this by the combined total "f" for these two groups. Then do the parallel calculation to obtain the mean for the entire white-collar group.

6. *Enter* the means for the variable computed by the other half of the class in the space provided below Table 1. (Your instructor will put these on the blackboard.)

Lab report

1. See Appendix A for general instructions on writing laboratory reports.

2. Report and discuss the findings for both participation indexes.

3. In the DISCUSSION section of the report, evaluate the findings for the farm group in light of the fact that only the children of farmers with relatively high income and education are likely to be found in a sample of college students.

References

Axelrod, Morris, "Urban Structure and Social Participation," *American Sociological Review, 21* (February 1956), pp. 13–18.

Bell, Wendell and Marion D. Boat, "Urban Neighborhood and Informal Social Relations," *American Journal of Sociology, 62* (January 1957), pp. 391–398.

Burchinal, Lee G., ed., *Rural Youth in Crisis: Facts, Myths, and Social Change*. Washington, D.C.: Department of

Health, Education and Welfare, U.S. Government Printing Office, 1966.

Faris, R. E. L. and Warren H. Dunham, *Mental Disorders in Urban Areas*. Chicago: University of Chicago Press, 1939.

Litwak, Eugene, "Occupational Mobility and Family Cohesion," *American Sociological Review*, 25 (February 1960), pp. 9–21.

Mills, C. Wright, "The Professional Ideology of Social Pathologists," *American Journal of Sociology*, 49 (September 1943), pp. 165–180.

Nye, F. Ivan, "Adolescent-Parent Adjustment: Rurality as a Variable," *Rural Sociology*, 15 (December 1950), pp. 334–339.

Redfield, Robert, "The Folk Society," *American Journal of Sociology*, 52 (January 1947), pp. 293–308.

Shaw, Clifford and H. D. McKay, *Juvenile Delinquency and Urban Areas*. Chicago: University of Chicago Press, 1942.

Simmel, Georg, "The Metropolis and Mental Life," Paul K. Hatt and Albert J. Reiss, Jr., eds. *Cities and Society*. New York: Free Press, 1957, pp. 635–646.

Stone, Gregory P., "City Shoppers and Urban Identification: Observations on the Social Psychology of City Life," *American Journal of Sociology*, 60 (July 1954), pp. 36–45.

Straus, Murray A., "Work Roles and Financial Responsibility in the Socialization of Farm, Fringe, and Town Boys," *Rural Sociology*, 24 (February 1962), pp. 17–25.

Sutcliffe, J. P. and B. D. Crabbe, "Incidence and Degree of Friendship in Rural and Urban Areas," *Social Forces*, 42 (October 1963), pp. 60–67.

Tonnies, Ferdinand, *Fundamental Concepts of Sociology*. New York: American Book Company, 1940.

Wirth, Louis, "Urbanism as a Way of Life," in Paul K. Hatt and Albert J. Reiss, Jr., eds., *Cities and Society*. New York: Free Press, 1957, pp. 46–63.

Name____________________

Date____________________

TABLE 1. Primary group (or organizational) participation index by residence and occupational class

PRIMARY GROUP PARTIC. INDEX (Box 26t) OR ORGANIZATIONAL PARTIC. INDEX (Box 28t) x	Farm (1 in Box 38)		WHITE COLLAR (1, 2, 3, or 4 in Box 11)				BLUE COLLAR (6 or 7 in Box 11)			
			Rural non-farm (2 in Box 38)		Suburb, city (3, 4 in Box 38)		Rural non-farm (2 in Box 38)		Suburb, city (3, 4 in Box 38)	
	f	fx	f	fx	f	fx	f	fx	f	fx
0 to 2										
3 to 4										
5 to 6										
7 to 8										
9 to 10										
11 to 12										
13 to 14										
15 to 16										
17 to 18										
19 to 20										
21 to 22										
23 & over										
TOTAL										
Mean =										
+ (No info.)										

________________ Mean of All White Collar

________________ Mean of All Blue Collar

LABORATORY REPORT FOR PROBLEM ____________

Course or Section ____________ Date ____________ Name ____________

HYPOTHESIS: ____________

SAMPLE: ____________

INDEPENDENT VARIABLE(S): ____________

DEPENDENT VARIABLE(S): ____________

OTHER FACTORS: ____________

LABORATORY REPORT FOR PROBLEM ____________

SUMMARY OF FINDINGS: ____________

DISCUSSION: ____________

Institutions VII

PROBLEM 15
FAMILY

Despite the apparent universality of the nuclear family, families differ markedly in the functions they perform for the society as well as for their own members. In some societies, for example, nuclear families are expected to maintain rigid and formal relationships: gossip, informality, joking are carried out with friends, not kin (Bott, 1957). In other societies, especially mobile urban-industrial societies, the expectation is reversed: love, companionship, informality are the very things thought to bind family members together.

The emotional tenor of family life is important, for it raises questions about the roles families play in socializing as well as stabilizing the personalities of adult members of the family. Clearly, if families are rigid and formal, members will tend to go elsewhere for primary group support. Arensberg and Kimball, for example, noted in rural Ireland the relationship between a traditional and rigid family system and participation in the *cuaird*—an age-graded informal network of friends (Arensberg and Kimball, 1961). Similarly, an analysis of lower-class families in New Haven, Connecticut, found that involvement in a network of informal relations tended to be associated with a traditional orientation to family life, and the absence of such networks tended to be associated with an emotionally charged, love-oriented family system (Nelson, 1966).

As important as the role of socializing and stabilizing adults, is the function of socializing the young. In nearly all societies the family is the most influential and important agency for socializing children. Some theorists have speculated that marriage is really a legitimation of parenthood (Malinowski, 1955). It appears, in fact, that many of the norms surrounding marriage have the consequence of fixing responsibility for socialization on the family and maintaining it as an efficient socializing agent: prohibitions against divorce enhance its stability; incest taboos between parents and children clarify the lines of power and influence; the condemnation of illegitimacy highlights the universal dictum that "every child should have a parent."

Unlike other groups which recruit members, families reproduce. Therefore an important issue in understanding the socializing function of the family is some sociological explanation of the conditions underlying reproduction rates. Research has adequately demonstrated that fertility rates do fluctuate under different social conditions: nonindustrialized societies have higher fertility rates than industrialized societies (Coale, 1963); lower-class persons have higher rates than middle-class persons (Wrong, 1956); and Catholics have higher rates than Protestants or Jews (Westoff, 1961). One interesting impetus for increased fertility is introduced in the reading for the present problem: the sexual composition of the children in the family. The authors argue that, in most circumstances, couples will enjoy having both a boy and a girl. In the event that their first two children are of the same sex, some pressure will therefore develop to have a third child in the hope that the new baby will be of the opposite sex. This pressure, of course, should not exist in families that have children of opposite sexes. To test this intriguing hypothesis, the authors show that intentions to have additional children are usually greater in families with same sex children than in families with opposite sex children. Finally, it is interesting to note that the research treats the family as a self-contained entity where a structural characteristic of the family, the sexual composition of children, influences the family decision to have additional children.

SIZE OF FAMILY AND PREFERENCE FOR CHILDREN OF EACH SEX / *Deborah S. Freedman, Ronald Freedman, and Pascal K. Whelpton*

Preference for at least one child of each sex has a minor, but significant, influence in determining whether couples with two, three, or four children expect to have and do have an additional child. This relationship was found to persist with a number of socioeconomic and demographic controls. Its importance increases with the number of children of identical sex. The analysis is based on the data from a national probability sample of white married women in the child-bearing years.

This paper deals with the question whether the number of children Americans expect and have is influenced by their desire to have at least one child of each sex. The maintenance of every society depends on a reasonable balance of the sexes. Preference for one or the other sex and the desired ratio between the sexes probably will vary with the nature of the society, particularly with reference to the difference between male and female roles at various stages of the life-cycle and how the sex of a member affects ability to discharge certain responsibilities in the family.

In Western society, preferences for male or female children are not, to any important extent, dependent on economic considerations. The economic significance of children of either sex has declined with the disappearance of child labor, the separation of economic activity from the family, and the relative economic independence of new families of their parents. Nevertheless, it is a common observation that a majority of couples want children of each sex. Presumably, this is because boys and girls play different roles in the family apart from any economic considerations.

From one point of view, children can be regarded as consumer goods—yielding direct satisfactions which will vary according to whether they are boys or girls; hence, some value is involved in having at least one of each. For example, boys bring about relations of their parents to outside groups which differ from those effected by girls; they involve their parents in different kinds of leisure pursuits (e.g., hunting and certain sports for a boy and his father as contrasted with dolls and an interest in clothes for mother and daughter), and children of either sex permit the parents to relive vicariously their childhood experiences, or experiences they wish they had had. (The parent may derive satisfaction from vicarious participation in the childhood role of the opposite sex: the mother who really wanted to be a boy may get special satisfaction from a son's activities.) If such differential satisfactions are enjoyed by couples with any given number of children, those with children all of the same sex will be more likely than will others to have an additional child. Whether it is, in fact, the case that couples whose children are all boys or all girls are more likely to go on to have more children is reported in this paper, on the basis of data for a national sample.

Reprinted with permission of the authors and publisher from the *American Journal of Sociology, 66* (September 1960), pp. 141–145.

Previous studies

There have been some previous studies of this problem, with more limited samples. Clare and Kiser analyzed ex post facto statements by married couples in the Indianapolis Study[1] as to how important the desire for a child of each sex was in their decision to have their last child. They found that it was important to a small group at each parity. However, as the authors indicate, this kind of ex post facto statement of reasons for actions is suspect as rationalization. In the Princeton American Family Study of two-child couples in large metropolitan areas, Westoff[2] used factor analysis to isolate the variables which are related to the desire for another child. He found sex preference to be important to Protestants but not to Catholics or Jews.

Results similar to Westoff's are reported by de Wolff and Meerdink[3] in a study of births in Amsterdam between 1948 and 1955. They found that the first two children of couples having a third child in those years were more likely to be of the same sex among Protestants and those professing no religion than among Catholics. In families with a third birth, the first two children were of one sex in 50 per cent of the Catholic and 52 per cent of the non-Catholic. (A considerable proportion of both Protestants and Catholics stopped at the second child.) These differences are not large, but they are statistically significant.

All these studies show that the desire to have a child of each sex is a relevant but not decisive factor determining the size of a family. Given the current

[1] Jeanne E. Clare and Clyde V. Kiser, "Preference for Children of Given Sex in Relation to Fertility," *Milbank Memorial Fund Quarterly,* XXIX, No. 4 (October, 1951), 440–92.

[2] Charles F. Westoff, "The Social-Psychological Structure of Fertility," in *International Population Conference* (Vienna: International Union for the Scientific Study of Population, 1959), pp. 355–66.

[3] P. de Wolff and S. Meerdink, "La Fécondité des marriages à Amsterdam selon l'appartenance sociale et religieuse," *Population,* XII, No. 2 (1957), 289–318.

norm of two, three, or four children in American families,[4] it is inevitable that this will affect only a small percentage of the families. By virtue of the nearly equal sex ratio at birth, most families will have children of both sexes in the course of having the moderate size of family they desire. On a chance basis, about 50 per cent of the two-child families, 75 per cent of the three-child families, and 87 per cent of the four-child families will have at least one child of each sex.

The data for this paper come from the Growth of American Families Study.[5] That study included 2,713 wives, chosen to constitute a national probability sample of all white wives who, in 1955, were eighteen to thirty-nine years old, married, and living with their husbands. The present investigation is limited to a subsample: those classified as fecund,[6] in their first marriage, having borne two, three, or four children to date, all still living. This involves 889 couples—521 with two children, 266 with three, and 102 with four.

Only fecund couples were studied, which seemed reasonable in an analysis of expectations of additional children. The investigation is limited to women who had been married only once, to eliminate the influence a second marriage might have on expectations of additional children, and to those who have never had a child who died, since when a child dies the parents frequently desire to replace it and there are too few such cases for proper assessment.

In analyzing preferences in size of family, the variable we have used is the expected, instead of desired, number of children. The stated desires in size do not necessarily represent a couple's probable performance; nor are expectations of size of family to be equated with the desires, intentions, or plans of a family. Many parents do not plan the size of their families; others have attempted to plan, but have been unsuccessful. Such families may not want more children and may not intend to have more, but a realistic appraisal leads them to expect a certain number of additional children. The expectations of a couple with regard to size of family reflect not just their hopes or intentions but also a more or less realistic appraisal of their future fertility. For most couples, expectations and desires will be identical, but the minority for whom there is a discrepancy is substantial.

Findings

For our subsample of 889 families, the hypothesis investigated is that, at a particular parity, couples with only boys or only girls are more likely than others (1) to expect to have additional children in the future and (2) actually to have gone on to have additional children in the past. We deal first with what people expect and then with actual behavior at each parity.

Two types of data were used to test the two parts of this hypothesis: (*a*) The sex composition of the family—whether or not the children were both (or all) of one sex—was related to the expressed expectation of additional children. This was done separately for two-child, three-child, and four-child families. The question is whether the proportion expecting additional children is larger among couples who, to date, had had just girls or just boys, or among those who already had at least one child of each sex. We are also interested in whether this relationship, if it exists, is more pronounced in larger than in smaller families. (*b*) The sex composition of the first two children of the three-child families was compared to that of completed two-child families—that is, those in which additional children were not expected. Here the question is whether couples with two children who actually went on to have three children might have been influenced by the fact that their first two children were of the same sex. This influence was measured by comparing the proportion of such couples whose first two children were of the same sex with the comparable proportion among completed two-child families. The same comparison was made for the first three children of four-child families and of the completed three-child families.

The relationship of sex of the children already born to expectations of additional children is shown in Table 1 separately for two-, three-, and four-child families.

TABLE 1. Expectations of additional children of two-child, three-child, and four-child couples, by sex distribution of children already born

	COUPLES EXPECTING AN ADDITIONAL CHILD			
	Families with children of just one sex		Families with children of both sexes	
No. of children already born	Per cent	N[a]	Per cent	N[a]
Two	63	259	59	261
Three	61	69	53	197
Four	76	17	49	85

[a] Total sample on which the percentage figure was based.

At each parity level the mothers with children of the same sex are more likely to expect additional children than are the other mothers. Among the two-child mothers, 63 per cent of those who had had only boys or only girls expected additional children, as against 59 per cent of those who had both boys and girls—a difference of four percentage points.

For mothers of three children, 61 per cent of those with children of just one sex expect additional children,

[4] For evidence on the marked consensus on the two-, three-, or four-child family, see Ronald Freedman, "Social Values about Family Size in the United States" (*International Population Conference, op. cit.*, pp. 173–83).

[5] The methodology and major findings of this study are reported in R. Freedman, P. K. Whelpton, and A. Campbell, *Family Planning, Sterility, and Population Growth* (New York: McGraw-Hill Book Co., 1959).

[6] The "fecund" wives are those in couples for whom there is no reason to suspect any physical limitation to the ability to have additional children (for a more complete operational definition, see Freedman *et al., op. cit.*, chap. ii).

compared to 53 per cent of those with children of both sexes—a difference of eight percentage points.

When mothers of four children are considered, the difference becomes much larger. Seventy-six per cent of the mothers with children of just one sex hope for additional children, as compared to 49 per cent of those families with children of both sexes—a difference of twenty-seven percentage points.

For both the two- and the three-child families the differences are small.[7] Though the difference is large for the four-child families, the number of cases is too small to yield a statistically significant difference. However, in all three cases the differences are in the expected direction and increase progressively with size of family.

A comparison was also made between the sex composition of completed two-child families and that of the first two children of those couples who had had a third child. The same comparison was made between the sex distribution of completed three-child families and that of the first three children of four-child families. In both comparisons a higher proportion of couples who actually had the additional child earlier had had children of only one sex. Among the 266 couples with three children, 55 per cent had only boys or only girls among their first two, compared with 47 per cent of the 203 couples stopping at two. Among the 102 couples with four children, 31 per cent had children of only one sex among the first three, as compared with 23 per cent among the 119 couples stopping at three.

Thus, five comparisons have been made between couples with children of both sexes and couples with children of just one sex—three comparisons of expectations to have additional children and two of the sex composition of groups of differing performance. In all five comparisons, whether the couples have children of only one sex is consistently related to expecting or having an additional child. The relationship is admittedly small, but it is consistent throughout and becomes larger as the family increases. It is reasonable to infer that this relationship demonstrates a preference for children of both sexes.

Given this small but consistent relationship between sex preferences and fertility expectations and behavior, a next step is to determine whether the relationship persists if controls are used for certain variables which are related to size of family. As control variables, four characteristics were used which, in the Growth of American Families Study, were found to have a significant relationship to size of family: number of years wife worked, education of wife, religion of wife, and duration of marriage. Since the number of cases was limited, each control variable was simply dichotomized, and the relationship between sex distribution and fertility expectations or achievements was investigated within the two categories of each control variable. The two types of comparisons made for each pair of subgroups were identical with those discussed previously, namely, (1) between those couples at each parity (two, three, or four) who do and those who do not expect to have additional children, and (2) between those couples who had complete families of two (or three) children and those who had at least one additional child. Thus, for each control variable ten comparisons were made of fertility as related to sex distribution.

The results are as follows:

1. *Years wife worked.*—This control does not change the relationship previously found between sex distribution and fertility. The differences in eight out of ten cases are in the expected direction. There is no apparent relationship between the size of the differences and the length of work experience.
2. *Education of the wife.*—This does not change the relationship. In eight out of ten comparisons the differences are in the expected direction. The amount of education has no consistent relationship with the size of the differences.
3. *Duration of marriage.*—In all ten comparisons, the differences are in the expected direction. Duration of marriage does not affect the size of differences consistently.
4. *Religion of the wife.*—This variable affects the size of the relationship but not its direction. The validity of the general findings is not altered in that the differences are in the expected direction in five out of five comparisons for Protestants and in four out of five comparisons for Catholics. But the size of the differences is greater for Protestants than for Catholics in all five comparisons. It seems that a desired sex distribution is more important to Protestants than it is to Catholics. This is consistent with the findings of Westoff and of de Wolff and Meerdink.

The relationship between sex preference and fertility was investigated with another control—success in family planning—but in a different manner. For this analysis the sample was restricted to couples who said they had wanted all their children and who had never had an "accidental conception" (a conception occurring when the couple was practicing contraception to avoid a pregnancy). In four of the five comparisons made for this group, the differences are still in the expected direction and are about the same size as those for the total sample. For these couples who have planned size of family successfully, expectations and desires are most likely to be identical, so this particular test indicates that the discrepancy between expectations and desires does not affect the relationship under study.

Thus, a total of forty-four comparisons were made within control categories of various kinds. In thirty-nine of the forty-four, the difference is in the direction consistent with the hypothesis. While the overlapping samples and the interdependence of control characteristics make it improper to use a sign test to evaluate exactly the statistical significance of the pattern of differences, the cumulative evidence certainly supports the statement that the preference for children of both sexes persists in a wide variety of important subgroups in the population.

None of the evidence considered up to this point depends on statements by respondents about their

[7] Tests for significance, allowing for the clustered character of the sample, show the relationships to be significant at about the .10 level. The numbers in our sample are so small that a relatively large percentage difference is necessary for statistical significance at the .05 level. However, the consistency of the results at all three parities makes it unlikely that the results are due to chance fluctuations in sampling.

reasons for having any given number of children. We have simply considered whether the failure to have a child of each sex is associated in fact with expecting or having additional children. This seems to us to be the best kind of evidence in view of the large element of rationalization and the unconscious motivations affecting a respondent's statement of reasons why she has or expects to have a family of a certain size. Nevertheless, we have examined statements by respondents as to why they wanted to have at least a certain number of children.

In the complete sample of the Growth of American Families Study, among all the respondents giving reasons for having at least a certain number of children, 10 per cent mentioned sex preference among other reasons. This is consistent with our earlier findings that sex preference is relevant for a small but significant minority. Clearly, it is not perceived as important by any large number.

For the special subsample analyzed in this paper, a further check was made by considering the reasons given by couples with three or four children who had children of only one sex and did expect to go on to a fourth or fifth child. Did such couples explicitly recognize a desire for a child of the sex they did not have? Among 42 such couples who had three children, 15 gave this reason among others for expecting to go on to a fourth child. A significant minority of the wives told us that they expected more children but did not want them. If we eliminate from the comparison these 9 couples who did not want the additional children expected, 15 out of 33—almost 50 per cent—gave this reason. Among the corresponding 13 four-child families of boys only or girls only expecting to have a fifth child, 7 gave sex preference as a reason. If we eliminate the 3 couples who did not want the additional child expected, the proportion rises to seven out of ten. Though these wives mentioned other reasons for wanting additional children, it was clear from the interviews that, for the majority, sex preference was the most important reason.

We have considered here the reasons given by only a small number of couples of the third and fourth parities because most couples reaching these parities have children of each sex and some of the others can not or will not have additional children for a variety of other reasons.

Preference for a child of each sex appears to be a significant, if minor, influence in determining the size of a family in the United States. Such a preference exists in a variety of subgroups in the population. With the limited data available only one characteristic was found which affected the magnitude of this influence —religion. The preference apparently exists among both Catholics and Protestants, but it is less pronounced among Catholics. We may ask whether the special religious values attached to size of family and family planning for Catholics reduce the relevance of such matters.

The influence of sex preference was found to increase with size of family within the two- to four-child range considered. Although this needs confirmation with a larger sample, if it persists in replication it has interesting implications. One possible explanation is that, with increasing family size, those with children of only one sex are more and more "deviant" if they take as a reference group persons with families of similar size. Three-fourths of the couples will satisfy the preference if they have three children. Another possibility is that, within the range of two to four children desired and expected by most Americans, most of the gains derived from children can be realized with the smaller number. Those who go on to or beyond the upper end of the range may be increasingly those with special reasons, such as the desire for children of each sex.

There appears to be enough support for the idea that Americans do value having children of each sex to justify research on the differential functions of boys and girls in American family life.

Replication

SEX OF CHILDREN AS A DETERMINANT OF FAMILY SIZE

The data for our replication of Freedman, Freedman, and Whelpton's study will be drawn from characteristics of your family of orientation—your parents, your siblings. Such families have nearly all been established eighteen or more years, and most are therefore "completed families" in the sense that no further children are likely to be born. This characteristic of our sample enables a better test of Freedman, Freedman, and Whelpton's hypothesis than was possible with their sample, many of whom were still in the early years of marriage. Specifically because our sample for the most part consists of completed families, we do not have to depend on plans and expectations, some of which might not be borne out. Rather, we can directly test the hypothesis that a desire for children of both sexes leads couples with children of only one sex to have additional children in the hope of securing the desired sex composition.

The authors suggest that in modern Western society it is deemed desirable to have children of both sexes; it is this preference which they feel accounts for their results. However, there is other evidence to suggest that despite the lack of any real economic advantage of having male children, and despite equalitarian norms regarding women, male children are nonetheless still preferred (Dinitz, Dynes, and Clark, 1954). Consequently, our replication will go beyond the original study to test the additional idea that having all *female* children results in greater pressure to have an additional child than is the case when the children are all males. Also, in that there are known differences in the fertility rates of Protestants, Catholics, and Jews, we have provided a control for religion.

Hypothesis

1. State which of the following types of families have the smallest and largest average number of children: those with children of both sexes, those with only male children, and those with only female children.

2. State whether you expect these findings to be similar or different for Protestants, Catholics, and Jews.

Empirical indicators for this problem

8. My mother's religious preference is:

   1. Roman Catholic or Eastern Orthodox
   2. Baptist
   3. Lutheran
   4. Methodist
   5. Presbyterian
   6. Other Protestant, please specify:
   7. Jewish
   8. Other: ______________________
   9. None

35t. How many brothers and sisters do you have?_____

36. Including myself, the children in my family are:

   1. All girls
   2. All boys
   3. Some boys and some girls

Data analysis

1. *Sort* the code sheets on the basis of box 8 into the following three religious affiliation groups:

   Catholic = 1
   Protestant = 2, 3, 4, 5, and 6
   Jewish = 7
   Other = 8 and 9 (do not include these in the analysis from here on)

2. *Sub-sort* each of the religious groups into sex composition groups, as coded in box 36:

   Girls only = 1
   Boys only = 2
   Mixed = 3

3. *Tally* onto Table 1 the number of siblings per family in each of these nine groups, as coded in box 35t; *discard from the tally any cases coded as "O".*

4. *Compute* the mean number of siblings per family in each group. See Appendix C for instructions on computing the mean from grouped data of this type.

Lab report

1. The main emphasis of your report should be on a comparison of differences between sex composition groups. However, you should also pay attention to whether similar or different results were obtained within each religious group.

2. Bear in mind that it was necessary to divide our limited-size sample into nine groups. Consequently, there may be only two or three cases in certain groups. Results based on numbers this small are likely to be unreliable.

References

Arensberg, Conrad M. and Solon T. Kimball, *Family and Community in Ireland*. Gloucester, Mass.: Peter Smith, 1961.

Bott, Elizabeth, *Family and Social Network*. London: Tavistock Publications Ltd., 1957.

Coale, Ansley, "World Population Problems," in *The Growth of World Population*, National Academy of Sciences, 1963, pp. 18–19.

Dinitz, Simon, Russell R. Dynes, and Alfred C. Clark, "Preferences for Male or Female Children: Traditional or Affectional," *Marriage and Family Living, 16* (May 1954), pp. 128–130.

Malinowski, Bronislow, "Parenthood—The Basis of Social Structure," in Marvin B. Sussman, ed., *Sourcebook in Marriage and the Family*. Cambridge, Mass.: The Riverside Press, 1955, pp. 21–30.

Nelson, Joel I., "Clique Contacts and Family Orientations," *American Sociological Review, 31* (October 1966), pp. 663–672.

Westoff, Charles et al., *Family Growth in Metropolitan America*. Princeton, N. J.: Princeton University Press, 1961.

Wrong, Dennis H., *Population*. New York: Random House, 1956.

Name____________________

Date____________________

TABLE 1. Mean number of children per family by sex composition of sibling group and religion

X NUMBER OF SIBLINGS (Box 35t)	CATHOLIC (Box 8 = 1)						PROTESTANT (Box 8 = 2, 3, 4, 5 or 6)						JEWISH (Box 8 = 7)					
	Girls only (Box 36 = 1)		Boys only (Box 36 = 2)		Mixed (Box 36 = 3)		Girls only (Box 36 = 1)		Boys only (Box 36 = 2)		Mixed (Box 36 = 3)		Girls only (Box 36 = 1)		Boys only (Box 36 = 2)		Mixed (Box 36 = 3)	
	f	fx	f	fx	f	fx	f	fx	f	fx	f	fx	f	fx	f	fx	f	fx
1																		
2																		
3																		
4																		
5																		
6																		
7																		
8																		
9																		
10 and over																		
TOTAL																		
Mean																		
0 & + (No info.)		X		X		X		X		X		X		X		X		X

LABORATORY REPORT FOR PROBLEM ______

Course or Section ______ Date ______ Name ______

HYPOTHESIS: ______

SAMPLE: ______

INDEPENDENT VARIABLE(S): ______

DEPENDENT VARIABLE(S): ______

OTHER FACTORS: ______

LABORATORY REPORT FOR PROBLEM __________

SUMMARY OF FINDINGS: __________

DISCUSSION: __________

PROBLEM 16 RELIGION

To the layman, religion represents an expression of principles—a commitment to a way of life, a belief in a god. To the sociologist, religion is a fertile laboratory for studying a variety of concerns: as a church, religion is an example of a social organization; as a set of religious scriptures, it is a form of cultural belief; as a group of clergymen, it is an illustration of an occupation. There is nothing in the scientific concerns of sociology which affirms or denies the validity of religion. Religion rests on ideological preferences, sociology on empirical facts (Parsons, 1964). Although a sociological analysis of religion may provide insights disturbing to the layman (and to the sociologist), it cannot alter, with any scientific rigor, the tenets of religion (Kolb, 1953).

In the history of sociology, interest in the religious institution gained its force from two classic studies: Emile Durkheim's *Elementary Forms of Religious Life* and Max Weber's series on world religions (Weber, 1930, 1951, 1958). Although Weber's works are of primary concern for this problem, it should be noted that both Weber and Durkheim were concerned with the impact of sacred, transcendental values on secular beliefs and activities.

In systematically bringing to bear historical materials on an understanding of religion and society, Weber's work represents one of the most impressive intellectual efforts of this century. If there is any key to understanding Weber's complex analysis, it is that much of it was waged as a polemic against the sociological perspectives of Karl Marx. Marx's argument essentially stated that social life could best be understood as a direct function of the society's economic structure. Family forms, philosophy, and art were all reflections of stages in economic development. Weber's contribution to this perspective stemmed from his outright rejection of simple economic determinism. To this end he carried out extensive historical research to show that even a seemingly unlikely variable such as religion influenced the economic system. In one particular inquiry, *The Protestant Ethic and the Spirit of Capitalism*, Weber argued that Protestant Calvinist theology, with its emphasis on individual initiative and hard work as the key to eternal salvation, was instrumental in the development of modern capitalism. Catholicism, alternatively, ranked materialism and individual work as worldly evils and to this extent provided little in the way of a moral foundation for what Weber viewed as the "spirit" of capitalism.

It is a credit to Weber's genius that the thesis regarding religion and economic motivation has continually fascinated social scientists. Despite his disclaimer that in contemporary Western society a secular ethic may *replace* religiously based economic motivation, research on religious differences in economic activities persists. Some of the research has provided evidence consonant with Weber's theory (Lenski, 1961) while other research has provided negative evidence (Mack, Murphy, and Yellin, 1956; Greeley, 1963).

The study you will read for this problem does not deal directly with Weber's theory, or even directly with its contemporary applicability. Rather, the study secures evidence on one of the possible mediating links between religion and economic activity. This link is a difference in the extent to which Catholic and Protestant parents train their children for independence. Variations in such socialization experience could lead to differences in the kind of individualistic economic striving behavior which is so critical for Weber's theory. Consequently, the research to be replicated is essentially a study of religious group differences in socialization practices, but a difference which bears on Weber's theoretical concerns.

RELIGIOUS AND OTHER SOURCES OF PARENTAL ATTITUDES TOWARD INDEPENDENCE TRAINING /

David C. McClelland, A. Rindlisbacher, and Richard deCharms

Half a century ago Max Weber first formulated his hypothesis that the spirit of modern capitalism is intimately connected with the Protestant ethic (6). [See references at end of reading.] Ever since, the idea has been taken for granted by some or argued away by others as an artifact due to other causes. But all agree that this is one of the major hypotheses of modern social science. Weber's original presentation makes the problem seem very much like one in basic personality structure or in psychology, yet psychologists, by and large, have ignored the question, or at least done very little to test the hypothesis empirically. This paper represents a first step toward trying to check some of its implications at the behavioral level.

In brief, Weber's argument runs as follows: he first notes that Protestants in Germany, and generally in Europe, were more likely to go into business or to schools preparing for business than Catholics. He then deals with some of the more obvious easy explanations for this fact. For example, could it be because Protestants are a minority group and, like Jews perhaps, go into business because prevented from succeeding in other spheres of activity? This does not seem likely to him because Catholics, as persecuted minorities in Holland and England, did not similarly go into business. Or could it be that Protestantism simply represents a further stage of secularization to Catholicism, making it more possible for individuals to engage in materialistic economic affairs rather than spiritual enterprises? He feels this explanation is highly unlikely also because Protestant church control in some countries was *more* rigid than Catholic church control had been, and yet it was in these very countries that the most marked economic development occurred.

From considerations such as these and others he was led to the conclusion that the connection between Protestantism and energetic economic activity is ideological in nature. That is, he contends that it was the very nature of the Protestant view of salvation which forced devout Protestants into capitalistic enterprises conducted in a new and more strenuous manner. He quotes from Benjamin Franklin to illustrate the new spirit he has in mind: "Remember that *time* is money. He that can earn ten shillings today by his labor, and goes abroad, or sits idle, one-half of that day, though he spends but sixpence during his diversion or idleness, ought not to reckon *that* the only expense; he has really spent, or rather thrown away, five shillings besides." (6, p. 48). This new spirit changed entrepreneurs from leisurely business men carrying on middleman functions in a traditional way, into dynamos of energy, but "above all temperate and reliable, shrewd and completely devoted to their business." (6, p. 69). He further notes that this energy did not seem to be directed at the amassing of wealth because many of these business men did not feel that they could or should enjoy their money even after they had it. Instead they plowed it back into the business. In fact, as Weber sums it up, such a man "gets nothing out of his wealth for himself, except the irrational sense of having done his job well." (6, p. 71).

This seems to be the way in which these men behaved. Now in what sense does Weber feel their religion made them that way? First, he devotes considerable space to demonstrating how Protestantism, as contrasted with Catholicism, had managed to make "the evaluation of the fulfilment of duty in worldly affairs as the highest form which the moral activity of the individual could assume." (6, p. 80). This was new because previously the highest form of moral activity had tended to lead the individual out of the world into the monastery. Weber connects this shift in emphasis in particular with Luther's concept of one's calling or vocation as something required by God. Secondly, he argues that Protestantism in general and the Calvinistic doctrine of predestination in particular tended to put the individual on his own in relation to God with nothing—neither priest nor sacrament, nor good works—to help him gain salvation. Since, according to Calvin, a man could not "earn" his way into heaven, all that he could do was to create in himself the *conviction* that he was one of those whom God had elected and the chief way to create this conviction was never to err but always, in life's every detail, to perform one's highest moral duties. "There was no place for the very human Catholic cycle of sin, repentance, atonement, release, followed by renewed sin." (6, p. 117). Thus, economic activity became just one more place where a person was obligated by the highest moral considerations to create the conviction of his own salvation by the excellence of his performance. "In practice this means that God helps those who help themselves." (6, p. 115).

In terms of recent research on human motivation (1), it would appear not too far-fetched to associate the new "spirit of capitalism" (e.g., "the irrational sense of having done his job well") with an increase in achievement motivation (*n* Achievement) and the Protestant emphasis on "self-help" for salvation with an increased stress on independence training for young children. Stated in this way, the hypothesis can easily be checked empirically in terms of measuring instruments now available. That is, the prediction would be that Protestants should have higher achievement motivation than Catholics and that Protestant families should emphasize independence training more.

Reprinted with permission of the author and publisher from David C. McClelland, ed., *Studies in Motivation.* New York: Appleton-Century-Croft, Inc. Division of Meredith Publishing Company. Copyright, 1955. pp. 389–397.

This way of stating the problem tends to provide some further support for Weber's line of reasoning because Winterbottom (7) and McClelland and Friedman (2) have already demonstrated an empirical connection between emphasis on independence training and *n* Achievement. The full argument relating Weber's hypotheses to these two factors involves the following steps: (1) Protestant families tend to emphasize independence training more than Catholic families; (2) independence training leads to higher *n* Achievement; (3) Protestants have higher *n* Achievement than Catholics; (4) higher *n* Achievement leads to more vigorous economic activity if coupled with other belief systems such as those involved in Protestantism; (5) economic development is greater in Protestant groups and countries than in Catholic groups and countries. This paper is concerned only with the first step in this chain of reasoning—with the prediction that Protestant parents will emphasize early independence for their children more than Catholic parents will. Since Weber also suggests (6, p. 117) that Jews like Protestants have largely "rationalized" the world and "eliminated magic as a means to salvation," we will also check the attitudes of Jewish parents with the expectation that they too will emphasize independence training more than Catholic parents.

Procedure

The measuring instrument was a questionnaire administered as part of a larger study to be reported elsewhere which included among other things the items used by Winterbottom to measure parental attitude toward independence training. The instructions and some of the items used will serve to define most quickly what is meant by independence training:

> Beside each statement there are two blanks. In the first one put a check mark if it is one of the things you want in your child by the time he is ten years old. In the second one, put the approximate age by which you think your child should have learned this behavior . . .
>
> To know his way around the city.
> To try new things for himself.
> To do well in competition.
> To make his own friends.

These items are four of the thirteen which Winterbottom (7) found were associated significantly with higher achievement motivation in the sons of those mothers who tended to want these things early in their children. There were other "caretaking" items which also involved learning to do things for oneself, but which were not included in the scores computed for our purposes because they were not associated with higher achievement motivation. These included such items as:

> To eat well alone.
> To look after his own possessions.
> To go to bed by himself.
> To do tasks around the house.

These items seem to reflect things that the child should do for the *parent* rather than for his own welfare which may explain why they were not associated with higher achievement motivation.

The questionnaires were administered occasionally in church groups but more often individually in two or three medium-sized cities in Connecticut. The four religious groups of parents studied were Protestant, Jewish, Irish-Catholic, and Italian-Catholic. An attempt was made to get an equal number of fathers and mothers in each group and an equal number from three social class groups. As a rough check on the class status of our respondents, we obtained the years of schooling which the parent had completed since this was easier to obtain than other measures like income level, and since it correlates fairly highly with other indexes of class status (5). To avoid such complicating features as generational differences, volunteer errors and the like, we selected most of the parents on the basis of data provided by their children in a large questionnaire survey conducted in a city high school. This meant that we often picked parents on the basis of their religious and educational characteristics and went and asked them directly to fill out the questionnaire. Consequently we could restrict our sample to parents roughly between the ages of 30 and 50 who had at least one child at the present time between the ages of 6 and 18 (with the exception of four cases where the child was between 2½ and 6 years of age).

Results

The major findings are presented in Table 1 which shows the average ages, cross-classified by religious and educational status, at which fathers and mothers expected their children to have mastered the 13 independence training items. The means in this table represent varying numbers of cases in individual cells because it was easy to get some types of cases and hard to get others. For example, the means for the lowest educational level Italians are based on 10 fathers and 11 mothers, whereas the lowest educational level Protestant means are based on 2 fathers and 4 mothers because it was hard to find Protestant parents in this age range who had not graduated from high school. Consequently the means for the religious groups are not necessarily equivalent to what they would be for a representative sample of cases from each group, but it seemed better to equalize educational differences by using the means in the analysis, since otherwise the differences might be wholly due to the generally lower educational level of the Italian group. There were at least 4 cases in 20 of the 24 cells, 3 cases in 3 of the cells, and 2 cases in 1 cell. The total number of cases is 152. (See page 255.)

The results of an analysis of variance on these means are also presented in Table 1. The conclusions are clear-cut. Religion, sex of parent, and educational level all contribute significantly to the variance as tested against an error term based on individual cases in the total sample. The two Catholic groups expect independence in their children later than the Protestant or

Jewish groups. Fathers are generally more lenient than mothers—expecting independence nearly a year later on the average—and, as the educational level (and associated socioeconomic status) increases, parents expect earlier independence although this last factor is somewhat less important than the other two. There are also some interesting interaction effects among the three primary variables. For instance, education affects the reactions of Italian fathers and mothers quite differently from the way it affects parents in the other religious groups. This third-order interaction shows up as significant in the full analysis of variance (which incidentally appears to preclude using the interaction term as an estimate of error), but its meaning cannot be pursued here as beyond the scope of a preliminary analysis.

It is also possible to make comparisons between individual pairs of religious groups. For example, the Irish and Italians may be compared to note the effects of cultural differences with religion held constant. If this is done using the means in Table 1 and assigning their difference its appropriate mean square estimate by the method described by Snedecor (3, p. 400), an F ratio based on the error estimate in Table 1 may be obtained which is significant at less than the 2% level. That is, the Irish mean of 7.66 appears to be significantly lower than the Italian mean of 8.42. If samples matched for educational status and sex of parent are drawn at random from the Irish and Italian groups ($N = 23$ in each case), the Irish mean is lower than the Italian mean as in Table 1 but at a lower level of significance ($t = 1.65$, $p < .11$). Thus the analysis supports the contention that culture has an influence on age of independence training over and beyond religion, although not unequivocally if one chooses to pay attention to the results from the smaller, matched sample of cases. A similar analysis can be made of two similar cultures which differ in religion. This involves the Protestant vs. Irish comparison which shows by either method of statistical analysis that the Irish expect independence significantly later than the Protestants. That is, whether the significance test is run using variance estimates based on Table 1 or matched samples drawn from each group ($N = 26$ in each case), it reaches the 1% level of confidence. In short it looks as if the Irish are in between, being influenced toward earlier independence training by cultural factors and toward later independence training by religious factors. They expect independence significantly later than the Protestants and probably significantly earlier than the Italian Catholics.

Discussion

The hypothesis is clearly borne out by the facts. Protestant and Jewish parents expect independence earlier on the part of their children than do Irish- or Italian-Catholics. The first step toward attempting to check Weber's hypothesis at the empirical level has produced support for it. Religious factors do seem to condition parental attitudes toward independence training. However, there are many other steps to take before the general hypothesis can be considered verified. We know from Winterbottom's results that independence training is likely to lead to higher achievement motivation, but we have yet to demonstrate that Protestant and Catholic groups differ in this predicted way. Furthermore, we have shown that these expected differences in attitudes toward independence exist only within a given country, namely the U. S., and we have not as yet shown that they likewise exist in the same way in other countries which are predominantly Catholic or Protestant. Finally, of course, we have not demonstrated any empirical relationship between higher achievement motivation and greater economic activity, although here, as is the case with the other links in the chain of reasoning, the presumptive evidence seems fairly strong.

The data also shed light on other factors which have been alleged to be of importance in conditioning general value attitudes. For the Freudians the all-important source of values and motives is the family. We have shown that fathers and mothers differ in the age at which they expect independence of their children across cultural, religious, and educational-economic differences. To this extent our data provide some support for the general Freudian position that there are certain universal constants in the family equation which may be invoked to explain the motivational development of the individual. We know of no psychoanalytic attempt to make use of the possibly universal differential between father and mother that we have just demonstrated, but we see no reason in principle why it could not be used to explain motivational development in much the same way as they use the allegedly universal tendency for sons to fall in love with their mothers.

Our data also provide some support for the cultural anthropologists who have argued that traditional "patterns of culture" are of primary importance in determining the value structure of individuals. That is, we have evidence that the Irish and Italian groups despite their similarity of religion do differ in their attitude toward independence training. This strongly suggests that there is some source of this difference which lies in their own national or cultural history rather than in their religion as such.[1] Finally, we have a little evidence which is relevant to the hypothesis that economics is of primary importance in determining values. While it is true that our educational levels are not perfectly correlated with economic status by any means, it can scarcely be doubted that there is some connection between them. That is, certainly our parents who had not graduated from high school are less well-off

[1] Since the peak of Irish immigration to the United States occurred some 30 or 40 years before the peak of the Italian immigration, it might be argued that we are dealing here not with a cultural difference but with a difference in length of time the two groups have been exposed to American values. This interpretation is rendered somewhat unlikely by the fact that in the present instance we selected our informants from those parents whose children had at least one grandparent born in the "Old Country."

TABLE 1. Average ages at which parents expect children to have mastered various independence training items

	Less than high school graduate	High school graduate up to college graduate	College graduate or more	Means	Religious group means
Protestant					6.64
Father	8.04	6.41	6.90	7.12	
Mother	6.56	6.41	5.55	6.17	
Jewish					6.59
Father	7.65	7.12	6.48	7.08	
Mother	5.74	6.66	5.89	6.10	
Irish Catholic					7.66
Father	8.50	7.92	8.26	8.23	
Mother	7.23	7.61	6.40	7.08	
Italian Catholic					8.42
Father	9.05	10.43	6.51	8.66	
Mother	9.68	6.87	8.00	8.18	
Educational level means	7.81	7.43	6.75		
Fathers' mean	7.77				
Mothers' mean	6.88				

ANALYSIS OF VARIANCE

Source of variation	Sum of squares	*df.*	Mean square	F
1. Religion	13.91	3	4.64	12.21[a]
2. Educational level	4.60	2	2.30	6.05[a]
3. Sex of parent	4.74	1	4.74	12.47[a]
4. Interaction[c]	11.78	17	.69	1.82[b]
5. Error		128	.38	

[a] Significant at the 1% level.
[b] Significant at the 5% level.
[c] The primary sources of variation interact significantly, a fact which cannot be discussed here as being beyond a preliminary treatment of the results. For this reason it has also been necessary to compute an independent estimate of error based on the actual variation of the individual cases in the various cells following the approximation method described by Walker and Lev (4, pp. 381–382).

economically on the whole than those who had graduated from high school, and these in turn are less well-off on the average than those who had graduated from college. Roughly speaking also there are more "capitalists," entrepreneurs, and professional people in the most highly educated group and more "workers" in the least educated group. The types of economic activity in which these classes of people engage might be expected to influence their attitudes toward independence and initiative. And this is what our results show to be the case. Parents from the lower occupational levels encourage independence in their children less possibly because they see less opportunity for its being rewarded or less need for it in the type of work they engage in, while the reverse is true of parents who come more often from occupations requiring initiative, self-reliance, and the like. Actually in the present analysis the economic factor (as it is related to type of occupation) does not loom as large as religion or sex of parent—a fact which will give small comfort to those who see history as being determined primarily in economic terms. It is probably true that the design of the study tended to underplay the economic factor because it was measured indirectly through educational level rather than directly through type of occupation (or income level), but even so it appears to be only one determinant, along with others like religion, culture, and family structure, of attitude toward independence training which in turn influences the strength of achievement motivation and thus probably eventually the course of economic development and history.

References

1. McClelland, D. C., J. W. Atkinson, R. A. Clark, and E. L. Lowell. *The Achievement Motive*. New York: Appleton-Century-Crofts, 1953.
2. McClelland, D. C. and G. A. Friedman. A Cross-Cultural Study of the Relationship Between Child-Training Practices and Achievement Motivation Appearing in Folk Tales. In G. E. Swanson, T. M. Newcomb, and E. L. Hartley (Eds.), *Readings in Social Psychology*. New York: Holt, 1953. Pp. 243–248.
3. Snedecor, G. W. *Statistical Methods* (4th edition). Ames, Iowa: Iowa State College Press, 1946.
4. Walker, A. M. and J. Lev. *Statistical Inference*. New York: Holt, 1953.
5. Warner, W. L., M. Meeker and K. Eells. *Social Class in America: A Manual of Procedure for the Measurement of Social Status*. Chicago: Science Research Associates, 1949.
6. Weber, M. *The Protestant Ethic* (translated by Talcott Parsons). New York: Scribner's, 1930.
7. Winterbottom, M. The Sources of Achievement Motivation in Mothers' Attitudes Toward Independence Training. In D. C. McClelland *et al.*, *The Achievement Motive*. New York: Appleton-Century-Crofts, 1953. Pp. 297–304.

Replication

RELIGIOUS DIFFERENCES IN THE SOCIALIZATION OF CHILDREN

This replication will approximate the logic of McClelland, Rindlisbacher, and deCharms' design by comparing the independence behavior of the three major religious groupings. In addition, to rule out the possibility that differences observed between persons of different religious faiths are due to their place in the stratification structure rather than religious ideology, we will introduce a control for social class. The replication, however, departs from the original study in two significant ways. First, due to limitations in the size of the sample, it will be necessary to combine all Catholics into a single group. Second, the measurement of the dependent variable is somewhat different. McClelland and his colleagues used the ages at which children were expected to be independent in various activities. We will use a somewhat more general indicator: The extent to which parents place priorities on "thinking for oneself" (independence) or "obeying one's parents" (dependence). The two measures are not, of course, identical, but they do bear some conceptual affinity to each other.

Hypothesis

1. State whether Catholics or Protestants will place higher priorities on "thinking for oneself" as compared to "obedience to one's parents."
2. State whether you anticipate the above hypothesis will be equally applicable to the upper middle class, the lower middle class and the working class.

Empirical indicators for this problem

8. My mother's religious preference is:
   1. Roman Catholic or Eastern Orthodox
   2. Baptist
   3. Lutheran
   4. Methodist
   5. Presbyterian
   6. Other Protestant, please specify: ______________________
   7. Jewish
   8. Other: ______________________
   9. None

12. Occupational Prestige
   1. Proprietor of a large business (valued at $100,000 or more); Top-level executive in large organization; Top-level professional
   2. Proprietor of a medium business (valued at $35,000 to $100,000); Middle-level executive or official, or top level of a small organization; Lower-level professional; Sales representatives of manufacturers or wholesalers or other senior salesmen earning $10,000 or more per year; Farmer of farm worth $100,000+
   3. Proprietor of a small business (valued at $6,000 to $35,000); Lower-level official and manager; Semi-professional; Sales representative (as above) earning $7,000 to $10,000 per year; Farmer of farm worth $35,000 to $100,000
   4. Proprietor of a very small business (valued under $6,000); Technician; Sales Clerk and salesman earning *less* than $7,000 per year and clerical workers; Farmer of farm worth $15,000 to $35,000
   5. Farmer of farm worth under $15,000; Skilled manual worker and foreman
   6. Farmer, sharecropper or tenant with little stock or equipment; Semi-skilled worker and machine operator
   7. Unskilled worker

40. Which of the following characteristics did your mother think were the most important for you to have while you were in high school?
   Put a "1" next to the characteristics your mother felt was most important, a "2" for the second most important, etc., until you have ranked the whole set. The least important item should be numbered "8."

   ____a. that I work hard

   ____b. that I think for myself

   ____c. that I be considerate of others

   ____d. that I obey my parents well

   ____e. that I be dependable

   ____f. that I have self-control

   ____g. that I be popular with other children

   ____h. that I be able to defend myself

Data analysis

1. *Sort* the code sheets according to box 12 into the following occupational prestige groups:

   1 and 2 = upper middle class
   3 and 4 = lower middle class
   5 through 8 = working class

NOTE: The analysis can be facilitated if for steps 2 on, one third of the class is assigned the upper middle class, one third the lower middle class, and one third the working class.

2. *Sub-sort* the code sheets for the Occupational Prestige group assigned to you into religious groups on the basis of the mother's religion (Box 8):

1 = Catholic
2 through 6 = Protestant
7 = Jewish*
8 and 9 = Others: Put these aside for the remainder of this problem.

3. *Tally* for the Catholic group whether higher priority is given to "thinking for oneself" or to "obeying one's parents." This is to be accomplished by noting whether the number in box 40b is higher or lower than the number in box 40d. Remember that a rank of "1" indicates a *higher* priority than a rank of "4."

4. *Compute* the percentage giving priority to "thinking" and the percentage giving priority to "obedience." This should be done by dividing the number giving priority to thinking by the total number in the Catholic group, omitting those for whom there is no information. Use the percentage tables in Appendix B to save time.

5. *Repeat* steps 3 and 4 for the Protestant and Jewish groups.

Lab report

1. Summarize the findings for religious differences within each of the class groupings. If religious differences are not equal for each occupational group, speculate as to the possible reasons.
2. The discussion should attempt to relate your findings to Weber's theory.
3. See Appendix A for general information on writing laboratory reports.

References

Bendix, Reinhard, *Max Weber: An Intellectual Portrait.* Garden City, New York: Doubleday, 1960.

Durkheim, Emile, *The Elementary Forms of The Religious Life.* New York: Collier Books, 1961.

Greeley, Andrew W., "The Influence of The Religious Factor on Career Plans and Occupational Values of College Students," *American Journal of Sociology, 68* (May 1963), pp. 658–671.

Kohn, Melvin L., "Social Class and Parental Values," *American Journal of Sociology, 64* (January 1959), pp. 337–351.

Kolb, William, "Values, Positivism and the Functional Theory of Religion: The Growth of a Moral Dilemma," *Social Forces* 31 (May 1953), pp. 305–311.

Lenski, Gerhard, *The Religious Factor.* New York: Doubleday, 1961, esp. chapter 3.

Mack, Raymond W., Raymond J. Murphy, and Seymour Yellin, "The Protestant Ethic, Level of Aspiration, and Social Mobility: An Empirical Test," *American Sociological Review, 21* (June 1956), pp. 295–300.

Marx, Karl and Friedrich Engels, *The German Ideology.* New York: International Publishers, 1947.

Parsons, Talcott, "The Role of Ideas in Social Action," in Talcott Parson, *Essays in Sociological Theory.* New York: Free Press, 1964, pp. 19–33.

Weber, Max, *The Protestant Ethic and The Spirit of Capitalism.* New York: Scribner's, 1958.

* NOTE: If there are less than four cases in this group, add them to the "others."

Name________________________

Date________________________

TABLE 1. Value placed on autonomy by religion and social class

Value placed on AUTONOMY VS OBEDIENCE (Box 40b vs 40d)	UPPER MIDDLE CLASS (Box 12 = 1 or 2)					
	Catholic (Box 8 = 1)		Protestant (Box 8 = 2-6)		Jew (Box 8 = 7)	
	Tally	%	Tally	%	Tally	%
THINKING: Code in Box 40b is less than 40d						
OBEDIENCE: Code in 40b greater than 40d						
TOTAL		100%		100%		100%
+ (No info.)		X		X		X

LOWER MIDDLE CLASS (Box 12 = 3 or 4)

THINKING: Code in 40b is less than in 40d						
OBEDIENCE: Code in 40b is less than in 40d						
TOTAL		100%		100%		100%
+ (No info.)		X		X		X

WORKING CLASS (Box 12 = 5 through 7)

THINKING: Code in 40b is less than in 40d						
OBEDIENCE: Code in 40b greater than 40d						
TOTAL		100%		100%		100%
+ (No info.)		X		X		X

LABORATORY REPORT FOR PROBLEM ______

Course or Section ______ Date ______ Name ______

HYPOTHESIS: ______

SAMPLE: ______

INDEPENDENT VARIABLE(S): ______

DEPENDENT VARIABLE(S): ______

OTHER FACTORS: ______

LABORATORY REPORT FOR PROBLEM__________

SUMMARY OF FINDINGS:

DISCUSSION:

PROBLEM 17

EDUCATION

Formal education is an increasingly important vehicle of socialization in urban, industrialized societies. In the past, family units tended to fulfill many of the educational functions of the school; they were the most important and, at times, the only agents of socialization. Vital as the family may be in all societies, it is clear that the family is limited in its technical knowledge and thus limited in the scope of the cultural material it is able to transmit. To be a doctor, a pharmacist, an engineer requires highly specialized training by teams of experts; it requires, in brief, a formal education that families do not have the capacity to render.

There are many other issues arising from the role of formal education in modern societies, and sociologists have explored a variety of them. Some have raised questions about the educational institution as a bureaucracy and attempted to understand various social and community pressures on school administrators (Gross, 1958). Others have attempted to explore the role of education as a vehicle for social mobility (Lipset and Bendix, 1959). Still others have raised serious questions about discriminatory practices in schools (Hollingshead, 1949) and the extent to which they create major social problems by alienating economically deprived children (Cohen, 1955).

One interesting tradition has tried to understand the contribution of education to the development of mature and thoughtful intellectual capacities. The theme of this tradition can be summarized as follows: Education is usually, but not always, something more than digesting facts. To be an educated man is to be able to comprehend complexity, to apply general principles, to make subtle and informed judgments. Education, by challenging the shibboleths of previous generations, frequently requires persons to rethink and, if necessary, change their most fundamental postures and values.

The research findings emerging from this tradition are at times ambiguous; there is, however, some evidence to suggest that education indeed broadens the individual, for it appears to shape respect for one of the values most basic to the democratic process—tolerance of dissent (Trow, 1958; Selvin and Hagstrom, 1960; Goldsen *et al.*, 1960). It seems that the more educated the man, the more tolerant he will tend to be.

Part of this effect may be due to the liberal postures of the educators themselves (Newcomb, 1943). Part also may be attributed to the fact that tolerance requires an ability to understand and live with complexity. The uneducated man tends to see life along the stereotyped dimensions of black and white, good and bad. What is not white is bad and what is bad is not to be tolerated. Within the framework of the educated mind, such hard and fast distinctions cannot be readily drawn (Lipset, 1959). If it is not clear that some condition poses a threat, it is equally not clear whether the condition should be eradicated. Thus, the link between education and tolerance.

In brief, education indicates a degree of sophistication. While levels of education and sophistication are associated with occupational differences, the variables are conceptually distinct. In the reading for the present laboratory problem, the author's intent is to speculate about the impact of education on tolerance. He bases this in part on data from a study by Stouffer (in Table 1) on the effects of education on tolerance *within* occupational groups. By confining comparisons to educational levels within these occupational groups, he is able to rule out the effects of occupation and social class and thereby assess the distinctive contribution of education to civil liberties.

EDUCATION AS AN ACTIVE AGENT IN CULTURAL CHANGE / *Burton R. Clark*

The role of the school in transmitting culture and socializing the young[1] has led many observers to view education as largely a passive, dependent institution. If the school passes on a heritage to succeeding generations, it conserves existing society; if it forms the young in the image of previous generations, then traditional patterns of behavior are perpetuated. The school does society's bidding, and is indeed then largely a passive agent.

Sociologists have also long stressed that social institutions are interdependent and social change largely unplanned and evolutionary, a perspective that sees education as a dependent element in a slowly evolving web of institutions. This conception is best expressed in the statement by Emile Durkheim, the great French sociologist, that education is "a collection of practices and institutions that have been organized slowly in the course of time, which are comparable with all the other social institutions and which express them, and which, therefore, can no more be changed at will than the structure of the society itself."[2]

In this view, the school has little independence, little room to maneuver or innovate. Its teachers, administrators, and controlling boards cannot cause or "will" basic changes, but rather are themselves steered by the mores of the larger society and the nature of other institutions. Systems of education "depend upon religion, political organization, the degree of development of science, the state of industry, etc."[3] Society dictates to the school, the school cannot dictate to society.

This "conservative" view of the cultural role of education needs re-evaluation: Is it appropriate and adequate for advanced industrial societies in the middle of the twentieth century? We have already suggested that cultural transmission may be a weakening function, a theme to which we shall return later in the book. Here we will supplement the traditional perspective with a second view that the educational institution is now a prime contributor to change in society. Education is not purely dependent, always following the lead of other dominant institutions, for schools and colleges change society in a number of ways. These ways, at least in democratic societies, are not a result of the efforts of planners and reformers; deliberate attempts to use the schools for social transformation have made little headway. Rather, education is becoming an active center of cultural and social change as it grows in size and complexity and takes on new tasks. Its relation to other institutions as well as its own character changes as the technological society assigns it an increasingly important place. Much of its new significance stems from a vast broadening of its cultural role.

Education produces new culture

Education is portrayed as largely a conservator of society when it is seen as an enterprise devoted to preserving and transmitting the learnings of the past. This conception is still appropriate for elementary and secondary education, despite the innovations of progressive education, for these lower echelons remain a teaching establishment; but it is only part of the picture of higher education in modern society. True, colleges and universities still serve as custodians of the intellectual capital of mankind; but "they also serve as centers of innovation and change, of investigation of the application of knowledge to current needs, and of re-examination and criticism of society."[4]

The traditional conception of education particularly overlooks the increasingly large role of the university as an inventor of knowledge and technique.[5] While the university in this country engages in undergraduate education, it is, as elsewhere, centrally the home of graduate work and the professional school, of research and scholarship. Research is institutionalized in the American university, even massively bureaucratized there according to some critics.[6] The amount of research done within universities has increased enormously since the beginning of World War II. The amount spent on research in all American universities rose more than 2,600 per cent between 1939–40 and 1957–58, from $27,000,000 to $734,000,000. The Harvard Medical School alone, in 1959, had a research budget of over $5,000,000, compared to approximately $220,000 twenty-five years before.[7] The fruits of all this research—some bitter, some sweet—touch all institutions and lives. Research in physics and chemistry alters our technology which in turn affects the structure of industry, the distribution of population, the status of occupations, and even the tenor of international relations. Atomic research, of course, has been a prime mover in society since 1945, one that has worked out

[1] The individual is socialized through learning group-defined ways of acting, feeling, and thinking, internalizing the norms of the culture. Socialization takes place primarily in the family, the school, and the peer groups of the young; it also occurs in the learning of skills and in the performing of adult roles.

[2] Emile Durkheim, *Education and Sociology,* translated by Sherwood D. Fox (Glencoe, Illinois: The Free Press, 1956), p. 65. (Originally published in 1922.)

[3] Durkheim, *Education and Sociology,* p. 66.

[4] *The Price of Excellence,* Problems and Policies Committee, American Council on Education (Washington, D.C.: October, 1960), p. 1.

[5] A. H. Halsey, "The Changing Functions of Universities in Advanced Industrial Societies," *Harvard Educational Review,* Vol. 30 (Spring, 1960), pp. 118–127.

[6] William H. Whyte, Jr., *The Organization Man* (Garden City, New York: Doubleday & Co., Inc., 1957). Chapter 17.

[7] Nathan M. Pusey, "The American University Today," *School and Society,* Vol. 89 (Feb. 11, 1961), p. 49.

of the Universities of Chicago and California as well as such firms as General Electric. Polio vaccine and long-staple cotton, as examples, also have come out of the work of the university. Along with the research of physical and biological science, scholars in the humanities and the social sciences contribute new findings and perspectives to the understanding of history and the conditions of modern man. The *conservation* of knowledge has intermittently throughout the history of higher education led in modest degree to its *development;* in modern times, the point is, many more scholars spend much more time in the deliberate development of knowledge than ever before. Out of the old-time scholar emerges the likes of the researcher in linguistics, public administration, or food technology. Such latter-day academic specialists are primary producers of man's expanding supply of basic knowledge.

The university is not only a research center but also the place that trains the men who do the research wherever it is located. Of the highly trained men "produced" by the university, some remain in its own laboratories; but others in increasing number go out to staff the rapidly growing research facilities of industry and government.

The educational institution also provides some separation and protection for men devoted to critical assessment and innovation. Despite its ties to economic and political institutions, ties which in some respects grow ever tighter, education offers a base of operations in which men may be relatively independent. Some academic researchers and scholars remain *relatively* detached from the mores of the general culture, their freedom exceeded only by that of the few intellectuals who are detached from all establishments. Oriented to critical thought and set apart from many pressures of the market place, academic men can and do become free intellectuals, critical and innovating.[8] With the major, especially the best, universities quasi-autonomous and committed to inquiry, the initiative in social change rests in the hands of men of thought as well as men of action.

Colleges and universities, too, increasingly support groups that innovate in the arts. The artist of the medieval past was usually subsidized by a duke, a bishop, a wealthy family; later in history, writers gained a livelihood by means of sales to the small public of educated men. But in modern mass markets, there are few patron-sponsors and livelihood by sales depends on a wide popularity. Those whose painting or writing is not in heavy demand need other work for support, such as book reviewing, working in a bank or a publishing house, or teaching students; and artists and writers have been attracted to employment in higher education in increasing numbers. Intellectual magazines are often located around campuses, edited by professors or men with one foot in the academic door. The *Antioch Review*, *Sewanee Review*, and *Kenyon Review* are examples of the campus-based "little mag." Novelists, musicians, and painters become professors or artists in residence at the colleges. The campus is by no means a perfect location, for the burdens of teaching and the conventions of the academic community can stultify and limit artistry. But for many it is the least of the evils, with the man released from the economic necessity of writing for wide acceptance or painting for the specifications of a client. With the campus as shelter, artistic and literary coteries are subsidized and given time to develop their styles. Colleges and universities have become massive patrons of the arts.

Education liberalizes attitudes

A second way in which education shapes society is through its effect on the minds of those it trains. This effect is by no means a simple transmission of a traditional consensus, but is quite differentiated and often at the leading edge of the society. A growing body of evidence indicates that education leads toward tolerant and humanitarian attitudes. Consistently it has been shown that the higher the level of educational attainment, the greater the degree to which "democratic" attitudes are held. Similarly, education is a prime correlate of interest in politics and of cultural awareness or sophistication. College graduates are more tolerant than high-school graduates in their attitudes toward ethnic and racial groups; they are more supportive of democratic norms such as having a multiparty political system; they listen more to serious programs and read more magazines. High-school graduates, in turn, are more tolerant and more involved culturally and politically than are those with only grammar-school education. Level of education is related this way even when the influence of age, occupation, and income is "controlled" or ruled out.

Table 1 shows that political tolerance in the United States is closely related to education. The percentage of adults who showed a tolerant attitude toward political nonconformists, in a 1955 nation-wide poll, varied considerably when the respondents were grouped according to the amount of education they had received. Even when persons are grouped according to similar occupations, amount of education makes a great deal of difference. For example, the last row in the table reports for persons in high "white-collar" occupations (business executives, owners, and professionals) according to how much education they have had. Only 26 per cent of those with a grade-school education exhibited tolerant attitudes (on questions about civil liberties), compared to 83 per cent tolerant among those who had graduated from college, an imposing difference of 57 per cent. Between these extremes, each higher level of education shows more tolerance. The other rows of the table report a similar relationship, each for a set of occupations.

Table 2 suggests this relationship is not solely American. A national survey in Germany in 1953 asked citizens whether they favored the existence of several

[8] For a view that academic men are today less free, critical, and innovating than they were in the past, see C. Wright Mills, *White Collar* (New York: Oxford University Press, 1951), pp. 129–136.

TABLE 1. Education and political tolerance (percentage of American adults in 1955 nation-wide poll who showed a tolerant attitude toward political nonconformists, analyzed by level of education and type of occupation of the respondents)[a]

Occupation of respondents	EDUCATION OF RESPONDENTS: Grade school	Some high school	High-school graduate	Some college	College graduate
Low blue-collar	13[b]	32	40	—	—
High blue-collar	21	33	48	64	—
Low white-collar	23	29	47	64	74
High white-collar	26	46	56	65	85

[a] Each respondent was ranked on degree of tolerance according to his answers to a series of questions on willingness to tolerate nonconformists. (For example, "Should an admitted Communist be put in jail, or not?") The percentages report the share of respondents who fell in the upper two of six categories.
[b] Read: 13 per cent of respondents with grade-school education and "low" blue-collar occupation (unskilled labor) had a tolerant attitude. Rows and columns do not add to 100 per cent.
Source: Seymour Martin Lipset, *Political Man* (Garden City, N. Y.: Doubleday & Company, Inc., 1960), p. 109; figures computed by Lipset from data collected by Samuel Stouffer for his study, *Communism, Conformity and Civil Liberties* (Garden City, N. Y.: Doubleday & Co., Inc., 1955).

TABLE 2. Education and support of democratic party system (percentage of German adults in 1953 UNESCO survey of opinion who favored a system with several political parties instead of one; analyzed by occupation and education of the respondents)

Occupation of respondents	PER CENT OF RESPONDENTS FAVORING A MULTIPARTY SYSTEM: Elementary school educated	High-school or higher educated
Farm laborers	29	—
Manual workers	43	52
Farmers	43	67
Lower white-collar	50	68
Self-employed business	53	65
Upper white-collar	58	69
Officials (government)	59	78
Professions	56	68

Source: Seymour Martin Lipset, *Political Man* (Garden City, N. Y.: Doubleday & Company, Inc., 1960), p. 110; percentages computed by Lipset from the UNESCO survey.

political parties over a one-party system; that is, a democratic structure over a nondemocratic one. Education was here divided into only two categories—elementary, or high-school and higher—and the differences by education within each occupation are not huge, but they consistently show the higher level of education to be related to democratic attitude.

Such differences hold, for example, in knowledge and attitude on issues of foreign policy. A review in 1950 of a number of polls in the United States on foreign-policy issues showed greater contrasts between the college-educated and the grade-school-educated than between upper- and lower-income groups. *Interest* in international affairs correlated more highly with education than with any other factor. The lower-educated were characterized by lack of information, limited intellectual horizons, rudimentary analytical skills, and apathy. There were two or three times as many "don't know's" and "no opinion's" among them as among the college-educated. Table 3 illustrates these results.

The results from these opinion surveys show the impact of education on opinions at a general level. Specific information can be added through another approach; namely, studies made of changes in the attitudes of students during the college years. These studies generally show a widening of perspective along with increasing liberality; students tend to change toward the attitudes of academic men. The changes often, but not always, include a weakening of religious belief, indicating that college education is a secularizing influence. While these changes have been reported mainly from studies of small, leading liberal-arts colleges (Bennington, Vassar, for example), they have also recently been found to hold true in large state universities.

For example, a study at the University of California, Berkeley, suggests that students on this large state-university campus become more supportive of civil liberties as they go through the four undergraduate years. On the basis of students' attitudes on fifteen issues, such as refusing a passport to a Socialist, students were tagged as slightly, moderately, or highly libertarian. The proportion highly libertarian almost doubled from the freshmen to the senior years; as seen in Table 4, it went from 21 to 40 per cent. The proportion only slightly libertarian dropped from 32 to 14 per cent.

Another study shows that in *both* Ivy League and state-supported colleges, students become more supportive of civil rights as they go through the undergraduate years. (See Table 5.) The Ivy schools have a student body that is initially more supportive of civil rights and shows greater change over the four years. But the move in student attitude is in the same direction in both cases.

Thus the further the young progress through the educational mill, the greater is the liberalization of attitudes. The change in attitude results partly from greater knowledge, or the content of instruction, and in part from being socialized to new perspectives through contact with faculties and other students and through anticipation of one's future career. In any case, education is here an active cultural agent, working to change the balance of different attitudes and values in the population, and thus affecting the fortunes of different political and economic interests. At a minimum, education in modern democratic society consolidates and extends some of the liberal attitudes of the immediate past, providing a base for further liberality.

TABLE 3. Education and information and attitude on foreign policy (American adults, as reported in nation-wide public opinion polls)

Percentage of respondents	EDUCATION OF RESPONDENTS Grade school	High school	College
Who show a reasonably correct understanding of what a tariff is (Aug. '46).	22	50	64
Who belong to groups or organizations which discuss national and international problems (May '47).	7	15	32
Who are dissatisfied with the progress the United Nations has made so far (June '46).	42	53	69
Who gave "No Opinion" or "Don't Know" answers to the question concerning the progress the United Nations has made so far.	32	21	8
Who feel it would be a good idea to have reciprocal trade agreements with foreign countries (June '45).	43	67	81
Who gave "No Opinion" or "Don't Know" answers to the question of reciprocal trade agreements.	49	24	10

Source: Gabriel A. Almond, *The American People and Foreign Policy* (New York: Harcourt, Brace and Company, 1950), p. 129.

TABLE 4. Year in college and attitude on civil liberties (894 students at the University of California, Berkeley, 1957)

Student's attitude on civil liberties[a]	STUDENT'S YEAR IN COLLEGE Freshman	Sophomore	Junior	Senior
Highly libertarian	21	29	34	40
Moderately libertarian	47	44	50	46
Slightly libertarian	32	27	16	14
	100	100	100	100

[a] Classified into one of three categories on the basis of the student's answers to fifteen questions about civil liberties.

Source: Hanan C. Selvin and Warren O. Hagstrom, "Determinants of Support for Civil Liberties," *The British Journal of Sociology,* Vol. XI (March, 1960), pp. 51–73.

TABLE 5. Year in college and attitude on civil rights (percentage of students in each college class who were classified as supportive of civil rights;[a] based on 3,796 students in 4 Ivy League and 5 state-supported colleges, 1952)

Type of college	STUDENT'S YEAR IN COLLEGE Freshman	Sophomore	Junior	Senior
Ivy League college	45	57	58	68
State-supported college	31	40	41	44

[a] Each person received a composite score on the basis of his answers to four questions; for example, "It's unwise to give people with dangerous social and economic viewpoints a chance to be elected." (Agree or disagree.) The students were classified in five categories, from strongly pro-civil rights to strongly anti-civil rights, and those falling into the "upper" two categories were taken as supportive of civil rights.

Source: Norman Miller, "Academic Climate and Student Values," paper presented at the Fifty-Fourth Annual Meeting of the American Sociological Association, September, 1959.

Education's effects on habits and attitudes in the United States take place within a society that has little emphasized the life of the mind. The reading habits of Americans, for example, are always startling when compared to other advanced societies; and they seem at first glance to indict American education. In 1957, 17 per cent of a cross section of adults in the United States were able to answer yes to the question: "Do you happen to be reading a book at the present time?"[9] (This was a decrease from 21 per cent in 1949.) A similar poll in 1957 showed 55 per cent of adults in England reading a book, 34 per cent in West Germany, 33 per cent in Australia, and 31 per cent in Canada. The reading being reported covered "any kind of simple identification of black marks on white paper"—a paperback mystery story or a copy of the memoirs of a madam as well as a handsomely bound classic.

This makes the American educational system look completely ineffectual, since over two-thirds of the adult population has attended high school or college; whereas in England, "where three times as great a proportion of the adult population report book reading, only a negligible percentage has attended school beyond the age of fifteen." Yet it is clear that the source of little book reading lies largely in the general society, for the studies also show that education is the major correlate of reading in this country. On the above questions about current book reading, 6 per cent among the grade-school-educated were doing so, 19 per cent among those with a high-school education, and 43 per cent in the case of the college-educated. Or, when American adults were asked whether they had read a book *in the past year,* those who had *not* done so were 26 per cent of the college-educated, 57 per cent of those with a high-school education, and 82 per cent of those with only a grade-school education.

Such comparisons clearly indicate the considerable

[9] Lester Asheim, "A Survey of Recent Research," in Jacob M. Price (ed.), *Reading for Life* (Ann Arbor: University of Michigan Press, 1959), pp. 3–26. The data immediately following are also from Asheim's account.

effect of education on reading habits, even though the differentials stem in part from a weeding out of the poorer readers at the higher levels of education. The common man and the common reader are not the same person; the common man in the United States is essentially a nonreader, at least of books. Education apparently shapes very largely the chances of a person being exposed to the wide, wide world that is found on the printed page between hard or soft covers.

Replication

EDUCATION AND POLITICAL TOLERANCE

This problem will replicate the analysis of data collected by Stouffer and reported in Clark's article as Table 1. Our intention will be to observe the relationship between education and political tolerance independent of occupational differences. This will entail examining the association between tolerance and education within separate occupational groups. It should also be noted that the measure of political tolerance used in the replication is based on a report by the child of the father's *subjective* views. This could influence the replication since indirect reports of subjective factors are less likely to be reliable than reports of objective factors such as education and occupation.

Hypothesis

1. What relationship do you expect to find between level of education and degree of tolerance?

2. Do you think education will affect political tolerance more within the blue-collar, lower white-collar or upper white-collar groups?

Empirical indicators for this problem

6. Please circle the HIGHEST LEVEL of education completed by your FATHER.

   1. Some grade school
   2. Completed grade school
   3. Some high school
   4. Completed high school
   5. Completed high school and also had other training, but not college, e.g., technical
   6. Some college
   7. Completed college
   8. Some graduate work
   9. Graduate degree, M.D., M.A., Ph.D., etc.

12. Occupational Prestige

   1. Proprietor of a large business (valued at $100,000 or more); Top-level executive in large organization; Top-level professional

   2. Proprietor of a medium business (valued at $35,000 to $100,000); Middle-level executive or official, or top-level of a small organization; Lower-level professional; Sales representatives of manufacturers or wholesalers or other senior salesmen earning $10,000 or more per year; Farmer of farm worth $100,000+

   3. Proprietor of a small business (valued at $6,000 to $35,000); Lower-level official and manager; Semi-professional; Sales representative (as above) earning $7,000 to $10,000 per year; Farmer of farm worth $35,000 to $100,000

   4. Proprietor of a very small business (valued under $6,000); Technician; Sales clerk and salesman earning *less* than $7,000 per year and clerical workers; Farmer of farm worth $15,000 to $35,000

   5. Farmer of farm worth under $15,000; Skilled manual worker and foreman

   6. Farmer, sharecropper or tenant with little stock or equipment; Semi-skilled worker and machine operator

   7. Unskilled worker

Please answer each of the following three questions. Make the best guess you can about your father's opinion:

32f. An admitted Communist should not be allowed to make a speech in your community:

Father

1 Strongly agree
2 Agree
3 Not sure
4 Disagree
5 Strongly disagree

33f. Books written against churches and religion should be taken out of public libraries:

Father

1 Strongly agree
2 Agree
3 Not sure
4 Disagree
5 Strongly disagree

34f. Consider the case of a man whose loyalty has been questioned before a Congressional committee but who swears under oath he has never been a Communist. If he is teaching in a college or university, he should be fired.

Father

1 Strongly agree
2 Agree
3 Not sure
4 Disagree
5 Strongly disagree

Data analysis

1. *Sort* the code sheets according to box 12 into three groups:

Upper White Collar = all those coded 1 or 2
Lower White Collar = all those coded 3 or 4
Blue Collar = all those coded 5 through 7

2. To facilitate analysis, one third of the class may be assigned to analyze the data for the upper white-collar group, one third assigned to analyze the data for the lower white-collar group, and the final one third assigned to analyze the data for the blue-collar group.

3. *Sub-sort* the code sheets of the social class group which you were assigned according to the father's education (box 6) into the following five groups:

Some grade school or completed grade school = those coded 1 and 2
Some high school = those coded 3
Completed high school and others with additional technical training = those coded 4 and 5
Some college = those coded 6
Completed college and others with graduate training = those coded 7, 8 and 9

4. *Tally* onto the tabulation form the "Political Tolerance Index" of the father (box 34tf) for each of the five educational groupings into which you have just divided the code sheets.

5. *Compute* the average (e.g., the mean) Political Tolerance scores of each educational group. Use the "upper limit" as the "x" value in your calculation (see Appendix C).

6. *Compute* the mean for the entire social class group which you tabulated by adding together the four total "fx's" and dividing this by the grand total of the number of cases in your social class group (i.e., the sum of the four "f" columns).

7. *Graph* the means for the social class group you have tabulated onto Figure 1. Use either a dashed, solid, or dotted line depending on which group you are plotting. Then plot the means for the other two social class groups using the figures computed by the rest of the class. Your instructor will put these on the blackboard for you.

Lab report

1. Treat "occupational class" as a "control" variable. See the "Note on Interpreting Cause and Effect" in Appendix A.

2. Pay particular attention to interpreting the data for hypotheses two.

References

Cohen, A. K., *Delinquent Boys: The Culture of the Gang*. New York: Free Press, 1955.

Goldsen, Rose K., Morris Rosenberg, Robin M. Williams, and Edward A. Suchman, *What College Students Think*. Princeton, N. J.: Van Nostrand, 1960.

Gross, Neal, Ward S. Mason, and Alexander W. McEachern, *Explorations in Role Analysis: Studies of the School Superintendency Role*. New York: Wiley, 1958.

Hollingshead, August B., *Elmtown's Youth: The Impact of Social Class on Adolescents*. New York: Wiley, 1949.

Lipset, Seymour M., "Democracy and Working Class Authoritarianism," *American Sociological Review*, 24 (August 1959), pp. 482–502.

Lipset, Seymour M. and Reinhard Bendix, *Social Mobility in Industrial Society*. Berkeley and Los Angeles: University of California Press, 1959, esp. pp. 91–101.

Newcomb, Theodore, *Personality and Social Change*. New York: Dryden, 1943.

Selvin, Hanan C. and Warren O. Hagstrom, "Determinants of Support for Civil Liberties," *The British Journal of Sociology*, 11 (March 1960), pp. 51–73.

Stouffer, Samuel A., *Communism, Conformity, and Civil Liberties: A Cross-Section of the Nation Speaks Its Mind*. Garden City, N. Y.: Doubleday, 1955.

Trow, Martin, "Small Businessmen, Political Tolerance and Support for McCarthy," *The American Journal of Sociology*, 64 (November 1958), pp. 270–281.

Name______________________

Date______________________

TABLE 1. Political tolerance by education for ______________ class
FILL IN

FATHER'S POLITICAL TOLERANCE INDEX (Box 34tf)	FATHER'S EDUCATION (Box 6)									
	Grade school only (Box 6 = 1 or 2)		Some high school (Box 6 = 3)		High school & tech school (Box 6 = 4 or 5)		Some college (Box 6 = 6)		Complete college and over (Box 6 = 7, 8, or 9)	
x	f	fx	f	fx	f	fx	f	fx	f	fx
3										
4										
5										
6										
7										
8										
9										
10										
11										
12										
13										
14										
15										
TOTAL										
Mean										
++ (No info.)										

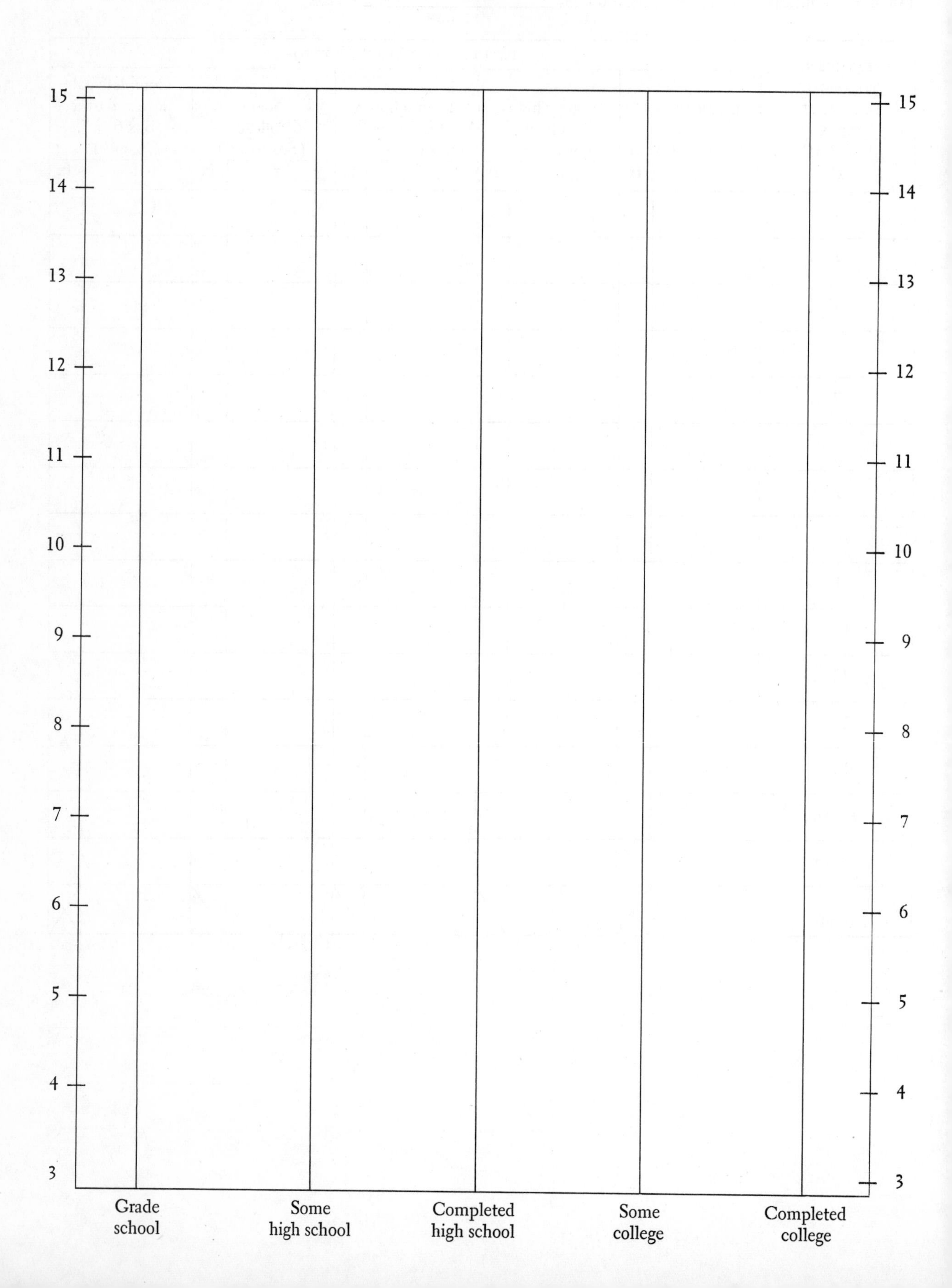

FIGURE 1. Political tolerance by education and social class

LABORATORY REPORT FOR PROBLEM ____________

Course or
Section ____________ Date ____________ Name ____________

HYPOTHESIS: ____________

SAMPLE: ____________

INDEPENDENT VARIABLE(S): ____________

DEPENDENT VARIABLE(S): ____________

OTHER FACTORS: ____________

LABORATORY REPORT FOR PROBLEM__________

SUMMARY OF FINDINGS:

DISCUSSION:

Social order and change VIII

PROBLEM 18 SOCIAL CHANGE

Change is a basic and normal characteristic of social life. Socialization changes individuals; the birth of children changes families; migration changes communities. Perhaps, however, the impact of change is most dramatically apparent at the level of society. Consider the case of the United States: Only two generations ago most of the population was scattered across farms and small rural towns, telephones and automobiles were not widely used, and industry was far less developed. Today, the face of America has shifted into a highly industrialized economy and to an urban society.

It can be readily accepted that change is a perennial feature of life. Less clear, however, is an adequate explanation of why change occurs. Despite the rich tradition in sociology devoted to the analysis of change—as evidenced by Marx's notions about the economy, Spencer's ideas regarding differentiation, Comte's thoughts on the stages of society—explaining change is still a persistent problem. Various theories of change have of course been advanced: cyclical theories, linear-evolutionary theories, equilibrium theories. But to this date none of these theories have gained widespread acceptance. At the present stage of knowledge, it appears that each theory is uniquely suited for explaining a specific set of circumstances. Hopefully, future work will develop a less fragmented and more general understanding of change (Moore, 1963).

The study of change is beset by other difficulties, some technical, others conceptual. For example, at what point does something change—when is one trait new and another old? Is the second trait a variation on the first, or actually different from the first? Or, can and should change be divorced from implicit value judgments? Is it possible to speak of maturity or modernization without introducing various preferences for certain situations?

An additional problem is that of obtaining accurate information about the past. Sometimes this problem is more imposing than at other times. Adequate census data, for example, are available in the United States for almost two centuries. But are there any good data available on the popular yet elusive question of shifts in attitude and beliefs? Countless attempts to contrast contemporary attitudes with the attitudes of an older, rural America have of course been made (Riesman, 1950; Mills, 1951; Whyte, 1956). Authors have spoken about the contemporary ascendance of "organization men," "cheerful robots," and "other-directed personalities." Admirable and interesting as these efforts may be, critics have justifiably noted that the prevailing attitudes of persons living generations ago have not been firmly established, and further, the sociologists who think they know this past may be dealing in stereotypes (Kluckhohn, 1958; Bell, 1961). Clearly, this kind of issue must be resolved empirically. But in the absence of reliable data on attitudes maintained in the past, an adequate analysis of social change is not easily sustained.

Nevertheless, certain kinds of data are available. For example, popular literature can be a source of data, provided one is willing to accept the assumption that such literature reflects the culture in which it circulates (Albrecht, 1956; Straus and Houghton,

1960). Occasionally it is possible to repeat studies done at an earlier time, using the original study as the base line for measuring change. The reading for this problem is one such instance for it provides reliable information dating back over a generation ago on an important area of American life: attitudes towards minority groups. In 1926, 1946, and 1956, Emory Bogardus administered to samples of college students the social distance scale, an attempt to measure attitudes towards various ethnic and racial groups. Although the author does not systematically account for the shifts he has observed over time, his research is a landmark in providing excellent data for an analysis of social change.

RACIAL DISTANCE / *Emory S. Bogardus*

The study of distance between racial groups is one of the best approaches to the study of racial relations, for it is an aspect of human relations that can be measured, and hence can be considered with a degree of precision. While "ethnic distance" might be a preferred term, the public for the most part thinks and acts in terms of racial groups; thus, in gathering data from the public, the concept of racial distance is used.

In this discussion of racial distance, the writer will draw upon three studies of the subject that he has made over a period of thirty years. His first sampling of racial distance in the United States included 1,725 persons and was made in 1926; the second included 1,950 persons and was conducted twenty years later in 1946; and the third involved 2,053 persons and took place after an interim of ten years, in 1956. In each of these studies the respondents were about equally divided between men and women.

In the three studies the same Social Distance Scale was used.[1] This scale was developed in 1924 with its seven gradations of social distance along a continuum. In 1932 extensive experiments were conducted in order to obtain as equal distances as possible between the different items of behavior that are described in the Scale.[2]

Regarding the reliability and validity of the Scale, many experiments have been conducted, including studies by a number of competent scholars working in different parts of the country. The results are summarized in Section 20 and appear to be satisfactory.

The simpler of two main methods of scoring the distance reactions of the subjects is generally used, for it has been found to be approximately as accurate as the more complicated procedure. The subject is asked to check as many of the seven columns of the Scale as his first feeling reactions for each racial group would indicate. One aim is to reduce rationalizing on his part as much as possible. The numbers of the columns nearest the left that are checked by each subject are added together and then divided by the number of subjects who have checked each race, in order to obtain a racial distance quotient, RDQ, for each racial group listed in the left-hand column of Chart B. The lowest RDQ possible would be 1.00 and the highest, 7.00.

The subjects in each of the 1926, the 1946, and the 1956 studies represented a specific sector of the general population, namely, persons with at least a high school education and about equally divided between college undergraduates and graduates most of whom were professionally employed while pursuing studies for an advanced diploma. In all three of these racial distance studies the subjects were enrolled in sociology and related social science courses. In each of the three nation-wide studies, the division between men and women was about equal, and the main ages ranged from 18 to 35.

The data were obtained in each of the studies through the same type of collaborators, namely, teachers of sociology and of the related social sciences in thirty different institutions of higher learning distributed widely throughout the United States, that is, somewhat equally in the northeast, the south, the north middle, and the Pacific western regions.

It may be noted that the respondents from each of the thirty universities and colleges came from many different parts of the United States. The lines that connected the places of residences of the respondents of any of the given institutions with the location of that institution crisscrossed with the lines connecting residences of the respondents from the university or college of all the other twenty-nine sets of lines connecting residence and institution. Thus, there was not only a similar but a rather comprehensive area distribution of the respondents of all three studies.

The administrators of each of the three studies were given a standard set of instructions, that was worded the same in each of the three years of 1926, 1946, and 1956. A marked degree of uniformity in administering the Scale was evident in all three studies.

In these studies about one half of those who had charge followed up administering the Scale with discussion periods and in a considerable number of cases with obtaining written statements from the respondents regarding their reactions to various racial groups

Reprinted with permission of the author from Emory S. Bogardus, *Social Distance*. Los Angeles: privately printed, 1959, pp. 30–40.

[1] The initial paper by the writer concerning this Scale was entitled "Measuring Social Distance," and it appeared in the March, 1925, issue of *Sociology and Social Research*, IX: 299–308.

[2] The procedure was described by the writer in "A Social Distance Scale," *Sociology and Social Research*, XVII: 265–71, January–February, 1933, but the results did not substantially differ from the original form of the Scale, but tended to support it.

CHART B—Social distance scale

1. In order to keep Scale anonymous, do not sign name, but give yourself as much freedom as possible; use only check marks.
2. Please give your *first feeling reactions* in every case.
3. Give your feeling reactions to each ethnic group in terms of the chief picture or stereotype you have of entire group. Mark each group even if you do not know it.
4. Check as many of seven columns in each case as your feelings dictate.
5. Work as rapidly as possible.

	1 Would marry into group	2 Would have as close friends	3 Would have as next door neighbors	4 Would work in same office	5 Have as speaking acquaintances only	6 Have as visitors only to my nation	7 Would debar from my nation
Armenians							
Americans (U.S. white)							
Canadians							
Chinese							
Czechs							
English							
Filipinos							
Finns							
French							
Germans							
Greeks							
Hollanders							
Indians (Americans)							
Indians (of India)							
Irish							

1. Please remember to give your *first feeling reactions* for every group.
2. Remember to give feeling reactions to your *chief picture* of each group as a *whole*.
3. Also, to check as many columns for each group as you can, and to work *rapidly*.

Italians							
Japanese							
Japanese Americans							
Jews							
Koreans							
Mexicans							
Mexican Americans							
Negroes							
Norwegians							
Poles							
Russians							
Scots							
Spanish							
Swedish							
Turks							

Please check. (1) Your ethnic backgrounds: Caucasian......, Mongoloid......, Negro......
(2) Your religious backgrounds: R. Catholic......, Jewish......, Protestant......, Other......
(3) Rural backgrounds......, urban backgrounds...... (4) Sex: male......, female......
(5) Education: 8th grade......, high school grad......, 2 yrs. coll......, coll. grad......, postgrad. work......
(6) Age: under 15......, 15 to 30......, 31 to 50......, 50 or over......
(7) Occupation: none......, student......, housewife......, unskilled worker......, skilled......, clerical or secretarial......, managerial......, executive......, professional......
(8) Annual income: none......, under $2500......, $2500 to $5000......, over $5000......

Changes in Racial Distance Quotients

I Racial Distance Quotients Given Racial Groups in 1926 by 1725 Selected Persons thruout the U.S.		II Racial Distance Quotients Given Racial Groups in 1946 by 1950 Selected Persons thruout the U.S.		III Racial Distance Quotients Given Racial Groups in 1956 by 2053 Selected Persons thruout the U.S.	
1. English	1.06	1. Americans (U.S. white)	1.04	1. Americans (U.S. white)	1.08
2. Americans (U.S. white)	1.10	2. Canadians	1.11	2. Canadians	1.16
3. Canadians	1.13	3. English	1.13	3. English	1.23
4. Scots	1.13	4. Irish	1.24	4. French	1.47
5. Irish	1.30	5. Scots	1.26	5. Irish	1.56
6. French	1.32	6. French	1.31	6. Swedish	1.57
7. Germans	1.46	7. Norwegians	1.35	7. Scots	1.60
8. Swedish	1.54	8. Hollanders	1.37	8. Germans	1.61
9. Hollanders	1.56	9. Swedish	1.40	9. Hollanders	1.63
10. Norwegians	1.59	10. Germans	1.59	10. Norwegians	1.56
11. Spanish	1.72	11. Finns	1.63	11. Finns	1.80
12. Finns	1.83	12. Czechs	1.76	12. Italians	1.89
13. Russians	1.88	13. Russians	1.83	13. Poles	2.07
14. Italians	1.94	14. Poles	1.84	14. Spanish	2.08
15. Poles	2.01	15. Spanish	1.94	15. Greeks	2.09
16. Armenians	2.06	16. Italians	2.28	16. Jews	2.15
17. Czechs	2.08	17. Armenians	2.29	17. Czechs	2.22
18. Indians (American)	2.38	18. Greeks	2.29	18. Armenians	2.33
19. Jews	2.39	19. Jews	2.32	19. Japanese Americans	2.34
20. Greeks	2.47	20. Indians (American)	2.45	20. Indians (American)	2.35
21. Mexicans	2.69	21. Chinese	2.50	21. Filipinos	2.46
22. Mexican Americans	—	22. Mexican Americans	2.52	22. Mexican Americans	2.51
23. Japanese	2.80	23. Filipinos	2.76	23. Turks	2.52
24. Japanese Americans	—	24. Mexicans	2.89	24. Russians	2.56
25. Filipinos	3.00	25. Turks	2.89	25. Chinese	2.68
26. Negroes	3.28	26. Japanese Americans	2.90	26. Japanese	2.70
27. Turks	3.30	27. Koreans	3.05	27. Negroes	2.74
28. Chinese	3.36	28. Indians (from India)	3.43	28. Mexicans	2.79
29. Koreans	3.60	29. Negroes	3.60	29. Indians (from India)	2.80
30. Indians (from India)	3.91	30. Japanese	3.61	30. Koreans	2.83
Arithmetic Mean of 48,300 Racial Reactions	2.14	Arithmetic Mean of 58,500 Racial Reactions	2.12	Arithmetic Mean of 61,590 Racial Reactions	2.08
Spread in Distance	2.85	Spread in Distance	2.57	Spread in Distance	1.75

given on the Scale. In many individual cases the respondent was carefully interviewed. In this way the author has received a large number of reports, which will be referred to hereafter as interview materials. While they were not complete enough to justify the drawing of general conclusions, they gave interesting explanations for further study regarding racial reactions.[3] This report does not pretend to represent a sampling of the population of the United States. It is distinctly limited to a selected sampling of undergraduate and college graduates, men and women about equal in number, chiefly between the ages of 18 and 35, and residing in 32 different overlapping regions of the United States.

These studies involve not all but selected racial and nationality groups in the United States. The same 28 groups appear in all three of the studies; and in addition, two others, Mexican American and Japanese American, appear in the 1946 and the 1956 studies.

The data on which the following observations rest are presented in Table 1 (above). Some of the points at which comparisons of the findings of these studies have been made will now be noted.

1. The same racial groups listed in the upper or nearness third of the total listing of racial groups are about the same for the three years, 1926, 1946, and 1956. In the main they represent racial groups of north European backgrounds.

2. While the distance scores for the racial groups in the nearness third are about the same for the years 1926 and 1946, they are a little greater for the same groups in the 1956 study. In order to obtain an explanation of this increase in distance reactions, the interview materials were examined with the result that at least one point came to the surface, namely, that in recent years the darker races seem to be developing an increasing degree of racial awareness and are reacting more than in earlier years against the "superior" attitudes of some members of the white race. Further study is needed in order to test this explanation.

3. In comparing the rank order of the 30 racial groups toward whom reactions were expressed by the respondents, it may be observed that the Germans went down in rank order (greater distance) in 1946 when compared with 1926, reflecting, according to in-

[3] The findings of the 1926 study were published in the writer's *Immigration and Race Attitudes* (Boston: D. C. Heath and Company, 1928), and the results of the 1946 study were published under the title of "Changes in Racial Distance," *International Journal of Attitude and Opinion Research,* 1:55–62, December, 1947.

terviews, attitudes developed toward them during World War II.

4. The Norwegians climbed up the nearness scale between 1926 and 1946, due in part to the courageous though losing stand of the nation against the nazis in World War II; but by 1956 this resistance seems to have been partly forgotten, as judged by interview materials.

5. The Spanish fell in both the rank order and the distance accorded them in 1946 when compared with the data for 1926. Interview data suggest that this increase was related to the association, in the minds of some respondents in 1946, of Franco with Mussolini and Hitler, as being a dictator.

6. In 1946 the Russians had maintained their rank order and their distance score of 1926, but by 1956 they had fallen decidedly. Interviews pointed definitely to the shift of the Russians from being allies in 1946 and earlier to the leading protagonists in the cold war that developed after 1946, as a major explanatory factor in the marked increase in distance score given them. Some respondents indicated that they would distinguish between Russians as people and Russians as communists, and that in the first instance they would give them a much greater nearness score than they would in the latter case, but that the friendly feeling toward the Russians as people was overcome by the type of government to which they were subject.

7. The Italians fell in rank order and in distance score in 1946. Interviews were uniform in accounting for this increase in distance reactions on the basis of the war and the fascist government under Mussolini. However, the antagonistic feeling reactions did not remain strong, for the 1956 data show that they were accorded a marked decrease in distance and that their rank order was also less.

8. The Czechs had risen in rank order and had been given a decrease in distance score by 1946 (they had fought against our opponents). By 1956 they had fallen in rank order and were given a greater distance score, because of "the communist regime to which they are subject."

9. The Jews received the same rank order and about the same social distance score in 1946 as they did twenty years earlier. However, the interview data showed two different sets of distance reactions by the respondents in 1946. In one type of interview materials deep sympathy was expressed for the Jews because in Europe they had been brutally persecuted by the nazis. In the other type of reactions, evidences of fear were expressed lest the immigration bars be lowered and Jewish immigrants by the thousands be admitted to the United States. It appeared that the friendly reactions and the unfriendly ones just about offset each other, for the distance scores toward Jews remained about the same.

In 1956 the Jews received a definitely higher rank order and an increased nearness score. According to the interviews, less marked distinctions between Jews and non-Jews were being drawn in 1956 by non-Jews than earlier, and to some respondents it seemed as though "Jews are undergoing assimilation into American life" and that "they are less conspicuous than they used to be."

10. The Mexicans fell in rank order and received an increased distance score in 1946. By 1956 they slipped down again in rank order, but were given a decreased distance score, which may mean that other racial groups received an even greater decrease in distance. The publicity given in the press in the western part of the United States to the large number of Mexicans who have allowed themselves in recent years to be enticed to come across the Border illegally to work on farms chiefly, and who had been labeled "wetbacks," aroused adverse reactions. Some respondents think of Mexicans as "wetbacks," "peons," and "unclean laborers."

11. The second-generation Mexican, that is, Americans of Mexican parentage received a higher rank order and a better nearness score in 1956 than they did ten years earlier. Many respondents distinguished between Mexicans and the second generation of Mexican Americans, in favor of the latter.

12. The Japanese fell greatly in rank order and in distance score in 1946 (following the attack on Pearl Harbor and the War). It is noticeable that the reactions toward them changed in the nearness direction after their defeat and their shift toward democracy, as evidenced by their rank order and their distance score in 1956.

13. The second-generation Japanese, that is, the Americans of Japanese parentage (Nisei), were for the first time included in the list of groups in the racial distance scale, as was also the case with the second-generation Mexican Americans in racial distance experiments, in 1934. At that time trial studies showed that they were given practically the same distance score as were the first generation (Issei), despite the fact that they were American citizens by birth, whereas their parents could not become citizens. By 1946 the second-generation Japanese Americans were given a higher rank order and a greater nearness score, showing that the respondents were distinguishing between the Issei and the Nisei, in favor of the latter. This nearness differential was related to the remarkable record for bravery in battle shown by the Nisei soldiers in the American military forces, especially in Italy. By 1956 the Americans of Japanese parentage had been accorded a still better rank order and a lesser distance score.

14. Filipinos moved up in rank order and in nearness score between 1926 and 1946. Their loyalty as a whole to the cause of independence and to the United States during the World War II is one explanatory factor, judging by the interviews. In the 1956 study the

Filipinos moved up in the rank order which was explained in part by some of the respondents as a result of the Filipinos' continued resistance to communism and to the continued friendliness of the Philippines under President Magsaysay for the United States.

15. In 1946 the Negroes were shown more distance than twenty years earlier, but in 1956 their distance score was decidedly less than in the preceding test years. In each of the three testing years some respondents showed resentment toward what they called the "increasing militancy" of some Negro leaders, but this resentment was more than offset in 1956 by the reactions of many respondents who were slowly becoming adjusted to the idea of integration, particularly in several areas in the United States, and who were in the 18 to 35 age group.

16. Sympathetic interest on the part of Americans in the Chinese prior to 1946 in their long defense against the Japanese military forces would explain in part the upward jump given them in rank order and in nearness reactions in the 1946 study. Their association with the United States in World War II suggests an added explanation. While the rank order and the distance score given them in 1956 shows a farness trend, due to the coming of the communist rule over China, yet there is evidence in the interview data that many persons are distinguishing between the Chinese as a people struggling toward democracy and the Chinese communist regime.

17. In looking at the greatest distance score given any racial group in each of the three years, 1926, 1946, and 1956, it will be noted that there is a decline in distance reactions represented by the figures, 3.91, 3.61, and 2.83. The aggravations affecting attitudes during World War II would seem to explain why the decline in distance score was limited between 1926 and 1946. It is seen that the large decrease in distance score for 1956 occurs in the reactions toward the races given the highest scores. This decrease more than offsets a small increase in distance scores accorded the races in the nearness third of the total list. The decrease given the darker races is found in interviews to be related to a greatly increased acquaintance with, understanding of, and interest in these racial groups that has developed in the last decade on the part of at least a considerable number of the 2,053 respondents in 1956.

18. The arithmetic means of the reactions toward all the racial groups by 1,725, 1,950, and 2,053 persons on the respective dates show a decline in distance reactions as follows, 2.14, 2.12, and 2.09. While these decreases may seem small, yet they take on significance when the total number of distance reactions that is represented by each arithmetic mean is considered, namely, 48,500, 58,500, and 61,590, respectively.

In this connection it may also be noted that the spread between the lowest and the highest distance scores decreased in the three tabulations as follows: 2.85, 2.57, and 1.74, which would seem to lend considerable support to the statement that racial distances in the United States were decreasing from 1926 to 1956. These scores indicate a decrease in racial awareness, a movement toward uniformity in population composition, a convergence of racial diversities, "a simplification in the formal structure of the population" and the development of what the Taeubers call "a national population."[4]

The foregoing data, based on the use of the Racial Distance Scale and on interview methods, suggest a number of hypotheses. They indicate fields for further research.

1. Racial distances during the years 1926 to 1956 in the United States have been measurably decreasing, although very slowly.

2. To the extent that there has been a decrease in the spread of racial distance, that is, in the difference between the scores of the racial groups receiving the lowest and highest scores, respectively, there has been an increase in the homogeneity of the population structure of the nation.

3. While racial distances are decreasing in one area of racial relations, they may at the same time be increasing in another area of the same field of racial relations, that is, with reference to the same racial group.

4. Racial distances are reduced more readily between racial groups of similar cultures than of dissimilar cultures, unless antagonistic competition for status and control has developed between them.

5. When racial groups of different cultures meet on their higher cultural levels rather than on their lower cultural levels, racial distance may be more easily reduced between them.

6. A racial distance situation usually includes a dominant group and a subordinate group, with the latter seeking opportunities similar to those enjoyed by the former.

7. The dominant group has yielded such opportunities from time to time when it felt that its own status and security were not seriously endangered.

8. When the dominant group has feared that it might lose its status and security, it has strenuously opposed the granting of opportunities desired by the subordinate group.

9. In periods of war, racial distances in the United States with reference to certain racial groups have greatly increased for a time, but, with the return of peace, a decrease in each case has occurred.

[4] Conrad Taeuber and Irene B. Taeuber, *"The Changing Population of the United States* (New York: John Wiley & Sons, 1958), p. 89.

10. Among the factors that account for decreasing racial distance are: (1) a decrease in a sense of insecurity, of fear, of loss of status on the part of the dominant group; (2) an increase in opportunities desired by the subordinate group; and (3) an increase in communication between the groups involved on the basis of interracial understanding.

11. In marked racial farness situations, a substantial decrease in racial distance calls for a long-term program of preparatory education for mutual understanding.

12. Racial distance may reflect a form of racial enclavement.[5] An enclaved group is one that cuts itself off from contacts with other groups. The group that enclaves itself uses social farness techniques in order to maintain its customs and traditions, and to protect them from what is considered to be an undesirable and dangerous invasion from outside people.

13. A racial distance scale is useful for measuring the amount of racial reactions at a given time in a given area, and of obtaining an idea of changes and trends in racial relations.[6]

14. The use of a racial distance scale needs to be supplemented by intensive interviewing that involves a representative sampling of the subjects in order to obtain accounts of racial experiences and, more important, to obtain explanations of why individuals react in the ways that they do in regard to their own racial experiences.

Replication

CHANGES IN RACE PREJUDICES SINCE 1956

In preceding laboratory problems the intent of the replication was to *duplicate* the results of the original study. For the present problem the focal point of analysis is the differences between the original study and the replication. Bogardus raised the question as to whether, for selected ethnic groups, there were shifts in rank and changes in mean social distance between 1926 and 1956. This replication raises the question whether those changes have stabilized, continued, or been reversed. The comparison will be between Bogardus' 1956 data and the data collected at the present time.

In the years since 1956 tremendous changes have been wrought in American race relations—Supreme Court decisions on the use of public facilities, growing equality in industry, the disappearance of first-generation immigrants, and the like. Have these shifts, however, been sufficient to reduce hostility towards minority groups, or to alter feelings towards one minority group at the expense of another? The present problem seeks to answer some of these questions. It does not, however, attempt to systematically explain and test why these changes come about.

The use of the replication data to document social change introduces a novel issue: Could the differences obtained in all the preceding problems between the original study and the replication be understood as a function of change in social conditions? Some attempt to deal with this problem should be offered in the discussion section of your laboratory report.

Hypothesis

1. In comparison with Bogardus' data for 1956, state which of the nine ethnic groups you think has increased the most and which has decreased the most in social distance scores.

2. As a second hypothesis, state whether you think either of these groups changed in *rank order* (in comparison with the 1956 data).

3. See Appendix A for general instructions on writing an hypothesis.

Empirical indicator for this problem

The Social Distance scale reprinted on page 277 provides the data for this problem. The version reprinted as question 59 of the questionnaire for this manual is identical to that given on page 277 except for it being restricted to the following ethnic groups:

a. Armenians
b. Chinese
c. French
d. Germans
e. Italians
f. Japanese
g. Jews
h. Negroes
i. Russians

Data analysis

NOTE: In order to cover a range of phenomena and at the same time facilitate analysis, your instructor will assign three different ethnic groups to each student for tabulation. Write the name of the ethnic groups as-

[5] E. S. Bogardus, "Racial Enclavement," *Sociology and Social Research*, 15: 460–65, May–June, 1941.

[6] Muzafer and Carolyn W. Sherif, *Groups in Harmony and Tension* (New York: Harper & Brothers, 1953), chap. 5.

signed to you and their corresponding box numbers in the space provided on the tabulation form. However, the laboratory report of the findings will consider all nine groups.

1. *Tally* onto the tabulation form the "Social Distance Scores" for the three ethnic groups assigned to you (three boxes from 59a to 59i. See NOTE above). All three scores can be tallied at one time from each code sheet.

2. *Compute* the mean social distance score for each of the three ethnic groups. See Appendix C for calculating instructions. The steps must be repeated three times to calculate the mean for each ethnic group (each column) of the table.

3. *Copy* the means for these nine ethnic groups into the left margin of the table on page 278. This will facilitate interpretation of your class study data.

Lab report

1. Summarize the findings and discuss the results for all nine ethnic groups, not just the three you tabulated.

2. In the discussion section, pay particular attention to the possible social conditions which may have affected the differences obtained between your scores and Bogardus' scores.

3. Remember that Bogardus' scores were obtained from a national sample of students whereas the scores you will use for this problem were more likely obtained from a specific region. Could the egional context of the sample be another source of variation? What problems does this pose for analyzing data in terms of social change?

4. See Appendix A for general information on writing laboratory reports.

References

Albrecht, Milton C., "Does Literature Reflect Common Values?" *American Sociological Review, 21* (December 1956), pp. 722–729.

Bell, Daniel, *The End of Ideology*. New York: Collier Books, 1961, chapter 1.

Kluckhohn, Clyde, "Have There Been Discernible Shifts in American Values During the Past Generation?" in Elting E. Morison, ed., *The American Style*. New York: Harper & Row, 1958, pp. 145–217.

Mills, C. Wright, *White Collar*. New York: Oxford University Press, 1951.

Moore, Wilbert E., *Social Change*. Englewood Cliffs, N. J.: Prentice-Hall, 1963.

Moore, Wilbert E. and Robert M. Cook, eds., *Readings on Social Change*. Englewood Cliffs, N. J.: Prentice-Hall, 1967.

Riesman, David, *The Lonely Crowd*. New Haven: Yale University Press, 1950.

Straus, Murray A. and Lawrence J. Houghton, "Achievement, Affiliation, and Cooperation Values as Clues to Trends in American Rural Society, 1924–1958," *Rural Sociology, 25* (December 1960), pp. 394–403.

Whyte, William H., Jr., *The Organization Man*. New York: Simon & Schuster, 1956.

Name____________________

Date____________________

TABLE 1. Social distance scores of selected ethnic groups

SOCIAL DISTANCE SCORES x	ETHNIC GROUP (3 assigned from Boxes 59a to 59i)					
	Ethnic group____: ________ Box #____		Ethnic group____: ________ Box #____		Ethnic group____: ________ Box #____	
	f	fx	f	fx	f	fx
1						
2						
3						
4						
5						
6						
7						
TOTAL						
Mean =						
+ (No info.)		X		X		X

LABORATORY REPORT FOR PROBLEM ________

Course or Section ________ Date ________ Name ________

HYPOTHESIS: ________

SAMPLE: ________

INDEPENDENT VARIABLE(S): ________

DEPENDENT VARIABLE(S): ________

OTHER FACTORS: ________

LABORATORY REPORT FOR PROBLEM____________

SUMMARY OF FINDINGS: ____________

DISCUSSION: ____________

PROBLEM 19

DEVIANCE

Society depends in large part on conformity to norms. If men failed to meet or contradicted what was expected of them, life would be chaotic: the foundations of society would collapse, behavior would become incomprehensible. In light of the critical role of conformity in maintaining the existence of society, it is little wonder that many early American sociologists placed clear value judgments on conformity and deviance. The formula they introduced was simple: deviant behavior was to be viewed as a sign of societal illness and conformity a sign of societal health (Mills, 1943).

However interesting such formulas may be, they introduce a host of problems into the analysis of deviant behavior. One problem is philosophical: To identify deviance with illness is to implicitly offer a model of what a "healthy society" is like. Now, it may be possible to identify a healthy man, but is it possible to identify a healthy society or a societal disease? The analogy between the dynamics of individual physiology and societal functioning is always dangerous to draw. Another problem is whether deviant behavior ever makes positive contributions to the functioning of society. The history of science, for example, contains many instances of the scientist who ignores, at some risk to himself, the conventional practices of society and boldly challenges existing knowledge. Less apparent examples may be the corrupt political boss who facilitates procedures in otherwise inert and bureaucratic governmental practices (Merton, 1957); or the prostitute who by catering to deprived men, as for example the frightfully ugly or pervert, reduces the likelihood of sexual violence and attack (Davis, 1961). Deviant behavior, in brief, appears to have consequences which are at times positively valued by society.

Another set of difficulties in analyzing deviant behavior is in separating the actual boundaries between deviance and conformity. In fact, when the two concepts are closely analyzed it becomes clear that the distinctions between them are not hard and fast; rather they are matters of subtle degree and circumstances. (See the discussion in Problem 4 [Roles] for examples.) The ambiguity between deviance and conformity stems primarily from the fact that few norms are rigid or specific. Rather, most have bands of tolerance which expand and contract in different situations, thereby lending a degree of flexibility and ambiguity to social life (Straus, 1966). Consider, for example, norms against stealing. It is clear that the norm in most instances is enforced; nonetheless, exceptions are abundant. A person stealing the possessions of another may be tolerated if other needs at the moment are defined as more important (e.g., the hungry boy stealing bread), if the situation is perceived as legitimate (the victorious army taking the property of the enemy), if the intent of the act was not serious (a friend taking a roommate's notes).

These illustrations suggest that there is latitude in judging deviance from norms. Some norms typically demand rather stringent compliance (e.g., norms against murder); other norms allow for a high degree of tolerance. The reading for the present problem focuses attention on a norm with a large band of tolerance: the prohibition against the widespread deviant practice of petty theft. The major purpose of the research is to identify how definitions of deviance shift in response to a particular characteristic of the victim, namely the size of the victim organization. The major research hypothesis offered is that persons are more likely to approve of stealing from large rather than small organizations. To test the hypothesis the author simply compares the frequencies of approval given to stealing from organizations of different sizes.

PUBLIC ATTITUDES TOWARD STEALING AS RELATED TO THE SIZE OF THE VICTIM ORGANIZATION /

Erwin O. Smigel

This study concerns attitudes toward stealing from each of three categories of organizations: small business, large business, and government. It was conducted in an effort to determine how size of the victim organization affects public attitudes toward stealing. The study seemed important not only for the immediate issue, but also for possible insights into attitudes toward bureaucracy, especially its impersonal aspects, and for what it could add to an understanding of the relationship between organizational size and attitudes in general. Usual assumptions pertaining to the effect of organizational size on attitudes suggest the following hypothesis: If obliged to choose, most individuals would prefer to steal from, and be more approving of others stealing from, large scale, impersonal rather than from small scale, personal organizations.[1]

To explore this hypothesis a systematic random sample of 212 non-transient adults of Bloomington, Indiana, was drawn and interviewed in their homes. These individuals in addition to background information queries were given fifteen hypothetic situational questions,[2] a set of five for each type of organization, involving stealing from government (GOV), large business (LB), and small business (SB).[3] The respondents were asked to approve or disapprove, using Likert scale categories, of stealing under a variety of circumstances. The first section of this paper analyzes situational question responses.[4] A second section examines responses to a forced choice hypothetical circumstance query. Respondents were requested to select the one organization— GOV, LB, or SB—from which they would prefer to steal if forced by necessity. They were then asked to give reasons for their selection or rejection of each organization.

The situational question analysis

Cross correlations between each of the organizations indicate that respondents generally disapprove of stealing regardless of the size of the organization. Despite this general disapproval, important differences in degree of disapproval were found. The Stealing Attitude Scores (Table 1) show greatest disapproval toward stealing from SB and lesser disapproval toward stealing from LB and GOV. Although differences in degree of disapproval between LB and GOV are negligible, the results, at least for the large versus small dichotomy, support the hypothesis.

When the Stealing Attitude Scores of people with various backgrounds are compared, some further differentiation is discovered. In terms of socio-economic status it was found that regardless of organizational size, the lower the SES, the greater the approval of stealing.[5] Similar results were obtained by separate analysis of occupation and education. In general, on Counts' occupational scale, respondents who rated lower were more approving than were those who rated higher. The same consistency was found in connection with level of education. Respondents with less than thirteen years of schooling were less disapproving of stealing than were those with more education.

Although relationships between approval or disapproval and social class exist, the various socio-economic levels seem to be affected differentially by the size of the victim organization. Table 2 demonstrates that lower socio-economic respondents show the greatest proportional difference in scores between government and small business.[6] A 77 per cent proportional difference resulted for lower SES as compared with 38 per

Reprinted with permission of the author and publisher from *American Sociological Review, 21* (June 1956), pp. 320–327.

Revision of a paper read at the Third International Congress on Criminology, September, 1955. This research was supported by a grant from the Graduate School of Indiana University.

[1] That individuals sometimes see large scale organizations as personal organizations is recognized. In the present study, however, this perception was seldom verbalized, due in part to the fact that the respondents were not given specific organizations to consider and so had to call on their generalized experience, rather than a specific name stimulus in order to visualize the types of organizations mentioned in the questionnaire.

[2] The situations were constructed so that respondents with a sixth grade education, or the equivalent, could read and understand them. Readability level was determined by the Flesch test and the usual interview pre-test. The entire questionnaire is available on request. A sample of the situational questions follows:

"Bill Terr, a World War II veteran, went to school on the GI Bill. While there, the government overpaid him $89 on his subsistence allowance. He did not report this error."

"Richard Smith's house burned. He is protected by fire insurance; however, when he filed his claim for insurance, he claimed damages greater than he actually had."

"John Charles went to his local cleaner to pick up a suit he had cleaned. The clerk was busy and asked John to find his own clothing. John found his suit and paid for it. He discovered later that he also had taken a pair of trousers that did not belong to him. He decided not to return them."

Many of the fifteen situational questions are usually regarded as crime from a legal standpoint but are often thought of as less serious than traditional crime and sometimes more lightly termed "chiseling."

[3] The questions concerning GOV, LB, and SB were rotated and mixed within each unit. No distinction arose because of the order of the questions.

[4] Three situational questions, one for each of the organizations under consideration, were judged to be equivalent. The other questions, designed to cover similar situations, make no claim for equivalence. The manner in which equivalence was determined is described in a previous article. See Erwin O. Smigel, "Public Attitudes Toward 'Chiseling' with Reference to Unemployment Compensation," *American Sociological Review,* 18 (February, 1953), p. 61.

[5] *Ibid.,* pp. 65–67. This finding is consistent with attitudes concerning "chiseling" unemployment compensation from the government. However, this lesser disapproval on the part of lower SES respondents probably does not justify any conclusions about a greater morality on the part of the upper classes.

[6] These figures were arrived at by taking the difference in scores between GOV and SB, and using the GOV score, which was usually the least disapproving, as the base.

TABLE 1. Attitudes toward stealing

Stealing attitude scores	Type of organization					
	Government		Large business		Small business	
	N	Per cent	N	Per cent	N	Per cent
6–10 (strongly approve to approve)	(0)	0	(2)	1	(0)	0
11–15 (approve to indifferent)	(13)	6	(7)	3	(5)	2
16–20 (indifferent to disapprove)	(133)	63	(129)	61	(101)	48
21–25 (disapprove to strongly disapprove)	(66)	31	(73)	34	(106)	50
Total	(212)	100	(212)[a]	100	(212)	100

[a] Includes one case not tabulated.

TABLE 2. Differences in attitudes of respondents from two socio-economic levels: percentages who strongly disapprove of stealing

SES level	Victim organization				
	N	SB	LB	GOV	Proportional difference[a]
		Per cent	Per cent	Per cent	
Upper	(62)	58	42	42	38
Lower	(146)	46	31	26	77
Both SES levels	(208)	50	34	31	61
Unclassified	(4)	—	—	—	—
Total sample	(212)				

[a] Difference between GOV and SB over GOV per cents times 100.

cent for upper respondents, indicating the differential effect of organizational size upon subjects' attitudes. Respondents, then, from lower socio-economic levels, are more affected by size of organization than are those from upper levels.

Comparable relationships of the following sort were also found.

1. *Sex.* Stealing Attitude Scores for the sample of 110 men and 102 women differ, with females more inclined to approve of stealing than males. However, men who approved did so to a greater degree than did women. Analysis of the differences in scores between GOV and SB, for both men and women, in the most disapproving column (21–25) testifies that size of the victim organization also affects men differently than women. Females, although more approving of stealing, showed the greatest proportional attitudinal difference against stealing when SB is the victim: 67 per cent compared to a 54 per cent difference for men.

2. *Religiosity.* Analysis of religiosity and Stealing Attitude Scores indicates nominally religious respondents as more critical of stealing than respondents not claiming religion. Examination of the most disapproving category reveals no change in the proportionate difference of attitude from GOV to SB. However, non-religious respondents were least disapproving of stealing from LB. Comparison between low disapproval and high disapproval scores for religious and non-religious respondents, using LB as the base for non-religious subjects in this instance, indicates that non-religious interviewees show the greatest proportional difference: 81 per cent as against 56 per cent for religious respondents.

3. *Veterans.* Although male veterans of World War II were more approving of stealing than were male non-veterans,[7] veterans were more affected by size of the victim organization. Comparison of differences between GOV scores and SB scores shows that veterans differed 86 per cent; non-veterans only 47 per cent.

Note has been taken that: (1) Nearly all respondents disapproved of the stealing behavior outlined in the situational questions, regardless of size of the victim organization. (2) Intensity of disapproval varied with size of the organization. Respondents were more disapproving of stealing from SB than from LB or GOV. (3) Further variations in attitudes were related to other social elements such as SES, sex, religiosity and group membership. (4) Additional differences in attitudes as affected by organizational size were observed within each of these social units. (5) The influence on stealing attitudes of any one background classification seems to depend on its relationship to one or more classifications.

Forced choice stealing preference

To arrive at the basis for these differences in attitudes, each respondent was asked to choose the type of organization from which he would rather steal if in need and he felt he had no other choice. Interviewees were then requested to explain their preference. In general respondents remained faithful to their strong disapproval of stealing from SB. However, the forced stealing question produced an altered order of stealing approval: LB now became the preferred first choice, then GOV and finally SB. The forced stealing choice reveals more than a change in order; of greater significance is the large number who preferred to steal

[7] This finding did not hold for veterans of previous wars whose resocialization to a civilian way of life is probably more complete.

from LB rather than from GOV as compared to the negligible difference in approval between LB and GOV when the situational questions were employed. Now 102 respondents preferred to steal from LB; 53 from GOV; and 10 from SB. Of the remaining subjects nine did not distinguish between LB and GOV, five did not differentiate at all, thirty refused to steal under any condition, and three would not answer the question.

Respondents who made a stealing choice used two basic lines of reasoning to explain their preference—these involved consideration of the principles of least evil and/or least risk. The majority had registered their disapproval of stealing when they answered the situational questions. The selection question forced them to make a stealing preference for themselves. This placed them in a situation many found objectionable. To modify this position, most respondents decided from which organization stealing was the lesser evil before choosing their victim.

The second major line of reasoning involved the principle of least risk. The possibility of being caught and punished for theft seems to have a strong influence on stealing preference. However, this reasoning often runs counter to the first. Respondents who conceive of the problem in terms of both concepts and who cannot integrate them must weigh and evaluate the principle of lesser evil against the principle of least risk. Although these themes run through most of the reasons advanced by respondents for their stealing, different categories of interviewees see these ideas in different ways. An analysis of these various categories of stealing preference and reasons advanced for stealing choice in its relationship to size of the victim organization follows.

SB AS THE PREFERRED VICTIM. Of the 212 respondents, only eight men and two women preferred to steal from SB. Their mean scores for the situational questions are slightly lower than those of subjects in other categories, and they show a greater predisposition toward cheating SB than do other respondents. This is the only category where the mean score for SB is not the most disapproving score. The order of mean scores from the most disapproving to least disapproving for these individuals is: LB 20.0, SB 19.5 and GOV 18.6 (the most disapproving score for each classification is 25).

Their reasons for choosing SB as the potential victim were relatively simple and direct. Selection was made mainly on the principle of the least risk. Even if caught, these respondents felt that the small businessman, who was on personal terms with his customers, would be more lenient than the managers of LB or GOV. A woman respondent put it: "The small businessman would be more human; he would give you a break. Big businessmen are cold-blooded and the government of course, might catch you."

The risk factor seemed to operate as a deterrent for these respondents. They did not feel more justified in cheating SB as against the other organizations, but they perceived the situation as involving the least risk. Only one respondent felt morally justified in stealing from SB. Most were afraid of the consequences of stealing from large scale organizations. Government especially inspired the fear of being caught and sentenced. The replies indicate that were it not for the fear of punishment, these individuals might have preferred to steal from the larger organizations. Their use of the principle of least risk seems to run counter to the original hypothesis which implies that the respondents would be more kindly disposed toward personal small business than toward impersonal large business. However, the findings revealed that though the personal element is recognized, it is evaluated in conjunction with fear of discovery and punishment. For these respondents the principle of least risk seems to have more importance for their decisions on stealing than the principle of least evil.

LB AS THE PREFERRED VICTIM. One hundred and two members of the sample preferred to steal from LB. The overwhelming popularity of this type of organization reverses the disapproval order elicited by the situational questions. The mean scores for these questions indicated only minor attitudinal differences, especially between GOV and LB: 20.8 for SB, 19.6 for LB and 19.4 for GOV.

The forces making for favorable attitudes toward stealing from large scale business seem more complex than those involved in creating similar attitudes toward small business. Many reasons for and against stealing from LB were offered. Some involved conflicts of values which were difficult to resolve. Most respondents based their choice of LB as the victim on the principle of lesser evil, feeling that stealing from big business was not as bad as stealing from small business because LB was impersonal, powerful and ruthless.[8]

While few respondents specifically mentioned the term "impersonal," they often implied it: "They're corporations." "Big business deals with you at arm's length; you can deal with it in the same way." For some, bigness and impersonality bred resentment and distrust. Two grounds were offered for this feeling; one concerned weakness generally associated with bureaucracy, the other the notion that big business is ruthless. Reasons advanced under the first classification claimed that LB wasted time, space, and energy. Second category reasons were more varied, for example: "I'm more callous toward big business because they're more ruthless." "After all they cheat you." "Why don't they pay a living wage?"

Many regarded big business profits as excessive and this belief was used by some as a basis for their resentment.[9] Examples are numerous: "They have the high-

[8] For an interesting article which distinguishes between stealing from impersonal organizations and the individual see: Harry Gersh, "The Code According to Mama-Tante-Mom," *Commentary,* 13 (March, 1952), pp. 264–270.

[9] For a larger picture of public attitudes toward big business see: Burton R. Fisher and Stephen B. Withey, *Big Business as the People See It,* The Survey Research Center Institute for Social Research, University of Michigan: 1951.

est margin of profits and can afford the loss better; besides they allow for it." "Big business has tremendous capital, a part of which they've cheated from me." Distrust and resentment of big business led 21 per cent of the individuals who would rather steal from LB to apply the "eye for an eye" principle in making their decision. They believed that big business robbed them either by outright theft, or by charging exhorbitant prices. In either event, this "behavior" on the part of LB provided justification for those who chose to steal from LB since they considered this decision the lesser evil. Another 68 per cent legitimated their preference for victimizing LB on a "Robin Hood" philosophy. For them robbing the rich to give to the poor—in this instance themselves—was a lesser evil.

TABLE 3. Primary reasons for preferring to steal from large business

Reasons for stealing choice	N	Per cent
Can afford it best, or has tremendous capital	(69)	67.7
Allows for it: raises prices, is insured	(13)	12.8
They cheat you; they're ruthless	(8)	7.8
Less chance of being caught	(4)	3.9
Provides the greatest opportunity	(3)	2.9
No reasons offered	(5)	4.9
Total	(102)	100.0

Some preferences appeared based mainly on the principle of least risk. In all, seven per cent believed that LB provided more opportunity for theft with less chance of discovery or punishment. The anonymity of big business is believed to offer greater opportunity for stealing from LB rather than SB. The choice between the two large scale organizations was made in favor of LB as the victim because of the respondents' greater fear of government. As one man expressed it: "There is no sense stealing from the government because the FBI is smarter than the police."

Grounds for stealing preference, even in the abstract, have been presented as if they were mutually exclusive, as if there were not a multiplicity of reasons which had to be considered and weighed before decision could be made. This is not so. The impersonality, the inconsiderate materialism, the opportunity offered by the anonymity big business provided were among the elements in favor of choosing LB. Many individuals who extended these reasons also had "cause" for not preferring LB, such as admiration for the big businessman, or intense dislike for government, or the belief that the small businessman might be more lenient if he caught them. Special difficulty arose when decision had to be made between LB and GOV where both organizations were considered big and both stand accused of bad bureaucratic practices.

Generally, however, grounds for preferring to steal from LB were related to reasons for not stealing from SB. One combination of reasons reads: "A man has to be very small to take from the little man. LB can afford it. If you clip government, you just clip yourself and what's more, you have a good chance of being caught." Table 4 shows the relative frequency of these reasons.

TABLE 4. Reasons for not stealing from government and small business, by respondents who chose large business as the victim[a]

GOVERNMENT		
Reasons for not stealing from government	N	Per cent
It's stealing from yourself	(23)	29.5
Would get caught by GOV and penalty might be stiffer	(18)	23.1
Needs its money	(15)	19.2
Stealing from GOV affects other citizens in the community	(13)	16.7
Patriotism	(7)	9.0
Lack of opportunity	(2)	2.5
Total	(78)	100.0
SMALL BUSINESS		
Reasons for not stealing from small business	N	Per cent
SB does not have too much money	(42)	76.3
Identification: Small like yourself, or member of community	(8)	14.6
Might know small businessman	(5)	9.1
Total	(55)	100.0

[a] Figures in this table do not equal 102 for each division GOV and SB since all respondents did not offer negative reasons for their stealing preference.

The data presented for this category again point out that while bigness and its corollaries play important parts in affecting the decision to steal from LB, these factors alone were often not sufficient to determine this choice. Many other reasons were offered. The pro and con of the particular choice appears to have been considered before final decision was made, and the principles of lesser evil and least risk run through the majority of the reasons proffered.

GOV AS THE PREFERRED VICTIM. Fifty-three members of the 212 sample chose to steal from government. Their mean scores (20.9 for SB, 20.2 for LB, and 19.5 for GOV) for the situational questions are slightly higher than those for respondents who chose SB or LB. The mean scores demonstrate that members of this category both preferred to steal from GOV and were less disapproving of others stealing from government.

The task of choosing a victim appears less complicated for these individuals than for those who preferred to steal from LB, but more complicated than for those who elected to steal from SB. Fewer secondary reasons for their choice were offered. Clear-cut primary reasons often coincided with reasons for not stealing from either SB or LB. Intense dislike for government also helped make for definite preferences.

All of the reasons for stealing listed in Table 5 involve the theme of lesser evil. Most of the 32 per cent who thought that government could best afford the loss felt also that what they might take would not hurt it to the extent that similar thefts would affect smaller organizations. This notion is subscribed to by an additional eight per cent who believed that stealing from GOV was the lesser evil because the loss was well distributed. The choice was further justified on grounds that a great deal of money was collected in taxes; some of this taxation, it was hinted, was unnecessary. Many argued then, that GOV was big and wealthy and stated their preference in terms of the "Robin Hood" principle.

TABLE 5. Respondents' primary reasons for preferring to steal from GOV

Reasons	N	Per cent
Can afford it best, or collects a great amount of tax money	(17)	32.1
Taking back own money	(8)	15.1
Government's function to take care of the needy	(7)	13.2
Against Democratic Administration[a]	(7)	13.2
Bureaucratic inefficiencies	(5)	9.4
Everybody does it	(5)	9.4
Distributes the loss	(4)	7.6
Total	(53)	100.0

[a] The data for this study were collected in 1951 and 1952 while the Democratic administration was in power.

Bureaucracy, which was equated to size and disfunctioning, was an additional justification for the choice of GOV as the victim. Although this type of criticism was leveled against LB, it was more frequently applied to GOV. Such items as waste and red tape were not uncommon grounds for stealing preference. Only 9 per cent of this category proffered this as their primary reason, but many others mentioned bureaucratic inefficiencies as a secondary reason. That bigness and its corollaries played a part in determining this choice is seen in the following examples: "Government is the bigger concern; it wouldn't hurt government as bad as an individual or smaller concern." "They waste anyhow; they throw away more than I would take."

Though GOV is generally conceived of as larger than LB, the section of Table 4 dealing with GOV indicates the importance of factors other than size as a determinant of choice for some respondents. Concepts of loyalty, patriotism and fear of government swayed many individuals to select LB rather than GOV. Yet, size was still important for many of those who chose to steal from government.

The bigness of GOV, however, does not account for all who elected it as the victim. Lesser evil may be premised on factors other than bigness, and the 13 per cent who were against the Democratic administration grounded their judgment on this theme. Their feelings are reflected in such statements as: "I'm anti-socialist." "It's a God damned government anyway—if it were O.K., I'd take from big business."

Another category felt that stealing from GOV was the lesser evil because the respondents were part of the government and had contributed to its support. They reasoned that stealing from GOV would be stealing from themselves, and so less criminal. These individuals were among the most difficult to force into a decision involving their possible stealing. Their scores on the situational questions were among the most disapproving. They selected GOV reluctantly and only because they felt this choice was the least dishonest.

An additional 13 per cent whose scores on the situational questions were also very disapproving, thought that it was government's function to take care of the needy. These individuals intimated that if government failed in its duty, they were then more justified in stealing from it.

The following generalizations seem to be indicated: (1) While bigness and impersonality played a part in determining the preference for GOV as the victim, these elements do not seem as important for this category as they did for LB. (2) Other factors with strong emotional overtones—loyalty, patriotism, even anti-administration sentiment—appear to affect the decisions of some of the respondents. (3) Making decisions for this category seems easier than for those who chose LB, but not as easy as for those who selected SB. (4) Enough reasons pro and con were advanced so that the weighing process noted in the selection of LB was evident once again. (5) Some of the same reasons for preferring to steal from LB were again in evidence for those who selected GOV.

Summary

While most respondents disapproved of stealing from any of the organizations, differences in intensity of disapproval exist. Attitudes against stealing from small business were the most intense. Differences in attitudes, however, were also found on the basis of other social elements: socio-economic status, sex, religiosity, and group membership. These differences were in turn variously affected by size of the victim organization. In general public attitudes toward a number of situational questions indicate that while size of organization does affect attitudes toward stealing, it is by no means the only factor.

When interviewees were "forced" to choose a victim organization, they weighted their selection in the following order: LB, GOV, and SB. The reasons offered for their decision generally involved the principles of least risk and lesser evil. Those who chose to steal from SB reasoned on the basis of least risk; those who preferred LB invoked both principles, but emphasized the lesser evil; while those who chose GOV overwhelmingly reasoned on the basis of the lesser evil.

Size and its concomitants, anonymity, impersonality, bureaucratic inefficiency, and power seem to play a major part in their decision. This supports the general hypothesis; yet other elements such as fear of capture and punishment, patriotism, and not wanting to cheat oneself also enter the picture. Further research in this area should prove fruitful. The relationship between size and stealing preference is not simple. No one-to-one correlation between size and stealing preference exists. The original hypothesis, based on the usual assumptions concerning the effect of organizational size on attitudes, needs modification, even though a relationship between size of the victim organization and stealing preference is confirmed.

Replication

SITUATIONAL VARIATION IN THE DEFINITION OF DEVIANCE

To replicate the present study an abbreviated version of Smigel's questions will be used: Two questions regarding approval of stealing from large organizations and two on stealing from small organizations. The items referring to government are omitted. The major focus of the analysis is on exploring the correlation between the varying size of the victim organization and approval of stealing. In addition, social class will be used as a control variable to replicate the finding on class differences in attitudes towards stealing.

Hypothesis

1. State whether there is less approval of stealing from small or large organizations.

2. Do you anticipate that the differences predicted in the above hypothesis are the same for the upper middle class, the lower middle class, and the working class?

Empirical indicators for this problem

12. Occupational Prestige

    1. Proprietor of a large business (valued at $100,000 or more); Top-level executive in large organization; Top-level professional
    2. Proprietor of a medium business (valued at $35,000 to $100,000); Middle-level executive or official, or top-level of a small organization; Lower-level professional; Sales representatives of manufacturers or wholesalers or other senior salesmen earning $10,000 or more per year; Farmer of farm worth $100,000+
    3. Proprietor of a small business (valued at $6,000 to $35,000); Lower-level official and manager; Semi-professional; Sales representative (as above) earning $7,000 to $10,000 per year; Farmer of farm worth $35,000 to $100,000
    4. Proprietor of a very small business (valued under $6,000); Technician; Sales clerk and salesman earning less than $7,000 per year and clerical workers; Farmer of farm worth $15,000 to $35,000
    5. Farmer of farm worth under $15,000; Skilled manual worker and foreman
    6. Farmer, sharecropper or tenant with little stock or equipment; Semi-skilled worker and machine operator
    7. Unskilled worker

69. John Green, an electrician, worked for a large steel corporation. He received overtime pay whenever he had to stay on at night to repair machinery for the operation of the next day. Sometimes John worked alone. When he did, he would add an hour to the time sheet he turned in to the company. What is your opinion?

    1. Strongly approve
    2. Approve
    3. Indifferent
    4. Disapprove
    5. Strongly disapprove

70. Richard Smith's house burned. He was protected by fire insurance. However, when he filed his claim for insurance he claimed damages greater than he actually had. What is your opinion?

    1. Strongly approve
    2. Approve
    3. Indifferent
    4. Disapprove
    5. Strongly disapprove

71. John Charles went to the local cleaners to pick up a suit he had had cleaned. John found his suit and paid for it. He discovered later that he had also taken a pair of trousers that did not belong to him. He decided not to return them. What is your opinion?

    1. Strongly approve
    2. Approve
    3. Indifferent
    4. Disapprove
    5. Strongly disapprove

72. Dan Thomas asked his local grocer to deliver a number of items to his home. When Dan checked the purchases he found that the grocer had mistakenly doubled his order, but charged only for the original order. Dan kept the entire order and did not report the mistake. What is your opinion?
   1. Strongly approve
   2. Approve
   3. Indifferent
   4. Disapprove
   5. Strongly disapprove

Data analysis

1. *Sort* the code sheets according to box 12 into the following three occupational groups:

   1 and 2 = Upper Middle Class
   3 and 4 = Lower Middle Class
   5 through 8 = Working Class

To facilitate analysis, one-third of the class may analyze the data for the upper middle class, one-third for the lower middle class, and one-third for the working class.

2. *Tally* onto the tabulation form the "Stealing Index—Large Business" (Box 70t) for the occupational group assigned to you. At the same time also tally the "Stealing Index—Small Business" (Box 72t).

3. *Add* the columns.

4. *Compute* the percentage "strongly disapprove," "somewhat disapprove," etc. by dividing the total for the column into the separate frequencies, or by using the percent tables in Appendix B.

5. *Add* the percentages for those with scores of 1 through 6 in each column, and enter these combined percentages in the space provided below the table. This is the percent giving some degree of approval.

6. *Copy* onto the tabulation sheet the corresponding percentages for the two other occupational groups. Your instructor will put these on the blackboard as soon as they have been calculated.

Lab report

1. Put the main emphasis of your report on differences between large and small organizations. However, you should also pay attention to any occupational class differences observed. Speculate as to whether there is anything in the context of the measures which could account for these differences—for example, class antagonisms to large and small business, occupational differences in perceiving the large scale organization as more tolerant of deviants, etc.

2. If your results differ from those of Smigel, could differences in the nature of your sample account for it? If so, explain how it could.

References

Davis, Kingsley, "Prostitution," in Robert K. Merton and Robert A. Nisbet, eds., *Contemporary Social Problems*. New York: Harcourt, Brace & World, Inc., 1961, pp. 262–288.

Merton, Robert K., *Social Theory and Social Structure*. New York: Free Press, 1957, pp. 71–82.

Mills, C. Wright, "The Professional Ideology of Social Pathologists," *American Journal of Sociology*, 49 (September 1943), pp. 165–180.

Straus, Murray A., "Westernization, Insecurity, and Sinhalese Social Structure," *International Journal of Social Psychiatry*, 12 (Spring 1966), pp. 130–138.

Name________________

Date________________

TABLE 1. Stealing attitude index for large and small business by social class

STEALING ATTITUDE INDEX	Upper Middle (Box 12 = 1 or 2)				Lower Middle (Box 12 = 3 or 4)				Working Class (Box 12 = 5, 6, or 7)			
	Stealing attitude for:				Stealing attitude for:				Stealing attitude for:			
	Large business (Box 70t)		Small business (Box 72t)		Large business (Box 70t)		Small business (Box 72t)		Large business (Box 70t)		Small business (Box 72t)	
	Number	%	Number	%	Number	%	Number	%	Number	%	Number	%
1 and 2 Strongly approve												
3 and 4 Approve												
5 and 6 Indifferent												
7 and 8 Disapprove												
9 and 10 Strongly disapprove												
TOTAL		100%		100%		100%		100%		100%		100%
+ (No info.)		X		X		X		X		X		X
Percent giving some degree of approval (scores of 1 through 6)	______		______		______		______		______		______	

LABORATORY REPORT FOR PROBLEM ____________

Course or
Section ____________ Date ____________ Name ____________

HYPOTHESIS: ____________

SAMPLE: ____________

INDEPENDENT VARIABLE(S): ____________

DEPENDENT VARIABLE(S): ____________

OTHER FACTORS: ____________

LABORATORY REPORT FOR PROBLEM ________

SUMMARY OF FINDINGS: ________

DISCUSSION: ________

PROBLEM 20

MASS SOCIETY

When sociologists discuss major features of social organization which influence human behavior, they almost inevitably turn to a consideration of social class. Such an analysis is typically based on a somewhat modified Marxian view of a class-oriented society. A number of critics, however, have raised serious questions about the wisdom of this approach. The evidence they present is often scanty, but their criticism in broad outline is clear: In industrial societies, differences in education and income between social strata tend to shrink. As this happens the middle class swells, and the older distinctions between lower and middle class become lost. To the extent that this happens, class differences and class conflict cannot account for behavior. The alternative offered to replace social class as a major structural determinant of behavior in modern societies is typically some variant of the mass society theme (Wilensky, 1964).

There are many versions of the concept of mass society, but for present purposes it may be defined as a society in which individuals have few meaningful and strong bonds with respect to each other. They are isolated and thus constitute little more than a sheer aggregate, a mass of persons. The mass society view gained much of its fire from the analysis of totalitarian regimes. As advanced by Hannah Arendt, the argument essentially stated that the atrocities of Nazi Germany could be understood only in terms of the extent to which post World War I Germany had become a mass society. Contemporary society, she argued, transformed the basis of social order: religious faiths were abandoned, kinship bonds disintegrated. Coupled with this isolation was a deep psychological sense of alienation, of being lost and left out from the larger society. To reestablish bonds, totalitarian movements become more attractive as a form of pseudo-community. Mass men enter into such movements to relieve the frustration, hostility, and alienation they feel (Arendt, 1951). While this argument is frequently sweeping and imprecise, there is some evidence to suggest that the view has merit. Careful research has documented that the alienated and the lonely are likely to be attracted to movements opposing fluoridation (Pinard, 1963), school bond issues (Horton and Thompson, 1962), the establishment of metropolitan communities (McDill and Ridley, 1962), and to support McCarthyism (Trow, 1958) as well as other forms of authoritarian activity.

It is of course not true that all persons in contemporary society are isolated or experience a deep sense of alienation, for there frequently tends to be mechanisms available which bind individuals to each other and hence integrate them into the larger society. The voluntary organization is one such mechanism. Voluntary organizations, particularly work organizations (unions, for example) or political organizations, occupy a unique position in large-scale industrial societies, for they offer ordinary citizens the opportunity to participate in decisions that affect not only their own lives but the destiny of their fellow men as well. As some theorists have noted, participation in such organizations should reduce the feeling of being left out of the larger society and hence reduce the sense of alienation that is the breeding ground for totalitarianism (Kornhauser, 1959).

The reading for the present problem examines the hypothesis that voluntary organizations are a vital factor in reducing powerlessness—a deep-rooted sense that events are beyond personal control. To test the hypothesis the authors first control for two factors they feel important to understanding powerlessness—mobility aspirations and class background—and then illustrate that participants in work organizations are generally less likely to manifest a sense of powerlessness.

ORGANIZATIONS AND POWERLESSNESS: A TEST OF THE MEDIATION HYPOTHESIS / *Arthur G. Neal and Melvin Seeman*

The theory of mass society proposes that organizations mediating between individual and state serve as a bulwark against the development of alienation. An empirical test of this proposition is presented, focusing on perceived powerlessness as a critical form of alienation. As predicted, members of work-related organizations are generally lower in powerlessness than non-members; this difference is sustained under appropriate controls for socio-economic status and mobility. The clearest associations between non-membership and powerlessness are found among the mobility-minded workers. Systematic exceptions to the mediation thesis are noted; and the problem of causal imputation (organization leads to a sense of mastery) is reviewed.

In his recent work on the political context of sociology, Bramson refers to ". . . the persistent parable of alienation that is the theory of the mass society."[1] The phrase is felicitous, for both the persistence of the theory and its alienation imagery are hardly debatable. An important theme concerns the organizational ties that must mediate between the isolated, hence potentially powerless individual and the massive state. This theme has been persistent, indeed; one may choose a statement of it from Durkheim or from a number of recent works in the same tradition.[2]

The mass society viewpoint holds that the destruction of the old community has separated the individual from binding social ties, and that this isolation produces a sense of powerlessness which can be both personally devastating and destructive of democratic processes. Thus, in a capsule, the mass society theory is an historically-oriented account of contemporary social structure; a set of assertions about the alienative effects of that structure; and some derived predictions about behavioral consequences (e.g., passive conformity, or volatile mass behavior). One of the clearest statements of this viewpoint is in Kornhauser's *The Politics of Mass Society*. "Meaningful and effective participation in the larger society," he writes, "requires a structure of groups intermediate between the family and the nation;" without such groups the individual cannot readily perceive himself "as having the capacity to determine his life and to affect the lives of his fellows."[3]

Naturally enough, the mass society interpretation has had its critics. It has been charged with romanticizing the pre-industrial order; with under-estimating the emancipating features of the new order; with falsifying the extent of contemporary isolation; and with disguising an ideology about society as a description of it.[4] These criticisms, whatever their merit on other grounds, do not touch the heart of the alienation parable embodied in the mass society thesis. They have not examined directly the presumed alienative consequences of the lack of organizations serving as the "dependable structure for mobilizing political opinion and action."[5]

Just how dependable that structure is at present is a matter for debate. In the eyes of some mass society theorists, the giant organizations to which people now belong are no longer agencies for expression and control, but agencies for further alienation. Thus, C. Wright Mills writes: "Voluntary associations . . . have lost their grip on the individual. As more people are drawn into the political arena, these associations become mass in scale; and as the power of the individual becomes more dependent upon such mass associations, they are less accessible to the individual's influence."[6] This is not only a dim view of the times; it is also a prediction that organizational affiliation as we know it will have little to do with developing the sense of mastery. It is to the test of these alienative consequences of membership and non-membership that our work is addressed.

The study design

While several variants of alienation are regularly implicated in discussions of the mass society, we are presently concerned only with the powerlessness aspect.[7] The hypothesis to be tested can be stated directly enough: we expected members of a work-based formal organization to exhibit less powerlessness than individuals without an organization to speak for them in the crucial area of occupation.

This hypothesis states the simple outline of the problem; but, unfortunately, things are rarely quite so

Reprinted with permission of the authors and publisher from *American Sociological Review*, 29 (April 1964), pp. 216–226.

The work on this paper was assisted by Contract No. AF 49 (638)–71, monitored by the Air Force of Scientific Research of the Office of Aerospace Research, and by a grant-in-aid from the University of California at Los Angeles. A related analysis of both powerlessness and normlessness can be found in Arthur G. Neal, "Stratification Concomitants of Powerlessness and Normlessness: A Study of Political and Economic Alienation," unpublished Ph.D. dissertation, The Ohio State University, 1959.

[1] Leon Bramson, *The Political Context of Sociology*, Princeton, N.J.: Princeton University Press, 1961, p. 72.

[2] See, for example, Emile Durkheim, *Professional Ethics and Civic Morals*, Glencoe, Ill.: The Free Press, 1958; and Robert A. Nisbet, *The Quest for Community*, New York: Oxford University Press, 1953.

[3] William Kornhauser, *The Politics of Mass Society*, Glencoe, Ill.: The Free Press, 1959, pp. 93, 110.

[4] See, especially, Daniel Bell, "America as a Mass Society: A Critique," in *The End of Ideology*, Glencoe, Ill.: The Free Press, 1960, pp. 21–36; and Joseph R. Gusfield, "Mass Society and Extremist Politics," *American Sociological Review*, 27 (February, 1962), pp. 19–30.

[5] Scott Greer and Peter Orleans, "The Mass Society and the Parapolitical Structure," *American Sociological Review*, 27 (October, 1962), pp. 634–46; p. 635.

[6] C. Wright Mills, *The Power Elite*, New York: Oxford University Press, 1956, p. 307.

[7] For a review of five alternative meanings of alienation, and a specification of powerlessness as an expectancy construct, see Melvin Seeman, "On the Meaning of Alienation," *American Sociological Review*, 24 (December, 1959), pp. 783–91. In Kornhauser's work (*op. cit.*) all five versions of alienation are woven into the fabric of the argument.

simple, and we must add several complications. The complications are of two kinds: structural and ideological.

We refer, in the first instance, to occupational mobility as a complication, and assume that in any work-based test of alienation it is essential to know the individual's inter-generational mobility. For example, the hypothesized connection between powerlessness and membership may well be weakest among those who have experienced upward mobility. These people, after all, have managed an important success in their world, and their sense of the manageability of events might be increased thereby, regardless of organizational affiliation.

The ideological complication focuses on attitudes toward mobility. In the first place, people who are striving to achieve higher status (as compared with non-strivers) may well take a different view of the need for, and the functions of, organization membership. Lipset has recently argued that the emphasis on individual achievement in the United States, as compared with the more ascriptive norms of Western Europe, accounts for major differences in union organization and tactics. In the achievement-oriented society "the lower status person is more likely to feel impelled to drive *himself* to get ahead," rather than trying to improve the situation "*collectively* through social movements."[8] Thus, mobility commitments presumably influence the meaning assigned to certain organizations.

Mobility ideology is also potentially relevant to the powerlessness side of our equation. Indeed, the twin values of mobility and mastery are commonly seen as part of a typically American orientation; they have been shown to be related in several empirical studies. Rosen, for example, has suggested that those who do not strive for success and whose achievement needs are low perceive the world as basically determined and unmanageable.[9] And Strodtbeck has shown that the relatively mobile Jews express greater commitment to the belief that "the world is orderly and amenable to rational mastery, and therefore a person can and should make plans which control his destiny."[10]

These studies by Rosen and Strodtbeck indicate that high powerlessness and low commitment to striving should be found together; but reasonable arguments to the contrary have been proposed. It has been asserted, for example, that an exaggerated concern for status and mobility reflects the absence of a fundamental sense of control. Such a connection between powerlessness and status striving is one element in Mills' notion of the "status panic" among white-collar workers; and in "the authoritarian personality" an underlying sense of low control is said to lead to excessive status concern.[11]

For the moment, we need not choose between these different versions of the relation between an individual's conceptions of mastery and mobility. Our main purpose is to argue that a strong presumptive tie exists between these values and the two key variables, organization membership and powerlessness. The mobility measure allows us to distinguish among persons who may attribute quite different meanings to organization, and to discover whether organization membership tells us less about an individual's sense of powerlessness than does his ideology.

Finally, one further complication concerns the specificity of our prediction that the absence of organizational ties will be associated with high powerlessness. In our view, this version of alienation is an expectancy construct regarding personal control, *not* an omnibus synonym for feelings of despair, maladjustment, unhappiness or generalized negativism. Low expectancies for control and generalized despair may be correlated to some degree under some circumstances, but they should not be equated. The mass society hypothesis predicts that the absence of organizational ties produces a sense of low control; though the literature from which this hypothesis derives is frequently sweeping and somewhat careless in its style, it does not necessarily follow that generalized despair or negativism will also ensue.

If powerlessness were shown to be a concomitant of lack of organizational ties, we wished also to discover whether *any* index of negative affect would show a similar association with membership. Accordingly, we included Srole's well-known "anomia" scale, taking it to be an index with a considerable loading of generalized despair.[12] We expected that anomia and powerlessness would not be very highly correlated, and that the predicted powerlessness differences would not be equally reflected in the anomia scores. These postulations concerning the character of alienation go contrary to the general trend in the relevant literature: we assume that powerlessness is a rather specific brand of alienation, susceptible to specific predictions in the terms of the theory of mass society.[13]

[8] Seymour M. Lipset, "Trade Unions and Social Structure," *Industrial Relations*, 1 (October, 1961), pp. 75–89 (emphasis in original).

[9] Bernard C. Rosen, "The Achievement Syndrome: A Psychocultural Dimension of Social Stratification," *American Sociological Review*, 21 (April, 1956), pp. 203–11; see also his "Personality and Economic Growth in Brazil," mimeographed, 1962.

[10] Fred L. Strodtbeck, "Family Interaction, Values and Achievement," in David C. McClelland *et al.*, *Talent and Society*, Princeton, N. J.: Van Nostrand, 1958, pp. 135–94.

[11] C. Wright Mills, *White Collar*, New York: Oxford University Press, 1951; and Theodore W. Adorno, *et al.*, *The Authoritarian Personality*, New York: Harper, 1950.

[12] See, especially, Edward L. McDill, "Anomie, Authoritarianism, Prejudice and Socio-economic Status: An Attempt at Clarification," *Social Forces*, 39 (March, 1961), pp. 239–45. McDill reports a factor analysis in which the major factor ". . . may be labelled as a Weltanschauung which is negative in nature, that is, a dim world view" (p. 244). All five of the anomia items have a high loading on this factor. See also, Dorothy L. Meier and Wendell Bell, "Anomia and Differential Access to the Achievement of Life Goals," *American Sociological Review*, 24 (April, 1959), pp. 189–202, especially for their remark, "We are convinced that these questions for the most part measure despair, that is, utter hopelessness and discouragement" (p. 191).

[13] The various brands of alienation are commonly viewed as a highly correlated syndrome, but relatively independent measures of various kinds of alienation can be developed; see, especially, Arthur G. Neal and Salomon Rettig, "Dimensions of Alienation Among Manual and Non-Manual Workers," *American Sociological Review*, 28 (August, 1963), pp. 599–608.

Methods

Our design for testing the hypothesis that membership in mediating work organizations minimizes the sense of powerlessness calls for measures of powerlessness, organization membership, mobility ideology, mobility history, and anomia. Each of these is described below, as is the sampling procedure.

The measures. The sense of powerlessness can occur in many contexts, ranging from powerlessness with respect to the intimate spheres of friendship and affection, to powerlessness in the domains of work or international affairs. The measure used here defines powerlessness as "low expectancies for control of events," and the events are those most directly relevant to the idea of the mass society—e.g., control over the political system, the industrial economy, and international affairs.

Twelve forced-choice items on powerlessness were included in the mailed questionnaire, and after testing for scalability, seven items were selected as the final measure.[14] These items, as illustrated below, present a dichotomous choice between mastery and powerlessness:

1. ——There's very little persons like myself can do to improve world opinion of the United States.
   ——I think each of us can do a great deal to improve world opinion of the United States.
2. ——Persons like myself have little chance of protecting our personal interests when they conflict with those of strong pressure groups.
   ——I feel that we have adequate ways of coping with pressure groups.

Membership in work organizations was determined through the question, "Are you a member of any of the following kinds of organizations?" The answer alternatives were: a labor or trade union (i.e., AFL-CIO); a business or professional association (i.e., Chamber of Commerce); a social fraternity or lodge. In the following analysis we have excluded those who reported membership in a social fraternity only. We are aware that this procedure defines organization membership in the barest possible way, since it tells nothing about the individual's degree of participation, his loyalty to the organization, or the value he places on it as an instrument for achieving work-related goals.

The respondent's attitude toward mobility was measured by means of a Likert-type scale which, in effect, offered a choice between occupational mobility and a series of other values—e.g., friendship ties, family values, intrinsic work satisfaction, or health. The scale is conceived as a measure of the relative reward value the individual places on occupational mobility. Examples of these items are:

1. I'd probably turn down a substantial advancement if it involved being away from the family a good deal.
2. I wouldn't let my friendship ties in a community stand in the way of moving on to a better job.

Fourteen such items were included in the questionnaire; eight of these were selected as a scalable measure of mobility orientation. In the following analysis, those scoring in the high half of the distribution on this scale are called "mobility-oriented," while the low scorers are designated as "non-strivers."[15]

The index of occupational mobility was based on a comparison of the respondent's own occupation and his father's, using the North-Hatt prestige scale as the scoring device.[16] The resulting distribution of vertical mobility scores was trichotomized to form upwardly mobile, stationary, and downwardly mobile groups. In the two mobile groups, respondents' occupational prestige differed by four or more points from their fathers' occupational ratings.

To obtain anomia scores, we used the well-known five-item Srole Scale.[17]

The sample. A sample of adult male residents of Columbus, Ohio was selected by taking every 200th name listed in the city directory. By means of a mailed questionnaire, the information described above was obtained from 609 respondents, ranging in occupational level from unemployed workers to top professionals. Of the 1094 questionnaires delivered, 57 per cent were completed and returned. Returning a questionnaire is, of course, directly related to socio-economic status. We were able to determine the magnitude of this relation for our study, since occupations were listed in the city directory. Questionnaires were returned by 66 per cent of the non-manual and 50 per cent of the manual workers.

We do not know, however, what relation (if any) exists between alienation and response to a mailed questionnaire. On *a priori* grounds, one would expect those high in alienation to be less likely to return the questionnaire. To assess this possible bias, we conducted personal interviews with 25 randomly selected

[14] This scale is a variant of the forced-choice instrument developed by the late Professor Shephard Liverant and his colleagues at The Ohio State University. For further descriptions of this method see, *inter alia,* Julian B. Rotter, Melvin Seeman, and Shephard Liverant, "Internal vs. External Control of Reinforcements: A Major Variable in Behavior Theory," in Norman F. Washburne (ed.), *Decisions, Values and Groups,* Vol. 2, London: Pergamon Press, 1962, pp. 473–516; and Melvin Seeman and John W. Evans, "Alienation and Learning in a Hospital Setting," *American Sociological Review,* 27 (December, 1962), pp. 772–82.

In the present study, 50 items were initially constructed, and after a series of pre-tests—first on college students and then on community samples—the seven items were selected as our final measure of powerlessness, taking into account both item content and scalability. The seven items yielded a reproducibility coefficient of .87 on the present sample. The scale items, along with information on their factor analytic structure, are presented fully in Neal and Rettig, *op. cit.*

[15] The reproducibility coefficient for these items was .89. Modified versions of this mobility attitude scale have proved useful in examining leadership style and ethnic prejudice; see, for example, Fred B. Silberstein and Melvin Seeman, "Social Mobility and Prejudice," *American Journal of Sociology,* 55 (November, 1959), pp. 258–64.

[16] See Albert J. Reiss, *Occupations and Social Status,* New York: The Free Press of Glencoe, 1961. We did not analyze *intra*-generational mobility because only 10 per cent of the sample reported an occupational change (on the North-Hatt scale) over the past five years.

[17] Leo Srole, "Social Integration and Certain Corollaries: An Exploratory Study," *American Sociological Review,* 21 (December, 1956), pp. 709–16.

non-respondents among the manual workers, and with 25 among the non-manual.

Prior to tabulating the interview responses, a comparison of alienation scores was made between those who had returned the mailed questionnaire on the first appeal, and those who returned it on subsequent appeals. It has been suggested that such a comparison of early and late returns approximates differences between respondents who return a questionnaire and those who do not.[18] We found no statistically significant difference in powerlessness between the early and late returns.

More important, in the subsequent comparison between those who were personally interviewed and those who returned the questionnaire, again no significant difference in powerlessness was found. Thus, while the rate of return from those relatively high in socioeconomic status was somewhat higher, there is no evidence of selectivity by degree of alienation.

Results

We predicted that members of work-related organizations will exhibit less powerlessness than those who are unorganized. The simplest comparison confirms this prediction. Taking all of the unorganized together, the mean score on the powerlessness scale was 2.94 ($N = 181$); while for the organized workers the mean was 2.54 ($N = 277$). The difference between these means is significant at the .01 level ($t = 2.94$), using the conservative two-tailed test.

But this is the grossest of comparisons, and we can proceed to the refinements by way of Table 1, where we hold constant the individual's occupational status, his mobility history, and his mobility attitude. Table 1, in effect, presents six replications of the comparison between organized and unorganized *manual* workers, controlling for the possible effects of mobility history and mobility orientation. The striking feature of Table 1 is the consistency with which the predicted differences in powerlessness are obtained. In all six comparisons, the unorganized manual workers are higher in alienation than their organized counterparts. The mean score for all the unorganized manual workers in Table 1 (regardless of mobility orientation) is 3.08, as compared to 2.64 for the organized, a difference significant at the .05 level ($t = 2.10$), again using the conservative two-tailed test. (See page 304.)

The parallel data for *non-manual* workers are presented in Table 2. For the mobility-oriented group, the pattern is again consistently in the predicted direction: in each of the three comparisons, the unorganized white-collar workers are higher in powerlessness. For the two mobile groups—both the upwardly and the downwardly mobile—the powerlessness differences are quite large indeed, and the overall difference (3.20 vs. 2.01) is significant at the .001 level.

[18] See Robert Ferber, "The Problem of Bias in Mail Returns: A Solution," *Public Opinion Quarterly*, 12 (Winter, 1948-9), pp. 669–76; but see also the discussion relevant to Ferber's paper in the subsequent volume of the *Public Opinion Quarterly* (especially, pp. 495–501 and 562–3).

But in the data for the non-striving white-collar workers, we find a consistent reversal, indicating that the consistency we have noted thus far is not to be taken for granted. Among the non-strivers, the organized are *higher* in powerlessness; and again the mean scores (2.03 vs. 3.06) are significantly different. Since this reversal among the non-strivers occurs consistently in all three mobility groups, it suggests that our argument for the relevance of mobility attitudes in understanding powerlessness and organization has merit. We must pursue the matter of mobility orientations further.

It is among the mobility-oriented that the lack of organization works most clearly to produce powerlessness. As we have seen, this is most dramatically true among the non-manual workers, but the trend is similar for the manual workers (see Table 1). The difference between the organized and unorganized manual workers is considerably greater among the mobility-oriented than among the non-strivers, and among the strivers the most striking differences are again among those who have in fact been mobile. Thus, we begin to understand the relevance of mobility attitudes to the mediation hypothesis: the thesis regarding organizational ties is particularly applicable to the strivers.

But are mobility attitudes related to powerlessness in a more direct way? The possibility that mastery beliefs and mobility beliefs constitute an ideological syndrome has been suggested. Yet, such a syndrome is not found in our data. For the sample as a whole, the powerlessness scores of the mobility-oriented and the non-strivers are not significantly different (2.61 vs. 2.82); a correlation of $-.07$ was obtained between powerlessness and mobility orientation. Presumably, the individual's mobility attitude is relevant to powerlessness not directly but because the attitude mediates the meaning of organization membership.

Is the alienation connected with non-membership a relatively specific phenomenon, or is it a more diffuse and generalized disaffection? The answer is important both for our conception of alienation and for our understanding of generality in human attitudes. Our data on anomia recommend caution in assuming a high level of generality: low expectancies for control are not closely tied to anomia, and the anomia scores are not systematically patterned after the powerlessness data.

Table 3 illustrates the basis for these conclusions. The table is parallel to Table 1, but the anomia scores of the manual workers are substituted for powerlessness. The data for the non-manual workers (the parallel of Table 2, not presented here) are similar in character. That character is best summarized as follows. First, the unorganized tend to be higher in anomia, but the tendency is sometimes very slight indeed (note the mean scores of 13.64 and 13.21 among the non-strivers). Second, the anomia differences do not show the consistency that we found for powerlessness (note, for example, the considerably higher anomia scores of the organized workers in two of the six comparisons in Table 3). Third, none of the four main comparisons between organized and unorganized workers (paralleling the "totals" in Tables 1 and 2) yields a significant

TABLE 1. Mean scores on powerlessness,[a] for unorganized and organized manual workers, with mobility history and mobility attitude controlled (N=245)

		Mobility-oriented		Non-strivers	
Mobility history		Unorganized	Organized	Unorganized	Organized
Downwardly mobile		3.08	2.38	3.00	2.56
		(25)	(21)	(15)	(34)
Stationary		2.70	2.61	3.23	2.96
		(10)	(21)	(13)	(26)
Upwardly mobile		3.00	2.31	3.29	2.95
		(15)	(29)	(14)	(22)
Total	Mean	2.98	2.42	3.17	2.79
	N	(50)	(71)	(42)	(82)
	S.D.	1.4	1.8	1.7	1.6

[a] The obtained scores on the powerlessness scale ranged from 0 to 7.

TABLE 2. Mean scores on powerlessness for unorganized and organized non-manual workers, with mobility history and mobility attitude controlled (N=216)

		Mobility-oriented		Non-strivers	
Mobility history		Unorganized	Organized	Unorganized	Organized
Downwardly mobile		3.86	1.81	1.33	3.25
		(14)	(16)	(6)	(12)
Stationary		2.25	1.93	2.53	3.71
		(16)	(31)	(15)	(14)
Upwardly mobile		3.41	2.29	1.66	2.58
		(29)	(30)	(9)	(24)
Total	Mean	3.20	2.01	2.03	3.06
	N	(59)	(77)	(30)	(50)
	S.D.	1.8	2.0	1.6	1.9

TABLE 3. Mean scores on anomia[a] for unorganized and organized manual workers, with mobility history and mobility attitude controlled (N=245)

		Mobility-oriented		Non-strivers	
Mobility history		Unorganized	Organized	Unorganized	Organized
Downwardly mobile		13.52	11.28	14.27	12.85
		(25)	(29)	(15)	(34)
Stationary		10.30	12.12	13.85	12.88
		(10)	(21)	(13)	(26)
Upwardly mobile		12.87	11.43	12.79	14.25
		(15)	(21)	(14)	(22)
Total	Mean	12.68	11.60	13.64	13.21
	N	(50)	(71)	(42)	(82)
	S.D.	3.5	3.7	4.7	4.5

[a] The obtained scores on the anomia scale ranged from 5 to 25.

difference in anomia. These findings encourage the conclusion that a relatively specific test of the mediation hypothesis is at stake here.[19]

The problem of related factors

Still another kind of specificity must be demonstrated. We are obliged to make a reasonable case for the view that the powerlessness differences we have reported are a function of organization *per se*, and not of correlated characteristics of the unorganized: low education, relative youth, low income and skill level, or the like. This demonstration is not easy to make with finality, but we believe that the data argue well for dismissing these contaminating variables.

For example, the powerlessness differences could be a function of occupational prestige differences between organized and unorganized workers. The evidence suggests that such hidden differences are not critical. In Table 4, the occupational prestige scores do not follow the pattern presented in Tables 1 and 2 for powerlessness. Among the manual workers, the prestige differences between the organized and the unorganized are

[19] The correlation, over the entire sample, between anomia and powerlessness was .33. The correlation for our four main sub-groups (manual organized, manual unorganized, non-manual organized and non-manual unorganized), is in no case appreciably higher, and in one instance is considerably lower (namely, .14 among the non-manual unorganized), than the overall figure. Our data as a whole appear to conform to the pattern of *relative* independence postulated in the work of Neal and Rettig, *op. cit.*

TABLE 4. Mean occupational prestige[a] for unorganized and organized workers, with mobility history and mobility attitude controlled (manual and non-manual, N=461)

		MANUAL WORKERS				NON-MANUAL WORKERS			
		Mobility-oriented		Non-strivers		Mobility-oriented		Non-strivers	
Mobility history		Un-organ-ized	Organ-ized	Un-organ-ized	Organ-ized	Un-organ-ized	Un-ized	Organ-organ-ized	Organ-ized
Downwardly mobile		55.6	55.7	51.8	56.0	67.1	70.1	65.0	68.2
Stationary		60.7	60.2	63.3	60.7	69.5	73.8	70.2	80.2
Upwardly mobile		65.3	64.5	61.4	61.7	75.1	77.7	77.4	79.0
Total	Mean	59.5	59.7	58.6	58.9	71.7	74.6	71.3	76.7
	N	(50)	(71)	(42)	(82)	(59)	(77)	(30)	(50)
	S.D.	9.0	9.5	12.2	7.0	7.0	7.5	8.1	7.7

[a] The occupational prestige scores were based on the North-Hatt scale; the obtained range of scores was from 32 (unemployed laborer) to 93 (physician). The N's in the various cells of this table are the same as those given in Tables 1 and 2 above.

small, insignificant and not patterned systematically. The case of the non-manual workers is somewhat more complicated, for here the differences in prestige are relatively large and they systematically favor the organized. But even here it is difficult to argue that powerlessness is merely prestige in disguise: among the organized non-strivers, high prestige and *high* powerlessness are found together; while among the organized mobility-oriented group, high prestige and *low* powerlessness go together. The general independence of powerlessness and prestige is indicated by the low overall correlation of .05 between these two variables.

The case with education and age is quite similar. The correlation with powerlessness was .01 in both instances, and the detailed tables (not presented here) argue for the same independence when mobility and occupational level are controlled.

A more troublesome possibility of masked influence is found in the case of income. As one might expect, a systematic income differential favors the organized workers, and the difference obtains among both the manual and the non-manual. These income differences are not necessarily evidence of contamination. They may merely represent the predictable economic gain that goes with organization, a gain not so closely tied to powerlessness as to explain away the differences we have shown.

That this is a tenable view is suggested by two facts. First, the correlation between income and powerlessness is very low and insignificant (— .03), and it is not appreciably higher when the correlation is computed separately for each of the four main sub-samples. Second, if income is held constant, and the organized are compared with the unorganized, the powerlessness differences do not disappear. Table 5 shows that among the manual workers, regardless of income level, the unorganized manifest a higher degree of powerlessness.

TABLE 5. Mean scores on powerlessness for unorganized and organized manual workers, with income controlled (N=244)

Income		Unorganized	Organized
Under $3,000		2.50	2.20
		(14)	(5)
$3,000–4,999		3.20	2.81
		(46)	(52)
$5,000–6,999		3.20	2.55
		(25)	(75)
Over $7,000		3.00	2.65
		(4)	(20)
Total	Mean	3.08	2.64
	N	(89)	(153)
	S.D.	1.5	1.8

The imputation of cause

All this we take to be congruent with the mass society thesis that membership in mediating organization is an element in generating a fundamental sense that the person's social world is manageable. We say "fundamental" sense of control because the measure of powerlessness used here refers to a broad range of events: war and peace, world opinion of the United States, control of pressure groups, inflation, and the influence of the average citizen on government decisions.

But to say that the evidence is "congruent" with mass society theory is to recognize that the direction of causation implied in that theory has not been demonstrated. Does membership lead to low alienation, or is it rather that only the non-alienated join organizations whose essential purpose is to exercise control in the occupational sphere? Nothing in mass society theory would deny the motivational argument (i.e., that alienation in the powerlessness sense may lead to the avoidance of membership), but the theory certainly emphasizes the structural sources of powerlessness.

It is altogether likely that both processes are operative in producing our results. While a test for these two alternatives—the "structural" and the "motivational" interpretations—was not a part of our initial design, we were able to derive some clues on the matter by returning to the original sample and collecting supplementary data that allowed us to compare workers in open and closed shops, "maintenance of membership" firms, and situations where no union was available in the plant.[20]

If our data merely reflect the fact that those with a strong sense of control are prone to join work organizations, members of open-shop unions should be lower in powerlessness than members of closed shop unions, for in the latter the alienated as well as the unalienated are involuntarily drawn into membership. Further, if the element of choice is the prepotent fact, no difference in powerlessness should occur where there is no essential choice, even though there is a difference in organization—e.g., the closed shop as compared with the "no union available" category.

The data in Table 6 are enlightening if not demonstrative on these causal implications. Here the differences in powerlessness appear to be a pooled motivational and structural effect. Only a minor difference in powerlessness exists between the open-shop and the closed-shop union members (2.66 vs. 2.80). The direction of this difference (as with all of the open shop vs. closed shop comparisons in Table 6) is consistent with the motivational thesis. But the comparison of the "no choice" situations also produces differences, and these are in the expected direction if organization itself is a factor (closed shop = 2.80; no union = 3.04). The highest levels of powerlessness occur among the non-unionized workers, irrespective of whether they have chosen to remain non-members ("open shop" mean score = 3.14) or are in a situation where no union is available (3.04). The lowest degree of powerlessness is found in the "maintenance of membership" situation which is, in one sense, optimal ground for the operation of both the motivational and the structural factors: initial membership is voluntary, but the required maintenance of membership encourages the development of a strong organization. It is worth noting in Table 6 that the distinction between the mobility-oriented and the non-strivers shows again that the differences in powerlessness are most striking among the mobility-oriented workers.

Obviously, this argument concerning the causal processes must remain highly inferential, not least of all because the union situations are more complicated than we have made them appear. For example, the informal pressures in many open-shop plants may be quite as coercive as contract clauses, narrowing the element of choice in distinguishing the various union situations. But if not definitive, the data are reasonable and instructive, and the same may be said for our parallel data on individual unions. The number of cases, of course, becomes very small, but the data follow a reasonable pattern: for example, among the open-shop unions, the unionized government employees, whose organization is traditionally weak, were conspicuously high in powerlessness (mean = 3.16; N = 6). Among the closed-shop unions, the Teamsters, where member control is at a minimum, score highest in powerlessness (mean = 3.55; N = 18)—though the unorganized workers in the transportation industry score even higher (mean = 3.64; N = 11).

Conclusion

We have shown that membership in a work-based organization is associated with a relatively strong sense of control over events, and that the higher powerlessness of the unorganized worker is not simply a function of his socio-economic status. Presumably, powerlessness is related to the fact of organization or the lack of it, both as a motivational factor in the decision to join and as a product of the mediating structure that organization provides. Furthermore, we note that these differences refer to a relatively specific form of alienation; they are not attributable to generalized despair, or to general differences in response style, since the organized and unorganized do not differ in their response to the Srole anomia scale. Finally, we find that the predicted differences in powerlessness are largest among the mobility-minded workers, while among the non-striving white-collar workers the general pattern is consistently reversed—here, organization and *high* powerlessness are found together.

This reversal among the non-strivers requires a further word, since it constitutes a clear denial of the major hypothesis under test. In one sense, it is a welcome reversal: at the very least, it makes clear that the mediation thesis is not to be taken for granted. The key to the matter may lie in the different meaning attached to organizational life by the manual as compared with the non-manual workers, and by the strivers as compared with the non-strivers. For the white-collar group, organizations (e.g., the chamber of commerce, or the professional society) serve much more as instruments of personal mobility, whereas for the manual workers the union is largely an instrument of group security and shared economic welfare. And perhaps the non-striving white-collar workers—deviants among their predominantly status-oriented fellows—join organizations for reasons associated with the manifest purposes of the organizations: to *do* something, while the mobility-minded join organizations to *get* something. If so, the high powerlessness of the organized non-strivers is rather different from the high powerlessness of the unorganized strivers.

Clearly, this is only one of several possible lines of interpretation. To test such interpretations we need, for example, information on the person's involvement in membership, on the availability of other organizations not directly concerned with work, and on the meaning of work itself.[21]

It is important, of course, to pursue this unexpected

[20] Through the city directory and the information obtained from the returned questionnaires, we could identify, for most of our respondents, the specific firms in which they were employed. We are indebted to Professor Herbert Parnes and the staff of the Labor Education and Research Service at The Ohio State University for the information on the union situation in these firms.

[21] Examination of the proportions of professionals, business owners and managers, and clerical-sales workers among the white-collar non-strivers compared to the strivers indicates that the revelsal of our basic finding is not simply a function of occupational differences.

TABLE 6. Mean scores on powerlessness for manual workers, by union situation,[a] with mobility attitude controlled (N=228)

Mobility attitude		Unionized: Maintenance of membership	Unionized: Open shop	Unionized: Closed shop	Non-unionized: Open shop	Non-unionized: No union available
Mobility-oriented		1.90 (10)	2.50 (24)	2.63 (35)	3.22 (18)	2.85 (27)
Non-strivers		2.75 (8)	2.83 (23)	2.94 (47)	3.00 (11)	3.23 (26)
Total	Mean	2.28	2.66	2.80	3.14	3.04
	N	(18)	(47)	(82)	(29)	(53)
	S.D.	1.4	1.7	1.8	1.4	1.5

[a] "Union shops" were included in the closed-shop category since membership is necessary for continued employment, and the worker may not freely choose to join. The "no union available" category consists chiefly of workers employed in small firms.

turn in our data. But it is equally important to recognize the basic consistency in the findings and to assess their meaning. For us, that meaning is best summarized by returning to our opening theme. The theory of mass society postulates certain structural antecedents of alienation, and specifies a set of behavioral consequences of alination that will ensue. We have sought here to test the reasonableness of that theory, though not the theory *in toto*, by discovering whether the structural conditions do, in fact, lead to the psychological predicate,[22] and we find in the result some support for the notion that powerlessness is a function of the lack of mediating organizational ties. Thus, in its own measure, this study constitutes one step in the required effort to convert the alienation parable into a proposition.

Replication

ORGANIZATIONAL PARTICIPATION AND ALIENATION

Neal and Seeman study the relationship between organizational participation and alienation using three control variables: occupational status, occupational mobility, and mobility attitude. Such an analysis requires a larger sample and more time than is available for our replication. However, the essential findings of the study can be replicated using only a control for occupational status. This is possible because other evidence suggests that participation in many types of organizations affects several aspects of alienation, regardless of the respondent's mobility history and aspirations (Rose, 1962).

In discussing the concept of alienation, Neal and Seeman point out that it consists of several component dimensions. Their research used measures of two of these: the "powerlessness" and "anomia" dimensions. However, they found consistent support for their hypothesis only with the powerlessness measure. Our replication will also use the powerlessness dimension, but an abbreviated three-item version. For a second aspect of alienation we will substitute a measure of "normlessness" (Dean, 1961) for the anomia scale used in the original study. The reason for this substitution is, in part, the unclear findings from the use of the anomia scale in the original study. More important, however, is the fact that normlessness is conceptually the reciprocal of powerlessness and is of strategic importance for the maintenance of society. That is, while powerlessness reflects a belief that a person is impotent to influence the course of events in his society, normlessness reflects a belief that an individual is not closely bound by the norms or rules of the society. The combination of powerlessness and normlessness, if sufficiently widespread, would signal the end of human society as we know it.

Hypothesis

1. State the differences you expect to find in "powerlessness" and "normlessness" for persons who are high as opposed to those who are low in organizational participation.
2. See Appendix A for general instructions in writing a hypothesis.

Empirical indicators for this problem

27. My father attended meetings of organizations and clubs such as fraternal orders, church groups (but do not count Sunday services), business organizations, unions, recreation groups such as bowling

[22] For two related papers seeking to demonstrate the connection between alienation and its presumed behavioral consequences, see Melvin Seeman, "Alienation and Social Learning in a Reformatory," *American Journal of Sociology*, 59 (November, 1963), pp. 270–284; and Seeman and Evans, *op. cit.*

teams, scouts, and any other non-profit voluntary group having a recognized organization and officers:

0. Not at all
1. Only once a year
2. Two or three times a year
3. Four to eight times a year
4. About once a month (9 to 12 times)
5. Two or three times a month
6. About once a week
7. A few times a week (2 to 4 times)
8. Almost every day or more often

28. About how many different clubs and organizations did your *father* belong to when you were a high school senior: ____________ organizations

29. PLEASE ANSWER THE FOLLOWING SIX QUESTIONS TWICE: First, answer in terms of whether YOUR FATHER agrees or disagrees. Make a guess if you are not sure. Second, answer in terms of whether YOU agree or disagree. Use the following rating scale

1 = Strongly Disagree	4 = Slightly Agree
2 = Moderately Disagree	5 = Moderately Agree
3 = Slightly Disagree	6 = Strongly Agree

Father Me

60. ____ ____ a. Sometimes he (I) have the feeling that people are using him (me).

____ ____ b. There is little or nothing he (I) can do towards preventing a major "shooting" war.

____ ____ c. We are just so many cogs in the machinery of life.

61. ____ ____ a. Everything is relative, and there just aren't any definite rules to live by.

____ ____ b. The end often justifies the means.

____ ____ c. With so many religions abroad, one does not really know which to believe.

12. Occupational Prestige

1. Proprietor of a large business (valued at $100,-000 or more); Top-level executive in large organization; Top-level professional

2. Proprietor of a medium business (valued at $35,000 to $100,000); Middle-level executive or official, or top-level of a small organization; Lower-level professional; Sales representatives of manufacturers or wholesalers or other senior salesmen earning $10,000 or more per year; Farmer of farm worth $100,000+

3. Proprietor of a small business (valued at $6,000 to $35,000); Lower-level official and manager; Semi-professional; Sales representative (as above) earning $7,000 to $10,000 per year; Farmer of farm worth $35,000 to $100,000

4. Proprietor of a very small business (valued under $6,000); Technician; Sales clerk and salesman earning *less* than $7,000 per year and clerical workers; Farmer of farm worth $15,000 to $35,000

5. Farmer of farm worth under $15,000; Skilled manual worker and foreman

6. Farmer, sharecropper or tenant with little stock or equipment; Semi-skilled worker and machine operator

7. Unskilled worker

Data analysis

1. *Sort* the code sheets into two occupational status groups on the basis of box 11.

Non-manual = 1, 2, 3, or 4
Manual = 5, 6 or 7

2. *Sub-sort* each occupational status group into organizational participation groups on the basis of the Organizational Participation Index in box 28t.

Low = 0 to 4
Medium = 5 to 8
High = 9 and over

3. *Tally* onto Table 1 either the Powerlessness Index —Father (box 60tf) or the Normlessness Index—Father (box 61tf). Your instructor will assign half the class one of these indexes and the other half the other index.

4. *Compute* the mean Powerlessness Index or the Mean Normlessness Index. See Appendix C for directions concerning calculation of the mean from grouped data.

5. *Plot* your mean scores and those computed by the other half of the class onto Figure 1. Use a dashed line for the Powerlessness Index and a solid line for the Normlessness Index. Label each line as either Manual or Non-Manual. There should be a total of four lines on your graph.

Lab report

1. Put the main emphasis of your report on the question of what difference organizational participation makes in alienation. You should, however, also pay attention to occupational status differences in alienation, and whether the relationship between participation and alienation is similar in the two status groups.

2. See Appendix A for general information on writing laboratory reports.

References

Arendt, Hannah, *The Origins of Totalitarianism*. New York: Harcourt, Brace & World, 1951.

Dean, Dwight G., "Alienation: Its Meaning and Measurement," *American Sociological Review*, 26 (October 1961), pp. 753–758.

Horton, John E. and Wayne E. Thompson, "Powerlessness and Political Negativism: A Study of Defeated Local Referendums," *American Journal of Sociology*, 67 (March 1962), pp. 485–493.

Kornhauser, Arthur, *The Politics of Mass Society*. New York: Free Press, 1963.

McDill, Edward and Jeanne Ridley, "Status, Anomia, Political Alienation and Political Participation," *American Journal of Sociology*, 68 (September 1962), pp. 205–211.

Neal, Arthur G. and Salomon Rettig, "Dimensions of Alienation Among Manual and Non-Manual Workers," *American Sociological Review*, 28 (August 1963), pp. 599–608.

Pinard, Maurice, "Structural Attachments and Political Support in Urban Politics: The Case of Fluoridation Referendums," *American Journal of Sociology*, 68 (March 1963), pp. 513–526.

Rose, Arnold, "Alienation and Participation: A Study of Group Leaders and the Mass," *American Sociological Review*, 27 (December 1962), pp. 834–838.

Trow, Martin, "Small Businessmen, Political Tolerance and Support for McCarthy," *American Journal of Sociology*, 64 (November 1958), pp. 270–281.

Wilensky, Harold L., "Mass Society and Mass Culture," *American Sociological Review*, 29 (April 1964), pp. 173–197.

Name________________________

Date________________________

TABLE 1. Powerlessness or normlessness (circle one) by organizational participation and occupational class

POWERLESSNESS (Box 60tf) OR NORMLESSNESS (Box 61tf)	NON-MANUAL WORKERS (1, 2, 3, or 4 in Box 12)						MANUAL WORKERS (5, 6, or 7 in Box 12)					
	Low org. particip. (Box 28t = 0 to 4)		Med. org. particip. (Box 28t = 5 to 8)		High org. particip. (Box 28t = 9 & over)		Low org. particip. (Box 28t = 0 to 4)		Med. org. particip. (Box 28t = 5 to 8)		High org. particip. (Box 28t = 9 & over)	
	f	fx	f	fx	f	fx	f	fx	f	fx	f	fx
3												
4												
5												
6												
7												
8												
9												
10												
11												
12												
13												
14												
15												
16												
17												
18												
TOTAL												
Mean												
+ (No info.)												

– – – – – – – – = Powerlessness

———————— = Normlessness

FIGURE 1. Powerlessness or normlessness score

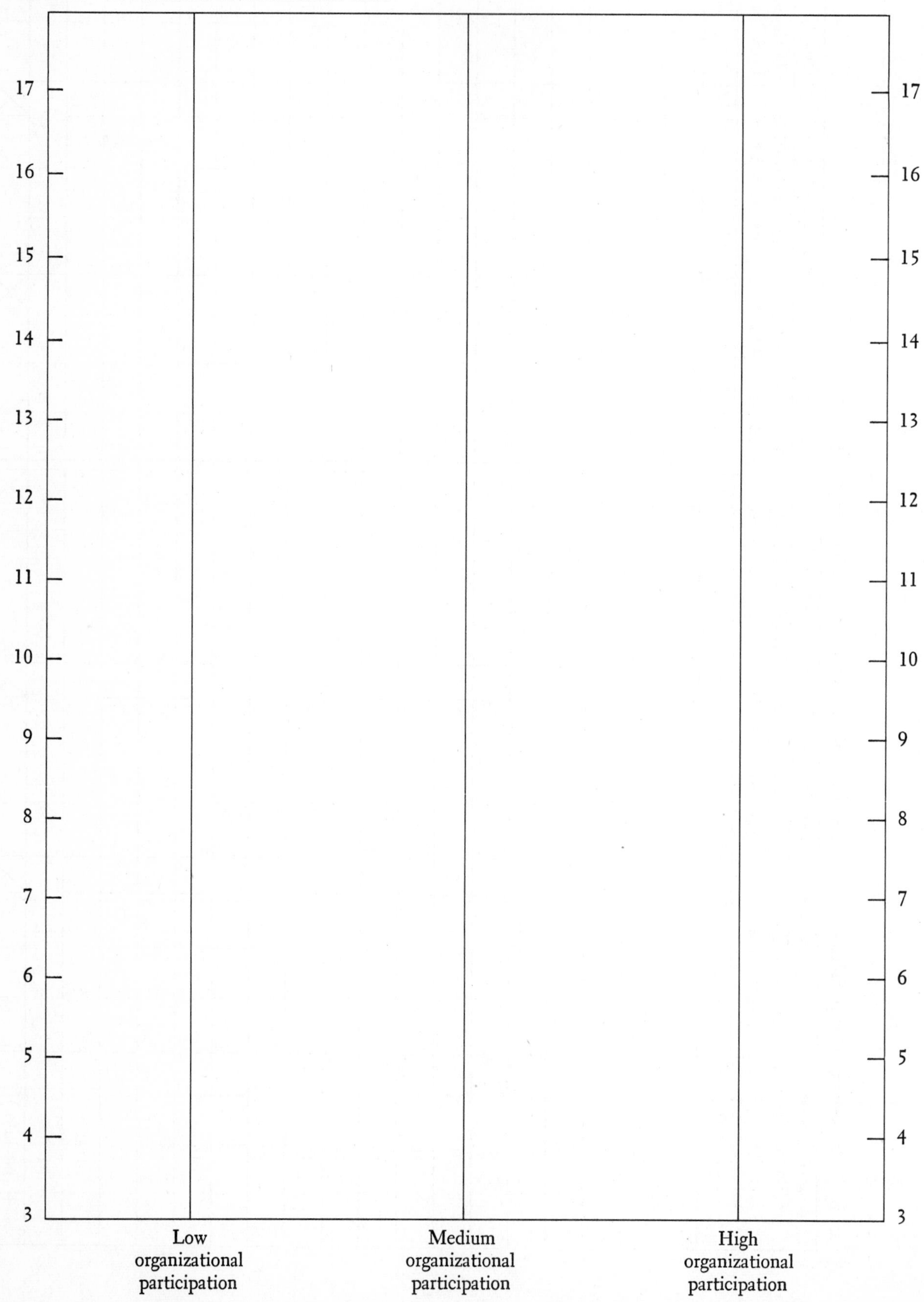

LABORATORY REPORT FOR PROBLEM ______

Course or
Section ______ Date ______ Name ______

HYPOTHESIS: ______

SAMPLE: ______

INDEPENDENT VARIABLE(S): ______

DEPENDENT VARIABLE(S): ______

OTHER FACTORS: ______

LABORATORY REPORT FOR PROBLEM____________

SUMMARY OF FINDINGS: ____________

DISCUSSION: ____________

Population IX

PROBLEM 21

POPULATION

Population research offers many vital perspectives for understanding society. Consider as an illustration the way population trends affect the possibilities of industrialization: An advancing technology requires a substantial base of manpower, i.e., a large number of persons. But the numbers cannot be so large that the resources of the society are wholly diverted to the production of food rather than machines (Davis, 1961). Consider also the research labeled "age cohort analysis." This is the analysis of the shared experiences of persons in a similar age group (Zeitlin, 1966; Ryder, 1965). Such research can reveal whether it makes a difference, for example, to be reared in a generation witnessing major upheavals such as war and depression as opposed to a generation experiencing relative stability and peace. These questions, and others like them, illustrate how the analysis of population can go well beyond the task of merely recording trends in births, deaths, and migration to help explain certain characteristics of a society.

Population is fundamental in another way to society and sociology: it not only sets constraints and potentials on social change but provides the very basis for society's existence and continuity. Obviously, society could not exist at all were there no people. It is therefore not surprising to find a number of studies, including the reading for the present problem, exploring the conditions affecting fertility plans and reproduction (Wrong, 1956).

One particular tradition has examined the finding that Jews tend to have lower rates of reproduction than Protestants, and Protestants lower than Catholics (Lenski, 1961; Westoff, 1959). Some have advanced an essentially cultural explanation of these differences. From this view, religious groups are regarded as possessing a relatively unique subculture with known differences in values and ideology—for example, Catholic disapproval of contraception on moral grounds. The greater fertility of Catholics as compared to Protestants is thus attributed to the effect of adherence to such a cultural norm.

This line of reasoning, however, encounters certain difficulties. France, for example, which is over 90 percent Catholic, has one of the world's lowest birth rates. To handle this disturbing fact, it is possible to adapt an alternative position and argue that in a modern urban society where all participate in the same mass culture, religious subcultures are not really important. This position would stress a "structural view" and argue that Catholic-Protestant-Jewish differences in fertility merely reflect the different positions in the social structure which tend to characterize the three major religious groups. Thus Jews in the United States are now predominantly middle class, whereas Catholics tend to have a disproportionately large number of working-class persons as compared to Protestants. Since working-class persons tend to have more children, and since Catholics are more often working class, it could be that the greater Catholic fertility does not occur because of anything intrinsic in the Catholic religion or values, but is simply a reflection of their particular socio-economic position.

This controversy reintroduces the theoretical issue of "structural" versus "cultural" determinants of social behavior which was the focus of Problem 3. It will be recalled that Problem 3 attempted to analyze the relative impact of class (a structural variable) and equalitarian ideology (a cultural variable) on the distribution of power in the family. The present reading essentially raises a similar question in regard to fertility decisions. Are the fertility plans of the three religious groupings a reflection of differences in class position or ideological preference or both? By controlling for socio-economic position through sampling Catholics, Protestants, and Jews with essentially identical class profiles, the authors are in a position to respond to this question.

SOCIO-ECONOMIC FACTORS IN RELIGIOUS DIFFERENTIALS IN FERTILITY / *Ronald Freedman, Pascal K. Whelpton, and John W. Smit*

Precision matching is used to test whether religious differences in fertility behavior result from socio-economic differences between the major religious groups. The 66 Jewish couples from a national sample survey of fertility are matched with Catholic and Protestant couples on duration of marriage and five socio-economic characteristics. These socio-economic controls eliminate most of the Protestant-Jewish differences for the fertility variables. However, the Catholic-Jewish differentials are not reduced. Apparently the distinctive Catholic fertility pattern cannot be explained by the combination of socio-economic characteristics considered. The significance of these results is discussed.

Jews, Protestants, and Catholics in the United States are known to differ in their behavior and values in the area of fertility and fertility planning. Several recent studies[1] have provided systematic descriptions of the nature of these differences. The recent data show that Jews: (1) have the lowest current fertility, (2) expect to have the fewest children, (3) want the smallest families, (4) approve the use of contraception most strongly, (5) are most likely to have used contraception, (6) are most likely to plan the number and spacing of all their children, and (7) are most likely to use the effective appliance methods of contraception. On all of these aspects of the fertility complex, Catholics differ most from the Jews, and Protestants have an intermediate position.

The fertility norms and behavior of the Jews appear to be consistent with their distinctive social and economic characteristics. They have the fertility characteristics we would expect to be associated with their high educational, occupational, and income status, their high concentration in white-collar occupations, their high concentration in metropolitan areas, and the small amount of farm background in their recent history. These social and economic characteristics have been associated generally in both theoretical discussions and in empirical work with low fertility, low fertility values, and high rationality in family planning. These social and economic characteristics of the Jews are those toward which the whole American population is moving as it becomes more completely urbanized, although we cannot expect such a concentration in the higher occupational and income positions to become typical of the whole population. But it has seemed reasonable in the past to speculate that the fertility behavior of the total population might develop in the future toward the present Jewish model, if the decisive factors in the present religious differences are related to differences in social and economic characteristics which will diminish. In earlier writing about higher Catholic fertility and associated behavior, the assumption has frequently been made that these differences would vanish as Catholics became similar to the general population in social and economic status.

Is it true that the fertility complex for Protestants and Catholics is different from that of Jews when they have similar social and economic characteristics, or is there a residual difference associated with religion even when these social and economic characteristics are taken into account? To provide some basis for answering this question a comparison is made below between the Jewish couples in a national sample and groups of Protestant and Catholic couples from the same sample who match the Jews on a set of relevant social and economic characteristics.

The 66 Jewish couples in the comparison include all the couples with both husband and wife Jewish in a national probability sample of white American couples with the wife 18 to 39 years old.[2] From the same national sample, 66 Protestant and 66 Catholic couples were selected to match the Jewish couples as closely

Reprinted with permission of the authors and publisher from the *American Sociological Review, 26* (August 1961), pp. 608–614.

A revised version of a paper presented at the annual meeting of the Population Association of America, May, 1960, Washington, D. C. The analysis was supported by the Program for Research in Population and Human Ecology of the University of Michigan.

[1] The general characterization of religious differentials and the data used in this paper are taken from the Growth of American Families study. The design and major findings from this study are reported in Ronald Freedman, Pascal K. Whelpton, and Arthur A. Campbell, *Family Planning, Sterility, and Population Growth,* New York: McGraw-Hill, 1959. The United States Census Bureau report on actual fertility differences between religious groups is consistent with the results of the Growth of American Families study. (See U.S. Bureau of the Census, *Statistical Abstract of the United States, 1958,* p. 41.) The original differences between religious groups reported here are consistent with those found in the Princeton Fertility study, although the measures used are not always the same. The Princeton study is limited to residents of the ten largest metropolitan areas who had a recent second birth. See Charles F. Westoff, "Religion and Fertility in Metropolitan America," in *Thirty Years of Research in Human Fertility,* New York: Milbank Memorial Fund, 1959, pp. 117–134. A major book-length report on the Princeton study will be published soon by Charles Westoff, Robert Potter, Philip Sagi, and Elliot Mishler.

[2] The sample for the larger study consisted of 2713 white, married women 18 to 39 years old, living with their husbands or temporarily separated because of his military service.

as possible on six characteristics: occupation of husband, education of wife, income of husband, duration of marriage, metropolitan character of present residence, and farm background.[3] Cases where husband and wife did not have the same religious affiliation were excluded. The procedure was to find all the Protestant couples in the sample who had the same combination of characteristics as a particular Jewish couple and then to select randomly one of the Protestant couples as a match. The same procedure was followed in matching 66 Catholic couples with the Jewish sample. The cluster of characteristics of the Jews was sufficiently distinctive so that the number of cases of multiple possibilities for matching was not great, despite the relatively large size of the Protestant and Catholic panels. In fact, in many cases it was not possible to match exactly in terms of the combined categories for all characteristics, and it was sometimes necessary to allow one and in a few cases two of the characteristics to be matched from the closest available category. When this was necessary the closest possible match was made. In some cases the match in an adjacent category was actually closer than possible within the category. Each of the Protestant and Catholic couples match the appropriate Jewish couple on occupation of husband, duration of marriage, and farm background. For Protestants, 45 of the 66 cases match exactly on all of the characteristics, 65 on at least five of the six characteristics, and all on at least four of the six. For Catholics, 35 of the 66 cases match exactly on all characteristics, 61 on at least five of the six, and all on at least four of the six. In carrying through the matching, income was the last criterion used and therefore most of the matching failures are with reference to income.

Since Catholics and Jews marry later than Protestants,[4] and since duration of marriage is significantly related to all of the variables of the fertility complex, it was considered important to match all the cases on number of years married. It was not possible with the number of cases available to match also on the wife's age. However, it seems quite unlikely that the fact that the matched Catholics are one year older than the Protestants and Jews could significantly affect the general results obtained. Leaving age uncontrolled while controlling on duration of marriage means that age at marriage has been permitted to vary. Within the controls imposed, there is some justification for permitting age at marriage to vary, since it is an important variable in the fertility complex being examined.

Comparisons between the matched groups can be summarized as indicating that the fertility complex for Protestants is very much like that for Jews when they have similar social and economic characteristics, but that this is not true for Catholics. On almost all of the comparisons, the difference between Jews and Catholics is as great or greater when the social and economic characteristics are controlled as when they are not. Apparently, the distinctiveness of Catholic fertility behavior as compared with that of Jews and Protestants cannot be explained by differences in the background characteristics considered here—at least not at the level set by taking the combination of characteristics of the Jews as a model. This broad summary of the results can be checked by comparing the results for the three religious groups in the original total sample and among the matched couples in Table 1.[5]

Several measures of fertility can be considered. The completed family size expected by wives in the total sample is significantly lower for Jews than for Catholics, and Protestants are in an intermediate position. In contrast among the matched couples, the Protestants expect the same low figure as the Jews, but the Catholic figure remains unchanged at the high level. In the total sample, actual mean number of births to date is lowest for the Jews and higher at the same level for Catholics and Protestants. (Fertility to date is the same for Catholics and Protestants in spite of the fact that the Catholics married later. They had the same number of children as the Protestants in a shorter period of time. There is reason to believe that Catholics will have more children than the Protestants by the end of the child-bearing period.[6]) In the matched groups, Protestant fertility to date is even lower than that for Jews, but Catholic fertility is high—considerably above that for either Protestants or Jews.

Each wife was asked several questions to ascertain how many children she wanted at the time of the interview in 1955. After matching, the mean value for Protestants is closer to the low Jewish figure, but the mean value for matched Catholics is even higher than that for all Catholics. Wives were also asked: "How many children would you choose to have if you could start your married life all over again and have just the number of children you would want by the time you are 45"? This was intended to give some indication of the respondents' personal ideals for family size in situations not too closely limited by their actual family history. Again here, the mean value for Protestants is identical with the lower figure for Jews after matching, while the Catholic mean value is even higher than it was before.

The measure for Catholics is close to that for Protestants and Jews for only one of the fertility values: the attitude on what is considered the ideal size of family for Americans in general. In this case, the mean values are very similar for the three matched groups, although they vary in the expected manner in the total sample.

Attitudes toward the use of family limitation by the general population are rather similar as between all Protestant and Jewish wives but Jews indicate the

[3] The categories used for matching were as follows: *occupation*—upper white collar, lower white collar, upper manual, lower manual, farm owner or worker; *education*—grade school only, one to three years of high school, four years of high school, college; *income of husband*—over $6000, $4000 to $6000, under $4000; *duration of marriage*—under five years, five to nine years, ten years or more; *present residence*—inside or outside of metropolitan area; *farm background*—either husband or wife has ever lived on a farm, neither has.

[4] There is direct evidence on this point from the national sample under study.

[5] See footnote 14.

[6] For a fuller discussion of this point, see Freedman, Whelpton, and Campbell, *op. cit.*, p. 275.

TABLE 1. Fertility behavior of all Protestant, Catholic, and Jewish couples in national sample and of Protestant and Catholic couples who match the Jewish couples on duration of marriage and selected socio-economic characteristics

Fertility and demographic characteristics	Total national sample			Matched groups		
	Protestants	Catholics	Jews	Protestants	Catholics	Jews
Number of cases	1684	628	66	66	66	66
Mean expected number of births, when family completed	2.9	3.4	2.4	2.4	3.4	2.4
Mean number of births to date	2.1	2.1	1.7	1.4	2.0	1.7
Mean number of children wanted when interviewed	3.0	3.5	2.6	2.8	3.7	2.6
Mean number of children wanted if could start life over	3.4	3.8	3.2	3.2	4.2	3.2
Mean number of children considered ideal for Americans	3.4	3.6	3.1	3.2	3.2	3.1
Mean duration of marriage in years	10.1	8.8	8.5	8.6	8.6	8.5
Mean age in years of wife	29.8	30.0	30.3	30.0	31.1	30.3
Mean age at marriage of wife	19.7	21.2	21.8	21.4	22.5	21.8
Attitude towards use of family limitation methods						
Percentage expressing:						
Unqualified approval	73%	32%	89%	92%	18%	89%
Qualified approval	13	12	5	4	12	5
Pro-con	3	6	3	—	3	3
Qualified disapproval	9	35	3	2	58	3
Unqualified disapproval	1	13	—	2	9	—
Not ascertained	1	2	—	—	—	—
Total	100	100	100	100	100	100
Percentage who have already used contraception (including rhythm)	75	57	86	83	59	86
Percentage who planned number and spacing of all pregnancies	22	9	47	33	14	47
Methods of contraception						
Percentage of all couples (including non-users) who have:						
Ever used an appliance or chemical method	67%	26%	83%	78%	15%	83%
Ever used a method unacceptable under Catholic church doctrine	69	29	84	80	15	84
Only used rhythm	5	29	1	3	44	1

strongest approval. Catholics are much more likely to express disapproval or to qualify their approval. After matching, the attitude distribution of Protestants is even more similar to that for the Jews, but the Catholics are even more different, a larger proportion expressing disapproval.

With respect to the proportion who have used contraception to date,[7] matching brings the Protestant figure much closer to the high Jewish figure but increases the Catholic figure very little.

[7] Many of the couples who have not used contraception will do so in the future if we judge either on the basis of their own reported intentions or on the basis of the experience of the older women in the sample. A significant number of the couples in all three religious groups have not used contraception because fecundity impairments made such control unnecessary. The term, contraception, is used here interchangeably with the term, "family limitation," to refer to any method of avoiding conception, including mechanical or chemical methods, coitus interruptus, or "rhythm." It does not include abortion.

In the total sample, the Jewish couples are much more likely than couples of either of the two other groups to have planned the spacing and number of all their children by means of contraception.[8] After matching, the proportion of such planned families rises sharply among the Protestants toward the Jewish figure but the Catholic proportion rises only slightly.

The types of contraception used also are more similar for the Jews and matched Protestants after controls, while the practices of matched Catholics are even more distinctive. Thus the matched Protestant and Jewish groups are much more similar in the proportions who have ever used an appliance or chemical method of contraception. These methods, forbidden to

[8] Here we are referring to couples who only conceived when they discontinued the use of contraception in order to have a child.

observant Catholics under church doctrine,[9] are even less frequently used in the matched Catholic group than in the original sample. The proportion of Catholics using any method forbidden under church doctrine is less than half as large in the matched group as in the total sample. This is certainly not consistent with the view that Catholic adherence to church doctrine on these issues results from their distinctive distribution in respect to the social and economic characteristics considered in this analysis.

The general results of this analysis appear to be consistent with the hypothesis that Protestant-Jewish differences in the variables of the fertility complex are a function of differences in a few strategic social and economic background variables. When these background differences are controlled, the differences in the fertility complex are greatly diminished, disappear, or are even reversed.

However, the unique values of the fertility complex of Catholics cannot be explained in this simple way. Not only do their characteristics persist, but the differences are more likely to be increased than decreased when the effect of the specific social and economic characteristics in this analysis is controlled.

We have not controlled for the degree of involvement in the religious community in the matched comparisons shown in Table 1. In this analysis the respondents are classified as Catholics, Protestants, or Jews simply on the basis of their self-identification with one of these major religious divisions in response to a rather simple question about religious preference. Strictly speaking, then, we have not examined the effect of the religious communities on their close adherents, because many more Catholics than Protestants or Jews are closely attached to the formal rites and institutions of their religion. We have been examining the effect of the religious groupings as they now operate in the United States on their broad constituencies—whether weakly or strongly identified. This seems to us to be a more significant approach than one which would center on a comparison of the large group of Catholics closely identified with their church and the much smaller groups of Jews and Protestants who are closely attached by comparable criteria.

Nevertheless, it is quite unlikely that the differences between Catholics, on the one hand, and Protestants and Jews, on the other, would disappear even if they were matched on such a criterion as frequency of church attendance. Neither the Princeton study nor the Growth of American Families study (GAF) found any significant variation in fertility behavior in relation to church attendance or indices of religious interest for non-Catholics. Among Protestants, major denominational differences are not related to major differentials in family planning practices. Catholic fertility and family planning do vary in relation to church attendance in the GAF study, but even the Catholics who report attending church "seldom or never" are markedly different (in "Catholic" directions) from non-Catholics for the major fertility variables considered in the GAF study.

The matching procedure used in our analysis does select Catholics more committed to the church; 86 per cent of the Catholic wives in the matched group reported regular attendance at church compared with 68 per cent in the original sample of Catholics. However, if we consider only the nine matched pairs for which the Catholics report less than regular church attendance, there are still very marked differences between Catholics and Jews: (1) the average expected number of children is 3.0 for Catholics and 1.9 for Jews, (2) live births to date average 2.3 for Catholics and 1.2 for Jews, and (3) 67 per cent of the Catholics and 88 per cent of the Jews approve the practice of family limitation without qualification.

Philip Sagi has pointed out,[10] on the basis of the findings of the Princeton study, that matching Catholics with the relatively well-educated Jewish group selects those Catholics who are most likely to be conforming to Catholic values about fertility, because: (1) Catholics who are well-educated are most likely to have most of their education in Catholic schools, and (2) Catholics who have extensive religious education are most likely to adhere to Catholic religious values about fertility.

Thus, Catholic religious education may be the factor which immediately explains the persistence of distinctive Catholic fertility patterns even under the impact of greater urbanization and higher status. While this explanation clarifies the problem, it does not eliminate it. We must still explain the strength of Catholic religious education. In the theory predicting elimination of Catholic-Protestant differentials, urbanization and increasing status for Catholics were expected to reduce their loyalty to distinctive Catholic values and institutions in general—not simply in the area of fertility. It may be that an explanation of the distinctiveness of Catholics with respect to fertility can be found only in a more general explanation of the continuing strength of American Catholic institutions and ideology.

The Catholic sub-culture involves an explicit and distinctive ideology about the fertility complex. In general, Jewish and Protestant groups have no special religious ideology on these issues. It may be that with more precise measurements of the variables for a larger sample,[11] or with the addition of other variables the distinctive Catholic position could be "explained

[9] Roman Catholic doctrine forbids the use of mechanical or chemical contraceptives or coitus interruptus. The "rhythm" method is permitted under certain conditions. For a fuller statement of the Catholic position, see Freedman, Whelpton, and Campbell, *op. cit.*, Appendix A, pp. 415–419.

[10] This interpretation was suggested by Philip Sagi in discussing this paper at the annual meetings of the Population Association of America in May, 1960, in Washington, D.C.

[11] The consistent results obtained in this study make this seem unlikely. As a check on the possible effect of matching more exactly on all the variables simultaneously, we considered only the 35 Catholics who matched the Jewish group on all the characteristics. The differences between Catholics and Jews were substantially the same for these 35 cases as for the larger group of 66 cases less completely matched. It is conceivable that the concentration of the Jewish population in New York City may influence the results.

away." The results obtained conceivably may depend on the particular weighting of the controls used for matching—those characterizing the Jewish group. This particular model was selected because it is the direction in which the general population appears to be moving with respect to urbanization and socio-economic status. Matching on the model of the Protestant or Catholic combination of background characteristics might produce different results. This will be explored in later work. But assuming that further work supports the results presented here, we are left with the question of why the specific Catholic ideology has arisen and has been maintained. Presumably it has an origin and a function which are not to be explained in any simple way by the variables treated here.

These results for the fertility complex are consistent with those for Catholic-Protestant differences in behavior and ideology obtained by Gerhard Lenski in a study in the Detroit area.[12] For a rather wide range of behavioral and attitudinal variables the Catholic-Protestant differences persist even when groups of similar social and economic status are compared.

Lenski finds that members of each major religious group tend to associate in primary groups mainly with people of their own faith. The existence of these partly closed religious communities within the larger community perpetuates and reinforces whatever unique values and ideologies the religion carries with it. In the case of the Catholics this no doubt includes distinctive values about family planning and fertility.

The Growth of American Families study calls attention to one subgroup in which Catholic-Protestant fertility and family planning differences are very small —the families in which the wife had worked a long time (at least five years) since marriage. In this subgroup, Protestants and Catholics tend to converge with respect to expected family size, attitude toward the use of family limitation methods, and the type of methods used.[13] If we interpret long work experience as facilitating the involvement of Catholic wives in groups outside the closed Catholic subcommunity, this result is consistent with the hypothesis that distinctive Catholic fertility behavior tends to disappear when the barriers between the religious subcommunities are reduced. However, this relationship may also be a matter of selection, at least in part, i.e., Catholic wives who previously have acquired non-Catholic fertility values will be most likely to work. The selection hypothesis is supported by the findings of the Princeton Fertility study that Catholic wives who have had little or none of their education in religious schools are most likely to work after marriage and resemble Protestants in their fertility behavior. Since only a small proportion of either Catholic or Protestant wives aged 18 to 39 years had worked five or more years since marriage, adding the wife's work history to the list of controls in the matching process would not have changed significantly the comparisons between the matched groups that are presented above.

We found earlier that controlling simultaneously on five socio-economic characteristics virtually eliminated the Protestant-Jewish differences on the fertility measures. To assess the extent to which each of the characteristics contributes to this result will require a different kind of analysis which we plan to carry out and report in a later paper. However, we can report some exploratory work in which matching procedures were used to test the hypothesis that one or a few of the characteristics could produce the observed results. This did not prove to be the case. When each of the socio-economic characteristics was controlled alone by matching, the Protestant values moved toward the Jewish values in a rather similar way, with income taken alone having the least effect and education and occupation taken alone having the most. However, when we matched simultaneously on all the characteristics except income we found that the Protestant values were not moved as closely to the Jewish as in our complete matching procedure. Apparently, income does have an effect not covered completely by the other variables. All of the characteristics appear to have some effect on the final result of close similarity but the independent effect of each cannot be assessed adequately by matching.

The emphasis in this analysis on the differences between Catholics and non-Catholics should not lead to an exaggeration of religious differentials in fertility and family planning. From some points of view the similarities are more striking than the differences. For example, none of the major religious groupings can be characterized as having very large or very small families. Like the other major strata of our population, they place a high value on moderate size families (two to four children). A large majority of Catholics as well as of Protestants and Jews use some form of conception control sometime during the child-bearing period, and many Catholics are using methods of contraception forbidden under Catholic church doctrine. Nevertheless, significant differences remain, and statements that Catholics are fully adopting the Protestant family planning practices are not correct. Moreover, the present analysis seems to indicate that the persistent differences are unlikely to disappear simply as a result of movement to higher socio-economic status among the Catholic population.[14]

[12] The results of Lenski's research, part of the continuing program of the Detroit Area Study of the University of Michigan, appear in Gerhard Lenski, *The Religious Factor: A Sociological Study of Religion's Impact on Politics, Economics, and Family Life,* Garden City, N. Y.: Doubleday & Co., 1961.

[13] Similar results were obtained in a study in West Germany. See R. Freedman, G. Baumert, and M. Bolte, "Expected Family Size and Family Size Values in West Germany," *Population Studies,* 13 (November, 1959), pp. 136–150.

[14] A final note on tests of significance may be in order. In both the total original national sample and the matched panels the differences between Protestants and Catholics, on the one hand, and Jews, on the other, were tested to determine whether they were statistically significant. In the initial sample the mean values for both Catholics and Protestants were significantly higher than for the Jews on all the fertility measures listed and the distribution of Jews was significantly different from that of Catholics and Protestants on the measures involving percentage distributions.

In testing the differences between the matched groups in Table 1 for sampling variability, the correlation between matched pairs was taken into account. In this instance the

Replication

RELIGIOUS AND SOCIAL CLASS DIFFERENCES IN FERTILITY

The replication of Freedman, Whelpton, and Smit's study will use two different measures of fertility: the mean number of children desired by respondents and the mean number of siblings they have. To estimate the influence social class and religious differences exert on actual or desired fertility, this replication will use the following procedure: first, a breakdown of respondents into social class groups; second, a breakdown of the respondents within each social class into three religious groups; third, a comparison of the fertility variables for each relevant breakdown. This procedure permits a separate comparison of religious effects on fertility within each social class—an advantage that Freedman, Whelpton, and Smit's study did not have. It should be noted, however, that the replication does not possess the same rigor in comparisons as existed in the original study for the simple reason that limitations in sample size preclude controlling for duration of marriage, community background, and other relevant characteristics.

Hypothesis

1. State which of the three religious groups has the largest and which the smallest number of siblings per family and which religious groups have the largest and which the smallest desired number of children.

2. State a similar hypothesis about the actual and desired fertility of working class, lower middle class, and upper middle class families.

3. Finally, state whether you think the religious group differences in fertility are independent of social class effects, i.e., when persons of roughly the same social class status are compared, will there still be differences in fertility between religious groups?

Empirical indicators for this problem

8. My mother's religious preference is:
   1. Roman Catholic or Eastern Orthodox
   2. Baptist
   3. Lutheran
   4. Methodist
   5. Presbyterian
   6. Other Protestant, please specify: ________________
   7. Jewish
   8. Other
   9. None

12. Occupational Prestige
   1. Proprietor of a large business (valued at $100,000 or more); Top-level executive in large organization; Top-level professional
   2. Proprietor of a medium business (valued at $35,000 to $100,000); Middle-level executive or official, or top-level of a small organization; Lower-level professional; Sales representatives of manufacturers or wholesalers or other senior salesmen earning $10,000 or more per year; Farmer of farm worth $100,000+
   3. Proprietor of a small business (valued at $6,000 to $35,000); Lower-level official and manager; Semi-professional; Sales representative (as above) earning $7,000 to $10,000 per year; Farmer of farm worth $35,000 to $100,000
   4. Proprietor of a very small business (valued under $6,000); Technician; Sales clerk and salesman earning less than $7,000 per year and clerical workers; Farmer of farm worth $15,000 to $35,000
   5. Farmer of farm worth under $15,000; Skilled manual worker and foreman
   6. Farmer, sharecropper or tenant with little stock or equipment; Semi-skilled worker and machine operator
   7. Unskilled worker

35. How many brothers and sisters do you have?

   __________ brothers __________ sisters

63. How many children do you want to have? ______

Data analysis

NOTE: Half the class will be assigned to do this problem using the data on the number of siblings in the respondent's family (box 35t). The other half of the class will do identical tabulations using the data on the number of children which the respondent desires to have (box 63). However, all figures will be put on the blackboard and everyone is to graph and write the laboratory report using both sets of data.

---

clustering in the original national sample was ignored since the selection procedure for matching eliminated the clustering effect. All the differences between Catholics and Jews remain significant at the .05 level, except for two cases. (The difference in number of births to date is significant at the .10 level and the difference for ideal family size is negligible.) *None* of the differences between Jews and Protestants is significant after matching, except the difference in the proportion who planned the number and spacing of all their pregnancies. In the matched groups all the differences between Protestants and Catholics are significant at the .05 level, except the two already noted for Jews.

1. *Sort* the code sheets into three social class groups on the basis of the father's occupation (box 12).

1 or 2 = Upper Middle Class (UM)
3 or 4 = Lower Middle Class (LM)
5, 6, or 7 = Working Class (W)

2. *Sub-sort* the code sheets for the Upper Middle Class group into three religious groups on the basis of the mother's religion (box 8):

1 = Catholic
2 through 6 = Protestant
7 = Jewish
8 or 9 = Others: Put these aside for the remainder of this problem.

3. *Tally* onto Table 1 of the Tabulation Form the number of siblings in the respondent's family (box 35t) or the number of children *desired* by the respondent (box 63).

4. Repeat steps 2 and 3 for the Lower Middle and Working Class groups.

5. *Compute* the mean number of siblings (or the mean number of children desired) of each religious group. See Appendix C for the short method of computing the mean from tabled data.

6. *Compute* the mean number of siblings (or the desired number of children) for the total of each religious group. To do this:

A. Add the total fx for the Upper Middle Class Catholics to the total fx for the Lower Middle and Working Class Catholics.
B. Do a similar addition for the three Catholic total f's.
C. Divide the grand total fx for Catholics (step A) by the grand total number of Catholics (step B).
D. Repeat steps A, B, and C for the Protestants and then for the Jews.

7. *Graph* the means for the variable you calculated onto Figure 1. Use a solid line for the number of siblings and a dashed line for desired number of children. Then graph the means for the variable calculated by the other half of the class. Your instructor will put them on the blackboard.

Lab report

1. The SUMMARY OF FINDINGS should answer the following questions: (A) Are there differences between religious groups in both actual fertility and planned fertility? (B) Are there differences between social class groups in these variables? (C) Do the religious group differences hold *within* each social class for these variables? (D) Does religion or social class make the greater difference in these two aspects of fertility?

2. The DISCUSSION can include such things as (A) the relative importance of religious ideology (i.e., a cultural factor) as compared to social class (a structural factor) in accounting for fertility differences. (B) The implications of the findings for predicting future religious group differences. Relate the findings to the reading for this problem and other studies you have read, but do not hesitate to advance your own reasoning as well.

References

Davis, Kingsley, "The World's Population Crisis," in Robert K. Merton and Robert A. Nisbet, eds., *Contemporary Social Problems*. New York: Harcourt Brace & World, 1961.

Freedman, Ronald, Pascal K. Whelpton, and Arthur A. Campbell, *Family Planning, Sterility, and Population Growth*. New York: McGraw-Hill, 1959.

Lenski, Gerhard, *The Religious Factor*. New York: Doubleday, 1961, esp. chapters 3 and 5.

Ryder, Norman B., "The Cohort as a Concept in the Study of Social Change," *American Sociological Review*, 30 (December 1965), pp. 843–861.

Westoff, Charles F., "Religion and Fertility in Metropolitan America," in *Thirty Years of Research in Human Fertility*. New York: Milbank Memorial Fund, 1959, pp. 117–134.

Wrong, Dennis, *Population and Society*. New York: Random House, 1956.

Zeitlin, Maurice, "Political Generations in the Cuban Working Class," *American Journal of Sociology*, 71 (March 1966), pp. 493–508.

TABLE 1. Actual OR desired fertility by religion and social class

NO. OF SIBLINGS (Box 35t) OR DESIRED NO. OF CHILDREN (Box 63)	UPPER MIDDLE (Box 12 = 1 or 2)						LOWER MIDDLE (Box 12 = 3 or 4)						WORKING (Box 12 = 5, 6, or 7)					
	Catholic (Box 8 = 1)		Protestant (Box 8 = 2-6)		Jew (Box 8 = 7)		Catholic (Box 8 = 1)		Protestant (Box 8 = 2-6)		Jew (Box 8 = 7)		Catholic (Box 8 = 1)		Protestant (Box 8 = 2-6)		Jew (Box 8 = 7)	
	f	fx	f	fx	f	fx	f	fx	f	fx	f	fx	f	fx	f	fx	f	fx
0																		
1																		
2																		
3																		
4																		
5																		
6																		
7																		
8																		
9 and over																		
TOTAL																		
Mean																		
+ (No info.)		X		X		X		X		X		X		X		X		X

Mean for all Catholics: _____ Mean for all Protestants: _____ Mean for all Jews: _____

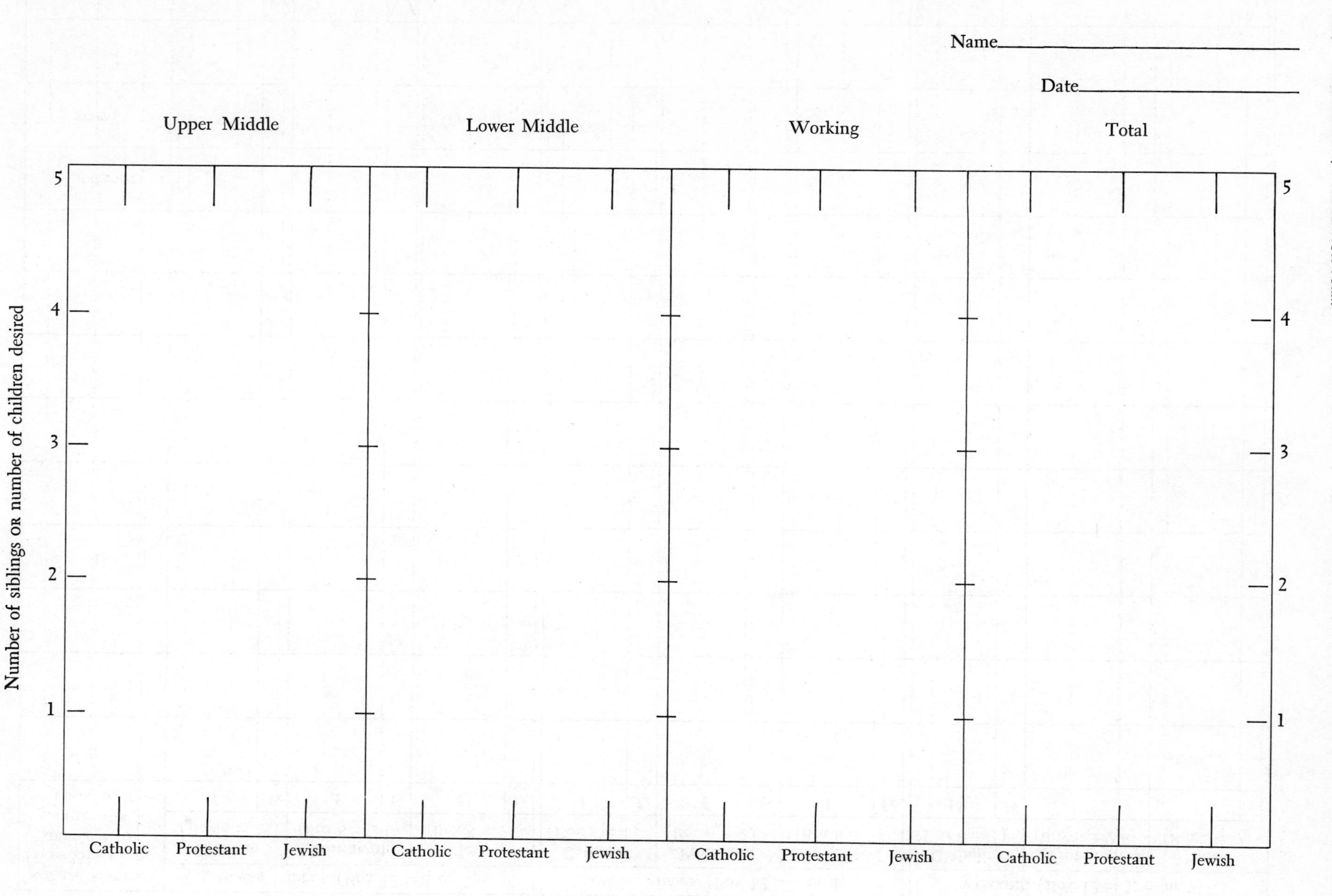
Name
Date
Upper Middle
Lower Middle
Working
Total
5
4
3
2
1
Number of siblings or number of children desired
Catholic
Protestant
Jewish
Catholic
Protestant
Jewish
Catholic
Protestant
Jewish
Catholic
Protestant
Jewish

LABORATORY REPORT FOR PROBLEM ________

Course or Section ________ Date ________ Name ________

HYPOTHESIS: ________

SAMPLE: ________

INDEPENDENT VARIABLE(S): ________

DEPENDENT VARIABLE(S): ________

OTHER FACTORS: ________

LABORATORY REPORT FOR PROBLEM__________

SUMMARY OF FINDINGS: __________

DISCUSSION: __________

Modern data analysis X

PROBLEM 22

CARDS AND COMPUTERS

Most sociological research is done with the aid of punched cards. A rapidly growing portion of this research also makes use of computers. In addition, as the ever-present punched card indicates, the use of computers is a technological development of profound and growing importance for all aspects of modern life. This problem is intended to give you an understanding and an appreciation of these techniques, but, of course, not to actually teach you how to use this equipment.

1. *The Cards.* An explanation and examples of punched-card recording are given in the reading for this problem. In addition, you should reread the portion of the article by Quinn (Problem 1) which describes the machines used to analyze punched cards. Note that one important difference between a code-sheet *box* and a punched-card *column* is that each column of the punched card usually contains only a single digit.

2. *Card Punch.* This machine is operated like a typewriter. However, instead of printing letters on a page, the keys punch holes in a card. Each card can record only 80 numbers or letters, so that it is often necessary to have several cards per respondent. For example, the information on the code sheets you have been using for this course would require at least three punched cards for each respondent.

3. *Counter-Sorter.* This machine was the basic tool for quantitative research in sociology until the introduction of computers, and it is still widely used today. It does exactly the operations you have been doing in sorting and tallying your code sheets. The difference between machine sorting and hand sorting is that whereas it took you about half an hour to cross-tabulate only 100 or so code sheets, the very slowest counter-sorters work at a speed of 250 cards a *minute*, and many run at 400 cards per minute.

4. *Reproducer.* Decks of cards wear out or jam in a machine and are spoiled. For these and other reasons it is usually necessary to have a second or third copy of the cards. These can easily be made in the reproducer. The punched deck of cards is placed in one hopper (the "read side") and a stack of blank cards is placed in the other hopper (the "punch side"). The start button is pressed and the two groups of cards are fed through the machine at the rate of 100 cards per minute. When they emerge into the two lower hoppers, the formerly blank cards will be punched in the same way as the original deck.

5. *Computer.* A computer is capable of an almost infinite variety of tasks. It is able to do the cross-tabulations which you have done by hand using code sheets and which can also be done on the counter-sorter using punched cards. Just as the counter-sorter could do the tabulations many times faster than you could do them by hand, the computer can do them many times faster than can be done on the counter-sorter. In addition, it will also calculate percentages and averages. Finally, it prints out the results in a neat and error-free form, as is shown in the example in the reading of a study of political party preference and voting.

RECORDING POLITICAL DATA ON PUNCHCARDS / *Kenneth Janda*

When a governmental official acts in an unexpected manner, computer-oriented political scientists may be taunted by the question, "How are you going to put *that* on punchcards?" This question, taken literally, suggests the existence of an important communications gap among political scientists. Some students of politics may be genuinely curious about "how" political data are put on punchcards. Knowledge of this process is basic for understanding the use of data processing equipment in political research, and this chapter describes ways in which various political data are recorded on punchcards.

The familiar "IBM card" will be discussed as an information-carrying medium. Next, standard procedures for recording different types of political information on punchcards will be briefly outlined—avoiding details that might confuse the beginner. . . .

The punchcard

Although several types of punchcards are in use today, the most popular type is the 80 column card pictured in Figure 1. Each of the 80 vertical columns contains 12 punching positions that appear as horizontal rows across the card. Numbers from 0 to 9 are printed across the bottom ten rows. Above the 0 row are two unmarked positions—the 12 and 11 rows. Information can be entered into a card by punching holes in the proper rows and columns. These holes then are "read" by data processing equipment and are interpreted as numbers, letters, or special characters according to the coding system devised by Herman Hollerith around 1900 and now referred to as "Hollerith code."

Any number from zero to nine can be represented by a single punch in the 0–9 positions in any given column. A single punch in the 12 row (for any column) is ordinarily interpreted as a plus sign; a punch in the 11 row ordinarily indicates a minus sign. Letters of the alphabet are produced by combining in a single column a "digit" punch (1–9) with a "zone" punch (12, 11, or 0). Special characters can be produced by certain combinations of two or more punches per column. The characters punched in the columns can be printed simultaneously at the top of the card at the time it is punched. Figure 1 shows the common punchboard characters printed above the hole combinations that produce them.

To understand how these holes in thin cardboard can contain political data, one must become familiar with the term "field." The 80 columns on a card can be allocated so that certain columns are reserved for one type of information and other columns for other types. A *field* is a group of adjacent columns reserved for a given type of information. A field may vary in width from one to eighty columns, depending on the number of columns needed to record the information. The arrangement or layout of fields for recording data is called the card *format*. The format for recording a particular type of information is determined before the data are punched into the card, and all cards in a given study generally follow the same format.

The manner in which these fields are used to record information depends on the nature of the data. *Quantitative* data, such as election returns or governmental expenditures, can be recorded on a card simply by punching the numerical value directly into the proper field. These punches can be given a literal interpretation: the digits "300" punched into a three-column field *mean* the number "three hundred."

Given the fact that a punchcard can carry alphabetical as well as numerical information, it may seem that *qualitative* data, which is of great interest to political scientists, could also be put on cards simply by punching directly into fields of adequate length. In truth, this can be done, but a number of technical problems exist in processing alphabetical information. These problems are not present in processing numerical data.

Using computing equipment to manipulate and analyze words and sentences is something called *information processing* or *information retrieval* instead of "data processing." . . . it is sufficient to say that qualitative data are not usually recorded directly on cards and instead are "coded" into numerical categories, which then are punched into appropriate fields. The punches in these fields defy literal interpretation, and their meaning must be deciphered with a code book that identifies punches that represent specified information.

Some concrete examples of political data in punchcard form will soon be presented to illustrate this discussion. But first, it is helpful to stress a basic similarity between the punchcards used by a researcher and the common 3 x 5 or 4 x 6 index cards. Punchcards and ordinary index cards both carry information. The main difference between the two lies in their representation of information. Information is carried on punchcards in the form of holes, while it is written or typed on index cards. The information on either type of card depends on the research problem and the researcher's decisions.

The researcher who uses index cards to study generals in battles must decide whether the data should be organized by generals or by battles. Whether he uses a different card for each general or a different card for each battle depends on the organization of information in his sources and the questions he wants to answer. He then has to decide what information to record, on what part of the card to record it, and how

Reprinted with permission of the author and publisher from Kenneth Janda, *Data Processing: Applications to Political Research.* Evanston, Ill.: Northwestern University Press, 1965, pp. 15–23.

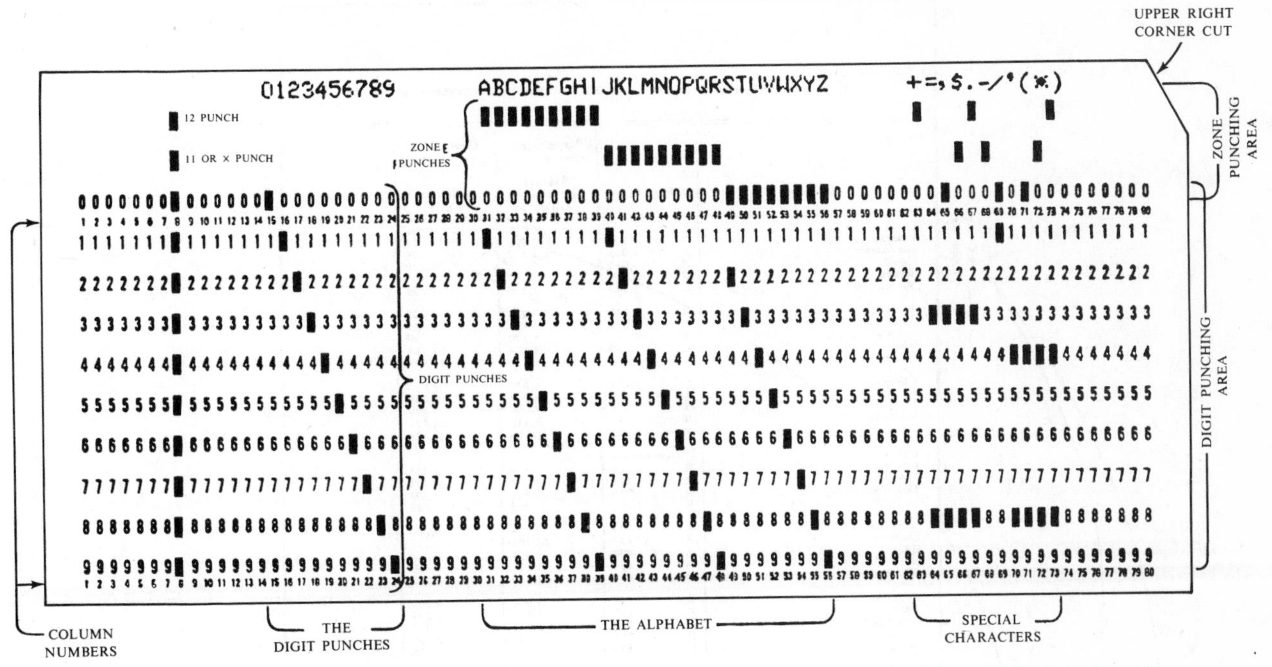

FIGURE 1. A punchcard and punching positions. Courtesy of International Business Machines Corporation.

to label or mark the cards so he can pull out the information he needs when he wants it.

These considerations also are involved when punchcards are used instead of index cards. The researcher still must decide how to organize his data, what to record, where to record it, and how to label his units of observation. Many decisions are similar because the *function* of both types of cards is similar when carrying research information. The punchcard's essential advantage as an information-carrying medium is that punchcards can be read, manipulated, and analyzed by machines; index cards cannot.

The payoffs from machine processing of punchcard data were enumerated in previously. Examples of computer analyses in political research will be given in later chapters. The following section illustrates how various types of political data can be put on punchcards. Election returns, responses to public opinion surveys, biographical information about political actors, characteristics of political institutions, roll call votes in legislative bodies, legislators' committee assignments, legislative histories of bills, instances of human conflict, and interactions in United Nations committee meetings have been selected as illustrations.

Election returns

The votes cast in precincts, wards, counties, and states for Democratic and Republican candidates are a basic source of data for students of American government and political behavior. Official election returns constitute one type of aggregate data—observations reported on groups of people living in a given area rather than on particular individuals. Familiar examples of aggregate data can be found in census-type information, such as the percentage of non-white population in a city block or the number of persons in a county engaged in farming. The same considerations and procedures involved in recording election returns on punchcards can be applied to various types of aggregate data. In general, aggregate data are easily put on punchcards and are especially suited to the powerful arithmetical capabilities of modern computers.

Voting returns for major state and national offices contested in recent elections are available in official state publications. In general, the county is the most common unit for reporting these returns. Figure 2 shows a page from the official Illinois publication of the 1962 vote by counties for the office of U.S. Senator. The counties are listed alphabetically along with the votes cast within each county for the Republican and Democratic candidates. Most states publish their official election reports in similar format.

The standard method of putting election returns on cards is to use different cards for votes cast in given areas for given offices. Figure 2 shows separate cards used in recording votes from Illinois' Adams and Alexander counties. Because Illinois has 102 counties, 102 cards are needed to record the votes from all counties for each statewide election. If it is considered desirable to break down the Cook County (Chicago and suburbs) vote by wards and townships, additional cards may be used to record votes in these subdivisions.

Transcribing information from official reports to punchcards involves both "direct" and "coded" punching. In Figure 2, three separate fields are arbitrarily laid out on the card for recording (1) the county identification code, (2) the Republican vote, and (3) the Democratic vote. The first field (columns 1–3) contains a simple three-digit code that assigns num-

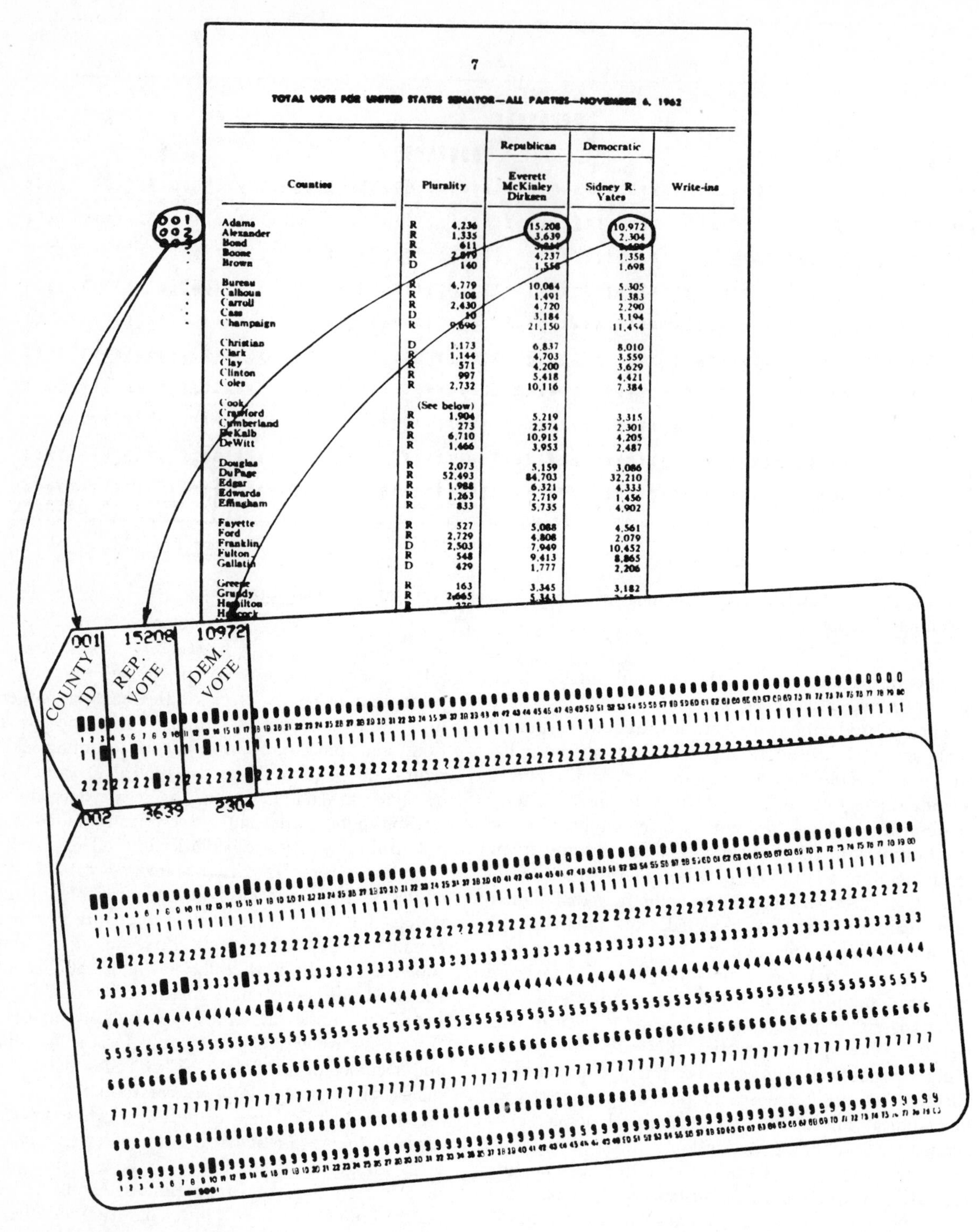

7

TOTAL VOTE FOR UNITED STATES SENATOR—ALL PARTIES—NOVEMBER 6, 1962

Counties	Plurality		Republican: Everett McKinley Dirksen	Democratic: Sidney R. Yates	Write-ins
Adams	R	4,236	15,208	10,972	
Alexander	R	1,335	3,639	2,304	
Bond	R	611	[illegible]	[illegible]	
Boone	R	[illegible]	4,237	1,358	
Brown	D	140	1,556	1,698	
Bureau	R	4,779	10,084	5,305	
Calhoun	R	108	1,491	1,383	
Carroll	R	2,430	4,720	2,290	
Cass	D	10	3,184	3,194	
Champaign	R	9,696	21,150	11,454	
Christian	D	1,173	6,837	8,010	
Clark	R	1,144	4,703	3,559	
Clay	R	571	4,200	3,629	
Clinton	R	997	5,418	4,421	
Coles	R	2,732	10,116	7,384	
Cook		(See below)			
Crawford	R	1,904	5,219	3,315	
Cumberland	R	273	2,574	2,301	
DeKalb	R	6,710	10,915	4,205	
DeWitt	R	1,466	3,953	2,487	
Douglas	R	2,073	5,159	3,086	
DuPage	R	52,493	84,703	32,210	
Edgar	R	1,988	6,321	4,333	
Edwards	R	1,263	2,719	1,456	
Effingham	R	833	5,735	4,902	
Fayette	R	527	5,088	4,561	
Ford	R	2,729	4,808	2,079	
Franklin	D	2,503	7,949	10,452	
Fulton	R	548	9,413	8,865	
Gallatin	D	429	1,777	2,206	
Greene	R	163	3,345	3,182	
Grundy	R	2,665	5,343	[illegible]	
Hamilton	[illegible]	[illegible]	[illegible]	[illegible]	
Hancock	[illegible]	[illegible]	[illegible]	[illegible]	

FIGURE 2. Recording election returns on punchcards.

bers to the counties according to their alphabetical order. The Republican vote is punched directly into the second field (columns 4–10) and the Democratic vote into the third field (columns 11–17). Note that the commas in official vote reports are not recorded on the card, and the figures are entered in the card fields with the units at the left. This is called a "right-justified" field. It is standard practice to right-justify numerical data entered in fields that are wider than the number of digits in the data. In general, card fields are made wide enough to accommodate the largest anticipated value, and the vote fields in Figure 2 were made seven digits wide to handle votes in the millions as might be cast in Cook County.

The simple card format discussed here captures only the most essential facts: the county identification codes and the party vote. The parties' pluralities in each county are not usually recorded because the computer can calculate pluralities from the vote totals far more easily and accurately than they can be recorded

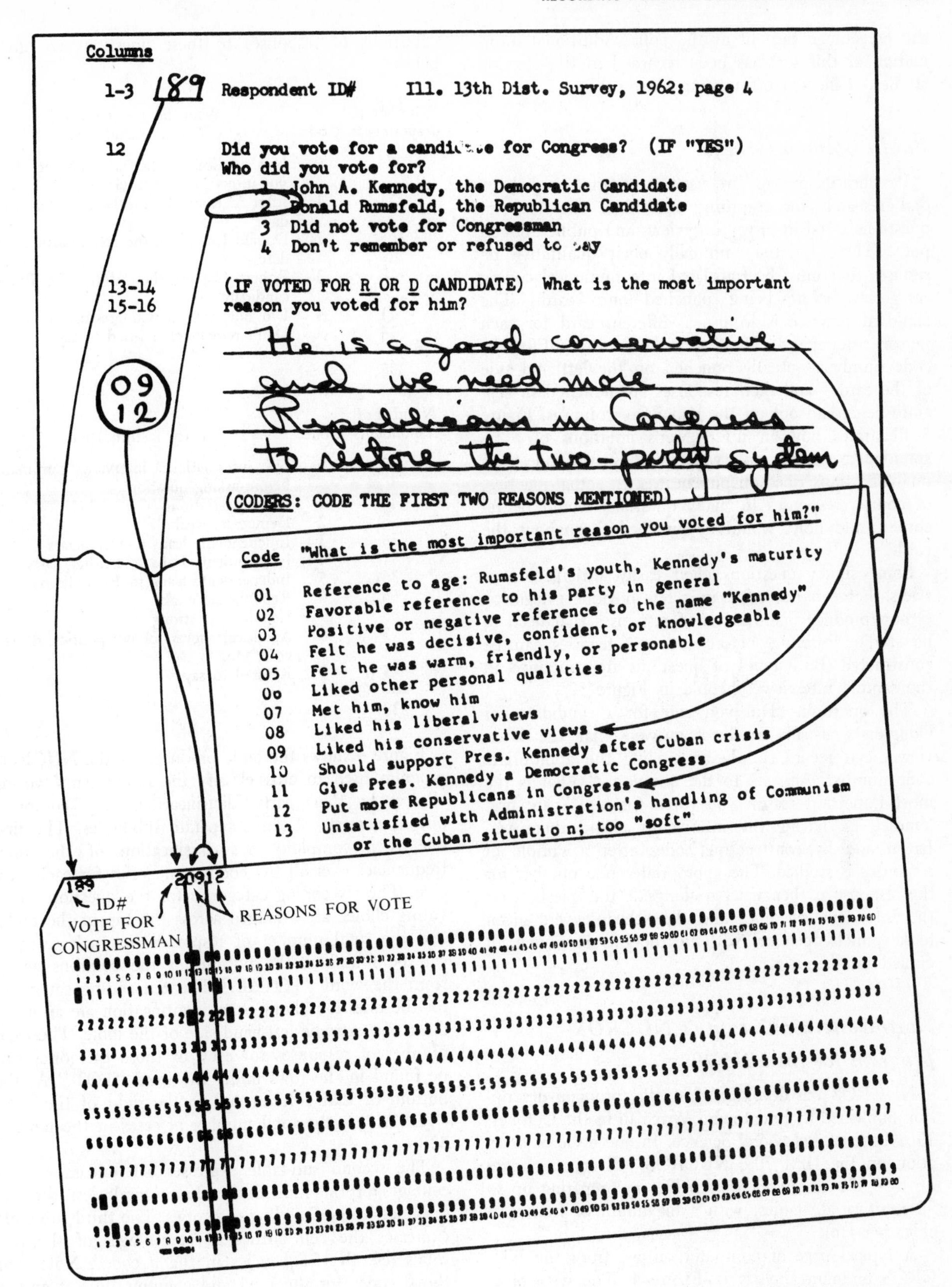

Columns

1-3 189 Respondent ID# Ill. 13th Dist. Survey, 1962: page 4

12 Did you vote for a candidate for Congress? (IF "YES") Who did you vote for?
1 John A. Kennedy, the Democratic Candidate
2 Donald Rumsfeld, the Republican Candidate
3 Did not vote for Congressman
4 Don't remember or refused to say

13-14
15-16 (IF VOTED FOR R OR D CANDIDATE) What is the most important reason you voted for him?

He is a good conservative and we need more Republicans in Congress to restore the two-party system

(CODERS: CODE THE FIRST TWO REASONS MENTIONED)

09
12

Code "What is the most important reason you voted for him?"

01 Reference to age: Rumsfeld's youth, Kennedy's maturity
02 Favorable reference to his party in general
03 Positive or negative reference to the name "Kennedy"
04 Felt he was decisive, confident, or knowledgeable
05 Felt he was warm, friendly, or personable
06 Liked other personal qualities
07 Met him, know him
08 Liked his liberal views
09 Liked his conservative views
10 Should support Pres. Kennedy after Cuban crisis
11 Give Pres. Kennedy a Democratic Congress
12 Put more Republicans in Congress
13 Unsatisfied with Administration's handling of Communism or the Cuban situation; too "soft"

FIGURE 3. Recording interview responses on punchcards.

on cards from the published report. It often is desirable, however, to punch other information in the cards while the raw data are being recorded. If the cards are to become part of a large library of punchcard holdings, it is useful to include codes for the offices being contested and for the election years. Estimates of the eligible electorate in each county should also be recorded if the computer is to calculate the percentage turnout at the polls. Additional information of this sort has been recorded in the election studies on file at Northwestern University. . . .

Public opinion surveys

Punchcards perhaps are used most often in behavioral research for recording individual responses to questions asked in survey interviews and public opinion polls. These questions normally elicit qualitative responses that must be translated into numerical coding categories before being punched onto cards. The standard practice is to use a different card for each person interviewed. The respondents are identified by code numbers—usually punched on the lefthand side of the cards—and their responses are punched in separate fields laid out on the remaining columns. Figure 3 illustrates how an interviewer's notations of a respondent's answers to two typical survey questions might be transcribed on punchcards. In actual practice, of course, responses to many questions would be recorded, and holes would be punched throughout the card.

Some survey questions elicit easily anticipated answers that can be coded in a few obvious categories. Others produce rich and varied responses that need to be studied carefully before coding categories can be constructed. Both types of questions are contained in the sample interview schedule in Figure 3.

The question, "Did you vote for a candidate for Congress?" usually produces answers that the interviewer can record simply by circling the appropriate code number. Answers to the question, "What is the most important reason you voted for him?" are best handled by having the interviewer record them verbatim and by constructing codes after a sample of responses is studied. The appropriate code number for the response is then written alongside the question on the interview schedule, and the schedules are given to keypunch operators with instructions to punch all circled numbers.

Northwestern university's NUCROS program for the IBM 709

NUCROS was developed from the program description published by Bonato and Waxman in the October, 1961 issue of *Behavioral Science*. In one cycle of operation on the IBM 709, NUCROS will accommodate up to 9,999 cases and 40 variables in preparing up to 72 *multivariate* tables, with a maximum of four variables per table.

A typical page of computer output from the NUCROS program appears in Figure 4. The data processed for this example were gathered from student interviews conducted both before and after the 1962 election in Illinois' 13th Congressional District. Two of the questions in the interview deal with the respondent's choice for Congressman and his party identification. The actual coding categories and distributions of responses to these questions are given below.

Number of respondents	*Code*	*Who did you vote for? (Congressional race)*
74	0	Not applicable: did not vote at all or not interviewed after election
71	1	John A. Kennedy, the Democratic candidate
165	2	Donald Rumsfeld, the Republican candidate
3	3	Robert Cosbey, the "Voters for Peace" candidate
11	4	Did not vote for Congressman
14	5	Don't remember, refused to say
338		

Number of respondents	*Code*	*Party identification*
2	0	No information: interview terminated before asking question
48	1	Democrat: strong
38	2	Democrat: weak
34	3	Independent: leans to Democrats
31	4	Independent: leans to neither party
36	5	Independent: leans to Republicans
56	6	Republican: weak
85	7	Republican: strong
3	8	Apolitical: never follows politics, doesn't vote, etc.
5	9	Refused to say
338		

Figure 4 shows the table produced by the NUCROS program used to cross-classify the respondents' voting choices by their party identifications. The computer output consists of three separate sub-tables. The first one is a complete cross-classification of the total frequencies over all the coding categories for each variable. The six coding categories for the question about voting choice are arranged across the top of the table, and the total number of responses for each category can be found at the bottom of the *columns* across from the word "TOTAL." The ten coding categories for the question about party identification are arranged down the extreme left-hand side of the table. The total number of responses for each of those categories can be found in the *rows* under the word "TOT." At the bottom of that column and to the right of the word "TOTAL" is the total number of cases in the table—338.

The second sub-table expresses cell entries as percentages of the individual *column* totals *less* the frequencies in the *0* coding categories. The third sub-table expresses the cell entries as percentages of the *row* totals less the frequencies in the *0* codes. Note that the *0* codes for the rows and columns do not appear at all in the two percentagized sub-tables. Note also that when the *0* categories are excluded from these sub-tables the total number of cases drops from 338 to 262. The 76 cases "lost" in the percentagizing process had been in one or the other of the *0* categories.

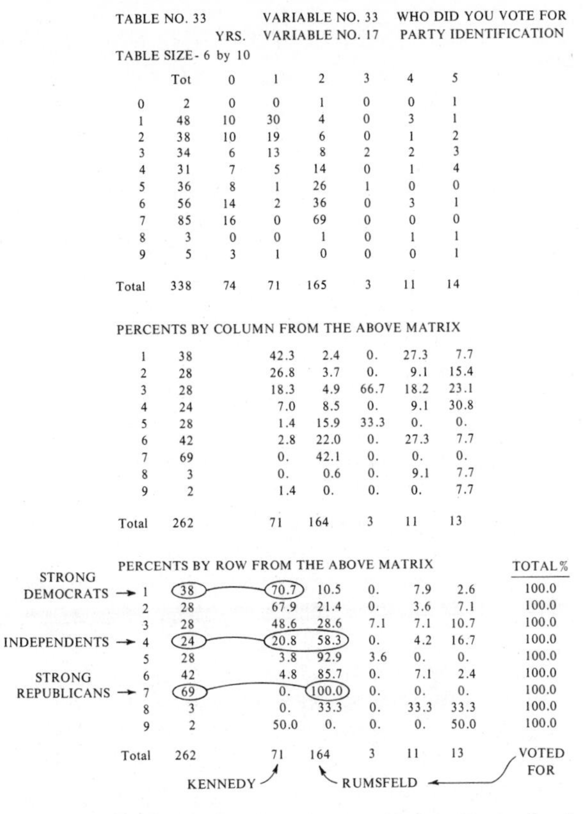

TABLE NO. 33 VARIABLE NO. 33 WHO DID YOU VOTE FOR
YRS. VARIABLE NO. 17 PARTY IDENTIFICATION
TABLE SIZE- 6 by 10

	Tot	0	1	2	3	4	5
0	2	0	0	1	0	0	1
1	48	10	30	4	0	3	1
2	38	10	19	6	0	1	2
3	34	6	13	8	2	2	3
4	31	7	5	14	0	1	4
5	36	8	1	26	1	0	0
6	56	14	2	36	0	3	1
7	85	16	0	69	0	0	0
8	3	0	0	1	0	1	1
9	5	3	1	0	0	0	1
Total	338	74	71	165	3	11	14

PERCENTS BY COLUMN FROM THE ABOVE MATRIX

1	38		42.3	2.4	0.	27.3	7.7
2	28		26.8	3.7	0.	9.1	15.4
3	28		18.3	4.9	66.7	18.2	23.1
4	24		7.0	8.5	0.	9.1	30.8
5	28		1.4	15.9	33.3	0.	0.
6	42		2.8	22.0	0.	27.3	7.7
7	69		0.	42.1	0.	0.	0.
8	3		0.	0.6	0.	9.1	7.7
9	2		1.4	0.	0.	0.	7.7
Total	262		71	164	3	11	13

PERCENTS BY ROW FROM THE ABOVE MATRIX

									TOTAL%
STRONG DEMOCRATS →	1	38		70.7	10.5	0.	7.9	2.6	100.0
	2	28		67.9	21.4	0.	3.6	7.1	100.0
	3	28		48.6	28.6	7.1	7.1	10.7	100.0
INDEPENDENTS →	4	24		20.8	58.3	0.	4.2	16.7	100.0
	5	28		3.8	92.9	3.6	0.	0.	100.0
STRONG	6	42		4.8	85.7	0.	7.1	2.4	100.0
REPUBLICANS →	7	69		0.	100.0	0.	0.	0.	100.0
	8	3		0.	33.3	0.	33.3	33.3	100.0
	9	2		50.0	0.	0.	0.	50.0	100.0
	Total	262		71	164	3	11	13	VOTED FOR

FIGURE 4. NUCROS computer output: cross-classifying voting choice by party.

The NUCROS program was designed to drop *0* codes in computing percentages (and in calculating statistics of association) in order to facilitate data analysis. It often is desirable to exclude cases of "no response" from analysis. If the *0* code is reserved for such "no information" or "not applicable" categories (as in the example), these cases are automatically kept out of statistical computations but are available for inspection in the frequency table. If it is desirable to include these categories for any variables in the computations, they can be included automatically through the recoding process by adding the value *1* to the codes for those variables. Although it was not used in the example, the NUCROS program also provides a method to exclude from analysis the eight respondents who could not be assigned a meaningful party identification (codes 8 and 9) and the twenty-eight respondents who did not report voting for the major party candidates (codes 3, 4, and 5).

The NUCROS program produces neatly printed tables that are easy to read and interpret. The strong relationship between party identification and voting choice can be seen clearly in the data of Figure 4. Democrats (codes 1 and 2) preferred the Democratic candidate John A. Kennedy (code 1), and Republicans (codes 6 and 7) favored the Republican candidate Donald Rumsfeld (code 2). Because we expect a person's party identification to affect his vote (not the other way around), "party identification" is referred to as an *independent* variable and "voting choice" as a *dependent* variable. Percentages usually have more meaning for the researcher if they are computed from the totals of the independent variable—in this case "party." When the data are percentagized by rows as in the third sub-table, we find that 78.9% of the strong Democrats in our sample voted for Kennedy, and 100% of the strong Republicans voted for Rumsfeld. Rumsfeld also did better with the pure Independents, getting 58.3% of their vote to Kennedy's 20.8%. (Our sample gave about 69% of the reported choices to Rumsfeld, who really got only about 62% of the total vote in the election. We were aware, however, that the sampling procedures used in this class project favored interviewing Republicans.)

Replication

DEMONSTRATION OF PUNCHED CARDS AND COMPUTERS

If time and facilities permit, your instructor may demonstrate the cards and equipment described above. For example, he might give each of you a punched card which has the same information punched on it as one of the code sheets. You can then compare the two and see how the numbers in the code sheet boxes correspond to the numbers punched out of the card. (If the class is small and the facilities are available, you might each be given the opportunity to punch some cards.) Similarly, besides demonstrating each of the machines described above, one of the cross-tabulations done for one of the laboratory problems might be repeated using the counter-sorter.

References

Adler, Irving, *Thinking Machines*. New York: New American Library, Signet Books, 1961.

Arnold, Robert R., Harold C. Hill, and Nicholas V. Alymer, *Introduction to Data Processing*. New York: Wiley, 1966.

Green, Bert L., *Digital Computers in Research: An Introduction for Behavioral and Social Scientists*. New York: McGraw-Hill, 1963.

Appendixes

APPENDIX A
OUTLINE FOR LABORATORY REPORTS

The following outline is a general set of directions to be used in writing laboratory reports. The reports are to be written on the perforated sheet appended to each problem. Obviously, a general set of directions cannot cover every possible contingency that may arise. If, for example, you consider something to be important and it is not covered in this outline, feel free to add it. These directions provide only a sketch of the minimum material to be covered in your reports. They are designed to guide your thoughts rather than straitjacket them.

HYPOTHESIS. (1) A hypothesis is a statement of an anticipated relationship between variables, as for example, "high income families have less children than low income families," or "persons with a college education are more tolerant than persons with a high school or grade school education." In phrasing the hypothesis, emphasize the way the independent variable is related to the dependent variable. You should base your hypothesis primarily on the findings of the original study which is reprinted as the reading for each problem. However, information available from other sources such as your textbook, lectures, previous courses, or the special characteristics of the replication (such as the nature of the sample) might lead you to pose a different hypothesis. (2) State the hypothesis in the present tense. This custom is followed because a hypothesis is a statement of what the investigator thinks is the actual present state of the real world and of the relationships which exist between variables. (3) Always be sure to give a brief justification or explanation for your hypothesis. (4) Write the hypothesis *before* coming to class to do the problem, or in any case before tabulating the data. Do *not* change the hypothesis to fit the findings. Hypotheses are often proved wrong by evidence, and this may be the basis for a new understanding of the issue being investigated. Bear in mind, however, that the hypothesis may be correct despite your findings. This could happen if the sample is inappropriate for the issue being tested or if the measurement of the variable used to test the hypothesis is inadequate.

SAMPLE. (1) Describe how the sample was chosen and how many cases are included. (2) Describe relevant characteristics of the sample such as age, sex, SES. (3) If there are any characteristics of the sample which might influence the findings, list and explain them. NOTE: After the first laboratory report only those characteristics of the sample which might affect the findings need be given.

INDEPENDENT VARIABLE (OR VARIABLES). The variable which is assumed to be causing change is the independent variable.[1] State what the variable is *and* how it is measured. It is important to specify how a variable is measured because different measurement procedures can produce different results, as in the case of an oral and rectal thermometer.

DEPENDENT VARIABLE (OR VARIABLES). The variable which is assumed to be caused by or influenced by changes or variations in the independent variable.[2] State what the variable is *and* how it is measured.

OTHER FACTORS. Confine the listing to those which are important for understanding the results of the research. If a *control variable* is employed, explain it here.

SUMMARY OF FINDINGS. Summarize the literal facts or relationships found. State the findings without using statistics: for example, "First born children are more often high in social responsibility than later born children." However, you may also use specific figures if these can be given briefly. You could, for example, add to the previous statement: ". . . as shown by the finding of 20% of first-born children with high responsibility scores as compared to only 10% of middle or youngest children." State whether your hypothesis is refuted, accepted, or partially accepted. Remember that your results can differ from those of the original study in certain ways yet still lead

[1] Although the terms "cause" and "influenced by" are used to describe the independent and dependent variables, it is important to note that most of the problems in this book do not provide clear evidence of cause and effect. See the "Note On Interpreting Cause and Effect" on page 336 for further explanation.

[2] See footnote 1.

to the same conclusion. For example, suppose the original study used a ten-point scale to measure a variable and found that group A had an average of 7.3 as compared to 5.8 for group B. Suppose further that your replication used a five-point scale rather than the original ten-point scale to measure this variable. If the analysis showed group A to have a mean score of 3.5 and group B to have a mean score of 2.4, you would conclude that the replication confirmed the finding of the original study because in both the original study and in your replication group A had a higher score than group B. In short, you should base your summary of the findings and acceptance or rejection of the hypothesis on what the statistics show about relationships between variables, rather than on the absolute values of the score.

DISCUSSION. This section should provide an *interpretation* of the findings, i.e., (1) what accounts for the findings, or (2) what do the findings mean, or (3) what is the importance of the findings. Example: "The findings are consistent with and support the theory that parents have stricter expectations for first-born children, and tend to let later born children get away with more. Thus first borns grow up. . . ." The discussion is one of the places where the scientist can (and should) be speculative and imaginative.

A note on interpreting cause and effect

The goal of all sciences is to discover cause-and-effect relationships. To establish causality, three criteria have to be met: It must be demonstrated first that there is a relationship between two variables; second, that this relationship is due to the variables under examination and not to some third, "confounding" variable; and third, that the presumed causal or independent variable occurs prior in time to the presumed effect, or the dependent variable (see Selltiz *et al.*, 1960).

The difficulties in establishing causal sequences in sociology stem primarily from the fact that much research is inadequately designed to provide information on the temporal sequence of variables. In most examples of sociological research, as in most of the problems contained in the present laboratory manual, data are gathered from a cross-section of some population at one particular point in time. Whatever the advantages of cross-sectional research may be in terms of minimizing the costs of data collection, the procedure imposes severe limitations on assessing causality: Information obtained at a single point in time provides few clues as to whether one variable occurred *prior* to the other. For example, if a "status concern" scale and also a "racial prejudice" scale were given to a sample, it might be found that those with high scores for status concern also have high prejudice scores. It would be plausible to maintain that status concern brings about feelings of insecurity that are eventually manifested in prejudice. However, this relationship, while interesting, would not constitute proof that status concern *causes* prejudice. It would be equally plausible to argue that persons already prejudiced develop an awareness of status to rationalize their racial views. With cross-sectional data the researcher may have little besides his own intuitive judgment to determine which alternative represents the correct causal sequence.

In some instances judgments about the temporal sequence may be easy to make and need not rest heavily on speculation. For example, if a relationship was demonstrated between religion and fertility plans, it would be relatively safe to say that religion, a status usually ascribed at birth, precedes fertility plans rather than vice versa. Even in this illustration, however, it is not legitimate to maintain that religion *causes* differences in fertility plans. Religious denominations and fertility plans are each known to differ by social class, and it may be that the observed relationship is due to the tendency of one religious group to be higher than the other group in social class standing, and the additional tendency of persons high in class standing to plan having fewer children. (See Problem 21.)

CONTROL VARIABLES. The problem just described can be handled with cross-sectional data by introducing "controls" for class. To do this, it would be necessary to divide the sample into relatively homogeneous social class groupings, and within each class group compare the relationship between religion and fertility plans. By confining comparisons to each homogeneous class group, the effects of social class are ruled out, or at least minimized. Two outcomes are relevant: If the original relationship between religion and fertility was not due to class, the relationship should persist for each comparison; if, however, the relationship was due to class, then holding class constant should make the relationship disappear. Again, however, the use of a control for class does not *prove* causality; it is always possible that class is the wrong variable to control. This additional difficulty illustrates the endless problems involved in establishing cause-and-effect relationships with data gathered from cross-sectional research designs.

The one research procedure capable of most clearly establishing cause and effect is the experimental method. In the experiment the researcher introduces a variable to one group, withholds it from another group, and then observes whether differences between groups emerge on some dependent variable. If differences do come about, the researcher can often attribute them to the experimental variable. Unlike cross-sectional research, experimental variables are introduced at a definite point in time prior to the emergence of the dependent variable, thus clarifying the temporal sequence. Also, it is possible in experiments to administer the experimental variable to a *randomly selected* group of persons. This method minimizes the possibility that other common characteristics and experiences of these persons may confound the relationship (Selltiz *et al.*, 1960). Because of these and other advantages, all sciences try to use the experimental method wherever possible. In sociology the use of this method is slowly gaining acceptance (Zelditch and Hopkins, 1961). The present manual contains three studies (Problems 4, 5, and 6) which approximate experimental designs.

References

Selltiz, Claire, Marie Jahoda, Morton Deutsch, and Stuart W. Cook, *Methods in Social Relations*. New York: Holt, Rinehart and Winston, 1960, chapter 4.

Rosenthal, Robert, *Experimenter Effects in Behavorial Research*. New York: Appleton-Century-Crofts, 1966.

Zelditch, Morris and Terrence K. Hopkins, "Experiments with Organizations," in Amati Etzioni, ed., *Complex Organizations*. New York: Holt, Rinehart and Winston, 1961.

APPENDIX B

PERCENTAGES OF INTEGERS FROM 1 TO 144

COMPUTING PERCENTAGES FOR BASE NUMBERS UP TO 72. To find what percent 7 is of 18, turn to the column headed 18. Look down the column to 7 and read the percentage to the right: 38.9%. For purposes of the problems in this book, round all decimals to whole percents; in the illustration above, 38.9% is rounded to 39%.

COMPUTING PERCENTAGES FOR BASE NUMBERS 73 TO 144. Divide in half both the base number and the figure to be converted to a percentage, and proceed as illustrated above. For example, to find what percent 66 is of 80, find the column headed 40 and read the percent to the left of 33, e.g. 82.5%, or rounded, 83%. In the case of odd-numbered figures, use the next higher number. For example, to find what percent 83 is of 141, find the column headed 71 and read the percent to the left of 42, e.g. 59.2%, or rounded, 59%.

	1	2	3	4	5	6	7	8	9
1	100.0	50.0	33.3	25.0	20.0	16.7	14.3	12.5	11.1
2		100.0	66.7	50.0	40.0	33.3	28.6	25.0	22.2
3			100.0	75.0	60.0	50.0	42.9	37.5	33.3
4				100.0	80.0	66.7	57.1	50.0	44.4
5					100.0	83.3	71.4	62.5	55.6
6						100.0	85.7	75.0	66.7
7							100.0	87.5	77.8
8								100.0	88.9
9									100.0

	10	11	12	13	14	15	16	17	18
1	10.0	9.1	8.3	7.7	7.1	6.7	6.3	5.9	5.6
2	20.0	18.2	16.7	15.4	14.3	13.3	12.5	11.8	11.1
3	30.0	27.3	25.0	23.1	21.4	20.0	18.8	17.6	16.7
4	40.0	36.4	33.3	30.8	28.6	26.7	25.0	23.5	22.2
5	50.0	45.5	41.7	38.5	35.7	33.3	31.3	29.4	27.8
6	60.0	54.5	50.0	46.2	42.9	40.0	37.5	35.3	33.3
7	70.0	63.6	58.3	53.8	50.0	46.7	43.8	41.2	38.9
8	80.0	72.7	66.7	61.5	57.1	53.3	50.0	47.1	44.4
9	90.0	81.8	75.0	69.2	64.3	60.0	56.3	52.9	50.0
10	100.0	90.9	83.3	76.9	71.4	66.7	62.5	58.8	55.6
11		100.0	91.7	84.6	78.6	73.3	68.8	64.7	61.1
12			100.0	92.3	85.7	80.0	75.0	70.6	66.7
13				100.0	92.9	86.7	81.3	76.5	72.2
14					100.0	93.3	87.5	82.4	77.8
15						100.0	93.8	88.2	83.3
16							100.0	94.1	88.9
17								100.0	94.4
18									100.0

	19	20	21	22	23	24	25	26	27
1	5.3	5.0	4.8	4.5	4.3	4.2	4.0	3.8	3.7
2	10.5	10.0	9.5	9.1	8.7	8.3	8.0	7.7	7.4
3	15.8	15.0	14.3	13.6	13.0	12.5	12.0	11.5	11.1
4	21.1	20.0	19.0	18.2	17.4	16.7	16.0	15.4	14.8
5	26.3	25.0	23.8	22.7	21.7	20.8	20.0	19.2	18.5
6	31.6	30.0	28.6	27.3	26.1	25.0	24.0	23.1	22.2
7	36.8	35.0	33.3	31.8	30.4	29.2	28.0	26.9	25.9
8	42.1	40.0	38.1	36.4	34.8	33.3	32.0	30.8	29.6
9	47.4	45.0	42.9	40.9	39.1	37.5	36.0	34.6	33.3
10	52.6	50.0	47.6	45.5	43.5	41.7	40.0	38.5	37.0
11	57.9	55.0	52.4	50.0	47.8	45.8	44.0	42.3	40.7
12	63.2	60.0	57.1	54.5	52.2	50.0	48.0	46.2	44.4
13	68.4	65.0	61.9	59.1	56.5	54.2	52.0	50.0	48.1
14	73.7	70.0	66.7	63.6	60.9	58.3	56.0	53.8	51.9
15	78.9	75.0	71.4	68.2	65.2	62.5	60.0	57.7	55.6
16	84.2	80.0	76.2	72.7	69.6	66.7	64.0	61.5	59.3
17	89.5	85.0	81.0	77.3	73.9	70.8	68.0	65.4	63.0
18	94.7	90.0	85.7	81.8	78.3	75.0	72.0	69.2	66.7
19	100.0	95.0	90.5	86.4	82.6	79.2	76.0	73.1	70.4
20		100.0	95.2	90.9	87.0	83.3	80.0	76.9	74.1
21			100.0	95.5	91.3	87.5	84.0	80.8	77.8
22				100.0	95.7	91.7	88.0	84.6	81.5
23					100.0	95.8	92.0	88.5	85.2
24						100.0	96.0	92.3	88.9
25							100.0	96.2	92.6
26								100.0	96.3
27									100.0

Reprinted from Carol L. Stone, *Percentages for Integers 1 to 399*. Pullman, Washington: Washington State University Agricultural Experiment Stations Circular 341, 1958, pp. 3–8.

	28	29	30	31	32	33	34	35	36
1	3.6	3.4	3.3	3.2	3.1	3.0	2.9	2.9	2.8
2	7.1	6.9	6.7	6.5	6.3	6.1	5.9	5.7	5.6
3	10.7	10.3	10.0	9.7	9.4	9.1	8.8	8.6	8.3
4	14.3	13.8	13.3	12.9	12.5	12.1	11.8	11.4	11.1
5	17.9	17.2	16.7	16.1	15.6	15.2	14.7	14.3	13.9
6	21.4	20.7	20.0	19.4	18.8	18.2	17.6	17.1	16.7
7	25.0	24.1	23.3	22.6	21.9	21.2	20.6	20.0	19.4
8	28.6	27.6	26.7	25.8	25.0	24.2	23.5	22.9	22.2
9	32.1	31.0	30.0	29.0	28.1	27.3	26.5	25.7	25.0
10	35.7	34.5	33.3	32.3	31.3	30.3	29.4	28.6	27.8
11	39.3	37.9	36.7	35.5	34.4	33.3	32.4	31.4	30.6
12	42.9	41.4	40.0	36.7	37.5	36.4	35.3	34.3	33.3
13	46.4	44.8	43.3	41.9	40.6	39.4	38.2	37.1	36.1
14	50.0	48.3	46.7	45.2	43.8	42.4	41.2	40.0	38.9
15	53.6	51.7	50.0	48.4	46.9	45.5	44.1	42.9	41.7
16	57.1	55.2	53.3	51.6	50.0	48.5	47.1	45.7	44.4
17	60.7	58.6	56.7	54.8	53.1	51.5	50.0	48.6	47.2
18	64.3	62.1	60.0	58.1	56.3	54.5	52.9	51.4	50.0
19	67.9	65.5	63.3	61.3	59.4	57.6	55.9	54.3	52.8
20	71.4	69.0	66.7	64.5	62.5	60.6	58.8	57.1	55.6
21	75.0	72.4	70.0	67.7	65.6	63.6	61.8	60.0	58.3
22	78.6	75.9	73.3	71.0	68.8	66.7	64.7	62.9	61.1
23	82.1	79.3	76.7	74.2	71.9	69.7	67.6	65.7	63.9
24	65.7	82.8	80.0	77.4	75.0	72.7	70.6	68.6	66.7
25	89.3	86.2	83.3	80.6	78.1	75.8	73.5	71.4	69.4
26	92.9	89.7	86.7	83.9	81.3	78.8	76.5	74.3	72.2
27	96.4	93.1	90.0	87.1	84.4	81.8	79.4	77.1	75.0
28	100.0	96.6	93.3	90.3	87.5	84.8	82.4	80.0	77.8
29		100.0	96.7	93.5	90.6	87.9	85.3	82.9	80.6
30			100.0	96.8	93.8	90.9	88.2	85.7	83.3
31				100.0	96.9	93.9	91.2	88.6	86.1
32					100.0	97.0	94.1	91.4	88.9
33						100.0	97.1	94.3	91.7
34							100.0	97.1	94.4
35								100.0	97.2
36									100.0

	37	38	39	40	41	42	43	44	45
1	2.7	2.6	2.6	2.5	2.4	2.4	2.3	2.3	2.2
2	5.4	5.3	5.1	5.0	4.9	4.8	4.7	4.5	4.4
3	8.1	7.9	7.7	7.5	7.3	7.1	7.0	6.8	6.7
4	10.8	10.5	10.3	10.0	9.8	9.5	9.3	9.1	8.9
5	13.5	13.2	12.8	12.5	12.2	11.9	11.6	11.4	11.1
6	16.2	15.8	15.4	15.0	14.6	14.3	14.0	13.6	13.3
7	18.9	18.4	17.9	17.5	17.1	16.7	16.3	15.9	15.6
8	21.6	21.1	20.5	20.0	19.5	19.0	18.6	18.2	17.8
9	24.3	23.7	23.1	22.5	22.0	21.4	20.9	20.5	20.0
10	27.0	26.3	25.6	25.0	24.4	23.8	23.3	22.7	22.2
11	29.7	28.9	28.2	27.5	26.8	26.2	25.6	25.0	24.4
12	32.4	31.6	30.8	30.0	29.3	28.6	27.9	27.3	26.7
13	35.1	34.2	33.3	32.5	31.7	31.0	30.2	29.5	28.9
14	37.8	36.8	35.9	35.0	34.1	33.3	32.6	31.8	31.1
15	40.5	39.5	38.5	37.5	36.6	35.7	34.9	34.1	33.3
16	43.2	42.1	41.0	40.0	39.0	38.1	37.2	36.4	35.6
17	45.9	44.7	43.6	42.5	41.5	40.5	39.5	38.6	37.8
18	48.6	47.4	46.2	45.0	43.9	42.9	41.9	40.9	40.0
19	51.4	50.0	48.7	47.5	46.3	45.2	44.2	43.2	42.2
20	54.1	52.6	51.3	50.0	48.8	47.6	46.5	45.5	44.4
21	56.8	55.3	53.8	52.5	51.2	50.0	48.8	47.7	46.7
22	59.5	57.9	56.4	55.0	53.7	52.4	51.2	50.0	48.9
23	62.2	60.5	59.0	57.5	56.1	54.8	53.5	52.3	51.1
24	64.9	63.2	61.5	60.0	58.5	57.1	55.8	54.5	53.3
25	67.6	65.8	64.1	62.5	61.0	59.5	58.1	56.8	55.6
26	70.3	68.4	66.7	65.0	63.4	61.9	60.5	59.1	57.8
27	73.0	71.1	69.2	67.5	65.9	64.3	62.8	61.4	60.0
28	75.7	73.7	71.8	70.0	68.3	66.7	65.1	63.6	62.2
29	78.4	76.3	74.4	72.5	70.7	69.0	67.4	65.9	64.4
30	81.1	78.9	76.9	75.0	73.2	71.4	69.8	68.2	66.7
31	83.8	81.6	79.5	77.5	75.6	73.8	72.1	70.5	68.9
32	86.5	84.2	82.1	80.0	78.0	76.2	74.4	72.7	71.1
33	89.2	86.8	84.6	82.5	80.5	78.6	76.7	75.0	73.3
34	91.9	89.5	87.2	85.0	82.9	81.0	79.1	77.3	75.6
35	94.6	92.1	89.7	87.5	85.4	83.3	81.4	79.5	77.8
36	97.3	94.7	90.0	92.3	87.8	85.7	83.7	81.8	80.0
37	100.0	97.4	94.9	92.5	90.2	88.1	86.0	84.1	82.2
38		100.0	97.4	95.0	92.7	90.5	88.4	86.4	84.4
39			100.0	97.5	95.1	92.9	90.7	88.6	86.7
40				100.0	97.6	95.2	93.0	90.9	88.9
41					100.0	97.6	95.3	93.2	91.1
42						100.0	97.7	95.5	93.3
43							100.0	97.7	95.6
44								100.0	97.8
45									100.0

	46	47	48	49	50	51	52	53	54
1	2.2	2.1	2.1	2.0	2.0	2.0	1.9	1.9	1.9
2	4.3	4.3	4.2	4.1	4.0	3.9	3.8	3.8	3.7
3	6.5	6.4	6.3	6.1	6.0	5.9	5.8	5.7	5.6
4	8.7	8.5	8.3	8.2	8.0	7.8	7.7	7.5	7.4
5	10.9	10.6	10.4	10.2	10.0	9.8	9.6	9.4	9.3
6	13.0	12.8	12.5	12.2	12.0	11.8	11.5	11.3	11.1
7	15.2	14.9	14.6	14.3	14.0	13.7	13.5	13.2	13.0
8	17.4	17.0	16.7	16.3	16.0	15.7	15.4	15.1	14.8
9	19.6	19.1	18.8	18.4	18.0	17.6	17.3	17.0	16.7
10	21.7	21.3	20.8	20.4	20.0	19.6	19.2	18.9	18.5
11	23.9	23.4	22.9	22.4	22.0	21.6	21.2	20.8	20.4
12	26.1	25.5	25.0	24.5	24.0	23.5	23.1	22.6	22.2
13	28.3	27.7	27.1	26.5	26.0	25.5	25.0	24.5	24.1
14	30.4	29.8	29.2	28.6	28.0	27.5	26.9	26.4	25.9
15	32.6	31.9	31.3	30.6	30.0	29.4	28.8	28.3	27.8
16	34.8	34.0	33.3	32.7	32.0	31.4	30.8	30.2	29.6
17	37.0	36.2	35.4	34.7	34.0	33.3	32.7	32.1	31.5
18	39.1	38.3	37.5	36.7	36.0	35.3	34.6	34.0	33.3
19	41.3	40.4	39.6	38.8	38.0	37.3	36.5	35.8	35.2
20	43.5	42.6	41.7	40.8	40.0	39.2	38.5	37.7	37.0
21	45.7	44.7	43.8	42.9	42.0	41.2	40.4	39.6	38.9
22	47.8	46.8	45.8	44.9	44.0	43.1	42.3	41.5	40.7
23	50.0	48.9	47.9	46.9	46.0	45.1	44.2	43.4	42.6
24	52.2	51.1	50.0	49.0	48.0	47.1	46.2	45.3	44.4
25	54.3	53.2	52.1	51.0	50.0	49.0	48.1	47.2	46.3
26	56.5	55.3	54.2	53.1	52.0	51.0	50.0	49.1	48.1
27	58.7	57.4	56.3	55.1	54.0	52.9	51.9	50.9	50.0
28	60.9	59.6	58.3	57.1	56.0	54.9	53.8	52.8	51.9
29	63.0	61.7	60.4	59.2	58.0	56.9	55.8	54.7	53.7
30	65.2	63.8	62.5	61.2	60.0	58.8	57.7	56.6	55.6
31	67.4	66.0	64.6	63.3	62.0	60.8	59.6	58.5	57.4
32	69.6	68.1	66.7	65.3	64.0	62.7	61.5	60.4	59.3
33	71.7	70.2	68.8	67.3	66.0	64.7	63.5	62.3	61.1
34	73.9	72.3	70.8	69.4	68.0	66.7	65.4	64.2	63.0
35	76.1	74.5	72.9	71.4	70.0	68.6	67.3	66.0	64.8
36	78.3	76.6	75.0	73.5	72.0	70.6	69.2	67.9	66.7
37	80.4	78.7	77.1	75.5	74.0	72.5	71.2	69.8	68.5
38	82.6	80.9	79.2	77.6	76.0	74.5	73.1	71.7	70.4
39	84.8	83.0	81.3	79.6	78.0	76.5	75.0	73.6	72.2
40	87.0	85.1	83.3	81.6	80.0	78.4	76.9	75.5	74.1
41	89.1	87.2	85.4	83.7	82.0	80.4	78.8	77.4	75.9
42	91.3	89.4	87.5	85.7	84.0	82.4	80.8	79.2	77.8
43	93.5	91.5	89.6	87.8	86.0	84.3	82.7	81.1	79.6
44	95.7	93.6	91.7	89.8	88.0	86.3	84.6	83.0	81.5
45	97.8	95.7	93.8	91.8	90.0	88.2	86.5	84.9	83.3
46	100.0	97.9	95.8	93.9	92.0	90.2	88.5	86.8	85.2
47		100.0	97.9	95.9	94.0	92.2	90.4	88.7	87.0
48			100.0	98.0	96.0	94.1	92.3	90.6	88.9
49				100.0	98.0	96.1	94.2	92.5	90.7
50					100.0	98.0	96.2	94.3	92.6
51						100.0	98.1	96.2	94.4
52							100.0	98.1	96.3
53								100.0	98.1
54									100.0

	55	56	57	58	59	60	61	62	63
1	1.8	1.8	1.8	1.7	1.7	1.7	1.6	1.6	1.6
2	3.6	3.6	3.5	3.4	3.4	3.3	3.3	3.2	3.2
3	5.5	5.4	5.3	5.2	5.1	5.0	4.9	4.8	4.8
4	7.3	7.1	7.0	6.9	6.8	6.7	6.6	6.5	6.3
5	9.1	8.9	8.8	8.6	8.5	8.3	8.2	8.1	7.9
6	10.9	10.7	10.5	10.3	10.2	10.0	9.8	9.7	9.5
7	12.7	12.5	12.3	12.1	11.9	11.7	11.5	11.3	11.1
8	14.5	14.3	14.0	13.8	13.6	13.3	13.1	12.9	12.7
9	16.4	16.1	15.8	15.5	15.3	15.0	14.8	14.5	14.3
10	18.2	17.9	17.5	17.2	16.9	16.7	16.4	16.1	15.9
11	20.0	19.6	19.3	19.0	18.6	18.3	18.0	17.7	17.5
12	21.8	21.4	21.1	20.7	20.3	20.0	19.7	19.4	19.0
13	23.6	23.2	22.8	22.4	22.0	21.7	21.3	21.0	20.6
14	25.5	25.0	24.6	24.1	23.7	23.3	23.0	22.6	22.2
15	27.3	26.8	26.3	25.9	25.4	25.0	24.6	24.2	23.8
16	29.1	28.6	28.1	27.6	27.1	26.7	26.2	25.8	25.4
17	30.9	30.4	29.8	29.3	28.8	28.3	27.9	27.4	27.0
18	32.7	32.1	31.6	31.0	30.5	30.0	29.5	29.0	28.6
19	34.5	33.9	33.3	32.8	32.2	31.7	31.1	30.6	30.2
20	36.4	35.7	35.1	34.5	33.9	33.3	32.8	32.3	31.7
21	38.2	37.5	36.8	36.2	35.6	35.0	34.4	33.9	33.3
22	40.0	39.3	38.6	37.9	37.3	36.7	36.1	35.5	34.9
23	41.8	41.1	40.4	39.7	39.0	38.3	37.7	37.1	36.5
24	43.6	42.9	42.1	41.4	40.7	40.0	39.3	38.7	38.1
25	45.5	44.6	43.9	43.1	42.4	41.7	41.0	40.3	39.7
26	47.3	46.4	45.6	44.8	44.1	43.3	42.6	41.9	41.3
27	49.1	48.2	47.4	46.6	45.8	45.0	44.3	43.5	42.9
28	50.9	50.0	49.1	48.3	47.5	46.7	45.9	45.2	44.4
29	52.7	51.8	50.9	50.0	49.2	48.3	47.5	46.8	46.0
30	54.5	53.6	52.6	51.7	50.8	50.0	49.2	48.4	47.6
31	56.4	55.4	54.4	53.4	52.5	51.7	50.8	50.0	49.2
32	58.2	57.1	56.1	55.2	54.2	53.3	52.5	51.6	50.8
33	60.0	58.9	57.9	56.9	55.9	55.0	54.1	53.2	52.4
34	61.8	60.7	59.6	58.6	57.6	56.7	55.7	54.8	54.0
35	63.6	62.5	61.4	60.3	59.3	58.3	57.4	56.5	55.6
36	65.5	64.3	63.2	62.1	61.0	60.0	59.0	58.1	57.1
37	67.3	66.1	64.9	63.8	62.7	61.7	60.7	59.7	58.7
38	69.1	67.9	66.7	65.5	64.4	63.3	62.3	61.3	60.3
39	70.9	69.6	68.4	67.2	66.1	65.0	63.9	62.9	61.9
40	72.7	71.4	70.2	69.0	67.8	66.7	65.6	64.5	63.5
41	74.5	73.2	71.9	70.7	69.5	68.3	67.2	66.1	65.1
42	76.4	75.0	73.7	72.4	71.2	70.0	68.9	67.7	66.7
43	78.2	76.8	75.4	74.1	72.9	71.7	70.5	69.4	68.3
44	80.0	78.6	77.2	75.9	74.6	73.3	72.1	71.0	69.8
45	81.8	80.4	78.9	77.6	76.3	75.0	73.8	72.6	71.4
46	83.6	82.1	80.7	79.3	78.0	76.7	75.4	74.2	73.0
47	85.5	83.9	82.5	81.0	79.7	78.3	77.0	75.8	74.6
48	87.3	85.7	84.2	82.8	81.4	80.0	78.7	77.4	76.2
49	89.1	87.5	86.0	84.5	83.1	81.7	80.3	79.0	77.8
50	90.9	89.3	87.7	86.2	84.7	83.3	82.0	80.6	79.4
51	92.7	91.1	89.5	87.9	86.4	85.0	83.6	82.3	81.0
52	94.5	92.9	91.2	89.7	88.1	86.7	85.2	83.9	82.5
53	96.4	94.6	93.0	91.4	89.8	88.3	86.9	85.5	84.1
54	98.2	96.4	94.7	93.1	91.5	90.0	88.5	87.1	85.7
55	100.0	98.2	96.5	94.8	93.2	91.7	90.2	88.7	87.3
56		100.0	98.2	96.6	94.9	93.3	91.8	90.3	88.9
57			100.0	98.3	96.6	95.0	93.4	91.9	90.5
58				100.0	98.3	96.7	95.1	93.5	92.1
59					100.0	98.3	96.7	95.2	93.7
60						100.0	98.4	96.8	95.2
61							100.0	98.4	96.8
62								100.0	98.4
63									100.0

	64	65	66	67	68	69	70	71	72
1	1.6	1.5	1.5	1.5	1.5	1.4	1.4	1.4	1.4
2	3.1	3.1	3.0	3.0	2.9	2.9	2.9	2.8	2.8
3	4.7	4.6	4.5	4.5	4.4	4.3	4.3	4.2	4.2
4	6.3	6.2	6.1	6.0	5.9	5.8	5.7	5.6	5.6
5	7.8	7.7	7.6	7.5	7.4	7.2	7.1	7.0	6.9
6	9.4	9.2	9.1	9.0	8.8	8.7	8.6	8.5	8.3
7	10.9	10.8	10.6	10.4	10.3	10.1	10.0	9.9	9.7
8	12.5	12.3	12.1	11.9	11.8	11.6	11.4	11.3	11.1
9	14.1	13.8	13.6	13.4	13.2	13.0	12.9	12.7	12.5
10	15.6	15.4	15.2	14.9	14.7	14.5	14.3	14.1	13.9
11	17.2	16.9	16.7	16.4	16.2	15.9	15.7	15.5	15.3
12	18.8	18.5	18.2	17.9	17.6	17.4	17.1	16.9	16.7
13	20.3	20.0	19.7	19.4	19.1	18.8	18.6	18.3	18.1
14	21.9	21.5	21.2	20.9	20.6	20.3	20.0	19.7	19.4
15	23.4	23.1	22.7	22.4	22.1	21.7	21.4	21.1	20.8
16	25.0	24.6	24.2	23.9	23.5	23.2	22.9	22.5	22.2
17	26.6	26.2	25.8	25.4	25.0	24.6	24.3	23.9	23.6
18	28.1	27.7	27.3	26.9	26.5	26.1	25.7	25.4	25.0
19	29.7	29.2	28.8	28.4	27.9	27.5	27.1	26.8	26.4
20	31.3	30.8	30.3	29.9	29.4	29.0	28.6	28.2	27.8
21	32.8	32.3	31.8	31.3	30.9	30.4	30.0	29.6	29.2
22	34.4	33.8	33.3	32.8	32.4	31.9	31.4	31.0	30.6
23	35.9	35.4	34.8	34.3	33.8	33.3	32.9	32.4	31.9
24	37.5	36.9	36.4	35.8	35.3	34.8	34.3	33.8	33.3
25	39.1	38.5	37.9	37.3	36.8	36.2	35.7	35.2	34.7
26	40.6	40.0	39.4	38.8	38.2	37.7	37.1	36.6	36.1
27	42.2	41.5	40.9	40.3	39.7	39.1	38.6	38.0	37.5
28	43.8	43.1	42.4	41.8	41.2	40.6	40.0	39.4	38.9
29	45.3	44.6	43.9	43.3	42.6	42.0	41.4	40.8	40.3
30	46.9	46.2	45.5	44.8	44.1	43.5	42.9	42.3	41.7
31	48.4	47.7	47.0	46.3	45.6	44.9	44.3	43.7	43.1
32	50.0	49.2	48.5	47.8	47.1	46.4	45.7	45.1	44.4
33	51.6	50.8	50.0	49.3	48.5	47.8	47.1	46.5	45.8
34	53.1	52.3	51.5	50.7	50.0	49.3	48.6	47.9	47.2
35	54.7	53.8	53.0	52.2	51.5	50.7	50.0	49.3	48.6
36	56.3	55.4	54.5	53.7	52.9	52.2	51.4	50.7	50.0
37	57.8	56.9	56.1	55.2	54.4	53.6	52.9	52.1	51.4
38	59.4	58.5	57.6	56.7	55.9	55.1	54.3	53.5	52.8
39	60.9	60.0	59.1	58.2	57.4	56.5	55.7	54.9	54.2
40	62.5	61.5	60.6	59.7	58.8	58.0	57.1	56.3	55.6
41	64.1	63.1	62.1	61.2	60.3	59.4	58.6	57.7	56.9
42	65.6	64.6	63.6	62.7	61.8	60.9	60.0	59.2	58.3
43	67.2	66.2	65.2	64.2	63.2	62.3	61.4	60.6	59.7
44	68.8	67.7	66.7	65.7	64.7	63.8	62.9	62.0	61.1
45	70.3	69.2	68.2	67.2	66.2	65.2	64.3	63.4	62.5
46	71.9	70.8	69.7	68.7	67.6	66.7	65.7	64.8	63.9
47	73.4	72.3	71.2	70.1	69.1	68.1	67.1	66.2	65.3
48	75.0	73.8	72.7	71.6	70.6	69.6	68.6	67.6	66.7
49	76.6	75.4	74.2	73.1	72.1	71.0	70.0	69.0	68.1
50	78.1	76.9	75.8	74.6	73.5	72.5	71.4	70.4	69.4
51	79.7	78.5	77.3	76.1	75.0	73.9	72.9	71.8	70.8
52	81.3	80.0	78.8	77.6	76.5	75.4	74.3	73.2	72.2
53	82.8	81.5	80.3	79.1	77.9	76.8	75.7	74.6	73.6
54	84.4	83.1	81.8	80.6	79.4	78.3	77.1	76.1	75.0
55	85.9	84.6	83.3	82.1	80.9	79.7	78.6	77.5	76.4
56	87.5	86.2	84.8	83.6	82.4	81.2	80.0	78.9	77.8
57	89.1	87.7	86.4	85.1	83.8	82.6	81.4	80.3	79.2
58	90.6	89.2	87.9	86.6	85.3	84.1	82.9	81.7	80.6
59	92.2	90.8	89.4	88.1	86.8	85.5	84.3	83.1	81.9
60	93.8	92.3	90.9	89.6	88.2	87.0	85.7	84.5	83.3
61	95.3	93.8	92.4	91.0	89.7	88.4	87.1	85.9	84.7
62	96.9	95.4	93.9	92.5	91.2	89.9	88.6	87.3	86.1
63	98.4	96.9	95.5	94.0	92.6	91.3	90.0	88.7	87.5
64	100.0	98.5	97.0	95.5	94.1	92.8	91.4	90.1	88.9
65		100.0	98.5	97.0	95.6	94.2	92.9	91.5	90.3
66			100.0	98.5	97.1	95.7	94.3	93.0	91.7
67				100.0	98.5	97.1	95.7	94.4	93.1
68					100.0	98.6	97.1	95.8	94.4
69						100.0	98.6	97.2	95.8
70							100.0	98.6	97.2
71								100.0	98.6
72									100.0

APPENDIX C

CALCULATION OF THE MEAN

An arithmetic mean is the most widely used measure to describe the "typical numerical value" in a group of scores. The following examples illustrate the possible methods for calculating the mean.

LONG METHOD. Suppose it was necessary to arrive at the mean score on an "ultimate power index" for the 22 cases or respondents reported in Table 1.

TABLE 1

Ultimate power index (Box 22t) x	Tally
6	//
7	///
8	~~////~~ //
9	~~////~~ /
10	
11	//
Total	20
+ (No answer)	//

One method for doing this would be to write out all the individual cases and add them as follows:

6	8
6	8
7	9
7	9
7	9
8	9
8	9
8	9
8	11
8	11
	165

Discounting the two cases for which there is no information, the mean in this sample of scores would be 165 ÷ 20, or 8.25. For the problems in this book, the figure can be rounded to 8.3.

SHORT METHOD. There is a quicker way to compute the mean when the cases are grouped, as they are in Table 1.

Table 1a illustrates the short method. The computations entail the following three steps:

(A) Multiply the number of cases (as indicated in the frequency or the "f" column of the table) by their respective value (as indicated in the "x" column), and write these products in the "fx" column.

TABLE 1a

Ultimate power index (Box 22t) x	Tally	f	fx
6	//	2	12
7	///	3	21
8	~~////~~ //	7	56
9	~~////~~ /	6	54
10		0	0
11	//	2	22
Total ⟶		20	165
Mean ⟶			8.3
+ No answer	//	2	

(B) Add the "f" column and then add the "fx" column. This yields the same values provided by the "long method" illustrated above.

(C) Divide the total of the "fx" column by the total of the "f" column to obtain the mean. The general formula for this is:

$$\text{Mean} = \frac{\text{Total fx}}{\text{Total f}} = \frac{165}{20} = 8.3$$

GROUPED DATA. In some instances the tables necessitate tallying together cases with similar but not identical scores, as for example, scores ranging from 3 to 6 or from 7 to 10. What should be the "x" value of the cases in each of these groups? The procedure to be followed in this book will be to always use the "upper limit" of a group of scores; if the category is 3 to 6, the "x" value will be taken as 6; if the category is 7 to 10, the "x" value will be taken as 10.

Correct statistical procedure actually requires using the "midpoint" of each group of scores rather than the upper limit. These midpoints, however, are often fractions (e.g., 4.5, 8.5, etc.) and therefore require considerable extra calculation to obtain the "fx" value. We can avoid this extra work because our interest is in determining differences between *groups*, and this is not affected by using the upper limit as the value for all the groups.

APPENDIX D
NOTES FOR INSTRUCTORS*

Hard and fast rules for the use of this book would be impossible and unrewarding. The following notes, culled from intensive pre-tests at a number of universities, should only be taken as suggestions.

Time requirements for problems

Some of the directions listed below are based on the assumption that the problems will be done in two-hour laboratory periods. Although this is preferable, the problems can also be done in several other ways: (1) The usual one-hour "quiz section" may be used by allowing students to complete their calculations and write-up as outside assignments. (2) The entire problem can be done as a home assignment. In this case sets of code sheets can be placed on reserve in the library or sets can be lent to students for use at home. (3) In a large lecture class without discussion sections, the cross-tabulation for the problem can be done in advance and presented on the blackboard. The students can then use these to compute means or percentages and write their laboratory report. If this procedure is followed it is recommended that the first one or two cross-tabulations be repeated as a demonstration in front of the class so that the students can visualize the actual mechanics of a cross-tabulation.[1]

Sampling

The laboratory problem method of this manual requires a sample of approximately 100 to 150 cases. In addition, the sample should, if possible, include both men and women respondents and should contain variation in social class level and religion. This does not mean that a sample containing equal numbers of men and women or of Protestants and Catholics is needed. However, there should be enough cases in each group to make computation of averages meaningful. In extreme instances even five or six cases will do. Where social class comparisons are needed, if there are not at least five farm families represented in your sample, those which are present should be included with either the white-collar or the blue-collar group. Which occupational group to combine them with depends on the socioeconomic level of the farm group which attends your institution.

These sample requirements do not rule out the use of this volume by an instructor teaching a class which cannot provide a sample meeting the criteria. An instructor in this situation could arrange to give the questionnaire to other groups of students in his own or nearby institutions. However, supplementing the sample by asking students to secure friends as respondents should be avoided because of the serious volunteer bias which this can introduce.

A difficulty with supplementing the sample lies in the time and labor costs of coding the supplemental group of questionnaires. If this is done, however, the most efficient procedure is to have each member of the class code two extra questionnaires. An extra lab period must then be allowed for coding, since coding the first questionnaire ordinarily requires a full two-hour laboratory period.

To provide a more convenient method of supplementing the sample, we have prepared a set of code sheets based on questionnaires completed by students in introductory sociology at the University of Minnesota. Each set contains 80 code sheets, selected so that there are approximately equal numbers of men and women; Catholics as well as Protestants; and children of farm, white-collar, and blue-collar fathers. Instructors wishing to supplement the sample obtained from their own class may purchase these code sheets.

Another method of supplementing the sample is to add the code sheets from previous classes. Within a short time more code sheets will be accumulated than are needed because a sample of over 150 cases takes up too much of the laboratory period with the clerical work of sorting and tabulating. However, larger sets of code sheets from Harper & Row can be put on reserve for use by students who wish to do more detailed analyses or write term papers.

It is always advisable to administer and code the questionnaire even if a sufficient number of code sheets have already been accumulated. These two steps are important parts of the laboratory experience. They give the student the opportunity to participate in data gathering and quantification as an integral part of the research process, and they lend a degree of saliency and reality to the materials which might otherwise not be experienced. If the addition of code sheets for a class makes the sample too large, it would be advisable to remove the code sheets from the previous class.

Mechanics of laboratory work

FIRST PERIOD: DATA GATHERING. The questionnaires should be answered in class. Students are *not* to sign their names. The questionnaire can be completed in 40 minutes by most students. As each completes his questionnaire, it should be turned in and the student may leave. It is important to number the questionnaires after they have been turned in.

SECOND PERIOD: PROBLEM 1, CODING. (A) Distribute the questionnaires in random order since it is important that no one code his own questionnaire. (B) The coding is to be done on the Coding Worksheet (page 33) and not on the ditto-master code

* See page 3 for an overview of procedures.

[1] Another alternative is an elective course for one or two credits. At the University of Minnesota we have done this with a course, Sociology Laboratory, which may be taken concurrently with the introductory sociology lecture course.

sheet. (C) If the coding is done in class, as recommended, have the students write in the code values for their questionnaire as you read out the items in the code. (D) After the coding has been completed, each student is to copy it onto the ditto-master code sheet. Make sure the students remove the tissue before starting to copy and that they write large, legible numbers and press hard while writing. It is advisable to have one or two razor blades available for those who need to make corrections. (E) Each student is to reinsert the protective tissue and hand in his ditto-master code sheet together with the questionnaire he has coded. Be sure to collect all questionnaires even if you are *not* going to check the coding or save the questionnaires: They should not be allowed to circulate on the campus and possibly influence the way a future class answers the questionnaires.

DITTOING CODE SHEETS. It is not necessary or desirable to run off a set of code sheets for every member of the class. It is preferable to have the students work in pairs when sorting and tabulating (the laboratory reports should, however, be written individually). Consequently, only *one* set of code sheets needs to be available for every *two* students. In addition, a set may be run off for your use and a set to put on library reserve for those who must make up a missed lab or who are writing term papers. Call for three or four volunteers to do the dittoing. Sets of code sheets can be assembled in class. Save the ditto-masters as you may later want to run more sets.

CHOICE OF PROBLEMS. Once the data have been coded, it is theoretically possible to do the laboratory problems in any sequence which fits the outline of the course. In practice, however, it is important to gradually build up familiarity and skill with the materials and the mode of analysis. For this reason it is recommended that Problem 2 or 4 be completed before any others, since each consists of simple frequency distributions rather than cross-tabulations. Most of the remaining problems are two-variable cross-tabulations. Some, however, involve the use of a third variable as a form of control, and it is advisable to avoid these until a two-variable problem has been completed.

Another factor to consider in the choice of problems is the desirability of varying the type of data used for the problem. Since most of the other problems use questionnaire data, it may be advisable, if possible, to work in Problem 5, which is an example of participant observation; Problem 6, which is a classroom experiment; Problem 11, which involves a content analysis of magazine stories; and Problem 13 which requires analysis of statistical data from library reference books. Problem 13, however, cannot be done with a large class unless sufficient copies of the needed reference books are put on reserve.

STUDENT PREPARATION FOR LAB PROBLEMS. The problem you select must be announced in advance so that students have an opportunity to read the study to be replicated and to write the hypothesis in advance. It is essential to stress the importance of also reading Appendix A ("Outline for Writing Laboratory Reports") before the first replication. If the mean is to be calculated, the students should also be alerted to read Appendix C.

CLASSROOM PROCEDURES. Summary statistics (means or percentages) should be put on a table drawn on the blackboard so that students may check the accuracy of their own work and make corrections if needed. Time will be saved and confusion minimized if you establish a pattern of having the first few students who complete their statistics walk up to the board and enter their figures. Differences between the statistics obtained by different students may be due to one or more code sheets getting lost or added from another set. These and the usual minor clerical errors which occur in most research studies will lead to small differences in the results. These small differences can be ignored if the general nature of the results are comparable. Select the mean or the mode of the figures put on the blackboard as the basis for the entire class to use in writing their laboratory reports.

THE LABORATORY REPORT. Appendix A contains general directions for preparing the lab reports. The instructions for the problems refer the student to these directions. However, for the first few problems additional reminders may be needed. The most difficult part of the preparation of these reports concerns the distinction between the Summary of Findings and the Discussion section. This is due to the tendency to repeat the summary of findings as the discussion, rather than to interpret the findings. Students need reassurance that it is permissible to interpret and speculate in a scientific report.

Although we have usually given grades to the lab reports, this should be secondary. We have found teaching and learning to be most rewarding when the laboratory reports are treated as a learning experience rather than as an examination. A helpful posture in answering questions and in aiding in the write-up is most likely to enhance such learning.

REDUCTION IN CLERICAL WORK. One difficulty with these laboratory problems is that a substantial part of each laboratory period is taken up with essentially clerical work: sorting, tabulating, adding, calculating percentages, etc. This is true of most research, but in the case of these laboratory problems there are two steps which can be taken to reduce the clerical work component:

(A) Students should work in pairs and divide up the work. For example, in a laboratory problem in which social class is an independent or control variable, one member of the pair might tabulate the code sheets for the middle-class part of the sample and the other person for the working-class part. Similarly, the work of figuring percentages and means can be divided. After each person has done his half, the results are traded and copied onto the relevant tabulation and calculation forms. Of course, the laboratory reports drawing on common data should be written individually by each student.

(B) It is possible to omit cross-tabulations by the class after four or five laboratory problems have been completed and students have thoroughly mastered the mechanics of cross tabulating data to test hypotheses. To do this the instructor can have two or three students cross tabulate the data in advance and post the statistics on the blackboard. This procedure is recommended not simply because it avoids the tedium of repeating a type of activity already thoroughly mastered, but because it allows more time for class discussion and for writing the laboratory reports.

Significance tests

The use of statistics in this manual is limited to means and percentages. There is no need for introductory classes to go beyond this. Since our purpose is purely illustrative, we assume that all differences are not due to chance. This is necessary if the labs are to be carried out by typical undergraduates within a two-hour period. While the assumption is not completely sound, it is made somewhat justifiable by the fact that each laboratory problem replicates an already established proposition. Statistically oriented instructors can, if they so desire, teach their students to apply inferential statistics to the data analyzed, and honors students writing term papers based on analysis of these data can be required to compute such measures.

Additional uses of these materials

The replications suggested in this volume by no means exhaust the possible modes for analyzing data. For example, the student interested in fertility could readily go beyond the suggested relationships with socioeconomic status and religion (Problem 21) and examine the impact of other variables including mobility, urban-rural residence, or the effects of large and small families on the personalities of children. It is also possible to use the relationships between variables not explored in the suggested problems as a base for empirically oriented term papers. Hopefully, the data collected are general enough to provide flexibility for a variety of concerns. Furthermore, if the aim of including a set of variables covering many key aspects of sociology has been achieved, then it should also be possible for instructors using this manual to develop their own laboratory problems. After some experience with the method and the questionnaire, articles can be chosen from the rapidly growing empirical literature and the necessary instructions and forms prepared for class replication.

In addition to new combinations of the data which were included for specific replications, data for a few laboratory problems which were not included within the book have been retained in the questionnaire. These permit interested students to work with the materials from the following studies.

Centers, Richard, "Occupational Endogamy in Marital Selection," *American Journal of Sociology, 54* (May 1949), pp. 530–535.

Dynes, Russel R., Alfred C. Clarke, and Simon Dinitz, "Levels of Occupational Aspirations: Some Aspects of Family Experience as a Variable," *American Sociological Review, 21* (April 1956), pp. 212–215.

Gurin, Gerald, Joseph Veroff, and Sheila Feld, "The Job," in *Americans View Their Mental Health.* New York: Basic Books, Inc., 1960, pp. 143–174.

Hoffman, Lois W., "Effects of the Employment of Mothers on Parental Power Relations and the Division of Household Tasks," *Marriage Family Living, 22* (1960), pp. 27–35.

Kohn, Melvin L., "Social Class and Parental Values," *American Journal of Sociology, 64* (January 1959), pp. 337–351.

Lenski, Gerhard E., "Social Participation and Status Crystallization," *American Sociological Review, 21* (August 1956), pp. 458–464.

Lenski, Gerhard E., "Status Crystallization: A Non-vertical Dimension of Social Status," *American Sociological Review, 19* (August 1954), pp. 405–413.

Nye, F. Ivan, "Employment Status of Mothers and Marital Conflict, Permanence, and Happiness," *Social Problems, 6* (1959), pp. 260–267.

Wright, Charles R. and Herbert H. Hyman, "Voluntary Association Memberships of American Adults: Evidence from National Sample Surveys," *American Sociological Review, 23* (June 1958), pp. 284–294.

Similarly, there are innumerable possibilities for "original research" laboratory problems. However, laboratory problems which are not replications, interesting as they may be to the instructor, miss one of the main pedagogical aims of the laboratory method: to permit the student to demonstrate for himself the validity of the empirical basis of sociology. Consequently, non-replicative laboratory problems are best avoided, except perhaps for term papers done by selected students.

Index

Questionnaire

SOCIOLOGICAL ANALYSIS QUESTIONNAIRE

Dear Student:

The attached questionnaire is designed to gather data about various aspects of American society. This data can contribute to our understanding of some important questions. We hope, therefore, that you will fill out the questionnaire with care.

Most of the questions are answered by circling a number. Others need a brief answer written in. Please be sure to answer every question. If you are not sure, but can make a reasonable guess, put that down.

The information in this questionnaire is strictly for research purposes. The only things which will be made public are group statistics such as averages and percentages. Do not sign your name.

The success of the study depends on your completing the questionnaire to the best of your ability. We appreciate your help with what we believe to be important research.

Date______________________________
Month Day Year

I. BACKGROUND INFORMATION

1. Sex: (Circle one number)
   1. Male
   2. Female

2. Age at my last birthday was: __________

3. Race:
   1. White
   2. Negro
   3. Oriental
   4. American Indian
   5. Other: ____________________

4. My present class standing is:
   1. Freshman, first quarter or term
   2. Freshman, second or third quarter
   3. Sophomore
   4. Junior
   5. Senior
   6. Graduate
   7. Other

II. MY FAMILY

5. At the time I finished high school, my parents were:
   1. Both living together
   2. Divorced
   3. Separated
   4. Father was dead
   5. Mother was dead
   6. Temporarily living apart for reasons other than marital problems, if for longer than 1 year

6. Please circle the HIGHEST LEVEL of education completed by your FATHER:
   1. Some grade school
   2. Completed grade school
   3. Some high school
   4. Completed high school
   5. Completed high school and also had other training, but not college, e.g., technical
   6. Some college
   7. Completed college
   8. Some graduate work
   9. Graduate degree, M.D., M.A., Ph.D., etc.

7. Please circle the HIGHEST LEVEL of education completed by your MOTHER:
   1. Some grade school
   2. Completed grade school
   3. Some high school
   4. Completed high school
   5. Completed high school, and also had other training, but not college, e.g., technical
   6. Some college
   7. Completed college
   8. Some graduate work
   9. Graduate degree, M.D., M.A., Ph.D., etc.

8. My mother's religious preference is:
   1. Roman Catholic or Eastern Orthodox
   2. Baptist
   3. Lutheran
   4. Methodist
   5. Presbyterian
   6. Other Protestant, please specify: ____________________
   7. Jewish
   8. Other: ____________________
   9. None

9. My father's father (i.e., paternal grandfather's) main occupation is (or was before retirement):

   ____
   What he did (or does)—not where he works

10. My mother's father (i.e., maternal grandfather's) main occupation is (or was before retirement):

    ____
    What he does (or did)—not where he works

11. My father's main occupation is (or was):

    ____
    Give the name of his job (i.e., "auto mechanic") or tell the kind of work he does—not where he works.

12. Please classify your father's occupation into one of the following six groups, AND THEN circle a number to show where it fits within that group.

Group A: Proprietors (business owners)

1. Proprietor of a LARGE business (valued at $100,000 or more)
2. Proprietor of a MEDIUM business (valued at $35,000 to $100,000)
3. Proprietor of a SMALL business (valued at $6,000 to $35,000)
4. Proprietor of a VERY SMALL business (valued under $6,000)

Group B: Executives and Officials

1. TOP LEVEL executive in LARGE ORGANIZATION: senior official of a large business, officer above the rank of major, mayor and city manager of a large city, head of a large government department, etc.
2. MIDDLE LEVEL executive or official, or TOP LEVEL OF A SMALL ORGANIZATION: district or branch manager, head of a small department, police chief of small city or sheriff, postmaster, personnel manager, etc.
3. LOWER LEVEL official and manager: credit manager, chief clerk, department or section manager, insurance agent or adjuster, shop manager, chain store manager, etc.

Group C: Professional and Technical

1. TOP LEVEL professional: CPA, architect, chemist, doctor, lawyer, college teacher, engineer (all must have college degree), etc.
2. LOWER LEVEL professional: accountant (not CPA), chiropractor, engineer (not college grad.), librarian, military officer up to major, nurse, optician, pharmacist, symphony musician, public health officer, research assistant, social worker, correctional officer, teacher (elementary or high school), etc.
3. SEMI-PROFESSIONAL: actor, M/Sgt., warrant officer, navy CPO, commercial artist, clergyman without seminary training, computer programmer, landscape planner, mortician, oral hygienist, photographer, physio-therapist, TV announcer, reporter, surveyor, tool designer, yard or station manager, interpreter, etc.
4. TECHNICIAN: dental technician, draftsman, driving teacher, inspector of weights & measures, investigator, lab technician, proofreader, RR tower operator, dispatcher, etc.

Group D: Clerical and Sales

2. SALES REPRESENTATIVES of manufacturers or wholesalers or other senior salesmen earning $10,000 or more per year
3. SALES REPRESENTATIVES (as above) earning $7,000 to $9,999 per year
4. SALES CLERK and salesman earning less than $7,000 per year and CLERICAL WORKERS: bookkeeper, business machine operator, RR conductor, interviewer, storekeeper, sales clerk, route salesman

Group E: Farmers

2. Farmer of farm worth $100,000+
3. Farmer of farm worth $35,000 to $100,000
4. Farmer of farm worth $15,000 to $35,000
5. Farmer of farm worth under $15,000
6. Sharecropper or tenant with little stock or equipment

Group F: Foremen and Manual Workers

5. SKILLED MANUAL WORKER AND FOREMAN: baker, barber, bookbinder, brakeman, heavy equipment operator, carpenter, cheesemaker, compositor, diemaker, auto repairman, engraver, plumber, fitter, hair stylist, horticulturist, lineman, machinist, policeman, postman, shoe repairman, tailor, watchmaker, welder, etc.
6. SEMI-SKILLED WORKER AND MACHINE OPERATOR: aids (hospital, etc.), bartender, truck driver, short order cook, delivery man, enlisted man in military, guard, watchman, meat cutter, practical nurse, roofer, waiter in high class restaurant
7. UNSKILLED WORKER: attendant, trash remover, restaurant worker and waiter in ordinary restaurant, cleaner, farm hand, freight handler, stevedore, unskilled factory worker (including assembly line), hog killer, janitor, laborer, porter, helper, window cleaner, etc.

3. Now classify your father's occupation according to the purpose of the organization or company for which he works. For example, if your father is a janitor for a bank circle Finance and Records; if he is an accountant for a shoe factory circle Manufacturing.
   0. Legal Authority: Organizations primarily concerned with the formulation, arbitration, interpretation, or enforcement of the custody of law-breakers
   1. Finance and Records: Organizations primarily concerned with the handling of monetary affairs or the processing of records, accounts, or correspondence
   2. Commerce: Organizations primarily concerned with the buying, selling, exchange, or marketing of goods or persons
   3. Manufacturing: Organizations primarily concerned with the fabrication of articles or the processing of raw materials on a production-line basis
   4. Transportation: Organizations primarily concerned with the movement of persons or goods from one location to another
   5. Extraction: Organizations primarily concerned with the extraction, procurement, or production of raw materials
   6. Building and Maintenance: Organizations primarily concerned with the construction of buildings or other nonmass produced units, or the installation, maintenance, or repair of equipment, property facilities
   7. Arts and Entertainment: Organizations primarily concerned with the creation of art forms or with the provision of entertainment, recreation, information or aesthetic satisfaction for the public
   8. Education and Research: Organizations primarily concerned with formal instruction or training or with the acquisition of knowledge as an end in itself
   9. Health and Welfare: Organizations primarily concerned with the detection, prevention, or alleviation of illness, hazard, or distress

14. For whom does your father work?
   1. Self-employed (own business or professional practice)
   2. Private business or industry
   3. Government or school
   4. Non-profit private organization (church, foundation, etc.)

15. About how many people are employed in the place your father works?
   1. 0-4
   2. 5-9
   3. 10-19
   4. 20-49
   5. 50-99
   6. 100-199
   7. 200-499
   8. 500-999
   9. 1,000 or more

16. About how many hours a week does your father work? (If he works from 8 A. M. to 5 P. M. five days a week, that would be 40 hours per week.)

   ____________ hours/week

17. How much would you say your father likes the kind of work he does?
   1. Dislikes his work extremely
   2. Dislikes his work considerably
   3. Dislikes his work somewhat
   4. Dislikes his work a little
   5. Likes his work a little
   6. Likes his work somewhat
   7. Likes his work considerably
   8. Likes his work extremely well

18. If your father were asked to use one of these five names for his social class, which one do you think he would be more likely to choose?
   1. The lower class
   2. The working class
   3. The lower middle class
   4. The upper middle class
   5. The upper class

19. Was your mother employed outside the home during your senior year in high school?
   0. No
   1. Part time: 1 to 4 hours per week
   2. Part time: 5 to 9 hours per week
   3. Part time: 10 to 14 hours per week
   4. Part time: 15 to 19 hours per week
   5. Part time: 20 to 24 hours per week
   6. Part time: 25 to 29 hours per week
   7. Part time: 30 to 34 hours per week
   8. Part time: 35 to 39 hours per week
   9. Full time: 40 or more hours per week

20. What kind of work did your mother do outside the home for the longest period during the time you were growing up?

____
If not employed, write "none."

21. Please estimate to the nearest $1,000 your father's yearly income (as opposed to total family income).

$__________ thousand dollars per year

22. During your last year in high school, WHICH PARENT HAD THE FINAL SAY on the things listed below? Circle one number for each of the decisions listed. If the decision never came up, guess which parent would have had the final say.

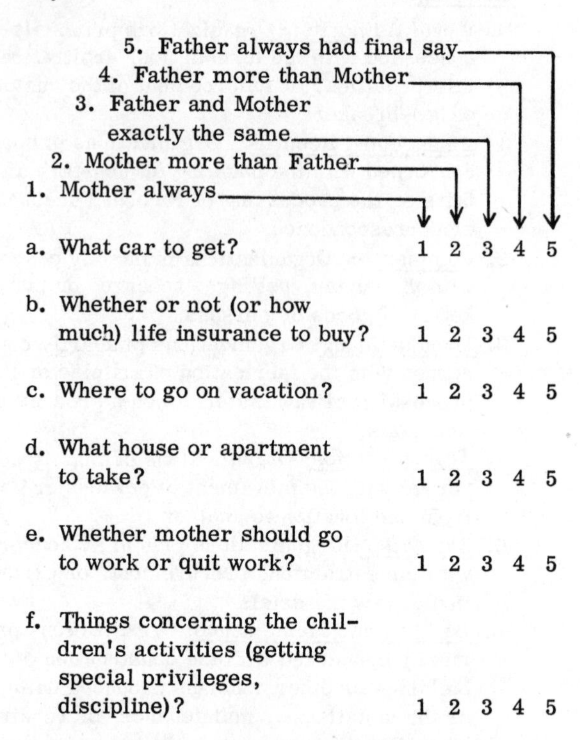

5. Father always had final say
4. Father more than Mother
3. Father and Mother exactly the same
2. Mother more than Father
1. Mother always

a. What car to get?	1	2	3	4	5
b. Whether or not (or how much) life insurance to buy?	1	2	3	4	5
c. Where to go on vacation?	1	2	3	4	5
d. What house or apartment to take?	1	2	3	4	5
e. Whether mother should go to work or quit work?	1	2	3	4	5
f. Things concerning the children's activities (getting special privileges, discipline)?	1	2	3	4	5

23. Taking all things together, how would you describe your parents' marriage? Would you say it was:
   1. Very unhappy
   2. Unhappy
   3. Not too happy
   4. Just about average
   5. A little happier than average
   6. Very happy
   7. Extremely happy

III. ABOUT MY FATHER

During the last year you were in high school, about how often did YOUR FATHER participate in each of the activities listed in the next four questions:

24. Visited his relatives (or had visits from them):
    0. Not at all
    1. Only once a year
    2. Two or three times a year
    3. Four to eight times a year
    4. About once a month (nine to twelve times)
    5. Two or three times a month
    6. About once a week
    7. A few times a week (two to four times)
    8. Almost every day or more often

25. Visited neighbors (or had visits from them):
    0. Not at all
    1. Only once a year
    2. Two or three times a year
    3. Four to eight times a year
    4. About once a month (nine to twelve times)
    5. Two or three times a month
    6. About once a week
    7. A few times a week (two to four times)
    8. Almost every day or more often

26. My father visited (or had visits from) his other friends:
    0. Not at all
    1. Only once a year
    2. Two or three times a year
    3. Four to eight times a year
    4. About once a month (nine to twelve times)
    5. Two or three times a month
    6. About once a week
    7. A few times a week (two to four times)
    8. Almost every day or more often

27. My father attended meetings of organizations and clubs such as fraternal orders, church groups (but do not count Sunday services), business organizations, unions, recreation groups such as bowling teams, scouts, and any other non-profit voluntary group having a recognized organization and officers:
    0. Not at all
    1. Only once a year
    2. Two or three times a year
    3. Four to eight times a year
    4. About once a month (nine to twelve times)
    5. Two or three times a month
    6. About once a week
    7. A few times a week (two to four times)
    8. Almost every day or more often

28. About how many different clubs and organizations did your father belong to when you were a high school senior?

    ____________ organizations

29. How much interest did your father take in politics during your last year in high school?
    1. None at all
    2. Very little interest
    3. Somewhat interested
    4. Moderately interested
    5. Very much interested

30. Which of the following comes closest to your FATHER'S political preference?
    1. Socialist
    2. Liberal Democrat
    3. Conservative Democrat
    4. Liberal Republican
    5. Conservative Republican

31. Which of the following comes closest to YOUR OWN political preference?
    1. Socialist
    2. Liberal Democrat
    3. Conservative Democrat
    4. Liberal Republican
    5. Conservative Republican

PLEASE ANSWER EACH OF THE FOLLOWING THREE QUESTIONS. IN THE LEFT-HAND COLUMN CIRCLE A NUMBER TO SHOW YOUR OPINION AND IN THE COLUMN TO THE RIGHT MAKE THE BEST GUESS YOU CAN ABOUT YOUR FATHER'S OPINION.

32. An admitted communist should not be allowed to make a speech in your community:

Me	Father	
1	1	Strongly Agree
2	2	Agree
3	3	Not sure
4	4	Disagree
5	5	Strongly Disagree

33. Books written against churches and religion should be taken out of public libraries:

Me	Father	
1	1	Strongly Agree
2	2	Agree
3	3	Not sure
4	4	Disagree
5	5	Strongly Disagree

34. Consider the case of a man whose loyalty has been questioned before a congressional committee but who swears under oath he has never been a Communist. If he is teaching in a college or university, he should be fired:

Me	Father	
1	1	Strongly Agree
2	2	Agree
3	3	Not sure
4	4	Disagree
5	5	Strongly Disagree

IV. CHILDHOOD AND ADOLESCENT EXPERIENCES

35. How many brothers and sisters do you have?

______ brothers ______ sisters

36. Taking yourself into account, are the children in your family:
1. All girls
2. All boys
3. Both boys and girls

37. Are you:
1. Only child
2. Youngest child
3. Middle child
4. Oldest child

38. What kind of place did you live in, for the most part, during your childhood and adolescence?
1. Farm (father was a farmer)
2. Fringe the open country but father was employed in non-farm work
3. Suburb or small town near a city where father worked
4. Within the city limits of a city, town, or village

39. How large was the town or city you lived in most of the time when you were growing up? (If you lived on a farm answer for the size of the place where you did most of your family shopping. If you lived in a suburb give the size of the city in which your father worked.)
1. Village or small town—up to 2,499
2. 2,500 to 24,999 population
3. 25,000 to 49,999
4. 50,000 to 99,999
5. 100,000 to 499,999
6. 500,000 and over

40. Which of the following characteristics did your mother think was the most important for you to have while you were in high school?

Put a "1" next to the characteristic your mother felt was most important, and a "2" for the second most important, etc., until you have ranked the whole set. The least important item should be numbered "8."

_____ a. that I work hard

_____ b. that I think for myself

_____ c. that I be considerate of others

_____ d. that I obey my parents well

_____ e. that I be dependable

_____ f. that I have self-control

_____ g. that I be popular with other children

_____ h. that I be able to defend myself

41. How close was the attachment between you and your father when you were in high school?
0. None at all
1. A little
2. Somewhat
3. Considerable
4. Very close
5. Extremely close

42. How close was the attachment between you and your mother when you were in high school?
0. None at all
1. A little
2. Somewhat
3. Considerable
4. Very close
5. Extremely close

43. Try to think back to when you were 13 to 14 years old. At this age did you usually:
1. Stay alone
2. Stay alone, but occasionally hang out with friends or a crowd
3. Hang out with brothers and sisters
4. Hang out with close friends or a crowd

44. At age 13 to 14, to what extent did you enjoy the things you did alone as much as the things you did playing with other children?
1. Enjoyed things alone more
2. About the same
3. Enjoyed things with other children more

45. At age 13 to 14, did you spend more or less time alone than most other children your age did?
1. More time alone than most
2. About average
3. Less time alone than most

46. During your senior year in high school, about how often did you visit friends (or have friends over to your house)?
0. Never
1. Only once that year
2. Two or three times
3. Four to eight times
4. About once a month (nine to twelve times)
5. Two or three times a month
6. About once a week
7. A few times a week (two to four times)
8. Almost every day or more often

47. About how often during your senior year in high school did you attend meetings of clubs and organizations?
0. Never
1. Only once that year
2. Two or three times
3. Four to eight times
4. About once a month (nine to twelve times)
5. Two or three times a month
6. About once a week
7. A few times a week (two to four times)
8. Almost every day or more often

48. During my last year of high school, my grade average was:
0. D- or lower
1. D Average
2. C- Average
3. C Average
4. C+ Average
5. B- Average
6. B Average
7. B+ Average
8. A- Average
9. All or almost all A's

HERE ARE SOME OTHER QUESTIONS ON THE THINGS YOU DID OR FELT WHEN YOU WERE A SENIOR IN HIGH SCHOOL

49. If a person didn't meet certain standards I didn't have too much to do with him (or her) even if I liked the person.
    0. Never
    1. Sometimes
    2. Frequently
    3. Usually
    4. Always

50. When you got angry with a person that year, to year, to what extent did you prefer to let your temper quiet down before trying to settle the argument?
    0. Never
    1. Sometimes
    2. Frequently
    3. Usually
    4. Always

51. When you were a high school senior, to what extent did the money you saved give you as good a feeling as the things you bought?
    0. Not at all
    1. A little
    2. Somewhat
    3. Almost as much
    4. As much or more

52. Taking all things together, how would you rate your childhood?
    1. Very unhappy
    2. Unhappy
    3. Not too happy
    4. Just about average
    5. A little happier than average
    6. Very happy
    7. Extremely happy

V. HEALTH AND PERSONAL PROBLEMS

53. Do you ever have any trouble getting to sleep or staying asleep?
    1. Never
    2. Not very much
    3. Pretty often
    4. Nearly all the time.

54. Have you ever been bothered by nervousness, feeling fidgety, or tense?
    1. Never
    2. Not very much
    3. Pretty often
    4. Nearly all the time

55. Have you ever been bothered by shortness of breath when you were not working hard or exercising?
    1. Never
    2. Hardly ever
    3. Sometimes
    4. Many times

56. Have you ever been bothered by your heart beating hard?
    1. Never
    2. Hardly ever
    3. Sometimes
    4. Many times

57. Do you find it difficult to get up in the morning?
    1. Never
    2. Not very much
    3. Pretty often
    4. Nearly all the time

58. Have there ever been times when you couldn't take care of things because you just couldn't get going?
    1. Never
    2. Hardly ever
    3. Sometimes
    4. Many times

VI. ATTITUDES AND OPINIONS

59. Please give your first feeling or reaction to each of the following groups. Base this on the general impression you have of each group. Mark each group even if you do not know it personally. For each group you may circle as many of the seven columns as your feelings dictate. Work as rapidly as possible so that you answer in terms of your first reaction or feeling.

	1 Would marry into group	2 Would have as close friends	3 Would have as next-door neighbors	4 Would work in same office	5 Have as speaking acquaint-ances only	6 Have as visitors only to my nation	7 Would bar from my nation
a. Armenians . .	1	2	3	4	5	6	7
b. Chinese	1	2	3	4	5	6	7
c. French	1	2	3	4	5	6	7
d. Germans . . .	1	2	3	4	5	6	7
e. Italians	1	2	3	4	5	6	7
f. Japanese . . .	1	2	3	4	5	6	7
g. Jews	1	2	3	4	5	6	7
h. Negroes	1	2	3	4	5	6	7
i. Russians . . .	1	2	3	4	5	6	7

PLEASE ANSWER THE FOLLOWING SIX QUESTIONS TWICE:
First, answer in terms of whether YOU agree or disagree.
Second, answer in terms of whether YOUR FATHER agrees or disagrees.
Please make a guess if you are not sure.

Use the following rating scale:

1 = Strongly Disagree	4 = Slightly Agree
2 = Moderately Disagree	5 = Moderately Agree
3 = Slightly Disagree	6 = Strongly Agree

↓ ↓

Me Father

Question 60

_____ _____ a. Sometimes he (I) have the feeling that people are using him (me).

_____ _____ b. There is little or nothing he (I) can do toward preventing a major "shooting" war.

_____ _____ c. We are just so many cogs in the machinery of life.

Question 61

_____ _____ a. Everything is relative, and there just aren't any definite rules to live by.

_____ _____ b. The end often justifies the means.

_____ _____ c. With so many religions abroad, one doesn't really know which to believe.

VII. FAMILY AND OCCUPATIONAL PLANS

62. Here is a list of things which some people consider important for their husband or wife. For each one, please circle a number to show the extent to which YOU agree or disagree.

4. Strongly agree
3. Agree
2. Not sure
1. Disagree
0. Strongly disagree

a. The person I marry must be sexually stimulating	0	1	2	3	4
b. Sometimes it is wise not to completely confide in your mate	0	1	2	3	4
c. Generally speaking, a woman has to sacrifice more in marriage than a man	0	1	2	3	4

63. How many children do you want to have?

____

64. Here is a list of five things or activities which can give a person satisfaction in life. Mark the item you feel will give you the most satisfaction as "1," the one which will give you the second most satisfaction as "2," and so on until all five have been marked.

____ a. Career or occupation

____ b. Leisure time recreational activity

____ c. Family relationships

____ d. Religious beliefs or activities

____ e. Participation as a citizen in the affairs of your community or nation

65. Assume that you have been married about ten years and that you (or your husband) are working in A LARGE CITY. In which of the following kinds of places would you prefer to live:
1. In or near the downtown area of the city
2. In a residential area within the city limits
3. In the suburbs or a nearby small town
4. In the open country

66. For whom would you prefer to work (assuming that income were the same)?
1. Self-employed (own business or private professional practice)
2. Private business or industry
3. Government or school
4. Non-profit private organization (church, foundation, etc.)

67. Try to think ahead to your situation when you are 40 years old. How much do you think you (or your husband) will be earning at that time (assume that the cost of living stays about the same as it is now)?

$__________ thousand dollars per year at age 40

68. Here is a list of things which might stop some people from taking a new job. Suppose you were offered an opportunity to make a substantial advance in a job or occupation. Circle a number for each item in the list to show how important it would be in stopping you from making that advance. (If you are a woman, please answer in terms of the advice you would give your husband.)

	0 Might stop me from making the change	1 Would be a serious consideration but wouldn't stop me	2 Wouldn't matter at all
a. Leave your family for some time	0	1	2
b. Move around the country a lot	0	1	2
c. Leave your community	0	1	2
d. Leave your friends	0	1	2
h. Learn a new routine	0	1	2
i. Take on more responsibility	0	1	2

VII. SOME PROBLEM SITUATIONS

The following situations all involve illegal action. However, many people disagree with the law and feel that the individuals concerned are justified in these instances for breaking it. What is your opinion?

69. John Green, an electrician, worked for a large steel corporation. He received overtime pay whenever he had to stay on at night to repair machinery for the operation of the next day. Sometimes John worked alone. When he did, he would add an hour or two to the time sheet he turned in to the company. What is your opinion?
    1. Strongly approve
    2. Approve
    3. Indifferent
    4. Disapprove
    5. Strongly disapprove

70. Richard Smith's house burned. He was protected by fire insurance. However, when he filed his claim for insurance he claimed damages greater than he actually had. What is your opinion?
    1. Strongly approve
    2. Approve
    3. Indifferent
    4. Disapprove
    5. Strongly disapprove

71. John Charles went to the local cleaners to pick up a suit he had cleaned. John found his suit and paid for it. He discovered later that he had also taken a pair of trousers that did not belong to him. He decided not to return them. What is your opinion?
    1. Strongly approve
    2. Approve
    3. Indifferent
    4. Disapprove
    5. Strongly disapprove

72. Dan Thomas asked his local grocer to deliver a number of items to his home. When Dan checked over the purchases, he found that the grocer had mistakenly doubled his order, but charged only for the original order. Dan kept the entire order and didn't report the mistake. What is your opinion?
    1. Strongly approve
    2. Approve
    3. Indifferent
    4. Disapprove
    5. Strongly disapprove

Imagine that you are proctoring an examination (i.e., in charge of keeping order during the exam) for a university course. About half way through the exam you see a fellow openly cheating. The student is copying his answers from notes. When he sees that you have seen the notes, he whispers quietly to you, "O.K., I'm caught. That's all there is to it." What would you do?

IMPORTANT: If your birthday is on an odd-numbered day, answer only for "Case A" (left-hand column) and skip "Case B." If your birthday is on an even-numbered day, skip "Case A" and answer "Case B" (right-hand column).

Case A (odd-birthdays only)

73. Assume that there would be very little chance that either the authorities or your friends would know about your part in the incident, and that you do not know the student who is cheating. What would you do? Circle as many of the following as you would do (i.e., more than one action may be circled).
   1. Nothing
   2. Tell him to stop copying
   3. Take away his notes
   4. Let him withdraw from the exam on some excuse such as sickness
   5. Dismiss him from the exam room
   6. Report him for cheating

74. In this situation which of these actions do you think the university authorities would most likely want you to take? (More than one action may be circled.)
   1. Nothing
   2. Tell him to stop copying
   3. Take away his notes
   4. Let him withdraw from the exam on some excuse such as sickness
   5. Dismiss him from the exam room
   6. Report him for cheating

Case B (even-birthdays only)

75. Assume that there would be very little chance that either the authorities or your friends would know about your part in the incident, and that the student who is cheating is your own roommate and close friend. You know that your friend is a hard working, though not a brilliant, student and desperately needs a good grade in this course. What would you do? Circle as many of the following as you would do (i.e., more than one action may be circled).
   1. Nothing
   2. Tell him to stop copying
   3. Take away his notes
   4. Let him withdraw from the exam on some excuse such as sickness
   5. Dismiss him from the exam room
   6. Report him for cheating

76. In this situation which of these actions do you think the university authorities would most likely want you to take? (More than one action may be circled.)
   1. Nothing
   2. Tell him to stop copying
   3. Take away his notes
   4. Let him withdraw from the exam on some excuse such as sickness
   5. Dismiss him from the exam room
   6. Report him for cheating

THANK YOU FOR YOUR HELP IN FILLING OUT THIS QUESTIONNAIRE.

69 70 7 6 5